Research in Social Work

Research in Social Work

THIRD EDITION

ANNE E. FORTUNE

WILLIAM J. REID

COLUMBIA UNIVERSITY PRESS

NEW YORK

Columbia University Press
Publishers Since 1893
New York   Chichester, West Sussex

Copyright © 1999 Columbia University Press

Library of Congress Cataloging-in-Publication Data
Fortune, Anne E.
    Research in social work / Anne E. Fortune, William J. Reid. 3d ed.
    p.   cm.
    Rev. ed. of: Research in social work / William J. Reid. 2d ed. c1989.
    Includes bibliographical references and index.
    ISBN   0-231-10812-5 (cl)
    1. Social service—Research. I. Reid, William James II. Reid, William James,
1928—Research in social work. III. Title. HV11. F678 1998
    361'.007'2—ddc21

                                                            99—37871
                                                            CIP

♾

Casebound editions of Columbia University Press books
are printed on permanent and durable acid-free paper.
Printed in the United States of America
c 10 9 8 7 6 5 4 3 2 1
p 10 9 8 7 6 5 4 3 2 1

To Michael Twentyman and Mary Fortune

Contents

Preface

We had two goals in mind in preparing the present (third) edition of this book. First, we wanted to increase its appeal to beginning (including undergraduate) students, particularly students not already familiar with social work practice. Revisions to this end included more definitions and examples to clarify concepts and several linking themes to provide better continuity and integration among chapters. A second goal was to update the text in light of recent developments in social work research and educational curricula (including content required by the 1992 Curriculum Policy Statement of the Council on Social Work Education). We thus included more content on epistemological issues, intervention research and program evaluation, computerized literature searches, qualitative methods, ethics, generalist practice, and cultural diversity. These changes resulted in substantial revisions in all existing chapters of the previous edition as well in the addition of three new chapters, a glossary, and appendixes on the library research process and writing research reports.

As in previous editions, we present research methodology as an instrument of professional social work practice. Our choice of research methods and our presentation of them have been guided by views of what social work is about and how research can best serve the interests of the profession. Accordingly, we give considerable attention to naturalistic and experimental designs that help understand phenomena of interest to social workers and help develop and test social work interventions. Chapters on problem formulation, sampling, measurement, data collection, data analysis, and qualitative methods include parallels to social work practice and are illustrated by practice studies. In addition, several chapters relate directly to social work practice: assessment of problems and needs, measurement of intervention characteristics, measurement of outcomes of social work methods, and the design and development of social work intervention.

If research is to be used to full advantage to advance the goals of social work, the profession needs to develop a climate in which both doing and consuming research are normal professional activities. Not that all social workers should necessarily do research or that all practice should be based on the results of research. We mean rather that an ability to carry out studies at some level and a facility in using scientifically based knowledge should be an integral part of the skills that social workers have and use.

Several features of the book attempt to foster the development such a climate. We provide stimulus and tools for carrying out modest studies—for example, through single case and exploratory experiments. More advanced methodology is presented to facilitate more complex studies and generally as a resource in the utilization of the sophisticated research that is increasingly appearing in print.

We also lay a basis for giving research a more persuasive and influential role in social work. In developing this theme, we set forth a scientific framework for practice and examine applications of research concepts and techniques to the practice arena. We also argue that more use can be made of "softer" studies if their limitations are properly evaluated, particularly when one considers that the yield of such studies may often be considerably "harder" than knowledge based on practice wisdom or untested theory. In developing this argument, we focus on the nature of social work knowledge—the epistemology of social work in effect. The discussion is not out of place in a book about research in a practice profession. In fact, the knowledge issues examined are, we think, fundamental in any consideration of research utilization.

An innovative feature retained from the previous edition merits comment. We present a multidimensional framework for classification of research design (chapter 4). The framework, we hope, provides a clearer, more comprehensive and more accurate approach to design typology than conventional conceptions. New in this edition is integrating the dimensions into discussions of particular designs and illustrations, to help students recognize the designs and their key characteristics.

We would like to express our gratitude to the many persons who facilitated our efforts to create the third edition. We are indebted to John Michel, Executive Editor, Columbia University Press, whose stimulation and guidance helped us launch the project. Lynn Videka-Sherman, the Dean of our School of Social Welfare at the University at Albany, created an optimal environment during our two years of effort in completing the revision. Work on this edition was assisted immeasurably by colleagues and students who used the book and who provided suggestions on how it could be improved. Special thanks are due to those who "pretested" portions of the manuscript in their classes: Jon Caspi, Mary Corrigan, and Valerie Massimo. Finally we owe thanks to a number of assistants who helped with library searches and editorial work: Lynn Bladek, Mary Ann Burke, James Golden, Lori Kinch-Ashley, Jungwon Kim, Michael O'Neill, and Pamela Zettergren.

Research in Social Work

1 Social Work and Research

Understanding the World

How do individuals make sense of the world around them? The physical world is made up of observable phenomena—raw unorganized data. If it were knowable, these unorganized data would constitute "reality." We organize these data into a conceptual framework that allows us to make sense of "reality." For most people individually, the conceptual framework is a rough and often inconsistent world view.

In trying to make sense of the raw data, most people use a combination of methods to understand phenomena. They rely on their personal knowledge from previous events (experience), trust their gut-level reactions (intuition), follow the assertions of others they admire (faith or values), consult acknowledged experts (authority), and test out assumptions systematically (scientific approach). For example, the first time a practitioner encounters a client with both mental illness and substance abuse problems, the practitioner may be at a loss about how to help. Influences on the practitioner's intervention might include the practitioner's previous case management work with mentally ill clients (experience), a "feeling" that this client needs a firm approach (intuition), a strong distaste for drunkenness (values), and the supervisor's advice to deal with the substance abuse first (authority). With knowledge from each of these sources, the practitioner may be comfortable beginning case management with the dually-diagnosed client.

But the intervention may not be the most effective, because knowledge from sources such as experience, intuition, and values is particularly prone to errors (Gibbs and Gambrill 1996). In this instance, the practitioner's experience is with women, but the new client is a male whose schizophrenic illness is greatly complicated by alcoholism. The practitioner's intuition about a firm approach does fit in well with the approach of the substance abuse agency the client attends, but the practitioner's belief that people willfully drink to drunkenness may limit ability to temper firmness with empathy. The supervisor's advice about sequence of intervention makes sense, but the client is unlikely to do well

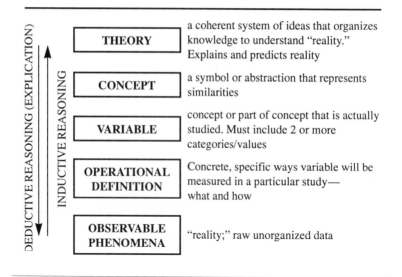

FIGURE 1.1

The language of research: The relation of theory to observable phenomena

unless treatment of substance abuse is coordinated with treatment of the mental illness.

Another approach to making sense of the world is the scientific approach. A scientific approach is characterized by reason—or systematic logic—and empiricism—or observation of the real world. The raw data are linked to a conceptual framework through a process that includes logical thought and testing of ideas. On the one hand, observation of the world leads to logical ideas about how that world is organized. On the other hand, reason is used to develop ideas about reality, and those ideas are tested empirically.

The way the scientific approach links observable phenomena to a conceptual framework for understanding the world is sketched in figure 1.1. At the level of conceptual framework, unlike the idiosyncratic individual world view where each individual has his or her own view, people following the scientific approach try to build consensus about the conceptual framework. The consensus is theory. Theory is a coherent system of ideas (concepts) that organizes knowledge. Theory both explains reality and helps us predict what is likely to happen. In the social work profession, important theories relate to human behavior and social work practice, for example, systems theory, psychodynamic theory, or learning theory.

Concepts, from which theory is built, are abstractions, or symbols, that represent similarities—common characteristics, the key properties, or shared experiences. For example, an important concept in social work practice is "relationship," which refers to the quality of the interpersonal interaction between clients and practitioners in a professional context. By using such a concept, practitioners—and researchers—communicate with each other about the professional interaction even when their own experiences with clients differ and, sometimes, when they are defining "relationship" differently.

Variables are concepts or parts of concepts that are actually included in a particular research study. Because they are actually studied, variables are the first direct link to observable phenomena. The final link is operational definitions, or the details of specifically how a variable is measured in a specific instance—which pieces of observable phenomena are to be included within a variable and how the phenomena are to be categorized. At this level, researchers may, and often do, have different definitions of a concept.

DIFFERENT OPERATIONAL DEFINITIONS FOR THE CONCEPT "RELATIONSHIP"

Shulman defines working relationship as "A professional relationship between the client and worker that is the medium through which the social worker influences the client. A positive working relationship is characterized by good rapport and a sense on the part of the client that he or she can trust the worker and that the worker cares for the client" (Shulman 1992:77). In one study in child welfare agencies, Shulman's interviewers asked parents directly what they thought about the social worker on two dimensions, trust and caring. For trust, interviewers asked "Do you feel you can talk openly to (social worker's name) about anything on your mind?" and "Does (social worker) make you feel comfortable to discuss your mistakes and failures as well as your successes?" For caring, interviewers asked "Did you get the feeling that your worker was helping you or just investigating your family?" and "Did you get the feeling that your worker was as interested and concerned about you as about your child?"(Shulman 1993)

Loneck, by contrast, defined the relationship, or working alliance, as "the extent to which the clinician and the client collaborate on the work at hand" (Loneck et al. 1996). Not only was his description different from Shulman's, but he measured it in an entirely different way. He tape recorded sessions between clients and their clinicians in a psychiatric emergency room. The tapes were transcribed and then trained assistants rated the interview using the Working Alliance Inventory (WAI) (Horvath and Greenberg 1989). The

WAI has 36 items grouped in three subscales: clinician-client agreement on goals, clinician-client agreement on tasks, and clinician-client bond. Each item is rated on a 7-point Likert scale and the items are added together for the final score of quality of working alliance.

Loneck used only the observer form of the WAI. However, three versions are available, one for an outside observer, one for the client, and one for the clinician. Thus, it is possible to secure three different perspectives even with the same definition of relationship.

The link between theory and observable phenomenon was just described "from the top down," from the most abstract to the most concrete. This type of reasoning is called deductive. Most people also think "from the bottom up," making observations, trying to find the similarities in their experience, developing operational definitions and linking them to broader concepts they can share with others. Reasoning from the concrete to abstract is inductive. In the social sciences, including social work, good research and theory development include both, as ideas generated from observation are formalized and tested in cycle.

Theory, as mentioned, involves organizing concepts in such a way that they describe and explain the world. In the scientific perspective, the accuracy of understanding and the relationship among concepts is tested systematically through hypothesis testing procedures. A hypothesis is a tentative statement about the relationship between variables. (In some instances, research questions that inquire about a relationship are used.) The hypothesis itself may be derived from deductive logic (from the theory), or from inductive logic (from observations). The hypothesis-testing procedure is laid out in figure 1.2, adapted from Bloom (1975).

The hypothesis-testing process parallels the broad outlines of the problem-solving practice approach (bottom half of figure 1.2). The investigator starts with a general orientation, a "scientific attitude." In the quantitative approach, the research is framed by a formal set of theory and concepts. The investigator defines the problem of interest, starting with previous literature, the investigator's own interests, and other influences such as agency needs or funding sources. Formal hypotheses or research questions which guide the rest of the research are generated. To test these hypotheses, the investigator develops a research design, which addresses such issues such as who to study (sampling), how many times to study them, and whether to actively experiment with variables. The investigator also plans the operational definitions or links between

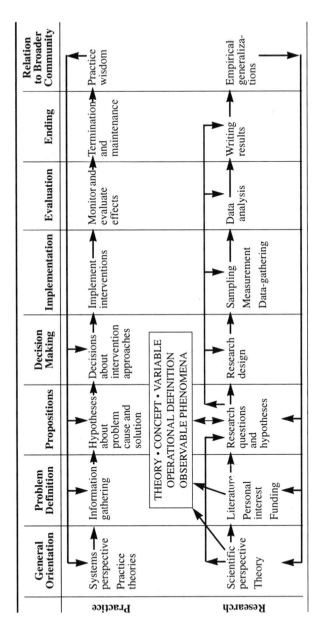

FIGURE 1.2
Parallels between practice and research. Adapted from Bloom 1975

the concepts and observable phenomena, which includes what to measure and how to measure it (measurement and data-gathering). The design is then put into effect and data are gathered according to the plan. The data are evaluated through data analysis methods, usually including statistical procedures. In the final steps, the investigator draws conclusions and disseminates them through reports and articles, thus contributing to knowledge for practitioners and the next researchers.

In the qualitative approach, the investigator starts with the same general orientation, a "scientific attitude," and with a formal theoretical framework to guide the research. At this point, however, instead of developing formal hypotheses to be tested, the investigator works inductively from the phenomena, observing and trying to develop new understandings of the data-concept link. The investigator develops a research design (who or what to study, how to study it), but these plans are flexible. Data analysis methods rely on logic and conceptualization, and are often simultaneous with data-gathering (rather than delayed as in statistical analyses). During the data-gathering and analysis, the investigator develops and tests explanations for the data, a reiterative process of hypothesis testing. As with a quantitative scientific approach, the final step is dissemination of the investigator's conclusions, adding to the empirical knowledge for others to draw on.

An example of a quantitative, deductive approach is McCall and Green's (1991) study of marital relationships. Drawing on theories that symmetrical, equal relations are competitive and unstable (both partners try to one-up each other) while complementary relations are reciprocal and stable, they hypothesized that symmetrical couples would report more marital instability than complementary couples. Statistical techniques were used to analyze questionnaires completed by 136 couples. Their analysis, which suggested that symmetrical and complementary couples did not differ on instability, failed to support their hypothesis. In an example of a qualitative, inductive approach, Gilgun (1992) interviewed individuals to investigate why some abused children become abusers as adults and some do not. She analyzed each interview for themes-e.g., using sex "to feel better." She selected people who differed on crucial factors, such as having a confidant available, to see if the themes were similar or if she needed new ways of conceptualizing the data. She concluded that early frequent sexual activity in order to feel good increases risk of becoming a perpetrator, while having confidants available (while being sexual abused) protects from becoming a perpetrator later.

In many respects, the hypothesis-testing procedure is similar to good social work practice (top half of figure 1.2). Like generalist social work practice, research follows a problem-solving approach. In practice, a practitioner starts with a general orientation that frames assessment and intervention; in generalist practice, this is a systems perspective. The practitioner also draws on sets of theories that explain practice phenomena, such as cognitive-behavioral or psychodynamic explanation of individual behavior, or group dynamics explanations of organizational behavior. The practitioner and clients define the problems to be addressed through information gathering that is directed in part by the systems perspective. The practitioner generates hypotheses about the causes of the problems and how they can be resolved; in the generalist systems perspective, this includes focus on multiple levels. Based on this information and on informed practice knowledge, the practitioner plans intervention, a sort of research design that includes where to intervene—at what systems, with whom, and with what interventions. The interventions are implemented and results monitored. If they are effective, the practitioner continues the interventions, builds on them, and implements other interventions that will maintain the gains once a case is ended. If the interventions are not successful, the practitioner and clients reevaluate, perhaps redefining the problem based on new observations, generating new hypotheses, and implementing new interventions. At termination, practitioner and client do a more formal evaluation and look at ways to maintain gains. Contact ends, and the practitioner adds the knowledge from this case to personal practice wisdom and occasionally to the social work literature. The process of logic in practice is an on-going loop of deductive and inductive thinking.

We will come back to the link between theory and observable phenomena in chapter 2 and to the steps in the research process in other chapters. Before continuing, however, we address the usefulness of a scientific perspective in social work.

The Contribution of the Scientific Approach to Social Work

How can a scientific approach contribute to the diverse and multifaceted activities of social work? Social work practitioners and researchers have struggled with answers to this question since the beginnings of the profession. We see two main components of the contribution of a scientific perspective to social work: empirical practice as a framework for constructing and directing intervention, and building knowledge for social work.

Empirical Practice

At a fundamental level, science can provide a framework for practice activities. Practitioners who take a "scientific attitude" toward their work will gather systematic and accurate data about their clients' problems, will be cautious in making inferences from the data, will try to resolve discrepancies in evidence through further inquiry, will make use of relevant research to increase their understanding of their cases, and so on.

At this level of generality there is little disagreement in social work that practice should be scientifically based. At the level of specific application, however, social workers disagree because there are differing views about what constitutes "good" science. Even when there is accord on that point, there may be conflict about the appropriateness or extent of application of a given scientific dictum to a practice situation. How precise do practice data need to be? How much inference is it reasonable to use in interpreting data? How much support from available research and from the case at hand is required before one can confidently develop a hypothesis for the case? To what extent should the demands of science be permitted to interfere with service requirements? How much weight should be given to "practice wisdom" or other sources of knowledge when making practice and program decisions? These are examples of the difficult questions that arise when an attempt is made to bring a scientific perspective to the realities of social work practice.

One's conception of scientifically based or empirical practice depends, of course, on how such questions are answered. We present our own conceptions of empirical practice by suggesting how an empirical practitioner approaches work with clients.

First of all, the practitioner relies primarily on an *empirical language* as a means of depicting intervention, goals, and processes. That is, language is clearly tied to empirical referents. Key terms can be spelled out or made operational—operational definitions—in the form of specific indicators that can he observed and adequately measured. The indicators might be in the form of descriptions of behavior, or if concepts refer to internal processes such as a client's self-image, the indicators might take the form of the client's statements or responses on a questionnaire. In any case, they are concrete pieces of evidence that can be communicated with sufficient clarity so that others can make their own assessment of them.

For example, if a couple complained that their communication was poor, the practitioner would try to help them define their poor communication in terms of specific behaviors, such as giving one another ambiguous messages or withholding information, and would try to specify these indicators through even more concrete referents. What characterizes an ambiguous message? What kinds of information are withheld? The indicators might be quantified through counts of frequencies or ratings of intensity, although quantification of this kind, while often desirable, is not seen as an essential requirement of empirical practice.

Reliance on empirical language does not, of course, preclude the use of abstract concepts; without them one can hardly speak of either professional or scientific knowledge. But unfortunately many abstractions used in social work have neither precise nor commonly accepted meanings. This fact can be appreciated when we reflect on possible definitions of concepts commonly used by social work practitioners: What is the meaning of concepts such as community power structure, group cohesion, family preservation, goal displacement, emotional neglect, permanency planning, ego strength, empathy, or advocacy? In empirical practice, abstractions of the kind just illustrated are assumed to convey only minimal information unless pinned to observable phenomena in the situation at hand. Thus, if a practitioner referred to a child as an "underachiever," the description might be specified by referring to a discrepancy between the child's scores on a scholastic aptitude test and academic performance as measured by grades. If a client is described as using the "defense of denial" to avoid recognizing internal hostility, the practitioner should be able to specify responses that could be reliably classified as hostile as well as instances of the denial of the hostile import of these responses.

In addition to relying on empirical language, a scientifically based practitioner makes use, whenever possible, of *well-explicated practice models*. In any intervention approach there are assumed connections between the practitioner's interventions and change. For example, one assumes that if the practitioner does X, then the client's functioning is likely to improve, a problem is likely to be alleviated, the agency will provide more resources, or some other desired change will probably occur. This statement is, of course, an oversimplification of complex formulations that make assumptions about the characteristics or actions of various systems and circumstances. For example, a fuller formulations is: if the practitioner does X with Y type of client, then the client is likely to respond in Z manner, while the client's support system will respond in V manner, leading to a certain kind of change. By integrating diverse elements into a coherent whole, such statements provide the theoretical structure of an intervention approach.

In well-explicated practice models, these connections are set forth in clear and specific terms so that it should be possible to obtain evidence that each link of the chain connects to another to produce a desired result. To the extent that such knowledge can be obtained, it becomes possible to demonstrate the effects of the approach with greater certainty and, perhaps of greater importance, to make specific improvements to increase its effectiveness or efficiency.

Examples of well-explicated models may be found in different types of social skill training programs (see, for example, LeCroy 1994). The absence of a skill, such as assertiveness, is identified; specific techniques—instruction, modeling, role play, coaching, and so on—are used to help the client learn the skill; and the client's performance of the skill is tested in simulated social situations. It becomes possible to trace clearly the process by which the skill is learned. As a result, weaknesses in the model can he identified and corrected through study of its operations. By contrast, processes of change may not be so readily discernible in an approach described only as "providing a nurturing relationship as a means of helping the client develop greater confidence in his own capacities." Such an approach may have great value, but, lacking better explication, the processes by which it achieves its effects would be difficult to sort out or study in a systematic way. It may be impossible to secure evidence on what leads to what and hence to bring about improvements based on scientific knowledge. To bring the approach within an empirical practice framework, one would need to spell out its concepts and processes. What are the ingredients of a nurturing relationship? By what means specifically can it be provided, how does it affect clients, and how can we detect these effects?

Increasingly, well-explicated practice methods are available for specific problems or situations, and more are being tested as federal funding sources have emphasized the development of practice protocols to guide practitioners implementing experimental research. Examples include: a range of manual-based approaches for treating problems of children and youth (LeCroy 1994), Jensen's (1994) model for the treatment of depression in women, Hogarty and Anderson's psychoeducation for families of mentally ill (Anderson, Reiss, and Hogarty 1986; Hogarty 1993); support groups for caregivers of frail or ill elderly (McCallion and Toseland 1995; Peak, Toseland, and Banks 1995); several approaches to family preservation that attempt to prevent removal of abused and neglected children from their homes (Fraser, Pecora, and Haapala 1991; Wells and Biegel 1991; Whittaker et al. 1990); and school-based case management for children with academic and attendance problems (Reid and Bailey-Dempsey 1995)

Such well-explicated models do not cover all—or even most—situations a practitioner may encounter. To provide a broader if idiosyncratic approach, by following principles set forth by Mullen (1983, 1994), practitioners can develop their own well-explicated personal practice models in which diverse methods are combined and adapted. Or such methods can be put together within frameworks for eclectic practice (Reid 1997a). And, as suggested, most practice approaches can be made more explicit. Explication, a characteristic of empirical practice, can be thought of as a matter of degree, and can be advanced by degrees.

A third characteristic of a scientifically based approach to social work is the relative stress placed on *research-based knowledge and technology* as a means of informing and molding practice activities. In attempting to assess the situation, identify the focus of intervention, and devise an intervention plan, the empirical practitioner makes use of a range of knowledge but gives priority to knowledge supported by research findings. The practitioner considers untested knowledge but regards it with skepticism. He or she avoids wholesale application of belief systems that lack empirical support. Even if the knowledge were backed by research findings, it is applied tentatively to the practice situation at hand and tested within that situation. The most that is expected from available knowledge is hypotheses that will be evaluated in the light of the realities of immediate concern to the practitioner. This is so because little of the research-based knowledge that social workers use can be cast in the form of laws. At best, such knowledge states what is true for most situations. The practitioner needs to determine if the immediate situation is one of the exceptions.

If such ad hoc testing for each case is needed in any event, why should the empirical practitioner give priority to research-supported knowledge? The priority can be justified on grounds that research support increases the probability that the knowledge in question does hold for the particular case. If there is evidence that a generalization has been found to be true in cases similar to the one at hand, one can posit that it is likely to be true in the present case. To accept this hypothesis, the practitioner may need to obtain only a small amount of confirming evidence from the case itself.

Suppose our practitioner is referred a child who has suddenly refused to go to school. This is the first time the child has had such a problem. The child had missed two days of school the previous week because of illness and had failed a recent examination. There is research-supported knowledge suggesting that a child with these characteristics has a particular type of school phobia—one apt to occur in anxious children who are afraid of failure because of having missed school (Kennedy 1995). If parents are able to return the child to school at once, the phobia is usually short-lived and does not return. The practitioner may entertain a strong hypothesis that the child's behavior fits the general picture of this type of school phobia and may attempt to help the parents return the child to school. If the child responds as predicted, then the practitioner has confirming evidence that the hypothesis is correct. If the child does not, then the practitioner might abandon this premise and search for another. It is also evident that ad hoc tests of hypotheses can be accomplished more effectively with research-based knowledge than with other kinds since the former knowledge is already expressed in researchable form; that is, concepts have been put in operational terms, measurement approaches have been worked out, and so on. While it is then true that each practice situation constitutes, for the empirical practitioner, a miniature study, the study is more likely to bear fruit if based on results of prior research.

Similarly, when selecting the intervention, the empirical practitioner gives priority to practice technology whose effectiveness has been demonstrated through research. But again, the interventions are tested cautiously in the immediate practice situation.

However much priority is given to it, research-based knowledge can provide only a limited amount of guidance to practitioners. In the complexities of practical situations, much knowledge and information cannot be readily connected to a research base. But in dealing with this information, practitioners can nevertheless employ the kind of logic that characterizes scientific work. A fourth attribute, then, of the empirical practitioner is the use of *scientific reasoning* to order phenomena encountered in practice—for example, to construct explanations for problems, for processes of change, and for the role of intervention in bringing change about.

One facet of scientific reasoning as it applies to practice activities—formulating and testing hypotheses derived from research-based knowledge—has already been described. More generally, the same process of testing theory and generalizations against the data in the situation at hand is used in applications of all forms of knowledge, whether the knowledge is derived from research, practice wisdom, or another source. Such deductive reasoning is combined with inductive approaches, in which one attempts to form generalizations from the particulars of a situation. Whether using inductive or deductive modes of reasoning, the empirical practitioner is concerned about the quality of the data and is cautious in making inferences about them. Moreover, the practitioner searches for alternative sources of explanation and considers several theoretical formulations. In considering alternative theoretical explanations, the empirical practitioner favors the one that can account for the data at hand in the most parsimonious fashion.

For example, if faced with a male client who is depressed for no apparent reason, the practitioner attempts to obtain data that might bear upon the causes of his depression and may consider a variety of possible theories to formulate an explanation. There may be some evidence to suggest that the client is harboring a good deal of resentment against his mother; other evidence may suggest that he has suffered a blow to his self-image at work. There may be indications that his wife is particularly attentive when he complains of feeling blue. There are hints that he has begun to question the meaningfulness of goals that were always important to him. Each piece of data points in different theoretical directions, none of which has convincing empirical support. Following a scientific mode of analysis, the practitioner would not form a hasty explanation on the basis of preconceived beliefs about the validity of a particular theory but would rather obtain further data in relation to different theoretical possibilities. With these data, the practitioner formulates a tentative explanation based on what best seemed to account for the data obtained, an explanation that might well be altered in the light of new evidence. Suppose further that the client's depression lifted during subsequent treatment. The practitioner would not necessarily assume that the remission was caused by the intervention nor that it proved the correctness of the explanation of the problem. The practitioner would evaluate these possibilities in relation to other possible explanations that might be suggested by the data of the case.

In applying research-based knowledge and technology and in using scientific reasoning, the practitioner, as we have noted, engages in forms of research activity such as data collection and hypothesis testing. More generally, a scientifically based approach can be characterized by its *use of research methods as an integral part* of practice (Blythe and Ivanoff, in press). In addition to gathering data to test hypotheses in practice situations, practitioners may use research instruments for assessing intervention targets or providing feedback on the immediate consequences of interventions. They may also conduct evaluative studies of single cases or of ongoing programs to improve practice operations. In other words, research is employed as a tool for gathering systematic knowledge about activities in the "here and now."

For example, working with a family referred for potential neglect of the two youngest children, the empirical practitioner may begin assessment with a measure of neglect potential such as the Family Assessment Scales (Magura, Moses, and Jones 1987). Interviews with the mother, boyfriend and father of some of the children, children, and school personnel may indicate problems with one child's academic performance and limited parenting skills among the adults. To keep track of change in these areas, the practitioner may ask the mother and boyfriend to complete the Parenting Stress Index (Abidin 1990) and may consult regularly with the children's teachers to gather data on attendance and test scores. In deciding at what level to intervene, the practitioner might use a structured assessment tool such as Vosler's Family Access to Basic Resources (FABR) (1990). Using such standardized measures is also a way of making operational links to specific referents, as well as use of research methods within practice.

Building Knowledge

Whether or not practice is scientifically based in the sense described, science can contribute to practice through generating knowledge relevant to its purposes. As we use the term, knowledge refers to generalizations about phenomena supported by evidence. Much of the core knowledge of social work consists of assertions about human behavior and methods of intervention. As we know, much of it is "soft," that is, based more on speculation than on hard data.

The central contribution of research to knowledge-building in social work is to develop generalizations based in empirical evidence. This objective may be achieved through studies that create or suggest generalizations supported by data or through studies that bring evidence to bear on generalizations derived from theory, practice wisdom, or other sources. In some cases, scientific study may buttress these generalizations, or in other cases it will qualify them; in still others it will reveal no support for the beliefs in question. In all these cases, research is contributing to knowledge building, even if its contribution takes the form of invalidating false assertions masquerading as knowledge.

From the perspective of empirical practice, preferred knowledge is knowledge backed by the strongest evidence, assumed to be evidence generated by research. This knowledge may be questionable by the usual standards of science, but it may be better—more likely to be true—than available alternatives.

This is so, we think, because the alternatives often offer only the promise of useful knowledge. Upon analysis they turn out to be not tested knowledge but rather what might be better called "unsubstantiated expertise." We refer here to statements that would be useful, if true, but their truth is not apparent and substantiating evidence is lacking. This is not to say that unsubstantiated expert opinion is necessarily wrong, but simply that it should be treated with skepticism, as it is knowledge based on authority. In social work, much of this expert opinion is presumably based on practice experience—in fact, the term *practice wisdom* (Klein and Bloom 1995), has been devised to describe it. Because practice wisdom has evolved to meet the knowledge needs of practitioners, it is generally highly relevant to practice, and since it is presumably based on the realities of practice, it seems to provide some assurance of validity. The empirical foundations of practice wisdom are often difficult to discern or evaluate, however, since they are seldom articulated. Some assertions may be backed by a considerable amount of carefully evaluated evidence sifted from practice experience; others may be based on biased impressions of unrepresentative examples.

Against this backdrop, generalizations for which some research evidence can be produced become more attractive. If the probing of a piece of practice wisdom reveals that it is based on some possibly biased impressions of a few cases, then a generalization grounded in a sizable number of cases studied systematically may offer a better basis for practice decisions, even though the research may be scarcely definitive.

This is not to say that knowledge presumably derived from research should be accepted with any less degree of skepticism or caution than practice wisdom. Research evidence can prove just as illusory as evidence gained from practice.

As subsequent chapters document, social work research is vulnerable to error from many sources. Most instruments provide at best crude and partial measures of complex social phenomena. The validity of data is inevitably threatened by at least two layers of human bias. At the level of data collection, the biases of subjects and their immediate observers may give false impressions of events under study. At the level of data analysis, interpretation, and reporting, biases of investigators may shape ambiguous findings in hoped-for directions. In what are probably the most frequent sins of all, generalizations may be unreasonably extended beyond the limits of available research findings or may ignore contradictory evidence.

Despite all this, knowledge produced by research retains crucial advantages over unsubstantiated expertise. Research builds knowledge through processes that are both self-corrective and cumulative. As experience is gathered, more effective methodologies evolve. As a body of research grows, convergences in findings do appear, and studies fraught with error fall to one side. Moreover, the shortcomings of research-based knowledge are more readily identified. If a statement claims some universal truth on the basis of a few equivocal studies of college sophomores, diligent readers are at least given the opportunity to search out the evidence and to form their own judgments about it.

Research evidence should be given the same hard look as any kind of evidence, but it should be looked at from the same vantage point from which other evidence is regarded. Thus one should not dismiss the evidence yielded by research because it fails to meet some absolute standard of scientific acceptability and at the same time embrace beliefs for which far less credible evidence exists.

If this position is accepted, then greater practical value can be placed on research that is highly relevant to the interests of practitioners but that may lack rigor in design and measurement—research that has sometimes been dismissed as "merely exploratory," or "soft." A study may be so characterized yet still make a useful contribution to the pool of knowledge used by practitioners, since it may deliver knowledge as good as can be obtained by other means or offer some knowledge where none exists. It may amount to the "the best attainable knowledge" (Reid 1994b).

We are not arguing for a shift from more rigorous research that may be of less immediate relevance to less rigorous investigations of pressing practice issues. We need more of both, particularly studies that are highly rigorous and relevant. Rather, we are arguing that studies of "low quality" by classical scientific standards be mined for useful knowledge rather than disregarded. Proper mining is, of course, the key. One must be able to distinguish between illumination and error, not an easy task in a study that may be fraught with the latter. But this is a task that social workers need to perfect in their quest for knowledge from whatever source.

To put the foregoing arguments into a realistic perspective, we must recognize that practitioners acquire knowledge from many sources. In fact, research and expert opinion are no more than contributions to a larger fund of "personal" knowledge that practitioners acquire from life and work experiences. At a practical level, the question becomes, how can research harden and expand these funds of knowledge? The task is not simple, since few research-based generalizations may fit the particulars of the situations practitioners face. Often the best knowledge available is practice wisdom. Still, an empirical orientation toward practice, the evaluation of practice wisdom and research against a common standard of evidence, and the active use of research at all levels of rigor should help further the process. As Klein and Bloom (1995:806) have so well put it, "if it's truly wise, practice wisdom incorporates information from a wide variety of sources, including those that are empirically based."

Research Utilization

The contribution of research to social work is dependent on how, and how much, the profession makes use of research. Studies of a particular question may have produced some definitive answers, but if the research is ignored by practicing social workers, its contribution is nil.

Researchers have long bemoaned the apparent lack of proper utilization of their work by program managers and practitioners. "Our studies are not read or used," researchers complain; to which program people may reply, "Your studies are likely to be off-target, incomprehensible, out of date, or otherwise uninformative." In an effort to move beyond the sterile acrimony of such disputes, researchers have increasingly turned their attention to the study of the utilization process itself (Grasso and Epstein 1992; Kirk 1990; Reid and Fortune 1992).

In earlier times research utilization in social work practice was considered a relatively straightforward process. Studies were conducted and their results disseminated to "program people" who then found ways to use them in their work with clients.

Although some research utilization does in fact occur this way, views that have come to the forefront in the past two decades suggest that the utilization process is far more varied, complex, subtle, and indirect (Albaek 1995; Beyer and Trice 1982; Greenberg and Mandell 1991; Pelz 1978; Rich 1977; Weiss and Bucuvalas 1980). Weiss and Bucavalas's (1980:213) observation about social science research states well the more contemporary positions: "Our understanding of research utilization has to go beyond the explicit adoption of research conclusions in discrete decisions to encompass the assimilation of social science information, generalizations, and ideas into agency perspectives as a basis for making sense of problems and providing strategies of action."

A key distinction that has emerged is between *instrumental utilization*—specific use of research "for decision-making or problem-solving purposes"—and *conceptual utilization*—"influencing thinking about an issue without putting information to any specific documentable use" (Rich 1977:200). Instrumental utilization preserves the classic, "strict constructionist" notion of utilization. In conceptual utilization a user's decisions may draw on some combination of their own beliefs and research findings.

These formulations help clarify two central issues in the utilization of effectiveness research in agency contexts. One of these issues concerns the low rate of instrumental utilization and the failure to develop means of facilitating it. A second issue concerns difficulties in sorting out the complexities of conceptual utilization and in constructing models to understand and study it. These issues can be combined if we view direct utilization of research findings relating to social work practice as essentially "conceptual." One can legitimately view virtually all such utilization of research data by program managers and practitioners in terms of complex cognitive and organizational processes in which the data constitute one of a variety of inputs. Research information is joined with such other considerations as the staff's own impressions of effectiveness, informal case reports, general knowledge, available alternatives, and cost factors. This process may produce new insight but, as Weiss and Bucuvalas (1980) have documented, seldom produces a clear-cut decision. Rather what is learned may affect program people in a collective decision-making process that is responsive to an even wider range of considerations.

A third type of utilization referred to by Leviton and Hughes (1981:528) as *persuasive utilization* involves "drawing on . . . evidence to support a position." Advocates, lobbyists, policy makers, and agency executives who marshal scientific findings to promote a cause or a program are making persuasive use of research. This kind of utilization, in which self-serving interests are rampant, might be seen as a political subversion of the research process. However, it can be useful if it follows a true adversarial model, that is, if there is opportunity for advocates of different sides of an issue to present scientific evidence supporting their position with an opportunity to critique evidence provided by their opponents. Resulting exchanges can be illuminating to decision-makers and to the public.

A fourth category is *methodological utilization*, or use of research tools such as single system designs or standardized tests (1992; Tripodi, Fellin, and Meyer 1983). This kind of utilization seems to be on the rise with the growing emphasis on routine outcome measurement in the human services (Mullen and Magnabosco 1997).

The final category is *indirect utilization*, which involves not the use of research studies or tools per se but rather the use of *products* of research. Modern life abounds with this kind of utilization. We need only think of our use of TVs, computers, and medical technology to appreciate our reliance on products of this kind. In social work, indirect utilization involves use of theories, practice models, or procedures that have been produced or shaped by research activities. Thus the practitioner who employs a form of social skills training that was itself shaped by a research process is utilizing research, albeit indirectly. Unlike other forms of utilization, indirect utilization requires no direct exposure to research. The practitioner's interface is not with the research itself but with the practice approach based on it.

Although indirect utilization is probably more common than any other kind and preferable to nonutilization, it may be less than ideal. Practitioners with knowledge of the research underlying an intervention model are likely to use that model in a more discriminating way than practitioners who do not (Rosen 1994). It is better for practitioners to be conceptual users—that is to take into account the empirical foundations of the methods they use—rather than simply to use the methods because they have passed a research litmus test.

In social work practice, these different forms of utilization interact over time to produce effects that are difficult to trace precisely. The dynamics can be best understood if one adopts a systemic view of the professional social work community, a community consisting of line practitioners, supervisors, program administrators, agency executives, researchers, educators, consultants, students, and so on, who interact through such media as publications, conferences, workshops, committee meetings, classes, consultations, and supervisory sessions.

This system draws on the broad domain of research and research-based practice methods in the social sciences and the helping professions. Although little is known about how this system processes these research products, we suggest that conceptual and indirect modes of utilization are the prevalent forms. It may be true that practitioners seldom turn to research studies to inform their practice, but their practice may be more influenced by research than is commonly thought—through what they learned in graduate school, through their use of empirical practice methods, through books and articles that draw on research, through program directors and supervisors who themselves are influenced by such literature, and through data generated by their agencies.

It is our thesis that these forms of utilization, often indirect and secondary, are cumulative and are beginning to make an imprint on direct social work services, modest as that imprint may yet be. As might be imagined, distortions of the truth are commonplace in these processes, and it is difficult to separate good from bad utilization. We must understand this complex processing, however, if we are to comprehend how research is utilized in social work practice.

Meanwhile we can make use of strategies to enhance research utilization. One approach is to enable service providers to become better users. These strategies might emphasize closer working relationships between providers and researchers. As utilization studies have suggested, agency staff members are more likely to use research that relates to immediate problems, is concerned with the effectiveness of program elements rather than overall effectiveness, and fits with their own fund of knowledge (Leviton and Boruch 1980; McNeece, DiNitto, and Johnson 1983).

Another approach would be to place greater stress on methodological and indirect utilization, at the same time trying to impart to practitioners the intellectual tools to be able to critically appraise the research foundations of what they are utilizing. Increased use of empirical practice would be one means of promoting these kinds of utilization. Another would be more reliance on research-based theory and intervention methods in practice courses in schools of social work (Task Force on Social Work Research 1991).

2   Generation of Inquiry

Research starts with a gap in understanding, with some sort of inquiry to fill that gap. The director of a program wonders about the changing needs of homeless women. A practitioner questions the effectiveness of including a child's sister in treatment. The policy analyst ponders how to differentiate parents who abuse their children from those who do not. In seeking answers to these questions, the empirical practitioner uses an intellectual process that is similar whether the inquiry involves formal theory-testing studies or quick efforts to gather knowledge for practice decisions. This chapter discusses the process of developing an inquiry: the contextual importance of theory, developing a research problem, ensuring that it is a useful problem, developing hypotheses or research questions to guide the research, and linking the concepts to variables suitable for the particular inquiry.

Theory

In a practice profession such as social work, inquiry begins with the need to generate knowledge to inform practice, whether that knowledge only guides efforts in an immediate situation or is added to the pool available to the field as a whole. But to be useful for this purpose, knowledge must be organized into coherent systems of ideas or theories. Knowledge may be thought of as providing the raw material from which theories are made.

An example will perhaps make this distinction clearer, as well as provide an introduction to our conception of theory. It has been found that clients want more advice than social workers usually provide (Davis 1975; Ewalt and Kutz 1976; Reid and Shapiro 1969). However, it is well known that clients frequently do not follow the advice they are given. Let us assume that these observations constitute pieces of knowledge. As disparate pieces, their value would be limited—in fact, they seem contradictory. They become more useful when organized into a system of ideas or theory. In the present case it can be theorized that clients want advice, usually more than they are given (even though they may not agree with it or may not use it), because advice seems to stimulate their own thinking about alternative actions that they might take to lessen their difficulties

As the example has shown, theory attempts to organize knowledge into thought systems by which reality can be better understood. Although the example illustrates the essential difference between knowledge and theory— and how theory may be formed from knowledge—it does not give the sense of a fully developed theory. One might begin to build such a theory, however, by incorporating additional pieces of knowledge about the giving and taking of advice in social work practice. For example, the theory might need to account for the finding (in one study) that professional social workers made greater use of advice than peer counselors (Smith, Tobin, and Toseland 1992). One would also soon wish to make distinctions between different types of advice and advice-giving and attempt to identify different consequences stemming from use of each.

As the example makes clear, theory is not the opposite of "fact," contrary to the popular distinction. Rather, theory organizes fact or knowledge into systems. It is true, however, that theory may contain hypotheses that have not yet been tested or verified. Such hypotheses may be derived (inferred) from knowledge incorporated in the theory or may be added to provide a more coherent system of explanation.

Formal Theory and Theory in Use

Theory is not limited to formal theories recorded on the printed page. Scratch any social worker and you will find a theoretician. A practitioner's perspectives about people and practice may be informed by theories in print (or formal theories), but each practitioner puts it together in a personal way with many modifications and additions growing out of professional and personal experience. This "theory in use" (Argyris and Schon 1974) is what actually guides practice; it is often also called "practice wisdom." In a practice profession, it is the theory in use that is critical because it is what influences practice. Often, however, it is not spelled out well enough to guide more than the individual practitioner who has developed it. To be useful to others as well, the theory in use needs to be explicated and shared. Much exploratory and descriptive research on practice, including social work's rich tradition of case studies, are in fact attempts to define and communicate theory in use so that it informs others and can be included in the conceptual frameworks that constitute formal theory. Indeed, one professional obligation acknowledged in the NASW Code of Ethics (1995) is contributing to theory through disseminating the social worker's pieces of knowledge and theory in use.

Definitional and Explanatory Functions

In general, then, a theory is a system of concepts and hypotheses that attempt to define (definitional role) or explain and predict phenomena (explanatory role). In its definitional role, theory organizes units of knowledge. It provides connective tissue that unites disparate elements of what is presumed to be true. This organization of knowledge serves functions that are essential to practitioners' efforts to comprehend and influence the realities with which they must deal.

At a basic level, theory provides a coherent way of defining and ordering complex events. In performing this "definitional" function, theory presents sets of concepts and terms that enable the practitioner to comprehend and describe aspects of reality that otherwise might be difficult to order or that might escape attention altogether. Thus Watzlawick, Beavin, and Jackson (1967), communication theorists, developed the notion that any interpersonal communication has both a "content" and "relationship" aspect—that is, it "not only conveys information, but . . . at the same time it imposes behavior" (p. 51). If a wife unexpectedly announces to her husband that they are going to the Lucas's for dinner on Friday, her message has "content" (concerning plans for Friday) but also reflects on their relationship (that she appears to assume a controlling position in social matters). These concepts help us examine communication processes in a systematic way and, more specifically, alert us to less obvious, but vital, facets of those processes (the relationship aspects). In this case, however, the function of theory here is definitional—no hypotheses that might explain or predict communication are contained in the distinction. Knowing that a wife controls social matters will not predict dinner arrangements, nor does the message about Friday dinner by itself explain their relationship.

Theory becomes potentially more useful if it can produce hypotheses that explain or predict events. In an earlier example a theory was developed containing a hypothesis that explained why clients might seek advice but not use it. Explanatory or causal hypotheses are at the heart of theories that practitioners find most valuable, since such hypotheses provide the "whys" of problems and behavior and the rationale for intervention. The thoughtful practitioner intervenes in a particular way because there is reason to suppose that the intervention will be effective. The "reason to suppose" is derived from a causal hypothesis existing in some form of theoretical structure. Thus, a practitioner who points out to the client the consequences of the client's behavior is being guided by a hypothesis that such awareness will have an impact on the client's behavior.

To say that a theory has an explanatory function says nothing about its actual power to explain. A theory is explanatory to the extent it contains causal hypotheses. Whether or not those hypotheses prove to be correct is another matter. While one may refer to the validity of a theory, it is perhaps more accurate to assess a theory in relation to its capacity to generate hypotheses that are confirmed when tested. In these terms a good theory is one that generates valid hypotheses.

Most explanatory theories that social workers use are rich in causal hypotheses, but relatively few of these hypotheses have been rigorously tested and, of those that have, even fewer have been consistently supported. In fact, with some of these theories—psychoanalytic theory is a prime example—it proved difficult even to extract hypotheses amenable to empirical testing.

Practice Theory

Of central interest to the profession is social work practice theory, which consists of hypotheses that guide the social worker's diagnostic and intervention activities. There are, of course, numerous practice theories in social work relating to different levels of practice (such as with families, groups, and communities), as well as systems theory which attempts to organize the different levels of practice. There are also many theoretical orientations (psychodynamic, cognitive-behavioral, family systems, and so on). Despite their variation, practice theories are similar in function. At their core are explanatory hypotheses that predict that certain kinds of interventions will result in certain changes in certain areas (personality, behaviors, support systems, and so on).

As can be surmised, practice theory organizes the knowledge base that underlies the practice principles, methods, models, interventions that social workers use. Thus, the hypothesis that replacing distorted thoughts about oneself with positive coping statements will reduce perfectionist behaviors (Ferguson and Rodway 1994) serves as the base for a practice principle or method that can be used with clients who have such problems. Note that practice theory serves as a base for technology but that practice theory and technology are not the same. In essence, practice theory says,"If X is done, Y will follow"; technology tells us "do X to achieve Y." As we move from theory to technology, we introduce desirable goals or values that convert "what we expect to happen" into "how to bring about what we want to happen."

Practice theory, then, occupies a pivotal role in social work. To be used in professional activities, theories from other domains need to be translated into practice theory, which in turn can be translated into practice technology. In the preceding example, cognitive theory states that beliefs about one's-self affect one's behavior. From this, we can hypothesize that A will lead to B (that changing one's thoughts will reduce the desire to be perfect and hence will reduce perfectionist behaviors). Then, to translate that practice theory into technology, we must construct principles and methods that state in effect "do A to achieve B." (To reduce perfectionist behaviors, the practitioner must change the way the client thinks about him or herself by using techniques of cognitive restructuring.)

The development of practice theory should command, we think, a first-order priority in social work research. There needs to be greater emphasis on the study of the impact of different kinds of interventions on different kinds of problems and populations. The development of theories in other domains, such as theories of human behavior and social organization, should be left largely to social scientists. The concern of social workers should be to apply such theories to social work problems. By the same token, study of social work practice should be conducted not simply to test bits of technology, although that is important, but also to inform a practice theory that may be helpful in identifying methods with a wide range of effective application.

Developing a Problem for Research

The first step in any research endeavor is developing a problem area for the research. As we have noted, research starts with a gap in understanding: a missing piece of knowledge, an inability to describe or explain coherently, or a desire to explain phenomena. At a pragmatic level, most research starts with a question or idea that intrigues the social worker: A practitioner asks, where should I intervene in this case? How will I know when to end with these clients? A social work student asks, what type of field placement will give me the best experience working with families? What will help me get a job? An evaluator asks, does requiring welfare recipients to work get them off welfare rolls? Does rehearsing skills like self-presentation really help the client in the real world, in a real job interview? And the scholar asks, which theory best explains why some adolescents engage in sexual activity—differential association theory (what their friends do), or social learning theory (what behaviors are reinforced?)?

Starting with an intriguing question, the potential researcher must define and explicate the problem until it is clear, delimited, and researchable. Because the research problem sets the stage for all the rest of the research process, it is essential to gain clarity early. Yet defining a problem is rarely straightforward, and often the investigator ends up in a very different place from the puzzling point that started the inquiry. Still, the process can be outlined simply enough: start with an interesting idea, find out what is known about it (including what people mean by it!), and define what is not known. Like any learning or creative process, it involves expanding one's view to incorporate new material and associations, then narrowing to a synthesized focus.

Most investigators begin by talking over ideas with colleagues—fellow investigators, other students, practitioners in the agency—batting ideas around until something begins to crystallize. A second, more formal step is conducting a literature review, discovering how others have conceptualized the problem, how they have defined the critical factors, what areas seem to be related. At this stage, one is trying to expand one's perception of the area, to assess its scope and complexity, to put the intriguing question in context. In doing so, the investigator begins to define the concepts central to the problem area. The concepts are the link between the investigator's interest and the profession's shared knowledge and theory. Pragmatically, these concepts are the keywords used in a bibliographic search, the access to what others have already explored (for further discussion of bibliographic search, see appendix 1).

Written material and discussion also convey how others have defined the key concepts, their operational definitions. When the investigator begins concentrating on the definitions, checking out the clever and pedantic ways people have defined their variables, then it is usually time to narrow the focus and to begin the formulation of the specific problem area. As will be discussed shortly, the process of refining the problem continues until the investigator has a clear explication that includes variables, definitions, hypothesized relations, and so on. In the process, the investigator continually assesses the problem against considerations for a useful research problem, against the literature, and against the initial starting point. Eventually, a working statement of the problem is developed, and this statement becomes the cornerstone for the research procedures in the investigator's study.

Considerations for a Useful Research Problem

Several considerations affect the quality and utility of a research problem in social work. We assume that the problem meets a crucial consideration of being of interest to the investigator. Although it is hard to discern from the literature, since they did not get published, a great many research studies end moldering in the "get to later" closet because the investigator could not sustain interest in them. Assuming, then, that the investigator has sufficient curiosity, some considerations are: whether enough is known, relevance to social work, importance, feasibility, and ethics. Even when a particular inquiry does not interest a reader of published research, these considerations are fair ways to evaluate the significance of a study's problem.

Current Knowledge

A first consideration is whether enough is yet known. In some areas, there has been a great deal of research and one is hard-put to say what another study might add. For example, much is known about people's reactions after loss and trauma, students' satisfaction with field placements, or adolescents' difficulty in projecting consequences of their actions. An exploratory or descriptive study in one of these areas is unlikely to add substantially to knowledge. Before beginning a study, it is essential to get a sense of what is known through literature searches, in both social work and other fields (where much of the descriptive research about human behavior is conducted).

In social work, however, more is unknown than known, especially about practice intervention and theory. For example, much less is known about effective interventions in grieving, what aspects of field instruction help students attain professional skills, or how to get teenagers to stop and think before they leap. Further, even when intervention research has been conducted, there may be question about the clients or situations in which the intervention is effective. For example, much initial research on family therapy was limited to well-educated middle-class families with relatively stable relations. Recent research demonstrates its application with a much broader range of people and problems, including schizophrenia, alcoholism, drug abuse, autism, chronic physical illness (Pinsof, Wynne, and Hambright 1996) and delinquency (Smith and Stern 1997). The importance of replication, with systematic variation in sample, situation, and so on, cannot be underestimated.

Relevance to Social Work

A second consideration for a useful research problem is its relevance to social work practice. Problems relevant to social work include a very broad range of issues related to human social behavior and social welfare, including incidence, etiology, prevention, and alleviation of social problems; content, creation, implementation, and effects of social policies; and types, processes, and outcomes of social intervention at levels from individual to community.

Despite the breadth, there are clearly problems that fall outside the domain of social work research. It is unlikely a social worker would be interested in the effects of agricultural crop rotation on production of food crops, or be competent to carry out research on retroviruses, as important as those topics are to society.

As discussed earlier, we put a premium on problems that are unique to social work and that contribute knowledge for social work practice. If other disciplines provide research on incidence or basic development, social work should "borrow" that knowledge (as it has done traditionally) and focus its research on neglected areas and on intervention. For example, the incidence, transmission, and prevention of HIV/AIDS are well-researched in other fields such as medicine and public health. Social work's contribution is in its focus on the neglected systems aspects—reactions of partners, for example—and on interventions that will alleviate interpersonal distress or increase compliance with preventive measures. For example, Greene, Kropf, and MacNair examined what happens to family structure and organization when a family member was diagnosed with HIV (1994), while Wiener and her colleagues evaluated the effect of telephone support groups on isolation among family members of HIV-infected children (1993).

Importance

Another consideration is whether the research problem is important enough to warrant the effort, what Rubin and Babbie call "so what?"(1993). What difference would the answer to the question make?

Clearly, research on alleviation of poverty addresses an important social issue, while research on whether clients are impressed by diplomas displayed on the wall is of less immediate relevance. The emphasis on "so what" is a characteristic of applied research, as opposed to basic research that cannot be applied immediately and may be undertaken purely for intellectual curiosity. In a profession such as social work, an important part of the "so what" question is whether the results will be of use—to clients, the agency, others. At times, investigators may focus too much on their own agendas or national issues and overlook projects that are more timely and relevant to practice needs (Schilling et al. 1988). Thus, while a needs assessment will not answer crucial questions about the prevention of clients' difficulties, it can benefit the agency's clients if service is then redirected to the greatest need.

The issue of significance is more complex when one tries to balance significance with resources. Most investigators do not have the resources for a comprehensive study of means to reduce poverty, yet they can make important contributions through small studies of readily available subjects, such as John Belcher's study of poor and homeless individuals visiting a health care facility (1991). Belcher and his colleagues spent three months as "researchers, volunteers, and concerned participants within the homeless community" (1994:127). They discovered three phases of homelessness: poor persons living with friends or relatives, individuals who were homeless for a relatively short time and still identified themselves as part of the mainstream of the community, and long-term homeless who were distanced from the mainstream community. These findings have important implications for social policy, for example, preventing homelessness by offering assistance to poor individuals who live with others but are not yet on the street.

Social workers are beginning to emulate other disciplines such as psychology and sociology and are learning to manage and fund large-scale projects that address important questions, such as Hogarty and Anderson's psycho-educational approach for families of the mentally ill to reduce relapse (Hogarty 1993), Schinke's prevention of substance abuse (1991), or Marx, Test, and Stein's Assertive Community Treatment for community-based treatment of mental illness (McGrew et al. 1995; Stein and Test 1980; Test 1980, 1996). But social workers also have a tradition of research that contributes at many levels of resource availability, from a practitioner conducting a series of single-case studies to agency evaluation of alcohol prevention programs to multiagency collaboration on prevention of school drop-out. Important contributions are possible whatever resources are available.

Feasibility

A fourth consideration is feasibility: given the restraints, is it possible to conduct the research? Potential constraints include ability to measure key variables, access to subjects or data, time involved, cooperation of others, and financial cost.

ACCEPTABLE MEASUREMENT An often overlooked constraint is whether the main variables can be measured in acceptable, ethical ways. For example, in a community organization project, is there an accepted instrument to measure the power of various actors such as the mayor, alderman, businessmen's association, or tenants' organization? In studying trauma, can the level of psychic distress be measured without increasing it through the measurement process? Often, important concepts cannot be measured directly and there may be question about the validity of indicators, for example, alcoholics' self-reports of drinking behavior or abusive partners' reports of violence.

ACCESS Another constraint may be difficulty of access to participants or data. Agencies struggling to meet their own institutional goals may be reluctant to allow access to their clients unless they can see how the research helps them meet their goals. Or agencies may need to respond to their constituents; for example, elementary schools are concerned about topics that upset parents, such as sex and drug education. Sometimes the desired participants are not easily available. Where, for example, should one recruit successful high school dropouts? Victims of incest who have not acknowledged being victims? Children of intact alcoholic families?

Similarly, access to existing data may be difficult because of agencies' reluctance to release it, often because of political considerations. What guarantees does an agency have that the investigator will not use the data to place it in a bad light? Or, existing data may not provide the type of information the investigator wanted. Case records may focus on information needed for insurance billing and progress reports, rather than on the investigator's interest, for example, the client's social system. And existing data are often incomplete; social workers, for example, are notorious for incomplete case records and notes.

TIME Another constraint to feasiblity is the time involved in a study. The time can be considerable, and is often underestimated. Time includes not only the hours the investigator (or hired assistants) put in, but the weeks involved in waiting for others to respond. The researcher's time includes planning the study, developing instruments, gathering data (by interviewing participants, reading case records, handing out questionnaires, or whatever), analyzing the data, and writing the results—all more or less time-consuming depending on the scope of the study and the skills of the researcher. Procedures that require waiting for others to respond include securing permission to conduct a study from agency personnel; approval by the local panel for protection of human subjects; recruitment of subjects particularly when new applicants for service are involved; responses to mailed questionnaires; and, once a manuscript is written, waiting for reviewers to critique it. An example that involves both the time of the investigator and time waiting is mail surveys: To get the largest response rate, Dillman (1978) recommends sending follow-up questionnaires one, three, and seven weeks after the initial mailing. An investigator who follows this procedure will have to wait at least nine weeks after the first mailing to be sure that most responses have been returned.

COOPERATION Another aspect of feasiblity is cooperation of others. Agency cooperation is often necessary for access to subjects and data. Such access requires convincing staff that the investigator is credible, that the research is useful to the agency, and that human subjects will be adequately protected. If agency staff are needed to refer clients or help gather data, they too will need to see the purpose and relevance, as well as have an incentive to cooperate. In one study, staff remembered to complete research forms after each client contact only when an investigator was present to remind them (Fortune and Reid 1973).

The cooperation of subjects is of course essential. Cooperation is easily gained when the topic is intriguing to subjects, for example, case analogs about what a practitioner should do with a withdrawn client, or a follow-up of clients' successes. Subject cooperation may be considerably more difficult if the topic is threatening, such as inquiries about child mistreatment or substance abuse. Many clients with problems of interest to social workers have good reason to distrust representatives of social welfare, for example, welfare recipients, the homeless, or court-mandated clients. On the other side of reluctance to cooperate, and sometimes as difficult to handle, is eagerness to please and say what the investigator would like to hear, called "social desirability."

COST A final aspect of feasibility is financial cost. Costs may include duplicating questionnaires, fees to use standard instruments such as McCarney's Attention Deficit Disorders Evaluation Scale (ADDES)(1995), postage for mail questionnaires, long-distance telephone calls, travel to interviews, payments to subjects for their time, computer analysis, or special equipment such as tape or video recorders. Many investigators trade off their own time for cost, for example, by hiring interviewers, coders, or data analysts to assist with the research. Or, investigators may seek funding from foundations or the government to cover such costs. Research conducted under such auspices is typically broader and richer in scope than unfunded research. However, because seeking funding is itself arduous and time-consuming, a new investigator or an agency-based investigator with delimited research questions may invest his or her time.

Ethics

A fifth consideration for a useful research problem is ethics. Is the study itself ethical? Blatantly unethical (harmful) research such as Naxi scientists' experiments to determine physical reactions to intense cold, or American doctors' attempts to chart the course of syphilis (the Tuskeegee Study) are fortunately relatively rare. In the United States, in reaction to such excesses, federal guidelines were developed to minimize the risk of harm from research, and most institutions have boards that review research proposals for procedures that protect human subjects. In social work, issues to consider in assessing whether a study is ethical include potentially harmful labeling of people, causing serious psychological distress, or withholding needed treatment.

However, it is often difficult to assess whether a study violates ethical guidelines. For example, in the Seattle Atlantic Street project, acting-out boys were identified as at risk for delinquency and given special services (Berleman and Steinbrun 1967). Today, we might question whether it was ethical to label children who, as yet, had not committed a delinquent act. Similarly, Milgram was interested in why German citizens did not protest the Nazi atrocities (1963; 1965). He studied susceptibility to authoritarianism by having a white-coated scientist ask American men to administer shocks to a learner who made mistakes. The shocks increased in intensity until they were "lethal." Despite the pain and protests of the learners, most subjects continued to administer the shocks until they were giving a lethal dose. In fact, the shocks were fake and the "learners" were confederates of the researcher. Was it ethical to deceive the subjects in this way? to create the psychological stress of making a lethal decision? Was the knowledge produced—that most men will indeed obey an authority figure and "kill" another person—worth the deception and stress to subjects? Would it be ethical to induce test anxiety among students, in order to study methods for dealing with test anxiety?

The knottiest ethical issue is undoubtedly giving or withholding treatment from one group of subjects while another group receives treatment, a common research practice that enhances confidence in the results of a study. For example, Dhooper and Schneider (1995) tested means of detecting and reducing child abuse through an educational program presented by puppets in some schools but not others. The programs were effective in increasing young children's knowledge of abuse and what to do about it. Was it ethical to withhold the program, which the children enjoyed, from some classrooms in order to make the test? What about the possibility of harming the children who saw the puppet shows, making them more anxious or fearful of their parents?

Formulating Hypotheses and Questions

Once a research problem has been conceptualized and deemed useful, the next step is developing a hypothesis to be tested or a formal question to be answered. A hypothesis is a tentative statement about the relationship among concepts; it requires some knowledge about the concepts and a theory to link them. A research question is a more general inquiry, before enough is known to generate hypotheses. We consider hypotheses first and in greater detail, since the principles of hypothesis construction include those of question formulation.

Hypotheses

A hypothesis is a conjecture about reality. It is a statement that one has reason to believe is true but for which adequate evidence is lacking.

Social work practitioners engage continually in hypothesis formulation in their day-to-day work. A program planner predicts (hypothesizes) that at least a quarter of the elderly citizens in the community would utilize a minibus service. A practitioner in a residential treatment center speculates (hypothesizes) that periodic expressions of aggression among members of a therapeutic group are related to flareups of overt conflict among center staff. Hypothesis formulation involves the same process in practice as it does in research studies. The chief difference is that these processes are usually carried out more deliberately in research than in practice.

SINGLE-VARIABLE AND MULTIVARIABLE HYPOTHESES These examples illustrate two forms that a hypothesis can take. In the first example, a certain level is predicted for a single factor or variable—the proportion of elderly clients who would use a service. In the second example, the hypothesis asserts a relation between variables—the conflict among staff members and the aggression expressed by members of a therapeutic group. The distinction is clearer if one thinks of the number of variables that are needed to test the hypothesis. In the first case, data are needed on the proportion of elderly citizens using the minibus service; it is a one-variable hypothesis. In the second case, data are needed on the occurrence of both staff conflict and expressions of aggression; it is a two-variable hypothesis.

Since most hypotheses are concerned with relations among different phenomena, hypotheses containing one variable are not common. In fact, some research methodologists require that at least two variables be present before a statement is considered to be a hypothesis (Kerlinger 1985). Although the notion of a single-variable hypothesis may strike some researchers as akin to the sound of one hand clapping, the notion does have value. Many predictions assume this form and do so legitimately. However, because of their greater importance and complexity, we will focus on hypotheses expressing relations between two or more variables.

HYPOTHESES OF ASSOCIATION AND DIFFERENCE Such two-variable hypotheses may be expressed as "hypotheses of association" and "hypotheses of difference" (Black and Champion 1976). In a hypothesis of association, one predicts that two variables "go together," or as one varies, the other varies in a systematic way. For example, one might predict that prolonged periods of maternal separation have damaging psychological effects on infants. A hypothesis of association might state that length of maternal separation is associated with ability to differentiate self from others. In a hypothesis of difference, one predicts that two (or more) groups or categories will differ in some systematic way. For example, one might compare a group of mothers who did not separate from their infants with another group who did. The hypothesis of difference might be that the children separated from their mothers would show less self-differentiation than the children who remained with their mothers.

Although expressed in the form of differences between groups, the hypothesis still asserts that maternal separation is related to psychological damage. Thus, two-variable relational hypotheses can be expressed in sentences that are variations of the following:

1. X will be associated with Y
   (Greater involvement of children's social systems will be associated with more durable outcome.)
2. Group A will differ from Group B in respect to Y
   (Children whose practitioners involved their teachers in treatment planning will continue completing homework longer than those whose teachers were not involved.)

Hypotheses predicting change in a single individual or group over time is basically a variation of the hypothesis of difference format ((2) above). For example, Jensen (1994) hypothesized that a woman would decrease her level of depression during treatment. The weekly level of depression for the three weeks before treatment began was compared to the seven weeks during which treatment took place. In other words, her hypothesis took the form: the woman's weekly depression levels during the no-treatment phase will differ from her depression levels during the treatment phase.

Hypotheses of association and hypotheses of difference can be thought of as different sides of the same coin, different ways to express a relationship. The form of the hypothesis has implications for testing the hypothesis, particularly the measurement and data analysis strategies. Consequently, in the process of developing a research problem and hypothesis, the final form of the hypothesis is often developed late, when other aspects of the research study are determined, and the final hypothesis often differs substantially from initial statements.

Often the researcher's predictions will involve more than one independent variable. In such cases the investigator may form a single hypothesis that asserts that some combination of factors will be associated with the dependent variable. Alternatively the researcher may put his or her predictions into separate hypotheses. For example in their study of burn-out among child protective workers, Drake and Yadama (1996:181) formulated several hypotheses. Two of them predicted that: (1) "emotionally exhausted workers will be more likely to leave their jobs"; (2) "depersonalized workers will be more likely to leave their jobs." Although these hypotheses may have been combined into a single statement (hypothesis), there is an advantage in keeping them separate. If one prediction is confirmed and the other not, it is clearer to say in discussing the findings that the evidence supported hypothesis 1 but not 2 than it is to say that the hypothesis was "partially supported."

ONE- AND TWO-TAILED HYPOTHESES Another way in which hypotheses differ is whether they predict what the systematic differences will be. One can hypothesize that client outcome will be associated with extent of social support network, or one can hypothesize that better client outcome will be associated with a larger support network. The first statement, which predicts only that there will be an association, is a nondirectional or two-tailed hypothesis. It is predicting that clients with larger support networks may have a worse outcome *or* a better outcome than clients with a smaller support network. We don't know which: supporters may interfere with attempts to change, or they may be a resource to resolve the situation; either is possible. The second statement, which predicts that better outcome "goes with" more support, is a directional or one-tailed hypothesis. The prediction rules out the possibility that clients with larger support networks will do worse and predicts that they will do better only, hence the one-tail or direction.

As we will see in chapter 11, the direction of the hypothesis has implications for how we assess the results. In essence, if one makes a directional hypothesis and the data then show that the opposite seems to be true, one cannot backtrack and say "oops, I want to change the hypothesis"; one can only admit that the hypothesis was false. Consequently, one-tailed hypotheses are normally reserved for situations in which there is preliminary evidence of the direction of association or difference.

EXAMPLES OF HYPOTHESES

Association, two-tailed: Clients' readiness to change varies with duration of the problem.
Association, one-tailed: The shorter the time clients have endured problems, the more ready they will be for change.

Difference, two-tailed: Families who receive psychoeducation about mental illness will differ from families who receive supportive family counseling in their attitudes toward the mentally ill family member.

Difference, one-tailed: Families who receive psychoeducation about mental illness will have more positive, accepting attitudes toward their mentally ill family member than families who receive supportive family counseling.

Criteria for "Good" Hypotheses

There are two main criteria of "good" hypotheses: testability and likelihood of confirmation. The criterion of testability requires that a hypothesis be stated in terms indicating how an empirical test could be conducted. The language of the hypothesis should be translatable into research operations; one can develop empirical or operational definitions for the terms of the hypothesis and it should be clear that a decision to accept or reject the hypothesis can be made on the basis of data obtained.

Hypotheses may fall short on the testability criterion for a variety of reasons. Two of the more common will be considered: statements of values and ambiguity. Trying to determine how an empirical test could be conducted may reveal that an "hypothesis" is really a statement of a practice principle or a point of view that cannot be accepted or rejected through an empirical test. Consider, for example, the assertion that "use of a systems perspective is essential to understand where to intervene effectively with juvenile delinquents." Although one might study the effect of practitioners' theoretical frameworks on their assessments, it is not possible to develop a way of testing for their "essentialness." What is essential, needed, desirable, and so forth, are in themselves questions of judgment or value that cannot be decided by data.

A second common error in constructing testable hypotheses is ambiguity. If an hypothesis contains terms that are too ambiguous or value laden, it may be hard to develop adequate empirical or operational definitions. Thus it may be hypothesized that marriages between partners at the same level of maturity will be more stable than marriages in which partners are at different levels of emotional maturity. Whereas acceptable empirical referents might be found for "stability," they may be difficult to identify for "emotional maturity" because of the multiple meanings and value connotations of that term. As Black and Champion (1976:139) observe, hypotheses may be evaluated "in terms of the amount of information they provide about phenomena." In the present example, the hypothesis provides so little real information that it is difficult to proceed with the specification of terms.

A second criterion for evaluating a hypothesis concerns the likelihood of its being confirmed when tested. To be worth testing, a hypothesis should have, as Ripple has observed (1960), an uncertain outcome. If an outcome is reasonably certain, there is little point in proceeding with a test. The hypothesis lacks interest because it is sure to be either accepted or rejected.

A variant of the uninteresting or "fail-safe" hypothesis is quasi-tautological statements, in which variables are by definition overlapping. Imagine, for example, a hypothesis: in bureaucratically organized social agencies there will be greater conflict among staff over formal division of labor than in social agencies that are not bureaucratically organized. Suppose, further, that among indicators used to identify bureaucratic organizations one, finds the "extent of formal division of labor." Support for the hypothesis as stated could be expected since bureaucratically organized agencies would have, by definition, greater division of labor and have greater opportunity for conflict. Such tautologies, like practice principles, may masquerade as hypotheses. With obvious tautologies, the statement is in fact testable, but it is not a hypothesis!

Sometimes the overlap between variables may not become apparent until methods for measuring them are examined. For example, James Forte and colleagues (1996) predicted that spousal abuse and social power in the marital relationship were associated. However, the measures of spousal abuse and power contained similar items. Spousal abuse included, for example, "my partner orders me around," ". . . demands obedience," ". . . acts like I'm his servant" (Hudson and McIntosh 1981, cited by Corcoran and Fischer 1987); social power included: who has more power, gets his or her way in disagreements, can force the other to do something (perceived social power, as described by Forte et al. 1996).

A more subtle version is a variation of the hypothesis that "reinforcement will increase some behavior (e.g., homework completion or use of appropriate social skills)." Since reinforcement is defined as an addition to the environment that will increase the rate of behavior, such statements are totally circular, assert nothing, and hence are really not hypotheses at all.

At the other end of the spectrum of ability to be confirmed are hypotheses that are almost certain to fail. Typically, such hypotheses occur when the study is too small or crude to detect the effects that are predicted. For example, suppose the hypothesis predicted that practitioner experience levels and client improvement were associated in a sample of twenty cases. The practitioners had between two and five years of experience, and "outcome" was a global rating of client functioning. Although it seems logical that experience might improve practitioners' effectiveness, the hypothesis is not likely to be upheld in this study in view of other factors that might affect improvement—the narrow range of practitioner experience, the imprecise measure of client outcome, the small number of cases, and prior research that practitioner experience is not a potent variable. As this example illustrates, it may be difficult to assess hypotheses without knowing something about the phenomena to be studied, the proposed method of testing, and the fate of similar hypotheses that have been tested in a similar manner.

Moreover, one should be reluctant to dismiss a hypothesis because it goes against the grain of what appears to be obvious. The history of social work is full examples of assumptions or practice edicts that, when finally tested, proved to be untenable: that the mother's interaction with the child causes schizophrenia ("schizophregenic mothers"); that giving advice to clients is futile or counterproductive; that group treatment is more cost-effective than individual treatment; and so on. In short, development of a good hypothesis relies on knowledge of the relevant theory and its empirical support (i.e., a good literature review).

HINTS FOR WRITING GOOD TWO-VARIABLE HYPOTHESES

Is the hypothesis complete: Are there two variables?
- NO: Clients benefit from treatment.
- YES: Length of treatment is associated with amount of improvement in social skills.
- YES: Practitioner empathy is associated with client self-disclosure.
- YES: Alcoholics confronted about their denial are more likely to stay in treatment than alcoholics who are not confronted.

Are the categories of the variables and the comparisons clear?
- NO: Girls will have high self-esteem.
- YES: Girls will have higher self-esteem than boys.
- YES: Girls who attend a skill-building class will have higher self-esteem than girls who do not attend.

Are the variables specific? Is it clear how they could be measured?
- NONSPECIFIC: Removal of a child from a family reported for maltreatment is related to type of abuse.
- SPECIFIC: A child's placement status (in home or removed from the home) will vary by type of abuse (physical abuse, sexual abuse or child neglect).
- NONSPECIFIC: Social workers who take into account the environment will be of more help to clients than those who focus only on the individual.
- SPECIFIC: Social workers who read a case summary that gives information about the client's family and work situations will include more envi-

ronmental factors in their written assessments of the case than workers
who read a summary that includes only developmental information about
the client.

Does the hypothesis avoid statements of causality?

- NO: Attending a parent education group makes parents better able to handle stress.
- YES: Parents who attend a parent education group will score lower on parenting stress than parents who read a manual about child-rearing.
- NO: Providing support groups for caretakers of ill elderly will reduce health care costs.
- YES: The costs for medical treatment for patients whose caretakers attend support groups will be lower than the costs for those whose caretakers do not attend support groups.

Research Questions

Research questions are used when not enough is known to formulate a reasonable hypothesis. Often, in social work research, not enough is known about the phenomena to be studied to justify the formulation of hypotheses. Or, convincing theory about the supposed relations among variables may be lacking. What is more, there may not even be sufficient knowledge to identify and define relevant variables. Before hypotheses can be formed and tested, there may be need to describe phenomena of interest, to locate promising variables and to explore relations among them. This is when research questions are merited.

Like hypotheses, questions may be concerned with a single variable or with the relationship among two or more. Thus a program planner may ask "What proportion of discharged patients will remain in our aftercare program for the first year after discharge?" A single-variable is of interest: the proportion of discharged patients. In a two-variable question, the planner might combine this variable with another in a question such as,"What patient characteristics are associated with continuance in the aftercare program?" An even more specific question might be: "Is there a difference in continuance between patients who live with family members and those patients who live alone?" As can be seen, the first of these two-variable questions could not be restated in the form of a meaningful hypothesis, since the range of possible characteristics that might be associated with continuance is not specified. The second question could be recast as a hypothesis, *if* there were reason to suppose that the continuance rate would differ among groups.

The criteria presented earlier for good hypotheses may be applied to questions. A good research question is testable—it can be answered by collecting data—and is not already known, i.e., its answer cannot be foreseen prior to the collection of the data. Nevertheless, questions may be couched in terms that cannot be precisely defined at the outset, and this use is common because questions are so often used to organize inquiry about relatively unknown phenomena. As we shall see, this "open" definition of terms may be all that is possible at the beginning of inquiry; more precise definitions may need to wait until more is learned about the subject. Thus an investigator studying a new program might ask "What benefits do clients see in the program?" The term *benefit* may be broadly defined because the investigator may not be sure what clients will perceive as benefits. The openness of the initial definition may be carried through to "open-ended" questions asked of clients. Thus, clients might be asked to cite what they saw as benefits they received from the program.

In some forms of inquiry, initial questions serve as points of entry into a subject, with recognition that the questions may be radically altered or replaced by more interesting questions as inquiry proceeds. For example, in his participant observation study of shelters for homeless women, Liebow began with a general question that asked what was "the world of homelessness as homeless women see and experience it" (1993:1). As he went along, he "realized that another of my aims was to explain both to myself and others how these women remained human in the face of inhuman conditions" (1). This gave rise to more specific questions about their relation to work, family, service providers, and each other, and then to even more specific questions, such as how to secure a job without an address or telephone for employers to contacts, or how to be presentable for a job interview.

Hypotheses Versus Questions

When one can choose to use questions or hypotheses, what considerations help one decide which to use? As mentioned, if little is known about a phenomena, then a question must be used. However, when a relationship between two or more variables can be predicted on theoretical grounds, stating the relationship in the form of a hypothesis has certain advantages. The confirmation of a hypothesis provides stronger evidence for the existence of the relationship than answering a question about its existence in the affirmative.

For this reason, a predicted relationship needs to pass a less stringent statistical test when inferential statistics are used to evaluate the role of chance factors in producing an observed relationship. Although the logic of this decision making is taken up subsequently (chapter 11), we can note at this point that stating a relationship as a hypothesis has the practical advantage of requiring less proof to establish its existence. Moreover, confirming a hypothesis drawn from a theory increases the probability that other hypotheses in the theory are confirmable, since the hypothesis is part of a network of assertions related to a common pool of knowledge. Hence the successful test of a hypothesis derived from theory has greater implications for a system of ideas than answering research questions.

Finally, a study that is organized around hypotheses generally has a more definitive structure than one organized around questions. Hypotheses provide a bounded framework for inquiry because the study concentrates on tests of relationships; the scope of work is well demarcated at the outset. While specific questions such as "Is X greater than Y?" are also limited, open queries such as "What are the characteristics of X?" have few boundaries. It is often difficult to know when an open question has been satisfactorily answered or even how it may be best answered. As a consequence, the more open the question, the more difficult it may be to focus and limit inquiry.

The full advantages of hypothesis testing can be reaped, however, only when the investigator can use a theory that yields hypotheses with a good chance of being confirmed or hypotheses that are generally believed to be true. In the first instance, a successful test can advance knowledge building by providing direct empirical support for a relationship between variables and indirect support for a theory. In the second instance, a test can raise doubts about a set of accepted but questionable beliefs and thus stimulate a search for something better.

But if the theory does not yield likely hypotheses, the special advantages offered by hypothesis testing may be lost. In fact, concentrating on the test of specific hypotheses may be dysfunctional when relevant theory is poorly developed or when little is known about the area under investigation. Since hypotheses narrow the focus of inquiry, it is possible that, without adequate theory or knowledge as a guide, the investigator may "look in the wrong place" or at least overlook aspects of greater interest. For example, Liebow found that, like other people, most homeless women organized their lives around work— going to a job, looking for a job, or preparing for a job (1993). Had he assumed, as many people do, that homelessness is tantamount to unemployment, he might have missed a key structure in the women's lives, and one that kept them connected to mainstream society.

Explication of the Problem

Once the problem is formulated and tentative hypotheses or questions are developed, the process of explicating or specifying what is meant begins. Research problems consist of sentences that assert hypotheses to be tested or pose questions to be answered. These sentences contain terms or concepts that usually can be understood in many different ways. These concepts are abstractions or symbols that allow those using them to communicate about shared meanings. However, the particular meanings given these concepts in the investigation at hand need to be made clear through explication that links the concepts to the phenomena studied.

Levels of Abstraction

In quantitative approaches to research, the process of explication moves down a "ladder of abstraction" (Phillips 1985). Concepts first need to be understood at an abstract level, as part of the theory or system of ideas to which the problem is related. Explications at this level are variously referred to as "nominal," "conceptual," "constitutive," or "theoretical" definitions; we will call them nominal definitions. Sometimes concepts are expressly defined. Thus, in her study of how mothers' behavior influences children's ability to develop a sense of time, Norton defines *seriation* as "the ordering of events in a temporal sequence"(1993:86). In other instances, terms are clarified in the course of presenting the theoretical framework pertaining to the problem. For example, in defining her notions of social environment for learning disabled schoolchildren, Hepler (1994) describes play interactions, social skill development, and social status accorded by other children.

Whereas precise nominal definitions may be desirable, precision in initial definitions of concepts is not always possible. A certain amount of openness is not only inevitable but is preferable to premature closure. At the beginning of an investigation, the researcher may not have the necessary knowledge to develop exact definitions, and it may turn out that terms can be much better defined in the light of the data obtained by the study. As Kaplan observes, definitions should be regarded as "successive" rather than fixed, with strict definitions the culmination rather than the precondition of scientific inquiry (Kaplan 1964:77). This position does not justify unnecessary vagueness; rather it suggests that nominal definitions evolve as inquiry proceeds. Indeed, the whole process of problem formulation, developing hypotheses, and explicating concepts is ongoing, with continual feedback and modification, not linear as it may seem when presented on paper.

With a first approximation of the general meaning of the concepts in mind, the investigator pushes toward greater specificity. Terms used to define abstractions may in turn need to be spelled out, linking them directly to observable phenomena. If "outcome" is said to be change in communication between parents and children, one needs to consider what is meant by "communication."

The process leads to the development of the indicators or phenomena that will actually be measured. At the lowest rung of the ladder, parent-child communication may be defined in terms of such specific characteristics as interruptions, disparaging remarks, approving comments, and the like. Such indicators are then used as the basis for instruments. For example, a coding scheme might be used to analyze characteristics of parent-child communication from tape-recorded samples of dialogue.

The process of moving from the abstract to the concrete and ultimately to instruments for data collection and measurement is often referred to as developing an "operational definition." In contemporary usage, an operational definition generally refers to the more specific indicators employed in concept measurement. Thus, an investigator studying practitioner productivity may say that "productivity was operationally defined as the number of interviews conducted by practitioners per week." The operational definition includes both what is to be defined—productivity as number of interviews—and how it is to be defined—here, implicitly, by counting number of interviews.

In the process of spelling out or operationalizing concepts, the investigator must deal with definitions of phenomena at different levels of abstraction and must be concerned with how these levels relate to one another. Ideally one hopes to define clearly concepts contained in the research problem and to select indicators that accurately and comprehensively reflect the key meanings of those concepts. This ideal is seldom attained, however, since concepts often cannot be defined with a high degree of precision at the outset. Indicators are likely to tap only aspects of these concepts and to do so imperfectly. Moreover, the indicators selected may measure phenomena that fall outside the scope of the concept.

Suppose an investigator wishes to study aggressive behavior exhibited by children on the playground during school recess. A nominal definition of aggression might be "actions done with the apparent intent of injuring another person." The definition is obviously less than clear-cut. "Apparent intent" is vague, but how should it be further explicated? There are problems in defining aggression strictly in terms of overt behavior. A child who accidentally injures another is not seen as behaving aggressively, but a child who tries to punch a peer but misses would probably be regarded as having been aggressive. Further dilemmas are encountered in relation to the scope of the concept. Should verbal aggression be included? The investigator may wish to do so since insults that may hurt a person psychologically are normally seen as aggressive acts, even though it may be difficult to define verbal aggression with any degree of precision.

The chances are that whatever definitions were formed would omit actions that would be considered aggressive under the circumstances. Thus, certain gestures or verbal expressions that may seem innocuous to the investigator may be interpreted by the children as aggressive acts. On the other hand, the indicators may result in classifying actions as aggressive when under the circumstances they would not be considered as such. For example, one investigator found with great dismay that observers using the carefully worked out descriptions of acts of physical aggression (shoving, jumping on, grabbing, and so on) were dutifully reporting as "aggressive actions"—the normal behaviors of boys in a football game!

As the foregoing suggests, operational definitions may suffer from both underinclusiveness and overinclusiveness. Parts of the concept may be neglected in the indicators, but at the same time the indicators may be in error and cover phenomena that are not a part of the concept.

Such problems are to some degree inevitable and may not be resolvable. However, the investigator must be aware of their existence and consequences. A common pseudosolution is to move directly from concepts to measurements, pretty much bypassing the sticky business of theoretical definitions. Although such naive operationalism may lead to convenient measures and neat data, the resulting findings are often of questionable significance. What has been measured may not add up to much that is meaningful, because problems of meaning were not adequately addressed in the formulation of the problem.

In qualitative approaches, the process of definition usually works in reverse order: from the phenomena, the investigator attempts to make sense and define at ever-increasing levels of abstraction, ultimately arriving at hypotheses and theory. Such an undertaking may seem monumental: how does one make sense of unrelated, disparate bits of knowledge with no framework or context in which to understand them? One approach is grounded theory, which uses "the constant comparative method of analysis": one asks questions about phenomena and makes comparisons between different bits of data (Glaser and Strauss 1967; Strauss and Corbin 1990). Mizrahi and Abramson (1994:140) describe the process they used to develop a typology of physician–social worker collaboration: "We reviewed a sample of ten transcripts, scrutinizing the responses . . . to produce provisional concepts that fitted the data. . . . The essential meaning of each response and related responses was compared with those already reviewed until the properties of characteristics of the concept became apparent and saturation was reached and no new ideas were emerging." While still interviewing people, they began to notice patterns in such areas as involvement in the research interview, definitions of the social work role, and the importance accorded psychosocial issues in medical care. Their final typology of collaboration included notions that had not been considered before, such as breadth of role and inclusion of psychosocial intervention, as well as traditional ideas about collaboration such as who controls decision-making.

Variables

The creation of variables is a part of the process of putting terms into operational form. A variable is a concept (or part of a concept) that is actually studied in an investigation. As the name implies, a variable is an entity expected to vary or to take on different quantities or categories in the investigation. Variables may be either continuous or categorical. Age is a variable commonly expressed in continuous form, as is amount of agreement with a statement. Gender, as a variable, inevitably takes on two categories, male and female; while child maltreatment may be placed in three categories, physical abuse, sexual abuse, and neglect.

As a step in problem explication, the creation of variables isolates the specific factors that will be investigated. There may be one or more variables for each concept that is a focus of the study. When the concepts in the problem are clear-cut, variables can be derived directly from them, such as gender and age. A complex concept, such as "outcome," may require a large array of separate variables, for example, questionnaires to measure different aspects of change in clients and their family members, observation of children's behavior, and reports from practitioners.

Not all key concepts in the research problem yield variables, however. Some terms refer to constants, factors that do not vary in the study. For example, suppose a problem states the following hypothesis: "Among the frail elderly, residential mobility (including moves from homes to institutions) will be associated with the rate of survival." "Residential mobility" and "rate of survival" would yield variables; each varies and has at least two categories, for example, moving and remaining in the same residence, and dying within a certain time and surviving that time. But "the frail elderly" would be a constant, since only this group of older people is to be studied in the problem as stated. It might be decided for another study, however, to treat "the frail elderly" as a variable; if so, different degrees of frailty would need to be distinguished, and the hypothesis might be revised: "the rate of survival among elderly is associated with degree of frailty and residential mobility."

> Forte and colleagues (1996) used Franks's interactional role-taking model (1989) to examine spousal violence against women. Role-taking involves the ability to take the perspective of the other in one's imagination. They spec-

ulated that in oppressive social situations, the less powerful person uses role-taking to try to understand the more powerful person, while the more powerful person does not tune in to the person with less power. The asymmetrical role-taking leads to differences in their behaviors in face-to-face interactions, which in turn affects emotional self-appraisal and coping strategies. What follows shows how they defined one of the concepts in the model, oppressive social situations.

CONCEPT	VARIABLES	OPERATIONAL DEFINITION
Oppressive social situations or oppressive contextual situations affecting likelihood of role-taking; includes (1) status and power differences, (2) structural and personal dependence, (3) lack of access to outside support or perspectives. Theoretical relevance—everyone performs role-taking to some degree. Oppressive situations affect people's role-taking. Oppressive situations include unbalanced status and power, one person depending on the other for resources, and lack of access to outside support or other perspectives.	1a. Spouse abuse. 1b. Social power—perception of relative power of husband and wife. 2. Structural and personal dependency. 3. Access to alternative perspectives: a) supportive others. b) profeminist ideology.	(All are questionnaires filled out by women) 1a. Index of spouse abuse 1b. Own questionnaire created for study. 2. Kalmuss and Strauss's Indices of Subjective and Objective Marital Dependency. 3. Number of outside groups belong to and frequency of meeting. Attitudes Toward Women scale

Types of Variables

Since explanation is a major goal of research, it is customary to classify variables according to their function in explanatory chains. *Independent variables* are presumed causative factors. Factors to be explained or presumed effects are referred to as *dependent variables*, since their variation is presumably dependent on the influence of an independent variable. In the preceding example about the frail elderly, "residential mobility" is an independent variable while "survival rate" is the dependent variable.

When more than one variable is involved, as is true of most social science research, additional variables can be classified in several ways. One classification is by time, or sequence. An *antecedent* variable operates prior in time to both independent and dependent variables. An antecedent variable is of particular interest if it can explain the relation between the independent and dependent variables. In the example of frail elderly, residential mobility and survival might be explained by an antecedent variable, health. The sicker elderly might move more for health reasons (particularly from home to institution), which in turn might be responsible for their lower survival rate. Sometimes the relation between an independent and dependent variable is influenced by a variable that occurs between them in time—an *intervening* variable. Residential mobility may have less impact on survival if the move is to a group foster home than to a nursing home. In other words, the type of move is an intervening variable that may alter the relation between mobility and survival.

Types of Variables in Time Sequence

ANTECEDENT	INDEPENDENT	INTERVENING	DEPENDENT
Health status	Residential mobility	Type of move	Survival
Worker skill	Client trust	Helpfulness	
Student and workstatus	Social support	Symptoms of stress	

As these examples suggest, a reason for interest in additional variables is because of their effect on the relationship between the independent and dependent variables. Another way to classify additional variables, then, is by the effect they have on that relationship. A *mediator* variable (also called mediating variable) is one that accounts for the effects of the independent variable, fully or in part (Gogineni, Alsup, and Gillespie 1995). In the example of frail elderly, the antecedent variable, health, is a mediator variable that accounts for the relationship between residential mobility and survival. Another example of a mediator is in Shulman's study of the working relationship (1993). The relationship between social workers' practice skill and clients' perception of helpfulness was mediated by the intervening variable, client perception of trust. In other words, practitioner skill led to trust which led to helpfulness, but skill did not lead directly to helpfulness.

A mediator variable may have a partial effect, when the relationship is increased or decreased. Or the mediator variable may have a full effect so that the original relationship between the independent and dependent variables disappears, as in these examples. In this case, the original independent variable is called *spurious*, or false; there appeared to be a relationship, but it was due to something else.

In mediation, the effect of the third variable is the same no matter the level of the independent variable, for example, health explains survival no matter what type of move the elderly individual makes, and perception of trust is important no matter how much skill the practitioner has. By contrast, if the relationship between the independent and dependent variables is different for differing values of the third variable, the third variable is called a *moderator* variable (also called modifier or specifier)(Coulton and Chow 1992; Koeske 1992). In the example of the frail elderly, the intervening variable, type of move, was a moderator variable because it specified that mobility and survival were more closely linked when the elderly person moved to a nursing home rather than another type of housing. The effects of a moderator variable are often called interaction effects because of the interaction between the variables. In another example, Koeske and Koeske found that social work students who were working part time while attending school full time showed more symptoms of stress than students who were not working or were attending school part time (1989). However, there was an interaction with social support, which acted as a buffer for some students but not others: the working full-time students showed fewer symptoms if they had high social support than if they had less, but amount of support did not affect stress for other students. Thus, social support was a moderator variable because it had different effects for different categories of student status.

A third type of classification of variables relates to whether the variable is an integral part of the hypothesis or not. Independent and dependent variables are essential parts of a hypothesis, and much research also specifies antecedent and intervening variables in the hypotheses. However, as we have seen, an apparent or hypothesized relationship may be due to some other variable. These other variables are called *extraneous* variables. Extraneous variables may be recognized and even studied, or they may not be imagined. For example, Koeske and Koeske (1989) included student status, social support, and stress in their hypothesis. They also examined a range of background variables such as age, income, number of credits already earned, and percent of tuition paid through loans in order to ensure that they did not affect the relationship among status, support, and stress. Despite their care, perhaps other extraneous variables they did not think of might affect that relationship, for example, intellectual ability or type of field placement.

The three types of classification discussed thus far relate to the roles of variables in explaining relationships. Another distinction among variables is whether they can be manipulated or changed. An *attribute* variable, such as a measure of socioeconomic status, is a measurement imposed on phenomena, leaving them as they already exist. An *active* variable, such as an experimental treatment, represents something done to affect phenomena (Kerlinger 1985). For example, a California welfare experiment allowed some families to work more hours before losing benefits, to see if it increased participation in the workforce (Hardina and Carley 1997). The active variable was the type of rules about working (some families were allowed to work more, some were under the usual stringent rules). Attribute variables, which the investigators did not manipulate but had to take into account, included ethnicity, type of employment, and education. The distinction is particularly important in social work. Attribute variables tend to measure phenomena we need to understand or to take into account in our change efforts. Active variables, such as social work intervention, represent our means of bringing change about.

Working Statement of the Problem

To recapitulate, the explication of a problem consists of translating general into specific terms. This translation, which includes the major concepts, variables, and operational definitions, becomes the working statement of the problem. Carried to its ultimate limits, the statement would be nothing less than a description of the entire research process, including who is to be studied, all the data collection procedures, data analysis, and, if relevant, the intervention program. At a practical level, the working statement of a problem is more usually a compact statement describing what is actually to be studied. Thus, in general form a hypothesis may be as follows: "Social work practitioners tend to view passivity as more problematic in male than in female clients." As the problem is explicated, it is decided to study social workers attending a workshop. The practitioners will be randomly divided into two groups. Both groups will receive a case summary portraying a passive client. The summaries will differ in only one respect: in the summaries given one group, the client will be described as a man (masculine form); for the other group, the client will be described as a woman (feminine form). All practitioners will complete a questionnaire called the Perceived Maladjustment Index, designed to measure a social worker's perception of degree of maladjustment in a client. The working statement of the hypothesis in such a study might be put as follows: the social workers receiving the "masculine" form of the case summary will have a higher mean score on the Perceived Maladjustment Index than those receiving the "feminine" form.

The working statement may not appear as such in a report, though a restatement of the problem at this level may often be helpful to the reader. Even if it remains in the mind of the investigator, the working statement is of value since it provides a way of comparing the research problem in the abstract with what will actually be studied. The gap between the meanings connoted by the abstract form and the information that can be expected from the working statement is a measure of the limitations of the study. The example of gender and perceived passivity illustrates this gap well, as the original general statement is much broader and inclusive than the working statement. The working statement makes clear the limitations—the passive client is fictitious, not real; practitioners report their perceptions of a case study, not their actual behaviors when confronted with a male or female passive client, and so on.

The working statement is the culmination of an interactive process that begins with problem formulation and ends with the hypotheses, variables, and operational definitions. Until the study is actually conducted, the working statement is in flux as the investigator explores the literature, takes into account the context of the research, tries out options for defining concepts, and examines phenomena in relation to theory. (In qualitative approaches, the working statement may not be complete until the data are analyzed, long after the study has begun.) Each piece of the working statement must relate to the others, and as one piece changes, the others usually change. For example, how does stress affect student performance? What is stress? How should it be measured? Most of the available measures of stress for students are self-perceptions. How do self-perceptions differ from actual stress? Stress theory suggests that external stressors are events or situations that stress most people, but the event may also be perceived as a growth-inducing challenge (Lazarus and Folkman 1984). It is the individual's perception of stress that mediates outcome. Is it important to distinguish stressors and stress when studying student performance? Perhaps both should be studied?—now there are three variables instead of two: stressors, stress, and performance.

The parts of a working statement, whether in its dynamic or "final" form, relate logically to each other. The concepts are integral to the theoretical framework; the variables are clearly part of those concepts and are relevant within the theory; the operational definitions are meaningful theoretically, and so on. As we shall see in later chapters, the problem formulation, theory, and hypotheses also set the framework for other steps in the research process. Are the people or things studied in fact relevant to the hypothesis? Is the way of measuring them relevant and theoretically consistent? Is the design strategy adequate to test the hypothesis or answer the question? Are potential explanatory variables included appropriately? Does the data analysis strategy take into account the explanatory function of the variables? Do the procedures capture the complexity of social phenomena?

Summary

Theory is a coherent system of ideas or concepts, a way of organizing knowledge so that it makes sense to us (definitional role) and so we can explain phenomena (explanatory role). In its explanatory role, theory permits us to develop hypotheses that can be tested; to the extent that the hypotheses are upheld, the theory is stronger and more useful. In research, theory is critical in the process of developing a problem, formulating testable hypotheses (derived from the theory and linking concepts important in the theory), and developing operational definitions that link the concepts to the raw data or phenomena under study. In addition to theory as the framework for research, a social work investigator must consider several other factors in developing a research problem: his or her own interest and curiosity, whether enough is known, relevance to social work, importance, feasibility, and ethics.

Research proceeds by developing hypotheses about the relationship among concepts, or if less is known, developing questions about the possible relationships. Hypotheses can state a relationship among concepts (or among the variables that represent the concepts), or they can state the difference one variable might make on the other. Hypotheses may be two-tailed—not stating what the differences or direction might be—or one-tailed—stating a direction. Whatever type an hypothesis takes, hypotheses and questions alike must meet the criteria of testability and likelihood of confirmation.

In order to test hypotheses, there must a link between the concepts and what is actually studied. The process of explicating or specifying is moving down (or up) through levels of abstraction to make this link. Nominal definitions (sometimes called conceptual definitions) are at the higher level of abstraction; they describe the meaning of the concept, usually in terms of other concepts. Variables are the parts of a concept that are actually used in a study. Operational definitions of variables are more specific and at the ultimate level of specificity—the working statement of the problem—are concrete statements about what will be measured as part of the concept, and how it will be measured.

Variables can be classified in several ways. In relation to their function in explanatory chains, they may be independent (the presumed "cause"), dependent (the outcome), antecedent (occurring before the independent variable), or intervening. The effect of a third variable on the relationship between two variables may be mediating (accounts for the relationship—in which case the original relationship is spurious) or moderating (having different effects for differing categories of the variable). Extraneous variables are other variables that might have an effect. Active variables are those that are manipulated, while attribute variables are ascribed.

3   The Context of Research

Research, like other endeavors, is carried out in a context that influences problem development and, indeed, the entire research process. A student assigned to write a research proposal for a study in a field agency is clearly constrained by numerous factors: the necessity to get something on paper by the due date, a topic relevant to the field agency, something the agency director will like and allow to be implemented, something the instructor will consider "social worky" enough for the course, and so on. All research, no matter its scope, is affected similarly. Such influences include the social work profession, theoretical frameworks, the agency or site in which the research is conducted, the social and political context, the need to protect participants from harm, and the need to guard against insensitivity and bias.

The Profession of Social Work

The social work profession is a powerful influence on the research problem and process. As already discussed, we—and most social workers—value research that is applied and useful to advance social work practice theory. This of course constrains the range of topics for a social work researcher. Even within that range, however, the social work profession influences the statement of the problem through its perspective, its preferred theories, and its values and ethics.

The social work perspective, or point of view, includes a whole cluster of beliefs that distinguish social work from other disciplines that deal with similar topics. Consider the topic of juvenile delinquency. An investigator in criminal justice might approach the topic from the point of view of crime control and policing technique. An investigator in urban studies might examine the physical layout of buildings, public space, and lighting for their effects on crime deterrence. An investigator in social work, by contrast, might study the effects of other persons—peers or family—on adolescent behavior.

Social work, like other disciplines, has its preferred theories that also influence how a problem is developed. Dominant theories may change over time. For example, social work derivatives of Freudian and Rankian theory, called psychosocial and functional, competed as "the" explanations for individual change from the 1940s well into the 1960s, when functionalism essentially disappeared. In the 1960s, behavioral learning theories were introduced into social work from psychology; metamorphosed into cognitive-behavioral approaches, they are now one of the most important paradigms. More recently, systems theories that incorporate ideas of multilevel, interactive effects have taken hold—and are the cornerstone of generalist practice. Other theories seem to make brief appearances on cycles, like comets: transactional analysis, neurolinguistic programming, rapid eye movement, and so on. Other theories of human behavior have a minimal impact on social work, for example, sociological theories of family functioning, biochemical ideas of mental illness, or anthropological ideas of symbolic meaning and communication.

Social work's professional values and ethics also influence the shape of a research study. Ethical principles included in the NASW Code of Ethics (1995) —service, social justice, dignity and worth of the person, and the importance of human relationships—clearly influence the types of problems a social worker might chose to investigate and how the investigation is carried out. The Code of Ethics is explicit that social workers have an obligation to evaluate policies, programs, and interventions, to share their knowledge, to give credit to others, and to facilitate research that contributes to the development of knowledge. It also includes guidelines for conducting research that mirror the federal guidelines for protection of human subjects in research studies, which will be discussed shortly.

Theory as Framework for Research

A second contextual factor that influences problem development and the research process is theory. Theory provides the matrix for the formulation of the questions and hypotheses that guide systematic inquiry. The generative role of theory is most obvious when a research problem is derived from a body of existing theory. As described in chapters 1 and 2, the scientific approach is a process of constructing and testing a theory that organizes knowledge.

In a quantitative approach, the key concepts, the general definitions of them, and their hypothesized relations, are derived from the theory. For example, an investigator looking at the causes of spouse abuse from a psychodynamic perspective might investigate the relation among such variables as dependency and self-esteem. A behaviorist might investigate events that precipitate and reinforce violent acts. A third investigator with a systems perspective might focus on variables such as external stressors, permeability of family boundaries, or the social acceptability of violence.

In a qualitative approach, where usually no hypotheses are developed and the investigator remains open to explore relations among data, theory is important in delimiting the boundaries of the investigation and in making sense of the connections among data. For example, Davis and Srinivasan (1994) used a feminist perspective to look at the operation of a battered women's shelter. Their feminist perspective emphasized the "politics of oppression and transformation" (p. 348) and the importance of control of social institutions to define reality for all. In their view, feminists running battered women's shelters should develop organizational environments that empower both staff and residents. Thus the theory framed their research question: did a feminist shelter in fact empower its members? Further, the theory directed them to look at organizational structure and at cues to power such as the formal hierarchy, the rules about who could do what, and who in fact did what. They conducted the study without hypotheses, observing carefully in the shelter and using their observations to suggest new lines of inquiry, but their theory framed the research question, the direction of their observations, and their understanding of what was relevant. Their results indicated that the shelter structure provided an empowering environment for its volunteer staff but not for the residents who were abused women.

Theory is less obvious, but still crucial, when inquiry arises from unknowns encountered in practice. For example, in one study (Garvin, Smith, and Reid 1978), the investigators were interested in determining if a monetary incentive ($30 a month) for participating in a federal work-training program was accomplishing its stated purpose of attracting recipients into the program. Various specific questions were posed for study. Did the recipients perceive the payment as an inducement to participate? Did they think it was adequate? Would they have participated without it? Although these questions seem very practical, and were, they were suggested by an informal theory of how the monetary incentive could be expected to operate. The theory suggested that welfare recipients would be influenced to participate in the program because of the incentive; if so, they would need to know about the incentive prior to the program and to view it as extra money that would result from the program. Further, other possible incentives, such as prospects of obtaining a better job, must not be so powerful as to nullify the effect of the "bonus" in the recipient's decision about entering the program. Thus a network of concepts and explanatory hypotheses—that is, the theory underlying this aspect of the program—could (and did) stimulate questions about the supposed incentive payment.

The Site of the Research

A third contextual factor affecting problem development and the research process is the agency or setting in which the research takes place. The topic and the problem formulation must be acceptable to the actors in the agency. In addition, as Weinbach (1988) points out, agencies operate with mandates for accountability, in social environments that often misunderstand or devalue their aims, and with scarce resources. These realities mean that, from agencies' points of view, the ideal research study should show agencies as productive, fulfilling socially desirable missions, and cost-effective, all without costing much to conduct the study! Fortunately, most social work agencies are also interested in improving professional knowledge and the quality of service to clients, and consequently are more open to research than the constraints of the environment might suggest. However, clearly the research must further the interests of the agency and major organizational actors to some extent. No board of directors would approve a study of clients who are not within the agency's mission, nor would they be receptive to a study intended to show their service is inadequate.

Within the agency, the organizational culture, beliefs, and practices shape the definitions and variables in the same way as does the social work profession. For example, the formal and informal decision-making structure affects who defines the research problem and how the data are gathered. An investigator interested in what factors affect decisions to remove a child from the family will first need to determine who makes the decision—the caseworker, the supervisor, or others. (Indeed, a study of factors influencing the decision-maker may be more interesting than a study of the characteristics of the child or family, and may explain more of the decision.) The organization's belief about who should receive service will affect the research. For example, if an agency defines the child as the case unit, its practice and research might be limited to the child's physical well-being, academic functioning, and psychological health. In another agency that defines the family as the case unit, research might focus on family structure, family problem-solving capacity, and community supports for families. Similarly, the approach to practice affects the research: It is not possible to compare family preservation to play therapy if the agency offers only one, and it would be difficult to find outcome measures that are equally appropriate to both.

Staff beliefs about service and the utility of research influence the conduct of the research. For example, Rubin recounts an agency director who privately viewed the experimental treatment as weak and consequently did not assign "tough" cases that needed "good" service to it (1997). Similarly, Schilling et al. (1988) cite an instance where practitioners did not refer clients to one research project because it was perceived as offering no benefit to clients, while another research project seen as providing valuable service received a flood of referrals.

The Social and Political Context

A fourth contextual factor affecting problem development and the research process is the social and political context—the gestalt of what is acceptable and of interest in the larger societal context. Some (by no means all) of the social and political considerations include overall social values, the current "hot topics," and the availability and interests of funders.

The overall social values influence what gets studied and how. For example, the United States currently places a great deal of emphasis on the individual and the individual's responsibility for "making it" or not in the economic and social arenas. Consequently, problems and solutions tend to be defined at the individual rather than larger systems level—research on training poor individuals to enter the current job market rather than on structural reforms such as integrating secondary education with work preparation; or research on stabilizing homeless families rather than on providing inexpensive housing stock. In another example, American attitudes toward women and their roles have changed dramatically since the 1950s. Whereas violence toward a marital partner was once unrecognized, it is now an important topic in social work research. And, as attitudes shifted, the subject of research on abuse has shifted. Where it was once focused on the dyadic interactive system, in which an abused woman bore equal (or more) responsibility for the violence, it shifted to focus on first one individual, the woman as victim, then to another individual, the man as perpetrator. Recently, the entire family as site and support of abuse has come into focus.

Another aspect of social values is conflict among values held by different groups—the political context, so to speak. Unopinionated research on the effects of abortion, for example, may be impossible in the United States of the 2000s, and certainly the interpretation and dissemination of results depends on which side of the debate one stands. Similarly, early research on acquired immune deficiency (AIDS) may have been hindered because the disease initially affected stigmatized groups such gay men and Haitian immigrants (Shilts 1987).

More fleeting than overall social values or political context, although influenced by them, are the current "hot topics," or ideas that suddenly become popular and influence both the public and the investigator's imaginations. Recent examples in social work include adult children of alcoholics (ACOA), repression of traumatic memory (especially of childhood abuse), kinship care, and total quality management. Sometimes the ideas are cutting edge and presage major breakthroughs in understanding of social interaction. Other times they are fads or lead to dead ends in research. In either case, for a time, they shape what investigators examine and how they approach them.

The availability of funding and the preferences of the funding sources also reflect social values and directly influence research. In the 1960s and 70s, for example, federal funding sources were interested in developing practice methods that could be applied in many different situations (Epstein, quoted by Coohey 1996). Hence studies tested the outcomes of behavior modification, short-term treatment, task-centered practice, and systems approaches to family therapy, without much attention to the type of problems treated. By contrast, in the 1990s, federal funding sources emphasized the problem—pragmatic and often eclectic approaches to specific, delimited problems, such as post-traumatic stress syndrome, child abuse, or dual diagnosis of mental illness and substance abuse. Even funding at less lofty levels than government affects research: a series of studies on prevention of school drop-out compared case management to monetary incentives because the funding source was convinced that adolescents, like employees, would respond directly to being paid for productive behavior (they did not) (Reid et al. 1994).

Protection of Human Subjects

A fifth factor affecting problem development and the research process is the need to protect participants from harm. In the United States, human participants have been protected since 1985 by the Public Health Service Act, P.L. 99–158, with current guidelines spelled out in the Code of Federal Regulations, Title 45 (Public Welfare) Part 46: Protection of Human Subjects (rev. June 18, 1991). The guidelines apply to all research involving human participants that is subject to regulation by the federal government. However, even a social work investigator working alone should follow the guidelines because the Code of

Ethics of the National Association of Social Workers (NASW 1995) requires social workers to implement similar protection procedures and to consult institutional review boards when appropriate.

The federal regulations require that each institution establish an Institutional Review Board (IRB). The IRB reviews research proposals to ensure that they provide adequate protection of human subjects. Universities, hospitals, public agencies, and most large social work agencies have IRBs; university-based investigators (students or faculty) who do research in social work agencies usually must receive approval from both the university and the agency IRB. Although certain types of research are exempt, most IRBs require that all research proposals be submitted. Thus, the IRB, not the investigator, determines the risk and the adequacy of protection from risk. IRBs vary in what they require submitted and in their interpretation of the guidelines, but the guidelines incorporate several general principles. These include protecting participants from risk, equitable selection of participants, confidentiality, and informed consent.

Protection from Undue Risk

The first principle in protection of human subjects is that participants be protected from undue risk, such as dangerous medical procedures or psychological harm. Much of the role of IRBs is determining how much risk is involved and whether the risk is warranted. For example, in incest, can a sexually abused child's safety be protected in an experimental family treatment where the abuser remains in the family while all receive treatment together? In studying welfare, what is the risk to poor families of withholding benefits so there is a control group for comparison?

The regulations require that risks must be minimized by using good research design and by using already-existing procedures when appropriate, for example, using questionnaires that are part of the intake procedure. IRBs then assess if "the risks to subjects are reasonable in relation to anticipated benefits, if any, to subjects, and the importance of the knowledge that may reasonably be expected to result." (45 CFR 46.111 (a) (2)). While some research is not approved, other research may be modified to reduce the risk to human participants. For example, in their study of the effects of monetary incentives and case management, Reid and his colleagues (Reid et al. 1994) wanted to include girls who did not receive treatment as a control group. The IRB ruled that it was too risky to interview girls who had not asked for service because contact by social workers might inadvertently label them as "problem girls." However, existing school records could be used, if kept confidential. Consequently, the study included grades and attendance for the no-treatment girls, but not the self-esteem measures that the other girls took.

Equitable Selection of Participants

A second principle in protecting human participants is equitable selection of subjects, particularly taking into account "the special problems of research involving vulnerable populations such as children, prisoners, pregnant women, mentally disabled persons, or economically or educationally disadvantaged persons" (45 CFR 46.111 (a) (3)). Research that could apply to anyone but selects such populations solely because they are easy to access or more likely to agree to participate is inappropriate. For example, if a study tested a controversial new approach with clients on Medicaid but excluded clients who were paying their own way, the selection is questionable.

Disclosure of Information About Participants

Another principle of protection of human subjects is that the individual should not be harmed by disclosure of information about that individual. Many social science studies rely on anonymity, where an individual's identity is never known. For example, Hawkins and Hawkins (1996) assessed the mental health problems of social work students, who for good reasons might not wish to be identified as having alcohol, depression, or other mental health problems. The investigators used an anonymous questionnaire that did not request the student's name and thus there was no way to track who said they had what problem.

Anonymity is not possible, however, if one wants to study change over time, for example, whether adolescents improve their independent living skills after attending a series of workshops. To assess the amount of change, the investigator must match each adolescent's skill level before the workshops with his or her skill after the workshops, that is, the individual must be identifiable at each time point. Usually, confidentiality is protected by assigning each individual a code number. The investigator guards a "key list" of names and code numbers (under lock and key). As soon as the data are collected and the responses are matched, the key list is destroyed so that no one, not even the investigator, can tell which individual was which.

Sometimes a key list approach is not seen as adequate protection of confidentiality. Massimo, for example, was evaluating the impact of training in computer use on how public child welfare workers did their jobs (1996). The workers were reluctant to answer a follow-up questionnaire because they feared the results would be used against them on their performance evaluations. Instead of keeping a key list, during the training, Massimo assigned each person a code number. Each worker put the code number on the first questionnaire, then self-addressed an envelope and sealed it with the code number inside. Six months later, Massimo mailed the follow-up questionnaire and the envelope. Each worker then put the same code number on the second questionnaire. The two questionnaires could be matched, but the investigator did not know to whom they belonged.

Even when participants respond anonymously, it is possible to violate confidentiality if the data are reported in such a way that individuals can be identified. In quantitative approaches, statistics that aggregate or group responses are used both to summarize the data and to protect individuals' responses. Thus, a report may include the average age for men and women, but not the ages of each individual. But investigators are often interested in refining the results to try to explain puzzling findings. For example, Fortune and McCarthy (1992) found that field instructors gave female social work students better performance ratings than male students. They suspected that field instructors might give harsher ratings to students of the opposite gender. Unfortunately, when the students and field instructors were grouped by gender pairs, there were very few male students with female instructors. Had the data been reported, anyone who knew the participants would immediately be able to identify the male students and their performance ratings. Consequently, the data were not reported because it would violate their confidentiality.

Confidentiality can be a critical issue in qualitative approaches where often a small group is studied and the data analysis consists of rich descriptions of roles and relationships. The researcher must disguise the participants and their situations while not distorting the data and their meaning. For example, Krassner (1986) interviewed five Mexican-American *curanderos*, or healers, to determine the effective features of their therapeutic healing. She describes in careful detail their practice settings (healing centers), their views of the cause of illness, and the processes they use to assess and treat people's problems. She quotes extensively from the interviews, grouping quotes around topics rather than relating an individual's full discussion. Clearly, she must alter identifying information and put the quotes in a new context in order to protect the *curanderos'* confidentiality.

Informed Consent

A fourth principle for protecting participants is informed consent, which means that the participants understand their part in the study and explicitly agree to participate. Informed consent also includes voluntary participation, with no penalties for refusing and with the right to withdraw at any time without penalty. Informed consent is particularly important in treatment research, when new forms of treatment with unknown effects are being tested. Clients who have come for help are particularly vulnerable to abuses of informed consent. They may fear loss of service if they refuse to participate, or they may not understand (or, for the moment, care) what the options are.

The IRB requirements for informed consent include, among other things, statements about the nature of the research: its purpose, procedures, duration, risks and benefits to participants, and so on. Thus, the investigator may not deceive the participants about the research. What about research that cannot be conducted if the participants know exactly what it is about? For example, many social psychology experiments test how people conform to social expectations, such as whether they will give an improbable answer when all others around them are giving the improbable answer. The study could not be done if the participants knew the purpose was to influence their answers. What about studies that observe how people behave under normal circumstances, for example, whether people living in cities will give change for a quarter (Levine et al. 1994)? If the investigator explained the study to each person ahead of time, their helping behavior certainly would not be normal. Studies like these, which include some form of deception, are acceptable *if approved by the IRB*. It is up to the local Institutional Review Board to determine the level of risk to participants and, if there is risk, whether the knowledge gained from the study offsets the risk. In most studies that do include such deception, once the participant has finished the research task, the investigator "debriefs" him or her by describing the real purpose and discussing the person's reactions.

BASIC ELEMENTS OF INFORMED CONSENT

(from Code of Federal Regulations, Title 45 (Public Welfare) Part 46 - Protection of Human Subjects (rev. June 18, 1991), 46.116 General requirements for informed consent)

(A) Basic elements of informed consent. . . . in seeking informed consent the following information shall be provided to each subject:

(1) a statement that the study involves research, an explanation of the purposes of the research and the expected duration of the subject's participation, a description of the procedures to be followed, and identification of any procedures which are experimental;

(2) a description of any reasonably foreseeable risks or discomforts to the subject;

(3) a description of any benefits to the subject or to others which may reasonably be expected from the research;

(4) a disclosure of appropriate alternative procedures or courses of treatment, if any, that might be advantageous to the subject;

(5) a statement describing the extent, if any, to which confidentiality of records identifying the subject will be maintained;

(6) for research involving more than minimal risk, an explanation as to whether any compensation and an explanation as to whether any medical treatments are available if injury occurs and if so, what they consist of, or where further information may be obtained;

(7) an explanation of whom to contact for answers to pertinent questions about the research and the research subject's rights, and whom to contact in the event of a research-related injury to the subject;

(8) a statement that participation is voluntary, refusal to participate will involve no penalty or loss of benefits to which the subject is otherwise entitled, and the subject may discontinue participation at any time without penalty or loss of benefits to which the subject is otherwise entitled.

(Additional elements of informed consent that may be added when appropriate include that treatment may involve unforeseeable risks, circumstances in which participation might be terminated by the investigator, additional costs to participants, consequences of a decision to withdraw, that new findings that might affect willingness to participate will be provided, and approximate number of subjects in the study. The language of an informed consent form must also be understandable to the subject.)

Insensitivity and Bias

A sixth contextual factor that affects problem development and the research process is the need to guard against insensitivity, bias, or stereotyping of a particular group on gender, racial, age, sexual orientation, cultural, or other factors. Such insensitivity can occur at any stage of research, from conceptualization to dissemination. In developing a research problem, for example, the investigator must ensure that the framework incorporates others' perceptions, not a single view that reinforces a stereotype. For example, during the 1960s and 1970s, research on poor urban blacks often focused on pathology, the negative effects of parental absence, and the "dysfunctions" of family life, ignoring the strengths and successful adaptations that enabled African Americans to survive in an oppressive society (Williams 1980). Similarly, early research on working mothers focused on the effects of maternal deprivation, under the assumption that only women nurture children. Research that does not stereo-type might look instead at role-sharing or at how several adults share tasks and provide each other emotional support. Often, taking another perspective is dif-ficult when cultural assumptions are unquestioned. Haizlip quotes an African proverb: "Until lions have their historians, tales of hunting will always glorify the hunter." (1994: 187)

Insensitivity also occurs if research procedures ignore gender, racial, or cul-tural differences that are critical to the research, for example, asking women but not men about doing household chores. Phrases on questionnaires may have different or unintended meanings among different cultures. For example, Briggs, Tovar, and Corcoran (1996), testing the Children's Action Tendency Scale (CATS), found that Anglo children but not Latino children distinguished between assertiveness and submissiveness.

Another source of insensitivity is overgeneralizing, or assuming that the results are applicable to "all" people when only a limited group was studied. For example, Martin and Christopher trained *mothers* in sex education techniques, but entitled their article "*Family* Guided Sex Education" and referred through-out to "*parents*" (1987). By contrast, McKay et al. (1996) studied how to engage urban African-American, Latino, and white families in mental health service; they are careful to use the phrase "inner city children and their families" in the title and throughout the article (even though it is cumbersome)!

In general, inappropriate language is insensitive and often perpetuates stereotypes, in research as well as normal discourse. Such language can occur throughout the research process: in the statement of the research question, in interviews, in questionnaires, in the written report, and so on. For example, referring to the study participants as "men and their wives" instead of "hus-bands and wives" mixes gender and role status and demeans the women. The terms should be parallel and equal, and if their gender is not germane to the research, a more generic term such as term "couples" might be more appropri-ate (Eichler 1988). Similarly, identifying a group by what they are not ("non-white") is insensitive because it implies that the referent is the standard; and identifying on the basis of a single characteristic ("disabled" or "mentally ill") implies that the person is only that characteristic.

SUGGESTIONS FOR AVOIDING INSENSITIVITY IN A RESEARCH STUDY

Become familiar with the culture of the group being studied: do participant observation, try out ("pre-test") questionnaires and other procedures with members of that group.

Collaborate with members of the group, involve representatives of the

group in the development and conduct of the research, help participants
benefit from the research in some way.

Frame the research in a balanced way: avoid one-sided conceptualizations
such as male-dominated (or female-dominated) notions of family functioning, the functional limitations of the elderly, or the inability of an
immigrant group to negotiate social services. Include the point of view of
those studied in the conceptualization.

Make sure research procedures are sensitive: mix qualitative and quantitative approaches to ensure you are getting participants' world views
(Becerra and Zambrana 1985); use questionnaires that have been tested
with representatives of the group and contain cultural- or gender-sensitive
wording; test whether your language is sensitive by substituting your own
group for the one you are discussing (American Psychological Association
1994); if appropriate, use bilingual interviewers or those familiar with the
culture.

Be explicit and accurate in describing the participants; avoid overgeneralizing to groups not studied (for example, "Vietnamese American" rather
than "Asian-American"); analyze and report differences by groups when
appropriate.

In language, use the appropriate level of specificity: specific terms for specific purposes and generic terms for generic purposes (American Psychological Association 1994; Eichler 1988), for example, if all the pupils in a
study are girls, do not call them "students" or "children"; if they include
both girls and boys, do not call them "boys."

Ensure participants get the results.

Summary

In sum, numerous factors influence the research process, some factors
immediately evident in a particular study, others more subtle. In the process of
developing a working statement, the investigator takes into account the context
for his or her study, often "trading off" an ideal approach for what is possible
in the context. While an investigator rarely spells out such trade-offs, an
informed reader should be able to detect them.

For example, in Forte et al.'s study of spousal abuse (1996), described in
chapter 2, the investigators' disciplines of social work and sociology influenced
their choice of spouse abuse as a topic and role-taking theory as a framework
(professional context). The topic, spouse abuse, is also recognized as a major

social problem, well worth studying (social and political context). The theoretical framework of role-taking suggests that the focus be on participants' perceptions of their own and their partners' perspectives—their ability to role-take —thus excluding (for this study) biological concerns or effects of parental modeling (the theoretical framework). The participants were women at shelters and social work students in two cities, reflecting the sites the researchers had access to (site of the research). The abusing partners were not included, possibly because they were not welcome at the shelters and would be hard to reach, possibly because of the difficulty of matching responses with the partner (site and protection of human subjects). Finally, the data were gathered using written questionnaires rather than observation of interaction, a concession to feasibility as well as to the theoretical framework, the possibilities at the sites, and concerns about confidentiality and safety.

4 Dimensions of Research Design

Research design refers to the overall plan or strategy by which questions are answered or hypotheses tested. It includes such considerations as when data are gathered and how many times, how many participants are involved, and whether variables are active or attribute. Although each study is done according to its own particular plan, we can think in terms of general features or principles of design used for different purposes or representing different approaches to inquiry. Although various frameworks have been developed, in our judgment no single scheme has proved adequate to the task of capturing the multidimensional qualities of research strategy. Consequently, we consider different dimensions used in analysis of design and propose ways they may be helpful in assessing and planning research strategy. After presenting the dimensions, we discuss the ability of various design dimensions to contribute to statements of causality, and introduce the ideas of alternative explanations (other than the hypothesized explanation) for the results.

The Investigator's Control Over Phenomena Studied

Naturalistic Versus Experimental Control

A key distinction in research strategy concerns what the investigator does with the phenomena under investigation. On the one hand, one can investigate phenomena "as they lie," that is, by studying events without trying to alter them. This approach to inquiry is commonly referred to as *naturalistic* research. On the other hand, one can deliberately seek to alter phenomena and then study the effects of the manipulations; the independent variable is active. This form of research is traditionally referred to as *experimental*. This distinction between naturalistic and experimental research is fundamental in the world of science. Some sciences, in which events of interest cannot be affected, are primarily naturalistic; astronomy is an example. Other sciences, such as nuclear physics, are primarily experimental. Most sciences make use of both methods, often as complementary means of advancing knowledge in the same area.

The purpose of both strategies is, of course, to gain knowledge, and ultimately this objective is achieved through observations of events. The key to the difference between naturalistic and experimental designs is that in naturalistic research the observed events would have taken place anyway; in experimental research the events were made to happen in order that they could be studied. In social work, naturalistic designs are common in studies that examine the status of phenomena at a point in time, for example, demographic characteristics of an agency's clients, the relation between marital status and health, or between organizational structure and service delivery. Experimental studies are common in intervention research, where the effects of treatment are assessed. However, intervention research could be either naturalistic or experimental depending on whether the investigator alters the phenomena (the intervention). For example, Reid and Strother (1988) analyzed interaction among "super problem solvers" to determine how the family and practitioner initiated successful change efforts. The research was naturalistic because they studied intervention without trying to alter it. In another study, Bradshaw (1996) assigned patients with a diagnosis of schizophrenia to one of two group treatments, one using a coping skills approach, the other a problem-solving approach. The intervention study was experimental because the investigator altered or manipulated the type of treatment by assigning people to the two groups. If the investigator sets out to test the effectiveness of a new technique, as in developmental research (Thomas 1978; Rothman and Thomas 1994), or deliberately varies treatments to compare outcomes, then it is experimental.

The reason for making events happen is to gain special knowledge. Experimentation provides a powerful means of acquiring knowledge about causal relations since the experimenter can observe what happens when one factor is changed and others are held constant. Through systematic manipulations, the investigator can build up bodies of knowledge that may be impossible to acquire if events were allowed to vary in their natural complexity.

Even when experimental methods cannot be applied directly to phenomena of interest, it is often possible to apply them to facsimiles or analogs of these phenomena. Such simulations, which are probably limited only by the researcher's ingenuity and resources, certainly span a wide range in science. The causes of local weather have been studied through computer simulations of ocean currents and air temperature. Experimental anthropologists have sought to explain historical events through sailing an ocean in a reconstruction of a primitive vessel and using ancient Egyptian technology to build a portion of a pyramid. More relevant to social work are experimental simulations of factors affecting human behavior. These include simulation games that model political forces governing a city, analog studies where social workers react to case summaries in which specific factors such as gender, race, or diagnosis are varied systematically; and laboratory studies where participants are asked to simulate tasks such as decision-making or conflict resolution. Most factors relevant to human behavior can be simulated for purposes of experimental study —for example, the effects of frustration, problem-solving, even intervention processes.

Some research writers limit experimental research to research that makes use of devices to isolate causative factors, for example, equivalent groups that do not receive the experimental intervention. In our view, such mechanisms of experimental control are not an essential characteristic of the experimental method. An experimenter may introduce and study an innovation without using control mechanisms. To experiment is to alter phenomena and then study the effect of that alteration. Additional devices are refinements on the study, refinements that define the type of experiment performed.

Types of Experiments

AMOUNT OF CONTROL Experimental designs may thus be subclassified according to whether they include additional groups as mechanisms that isolate causative factors. When one alters phenomena, one can see what happens, but then one may ask, what would have happened had there not been an alteration? Would the results be the same, or different? (To simplify matters, we limit our discussion of experimental design at this point to designs involving *groups* of individuals.)

Imagine that a social worker teaches parents to reinforce their children's completion of homework. The teachers' records indicate that the children turn in more homework. But what would have happened had there been no intervention? Would there be less homework, or the same amount, or more? To attempt to answer that question, many experimental designs include another group for comparison. If no alteration takes place, this group is usually called a control group. In the example, the control group would be children, perhaps in the same class, whose parents were not taught to reinforce their homework completion. The control group (or a comparison group if it receives a different form of intervention instead of no intervention) has various attributes that affect the ability of the design to isolate causative factors. An investigator's intent is to isolate or separate the intended cause (parent training, in this case) from other possible causes that might affect the phenomena (such as more interesting homework). This is often called ruling out or "controlling" alternative explanations (so that the most likely causative explanation is the intervention). The attributes of a control or comparison group that help to control alternative explanations will be discussed precisely later (a simplified guideline is that the more alike the experimental and control or comparison groups are, the better the control).

In general, experimental designs can be classified as uncontrolled, partially controlled, or substantially controlled, depending on the presence and type of groups. Experimental designs in which there is only one group, which is altered in some way, is uncontrolled since anything might have caused the results—one doesn't even know what might have happened without the alteration. Experimental designs in which participants are assigned to groups using random assignment are considered substantially controlled, because the procedure of random assignment is most likely to yield groups that are equivalent to each other. Experimental designs in which participants are assigned to groups in other ways are considered partially controlled. Beyond these general classifications, however, each study may vary substantially and the degree of control must be examined within the context of the specific study.

As noted earlier, we are defining the term *experiment* more broadly than do some research methodologists who have used "experiment" or "true experiment" to refer only to designs with equivalent groups produced by random assignment. These so-called experiments are, in our terms, substantially controlled experiments. What are sometimes referred to as quasi-experiments (those lacking equivalent groups) are in our lexicon uncontrolled (having no comparison group) or partially controlled (nonequivalent groups) experiments. Our broader definition incorporates the type of tryout and evaluation of service approaches that is typical of social work developmental research. It also encompasses newer approaches such as single-system experiments that include one system compared to itself.

FIELD VERSUS LABORATORY Another schema for classifying experiments, drawn from psychology, considers the site of the experiment. Those that are conducted in natural settings such as an agency are called field experiments, while those that are conducted in artificial settings are called laboratory experiments. For example, Bradshaw's (1996) comparison of coping skills and problem solving groups for patients with schizophrenia was a field experiment because it was conducted in an outpatient treatment facility, a normal setting for social work interventions. By contrast, Nugent (1992), looking at how practitioner verbal behavior affected client emotional reactions, asked participants to watch a role play of an interview in which the practitioner was sometimes facilitative and sometimes obstructive. This was a laboratory experiment because the interview was artificial; both the interview and the scenario were created for the experiment.

In general, laboratory experiments permit greater control over extraneous factors that might influence the results; one can be more precise about what conditions vary. For example, Nugent was able to control the practitioner's role-played behavior precisely, changing what the practitioner said, whether the client was interrupted, blamed, lectured, listened to and so on, while ensuring that only the practitioner's behavior and not other factors changed. However, the results from a laboratory experiment may not be strong enough to "hold up" in real life, where clients are influenced by many other factors. In Nugent's study, for example, perhaps a real client, distraught and focused on overwhelming problems, might not react strongly to the practitioner's behavior. In a field experiment, the independent variable must be more powerful if it is to affect phenomena given all the other influences on the phenomena. On the other hand, if a field experiment is successful, one has more confidence that the results will apply elsewhere, to other clients, because the setting itself is more natural and less controlled.

Some writers and funding sources distinguish effectiveness research—highly controlled clinical experiments typically in a near laboratory clinical setting—from effectiveness research conducted in more natural agency settings, without the strict controls of the laboratory (Pinsof, Wynne, and Hambright 1996). Although not identical, this distinction is similar to the idea of laboratory versus field. As we discuss later (chapter 6), the important considerations are how well results translate to other settings (generalization to other settings) and whether the results are worth reproducing (pragmatic generalization).

Purposes and Functions of Building Knowledge

Research is conducted to accomplish a range of purposes in building knowledge. An investigator may design a study to discover new ideas or hypotheses—an exploratory objective. A study may focus on developing tools for measurement. Another may seek to describe phenomena, or to produce explanations of relationships among variables. Before describing these purposes in more detail, we should note that although we can classify a study in terms of one main knowledge-building goal, many studies serve more than purpose. For example, it is hard to do an exploratory study without providing some descriptive information of the phenomena investigated.

In addition, it is useful to distinguish between purpose and function. Knowledge-building "purpose" reflects what the investigator intends to produce; "function" refers more broadly to what the study produces. A single-purpose study may serve a variety of functions, sometimes quite by accident. Experiments carefully designed to test an explanatory relationship may be remembered more for incidental discoveries having no connection with the purpose of the experiment. The unexpected exploratory function of research, known in science as serendipity, has been responsible for a host of discoveries including penicillin, Pavlov's conditioned reflex, REM sleep, the Rorschach test, and the Hawthorne effect. Moreover, a study may have different functions for different users. The investigator's purpose may have been largely descriptive but to another researcher the study's value lies in the evidence it provides for the validity of a particular attitude scale. Or, a theorist may combine the findings along with those of other studies to form the basis of an explanatory theory, as Durkheim did when using data on suicide rates to develop his explanatory theory of suicide.

This distinction between purpose and function suggests, first, that we should be alert for yields from research that fall outside its purpose, whether the research is one's own or someone else's. Second, the research one investigator does may have value to others in ways the investigator may not know, a notion that researchers may find comforting when the more straightforward results of their work appear to be ignored.

In what follows, we discuss knowledge-building primarily within the broader context of function. References to purpose will be made when we have the researcher's planning processes explicitly in mind.

Exploration

Research has an exploratory function when it is used to gain preliminary understanding of phenomena or to stimulate the development of concepts, hypotheses, theories, and technology.

Suppose that a community agency has established a new manpower program designed to provide on-the-job training and job placement services to unemployed youth. Within the first few months of operation a problem appears: many of the youths who entered the program are dropping out. The director requests a study of the problem as a basis for taking possible corrective action.

Assuming a researcher's role, a staff member contacts a dozen youths who have recently dropped out of the program—the first twelve who answered the phone and were willing to talk. As might be expected, the teenagers' reasons for leaving the program vary considerably, but almost half the youths mention that they were being used to carry out menial tasks at the training sites and were not being given the training they had been promised.

The staff member then contacts a coworker who had visited one of the youth's training sites. The second staff member recalls that the trainees did seem to spend a lot of time just helping out. Although the data are limited in scope and subject to bias, they provide a basis for a hypothesis about reasons for the dropout problem.

The hypothesis may serve as a basis for immediate action, such as requesting the trainers to increase the formal on-the-job training. The hypothesis also focuses further inquiry, which may be pursued through various means from collection of anecdotal data to a more elaborate study.

The example illustrates a study that served a primarily exploratory purpose. The investigator's intent was to gain an initial look at a piece of reality and to stimulate ideas about it. At this level, research yields a sense of what is possible, rather than what is probable. These possibilities may have generative effects. They may support other sources of evidence or may provoke new ways of construing reality.

Research done with exploratory purposes in mind requires, as the example indicates, only a modest investment of resources and allows considerable flexibility in method. Participants may be selected according to which sources of data will provide the most useful information most readily, and additional sources of data may be added to pursue leads. Data collection procedures may be similarly open to improvisation. Insightful analyses of one or a few cases may take precedence over an attempt to secure uniform measurements.

This is not to say that research must necessarily be "loose" to serve exploratory goals. More systematic studies may also have such purposes (often in addition to others, as we shall see). For example, the "super problem-solver" study of successful change process mentioned earlier (Reid and Strother 1988) was exploratory because its purpose (and function) was to generate new insights into how client change is initiated. The study used systematic procedures to scan and analyze case interviews, responses were formally coded, and frequencies of change-oriented responses were generated. On the other hand, clearly, worthwhile exploratory objectives can be achieved with research that is not highly systematic.

Measurement

Although most research contributes to ways of measuring phenomena, some studies are designed primarily to develop measurement tools. Most standardized instruments are the product of considerable methodological research. For example, in a series of studies to develop the Social Network Map, Tracy and colleagues first invited practitioners to use the map with clients, to test its feasibility and clinical usefulness (1990). They then gave the Map to 141 parents of children in Head Start and assessed its relationship to other acknowledged measures of support, including global social support, coping methods, and parental attitudes (Tracy and Abell 1994). Another common type of measurement study assesses whether a measure yields the same result at different times. Richman, Rosenfeld, and Hardy (1993), also developing a measure of social support, gave their instrument twice to 27 people, two to five weeks apart. Scores on most items were highly correlated, indicating that the measure was stable over a short period of time.

While the bulk of measurement studies assess the accuracy and utility of measurement instruments, measurement studies may also assess factors that affect measurement. For example, Tran and Williams (1994) studied the effect of language (Spanish or English) on Hispanic elderly persons' reports of their psychological well-being (the reports of positive affect were less reliable in Spanish), while Bowen (1994) assessed whether AFDC recipients who did not respond to a telephone interview would respond to a written, mailed questionnaire (they did not).

While the measurement function of research contributes to knowledge-building largely in an indirect manner by providing researchers with measurement tools, the measurement function makes a direct contribution as well. Through defining and spelling out variables for study, research can help clarify and specify key concepts within a body of knowledge. An excellent example of methodological research in social work is found in the work of Hudson and his associates to develop and validate a series of standardized instruments to measure different aspects of client functioning (Hudson 1982, 1990; Hudson and McMurtry 1997). The indirect contribution of this research to knowledge has been considerable: the "Hudson scales" have been widely used in social work research. Another example has been the efforts of Vosler to develop and validate measurement instruments that help practitioners assess larger systems that affect families, thus contributing to practitioner's ability to implement systems and generalist practice (Vosler 1990; 1996). Similarly, research has played a major role in developing a wide range of concepts used in the social sciences and social work—socioeconomic status, intelligence, anomie, self-concept, empathy, and so on.

Description

A third function of research is describing phenomena such as the characteristics of social systems, problems, and interventions. The descriptive function of research encompasses not only delineation of phenomena in a holistic fashion (a quarter of the families in East Town are single parent) but also specification of how different parts are related (the lower the income of East Town families, the more likely they are to be single parent). In fact, the logic of the descriptive function is to break wholes down into interconnected parts, to achieve as detailed a picture as possible. Thus, in describing the clientele of a family agency, we may wish to have initial breakdowns of the clients by age, sex, level of education, ethnicity, marital status, social class, presenting problem, and referral source. While some descriptive studies remain at the level of describing characteristics, most move toward determining associations among variables, for example, whether the presenting problem of the agency clientele differed by social class or whether ethnic background varied according to referral source. For example, O'Hare (1996) studied new clients at a New England mental health center. His study describes such characteristics as gender, age, income, and referral status, but the main function was to describe the relationship between referral source (court-ordered or voluntary), readiness to change, and problems such as family pathology and substance abuse.

Although investigation of these relations might stimulate (or even be guided by) speculations about causality, the descriptive function delivers only information about the presence of associations among factors. It does not point to causal connections. Thus, in the first example, we learn that income and single-parent status are related in a particular community, but we do not know if low income was a cause or consequence of single parenthood. In O'Hare's study, we learn that court-ordered clients were less ready to change than voluntary clients, but we do not know if they were ordered because of resistance, or resistant because they were ordered to go to the clinic.

Although any study can serve a descriptive function since it can provide at least some information about the characteristics of the phenomena studied, caution must be exercised about the capacity of a study to describe a population. The description may be misleading if applied inappropriately. For example, if a survey of the expressed needs of older residents were limited to participants in senior citizen centers, one could not reasonably claim that the results reflected an accurate description of the needs of all elderly in the community, since the less social and less mobile would not be adequately represented. Nevertheless, if this limitation were recognized, descriptive information concerning the needs of the elderly who were surveyed might still be useful, for example, in planning services for the kind of residents who do participate in senior citizen centers. Generally the more representative the sample and the more accurate the measurement, the better the resulting description.

Explanation

Probably the most esteemed function of research is its contribution to the explanation and prediction of phenomena. In social work considerable importance is attached to explanation, for example, in determining the etiology of problems, in understanding the dynamics of social systems, and in assessing the impact of different modes of intervention. At the core of such knowledge are assertions of cause-effect relations.

In a practice profession, explanation is of primary interest as a basis for prediction. We are interested in understanding causation so we can predict what is likely to happen—what kind of depressions are likely to lead to suicide, what kind of service programs are likely to have positive effects on certain types of clients. The better our capacities to predict, the more effectively we can intervene.

As we have seen, part of the descriptive function of research is to show how different factors are associated or occur together. The explanatory function takes this process a step further by providing evidence that factors are associated in a causal fashion. If it can be shown that factor A and factor B are associated, factor A has occurred prior to factor B, and that no other prior or concurrent (extraneous) factors are found to be associated with factor B, then it can be inferred that A is a cause of B. A key point in this chain of logic is that causal relations are not "proved" in a clear-cut fashion; rather, they are deduced through a process of elimination. Inferences are guided by theoretical expectations (chapter 2). We use theory to select and test those factors likely to provide alternative causal explanations. As a result, explanations offered by research always carry the qualification "as best as can be determined at this time." They are always open to the possibility that other explanatory factors, perhaps discovered by a novel theory, will be found.

Isolation of probable causative factors through elimination of other possibilities, variously called "alternative explanations," "rival hypotheses," "extraneous factors," or "threats to internal validity," is achieved through processes of "control" in research design and data analysis.

EXPLANATION IN EXPERIMENTAL RESEARCH The role of comparison groups in isolating and controlling factors was raised earlier in the discussion of experimental designs, which are usually explanatory in function. The most clear-cut and familiar example of control for the purpose of explanation is a substantially controlled design called the "classical experiment." In a classical experiment, equivalent groups are formed through random assignment; one group receives some form of treatment (the experimental group), the other does not (the control group). Attributes that might be expected to change as a result of the treatment are measured before and after treatment. If the treated group changes as predicted and the control group does not, and if it can be assumed that the groups differed in no other respect, then we may conclude that the treatment was the causative agent. (Note that the term *treatment* as used in discussions of experimental method refers generically to the independent or experimental variable, whatever it may be, and not simply to treatment in the clinical sense.)

An example of an experiment is a study of the effect of employment services for older unemployed workers (Rife and Belcher 1994). Fifty-two workers were randomly assigned to either the experimental group, a Job Club that met twice weekly to share leads and provide each other support, or to a control group that received the routine state government job referral service. The dependent variables, measured before and after the Job Club started, included levels of depression as well as employment measures. With random assignment, it is assumed that the experimental and control groups were equivalent on depression and employment as well as other extraneous variables that were not measured but might influence outcome, such as health, job skills, or self-presentation. Thus, when the experimental group gained employment more rapidly and decreased their depression, we have more confidence that the results may be attributed to the Job Club rather than to these other extraneous factors.

The same logic can be used in individual cases by comparing change during periods when no treatment is given with periods when treatment is applied (a single-system design). In both group and single-system experiments one attempts to "rule out" possible alternative explanations by holding them constant while treatment is introduced. In group experiments a control group is used to demonstrate the changes that occur as a result of maturation, ordinary environmental influences, or other factors that might happen anyway; presumably, both the experimental and control groups have been exposed to these factors while the experimental group differs only in receiving treatment. Thus any margin of difference in change between the two groups can be attributed to treatment, the independent variable. In the single-system experiment, the case serves as its "own control." "Control periods" (periods of time when treatment is withheld) are used to determine the effects of extraneous factors such as maturation or environmental influences. Change when treatment is added is ascribed to the effects of the treatment on the assumption that the extraneous factors will continue to operate as before. For example, a businesswoman recorded her perfectionist and irrational beliefs weekly for 3 weeks prior to treatment, for 8 weeks during treatment, and once after treatment (Ferguson and Rodway 1994). In comparing beliefs during the three time periods, we assume that her personal characteristics and external factors such as her stress at work or social life remain the same and are thus controlled. As we shall see, these assumptions may not in fact be true, but the logic of controlling extraneous factors while altering only the variable of interest is the basis for drawing conclusions about the effect of the independent variable. The implementation of this logic in the context of experimental design will be considered in detail in chapters 5 and 6.

EXPLANATION IN NATURALISTIC RESEARCH In naturalistic research, control of such extraneous variation through use of equivalent groups and "own control" devices is not possible because the investigator does not manipulate the independent variable. In naturalistic research, the investigator must deal with a complex web of associations among variables as they naturally occur. It may be difficult to determine which variables occur prior to another or to isolate any one factor as a cause of another. For example, a naturalistic study may reveal, as hypothesized, that adolescents exposed to harsh parental discipline engage in more antisocial behavior in the community than those whose parents are moderate in discipline. But does parental discipline provide an explanation for the behavior of the children? It may be that an antecedent variable, the antisocial behavior of some of the children (perhaps the result of peer group influences) preceded and, in fact, caused the harsh parental discipline. In short, it may not be possible to determine clearly the time order of the variables, and the flow of influence between variables may be in a direction quite the reverse from theoretical expectations.

Even when the time order of variables may be determined, other variables in a naturalistic study may provide competing explanations for a relationship. For example, suppose a researcher finds that young boys whose fathers are absent from the home because of marital separation or divorce have a poorer self-concept than boys whose fathers are present. Although one might reasonably assume that the self-concept of the child was not a cause of the father's leaving, it does not follow that the fathers' absence affected their sons' self-concepts. The presence of prior marital conflict in the home, an antecedent variable, may have caused both the parental separation and a lowering of the boys' self-concepts. Or socioeconomic circumstances may explain both father absence and low self-esteem. Compared to middle-class boys, lower-class boys may be more likely to lose their fathers and, given their more deprived socioeconomic circumstances, may be more likely to have a poorer self-concept.

If so, boys lacking fathers in the home would differ from boys whose fathers are present in respects other than the presence or absence of the father. Father-absent boys would have poorer self-images, be more likely to come from families with a history of marital conflict, and be lower class. Several factors which might cause poor self-esteem have been identified, and we do not know which of these variables are actually affecting self-concept. Worse, other influential factors may not have been identified.

To determine whether father's status affects the son's self-esteem would be relatively easy in a controlled experimental study. One would begin with a group of families randomly assigned to either an experimental or control group. In the experimental group, fathers would leave home (the experimental treatment); in the control group, they would stay put! If the self-concept of the experimental boys showed a greater worsening than those of the control boys, the fathers' absence could be regarded as a causative variable. Obviously an experiment that would so disrupt family life and threaten the mental health of children would never be done. But the example dramatizes what is required to determine explanations when variables are associated in naturalistic research. What is needed is to eliminate possible confounding differences between groups being compared—in other words, to control extraneous variation.

There are several ways to tackle this problem of ruling out alternative explanations in naturalistic research: restrictive sampling, adding a variable in the research design, matching, and statistical control. Each approach reflects the logic of controlled experimentation.

One means of reducing extraneous variation is through restrictive sampling, limiting the participants to those who are similar on one of the possible causes. If socioeconomic differences are thought to affect self-concept, a study may be confined to middle-class boys. By this means, father-absent and father-present boys are made equivalent in respect to social class; social class is controlled and cannot be an explanation for poor self-esteem. The drawback is that increasing the homogeneity of the participants limits the investigator's ability to generalize from the sample; it is not possible to say whether the finding holds true for lower-class boys, or for girls of any class.

A second means of controlling an extraneous variable is to incorporate it as part of the study. Instead of restricting the participants to middle-class boys, one could add a group of lower-class boys. The effect of father presence or absence on self-esteem can be examined separately for the middle-class and lower-class boys. Through this means, one obtains a more diversified sample and can isolate and hence control for (through statistical techniques discussed later) the influence of social class on the dependent variable.

An alternative to adding groups to the study is to use some form of matching, where pairs (or trios or quartets and so on) differ on the independent variable but are matched on the extraneous variables one wishes to control. Thus, if one wished to control for social class and age, each pair of boys would include one father-absent boy and one father-present boy who were the same class and age. Matching of this kind provides more precise control over extraneous variables than simply adding a group of boys of various classes and ages. However, matching on many variables is cumbersome and requires very large pools of potential participants. Usually the investigator can match on only a very small number of variables. Other variables that might be more important remain uncontrolled.

A fourth method of control for extraneous variation in naturalistic studies is statistical techniques. These techniques can be used in conjunction with the sampling and matching methods built into research design, or they can be applied post hoc, after the data are gathered. Suppose a predicted difference in self-concept is found between father-present and father-absent boys. However, class is also associated with self-concept, and the father-absent boys are more likely to be lower class. Statistical techniques can be used to try to separate out the effects of father status and class. One common technique using crosstabulation compares father status and self-concept for boys of different classes separately. The basic principle can be seen in tables 4.1 and 4.2.

TABLE 4.1

Self-Concept Ratings for 92 Boys by Presence of Father in Home (hypothetical data)

SELF-CONCEPT RATINGS	FATHER PRESENT	FATHER ABSENT
Good	62%	40%
Poor	28%	60%
Total percent	100%	100%
Number of boys	37	55

TABLE 4.2

Self-Concept Ratings for 92 Boys by Social Class and Presence of Father in Home
(hypothetical data, if father status is spurious)

	SOCIAL CLASS			
	LOWER CLASS		MIDDLE CLASS	
Self-Concept Rating	Father Present	Father Absent	Father Present	Father Absent
Good	25%	25%	80%	80%
Poor	75%	75%	20%	20%
Total	100%	100%	100%	100%
Number of boys	12	40	25	15

Imagine that the data show a moderately strong relation between presence of father and the self-concept rating (table 4.1). Boys whose fathers are present are far more likely to have a good self-concept (62 percent) than boys whose fathers are absent (40 percent).

However, when social class, an antecedent variable, is introduced into the analysis of the same data (table 4.2), we see that a different picture emerges. Lower-class boys are much more likely to have a poor self-concept (75 percent) than middle-class boys (20 percent). In both lower and upper classes, self-concept is not affected by the presence or absence of the father; that is, middle-class boys are likely to have a good self-concept regardless of father presence, while lower-class boys are likely to have a poor self-concept regardless of father presence. The statistical control in effect holds social class "constant" (or eliminates it as a source of variation) in the test of the relation between the father's presence and self-concept. When this is done, the apparent relation disappears. (Father's status is a spurious variable and social class is a mediator variable with a full effect.) The apparent relation in the first table is an artifact of having more lower-class than middle-class boys in the sample. Thus, social class emerges as a more promising explanatory variable.

LIMITATIONS ON THE ABILITY TO EXPLAIN Each of these four methods of ruling out extraneous variation in naturalistic studies attempts to perform the function of random assignment or "own control" comparisons in experimental research, that is, to make the subjects being compared as equivalent as possible on variables other than the presumed explanatory variable. As has been shown, none of these methods can, practically speaking, exhaust the range of possible variables that may provide plausible alternatives.

TABLE 4.3

Self-Concept Ratings for 92 Boys by Social Class and Presence of Father in Home (hypothetical data, if class is not explanatory)

	SOCIAL CLASS			
	MIDDLE CLASS		LOWER CLASS	
Self-Concept Rating	Father Present	Father Absent	Father Present	Father Absent
Good	58%	40%	64%	40%
Poor	32%	60%	26%	60%
Total percent	100%	100%	100%	100%
Number of boys	12	40	25	15

If social class had made no difference, both sides of table 4.2 would have mirrored the apparent relationship between father's presence and self-concept found in table 4.1. This is shown in table 4.3, where middle-class and lower-class boys are both more likely to have good self-concepts if their fathers are present (58% and 64%, compared to 40% if absent). In that case, we would conclude that the original relationship was true when social class was controlled; social class does not affect the relationship between father's status and self-concept. However, there might still be other mediator variables that do affect that relationship; we do not know. Like sampling and matching techniques, using statistical controls does not permit certainty that all possible relevant variables have been taken into account. Moreover, the simultaneous control of more than one variable, for example, to control for boys who are *both* of a particular class and age, requires samples of large size.

Moreover, these methods are limited in another important respect. Certain variables may be so inextricably linked with the presumed explanatory variable that they cannot be extracted through such methods of control. For example, history of prior marital conflict was identified earlier as a possible rival to presence of the fathers in explaining variation in self-concept. But control of such a variable in a naturalistic study would be extremely difficult because one would need to have boys who were exposed to the same degree and kind of prior marital conflict, whether the parents had separated or not. But a parental separation in itself suggests that the prior marital conflict was of a different order than it was if the parents remained together. If so, then father-absent boys inevitably differ from father-present boys in respect to a critical variable, conflict, that would explain differences in self-concept. Such fusion of variables introduces an irreducible amount of uncertainty into any naturalistic study that attempts to isolate explanatory variables, regardless of the type and sophistication of the controls used.

Although it is difficult to achieve explanation through naturalistic research, attempts to do so are justified. Knowledge in social work becomes gradually "hardened" through accretions of modest findings. Possible cause-and-effect relationships that hold when a number of variables are controlled gain some probability of providing valid explanations. Accumulations of evidence built up over a number of naturalistic studies in which most plausible rival hypotheses have been controlled can lead to persuasive evidence of cause-and-effect relations. For example, few now question the causal connection between cigarette smoking and lung cancer, a relation established almost entirely through naturalistic studies.

Although controlled experiments make it easier to achieve explanation, even experiments seldom provide perfect control over alternative explanations. Experiments are also limited because it is difficult to generalize from experiments to other situations given the inordinate amount of variation present in social phenomena and their tendency to change over time. While this variation and change can be addressed through repeated experimentation, cost limits and other practical constraints limit the amount of experimentation possible. Finally, experimentation cannot be applied at all to many questions; some variables, like parental presence, cannot be manipulated for ethical reasons, while others like gender cannot be manipulated at all.

Achieving the function of full explanation is also hindered by limitations in the scientific approach to knowledge itself. Whether explanation is attempted through naturalistic or experimental methods, the traditional approach has been to try to isolate one or at best a few independent variables as the cause of a solitary dependent variable or to view causation as proceeding in a single direction—from independent to dependent variables. This explanatory model is inadequate for many social phenomena, particularly those in which variables are likely to have reciprocal effects on one another. Interactions within social systems such as families, organizations, or communities provide the most obvious examples. Thus parental discipline and the behavior of children clearly affect one another, often in an escalating series of exchanges. Or, there may be simultaneous interactions among numerous variables. The loss of a steady source of income may trigger a host of reactions within an agency, affecting staff, program, and clients. These changes in turn may result in new responses from the agency's environment.

Many research methods attempt to study these interactions. One strategy, made possible by advances in the speed of computing, is to employ elaborate statistical techniques to tease out causal relationships and interactions within sets of variables. Another approach is to use qualitative approaches to piece together word pictures of the operation of complex systems, for example, through participant observation and other ways of accessing participants' worldviews. But the rigorous specification of causal patterns in social systems does not yet appear to be within the grasp of any available methodology.

In short, the scientific method cannot provide complete or certain explanations for the diverse phenomena with which social workers are concerned. It can provide evidence that certain factors may influence others in certain ways. In professional decision making, this evidence is a part of a complex web of various sources of knowledge, including an understanding of the particular characteristics of the situation at hand. Scientific knowledge may increase or decrease the probability that one factor is the cause of another under a given set of circumstances. A scientifically oriented practitioner normally gives greater weight to research evidence than to expert opinion in determining probable causes of phenomena but seldom finds that this evidence alone provides a sufficient base for decision making.

Size and Composition of Sample

A third basis for distinguishing among research strategies is the size and makeup of samples. A sample is the group studied—the participants. In social work research, the sample is generally composed of social systems—individuals, families, organizations, communities, and so on—although it may include objects such as case records or journal articles. Studies may focus on a *single unit* (single-system designs) or many units (group designs). Group samples may be further broken down into *homogeneous groups*, where the units are similar on key characteristics, *multiple groups*, where groups are formed based on categories of a key variable, or *heterogeneous groups*, that differ on many characteristics of interest. Each has comparative strengths and drawbacks.

A single unit selected for study may be an individual, or an aggregate such as a family, a treatment group, or a single organization, so long as the aggregate is studied as a single unit. The study of treatment of the perfectionist businesswoman mentioned earlier (Ferguson and Rodway 1994) is an example of an individual; a shelter for battered women was the unit of analysis for a study of the impact of feminist ideology on organizational dynamics (Davis and Srinivasan 1994).

A sample of a single system allows intensive and precise study but makes generalization to other systems difficult. To illustrate this, we will contrast a study involving a single subject with one involving a small group of twenty individuals. In our example, the general purpose of each study is the same: to learn more about the behavior of young, profoundly deaf children. With a sample of one, an investigator may do a highly intensive study in which a considerable amount of data are collected about one child: the child's physical and cognitive history, language ability, interaction with parents and siblings, and so on. In the group study, less is likely to be learned about any particular child, but the investigator may uncover behavior patterns that characterize the children, for example, patterns of a culture based on sign language. If so, there is basis for inferring that other deaf children will show that pattern. With a single child, the ability to generalize is limited because the child may be atypical, even though there may be more information to generalize about.

In this illustration, a group of individuals were selected because of common characteristics; all were young, profoundly deaf children. Such a group is an example of an homogeneous group, for its members are similar in respect to the variable of primary interest. Such groups are used when an investigator is interested in learning about other characteristics or patterns within the group. Do the children express aggression in a similar manner? Are there consistent themes in the kind of reactions they evoke from their parents? Studies confined to homogeneous groups serve useful exploratory and descriptive functions, but they are fundamentally limited in one major respect: they lack comparative data. If the children appear dependent on their parents and "clingy," is this behavior characteristic of deafness, or is it typical of children of this age? Descriptions of a single homogeneous group have an inevitable inconclusive quality since it is difficult to say if any pattern distinguishes this group from other groups. Generalizations about a single group do not "speak for themselves." However, those who interpret studies of homogeneous groups often make implicit comparisons that can lead to inappropriate and inaccurate assumptions. They may conclude, for example, that "deafness and dependency go together," even though the study has not provided any data on the reactions of hearing children of the same age, data necessary to provide evidence for the association inferred.

For this reason, investigations are typically not confined to a homogeneous group but rather involve comparisons between sets of subjects, for example, deaf children and children without this handicap. This multiple group strategy is used to investigate relationships between variables in both naturalistic and experimental research. The comparison of deaf and hearing children is an example in naturalistic research. In an experiment like the Job Club for unemployed workers, one group of clients receives treatment; a second group does not; and outcomes for both groups are compared. The results of the experiment may be expressed as differences between groups or as a relation between two variables: type of treatment and outcome (see chapter 3). In each example, groups differing on one variable are compared in relation to a second variable.

In much research, the interest is more complex than these examples, and more than two groups may be used. For example, Zuravin and DePanfilis (1997) selected and compared families who had entered the Child Protective Services for reasons of physical abuse, child neglect, and sexual abuse. The key to multiple group strategies is that the investigator selects distinct groups of subjects according to predetermined criteria, or forms groups through assigning subjects to treatment or control conditions. In short, the investigator sets out to build groups in order to compare them, deliberately building variation into the study.

Variation may be achieved by another means. A group may be selected that is sufficiently heterogeneous that one can reasonably expect sufficient variation to occur on independent variables of interest. In other words, separate groups are not built in from the outset, but one assumes (and hopes!) that the heterogeneous group will vary enough to permit examination of associations. Heterogeneous groups are used when there are too many key variables to select a group for each category, as in multiple-group samples. They are also used when it can reasonably be assumed that there is a large natural variation in a group. Thus, Loneck et al. included 39 cases in a study of the relationship between therapeutic process and client outcome (1996). In doing so, they assumed that there would be enough natural variation in therapeutic process to be able to compare cases with various levels of, for example, therapist warmth and friendliness, patient participation, and therapeutic alliance. The assumption was correct; cases varied considerably and they were able to show that some aspects of therapeutic process were more important to outcome than others. Had their assumption not been correct, and the levels of therapeutic process were the same among all cases, they could learn nothing about the association between process and outcome.

We have outlined a simple progression in sampling units—from the individual subject to a homogeneous group of subjects and then to multiple and heterogeneous groups. This progression involves considerations of both sample size and variability. As sample size is increased, the amount of attention that can be paid to the study of any given subject is decreased, if the resources of the researcher are assumed to be fixed. There will be loss of detail and may be loss of ability to generate new hypotheses. At the same time, an increase in size enhances the potential for generalization—we say potential, for how well one can generalize from data about a set of subjects depends also (and more importantly) on the representativeness of the sample (see chapter 8). Moreover, the larger the sample, the greater the chance that sufficient variability will occur to permit examination of relationships between variables.

Timing of Data Collection and Occurrence of the Independent Variable

The timing of data collection constitutes another dimension of research strategy. A fundamental distinction concerns whether data are first collected before or after the operation of the presumed causative or independent variable. If the initial data collection takes place prior in time, the study is referred to as *prospective* or *projected*. If the data are not collected until after the independent variables have exerted their influence, the research is designated as *retrospective* or *ex post facto*. If a study lacks an explanatory purpose, for example, if it is designed primarily to describe the current state of some phenomenon, the temporal distinction between independent and dependent variables may not be clear. In that case, a third category, which we term *undifferentiated*, is possible.

In experimental research, a prospective approach is common because the researcher controls the occurrence of the independent variable. By measuring the status before introducing the independent variable, the investigator can assess the amount of change. For example, in the Jobs Club study, the unemployed workers took the Geriatric Depression Scale before they were assigned to experimental or control groups (Rife and Belcher 1994). Thus, data collection was prospective. Twelve weeks after starting service (the Jobs Club or the control group of normal government unemployment service), they took the same scale and the investigators were able to compare the levels of depression before and after service. Although prospective data collection is usual in experiments, ex post facto data collection may be used for "after only" experiments in which measures of outcome are obtained after treatment has been completed. For example, in one study, inner city families were randomly assigned to practitioners who had or had not been trained in special techniques for engaging resistant clients during the first interview (McKay et al. 1996). Data collected after the first interview included whether the clients returned for a second interview and how long they stayed in treatment. Clearly, these data could only be collected ex post facto, after the initial interview with a trained or untrained practitioner. In other instances, prospective data collection may be possible but the investigator may chose to collect data only after the independent variable, for example, in evaluations of new intervention programs.

In naturalistic research, the choice of prospective or ex post facto strategies can be more difficult. Imagine a study of the effects of "mothering ability"—

warmth, attentiveness, cuddling, and the like—on the development of infants during the first six months of life. If a prospective strategy were used, a sample of women might be obtained prior to delivery and their mothering ability measured. Some time after birth, when the possible effects of mothering had time to show themselves, measures of the infants' development would be obtained —the child's attentiveness, interaction, and so on. Using an ex post facto strategy to address the same research question, an investigator would find a sample of women who had children about six months of age and collect data on both mothering abilities and the infants' developmental characteristics. Thus, data are collected ex post facto, after the independent variable had supposedly exerted its effects.

Clearly the prospective strategy is preferable, if feasible. One can establish that one variable occurred before the other, that is, one knows what mothering ability was before the birth (although of course it may change). In the ex post facto strategy, the passage of time alone would make it difficult to obtain adequate measures of independent (and control variables) and to secure baseline data. Some infants may have developed slowly for reasons unrelated to mothering abilities, but their retarded development may have adversely affected these abilities (a mother might react with less warmth to an unresponsive infant). It is difficult to reconstruct the past—to determine how one thing looked before another thing happened or to ascertain what preceded what in the time order of events. Further, the sample may be distorted because of the ex post facto strategy. Women with good mothering ability who have difficulty with their infants may choose not to participate in the ex post facto study, leaving only those with model infants to be compared to participants with poor mothering ability. Quite possibly, these women might have agreed to be subjects in the prospective study.

A naturalistic study that moves forward in time largely avoids this particular set of problems but encounters others. First of all, in a prospective study one must wait for events to happen. Many natural processes work slowly, too slowly for the circumstances of some researchers, students in particular. The longer the time period that must elapse before effects can be detected, the greater the likelihood that attrition in the original sample will occur (although in ex post facto studies, the equivalent of sample loss can occur in ways that cannot be detected). For example, Norton (1993) videotaped mother-child interaction over a nine-year span and lost 15 of the original 41 dyads. Perhaps the most serious limitation, however, is in range of application. For a prospective study to be practical, one must deal in effects that are likely to occur. Many effects of concern to social work are problems, such as child abuse or running away, whose occurrence can hardly be counted on for any given sample. A prospective strategy fits well to a study of maternal behavior and infant development, for all infants develop in one way or another. It might not be at all feasible for a study of maternal contribution to "failure-to-thrive" syndrome, for an inordinately large number of mothers would need to be sampled to ensure that the problem would occur with enough frequency to permit meaningful study of its relation to maternal behavior. Finally, a prospective strategy does not rectify the limitation of a naturalistic study in respect to lack of control over extraneous variables; for example, an observed relation between mothering ability and infant development would need to be considered in the light of shared genetic factors that might explain both phenomena.

In undifferentiated studies, there is only one period of data collection and either there is no predominant independent variable or it is not possible to determine which variable occurred first. Typically, undifferentiated studies are descriptive studies that may include attempts to ascertain association between key variables. For example, Abramson (1988) interviewed social workers about the participation of their elderly patients in decision-making about discharge from the hospital, a typical undifferentiated study. She found, among other things, that only a fourth of the patients who had the cognitive capacity to do so were in control of their own discharge planning. Although Abramson obtained data on several potential causal factors and explored their role, her interest was primarily in determining the amount of control over discharge planning exercised by cognitively competent patients rather than in determining possible explanations for the degree of control found.

As should be evident, the timing of data collection is critical to helping establish causation. Prospective data collection gives an assessment of the status of things before the independent variable occurs, as well as an estimate of change. Ex post facto data collection requires the investigator to rely on assumptions about change and temporal priority. In undifferentiated studies, causation is not of primary interest.

Repetition of Data Collection

A related dimension concerns the repetition of data collection. A variable may be measured on one, two, several, or numerous occasions as time passes.

If data collection is confined to a single occasion, the study may be referred to as cross-sectional (some writers also refer to it as a survey). The limitations of cross-sectional studies depend on the timing of data collection (ex post facto or undifferentiated), as discussed in the last section. In experiments, there are normally at least two measurement points, one prior to and one following the occurrence of the independent variable; the advantages of this prospective measurement was also discussed in the last section. Our focus in this section will be on longitudinal or time-series investigations in which measurements are repeated several times. Regardless of the number of occasions on which measures are taken or the terms used to describe the process, the repetition of data collection serves one fundamental purpose: to record variation of the same phenomena over time.

Single-system designs in which there are many data collection points are usually referred to as time-series designs. Naturalistic time-series designs are common although often unrecognized: newspaper charts of Consumer Price Index or unemployment rates over several years, agency directors' tables of client intake each month, practitioner's records of group attendance each week. In experimental time-series designs, data are collected at regular time points before and during intervention, and often after intervention is withdrawn. In the study of the perfectionist businesswoman, referred to earlier, the client completed measures of perfectionist and irrational beliefs each week for 3 weeks before treatment, 8 during, and once after (Ferguson and Rodway 1994). In another study, a family recorded the number of times during his study periods that their son sought attention instead of working independently; they recorded this for 10 study periods before treatment began, 30 during treatment, and 3 after treatment ended (Besa 1994).

Group designs, in which data is collected many times, are referred to as longitudinal designs. Some experimental designs involve several data collection points after the occurrence of the independent variable, usually to assess whether client changes are maintained over time. For example, Reid and Bailey-Dempsey (1995) collected data on girls for a year following their intervention to improve school performance; they measured grades and absences in the marking period before the intervention began, in the last period during intervention (the last of the school year), and in the first and last marking periods of the following school year.

An important use of naturalistic longitudinal designs is to record variations in phenomena as they might naturally occur. The most common, in which one group of people is studied many times over a period, are called panels. Norton's (1993) study of mother-child interaction, with videotaping every six months over nine years, is a panel. From a descriptive standpoint, knowledge of how phenomena change provides a foundation for prediction even if the causes of the change are not apparent. Longitudinal research can thus address a range of questions of considerable interest to social work practitioners: What kinds of troublesome behaviors are children likely to outgrow? How long does it take psychological crises to run their course? Is street crime increasing in a particular neighborhood? Answers to such questions provide data that help practitioners predict what is likely to happen in the case or situation at hand. With this knowledge, practitioners can attempt to devise interventions that may alter a predictable course of events, or they may decide that intervention is not warranted.

Longitudinal studies can serve explanatory functions if independent variables can be identified and their presumed effects assessed over time. For example, Carolyn Smith (1996) used data from the Rochester Youth Development Study, a panel study of the development of delinquent and drug abuse behavior among urban adolescents, to examine the effects of maltreatment on girls' pregnancy. She compared girls for whom the child protective services had records of maltreatment before the study began (when the girls were in 7th or 8th grade) to girls who had no such record. The girls were interviewed every six months; Smith used their self-reports of pregnancy at any time two to five years after the start of the panel. She also included control and mediating variables such as family structure, being on welfare, and race. Her findings indicated that maltreatment was related to pregnancy, primarily by predisposing the girls to high-risk behaviors such as substance use and search for sexual intimacy.

A drawback of longitudinal group designs is that because meaningful variation in most phenomena occurs at a slow pace, naturalistic research involving repeated data collection normally spans substantial periods of time, from months to years. Such studies are costly and often suffer from sample attrition. Their lengthy time spans pose feasibility problems for investigators, such as students who must complete their work within limited time periods, and require researchers to delay satisfaction of their curiosity. On the other hand, a good deal of longitudinal research makes use of available data, and many longitudinal researchers make their data sets available to other investigators through such archives as the Inter-University Consortium for Political Research (ICPSR) at the University of Michigan, the Social Science Research Council Data Archives at the University of Essex (England), or the U.S. Government's Bureau of the Census. For a guide to such data sets, see Kiecolt and Nathan, *Secondary Analysis of Survey Data* (1985).

One solution to the attrition problem in panels is another longitudinal design called a trend study, in which all the original participants are replaced by others who are comparable to them at the later time. For example, had the Rochester Youth Development Study been a trend study, instead of interviewing the same youths six months later, the investigator would draw a new sample of youths who were the same age now and had as many as possible of the same characteristics as the original sample. A new sample, six months older each time, would be drawn at each data collection time. While this solves the attrition problem, interpretations of trend studies may be complicated by shifts in the population base. The youth crime rate may increase because of increased numbers of youth in a community or because of changes in the makeup of the youth population resulting from in-migration, rather than because the youth committed more crimes.

Diagramming Designs

It is convention in research texts to describe or diagram designs in terms of the number of data collection points. The letter O is used to represent each time data are collected, to indicate an observation of the sample members. For example, a design using a single occasion for data collection is represented as one O, one with two occasions as O O, one with five as O O O O O. In naturalistic designs, the O stands for an observation of the entire sample, be it a homogeneous group, a heterogeneous group, or a single system. Common designs that we have just discussed are shown in diagram 4.1.

DIAGRAM 4.1
Design for Number of Data Collection Points

Survey or cross-sectional design with one data collection point

O

Naturalistic time series or longitudinal design with ten data collection points

OOOOOOOOOO

O = indicates data collection point.

In experimental designs, each group is indicated with its own O (as will be shown in chapter 7, data may be collected from each group at different times, so it is important to indicate when a group was observed). The Os are usually labeled as E (experimental) or C (control) to distinguish them from each other. A final convention is to indicate occurrence of a manipulated independent variable with an X. The X thus defines the timing of the data collection in relation to the independent variable. For example, an experimental design with a single group, two data collection points, and prospective data collection would be represented as O X O. Common experimental designs are shown in diagram 4.2.

DIAGRAM 4.2
Common Experimental Designs

Experimental design with two groups (experimental and control) and prospective measurement

E O X O
C O O

Experimental design with two contrasting treatment groups and prospective measurement

E_1 O X_1 O
E_2 O X_2 O

E = Experimental group.
C = Control group.
X = Indicates occurrence of manipulated independent variable.

Methodological Orientation

Our final distinction concerns differences between "quantitative" and "qualitative" strategies for investigating phenomena. This distinction sometimes refers simply to techniques of data collection and analysis. For example, quantitative analysis makes use of numbers; qualitative analysis relies on words. We think that distinction too simplistic, in part because most data collection techniques and analysis can be used with any type of research. Another distinction between quantitative and qualitative emphasizes marked differences in working assumptions and in approaches to conducting an investigation. Our focus will be on the second meaning of this distinction.

In our conceptualization, the primary distinction between qualitative and quantitative research refers to the starting point and the logical processes used to move between phenomena and theory. In qualitative methodology, the investigator usually starts with the phenomena and uses reason inductively, from the concrete and specific to the broader concepts and theory. This is so whether the purpose of the research is to understand another's worldview, to "deconstruct" current ways of thinking in order to gain new insights, or to explore new areas to generate hypotheses. In quantitative methodology, the investigator generally starts with the theory and concepts and uses reason deductively, from the theory to the phenomena. Quantitative research often emphasizes hypothesis-testing, although it encompasses a wide range of research that shares the assumption that the concepts and variables can be defined on an a priori basis, prior to observing phenomena.

From this basic distinction, we can derive several characteristic differences between quantitative and qualitative research. These include a) differences in the investigator's role—"outsider" or "insider," b) focus on a static hypothesis or question versus a general, flexible question, c) predetermined and uniform data collection procedures versus flexible, changing data collection methods, d) data analysis relying heavily on statistics applied after data collection versus on-going synthesis and logical analysis of data, and e) philosophical assumptions about how knowledge can be gained, from objective standards that control "bias" or from subjective, holistic experience.

Quantitative methodology can be said to describe the extension to the social sciences of the methodology of the natural sciences. In the canons of this methodology, the researcher's role is that of an objective observer whose involvement with phenomena being studied is limited to what is required to obtain necessary data. Studies are focused on relatively specific questions or hypotheses that remain constant throughout the investigation. Plans about research procedures—design, data collection methods, types of measurement, and so on—are developed before the study begins. Data collection procedures are applied in a standardized manner, for example, all participants may answer the same questionnaire. Data collectors, such as interviewers or observers, are expected to obtain only the data called for and to avoid adding their own impressions or interpretations. Measurement is normally focused on specific variables that are, if possible, quantified through rating scales, frequency counts, and other means. Analysis proceeds by obtaining statistical breakdowns of the distribution of variables and by using statistical methods to determine associations (or differences) between variables.

For example, an investigator using quantitative methods to examine the impact of hospital emergency rooms (ER) on psychiatric care might develop a hypothesis that admission to the psychiatric ward depended on previous psychiatric history and level of immediate psychiatric disturbance. Emergency room personnel might be trained to complete a short questionnaire on intensity of psychiatric symptoms and physical health each time a psychiatric patient was seen in the ER; the same questionnaire would be completed in much the same way for each patient. Coders might then examine patient records for information on previous psychiatric history; they would ignore other information on health. When the data were collected on a sufficient number of patients who met specified criteria, the investigator would apply statistical techniques to determine the frequencies and associations between admission, psychiatric history, and immediate disturbance.

Qualitative methodologists proceed from the premise that the methods of the natural sciences, while useful, are not ideal for understanding many social phenomena. In the qualitative approach, the investigator attempts to gain a firsthand, holistic understanding of phenomena of interest by means of a flexible strategy of problem formulation and data collection shaped as the investigation proceeds. Methods such as participant observation and unstructured interviewing are used to acquire an in-depth knowledge of how the persons involved construct their social world (the insider role). As more knowledge is gained, the research question may shift and the data collection methods adjusted accordingly. To do this, the investigator is constantly analyzing data using formal logical procedures, although final analysis is ordinarily completed after the early, immersion, phase of the study.

An investigator using qualitative approaches to examine the same research question, impact of ERs on psychiatric care, would start with a much broader focus than the quantitative methodologist. The investigator might have certain questions in mind—perhaps concerning reasons patients came for treatment when they did, and what outcomes they expected—but would regard a focus on a small set of specific questions or hypotheses as premature. Data collection methods might include taking the role of a patient (one kind of participant observation) or simply sitting in the waiting room and watching what happened (another kind of participant observation). Emphasis initially would be on observing as much raw phenomena with as little preconceived interpretation as possible. As patterns are discerned, however, the emphasis shifts to testing out inferences. For example, knowledge that certain patients were frequent users of the emergency services but were rarely admitted might lead to the hypothesis that some patients were using the service as a clinic. To check this out, the investigator might first talk informally to patients and staff, then perhaps conduct unstructured interviews and read through medical charts. Who was interviewed would depend on emerging knowledge of the situation and the questions it stimulated. Stress would be placed on understanding the system from the perspectives of the actors involved—psychiatric patients, other patients, ER staff—rather than through imposition of the researchers' views. Data would be analyzed when acquired and used to guide further inquiry; at the end of the study, the investigator would formalize the hypotheses and conclusions using supporting data from the study—examples, descriptions, accounts of incidents, perhaps some frequency counts.

An important element in this distinction of quantitative and qualitative— an element that has generated much discussion in the social work literature— is the philosophical assumptions about how knowledge is gained. As may be gathered from the example, qualitative methodology rests on the assumption that valid understanding can be gained through accumulated knowledge acquired firsthand by a single researcher. In the words of Glaser and Strauss, one puts "trust in one's own credible knowledge"(1970:294). Lincoln and Guba (1985:192) expand on this principle in their conception of the "human-as-instrument." As these authors point out, the human being possesses unique qualities as an instrument of research, including capacity to respond to a wide range of cues, to view phenomena within a holistic perspective while yet noting atypical features, to process data on the spot bringing a fund of knowledge to the task, and to test out new knowledge immediately.

Thus, in the qualitative approach, essential validity is accorded the investigator's understanding gained through variable methods of data collection and through the use of the human capacity for analysis and synthesis of complex events. In taking this position, qualitative methodologists assume that the investigator is able to make rigorous observations and to exercise control over the effects of biases on the events observed and on interpretations of them. Measures of reliability in the sense of determining how well independent observers agree on the same events are often not possible to obtain and, in view of assumptions about the validity of the researcher's knowledge, may not be seen as crucial.

By contrast a different set of assumptions underlies quantitative research. It is assumed that there is an objective reality that can be measured, albeit imperfectly, through instruments in which the researcher's role is that of an objective observer. However, both instruments and researchers are vulnerable to bias. Hence the measurement process needs to be systematically checked to determine if the observations obtained meet standards of consistency and truthfulness (reliability and validity). Further, complex phenomena can be best understood by breaking them down into very specific factors (variables) and studying the relations between such factors.

Do these assumptions rest on epistemological foundations that are essentially different from those of quantitative approaches? One school of thought —incompatibalism—would answer in the affirmative. Incompatabilists see qualitative methodology as the outgrowth of fundamental epistemological positions which clash with those that underlie mainstream, i.e., "quantitative," research (Smith and Heshusius 1986). Although they may acknowledge that qualitative and quantitative approaches may be fitted together at a procedural level, as Howe (1988:12) observes, "they would contend that this is only a misleading surface compatibility and that at a deeper epistemological level, at 'the logic of justification' or 'paradigm level,' qualitative and quantitative methods are indeed incompatible because of the different conceptions of reality, truth, the relationship between the investigator and object of investigation and so forth, that each assumes."

In taking a compatabilist position, we would argue that these assumptions can be modified to fit into the same epistemological framework that underlies quantitative methodology. Thus in doing qualitative research it is possible to assume that valid knowledge can be gained firsthand by a single researcher but with the awareness that this knowledge may be flawed by the researcher's biases despite efforts to control for them. Reliability tests may be sacrificed, but at the possible cost of not knowing if similar perceptions would be made by another investigator. In essence, both quantitative and qualitative approaches can be viewed as ultimately having to meet the same standards of truth (Phillips 1987; Reid 1994b). Here, as elsewhere in research, choice of methodology involves trade-offs. Qualitative methodology can yield insights beyond the reach of quantitative approaches, but at risks of error. The real question is, "How can these two methods be best used to advance knowledge?"

Perhaps the answer lies in knowing when to use each. For example, the "rules" of quantitative research do not apply when trying to discern patterns in raw data or to reconstruct another's worldview. Conversely, the total immersion and holistic experiencing of a qualitative approach is not helpful when trying to establish generalities that may apply beyond the particular case. The two methods complement each other, and the choice depends on the purpose and question.

The knowledge gained by an investigator using qualitative methods may be skewed by that investigator's personal experience, but it reveals a richness and depth of understanding of complex situations that is simply beyond the capacity of quantitative methods, no matter how rigorously and artfully applied. Firsthand involvement in data collection, a holistic viewpoint, and the gradual synthesis of data from many sources can result in a grasp of relationships that might never emerge in fragmented quantitative analysis. Qualitative approaches have particular strengths as a means of acquiring holistic knowledge of complex social systems, including service networks, organizations, small groups, families, and the social systems of different kinds of people—for example, the worlds of the drug addict or the welfare recipient. The need for such knowledge is of unquestioned importance in social work.

Quantitative methods have particular strengths in ascertaining generalities—for example, the incidence of mental illness in urban cities—and establishing causality. Control over extraneous variables, systematic measurement, precision in analysis, and the capacity to study large numbers of subjects enable investigators using quantitative methods to acquire knowledge beyond the scope of qualitative investigations. The need for both kinds of approaches can be justified and, indeed, may be incorporated in a single study to address different questions.

TABLE 4.4
A Listing of Dimensions in Combination

I. The Researcher's Control over Phenomena Studied
   A. Experimental
      1. Field
         a. Substantially controlled
         b. Partially controlled
         c. Uncontrolled
      2. Laboratory
         a. Substantially controlled
         b. Partially controlled
         c. Uncontrolled
   B. Naturalistic
II. Function in Relation to Type of Knowledge Produced
   A. Exploratory
   B. Measurement
   C. Descriptive
   D. Explanation
III. Size and Composition of Sample
   A. Single System
   B. Homogeneous Group
   C. Multiple Groups
   D. Heterogeneous Group
IV. Timing of Data Collection and Occurrence of Independent Variable
   A. Ex Post Facto
   B. Prospective
   C. Undifferentiated
V. Repetition of Data Collection
   A. Single Occasion
   B. Two Occasions (e.g., before and after intervention)
   C. Repeated Occasions (time series, longitudinal (panel, trend))
VI. Methodological Orientation
   A. Quantitative
   B. Qualitative

Establishing Causality

The theme of causality has run through our description of the six dimensions of design. A major purpose of research is explanation, or assertion of cause-effect relations. For example, we wish to be able to say that community prevention efforts (the independent variable) cause a reduction in delinquency (the dependent variable). But, as should be evident, establishing causality is not a simple matter. Before turning to specific design examples in the next several chapters, we will summarize the principles for establishing causality. In later chapters, we will link these principles more directly to combinations of design.

What does it take to attempt to establish causality? The process is complicated and involves the entire research process. Ultimately, the best we can conclude is that we have increased the likelihood that one variable influences another; in the scientific approach, absolute "proof" is impossible. Nevertheless, the general principles for attempting to establish causality are brief. In the order in which they must be done, the steps are: (1) establish association between two variables; (2) establish that the independent variable occurred before the dependent variable; (3) rule out alternative explanations for the association; and (4) link the results to theory.

Association

Association, or covariation, means that two variables "go together," or vary systematically in relation to each other; X is related to Y (this includes the hypothesis of difference, which is another way of stating association). For example, parents who abuse their children are more likely than nonabusing parents to have been abused as children. Family treatment begins and the interaction between mother and sons improves. The recuperation of elderly patients is related to their participation in health care decisions. Without covariation, it makes no sense to ask if X caused Y, to ask whether experiencing abuse leads to perpetrating abuse on others, when those abused do not abuse others; to ask whether family treatment caused improvement when there was no improvement; to ask whether participation aids recovery when active and inactive patients heal equally rapidly. Thus, showing that two variables are associated is the first step in demonstrating causality.

To establish association requires two or more variables in a study, each of which varies systematically in relation to the other. This is why single-variable hypotheses are rarely of interest; one cannot establish association solely by predicting that some children will be abused by their parents. Similarly, homogeneous group samples preclude establishing association, because there is not another group to compare, here, parents who were not abused as children. (Technically speaking, there is not a true variable, since there is only one category of the variable "parental abuse.") In looking for association, we must recognize that relationships are rarely perfect—not every abused child becomes an abuser (in fact, the vast majority do not go on to abuse their children). To help detect association in quantitative studies, one can use inferential statistics, although visual and logical examination of data may be appropriate. In qualitative studies, the search for patterns and meanings is in fact the search for association.

Time Priority

If association can be demonstrated, the next step is to determine whether one variable could have occurred before the other, or to establish time priority. A parent's experience of abuse as a child clearly precedes the individual's actions as an adult; the onset of treatment probably preceded change in the family system, although we can't be sure; but, did the patients participate more because they were healthier before the decision-making, or did the decision-making precede their improvement? The timing of data collection can help to answer questions of time priority, as does experimental control, but often the answer is inferential.

An important approach to establishing time priority is through measuring phenomena at several points in time. If at Time 1, A is present but not B, while at Time 2, both A and B are present, we have some confidence that A preceded B. This is the logic behind studies that use prospective measurement or repeated occasions of data collection. For example, children could be studied over time to see if they were abused while young, and then their behavior assessed as adults. If the mother-son relationship is poor before treatment, treatment occurs, and the mother-son relationship is better after treatment, we have some evidence that the family's treatment occurred before the improvement in relationship.

Of course, establishing that A precedes B does not establish that A caused B, or that the parental abuse caused child abuse, but it does make it unlikely that B could have caused A. A more convincing demonstration of time priority comes from experimental designs, where the investigator alters one variable while trying to keep everything else constant. Thus, in the family treatment example, a longitudinal study might establish that treatment occurred before change in the relationship, but much more powerful evidence of time priority is an experiment in which some families receive treatment and some do not.

Ruling Out Alternative Explanations

Once association and time priority are established, the third step is ruling out alternative explanations for the results, other factors that might have caused both phenomena to begin with. Does the family seek treatment because the son attempted suicide, an event that also led the mother to pay attention to him? Does higher education among the elderly mean that they both take care of their health and act proactively in decision-making situations? Were abusive families—both parents and children—exposed to television violence that glorified physical solutions to problems?

As discussed earlier, ruling out such other explanations for association is aided by research designs that include comparison groups, by statistical techniques, and by repeated occasions of data collecting. However, it is a never-ending quest because there may be other explanations we did not think of to begin with. For example, is childhood abuse associated with being an abusive parent because of poverty? nutritional deficits handed down in family culture? a genetic predisposition to aggression and short tempers?

Theoretical Explanation: Linking Results to Theory

A final step in establishing causality, a plausible explanation for the results, ties the inferential process back to theory. In sciences such as biology or medicine, investigators are rarely satisfied that they have the "cause" until they can isolate the mechanism, the gene that causes an hereditary disease, for example. In the social sciences, such certainty is elusive and perhaps impossible. Instead, we live with probabilities and tentative explanations. If an association can be explained by the theory, we have more confidence in its accuracy to describe the phenomena. At the same time, we have more confidence in the theory to explain phenomena. For example, if our theory of socialization predicts that children learn possible coping responses from the adults around them, it is a reasonable explanation of the association between abuse as a child and abusing one's own children and strengthens our assertion that abuse is one causal link in becoming an abuser.

As is evident from this discussion of establishing causality, a single study or even a series of studies cannot establish causality. Indeed, the best that can be hoped for is making causality more likely through building systematically on previous knowledge. An individual study may be assessed on whether it contributes to each of these steps—and our earlier classification of studies as exploratory, descriptive, or explanatory is one way of doing so—but any particular piece of knowledge may be assessed for the amount of evidence available to establish its validity.

Threats to Internal Validity

We have referred consistently to alternative explanations—explanations other than the independent variable that might cause the relationship between an independent and a dependent variable. In discussing research design, it is useful to classify possible alternative explanations by their source. When discussing alternative explanations in this context, they are customarily called "threats to internal validity," because they compromise the ability of a design to give "valid" knowledge. We introduce these threats here in preparation for discussion in the next few chapters of how various designs may offer more or less control over the type of threat. In this analysis, we draw upon the work of Campbell and his associates (Campbell and Stanley 1963; Cook and Campbell 1979) and an extension of this work by Krathwohl (1985). Although they developed the classifications for experimental designs, the threats as alternative explanations can be extended to naturalistic designs as well.

One threat to internal validity is *maturation*, any effects due to the passage of time, for example, reduction in grief over time, the client's self-generated problem-solving actions, or normal growth among adolescents. A second threat, *history*, comprises specific environmental events that might influence the outcome state, such as a change in the client's situation or the actions of others, for example, a father returns home at the same time as a child starts treatment. A third source of alternative explanation—*statistical regression*— refers to the tendency of extreme scores to move toward the middle, for example, people who score very high on the SAT or GRE the first time tend to score lower the second time (or vice versa). A group of clients with extreme scores on some clinical measure such as depression will tend to be less extreme at a second point of data collection. In particular, if one is comparing two groups with very different levels of depression at initial testing, they will tend to move toward each other at the second testing, due solely to statistical regression. These regression artifacts are of particular concern in research on intervention, for intervention (and hence studies of it) is likely to begin when problems are at or close to their peak level. Hence, some positive change can often be expected as a result of regression alone. Some problems are, of course, more susceptible to regression effects than others: if a problem shows little variation over time—e.g., a stabilized pattern of heavy drinking—regression may not be a major source of concern.

Another threat to internal validity is apparent differences that reflect the operation of chance. All measurements exhibit some degree of fluctuation caused by unidentifiable factors that, for want of knowledge of them, are referred to as chance or random influences. This *instability* must therefore be taken into account in evaluating differences among groups or over time. If the number of a child's temper tantrums is fluctuating wildly, for example, a string of "good days" may be due to random fluctuation, not to the intervention as we might hope. As will be shown later, the role of instability can be evaluated through inspection of the data and through statistical tests of significance.

The factors described thus far, maturation, history, regression, and instability, relate to changes in problems that may occur independent of efforts to measure or treat them. Additional sources of alternative explanations are related to the measurement processes used to determine if change has occurred.

First, *instrumentation* refers to systematic biases introduced by the measuring instruments, for example, "decay" in instruments, or changes over time in the data collection procedures themselves. For example, observers recording a child's acting out behaviors may get inured to the behavior and record it less often, leading to the impression that the noxious behavior had decreased. Or interviewers may unconsciously but systematically present questions in a different way to women than to men. Of particular concern in research on intervention are systematic biases in measurement that may erroneously suggest that changes have occurred in response to intervention. Those responsible for data collection, and the clients who may provide the data, usually hope that the practice methods will in fact prove helpful, and these hopes may lead to exaggeration in reports of gains and underestimates of continued problems. This bias in favor of the experimental hypothesis, called experimental "demand" (Rosenthal 1966), may affect not only measurement, but any phase of a project from selection of subjects to analysis of data.

A second source related to measurement is *testing*, effects due to the subjects' reactions to being tested (measured), for example, a questionnaire motivates someone to study the subject matter. Put another way, the devices used to collect initial assessment data may themselves contribute to change or apparent change. For example, in a study of a parent-skills training program, a parent's skills before training may be tested with paper-and-pencil inventory. The items of the test may provide the parent with clues about his skill deficiencies and he may take steps to correct them. Observations of behavior may cause individuals observed, if they are aware of being observed, to alter their behavior. Sometimes these effects are so strong that they may be used as part of intervention, for example, asking smokers to keep a record of each time they light up.

Another set of threats to internal validity, nonspecific effects and reactive effects, relate to an active independent variable, usually intervention in experiments. *Nonspecific effects* are elements that go along with categories of the independent variable but are not part of them. For example, a client on a ward might be moved to another location to receive the intervention, or one type of treatment might be conducted in a cheerful room, a contrasting treatment in a shabby room.

Nonspecific effects are of particular concern in social work because of inevitable difficulty in defining what an intervention is. The difficulty arises from the complexity and elusiveness of helping processes. Interventions seldom come in the form of specific, clear-cut methods but rather take the shape of messy gestalts—like "family therapy," for example—that are difficult to define. Even when intervention is defined explicitly, as it is increasingly with protocol-driven research, alternative explanations can be found in other activities that may have accompanied the interventions but may not have been defined as a central part of it. For instance, focusing the client's attention on a problem, conveying expectations that help will be provided and that change will occur, or simply allowing the client to ventilate concerns might be the cause of change. Consequently, such nonspecific components—or what are sometimes referred to as placebo effects—are a potential source of alternative explanations. A special case of nonspecific effects is *multiple intervention interference*, which occurs when it is impossible to disentangle the effects of two or more interventions used simultaneously or in sequence.

Another alternative explanation related to an active independent variable is *reactive effects* or reactivity. These are effects due to an interaction of being measured (testing) and receiving the intervention, for example, treatment is effective only because the clients' anxiety was reduced by pretest interviews. Observing a child in order to collect baseline data on his behavior may suggest to him that his behavior is amiss, which may make him more receptive to the subsequent intervention. Note that testing is not directly responsible for a change in outcome measures, as is the case when testing is a source of extraneous variation or threat to internal validity; it is rather that testing increases the potency of the intervention. Hence, the intervention may not produce the same effects when it is used in the absence of prior measurement.

Two final sources of alternative explanation apply to multiple group designs only. *Selection* refers to unintended systematic differences in the characteristics of the groups that are being compared, differences that affect the dependent variable; for example, the experimental group may have more motivated clients. This problem was discussed earlier under Explanation in the section on Knowledge-Building Purposes and Functions where it was framed as getting the groups as similar as possible on factors other than the independent variable.

In experiments, not only must groups be equivalent at the outset in characteristics that may affect outcome, but also this equivalence must be maintained during the experiment. The only differences should be those produced by the intervention program. Equivalence can be jeopardized by *mortality*—if clients drop out of either the experimental or control groups at different rates, or if different types of clients drop out of the groups compared. Suppose, for example, that clients with little capacity for improvement become discouraged and leave the program while their counterparts remain in the control group in anticipation of being helped subsequently. If these experimental dropouts are not accessible for the later data collection, the experimental group may surpass the control group only because the former has lost its "worse" cases.

To illustrate how alternative explanations may be identified and appraised, let us consider a study that evaluated the effects of a family preservation approach with families of newborns who had been exposed to substance abuse before birth (Potocky and McDonald 1996). The program offered a wide variety of services including home visits to focus on parenting and housekeeping skills, early childhood education, nursing services, parent education groups, parent/child groups to practice interaction, and a crisis nursery. The social worker assessed the families on the Child Well-being Scales (Magura and Moses 1986) before the program began, three months into the program, and at the end of the six-month program. Of the 27 families who began the program, 6 had their children placed in foster care within six months, 1 child was placed with other relatives, 1 died, and 19 remained with their families, the goal of the program. For these 19, there were slight improvements on the Child Well-being Scales.

In assessing this example for the threats to internal validity, we can readily see that the family preservation approach is not the only plausible explanation of the outcomes. The families might have been motivated to improve their child-care practices by the referral to the social worker, or they may have been in the process of learning health care, child care, and coping skills in response to any number of internal or external influences, including the effects of having a newborn (maturation). Any number of changes occurring in the community might have caused improvement in the families' coping, such as an antidrug campaign or an increase in support to families with children (history). Because the families were referred at a probable low-point in the mothers' functioning—shortly after giving birth and having their infant identified as drug-exposed—their functioning scores would be low and might increase due solely to the tendency of extreme scores to move toward the middle, that is, statistical regression.

Apparent improvement might also be due to instability in the Child Well-being Scales; indeed, when the investigators applied statistical tests to the data, they found that the results were not significant, that is, the apparent improvement was not great enough to rule out instability as the cause. However, instrumentation error also needs to be considered, especially since the social workers who provided the service did the ratings; they might unintentionally rate the families as better functioning because of the intensive time and effort they themselves had put in. Perhaps being observed intently by the social workers as they make the ratings may have motivated the families to focus on improving the areas that they believed the workers were rating (testing), or they would not have responded well to the family preservation efforts unless they had been observed first (reactive effects). Nonspecific effects could have been operative: perhaps the families enjoyed the friendships of the support groups, or the interaction with service providers, and it was this rather than the service per se which affected them. Although these factors have been presented one by one, it is obvious that they can interact in various ways. For example, an improvement in the families' coping capacity resulting from maturation could cause the social worker to act differently toward them.

This study of family preservation was in fact a homogeneous group design—only one, experimental, group was studied. A second, control, group might have been included, for example, families who were referred for the family preservation program but who declined to participate. Including a second group would help rule out many of these alternative explanations. For example, if the control group were assessed at the same time, they would be exposed to the same external events as the experimental group, and consequently history would be an unlikely alternative explanation. However, the second group of families must be assessed for its equivalence to the family preservation group. If indeed a control group were composed of families who refused service, it is highly likely they would differ on important characteristics such as receptivity to intervention and motivation to change! (selection) Finally, the participants who were assessed at later time points would need to be checked to ensure that there were not different drop-out rates, or different types of mothers dropping out (mortality).

Summary

In summary, research designs can be assessed along six dimensions, as outlined in table 4.4. At one level, these dimensions are ways of describing the research plans, for example, how many groups are studied, how often data are collected, whether qualitative or quantitative methods are used, and so on. On another level, these dimensions determine how well the research plans can help answer the questions posed or hypotheses developed. One cannot assess a culture's worldview through quantitative methods, measure changes over time using a single-occasion of data gathering, or assess "before and after" differences with ex post facto data collection. If the search is for causal elements, some types of design contribute to greater certainty about causality than others, in part by ruling out rival hypotheses such as maturation, history, or statistical regression. Although for pragmatic reasons, investigators sometimes use designs that are not ideal for their purposes, there is usually a combination of design elements that is optimal for a particular question. In the following three chapters, we will take up some of these issues in discussing specific designs.

5   Naturalistic Designs

In this chapter we shall discuss and illustrate some types of naturalistic designs, where there is no attempt to alter phenomena. These designs are among the most common in social work. They are simultaneously important in generating social work knowledge and feasible for use in student research. We group the studies into two major categories of knowledge-building function, exploratory-descriptive and explanatory, and discuss them in terms of the design dimensions introduced in the previous chapter. Designs whose purpose is measurement will be taken up briefly in chapter 9, measurement, although they are almost exclusively naturalistic.

Designs with Exploratory-Descriptive Functions

Many social work research studies combine both exploratory and descriptive functions. They aim to gain preliminary understanding, develop hypotheses, and also to provide descriptive data, especially in areas where little empirically based knowledge is available. Common applications include studies of characteristics of clients or at-risk groups and studies of community, agency practitioner and service characteristics. Such exploratory and descriptive studies, as a rule, are neither prospective nor use repeated measures. They include measurement on a single occasion and are often undifferentiated with respect to timing of the independent variable. They can be differentiated by dimensions relating to size and composition of sample and to methodological orientation. Here, we discuss two common naturalistic designs that have exploratory-descriptive functions, a homogeneous group design using a qualitative approach and a heterogeneous group design using a quantitative approach.

Homogeneous Group, Qualitative, Single Occasion of Data Gathering

A naturalistic design with an exploratory-descriptive function is a homogeneous group design using qualitative methods. Studies of this type have a time-honored tradition in anthropology and sociology. Classics include *Street Corner Society* (Whyte 1981) and *Five Families* (Lewis 1959); more recent examples include a study of boys growing up in the projects in Chicago (*There Are No Children Here* (Kotlowitz 1991)), of homeless women in a shelter (*Tell Them Who I Am* (Liebow 1993)), and of gay and lesbian adolescents coming out (Due 1995). Basically, this kind of investigation consists of in-depth study of a homogeneous group of subjects or a single system, usually selected because it is of interest or is considered "typical." Methods often include semistructured interviews, participant observation, and other qualitative data-gathering methods. The purpose is to provide a "thick description" (Geertz 1973; Lincoln and Guba 1985) of the complexities that characterize the objects of study. Although the data collection may take considerable time, measurement is considered to have taken place once.

A social work example is Krassner's (1986) study of *curanderismo*, a form of faith healing common among Mexican Americans. Krassner's research question was: What are "the effective ingredients of the form of healing known as *curanderismo*, as seen by the healers themselves?" (164). Her theoretical framework included a cross-cultural view of "universal therapeutic techniques" that vary by culture but exist everywhere. The techniques include a shared worldview between helped and helper, a shared faith in the healing system including a relationship between helped and helper, the role of group processes, the importance of "naming" the problem as a way of understanding it and making it culturally acceptable, and the influence of therapist (high prestige, expectations, the power of suggestion, emotional arousal). To investigate these areas, she conducted in-depth interviews (from one to six hours) with five experienced practitioners of *curanderismo* (*curanderos*). The *curanderos* were selected because they shared the key characteristic of interest: they were recognized as active healers in the Mexican-American community.

Using an unstructured format, Krassner asked questions that might be asked of any therapist: questions concerning training, how they obtained their theories of illness, and methods of diagnosis and treatment. She also observed their healing settings and the materials used in healing, although she did not participate in therapeutic consultations. Her report was a description of the *curanderos'* beliefs and practices empirically grounded with liberal quotes from the interviews and conceptualized in a way to facilitate comparison with mainstream "anglo" therapists. In doing so, she relied on her ability to understand and synthesize their answers. Thus, she was able to provide an account of how *curanderos* used the client's religious faith to heighten expectations that the treatment experience would be beneficial, just as Western therapists use their client's faith in the expertise of professionals. Although variations among the *curanderos* are discussed, her stress is on themes that characterize them as a group.

The purpose of Krassner's study is exploratory and descriptive because it examined an important belief system unfamiliar to most social workers. It depicts a "therapy culture" that can enhance our understanding of dominant western practices and it provides insight into a helping system widely used by Mexican Americans. Krassner was not interested in associational or causative factors, such as who benefits from this form of therapy or whether belief in the system is necessary for healing to take place. However, the study clearly has important implications for generating such hypotheses.

How representative are the five *curanderos*? The question is important if one wishes to describe the practices of all *curanderos* or to understand the interrelationship of healing systems used by Mexican Americans. When the purpose is to gain a beginning understanding of a poorly understood phenomena, as in Krassner's study, the question of representativeness is less important. Indeed, the outcome of the study is as much a better understanding of other (Western) therapeutic systems as it is a description of *curanderismo* itself.

The study also illustrates a type of design that is feasible for student research. In fact, Krassner completed the study as a thesis requirement for her MSW. We think this kind of design deserves to be used more than it is, especially for exploratory research and when the phenomena to be studied do not lend themselves to other research methods.

Heterogeneous Group, Quantitative

A second common type of naturalistic, single-occasion study is heterogeneous group studies that explore and describe the characteristics of client or at-risk populations. Although a particular population may be the focus, sample size and selection usually permits some comparisons of subgroups.

For example, Lyman and Bird (1996) addressed the self-images of male adolescents in foster care. Their research questions focused on the adolescents' self-images in comparison with a normative population and the extent that "individual background characteristics in conjunction with characteristics of the foster care experience explain the self-image of adolescents in foster care" (87). Thus their research questions asked for a description of the client population and for association of various characteristics with self-image. At the same time, the investigators hoped to gain preliminary understanding that could lead to hypotheses for practice and research, for example, possible attributes of the foster care system that might enhance or deflate self-image.

To answer these questions, they identified a group of youths who were believed to be typical foster care youth—58 boys, aged 12 to 19 years, who resided in a local residential group home (one that allowed the investigators to conduct the study). Their research design involved collecting data once using quantitative methods to gather and analyze the data. The youths completed the Offer Self-Image Questionnaire (Offer, Ostrov, and Howard 1982), a typical quantitative instrument that measures self-image in such areas as impulse control, body image, family relations, and mastery of the external world. The investigators also gathered background data from the boys' foster care records. Although the boys were homogeneous on several characteristics (gender, being in foster care), they differed on the key characteristics of interest (self-image, background characteristics, and foster care experiences), thus making the sample heterogeneous.

The overall self-image of the foster care youths was similar to that of norms established by testing large samples of presumably normal youth. This was an unexpected finding and a good example of why research questions are appropriate when there are few previous empirical data! However, on subscales, the foster care boys were lower than norms on family relations and emotional health. In looking at factors associated with self-image, several subscales were associated with background and foster care experiences. For example, white boys had poorer family relations than boys of other races. And boys with more placements had poorer family relations.

Did having multiple placements "cause" the boys to have poor self-image related to family and morals? Because the design is naturalistic, it is impossible to determine what was the cause. However, the authors used several procedures to rule out some alternative explanations. For example, selection is an important threat: did the low self-image boys differ systematically from the higher self-image boys on some characteristic other than number of placements? By including only boys, the investigators ensured that any variations in self-image could not be due to differences between boys and girls. Because race was important and the sample included boys of several races, they used a statistical technique (multiple regression) to control for race when examining the association between number of placements and self-image. Age, academic achievement, and time in current placement were also controlled in similar analyses; the association between number of placements and self-image is not due to those factors. However, there may be other factors that explain the association. Thus, the study has ruled out several possible alternative explanations, but cannot rule out all. This incremental approach to establishing causality is typical of a quantitative approach to research.

Further, because the study design included a single measurement and was undifferentiated in terms of timing, one cannot determine when the self-image problems occurred, before or after the boys were removed from their homes. The authors conclude, with appropriate caution, "foster care placement may serve to reduce the sense of belonging and support that an adolescent can get from his or her family, but in all likelihood the removal of the youth from the home also reflects some family deficit or dysfunction that influenced the family's ability to provide support" (Lyman and Bird 1996:92)

A major limitation of the study, as descriptive research, had to do with potential biases. The authors carefully compared the sample to regional and national data and believed it was representative on most characteristics. However, there were more whites than are represented in foster care nationally. Thus, it is difficult to estimate how well this group of boys represents all boys in foster care. To do so would require a more "scientific" sample, as will be described in chapter 8. Nevertheless, the results suggest hypotheses that can be tested in studies with more representative samples. They also suggest directions for program planning or other service initiatives that are directed at boys with similar characteristics.

Designs with Explanatory Functions

Many naturalistic studies are designed to help explain phenomena. To do so, they must first establish some form of association between variables as they naturally occur, while attempting to establish temporal sequences. Then the investigator attempts to make the case that one variable provides a possible explanation or prediction of another using techniques for ruling out alternative explanations such as matching, statistical control, explanation credibility, and so on. Such techniques are usually planned carefully in advance, which can distinguish explanatory designs from ostensibly similar descriptive designs such as the Lyman and Bird study just described (1996). The case for explanation is usually made with considerable qualification, as it should be, because naturalistic designs are limited in their ability to control those alternative explanations. This section examines three common quantitative designs: an ex post facto design where measurement is taken after the presumed causative variable has occurred, a longitudinal panel design which offers better ability to establish temporal sequencing, and a single-system time series design with many data collection points.

Multiple Group, Ex Post Facto

A frequently used design in naturalistic research is a multiple group ex post facto quantitative comparison that attempts to identify factors responsible for a problem or characteristic. In brief, a group that has the problem or characteristic is compared with one that does not. Differences, if any, are discovered, and an attempt is made to use the differences for explanatory purposes. One can begin with groups defined by a presumed causative factor and treat differences as presumed effects, or one can start with groups identified by possible effects and treat differences as potential causes. An example of the first type of study, which Chapin (1955) has referred to as "cause-to-effect," would be a comparison of cohesive versus noncohesive communities with the hypothesis that the crime rates would differ. "Cohesiveness" would be the cause and "crime rates" the effect. The second type, or "effect-to-cause," is illustrated by a study that compares addicted and nonaddicted children in terms of differences in family structure. Addiction of children would be the effect and family structure, the cause. In both types, the researcher must be concerned with the time order of variables, unwanted variation between groups, and the possibility of alternative explanations.

An example of a multigroup ex post facto study that uses both "effect-to-cause" and "cause-to-effect" reasoning is an effort by Marcenko and Spence (1995) to investigate attributes associated with substance abuse among pregnant women. Starting with a very broad research question, "to identify the social and psychological attributes of pregnant women with substance abuse histories compared to demographically similar women who denied substance abuse" (1995:103), they included two types of variables, those that logically preceded substance abuse, and those that might be presumed to derive from the drug abuse. "Preceding" variables included having parents who were substance abusers and being physically or sexually abused as a child, while variables that might be the effect of drug abuse included self-esteem, psychological symptoms, and current social support. They used quantitative methods to gather data: in a face-to-face interview, women were asked to complete a set of questionnaires that included standardized instruments measuring the variables mentioned.

Because the key variable of interest was substance abuse, Marcenko and Spence recruited a sample of women who differed on that characteristic. However, to control for other variables, they sought groups of abusing and nonabusing women that were as similar as possible on all other characteristics. To do so, they recruited women from an obstetrics outpatient clinic that served poor, urban women, predominantly African Americans. Indeed, when compared, the abusing and nonabusing groups were similar on race, educational level, income, and living arrangements, so these factors could not be alternative explanations for the results. (While the restrictive sampling strengthens the research design, it makes it more difficult to generalize the results to persons of other races, education, income, etc.) However, despite their best efforts, the two groups differed on an important characteristic, age, and consequently statistical techniques were used to control for this difference.

The results indicated that the women who abused drugs were more likely to have experienced abuse and to have a family history of substance abuse, variables that occurred before their own substance use. The abusing women also had less social support, especially from parents, and greater psychological distress. While one might like to assert that substance abuse caused the psychological distress and lack of support, it is difficult given the ex post facto nature of the study to establish the temporal sequencing of events. As Marcenko and Spence comment, "women with a history of substance abuse may have alienated family members because of their drug-related behaviors. . . . [or the] women may have fewer family resources to draw on because of the substance abuse of family members" (1995:108).

The multiple group ex post facto design can be diagrammed as a single O. This diagram is the same as for the previous two designs, the homogeneous quantitative design and the heterogeneous quantitative design, because there was only one occasion of data collection in each of the designs. Other important distinctions among the designs are not captured by the diagramming convention.

Prospective, Multiple Occasions, Longitudinal (Panel)

In the Marcenko and Spence study, where data collection was undertaken once, it is difficult to assure that substance abuse occurred before lack of family support. Another naturalistic design improves the ability to establish temporal sequencing by studying a sample prospectively through repeated data collection over a period of time. In respect to sample size and composition, these longitudinal studies normally use heterogeneous groups of at least moderate size. Even if the group is originally identified as homogeneous at the outset, it is expected that differentiation will occur as time progresses. These designs attain the explanatory function through analysis of factors that are apparently predictions of subsequent changes.

An example of a relatively simple longitudinal study is Lewis, Giovannoni, and Leake's (1997) study of the effects of mothers' substance abuse on infants placed in foster care. At the time of birth, the children were classified as exposed to street drugs in utero or not drug exposed; two years later their status in the foster care system was evaluated. (All children included in the study had been separated from their mothers at birth by the local juvenile court.) The first data collection clearly establishes that some factors occurred first. This may be obvious for prenatal drug exposure, but might be less clear for other variables measured at that time, such as the infant's health, maternal neglect, or mother's prostitution activity. Two years after birth, more drug-exposed than nondrug-exposed children remained in foster care. However, statistical analysis indicated that it was not the drug use per se that contributed to the result. Among both groups, the children were more likely to stay in foster care if the mother were homeless or not living with the child's father, if the mother neglected other children, and if the mother were promiscuous. Not surprisingly, the drug-using mothers had more of these problems.

One observation from the Lewis et al. study was that the predictors of remaining in foster care were all characteristics of the mother that were measured at the time of removal of the child (none of the children's characteristics predicted time in foster care). As the authors suggest, this has implications for policies about how early to make permanent plans for the children (Lewis, Giovannoni, and Leake 1997:89). This understanding of timing would not be possible without a longitudinal design.

DIAGRAM 5.1

Diagrams of Example Longitudinal Designs

Foster children exposed to drugs in utero, or not (Lewis, Giovannoni, and Leake 1997).

O O

Early problem behaviors predicting antisocial behavior at age 21 (Pakiz, Reinherz, and Giaconia 1997).

O O O O O O

Peers, beliefs, and drug use among adolescents in the Rochester Youth Development Study (Krohn et al. 1996).

O O O O O

O = indicates data collection point.

Another example is a prospective panel study of predictors of antisocial behavior in youth in a northeastern city (Pakiz, Reinherz, and Giaconia 1997). The sample was children who enrolled in a public school kindergarten in 1977, who had been followed for 18 years at the time of the report. Although they accepted all eligible children into the study, the investigators assumed that the sample would be heterogeneous on variables of interest, both current and future problems, and antisocial behavior. Data included measures completed at ages 5, 6, 9, 15, 18, and 21, and included questionnaires and reports from teachers and parents as well as the youths. Pakiz et al. hypothesized "the following early factors would be associated with an increased risk for antisocial behavior at age 21: male gender; early behavior problems, aggression, or hostility; negative family environment; academic problems; and lack of social support and low self-esteem" (93). Pakiz et al. used a statistical technique called multiple regression that determines which factors (from any age) are most associated with antisocial behavior while taking into account the effects of the other factors. Because they expected predictors to be different for boys and girls, they examined the two groups separately. Early problems did indeed predict antisocial behavior at early adulthood, but the strongest predictors were problems at age 18. The predictive behaviors and the timing of them were different for boys and girls, with relevant boys' problems surfacing at an earlier age.

An example of an even more complex longitudinal study is an investigation of how adolescents become involved in drug use, drawn from the Rochester Youth Development Study (RYDS) (Krohn et al. 1996). Beginning when the youths were in the 8th or 9th grade, project staff interviewed 1,000 youths and their adult caretakers every six months, a typical panel design using quantitative methods. Because they were interested in delinquency, the investigators oversampled high-risk youth, but the type of selection procedures ensured that the participants were representative of all adolescents in those grades in the Rochester public schools at the time the study began. Although the youths were similar on age and schooling, it was assumed that they differed on other characteristics of interest (such as delinquent behavior) and, furthermore, that they would differ in their behavioral patterns over time (heterogeneous sample).

In the analysis of drug use among the RYDS youths, Krohn et al. (1996) used interactional theory to posit a model of how peers, beliefs, and drug use are interrelated. Rather than assuming one-directional causality, as most models do (for example, associating with drug-using peers leads to drug use), they assumed interactions (for example, one is influenced by peers and also chooses peers who have similar behaviors). In their model, "association with drug-using peers is hypothesized to cause increases in drug use [over time] and drug use is viewed as having a reciprocal effect on associating with drug-using friends. Initially, having beliefs that are conductive to drug use is hypothesized to be primarily a consequence, rather than a cause, of drug use and associating with other drug users. Over time, however, as a deviant belief system becomes more fully articulated, beliefs exert a stronger influence on the other variables"(Krohn et al. 1996:408).

At each data collection period (called "waves"), the investigators asked the

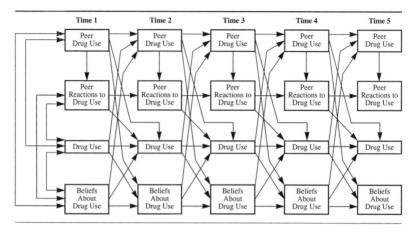

FIGURE 5.1

Lagged model of casual relationships among peer drug use, peer reactions to drug use, beliefs about drug use, and drug use (Model 2). Source: Krohn et al. 1996:415

youths questions about peer drug use, peer reactions to drug use, beliefs about drug use, and the youth's own drug use. The drug-use article used five time points (labeled Time 1 through Time 5 in figure 5.1), from waves 2 through 6, or over a two-year period. Employing complex statistical models, the investigators looked at the associations between variables at each time period and the association from each time to the next. For example, peer drug use and the youth's own drug use were associated at each time, and drug use at time 1 was associated with use at time 2. Having multiple times allowed the investigators to plot changes in associations over time to see what changed first (or not at all). For example, if youths used drugs, over time their attitudes changed, but their attitudes at one time did not predict drug use until later times. The investigators conclude: "As adolescents become further integrated into a drug-using peer network, they are more likely to adopt the attitudes consistent with their friends' behavior, and then those beliefs play a role in the maintenance of drug using behavior"(Krohn et al. 1996:423).

Do other factors than peers and beliefs explain drug use? To eliminate some of the most important rival hypotheses, the investigators used statistical techniques to control for variables that previous research indicated were important in drug use, such as gender, race, and social class. Still, other factors such as drug availability, deteriorating neighborhoods, or parental attachment may explain some of the observed patterns. Indeed, the investigators note that they were testing only one portion of interactional theory, which also specifies that weakening in parental bonds, lack of commitment to conventional values, and other breakdowns in socialization increase the likelihood of deviant behavior.

Confidence in the results of Krohn et al.'s (1996) study is enhanced because the results support hypotheses that were carefully specified from a well-articulated and previously tested theory. At the same time, the findings support the validity of interactional theory, that behaviors influence each other reciprocally. The study thus illustrates the important interaction between theory and research, where well-developed theory contributes to research and research to theory-building.

The study also demonstrates a welcome trend in social science and social work research, a move away from linear models of thinking about causality (A leads to B) to interactive models (A and B interact and affect each other). Interactive models seem to fit human behavior and social systems better than linear models. For example, adolescent substance abuse affects the family, and the family's reaction influences the youth as well. However, until recently, statistical techniques to test interactive models were not readily available. Now, thanks in part to the speed of modern computers and in part to a change in conceptual thinking to interactive systems perspectives, such statistical techniques are accessible (Krohn et al. used FIML covariance structure analysis on a computer program called LISREL.)

On the other hand, both the Pakiz et al. (1997) study of antisocial behavior and the Krohn et al. (1996) study of delinquency illustrate some of the disadvantages of group longitudinal designs: the lengthy span of data collection, the cost of repeated data collection, the complexity of the analysis, and the inevitable problem of sample attrition. The Pakiz et al. study retained 73% of its subjects after 18 years. Krohn's RYDS is considered exceptional in terms of retaining its subjects, with a low overall attrition rate of only 10% by wave 6 (see Thornberry et al. (1993) for discussion of issues and methods of retention in this and other panel studies). Nevertheless, in the drug study, only 771 of the original 1000 youths were included; the others either were not interviewed at each wave or did not answer questions about drug use. In both cases, we cannot be assured that the pattern of associations among variables would be the same had all the original subjects been in the final sample. A sample of continuers can overrepresent the subjects who are less transient, more cooperative, and better functioning. In the Pakiz et al. study, most of the dropouts were pupils who transferred from public to parochial schools; thus the dropouts were likely to be more religious and less satisfied with the school system. Still, despite panel attrition and other limitations, longitudinal studies can provide

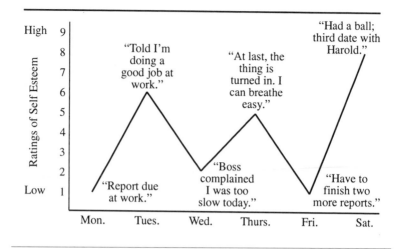

FIGURE 5.2

Example of a chart including ratings of feelings and data from a client log, as well as annotations of concomitant events. Source: Bloom, Fischer, and Orme 1995:250

a useful picture of the process of change over time, and some, like the Krohn et al. study, provide sophisticated tests of theory and causal explanations for behavior.

Prospective, Multiple Occasions, Single-System Time Series

A very different type of naturalistic design is a time series design that takes repeated measures of a single system. As with other longitudinal designs, its purpose is to determine what variations occur normally over time. As with group longitudinal designs, these designs can be diagrammed with a series of Os, one for each data collection point. The most familiar example, albeit not a social work one, is performance indicators in business—line charts of Gross National Product, Consumer Price Index, unemployment figures, corporate earnings, and so on. Like longitudinal panel designs, naturalistic time series designs may be used exclusively for descriptive purposes, but they are increasingly used in attempts to explain or predict phenomena. The logic behind explanation is the same as with the group longitudinal designs: events or effects which occur earlier in the series of measurements are presumed to affect later events, that is, temporal priority and association are established.

A simple time series design used to aid in assessment for clinical practice is suggested by Bloom, Fischer, and Orme (1995). Data about the client's acknowledged problem, in this instance poor self-esteem, are collected and the level of self-esteem is plotted on a graph over time (see figure 5.2). Simultaneously, the client keeps a log of events. Noting the events on the chart enables the client and practitioner to estimate visually whether some events or type of events seem to be associated with highs or lows of self-esteem, either simultaneously or shortly thereafter. In their example, instances of low self-esteem coincide with criticism at work, high self-esteem with praise at work or pleasant social interaction. (If the log and graph were continued after treatment began, the design would become an experimental single-system design; see chapter 6.)

One limitation of such an approach is that the human mind tends to see patterns in data, even when they may not exist. This may not be a problem with a single client, who may improve because he or she believes the cause has been found and changed, but it poses difficulties when the purpose is to describe or explain relationships. Moreover, "true" patterns may not be visible to the eye on a graph because the relationships are obscured by random or systematic variations due to other factors. As with other naturalistic designs, statistical techniques can be used to discover association and to minimize such outside influences (see chapter 11).

DIAGRAM 5.2
Diagrams of Example Prospective Single-System Time Series Designs

Woman with feelings of low self-esteem (Bloom, Fischer, and Orme 1995).

O O O O O O

M and Dr. X: Data collection is analysis of 53 sessions over the 208 sessions of treatment (Jones et al. 1993).

OOOOOOOOOOOOOOOOOOOOOOOOOOOOOOOOOOOOOOOOOOOOOOOOOOOOOOO
O = data collection point.

A study using sophisticated statistical techniques to try to establish causality in a naturalistic times series design is one by Jones et al. of the therapeutic process in a single case of a woman treated for depression (1993). M, a 35-year-old woman, was seen twice a week for two and a half years by Dr. X, who used an ego psychological perspective that included active support, direct encouragement, focus on feelings, interpretation that linked feelings and experiences to the past, and identification of recurrent patterns. Every 16 weeks, M recorded her level of depression, general symptoms, and severity of automatic thoughts on standard questionnaires characteristic of quantitative research. Each therapy session was videotaped and every fourth session was analyzed using the Psychotherapy Process Q-set, a procedure that allowed trained coders to determine which client and practitioner behaviors were characteristic of each session. To control any systematic expectations the coders might have about the development of therapeutic process, the sessions were rated in a random order.

Analysis of the Q-set data yielded four dimensions or groupings of therapist, client, and interactive behaviors that clustered together. For example, Therapist Acceptance/Neutrality included such descriptions as "therapist conveys a sense of nonjudgmental acceptance" and "therapist is sensitive to the patient's feelings, is attuned to the patient, and is empathic"; if one was typical in a session, the other was also likely to be typical. Other dimensions included Therapist Interactive (examples: "therapist's own emotional conflicts intrude into the relationship," "therapist behaves in a teacher-like (didactic) manner"; "patient has difficulty understanding the therapist's comments"), Patient Dysphoric Affect ("patient feels sad or depressed, patient struggles to control feelings or impulses," "humor is used"), and Psychodynamic Technique ("therapist interprets warded-off or unconscious wishes, feelings, or ideas," "therapist points out patient's use of defensive maneuvers (e.g., undoing, denial)").

The scores for each dimension and the outcome scores were graphed over the 208 therapy sessions. Before analyzing association between the therapeutic processes and client symptoms, the investigators processed the data to rule out a rival hypothesis called autocorrelation (the association between a score at one point in time with the score at the next point), which can cause spurious associations among measures in time series designs.

As with the Krohn et al. youth study (1996), the investigators applied a statistical modeling procedure which looked at how each variable at one time was associated with itself and other variables at later times. Unlike that study, they did not limit the point in time to the very next one, but also looked at the next 10 data collection points (that is, the next 20 weeks of therapy). This procedure permits assessment of which therapeutic processes affect later symptoms, which symptoms affect later process, and whether there is reciprocal interaction.

In M's therapy, there were indeed both one-way and two-directional effects (Jones et al. 1993). Most of the therapeutic processes had bi-directional relations with each other, that is "therapist and patient mutually influenced one another" (392). However, in one-directional results, Patient Dysphoric Affect predicted Therapist Acceptance/Neutrality which predicted Psychodynamic Technique; in other words, M's expression of distressed feelings predicted Dr. X's use of facilitative activity and that predicted use of psychodynamic interpretive techniques. In looking at outcome, they found that lower levels of

Therapist Acceptance/Neutrality led to symptom improvement, as did lower Patient Dysphoric Affect. Given the interrelationships, they concluded "during the beginning phase of treatment, . . . Dr. X was more nonjudgmental, facilitative, and neutral and that M's depressive affect during the therapy sessions seems to have gradually 'pulled' Dr. X toward a more authoritative and emotionally reactive and involved posture. This change in the nature of the process was predictive of M's gradual reduction in symptom level" (Jones et al. 1993:392).

The interpretation that Dr. X's switch from supportive to directive interventions "caused" a decrease in M's depression must be made with a great deal of caution. The design does allow the investigators to establish temporal sequence (less support precedes more active therapist involvement and both precede a decrease in depressive symptoms). The statistical control for autocorrelation rules out one important alternative explanation and also helps control for random errors (instability). On the other hand, there is no control over coincident external events that might have affected both Dr. X and M, for example, holidays that put both under pressure (history). Perhaps, as might be typical of the beginning of treatment, M started at an extreme of depression and Dr. X at an extreme of support, and both moved inevitably toward middle ground (statistical regression). Or perhaps the combination of high support and directive structure are the critical elements (multiple intervention effects, a specific form of nonspecific effect). As sophisticated as the design and data analyses are in this instance, they cannot rule out many plausible rival hypotheses.

Even though the Jones et al. study (1993) looked at therapeutic interventions, it is not an experimental design. This is because the investigators did not try to alter the treatment itself; they just studied its normal process. Had they asked Dr. X to change her interventions, for example, to increase her use of Therapist Acceptance/Neutrality to see whether the depression then increased, then the design would be experimental. Such alteration of the independent variable would also give more confidence in any causal interpretation of the relation between acceptance/neutrality and depression.

What does the M/Dr. X case say about principles of good treatment? As is typical of a single-system design, we have a great deal of precise and interesting information about one case, but little ability to apply it to other cases. As the authors note, only replication can determine if the same types of reciprocal processes and effects on outcome occur in other cases (Jones et al. 1993:392). The study is provocative and suggests fruitful areas for future research, but does not permit conclusions about other cases.

Summary

Naturalistic designs may be used for exploratory-descriptive functions, where the purpose is to map out new areas, describe characteristics of a phenomenon, or explore associations among variables. They are ideal for determining natural fluctuations over time. And they may be used for explanatory functions, where the purpose is to gather evidence of a causal link. As has been demonstrated, naturalistic designs may combine many other design elements, particularly size of sample, timing and repetition of data collection, and quantitative vs. qualitative methodology. The combinations selected reflect the research questions or hypotheses and the function of the research. We have illustrated the most common combinations in social work research. From the illustrations, it is evident that designs which attempt to establish association (the first step in showing causality) must include multiple or heterogeneous groups or, in the instance of single-system designs, must collect data on two or more variables. This is so whether their purpose is exploratory-descriptive or explanatory. Adding more than one data collection point permits tracking variation over time, and if measurement is prospective, one may be able to establish a temporal sequence of which event occurs first. However, no naturalistic design gives as convincing a demonstration of time priority (the second step in establishing causality) as does an experimental design. Further, none of the naturalistic designs by themselves can rule out rival hypotheses, although the inclusion of data on possible alternative explanations and the use of statistical techniques can eliminate some likely explanations.

Despite these generalizations about naturalistic designs, each study must be examined carefully to determine how effective the design is in carrying out the investigators' purpose. As we have shown, ostensibly similar designs can have very different functions—and conclusions about causality—depending on how well grounded the study is in theory and on how the investigator handles elements of the design such as timing of measurement and use of statistical controls.

6   Single-System Experiments

In previous chapters, we argued that research that helps develop social work intervention is of particular importance to the profession. Experimental designs where the investigator planfully alters phenomena (the intervention) to study the effects are of particular importance because they provide a direct and powerful means of developing methods of social work intervention. Hence, we examine experimental strategies in the context of intervention. We begin with single-system experiments because they provide, we think, a convenient way to present and understand basic features of experimental research, which can then be applied to more complex group undertakings. In discussing single-system experiments, we mean a single client or aggregate of individuals that is treated as a single unit for purposes of analysis. For example, a family, a treatment group, even a community, may be studied in a single-system design if the unit of attention is the whole family, group, or community.

The Case Study

The most elementary form of the single-system design is the case study. The case study consists of collection of data on case characteristics and change, and on interventions that presumably were influential in producing change. The research strategy may include qualitative methods (many student papers written for practice classes are qualitative case studies), or it may be quantitative with systematic observations such as a time series design. Such a time series design might appear similar to the naturalistic study illustrated in chapter 5 with the study of M and Dr. X. The difference is that in the case study, treatment—the independent variable—is introduced with the explicit purpose of studying its effect on outcome—the dependent variable. The case study design is "uncontrolled" in the sense that intervention is not systematically withheld or varied.

Although the case study is severely limited in its capacity to isolate treatment effects, it is of interest for several reasons. It is the most feasible and readily applied of any design that might be used to study the effects of intervention. It can be very useful clinically to tell the practitioner when change has occurred and when termination or a new intervention should be considered. From a research point of view, it can serve an important exploratory function in pre-liminary tests of service approaches. Although it may not be able to determine effects of intervention in a definitive way, it can be used to generate hypotheses about these effects. And, as we shall see, in some studies this design can provide strongly suggestive, if not persuasive, evidence about the accomplishments of service. Finally, the case study makes clear the need for the kind of controls used in more sophisticated single system designs, and we shall use it to illustrate the function of these controls.

An example of a case study is the treatment of a family with teenage sons who would beat each other up (Reid and Donovan 1990). Finding little in the literature about treating sibling violence, the investigators conjectured that the family lacked a structure of rules to guide interactions within and between sub-systems. Using a task-centered and family systems framework, they developed an intervention that focused on establishing generationally appropriate sub-systems and rules for interaction. The effectiveness of the intervention was monitored by tracking episodes of violence and having the family take a stan-dardized measure of family relations on a regular basis. Initially, the practi-tioner attempted to develop the parental alliance by seeing the parents together and having them develop and implement rules about how to discipline the children and how to support each other when doing so. There was no change in the boys' fighting. Then the children were invited in to learn problem-solv-ing and to set their own rules for governing conflict. After about five sessions, the physical violence between the boys stopped. It did not recur during the remainder of treatment nor by a follow-up four months after.

Problems in Determining Effectiveness

Why did the boys stop fighting? The case study is confronted with inherent problems in determining the contribution of intervention to change. Changes in client systems that *follow* the introduction of intervention may or may not be the *result* of the intervention. We return here to the problem of isolating causative factors that we considered in chapter 4. Now we examine this problem within the context of single-system experimental trials of social work intervention.

What other factors than the intervention might have caused the change in the siblings' violence (and the improvement in overall family relations, we should add)? Maturation is a possibility: with the passage of time, as they turned to peer interactions, the boys may have outgrown their tendency to feud with each other. Another factor might be history: perhaps, unbeknownst to the practitioner, Mr. T, who acknowledged a drinking problem, had beaten the boys into submission. A third possibility, statistical regression, suggests that the boys were at an extreme of conflict when treatment started and "retreated" to their normal ranges over time (this does not explain prolonged cessation, however). A fourth possibility is instability—the boys' fighting behavior fluctuates dramatically under the best of circumstances, and the highs and lows of fighting are just part of this fluctuation. Another is instrumentation, or changes in the measurement procedures; since the practitioner was relying on family members' reports of fighting episodes, perhaps something happened to make them conceal continued incidents—perhaps they were afraid of disappointing the practitioner, or feared a court-ordered removal of the boys. Similarly, testing might be a possible cause of the change— having to chronicle their fights weekly embarrassed the boys and, as a reaction to the reporting, they stopped fighting. A seventh possibility is nonspecific effects that go along with intervention: it was not the task-centered family systems intervention that worked as the investigators had hoped, but the role modeling of nonphysical interaction that the practitioner unconsciously provided each week. Finally, the changes might be due to reactive effects (the combined effect of testing and intervention): because the fights were recorded, the boys became sensitive to what they were doing and were receptive to the problem-solving efforts; without the recording as well as the intervention, they would not have changed. Although these threats to internal validity have been presented one by one, it is obvious that they can interact in various ways. For example, an improvement in the boys' behavior resulting from maturation, combined with the parents' greater marital satisfaction from the first phase of treatment (reactive effects), could cause the parents to under-report incidents of fighting (instrumentation).

Strengthening the Design

ADDING A BASELINE In the cited example, and in most case studies, it is difficult to draw definitive conclusions about the effects of intervention. However, when sufficiently strengthened, the design may provide valuable evidence on effects of intervention. Because variation in the clients' problems is a major source of alternative explanations, the first step in strengthening a case study is to obtain baseline data on variations before intervention. If research considerations were paramount, the data would be obtained prospectively; that is, one would collect data on the problem through observation or other means over a period of time, perhaps as long as several weeks, before intervention. For example, in the case of sibling violence, the family might record the violence and marital relations for several weeks before starting the sessions with the parents. (The design would then become a basic time series design, which we will discuss in the section following.) If clinical considerations are paramount (for example, it is not feasible to delay intervention), retrospective baseline data may be collected in initial interviews or from available records. Thus, the parents and children might be asked to estimate the number of violent episodes each day for the previous week.

The availability of such baseline data, whether prospective or retrospective, allows the investigator to assess how the problem has varied prior to intervention. The investigator's concern is how much such threats as instability, maturation, and regression complicate interpretation of the effects of intervention. For certain problems, it may be possible to establish that little fluctuation has occurred, thus ruling out instability as a likely cause of any observed changes. Similarly, a baseline that shows no decreasing or increasing problems suggests that, in the past, maturation and regression were unlikely to be operating and thus are unlikely explanations of current change. In the example of sibling violence, for example, interviews with other relatives and neighbors might have established that the boys' fights had occurred at a relatively stable rate for the past several months and did not seem to be either escalating or decreasing. In some cases, baseline stability can be readily determined: a man has been unemployed for the past two years, or for the last six months a landlord has done nothing to fix a rundown apartment. Establishing the chronicity of a problem obviously "helps" an uncontrolled design since changes following intervention cannot be readily attributed to maturation or regression. On the other hand, if the baseline pattern reveals considerable variation in the problem or a trend toward alleviation, then instability, maturation, and regression cannot be ruled out. In such a case, an uncontrolled case study design may provide little information about treatment effects.

AVOIDING SIMULTANEOUS INFLUENCES A case study design can also be strengthened somewhat by being alert for history during the intervention. Although such environmental influences cannot be completely controlled, the investigator can collect data on the occurrence of more obvious events that might have affected problem change. Moreover, the investigator may be able to take action to avoid the occurrence of confounding environmental events; accordingly, the parents in our example might have been asked to postpone a plan to enroll the boys in martial arts until after intervention was completed.

TESTING WELL-DEFINED PRACTICE APPROACHES As we noted in chapter 2, the capacity of research to inform practice is enhanced if the practice is well explicated. This principle also applies to the utility of the case study. For example, if practice events and outcomes are explicated in terms of specific, observable indicators, they can be more precisely measured. Although any data collection procedure can be biased, if specific details are measured, the bias is less likely than if outcomes are based on general impressions. What is more, the specificity of the connections between problem intervention and change found in well-explicated approaches may help rule out effects of maturation and history. The more globally a problem is defined, the broader the range of factors that may affect it. For example, there is a host of maturational and historical influences that might affect a problem as broadly defined as a mother's inability to cope with her children. If the problem is narrowed to the mother's habit of slapping her infant son when he cries, the range of such influences is narrower.

The specificity and directness of the intervention also become important considerations in assessing rival hypotheses. If the intervention is aimed at general changes that are difficult to delineate, if it operates indirectly, and if its processes are not clearly demonstrable, then alternative explanations become more attractive. For instance, to attribute a change in the mother's slapping her son to her participation in an unstructured parents' discussion group requires a chain of inferences that connects presumed benefits derived from the group experience—such as emotional support from other parents—to the change in mother's slapping behavior. Although such a plausible explanation can be constructed, a certain amount of speculation would be required and it is hard to assert that this speculation is more convincing than other speculations based on changes in the mother's motivation, family circumstances, or other factors that might not be the result of intervention.

By contrast, an intervention consisting of direct, explicit efforts to change the problem, through means such as having the mother rehearse and practice other responses when her son cries, could be more plausibly connected to the change. The link between intervention and change requires fewer assumptions; the process by which intervention may produce change is more apparent. The plausibility of the connection can be further strengthened by documenting the change process, for example, by showing that a problem changes immediately following an intervention and in a way specifically suggested by the intervention. The mother in our example might have one of her older children attend to the infant if she felt she were losing control. If it could be shown that she in fact then behaved in this manner, the case that she did so because of the intervention becomes more persuasive.

SIGNED CAUSES AND SLAM-BANG EFFECTS Another way to increase the plausibility of the case for an intervention's effect is through its characteristic signature. As Cook and Campbell (1979) observe, a cause may operate with such
specificity that it leaves a unique "signature" in its effects. For example, the
identity of a criminal may be revealed by the modus operandi of the crime, or
characteristics of a trainee's performance may tell us who trained him. Social
work may likewise assume properties of such "signed causes," as perhaps in the
example of the slapping mother just cited. In these cases, plausible alternative
explanations may not arise and controls may not be necessary to rule them out
in order to establish the effectiveness of the intervention.

Kazdin (1981) has cited several conditions that can be used to argue for
treatment effectiveness in single-system studies even if design controls are lacking: reliance on objective measurement, a problem that has followed a stable
course prior to treatment, the use of continuous assessment to monitor problem change before and after treatment, the occurrence of immediate and
marked effects after the intervention is introduced, and the replication of
effects with multiple cases. Not all of these conditions need be present. For
example, a large, dramatic, and predicted effect following an intervention—a
slam-bang effect—may obviate the need for objective measurement (Gilbert,
Light, and Mosteller 1975). Applications of these ideas in case studies may be
found in Reid (1994a).

Strengthening of the case study has been discussed at length because it is a
widely applicable design and because it demonstrates the thinking used in considering the possible effects of treatment in any design. Whether uncontrolled
or controlled, or whether it uses single cases or groups of cases, a study of the
effects of intervention must be evaluated through careful comparison of the
plausibility of hypotheses asserting that intervention is a causal agent against
the plausibility of alternative hypotheses. Design controls never provide a substitute for logic and judgment.

The Basic Time Series (AB) Design

Definition

In considering ways in which the case study might be strengthened, we
cited the value of baseline measurements as a means of providing some control
over extraneous factors. If the researcher obtains measures before intervention
and continues to obtain them after intervention is begun, it becomes possible
to obtain a continuous reading of problem occurrence or severity and to deter-

mine what happens when intervention is introduced. This design is called a *basic time series design*. Using our notation for designs, it could be represented as a series of Os, followed by Os simultaneous with Xs to indicate continued observation while the intervention is implemented. However, a shorthand notation for experimental time series designs uses letters, with the A symbolizing the series of measurements obtained during a baseline period before intervention and the B standing for the measurements taken during intervention (see diagram 6.1). Thus, the basic time series design is also called the AB design (baseline and intervention). The basic time series design has considerable utility in its own right and serves as a foundation for understanding the more complex single-system designs to be considered subsequently.

DIAGRAM 6.1
Diagram of the Basic Time Series (AB) Design

A   B

OOOOOOOOOO⊗⊗⊗⊗⊗⊗⊗⊗⊗⊗

A = Measurements obtained during baseline period before intervention.
B = Measurements taken during intervention.
O = Observation—data collection point.
X = Continued observation, occurrence of manipulated independent variable.

The essential features of the design can be grasped from figure 6.1, which presents the results of a hypothetical case in which modeling and coaching were used to increase the frequency of "positive messages" (expressions of approval, praise, etc.) imparted by a mother to her ten-year-old son during a series of tape-recorded interactions between them. As the graph indicates, the design yields data on change coincident with the introduction of intervention. In this design, the mother acts as her own control, so to speak, in comparing her positive messages before and during treatment. Hence, selection as a rival hypothesis is not an issue. The pretreatment baseline helps reduce the plausibility of maturation and regression as alternative explanations but does not rule them out completely. If maturation or regression were present, we would expect a gradual increase in the number of positive messages over time, rather than the stable low level of positive messages actually observed. The design provides only weak control over the operation of history (contemporaneous events); it is possible, for example, that the mother discussed more pleasant topics when intervention occurred, and the topic rather than intervention caused the change in mother's behavior.

To use an AB design, at least three requirements must be met. First, it must be possible to delay intervention until baseline data can be obtained (although,

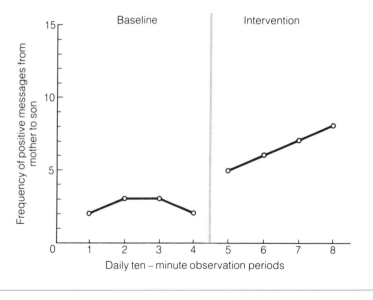

FIGURE 6.1

Illustration of basic time series design (hypothetical data)

as we shall discuss, retrospective baselines may be adequate alternatives). Second, the desired outcome must be so defined that variation in its characteristics—usually frequency or severity—can be measured at different points of time. Finally, it must be possible to obtain adequate measurement of these variations. (These requirements make clear that the time series designs are quantitative: they require planning of the data gathering strategy, the data is collected in similar ways at each time point, analysis of the data is done using numerical techniques that can include statistics.)

Once the requirements for an AB design are met, the time series measurements must have a pattern that permits some reasonable interpretation of change, if any. We now turn to some considerations for developing time series that can demonstrate change: keys to interpretation, planning baselines, and assessing change.

Time Series Measurement

Central to the basic time series design, as well as to more elaborate variations of single system studies, is the notion of time series measurement. As previously indicated, a time series consists of repeated data collection of a given variable over time. At least three fundamental features of a time series need to be taken into account in planning studies and in analyzing their results: variability, trend, and level. *Variability* is the extent to which repeated measurements (data points) fluctuate over time. *Trend* refers to tendencies of the series to move either upward or downward. For instance, in figure 6.1 the graph shows an ascending trend following the beginning of intervention. *Level* describes the location of a data point on the scale used to measure the variable—in figure 6.1 there is also a noticeable change in level after the intervention is introduced (the mother makes more statements). To interpret changes in trend and level, one must, obviously, know what is being measured and whether it is desirable to increase or decrease it. In figure 6.1, for example, the dependent variable is frequency of positive messages (to the son) and, we assume, the mother wishes to increase them.

In order to make inferences about the effects of intervention, the investigator must establish a baseline that permits interpretation of any changes in variability, trend, or level once intervention begins (see figure 6.2). While single-system designs are, by definition, idiosyncratic, some principles about planning baselines are relevant.

BASELINES A perhaps unattainable ideal is a stable, flat baseline with little or no variability. Any change from such an ideal baseline is immediately apparent. In most cases, however, human behavior is more or less variable; consequently, it is important to recognize any patterns that exist during the baseline.

In general, the lengthier and less variable the baseline, the better the capacity of the design to demonstrate possible effects of intervention. Although a time series can be established with only three data collection points, the desired number depends on the variability exhibited by the target: the greater its variability, the more data points required to establish a pretreatment pattern.

Traditional advice is to extend the baseline period until a stable pattern has been attained. Unfortunately, many client problems display such erratic variability that baselines would need to be extended an inordinate length of time, raising practical and ethical problems. Clients or referral sources may not be willing to wait or a practitioner may not have the time. A practical alternative is to limit the length of the baseline periods in advance of the experiment, perhaps after a brief exploration that provides some basis for estimating the time needed to establish stability. Planning baseline length ahead of time has the advantage of eliminating arbitrary and possibly biased decisions by the investigator about the length of the period.

The length of baseline and intervention phases is also related to the potency of the intervention. Generally, more potent interventions require less stability

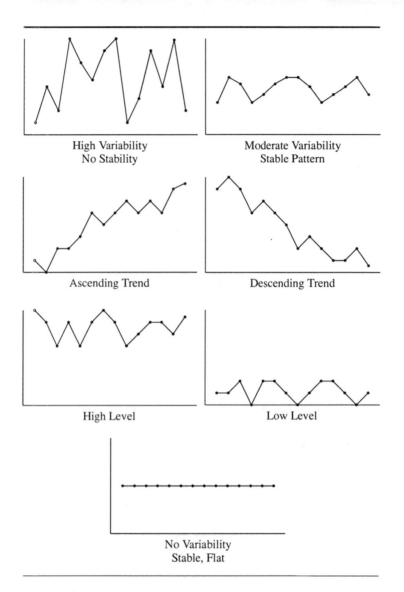

High Variability
No Stability

Moderate Variability
Stable Pattern

Ascending Trend

Descending Trend

High Level

Low Level

No Variability
Stable, Flat

FIGURE 6.2
Examples of variability, trend, and level in time series

in baselines to show effects. This point can be appreciated by comparing the two hypothetical time series presented in figure 6.3. Although the baseline for client A is less variable than that for client B, the data during the intervention phase provide more convincing evidence for an effect with client B. The change in level for client B after intervention is begun is great enough to "override" the variability in baseline.

The same principle also applies to another kind of troublesome baseline pattern: when the baseline shows a trend toward improvement in the target. Consider the baselines in figure 6.4. Both baselines show an accelerating trend, which is, of course, fine from the standpoint of client recovery but complicates interpretation of the data. In the case of client C, it is virtually impossible to rule out the possibility of spontaneous improvement (maturation), for change during the intervention could be predicted by extending the baseline trend. In the case of client D, we have a similar positive trend in baseline but a marked acceleration of the trend during the intervention period. Although the positive trend creates difficulties for any interpretation, the data for client D present a pattern more consistent with an intervention effect. For more extended discussion of baseline issues, see Bloom, Fischer, and Orme (1995).

ASSESSING CHANGE As the preceding discussion has suggested, it may be difficult in time series designs to determine if the pattern of change during the intervention period in fact differed in any meaningful way from that during the baseline period. Decisions about presence and magnitude of change in time series designs are customarily made on the basis of visual inspection ("eyeballing") of graphs or other data displays. For example, in figure 6.1, of the mother giving positive messages to her son, there is clearly a desirable change in level and trend between the baseline and the intervention period. Figure 6.5 illustrates other patterns where the eyeball method is effective in determining whether change has occurred.

The eyeball method works reasonably well when differences between baseline and intervention periods are relatively clear-cut (as in figures 6.1 and 6.5), but it does not work so well when the data is more ambiguous as in figures 6.3 and 6.4. Determining how much change is "meaningful"—that is, worth considering as a possible intervention effect—is always difficult. At the very least, the investigator would like to exclude change that may occur as a result of random variation or instability. In group experiments the problem of random variation is tackled through statistical tests of significance.

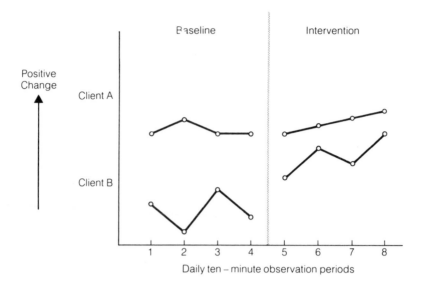

FIGURE 6.3

Contrasts in baseline stability and apparent treatment efforts (hypothetical data)

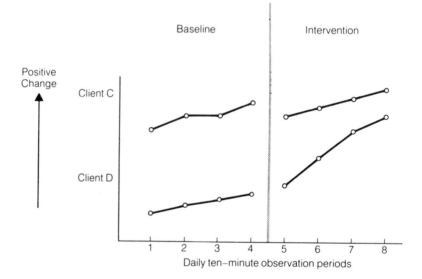

FIGURE 6.4

Ascending baselines followed by different trends during intervention (hypothetical data)

In time series designs, similar statistical tests can assess variability while comparing levels and differences in slopes from baseline to intervention periods. However, statistical analysis in time series designs is complicated by the interdependencies (autocorrelation) that occur in repeated measurement. Because the measurements are taken on one system, they are often related to each other, that is, a score at one time predicts the next score(s). This autocorrelation requires special and by no means simple adaptations of tests of significance. We will take up some of the statistical analyses in chapter 11. Here, we note that there is some controversy about the utility of statistical tests in time series designs. Some skeptics say that if a test is needed to tell whether "real" change has occurred, then there is not enough change to get excited about. Others have argued that without statistical tests, there is no criteria for ruling out instability as an explanation of change. In either case, simple tests of significance are not very useful when there is marginal change. A fairly large amount of change is needed to make a convincing case that random fluctuation can be discounted as a possible explanation.

Variations on the Basic Time Series Design

Certain variations of the AB design may be particularly useful in social work applications because they are easy to use and clinically relevant. As we shall see, these variations provide some additional elements of control.

In the changing criterion design (Hall 1971), the practitioner and client work toward achievement of a particular goal (criterion); once this is achieved, another is set at a higher level. Thus a child reluctant to read out loud in class may have reading two sentences out loud as a first goal, a paragraph as a second goal, and, once the second goal is achieved, then two paragraphs. If the client moves ahead in this predicted fashion, the design can provide persuasive evidence that intervention is the influencing variable. The range of application of the design is, of course, limited to situations in which performance goals can be "laddered" in the manner suggested in the example, and it may require slowing down the pace of change to demonstrate experimental control.

Another approach is to vary the treatment in successive phases. This design is usually represented as $AB^1B^2B^3$ if the interventions are similar (for example, various redemption levels in a token economy) or ABCD if the interventions are different. Combinations of interventions may also be tested. For example, Nugent used cognitive behavioral treatment and an Eriksonian hypnotic sequence with a woman who had severe panic attacks (1993). After measuring

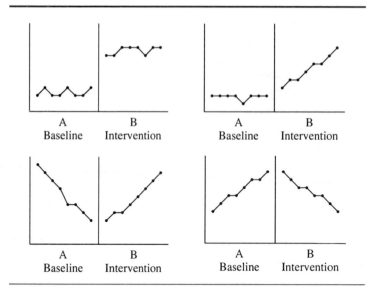

FIGURE 6.5

Patterns illustrating differences in level or trend between baseline and intervention phases

her panic attacks for one week (A), she received the hypnotic intervention one week (B), the cognitive-behavioral instruction the next week (C) and both interventions the third week (BC). In this design, each treatment phase is compared to the preceding one as well as to the original baseline. However, it may be difficult to separate out the interaction effects between treatments—an improvement in the C phase, for example, may be due to intervention C or to the combination of B followed by C or indeed to the triple combination of AB and then C (this is a particularly complex form of reactivity). On the other hand, this design is particularly useful in practice; if the first intervention is not working as desired, the practitioner may switch to another intervention while continuing to collect data on the dependent variable.

In a variation discussed by Barlow and Hersen (1984), an extended follow-up and "booster" treatment is employed. An AB design may have demonstrated that positive change occurred during treatment, but it may not have been possible to rule out alternative explanations. A follow-up several weeks after the termination of intervention may reveal that some backsliding has occurred. A second brief course of treatment is made. If the client's problem again shows positive change, evidence that treatment is effective is strengthened, though nonspecific effects would still need to be considered. As will be seen, this variation of the AB design is based on the logic of the withdrawal-reversal design and in fact can be seen as a somewhat adventitious form of that design.

Finally, repetitions of the AB design with different subjects and in different settings can result in an accumulation of evidence of effectiveness if it can be shown that consistent results are achieved across such variations. Planned variations in different settings could be used as a control for history, and use of baselines of different lengths would provide additional control for maturation.

Summary of Basic Time Series Design

In summary, the basic time series or AB design is a useful clinical design for establishing the presence of change. If the baseline is stable, or has an identifiable pattern, any change that occurs with the introduction of intervention is evident. If the baseline is stable, the design also helps rule out maturation, regression, testing, and instability as rival hypotheses. However, it is most useful for developing interventions and evaluating practice, for example, telling a practitioner when change has occurred and when termination might be considered, rather than for establishing that intervention is the cause of that change.

Withdrawal-Reversal Designs

Although the basic time series design is useful in evaluating practice, it lacks controls for most rival hypotheses. The withdrawal-reversal design is based on the fairly simple premise that one can determine the effects of any agent if one can show that effects occur after the agent is applied but do not occur when the agent is withheld. That is, differences in the outcome measure are associated with the presence or absence of intervention. This is the same logic that is used if a person wishes to make sure that a particular appliance, and not other causes, is responsible for static in a radio. To make sure, the individual might turn the appliance on and off several times. If the static appears when the appliance is turned on but disappears when it is turned off, then there is little doubt that it is the cause. Similarly, if an investigator applies an intervention, withholds it, and applies it again, and change occurs when the intervention is applied but vanishes as soon as it is withheld, the intervention may be logically regarded as a cause of this change.

Description

In the ABAB or withdrawal-reversal design, a pretreatment baseline (A) is taken while problem occurrence is measured; an intervention is administered(B); the original intervention is stopped for a period (A) and then reinstated (B). Data collection continues throughout. Although we refer to these designs generically as "withdrawal-reversal," a distinction can be made between designs in which treatment is simply withdrawn and those in which it is reversed. In withdrawal designs, intervention is simply suspended and reinstated. In reversal designs, intervention is not simply withheld but rather an active effort is made to restore the target condition.

A reversal design is illustrated in a study of Anne, a 69-year-old widow who was overwhelmed by the care of her 99-year-old mother (Richey and Hodges 1992). The hypothesis was that respite care—a substitute caregiver in the home five days a week—would alleviate Anne's burden. Social work intervention consisted of case management to arrange caregiving (no small task, especially since public assistance was involved) and work with Anne to alleviate her guilt about being unable to provide all her mother's care. Data were collected on Anne's time away from home, her level of enjoyment when away from home, and her attitude toward her mother, on a standardized questionnaire called the Child's Attitude toward Mother (CAM) (Hudson 1982). The baseline was two weeks (A), respite care lasted three weeks (B), and then stopped with Anne

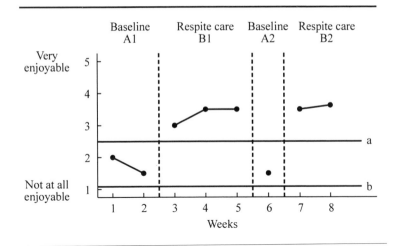

FIGURE 6.6

Weekly averages of caregiver enjoyment when away from home. Source: Richey and Hodges 1992

A. Upper two standard deviation band = 2.45.

B. Lower two standard deviation band = 1.05.

resuming all care for her mother (A), and finally respite was reinstated while data collection continued for another four weeks (B). The outcomes were as hypothesized: Anne's time away from home was low during the baseline (less than an hour a day), higher during the first intervention (about two hours a day), dropped to under an hour during the reversal, and rose again to about two hours during the second intervention. Similarly, Anne's enjoyment while out of the home was low during the baseline and reversal, higher during respite, while her attitude toward her mother was more positive during intervention.

Because Anne's baseline was relatively stable, maturation, statistical regression, and instability are unlikely rival hypotheses. History—some event simultaneous with the introduction of respite care—is possible but its likelihood is reduced because such events would have to occur twice to explain the change in outcome, once at the beginning of the first respite period, again at the beginning of the second. Testing is pretty well ruled out because if Anne were responding solely to recording her behavior and attitudes, the changes should occur during the baseline and should not coincide with intervention. However, reactivity, the interaction of testing and intervention, is still a plausible rival hypothesis. Similarly, nonspecific effects cannot be ruled out; for example, Anne's burden might be reduced because she enjoyed the companionship of the caregiver, not because she had fewer caretaking responsibilities. Finally, instrumentation is a potent explanation rivaling intervention: Anne recorded her own attitudes and might helpfully record less burden whenever intervention occurred, just to please the social worker. In sum, the withdrawal-reversal design provides considerably more control over alternative explanations than does the basic time series design, but like most designs cannot automatically rule out all such explanations.

In the study of Anne, the intervention was reversed, with Anne's workload and her interaction with her mother returning to baseline conditions. In a withdrawal design, intervention is withdrawn but conditions are not deliberately returned to baseline conditions. For example, a school principal, modeling for the classroom teacher, attempted to increase children's performances through setting goals and reinforcing the children's accomplishments (Gillat and Sulzer-Azaroff 1994). During the baseline (A), the principal met with the pupils and talked about the importance of math. During the first intervention period (B), the principal set goals with each child and used verbal praise and nonverbal gestures of approval. During the withdrawal phase, the principal continued to interact with the children but was asked not to set goals or use praise; however, there was no attempt to go back to the earlier, relatively impersonal, exhortations of the baseline. Analysis of the principal's behavior indicated that during the withdrawal phase, she reduced but did not totally eliminate her praise and goal setting. Thus the withdrawal design is not as "clean" as the reversal in terms of differentiating the intervention and nonintervention phases, but in many instances it is far more practical. In practice, it may be hard to distinguish between the two, so we, like other texts, refer to the two generically as withdrawal-reversal or ABAB designs.

Although the withdrawal-reversal design can provide strong evidence on the effectiveness of an intervention, it may be difficult to do for practical and ethical reasons. For example, withdrawing intervention may raise ethical questions. Social work investigators have recommended several modifications of time series designs to accommodate such practice constraints. Such modifications include uneven lengths of A and B phases, beginning new phases at natural transition points, reconstructing missing data, and using nonstandardized measures such as self-ratings (Blythe and Rodgers 1993; Reid 1993). The case of Anne and her mother (Richey and Hodges 1992), just discussed, illustrates a number of these adaptations. The A and B phases differed in length and their length was determined by practice considerations. The baseline lasted as long as it took the social worker to arrange respite care. The reversal phase was serendipitous: the caretaker was unable to continue so there was a hiatus while a second caretaker was found. Outcome measures included both an individualized measure (level of enjoyment) and a standardized measure (the CAM). Such modifications weaken the design somewhat but nevertheless make it easier to balance the needs of research and practice.

In the case of Anne, the design modifications were possible because the situation "worked:" the shortened baseline was stable and there were visually clear and predicted changes in the levels of all three dependent variables during each phase. A common difficulty in withdrawal-reversal designs is the failure of outcome measures to return to previous levels during the second or subsequent A phases. An example is a study of intervention with a child afraid of dogs (Secret and Bloom 1994). During the baseline, the child, Sally, reported high levels of fear in situations such as being in the same room as the dog or sitting near it. Intervention was in vivo desensitization, or gradual exposure to a dog under relaxed, self-controlled situations. Almost immediately, Sally's fear of the dog disappeared in all situations except letting it jump on her. When intervention was withdrawn, the fears did not return. This outcome, while ideal from the point of view of Sally and the practitioner, poses difficulties for the researcher who wants to know if it were the intervention that caused the disappearance of fear. Because fear and intervention no longer covary, we cannot rule out such explanations as maturation (Sally outgrew the fear) or history (she saw a movie with a cuddly dog as hero).

Variations on the Withdrawal-Reversal Design

The basic principle of the withdrawal-reversal design can be used to generate a variety of strategies for study of intervention in the single case. Two are considered here. More extensive discussion of variations can be found in Bloom, Fischer, and Orme (1995).

An ethical issue can arise in testing a new intervention if a client is already in treatment: should treatment be withdrawn to create a baseline without any intervention? Instead of doing so, the investigator may use the current or standard treatment as the baseline, thus creating a "comparative treatment" rather than "no treatment" control condition. For example, a practitioner treating families with a problem adolescent attempted to shift the family's interaction pattern of blaming each other to a supportive, positive interaction (Melidonis and Bry 1995). To do so, during the intervention phases (B), the practitioner used the "exceptions technique": whenever blaming about a problem occurred, the practitioner asked the family a series of questions about exceptions to the problem, when the problem was expected to occur and did not, what was different, why, and so on. The practitioner acted interested and surprised at the exceptions, and asked for specific details. This intervention was compared to baseline conditions of normal treatment (A), which was defined as standard behavioral family therapy following a published treatment manual. The investigators found that the family members made fewer blaming statements and more positive statements in-session during the period of "exceptions intervention" than during standard treatment. In making the comparison with another treatment, such a withdrawal reversal design has similar control over alternative explanations as does a regular no-treatment withdrawal reversal design. However, one does not know what the situation would be like if there were no intervention. For example, the family might ordinarily make few blaming statements, and the high number was precipitated by the treatment itself!

Another variation, an ABACAD or $AB^1AB^2AB^3$ design, permits comparison of the effects of two or more intervention methods. This is similar to the ABCD model discussed under the basic time series design, except intervention is reversed or withdrawn before a new intervention is begun. This permits comparison of each intervention to a no-treatment condition. A drawback is that an new rival hypothesis is possible: the interaction of previous phases with the current intervention phase. Variations of this design may be used to test the relative effectiveness of different components of complex intervention packages; each component or method making up the package can be tested in turn. For example, components of a case management package might be tested sequentially: the first intervention period might include the case manager coordinating the client's services, the second might include meeting with the client to discuss services and progress (without the coordination), and the third might include the combination of the two.

Summary of Withdrawal-Reversal (ABAB) Design

In summary, the withdrawal-reversal design (ABAB) generally provides good control over maturation, history, instability, testing, and regression because it is usually unlikely that these sources would produce an ebb and flow of change coincident with the use and suspension of intervention. Because of its greater control over rival hypotheses, it is superior to the AB design for testing whether intervention has caused a change. In fact, the AB design is really an evaluation of whether change has occurred, whereas the ABAB designs permits inferences about the cause of the change.

Despite its powerful controls, the withdrawal-reversal design presents certain limitations as a strategy for testing the effects of intervention. Its most serious drawback is its limited range of application. To use it, one must have an intervention whose effects will not persist after it is withdrawn or can be readily undone. As we have seen, often this criterion cannot be met; in fact, as practitioners, we usually hope for the opposite. For example, cognitive interventions are expected to have effects that are persistent and irreversible; one does not expect insight or altered beliefs to vanish when treatment stops—the reason perhaps why researchers are advised to "reverse early." Second, the withdrawal-reversal design may be particularly susceptible to agency constraints, particularly ethical concerns about withdrawing treatment. However, if reversals are kept short, just long enough to demonstrate that problems return toward baseline levels, harm to clients is unlikely. A little creativity can enable practitioners to use naturally occurring withdrawal periods, for example, vacations or holidays when treatment is suspended anyway. Moreover, the withdrawal-reversal feature can provide clients with graphic demonstrations of how their problems arise and how they can be controlled.

The Multiple Baseline Design

In the reversal-withdrawal design, control over extraneous variations was achieved by *interruption*—for example, by turning intervention "on and off." In the multiple baseline design, one attempts to attain this control through *replication,* that is, through repeating the same intervention across different targets to determine if change consistently follows the introduction of the intervention. Control is further strengthened by successively increasing the length of the baseline for each target before introducing the intervention. By so staggering the inception of the intervention, one attempts to rule out the possibility that change simply coincides with intervention and actually results from maturation, history, or other extraneous factors. In other words, by staggering the inception of intervention across a series of targets, a researcher can demonstrate that change occurs only when intervention is introduced and hence is the result of the intervention. The pattern could theoretically, of course, be produced by a series of coincidences, but such an explanation begins to sound implausible when the investigator has been able to predict the result repeatedly.

The strategy is illustrated by figure 6.7. The targets, which could be behav-

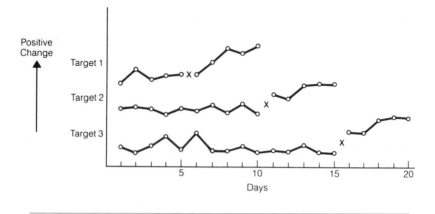

FIGURE 6.7
Illustration of general form of multiple baseline design. The targets can stand for different clients or for different problems or situations involving the same client.

iors, problems, situations, or clients or other systems, are monitored over time with intervention introduced successively in each. (When the targets consist of clients, the design, technically speaking, is no longer a single-system experiment though it is convenient to present it within this general category of design.)

Multiple Baseline Design Across Systems

Because its utility in social work is perhaps greater than other multiple baseline designs, the multiple baseline across systems is considered first and in greater detail. We begin with a review of basic procedures and considerations involved in this time series design, using an across clients design to illustrate.

To conduct a study using the multiple baseline design across clients, the investigator selects a set of clients as closely matched as possible. Usually the clients share the same type of problem and are similar in respect to other important characteristics, such as age, that might influence the intervention. If clients are similar, it is possible to design an intervention program expressly suited for clients of that particular type. Additionally, baselines are more likely to show similar patterns, and this makes it easier to detect changes associated with treatment and to generalize about a set of similar clients. Precision matching is not essential, however, for equivalence among clients is not a required assumption. Differences in initial characteristics are presumably controlled by determining patterns of change within each client over time. The crucial comparison involves differences in these *patterns*, differences that are presumably a function of *when* intervention is introduced.

Data collection on each client's behavior or problem is begun simultaneously. Intervention is then introduced in staggered fashion. For example, when intervention begins for the first client, baseline data collection is continued for the other clients; when intervention begins for the second client, the baseline continues for the third, and so on. The design looks like a series of AB designs, except that they are conducted simultaneously and the baselines are progressively longer. It is expected that, if the intervention is effective, each time series will show systematic improvement over its own baseline only after intervention is introduced.

The design is illustrated by an experiment conducted by Gamache, Edleson, and Schock (1988), who were studying the effects of coordinating the reponses of police, the judicial system, and social services when women were battered. Rather than individual clients, they selected three communities, which were matched as closely as possible on suburban locale, size, racial composition, income, and types of employment. Intervention consisted of requiring police officers to make arrests in domestic assault situations, sending advocates to work immediately with both partners upon arrest, having attorneys actively prosecute cases, and instituting a strong social service program for batterers. In each community, the investigators monitored arrests and prosecutions for domestic violence. After a 6-month baseline, the coordinated program was started in the first community, 3 months later in the second, and another 3 months after in the third community. In all three communities, arrests and prosecutions were low until the program was started, and then increased. The authors concluded that, at least for the short run, the program was effective in mobilizing the police and courts to intervene actively in domestic violence cases. (See figure 6.8.)

Like the previous time series designs, stable baselines rule out the likelihood that maturation, statistical regression, instability, or testing could cause the changes rather than the intervention. If the baselines for other systems are stable while intervention begins in the first system (and remains stable in the third when intervention is begun in the second), there is good evidence that history is not the cause. In this example, if some event such as a television special on violence caused the increase in arrests and prosecutions, then we would expect to see a simultaneous increase in all three communities. Instrumentation is unlikely to be a rival hypothesis since standard, public data (arrests and prosecutions) were used. However, had the outcome measure been recorded by one person who knew when all the interventions began, say, an investigator rating

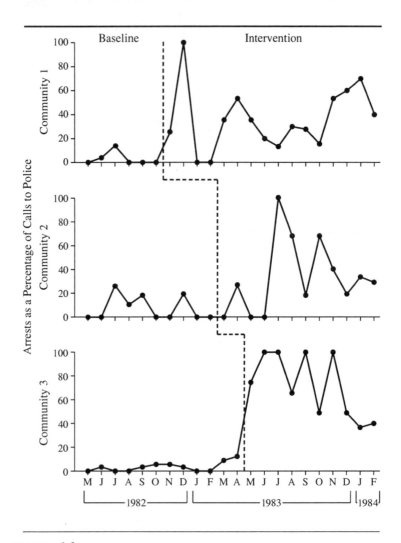

FIGURE 6.8

Arrests as a percentage of the total number of male-female domestic violence calls received each month by police from May 1982 to February 1984, across three target communities. Source: Gamache, Edleson, and Schock 1988:202.

the community's overall attitude toward domestic violence, instrumentation might have been a possibility. Reactivity is not ruled out, but if it occurred, its presence in all three systems suggests that it might well be considered a non-specific effect, an effect that goes along with intervention even if unintended.

In planning a multiple baseline design, the length of the baseline periods and the timing of the inception of intervention are affected by certain requirements of the design. Because the baselines must be staggered, their lengths are progressively increased—an argument for keeping the initial baseline as short as possible and for limiting the duration in advance of the study. The length of the second and subsequent baselines is also a function of the time required to produce an intervention effect. Hence, if the initial baseline runs for a ten-day period, the second for twenty days, and the third for thirty days, the intervention must show a change over baseline within a ten-day period. Some interventions that are not expected to show results for long periods of time may not be suitable for testing in this design.

In discussion of the multiple baseline design so far, we have used three targets as a norm. This figure is somewhat arbitrary, although it is frequently suggested as a minimum number to provide evidence on the effectiveness of intervention (Bloom, Fischer, and Orme 1995). A larger number of clients or systems may be advantageous, but a practical problem unique to this design is encountered as the sample size increases. Because each client added has to wait progressively longer, the last client in a set of, say, five clients may be required to spend a rather lengthy period of time in baseline, possibly too long if the client is anxious to receive help.

As in any service experiment, the size of the sample needed to demonstrate an intervention effect depends on the strength of the intervention. The "rule of three" used in multiple baseline designs seems to be based on the assumption that if a change in the target follows the introduction of treatment that many times, then the case for a treatment effect becomes persuasive. This assumption may be reasonable if the pattern of change conforms to the ideal expected results presented in figure 6.7. These results are not, however, always obtained. For example, Miller and Kelley (1994) used parental goal setting and contingency contracting to improve children's performance of homework. Although the children all improved their accuracy when intervention began, only two of the four substantially increased the amount of time they spend "on-task" actually doing the homework. The findings are no longer so convincing. In social work, most interventions are not so potent as to produce dramatic effects in an unbroken succession of cases. Consequently, more than three cases is usually desirable for this reason, although as noted, there may be practical problems in expanding the number beyond this limit.

One solution is to have more than one client for each baseline condition. For example, by pairing clients, six clients can be treated within the time period that would be normally consumed by three. It is not even necessary to use pairs, or even to be consistent about the number of clients bunched together. Clients can be paired only in relation to length of baseline; otherwise they are treated independently. This design can yield a greater amount of information about intervention than the three-client multiple baseline but it is not as strong as six baselines each of varied length. As an example, Jensen (1994) randomly assigned 9 depressed women to baselines of 3, 4, or 5 weeks. Thus, 3 women had 3-week baselines, 3 had 4-week baselines, and 3 had 5-week baselines. All nine clients showed an immediate and continued decrease in symptoms when intervention began, regardless of length of baseline. Thus it is clear that length of time in treatment is not an alternative explanation, and it is unlikely that history, other aspects of maturation, or regression explain the results in all nine clients.

The across-systems design has a broad range of application in tests of social work intervention. It can be used with "nonreversible" methods that are difficult to test with withdrawal-reversal designs. Clients can be treated in a holistic manner; that is, one does not need to concentrate on one problem or situation at a time. For these reasons, it may be more suitable than other controlled single system designs for studying interventions based on psychodynamic or systems theories, which treat client problems as indivisible.

Multiple Baseline Across Problems

In the multiple baseline design across problems the researcher tests the efficacy of an intervention method with different problems of one client system. In other respects the design is equivalent in structure to the across-systems multiple baseline; that is, baselines are taken on different problems and the timing of intervention is staggered across the set of problems.

The control over rival hypotheses of the across-problems design is similar to the across-systems multiple baseline. If the experiment works as intended, with a stable baseline and the desired change in each problem beginning only when the staggered intervention is initiated, then it is unlikely that maturation, regression, instability, testing, or history could be alternative explanations. Further, because the same system is involved, reactivity is less likely. Nonspecific effects are still a plausible explanation, and instrumentation depends on how the dependent variable is measured.

For example, Acierno and Last (1995) treated a man with obsessive symptoms: to counteract his fears of a physical catastrophe like a heart attack, the

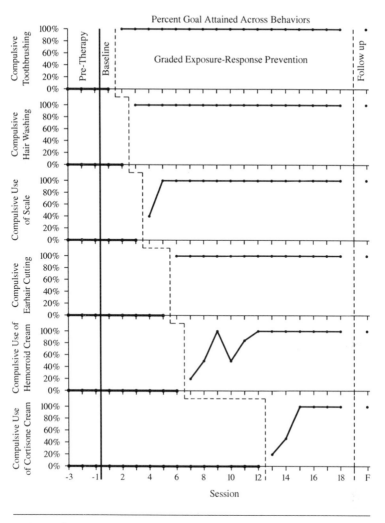

FIGURE 6.9

Man with obsessive symptoms: Behavioral gains reported as percentages of pre-determined performance goals for each compulsive area. Source: Acierno and Last 1995:8.

man spent nearly three hours a day in ritualistic grooming. While baselines were begun on 6 compulsive cleaning behaviors, the man was taught methods to reduce anxiety and prevent the ritual behavior. Then, he applied these methods first to brushing his teeth, then to compulsive hair washing, then to compulsive weighing himself, and so on. Each of the 6 behaviors decreased dramatically to appropriate levels when the intervention was applied to it, convincing evidence that most rival hypotheses were unlikely. (See figure 6.9.)

The principal advantage of the multiple baseline design across problems or behaviors over its across-systems counterpart is that an experiment requires only one system, rather than several concomitantly. Clients or others do not need to be kept waiting lengthy periods in baseline conditions before service is started.

Certain prices are paid for this advantage. A single-client system provides less basis for generalization than several clients; that is, it is hard to say what might happen with other clients. Further, the interdependency that usually exists among different problems in the same system is almost always a matter of concern. The obsessive man was unusual in that his behaviors were not interrelated. Treatment of one problem is likely to affect another, or spontaneous recovery may occur in all problems simultaneously. If all problems show positive change at the same time, we cannot determine whether treatment or extraneous factors are responsible. On the other hand, the intervention may be responsible or "carry over" and affect all problems. To avoid such carry-over effects, the intervention must be problem specific, which may make it unsuitable for all the problems baselined.

For example, in a multiple baseline design across behaviors, Aylward et al. (1995) sought to improve skills of direct-care staff members at a residential treatment facility for retarded children; these skills were controlling physical aggression, controlling verbal aggression, giving adequate guidelines to residents, and giving residents feedback on their performance. The staff were treated as a unit for analysis. For two skill areas, staff consistency improved as predicted when intervention began on each. However, when intervention began on controlling physical aggression, consistency for both physical aggression and verbal aggression shot up. We may suspect that staff had difficulty distinguishing physical and verbal aggression, or because the skills were similar, they immediately generalized the application of one skill to the other. Still, we cannot rule out other explanations such an external event having improved consistency across all situations. In other words, there may not have been a carryover effect.

On the other hand, the study of staff behaviors is enhanced by the inclusion of four rather than three behaviors, and the fact that three of them did change

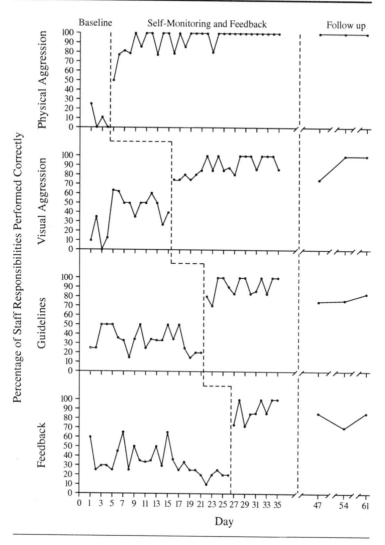

FIGURE 6.10

Percentage of staff responsibilities performed correctly Source: Aylward et al.
1995:57

only when the intervention occurred gives some confidence that rival hypotheses are unlikely. Further, although the design treated the staff as a single unit, there were in fact 12 staff involved. We might question whether the same patterns occurred for all 12—an alternative design choice would be 12 basic time series (AB) designs. If so, we have greater confidence that the intervention might work with other staff as well. (See figure 6.10.)

Multiple Baseline Design Across Situations

In the multiple baseline design across situations, the investigator is concerned with separate locations of the same problem within a single client system. A child's problem of aggressive behavior may be expressed in the classroom, in play with peers, and at home. Separate problem baselines are taken for each situation, and the inception of intervention is staggered across situations. In one study, for example, the investigators tried to increase recycling of office paper at a human service agency by providing convenient recycling bins and sending reminder memos (Brothers, Krantz, and McClannahan 1994). The intervention was staggered in the administrative area, the instructional classrooms, and therapeutic office area. The amount of paper recycled and the quality of sorting improved in each area only when the recycling containers were made convenient in that area. (See Figure 6.11.)

The limitations of the multiple baseline across situations parallel those cited for the across-problems design. A problem that occurs in different situations is required; treatment of the problem and resulting change need to be situation specific, the design is easier to use with highly specific treatment approaches, and so on. It does, however, provide a means of using a controlled design with a single system and single problem.

Variations of the Multiple Baseline Design

A powerful variation of the multiple baseline design is to withdraw or reverse treatment for each of the systems, problems, or situations. This design thus looks like a series of concurrent ABAB designs, with the intervention, withdrawal-reversal, and reintervention at staggered intervals. For example, Sternberg and Bry (1994) studied three families in treatment for problems with their adolescents. The baseline condition was in fact the normal problem-solving treatment, while the intervention was the same treatment augmented by the practitioner's explicit acknowledgment of each solution proposed by a family member. Intervention was staggered on the three families, then withdrawn (the therapist did not systematically acknowledge solutions), then instituted, withdrawn, and reinstated (ABABAB), all with staggered timing. In two

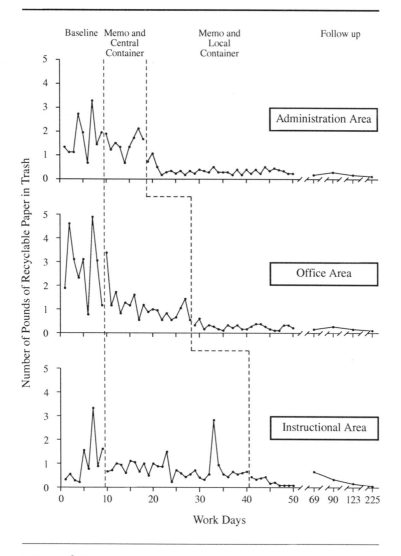

FIGURE 6.11

Number of pounds of recyclable paper in trash Source: Brothers et al. 1994:158

of the three families, members generated more problem solutions when the practitioner acknowledged their solutions. (See figure 6.12)

The ABAB multiple baseline combines the strengths of the withdrawal reversal with those of the multiple baseline. The withdrawal-reversal design establishes that intervention and outcome are associated, that is, that improved functioning occurs when intervention is present and disappears when it is not present. The multiple baseline strengthens the demonstration that time is not a factor (through the staggered baselines), shows that intervention and outcome are associated with several systems, problems, or situations; and may provide some evidence that reactivity is not a factor. Disadvantages of the design are that it requires interventions and outcome measures that can be reversed (for the ABAB part) and interventions that are nonspecific enough to apply to several targets. Further, if the results are not exactly as predicted, interpreting the results can be quite difficult.

Summary of Multiple Baseline Designs

In summary, multiple baseline designs attempt to control rival hypotheses through replicating an intervention and (hopefully) its results over a series of targets, staggering the timing of intervention to demonstrate that change occurs only when intervention does. The intervention may be repeated in three or more systems that have similar problems—clients, families, communities, etc. (multiple baseline across systems or across clients)—in one system with several problems (across problems), or in one system with problem-behavior that occurs in several settings (across situations). Each design makes implausible the threats to internal validity called maturation, regression, history, testing, and instability. The across systems design also provides control over reactivity if we assume that reactive effects would "leak" to other problem areas. All of these controls are with the caveats usual to time series designs: if the baseline is relatively stable, if the outcome changes in the desired direction at the right time; if changes replicate themselves across systems, problems or settings, and so on.

The multiple baseline designs have the advantage of being useful for interventions whose effects cannot be reversed. Disadvantages include that clients or problems may have to wait for treatment, perhaps an unacceptably long time, and effects from the intervention must be rather quick. In the across-problems and across-situations designs, the interdependence of problems and the possibility of "leakage" of treatment effects are practical constraints.

The multiple baseline designs also have an important advantage over other single-system designs in that they can demonstrate that intervention has worked in more than one situation—with several systems, several problems, or

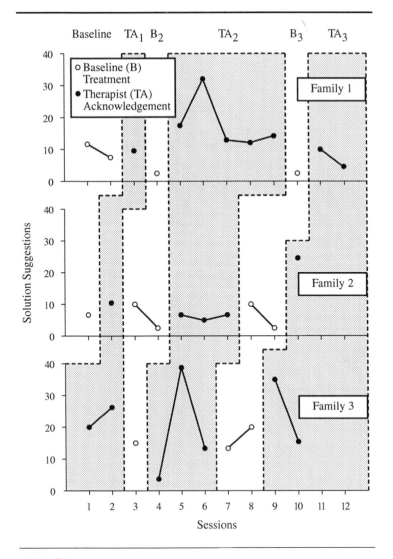

FIGURE 6.12

Solution suggestions generated by session and treatment. Source: Sternberg and Bry 1994:11

several settings. The issue of whether intervention would work in a different situation is a crucial one, which we take up in the next section.

Generalization (External Validity)

Thus far, in describing types of time series designs, we have paid particular attention to the "control" features or "internal validity" of a design—the capacity of the design to isolate the effects of the experimental intervention by controlling for extraneous variables. We now take up a contrasting aspect—the extent to which a research design offers a basis for generalization to other situations. This aspect, which Campbell and Stanley (1963) refer to as the "external validity" of an experiment, is taken up for single-system experiments as a whole. The basic ideas will later be applied to group experiments.

In social work experiments, two questions are at issue in generalization. One question asks, in effect: "Will the interventions tested produce similar results in other situations?" The interventions may have worked in a given experiment, but will they work well if applied to other clients, used by other practitioners, and in a nonexperimental context? These are the classical questions posed in thinking about generalization. They may be thought of as relating to the "reproducibility" aspects of generalization. As important as this aspect is, it leaves out a dimension of particular importance in a practice profession: the pragmatic aspects of applying an intervention. Thus the second question: "Are the results worth reproducing?" An intervention may be reproducible, but it may also be difficult and costly to deliver and its payoff may not be commensurate with the difficulties and costs. These might be called the "pragmatic" aspects of generalization.

Generalization to Other Situations

In considering whether results can be reproduced, our starting point is a unique event involving particular problems, interventions, research methodology, and so on. Although any such facet may limit generalization, we will illustrate the issues in generalization by focusing on the interventions tested as they relate to other facets. The same points can be made for practitioners, agencies, and so on.

A key issue in generalization, of course, is the system on which the intervention was tested—the client, family, group, agency, and so on. To what extent can one system be considered representative of some larger group of systems with which the intervention might be used? A single system study can provide little assurance about representativeness of this kind. (In this discussion, we continue to use "single system" to include across-systems designs. Because they involve several systems, these designs usually provide a slightly better basis for generalization than the "pure" single client study.) Generalizability is often further limited by the nature of case selection: the case(s) treated may be particularly well suited to the intervention. And, the investigator may be further selective about the case chosen to write about. Consequently, we may be presented with the one case in which the intervention worked best; while half a dozen less successful cases are buried in the experimenter's files. Further, in a single system design, the investigator can tailor the interventions to suit the particular characteristics of the case. This plasticity is an advantage in achieving effects in the case (internal validity) but may create an idiosyncratic mesh that is hard to generalize to other cases.

However, the single system design does have one special strength in respect to generalization: one can generalize from a base of a considerable amount of detailed knowledge about the system studied. Generalization from group experiments must inevitably be based on averages of one kind or another, which may mask specific relationships between certain outcomes and treatment variables. For example, in a group experiment, ten children may be treated for a school phobia. All may recover except one who gets worse. In a group design, one cannot say if that particular child would have become worse anyway or was made worse by the intervention, since the effects of the intervention are not tested on a case-by-case basis. In a single-system design, more precise information is available about each case. If the child was affected by a particular type of school phobia that was made worse by the intervention, this important fact would be more likely to come to light in a single system study. In this sort of situation, not uncommon in clinical practice, a series of single system studies might provide a basis for discriminating generalizations; for example, the intervention works well with type X phobia but may aggravate type Y.

Characteristics of practitioners and more generally the setting of the experiment must also be taken into account. The experience and skill of the practitioner, caseload size, the quality of supervision, and the cooperation of agency staff are among the more specific factors that may limit generalizations. Special consideration must be given to the knowledge and experience that a practitioner-researcher may accrue in the course of efforts to perfect methods of treating a particular type of case. Such accumulated expertise, which may not be exportable, may have been decisive in the success of the methods. A similar issue arises in attempts to disseminate the methods of celebrated "super practitioners" who, by all accounts, are remarkably successful but whose methods defy emulation because they may be so much a part of the practitioner's special knowledge or personal qualities.

The very act of studying intervention may affect the results. The effectiveness of an intervention may be attributable in part to the procedures used to study it. We referred to this earlier as the threat to internal validity called reactive effects. Observing a girl in order to collect baseline data on her timid behavior may give her a clue that her behavior is amiss, which may make her more receptive to the subsequent intervention. Hence, the intervention may not produce the same effects when it is used in the absence of prior measurement.

Another phenomenon, called the Heisenberg principle or Hawthorne effect, is that simply being a part of an experiment may affect the practitioner or client in additional ways. The practitioner may put forth extra effort because of commitment to the method and desire to demonstrate its effectiveness. The client may be stimulated by the worker's enthusiasm. Both may try harder simply because they are the focus of study. Such "reactive effects of experimental arrangements" (Campbell and Stanley 1963) may then produce an extra impact that may vanish when the intervention is used under ordinary practice conditions.

These limits on generalization, which apply to all experiments but with greater force to the single system design, may seem so restrictive that one might question whether one study has anything to say for other situations. Our intent is to make clear factors that should be taken into account in generalization, not to discourage it. On a more positive note, any set of valid findings affects to some extent our assessment of the validity of general propositions. If we can learn some truth about a slice of reality, even a single case, our knowledge of the world is increased.

There are other reasons why generalization from limited evidence need not be a fool's mission. The findings of an experiment may be consistent with findings from other studies—that is, grounds for generalization may already exist. In the context of operations research, we may not need to generalize very far. We may need only to know if an agency is reaching its intended clientele, or if an intervention method is effective for the type of clients in one's own circumscribed caseload.

Pragmatic Generalization

The pragmatic aspects of generalization involve two related considerations: feasibility and cost-effectiveness. Feasibility problems arise if the intervention would be difficult to implement on a broader scale. For example, an intervention may run counter to the norms of practitioners, require apparatus not usually available, or demand that staff perform tasks that might interfere with other responsibilities. Cost-effectiveness in the strict sense refers to the comparative monetary costs of alternative means of achieving a given goal or effect; we use the notion more broadly to refer to the probable effects and costs of an intervention in relation to possible alternatives. If we appraise the results of an experiment from a cost-effectiveness standpoint, we ask "How much of an effect was achieved at what cost (at least in terms of practitioner and client time) and could a comparable effect be achieved by other means at less cost?" (see chapter 14 for additional discussion of cost-effectiveness).

Suppose we learn from a single-system study that an individualized remedial reading program enabled an adult studying for the GED to increase his or her score on a reading test by ten points and further that it took ten one-hour sessions to achieve this gain. If we have information suggesting that an available group approach (that could reach more sstudents with no greater expenditure of practitioner time) produces results almost as good on the average, we would have questions about the cost-effectiveness of the individualized methods. These questions would prompt further inquiry: Is there another reason to treat the learner using individual methods, such as evidence that that this type of student would not have responded to the group approach? If the individualized program seemed to be a little more effective than the group approach, is the slight margin of difference worth the investment if we consider that more learners could be helped by group methods?

Use of pragmatic criteria need not necessarily constrain generalization. An intervention may produce only a modest effect but may be simple to learn and may be applied easily and quickly—factors that would enhance its generalizability. Further, in developmental research, a modest effect may suggest more potent variations that ultimately lead to effective treatment packages.

Improving Generalizability

Although the generalizability of single-system studies is inherently quite limited, steps can be taken to improve it. An experimental case can be selected from a well-defined population using more "scientific" sampling methods such as random sampling (see chapter 8 for a description of sampling methods). This would avoid a tendency to hand-pick a case because it seemed well suited to the intervention. Although a report might feature the study of a single case, reference can be made to other single case tests of the intervention if these have been conducted by the investigator. Of particular relevance would be information concerning cases in which the approach had been tried but found unsuitable. Finally, more emphasis could be placed on developing intervention models for particular types of clients or problems and on testing them with representative cases. Single case studies in which interventions are molded to meet various requirements of the case at hand have considerable value within the context of developmental and operations research, but they provide a poor basis for generalization. In short, those interested in how the results apply to other situations must speculate based on logical and untestable considerations such as similarity of clients, practitioners, agency setting, and so on.

Replication

So far in our discussion of external validity of single system studies, we have considered one strategy for attempting to develop general knowledge from single system approaches: extrapolation of the results of a given study to other situations. A second, and more powerful, strategy is replication, or repeating, with variations, previous studies to build generalizations through empirical means. In single-system research, replication has been seen as especially important because of limitations on generalizations inherent in a study based on only one system. At the same time, replication is more readily accomplished in single-system research than in research involving groups.

Two types of replication in single-system experiments can be distinguished: direct and systematic (Barlow and Hersen 1984). In direct replication, an investigator (or research team) retests an intervention with the same type of subject and problem and setting. For example, Ferguson and Rodway (1994) used the same cluster of cognitive behavioral interventions to treat perfectionism in nine women. In all nine, both standardized and personalized measures of perfectionism were stable during baseline (A), decreased during intervention (B), and remained low when intervention was withdrawn (A). (A final intervention (B) period was unnecessary because the problem had not returned; there was no reversal.) They concluded that intervention caused the changes, using the logic that because the same intervention had the same effect on so many different clients, rival hypotheses such as maturation or history are unlikely alternatives to intervention as the causal agent.

Such direct replication is considered to be the first step, since it can establish that the treatment and research procedures used by a particular investigator achieve consistent results with the same kind of client, problem, and so on. In other words, it can show that the success of a single study was not a fluke occasioned, for example, by a client with an exceptional capacity for change. Direct replication provides only a very narrow base for generalization, however. After it has accomplished its objectives—Barlow and Hersen (1984) suggest that three successful replications of an experiment should be sufficient—systematic replication becomes the next logical step.

In systematic replication, an attempt is made to broaden the scope of generalization by systematically varying practitioners, clients, problems, and settings. If a case management program has been found to work (through direct replication) with preadolescents, it may be tried with adolescents. If it has proved successful with academic problems, it may be applied to classroom behavior problems, and so on. In this way the range of successful application of a method can be incrementally established.

In this process it is vital to have replication by investigators who were not involved in the original experiment nor in direct replication of it; ideally, they have no involvement or personal investment in its success. Such independent replication can help ensure that effects were not due to biases resulting from a developer's stake in demonstrating its efficacy. From such replications, one accumulates evidence on how well combinations of interventions appear to work with particular kinds of clients and on problems and factors that differentiate more successful from less successful applications.

Summary

Single-system experiments using quantitative time series designs provide a means of assessing outcome systematically. They may be used on any system where the unit—individual, client, group, community, or other aggregate—can be treated as a unit for data analysis. Single-system designs are the designs of choice in small-scale practice evaluation or where information about specific cases is an asset.

Baseline measurements over time establish the pattern of variation or stability of the problem (the dependent variable) prior to intervention. Data collection continues once intervention (the independent variable) is introduced. To assess change, the intervention-phase (B phase) patterns are compared to the baseline (A phase) patterns. In doing so, one assumes that the baseline patterns would have continued if intervention had not begun.

The three core time series designs are the basic time series or AB design, the withdrawal-reversal or ABAB design, and the multiple baseline design. Interpretation of all three requires a relatively stable baseline and a difference between A- and B-phase patterns that can be detected using "eyeball" or statistical methods.

The basic time series (AB) design is useful for establishing the presence of change, but has limited control over rival hypotheses. The withdrawal-reversal design (ABAB) adds to the basic times series design by withdrawing treatment (or reversing to the original baseline conditions) and then reinstating treatment. It can demonstrate directly that outcome is associated with intervention, and it generally provides good control over threats to internal validity such as maturation, history, instability, regression, and testing.

Multiple baseline designs replicate an intervention over a series of targets, staggering the timing of intervention to demonstrate that change occurs only when intervention does. The across-systems design repeats the same intervention in several systems that have similar problems—clients, families, communities, etc.—while the across-problems and across-situations designs repeat the intervention in one system with several problems or one problem that occurs in several settings. The multiple baseline designs also have good control over maturation, regression, history, testing, and instability (and possibly reactivity). In addition, the multiple baseline designs have a distinct advantage of demonstrating that the change occurs in more than one system, problem or situation. In any study, however, one cannot assume that the design eliminates alternative hypotheses when making causal attributions. One must use logic and judgment to assess each study individually.

In all single-system designs, generalization, or whether intervention would work with other clients or situations, is a crucial issue. Although one can be precise about what was done in what context, it is rarely possible to say what clients, systems, situations or even interventions the study represents, and this is a major drawback. To demonstrate generalization from single system designs requires replication, or repeating the experiment, either in the same way (direct replication) or with planned variations (systematic replication).

7 Group Experiments

In this chapter we take up strategies for group experiments, still staying within the context of social work intervention. Group experiments are quantitative designs that involve one or more groups of participants and an active independent variable (the experimental intervention). Their purpose is explanation—to attempt to show a causal link between variables: the hypothesis, whether stated formally or not, is almost always that the experimental intervention will be superior to no intervention or to a comparison intervention. As with other designs, establishing that link relies on the process of eliminating rival hypotheses. As in the preceding chapter, we begin with the most elementary form of group experiment—a design confined to a single group and lacking in control over extraneous factors.

Uncontrolled Single Group Experiment

Perhaps the most frequently used evaluative design in social work, the uncontrolled single group experiment involves a single group that receives the intervention. Its uses range from modest tests of a specific intervention with a handful of cases to studies of hundreds of cases exposed to a multifaceted program. The logic of the design is, however, no different from that of the uncontrolled single-system study. An intervention is conducted without further research manipulation, that is, without delay, interruption, withholding, or other means of determining change in the absence of intervention. Nor is another group available to assess what might happen without intervention.

Assessing Intervention Effects

In the uncontrolled single group experiment, a characteristic is measured before and after the intervention, or an estimate of change is derived from data obtained following the intervention. The guiding hypothesis is that intervention was responsible for observed changes. However, it is usually not possible to test this hypothesis adequately, because the design does not control for alternative explanations.

An example of an uncontrolled experiment with post hoc data collection is a study of a training program by DePoy and colleagues (1992) (diagram 7.1). Called "Train the Trainers," the program taught agency staff how to train community persons to work with children and families with HIV/AIDS. Four one-variable hypotheses guided the research, for example, "Posttraining, trainees will demonstrate a high degree of knowledge of AIDS and of families with children with AIDS"(47). Participants attended a training conference and a follow-up session after they had had a chance to recruit and train volunteers. Data were collected at the follow-up session. As hypothesized, the trainers were knowledgeable about HIV/AIDS, had positive attitudes toward working with ill persons, and had been able to recruit and train volunteers.

DIAGRAM 7.1
Design Used in Train the Trainers Project (post hoc uncontrolled single group experiment)

    E O X
    E = Experimental group.
    O = Data collection point.
    X = Occurrence of manipulated independent variable.

DePoy, Burke, and Sherwen 1992.

The question with such an uncontrolled experiment is whether the training had any effect on the trainers. The design cannot control rival hypotheses that might explain what affected their knowledge and attitudes. For example, in terms of the participants' good knowledge of AIDS/HIV, perhaps most read a recent newspaper article (history), perhaps their experience serving ill children gave them knowledge (maturation), perhaps the investigators homemade questionnaire overinflated all responses (instrumentation), perhaps they learned because the trainers were attractive role models (nonspecific effects), and so on.

The post hoc design also raises another important issue, because we do not know if there was any change from before to after the training. The participants were recruited from agencies that served families with children with HIV/AIDS, so it is likely that they already had knowledge and a commitment to serve such families, and we simply do not know if they had trained volunteers prior to the conference. A prospective design (pre-/post-) with measurement of knowledge and attitudes at the beginning of the conference would have permitted assessment of any change.

Whether measures of change are derived ex post facto or from comparison of before and after assessments, the design is generally (and correctly) considered to be a questionable strategy for assessing intervention effects. Because many types of social work problems tend to improve over time without intervention, studies using the design may in fact give a misleading picture of intervention effects. Persons with a stake in the success of a program expect "positive results" and hope to achieve them. Thus when they learn that two-thirds of the clients receiving a service have improved, they are quite ready to interpret the causes of the improvement to the program and may become impatient with caveats about "alternative explanations."

Such misinterpretations can have unfortunate results. For example, during the late 1950s, a number of demonstrations of casework programs with "multiproblem" families receiving public assistance were conducted. These studies, which generally used uncontrolled single group designs, were used as the basis for claims about the effectiveness of intensive casework to reduce multiproblem families' "dependency on welfare" (May 1964). However, when controlled studies of these programs were subsequently conducted (Mullen, Chazin, and Feldstein 1972; Wallace 1967), it was found that families receiving intensive casework did not improve at a significantly greater rate than control families who did not receive this form of service. In retrospect, the service had been oversold with the help of overinterpreted studies.

Although the risk of drawing false conclusions about the effectiveness of intervention is omnipresent in uncontrolled group experiments, such designs can provide rather persuasive evidence on the presence of interventive effects under certain conditions. These conditions are similar to those described for the uncontrolled single-system study (chapter 6): intervention addressed to stable targets, use of well-explicated practice models, pre- and post-measurement of change, and interventions which leave a typical "signature." For example, programs designed to teach specific knowledge or skills are often evaluated by simple pre-post designs. If it can be demonstrated through "before" and "after" measures that recipients acquired the knowledge or skills taught and if it can be safely assumed that they could not have acquired them by any other means, then program effects can be legitimately claimed. Pre-post designs are also useful as exploratory experiments in developmental research, as will be described in chapter 16.

Strengthening the Group Design

In the single-system design, control over alternative explanation was achieved by within-case tracking of variation in outcomes; variation occurring during periods of intervention was compared with variation when intervention was not used. In group designs, control is usually attained by comparing variation in outcomes between groups. One group may receive the intervention while another group does not, or two groups may each receive different interventions. (Of course, many other patterns are possible, as we shall see.)

Such designs, which are quantitative, may vary in two important ways: the equivalence of the groups compared, and the timing of the data collection. If groups are equivalent to each other, then differences among group members (selection) cannot be an explanation of differences in outcomes. By convention, designs are considered "equivalent group designs" if the participants are assigned to groups using random assignment. Designs are considered "nonequivalent group designs" (sometimes called quasi-experiments) if participants are placed in groups using some other method such as selecting natural groupings (a classroom, community, or hospital ward) or alternating assignment. The timing of data collection may be ex post facto (in which case it is not possible to measure change) or prospective, with data collected for the first time before the experimental manipulation.

Equivalent Groups and Random Assignment

Equivalence between groups is achieved basically through random assignment of cases. When we say that cases are randomly assigned to different groups, we mean simply that assignment is determined by chance rather than by other criteria, such as diagnosis or preference of the client. In random assignment, each participant has an equal change of being assigned to each group, and every possible combination of individuals has an equal chance of being in any group. Theoretically, when random assignment is used, the probability is high that characteristics that might influence outcome will be equally distributed among the groups. Thus, whether we can guess what might affect outcome or not, such characteristics are unlikely to affect one group more than another.

In using random assignment, a set of participants is first selected according to whatever criteria are used to define the sample on which the intervention will be tested; for example, criteria may include persons of a particular age, gender, with specific types of problems, and so on. Once the participants are selected, they are assigned to groups randomly, using some device such as a table of random numbers (see chapter 8). For example, if there are two groups, an experimental and control group, the end result is the same as if a coin were flipped fairly for each case, with "heads" going to the experimental group and "tails" to the control group. If random assignment "works," the original set of cases will be divided into similar, roughly equivalent, sets. How well random assignment works is largely a function of the size of the pool of cases to which it is applied. If this pool is large, say a hundred or more cases, it is highly likely that the resulting groups will be equivalent. As the pool shrinks, so does this likelihood. With a pool of fifty cases, "straight" random assignment may still work reasonably well, but with twenty cases it may well fail to "deliver" comparable groups. This is so because, with small numbers, short-term chance effects can produce inequities. (If a coin is flipped a large number of times, a roughly equal distribution of heads and tails will result, but one flipped only ten times might well produce an 8/2 split.)

To avoid such "bad breaks," investigators may resort to precision *matching* when samples are small. Before random assignment, pairs of cases are matched according to one or more variables thought to affect outcome. The two cases in each pair are then randomly assigned, one to the experimental group and the other to the control group. This ensures that each group will have equal numbers of cases characterized by the variables matched. For example, if we think that girls may react differently from boys (gender is thought to be an important variable) pairs would be formed in the following manner: MM, FF, MM, FF, and so on. The two males in the first pair would be allocated using random assignment, one to each group; the process is repeated with the second pair, and so on. The experimental and control groups would then be identical in respect to sex distribution. (If three groups are involved, then there would be matched trios; four groups, quartets; and so on.)

Subjects may be matched on more than one variable. For instance, if age were added to the previous example, the pairs might look as follows: M 10 yr, M 10 yr; F 8 yr, F 8 yr. It is obvious that the more variables are added, the more difficult it is to find cases with the necessary combination of characteristics. Thus, precision matching on more than three variables is rare. Less precise forms of matching (which will not be dealt with here) are also available. Whatever form is selected, random assignment must be used to ensure equivalence of groups. The random assignment makes it probable that other characteristics besides those included in the match are also evenly distributed among groups.

Even when random assignment is used, there is a possibility the groups might not be equivalent. How does one decide if they really are equivalent? A common method is to compare the groups on available measures and to apply a test of significance (chapter 11) to any differences to determine if they are within the limits of random variation. If they are not, the investigator may be the victim of a bad break. Further, initial differences between the two groups that are within the limits of reasonable chance variation, that is, not statistically significant, may still work in the favor of one group or the other. Consequently, if there appear to be initial differences between groups, whether significant or not, a common procedure when analyzing the outcome data is to use statistical procedures that take into account the variations in initial scores (chapter 11). Nevertheless, equivalent-group experiments that have encountered such bad breaks in the results of random assignment must be interpreted cautiously; like nonequivalent group designs, selection cannot be eliminated as an alternative explanation.

In diagramming equivalent group designs, we use the symbol R before the groups to indicate random assignment (or matching with random assignment). See diagram 7.14 for summary sketches of the designs in this chapter.

The Timing of Data Collection

The timing of data collection in experimental designs affects both the investigator's ability to assess selection and the measurement of change. In pre-post designs, with the first data collection before intervention, it is possible to compare the groups to see if they differ systematically on key variables before they receive the intervention, as was just described. In posttest only designs, where the first data collection is after intervention has occurred, we cannot make that assessment. Any differences between groups may be due solely to initial differences, not to the intervention as we hope. However, if groups have been randomly assigned, are sufficiently large, and are similar on demographic characteristics (which can be checked post-intervention), one can assume initial equivalence and ascribe posttest differences to the intervention.

In many studies, the differences over time are important. For example, in the study of the Train the Trainer project referred to earlier (DePoy, Burke, and Sherwen 1992), it was not possible to tell if participants had improved their attitudes during the program or if they had held positive attitudes to begin with. Clearly, prospective designs, with one data collection before intervention and a second after intervention, are necessary to establish that there has been change. Ex post facto designs with data collection only after intervention does not allow assessment of change. For example, suppose the after-treatment problems of families who received treatment are better than those who received no treatment. Possibly both groups were better off before the intervention began. Treatment may have retarded deterioration—a positive result, but not the improvement that the investigator might wish to claim.

Despite this limitation, posttest only designs have certain strengths when initial equivalence between groups is likely because of random assignment. Because there is no data collection before intervention, testing and reactivity are not possible alternative explanations; family members did not change solely because they took a questionnaire, for example. Nor did taking a questionnaire make them more receptive to the treatment, so if we wish to apply the intervention to other clients, we know we do not need to pretest them to sensitize them to treatment. Further, changes in the data collection procedures over time (instrumentation) cannot be an explanation.

Ex post facto designs are useful in social work because of their ease and the ability to apply them even after intervention has begun. At times, posttest only measurement is sufficient to accomplish the purpose, or even desirable, because it avoids reactivity. For example, in a study of the effects of racial composition on people's comfort in groups, Davis, Cheng, and Strube (1996) randomly assigned black and white students to groups that had black-white ratios of 1:3, 2:2, 3:1 (diagram 7.2). To control for gender differences, the groups were all men or all women. After the groups completed their assigned tasks, members filled out questionnaires about the group's decision-making ability and their comfort in the group. In this instance, such assessments would be meaningless before the group began its work; worse, having the members complete an assessment ahead of time would alert them to the important variables being studied and change the natural group processes that the investigators wished to study.

DIAGRAM 7.2

Design Used in Study of Effect of Racial Composition in (equivalent comparison) Groups

			Posttest
R	E_1	X_1	O
	E_2	X_2	O
	E_3	X_3	O

E_1 = Experimental group: 1:3 black-white composition.
E_2 = Experimental group: 2:2 black-white composition.
E_3 = Experimental group: 3:1 black-white composition.
R = Random assignment to groups.

Davis, Cheng, and Strube 1996.

Experimental designs may also differ on repetition of measurement after the intervention. Many studies of treatment include follow-up data collection months and years after the end of treatment. For example, in Reid and Bailey-Dempsey's (1995) study of case management and monetary incentives to improve girls' school performance, the girls' grades were collected for the marking period before the program began, the last marking period of the school year, the first period of the following year, and the last period of the following year (diagram 7.3). The effects of the interventions diminished over time, especially among the girls who received monetary incentives for improved performance. Such follow-ups are essential to demonstrate that any changes can be maintained over time—a limitation of many interventions is that the effect is not durable. However, as important as follow-ups can be, their presence does not affect the ability to rule out alternative explanations. The critical design elements in assessing alternative explanations in experiments are whether the groups are equivalent and whether data collection is prospective. These are also the core elements that are used to differentiate among group experiments.

DIAGRAM 7.3

Design Used in Comparison of Case Management and Monetary Incentives to Improve Girls' School Performance (comparative groups with control group)

		Pretest		Posttest	Follow-up 3 MO.	Follow-up 1 YEAR
R	E_1	O	X_1	O	O	O
	E_2	O	X_2	O	O	O
	C	O		O	O	O

E_1 = Case management.
E_2 = Monetary incentives.
R = Random assignment to groups
C = No contact control group (not randomly assigned).
Source: Reid and Bailey-Dempsey 1995.

We now take a closer look at the most controlled group experiments, the equivalent group experiments.

Equivalent Group Designs

The Classical Experimental Design

The expression "classical experimental design" is commonly used to designate an experiment with prospective measurement and two equivalent groups of clients who are randomly assigned to groups: one group (the experimental group) receives some form of intervention; the other group (the control group) does not. For obvious reasons, this design is also called the pretest-posttest control group design.

An example of a classical experimental design is a study of individual counseling sessions for the spouses of cancer patients conducted by Toseland, Blanchard, and McCallion (1995) (diagram 7.4). The investigators recruited participants in the waiting room at a regional oncology clinic, being careful to get a balance of men and women. The eligible participants were randomly assigned to treatment or control conditions, with men and women assigned separately to ensure equal numbers in each condition. Spouses in the experimental group received six 1-hour individual counseling sessions, conducted by an experienced oncology social worker and focusing on support, problem-solving, and coping skills. The control group members were not offered counseling services (about a quarter used some other helping services on their own). At the beginning of the study, before they were assigned to conditions, all caregivers and the patients took an extensive series of questionnaires measuring such attributes as depression, anxiety, quality of the marital relationship, social support, perceptions of caregiving burden, and so on. Two weeks after their counseling sessions ended, the experimental group completed the same questionnaires. The control group members also completed the questionnaires at the same time period, approximately 10 weeks after taking the pretest. In this study, because previous research had been equivocal, the authors did not make a formal hypothesis about superiority of the counseling, and indeed the results found no significant difference between the experimental and control groups.

DIAGRAM 7.4
Diagram of Design Used in Study of Supportive Counseling for Spouses of Cancer Patients (classical experimental pretest-posttest control group design)

		Pretest		Posttest
R	E	O	X	O
	C	O		O

E = Experimental group: individual counseling including support, problem-solving, and coping skills.
C = Control group: no treatment control.
R = Random assignment to groups.
Source: Toseland, Blanchard, and McCallion 1995.

In planning or assessing the classical experimental design—indeed, any experimental design—several aspects should be considered. These are the function and nature of the control group, the size and composition of the sample (participants), and how to evaluate alternative explanations. We will discuss these briefly before going on to other equivalent group designs.

THE CONTROL GROUP The function of the control group in the classical experimental design is to provide an estimate of change produced by nonintervention variables, or how much change would occur naturally, without intervention. The logic is that if the experimental group changes more than the control group, the difference may be attributed to the intervention (as we shall see, reality isn't this simple). Ideally the members of the control group should not receive any form of intervention (or have any experience) that resembles the interventions received by the members of the experimental group. In social work research, this ideal is seldom, if ever, achieved.

In thinking about control groups, it is helpful to distinguish between two types of clients; those who are actively seeking service and those who are not in the market for service but who would be willing to accept it if offered. With help-seeking clients, a "no-intervention" control group is especially difficult to achieve. Agencies are reluctant to withhold service from people who come to their doors. Moreover, assigning such clients to control groups is no guarantee they will remain isolated from experiences that may compete with the intervention program. Some may seek comparable forms of service elsewhere; others may obtain help from friends, clergymen, physicians, and the like.

Nevertheless, some workable solutions are possible. Perhaps the most satisfactory is to use a control condition in which clients are requested to *wait* for service. This solution works best, of course, if the agency has some form of waiting list anyway and if the waiting period for clients assigned to the control group is kept relatively brief. In one successful use of this strategy, Subramanian (1991) (diagram 7.5) hypothesized that patients with long-term chronic pain who were taught pain management techniques would have less pain, better mood, and less disability than patients not taught the techniques. She assigned half of the patients to a wait-list control group while half attended 10 weeks of group sessions. After posttest data collection was completed, the control group was offered the treatment (which was effective). Interestingly, 30 percent declined treatment; perhaps they felt they had learned to manage on their own.

Another form of control group is a *placebo* treatment. Its purpose is to provide control for the nonspecific effects of intervention—sympathetic listening and so forth. It has the additional advantage of keeping clients connected with the agency should treatment be offered later. For example, Frey et al. (1992), seeking to improve self-esteem among men in a Veterans' Affairs nursing home,

DIAGRAM 7.5

Design in a Test of Group Training in Pain Management Techniques (partial crossover design with follow-up)

R		Pretest		Posttest		Follow-up 6 MOS.	Follow-up 20 MOS.
	E	O	X	O		O	O
	C	O		O	X	O	O

E = Experimental group sessions in pain management.
C = Control group wait-list that receives training after E group posttest.
R = Random assignment to groups.
Source: Subramanian 1991.

compared a structured group counseling program to a current events discussion group that met the same length of time.

There are, however, some difficulties with placebo control groups. Because it is sometimes difficult to separate the placebo effects from those of the intended intervention, the placebo treatment may compete with the experimental intervention; its control function may become somewhat cloudy. In addition, practitioners may have qualms about having clients participate for any length of time in a pseudo-treatment. Moreover, there is the delicate problem of informing clients about it—and securing their consent to participate in it—in such a way so as to preserve their expectation that it may have some value for them, as it well might, without leading them to think that it is all the agency has to offer.

Whatever type of control group is used, it is important to remember that any client selected for the study has a chance of being assigned to the control group. Initial interpretations to clients about what might be in store for them must be made accordingly, and there may be difficulty if some clients refuse to participate or drop out later because they do not wish to be assigned to a control group. Also some provision needs to be made for emergencies—situations that cannot wait. In such cases, probably the best solution is to proceed with random assignment but to have an "escape clause" that permits intervention to take place in any control case needing emergency services. Fortunately, in most projects such emergencies do not arise with sufficient frequency to jeopardize the purpose of the control group.

The situation is somewhat different when clients are not seeking anything resembling the kind of service to be tested. The experimenter offers to provide a possibly useful program to a population that would ordinarily not receive it, on condition that the people participate in a controlled study. Under such circumstances, the complaint that service is being unnecessarily withheld if a control group is used is less likely to arise, and control clients are less likely to feel deprived or to seek alternative forms of service. Usually such groups are found in settings—such as schools, hospitals, courts, welfare agencies, or residential institutions—that can facilitate recruitment of potential clients and that can help avoid exposure of controls to competing programs. However, many investigators regularly recruit volunteers through advertising. For example, in one experiment comparing approaches to treating aggressive children, Magen and Rose (1994) recruited parents by advertising in newspapers, at schools, social service agencies, physicians, and churches.

There are, of course, certain drawbacks in soliciting the participation of clients in tests of social work interventions. Because they have not sought help, clients may not be motivated to receive it, a factor that may weaken the effectiveness of social work services, which are usually based on the assumption that clients are genuinely interested in receiving them. Further, those who volunteer or agree when recruited may differ systematically from those who seek help in other ways as well. This is an issue of generalization; the experimental effects may not generalize to real clients.

In some situations, the population to be offered the experimental program may be already receiving some form of "lesser" service, such as routine supervision by a probation officer. The control group may then consist of clients so served. In fact, these services are often "mandatory," that is, required by law or regulation, and cannot be withheld. A number of experiments in social work have used some form of lesser treatment "controls" under the assumption that they were receiving little real help—at least not enough to compete with the experimental program. Often, results for both groups were similar, which raises questions about this assumption. Although perhaps neither experimental nor control clients were helped, possibly both types of clients received comparable benefit. It may therefore be more appropriate to view lesser programs as alternate forms of service, as in a comparative design (discussed later) rather than as performing something equivalent to a "no-service" control function.

Fundamentally, a "no-treatment" control group, whether it consists of help-seeking or specially recruited clients, gives a picture of what can be expected to happen in the lives of a group of clients who do not receive a systematic intervention similar to that of the experimental program. The functions of this form of control are not necessarily wiped out if clients receive some help, but it is good to know what this help has amounted to in order to make a valid assessment of the accomplishments of the experimental service.

In the preceding discussion, reference was made to ethical questions concerning use of control groups. These questions merit additional comment in view of the regularity with which they are raised, particularly by persons with program responsibilities. The usual argument is that it is unethical to withhold a service from clients who would benefit from it. The key assumption here is that the service is effective and that if provided would lead to some benefit for the client. A program administrator may claim that a service is (or will be) effective and should not be denied people who need it. From the researcher's standpoint, however, the effectiveness of the service has not been demonstrated—otherwise there would be no point in conducting an experiment to test it. Until evidence for effectiveness has been obtained, one cannot say that clients in a control group are necessarily being deprived of any benefit. They may do as well as clients who receive the service and, as some studies have demonstrated, may do better (see, for example, reviews by Fischer (1973) and Lambert and Bergin (1994)). This argument may be taken a step further: the ethics of providing a client with a service that has *not* been adequately tested may themselves be questioned.

SIZE AND COMPOSITION OF SAMPLES Since experiments are costly and it is often difficult to find suitable clients willing to participate, questions concerning the number of participants assume considerable importance in the planning stage. Here, as in any group study, a simple answer to the question of "how many" is "the more, the better." Although true, the answer is not terribly helpful. Although very large samples are almost always desirable, practical constraints usually force us to consider what minimum number is needed to achieve the central purpose of the experiment.

The number of clients in the experimental and control groups needs to be at least great enough so that differences in outcomes can be detected. Customarily, in group experiments these differences are evaluated through statistical tests of significance (chapter 11), which are used to discount or rule out variation in outcome that may be due to chance. Unless differences are great enough to "pass" these tests at acceptable levels, it is usually concluded that the intervention has failed to demonstrate its effectiveness.

Significance tests tend to be conservative: a rather large difference in a small sample may be discounted as an occurrence that is too likely to be due to chance to be taken seriously. Suppose, for example, that an investigator tested a social work intervention in a project with twenty clients, divided equally at random into experimental and control groups. Nine of the ten clients in the experimental group have improved as opposed to only half the clients in the control group. Although this result may be exciting, it would not "pass" a test of significance at a customary level (the .05 level). Under the conventional rules of interpretation, we are forced to conclude that the differences might have been due to chance; we could not claim that the experiment had demonstrated the effectiveness of the intervention. (Because the sample is small, to be statistically significant, if half the clients in the control group improved, all the clients in the experimental group would have to improve.)

The size of the sample needed to demonstrate the effects of an intervention (at a given level of significance) depends on the strength of the intervention and the amount of natural variability in the problem—or more simply, on the expected variability of the problem under control and experimental conditions. We are dealing basically with the same factors considered in single subject designs to determine the number of data collection points (the single subject equivalent to sample size); the greater the variability, the greater the number of data points or sample size.

If we can determine the expected variability of the problem, we can estimate the size of the sample needed to demonstrate effects through a procedure known as *statistical power analysis* (Orme and Combs-Orme 1986; Cohen 1960; Rubin and Babbie 1997), elements of which were in fact applied in analysis of the foregoing example. Even though expected variability in an outcome is usually not known, some educated guesses can often be made on the basis of available research.

If there is no empirical basis for making such estimates of variability, a guideline might be to use a minimum of thirty subjects divided between experimental and control groups. (Recall the difficulty in demonstrating statistical significance with a sample of twenty in the example presented earlier.) The thirty subjects need not necessarily be divided equally between experimental and control groups; there are usually advantages in having the experimental group the larger of the two, for more clients can be given service and more meaningful analyses of change within the experimental group can be conducted.

Some steps can be taken to reduce the variability when small sample sizes are needed. Matching subjects before random assignment has already been mentioned. Effective matching reduces extraneous variation between experimental and control groups. Another approach, when possible, is to limit the participants to those with similar problems, so that differences in problems do not contribute to additional variability. In fact, many studies set criteria that participants must meet to be included; this screening is an attempt to limit the unwanted variability so that one has a better chance of detecting differences due to the experimental intervention (if any). In the experiment where parents were recruited through advertising (Magen and Rose 1994), for example, parents had to meet several criteria designed to limit variability: that the child had aggressive or noncompliant behavior and was between 5 and 11 years, and neither parents nor child had a developmental disability. Similarly, in the classical experiment with counseling for spouses of cancer patients, the patients had particular types of cancer, had known it at least three months, and were not in hospice programs, while the caregivers were experiencing some difficulty coping but were not receiving social services (Toseland, Blanchard, and McCallion 1995). The principle of restrictive sampling to reduce extraneous variation is the same as that discussed in chapter 4, in the context of reducing possible alternative explanations in naturalistic research.

EVALUATING ALTERNATIVE EXPLANATIONS A key factor in evaluating the possible effects of extraneous factors in the classical experimental design is selection. As discussed, if random assignment "works," then the experimental and control groups are the same on characteristics that might affect outcome. Further, they should be the same on characteristics that might affect certain other threats to internal validity. For example, there should be equal numbers of high and low scorers, so that statistical regression should not be an explanation of any differences between the groups. And whatever characteristics might make a person more susceptible to the passage of time should be evenly distributed, so maturation should not be an explanation. Instability should be controlled because it is equally likely to occur in both groups (and, as mentioned, statistical significance testing assesses its effects). Similarly, testing is an unlikely alternative explanation because both groups should react similarly to the data collection procedures.

However, as noted, random assignment does not guarantee equivalence. Initial differences between experimental and control group clients can then pose a threat to the internal validity of the experiment. For example, hypothetically, in the study of counseling for spouses of cancer patients (Toseland, Blanchard, and McCallion 1995), had the caregivers assigned to the experimental group been more depressed and burdened to begin with and then improved dramatically, we would not be able to rule out statistical regression as a possible alternative explanation for a superior showing of the experimental clients. Or had the experimental group received a higher proportion of better motivated caregivers, we could not rule out a combination of selection and maturation as an alternative explanation. Even when random assignment is used, the results of each study, particularly the pretest scores, must be examined carefully for possible inequivalencies that affect internal validity.

Not only must groups be equivalent at the outset in characteristics that may affect outcome, but also this equivalence must be maintained during the experiment. The only differences should be those produced by the intervention program. Equivalence can be jeopardized if clients drop out of either the experimental or control groups—mortality. For example, clients assigned to the control group might drop out because they do not wish to wait for service and thus the control group loses those most motivated and ready for change. If such dropouts do not participate in posttesting, the experimental group may surpass the control group only because the best cases have dropped from the control group.

When dropouts do receive a postprogram assessment, there are two approaches to using the information. Including the dropouts in the data provides a conservative estimation of program effects by demonstrating what the effects might be if any client similar to the sample were considered. This approach lumps together cases that have completed the program with cases that may have received no service at all; the latter could hardly expect, of course, to show program effects. The less conservative approach includes only the participate—those who were motivated to complete the experiment (and their motivations may differ since the conditions are different!).

Neither solution is completely satisfactory: to exclude the dropouts may lead to overrating program effects; to include them, particularly if there are many who have received little service, puts the program to a test that may be unfair and overdemanding. One way out of the dilemma is to present the data both ways (including and excluding dropouts) and let readers draw their own conclusions. The ideal solution is, of course, to avoid dropouts in the first place.

A somewhat different form of mortality occurs when clients complete a program but cannot be located or prove uncooperative for purposes of a postprogram assessment. There are grounds for assuming that such "assessment dropouts" tend to have poor outcomes, for they are likely to include "drifters" and dissatisfied customers. Hence, the higher the rate of missing outcome data the more likely it is that program effects will be overstated

As with other threats to internal validity, mortality must be assessed in each study. Most research reports include information on mortality. An example of a study that is difficult to evaluate because of mortality is Subramanian's study of training for pain management. The study began with 39 pain victims: 5 of 24 clients in the experimental group dropped out during treatment while none of the 20 wait-list controls dropped out by the posttest (Subramanian 1991). However, when the control clients were offered treatment, 6 declined; of the 14 who started the delayed treatment, 3 dropped out. In the follow-up nearly two years later, only 22 clients could be located (Subramanian 1994).

History as a rival hypothesis is controlled if data are collected from both groups at the same time, since any events are likely to affect both groups equally. Errors of instrumentation are controlled only if they apply equally to both experimental and control groups. For example, if interviewers or judges know which clients received intervention and which did not, there is reason to doubt that change in the groups has been assessed in an equitable fashion; the judges may well have a proexperimental bias in how they collect or assess the data. To avoid this problem, judges or coders are often "blinded," meaning they do not know which group a participant has been assigned to. In medicine, a more complex procedure is called the double-blind—neither the experimenter/judge nor the patient know whether the medication is real or a placebo dosage. In social work intervention research, such double-blinds are, obviously, impossible, since the client and practitioner—if not the judge—must know whether the client is receiving intervention.

Two threats to internal validity cannot be ruled out in the classical experimental design—reactive effects and nonspecific effects. Clients in the experimental group may improve more than the control group because the initial data collection prepared them to make good use of treatment, or because some unintended aspect of the intervention affected them. For example, hypothetically, the spouses of the cancer patients in Toseland et al.'s (1995) experimental group may have done well because getting out of the house to attend counseling gave them a needed break from caregiving, not because of the counseling itself.

Partial Crossover Design

Some equivalent group designs are particularly useful in social work given the exigencies of practice and problems inherent in using no-treatment control groups. An example is the partial crossover design, in which clients are given the experimental intervention after they have been a control group; data about their progress are collected once again after they have received the intervention.

The partial crossover design not only ensures that control clients will receive the benefit of the experimental treatment but also provides an additional test of intervention. Changes in the control clients during the no-treatment condition (Time 1–Time 2) can be compared with changes in these clients during the intervention period (Time 2–Time 3). In this kind of comparison, which would be similar to the kind made in an AB design, it would be predicted that the control clients' rate of problem change would increase after their "crossover" into the treatment condition. Although this use of clients as their "own controls" does not permit one to rule out maturation and other extraneous factors as possible causes of change, it does provide a useful supplement to the more definitive comparisons between experimental and control groups. It can provide confirming evidence that an intervention effect has occurred and can provide additional data on the nature of this effect.

The study of training in pain management by Subramanian (1991, 1994) was a partial crossover design with prospective measurement. Another example, a partial crossover design with ex post facto data collection, is an evaluation of a video designed to reduce resistance among spouse abusers (Stosny 1994) (diagram 7.6). Men who were beginning treatment for spouse abuse at seven agencies were randomly assigned to experimental and control groups. The experimental group saw a video and participated in a discussion designed to validate their feelings of anger and humiliation while teaching them compassion for other family members. The control group attended a regular meeting of the agency's spouse abuse treatment group. Dependent variables included staying after the session to continue discussion, participation at the next meeting (a regular spouse abuse treatment group), and a measure of verbal and physical aggression. At the end of the next meeting, the control group was shown the same video, and their staying after and participation levels were measured.

DIAGRAM 7.6

Design Used in Study of Effects of a Video on Treatment Resistance in Spouse Abusers (an ex post facto partial crossover design)

			Posttest		Posttest
R	E	X	O		
	C		O	X	O

E = Experimental group, video and discussion to reduce treatment resistance.
C = Control group.
R = Random assignment to groups.
Source: Stosny 1994.

In terms of threats to internal validity, the partial crossover design has the same strengths and weaknesses as its comparable equivalent group design. In this example, random assignment appeared to work: there were no statistically significant differences between the experimental and control groups on critical characteristics as race, employment, drinking behavior, previous treatment history, and violence level (Stosny 1994). Because there was no initial data collection, we do not know if the groups were comparable on the dependent variables; we are left to assume they were. If so, selection is not a likely alternative explanation, nor are history, instability, maturation, and statistical regression. Testing and reactivity are not issues because data collection was ex post facto.

Mortality was cleverly built into the outcome measurement, since attendance at subsequent meetings was a dependent variable.

Instrumentation is a possible threat to internal validity in this study because the investigator himself recorded the participation data in the subsequent group meeting and acknowledged recognizing some of the men from the video experimental group. (While the design would have been stronger had Stosny been able to recruit an assistant who did not know the men, it does demonstrate that creative, useful research can be conducted by a single investigator-practitioner.) Finally, nonspecific effects such as the pure novelty of seeing a "film" during treatment cannot be ruled out as an alternative explanation.

Solomon Four Groups Design

In the classical experimental design, reactive effects could not be ruled out. One design provides information on the possibility of this alternative explanation for outcome, the Solomon Four Groups Design (Solomon 1947). As the name implies, there are four groups, two experimental groups and two control groups, with random assignment to groups. In each pair, the groups differ in whether data collection is prospective or ex post facto, that is, one experimental and one control group have a pretest, the other does not.

DIAGRAM 7.7
The Solomon Four Groups Design

			Pretest		Posttest
	i	E	O	X	O
R	ii	E		X	O
	iii	C	O		O
	iv	C			O

E = Experimental group.
C = Control group.
R = Random assignment to groups.

The Solomon Four Groups design permits comparisons that can assess the effects of testing and reactivity, as well as differences between the experimental and control conditions. We assume that the posttest-only control group (group iv) represents the participants' situation if there were no intervention and no initial data collection. We also assume that random assignment has "worked" and other threats to internal validity affect the groups equally. Comparing the posttest scores of the two control groups (groups iii and iv) assesses what might happen with data collection but no intervention, that is, the difference represents the effects of testing. Comparison of the posttests of the two experimental groups (i and ii) assesses the effect of a pretest combined with intervention, that is, the effects of testing and reactivity together. Thus, the difference between those two comparisons is the effect due to reactivity. If it can be shown that the experimental intervention works even in the absence of a pretest, it means that the intervention can be used by itself, that is, can be generalized to clients who have not been pretested (Frankfort-Nachmias and Nachmias 1992).

Conversely, if the pretest alone (iii) has the same effects as the combined intervention and pretest (i), then only the pretest measurement instruments need be given to clients to achieve the same effects. Meadow (1988) sought to take advantage of this feature of the design in a test of pre-group interviews to prepare clients for group treatment. She reasoned that if the pretest questionnaire about group expectations and treatment goals sensitized clients to group processes, the agency could save money and staff time by giving the clients the questionnaire in lieu of an individual interview before the group began. In fact, the questionnaire had little effect, while the interviews did help prepare clients for the groups.

An example of a Solomon Four Groups design is a large-scale evaluation of the D.A.R.E. (Drug Abuse Resistance Education) program in Colorado Springs, Colorado (Dukes, Ullman, and Stein 1995) (diagram 7.8). D.A.R.E. is a weekly education program conducted by police officers in over half the elementary school classrooms in the United States. In this study, Dukes, Ullman, and Stein used classrooms rather than individuals as the unit of analysis—480 classrooms (with 9,552 pupils) were randomly assigned to one of four groups: D.A.R.E. program with a pretest and posttest (group i); D.A.R.E. program with posttest only (group ii); no D.A.R.E. program but both pretest and posttest (group iii); and posttest only (group iv). Comparing the two control groups permits an assessment of maturation, and Dukes et al. discovered that self-esteem and bonds to family, police, and teachers decreased significantly over time in the untreated control youngsters. Checking for the effects of taking the pretest, they found that the pretest sensitized youngsters to the measures of resisting peer pressure, but there was no interaction with the D.A.R.E. program. Finally, their overall results indicated that the D.A.R.E. program had a moderate positive effect on all four dependent variables, self-esteem, bonds to societal institutions, resistance to peer pressure, and acceptance of risky behaviors. These positive effects persisted to the end of the school year but had diminished by a longer-term follow-up.

DIAGRAM 7.8

Design Used in Evaluation of City Drug Abuse Resistance Program
(Solomon Four Groups Design)

			Pretest		Posttest	End of school year	Long-term Followup
R	i	E	O	X	O	O	O
	ii	E		X	O	O	O
	iii	C			O	O	O
	iv	C	O		O	O	O

i = D.A.R.E. program with pretest and posttest.
ii = D.A.R.E. program with posttest only.
iii = No D.A.R.E. program but both pretest and postest.
iv = Posttest only.
R = Random assignment to groups.
Source: Dukes, Ullman, and Stein 1995.

Because it includes within it a classical experimental design, the Solomon Four Groups design has the same advantages as that design. If random assignment if effective, selection is not a likely alternative explanation, nor are history, testing, instability, maturation, and statistical regression. Reactivity is controlled by the presence of the additional ex post facto control and experimental groups. Mortality and instrumentation must be assessed carefully for each study, while nonspecific effects cannot be ruled out as an alternative explanation.

The primary drawback is the difficulty of recruiting the additional participants needed for the extra groups; if the minimum number is used in each group, the design requires twice as many participants as a classical experimental design. In many settings, recruiting the additional clients within a reasonable time period is difficult. Additionally, twice as many clients must be assigned to the control group, an issue if there is concern with withholding treatment. For these reasons, despite the additional information and control offered by the Solomon Four Groups design, it is not commonly used in field research.

Comparative Design

In the comparative or "contrast" group design, two or more experimental interventions are assessed: its purpose is to test the *relative* effectiveness of the interventions, that is, to determine which is the more (or most) effective of those tested. As in the classical experiment, clients are randomly assigned to different conditions. Each condition consists, however, of some form of intervention. (To simplify discussion, we assume that two interventions are being compared, which is the usual case; the same design principles apply to comparisons of several interventions.) The interventions are considered to be alternative means of achieving common goals in respect to client outcome. Although investigators may *hypothesize* that one intervention is superior to the other, it is not assumed, or taken for granted, that one will do better.

An example of a comparative group design with prospective data collection is a study of couples groups and gender-specific groups for intervention in spousal abuse (Brannen and Rubin 1996) (diagram 7.9). Using a systems perspective that spousal abuse includes communication and interactional problems, the investigators hypothesized that the couples group intervention would be more effective than the gender-specific groups in reducing violence and in enhancing communication, problem-solving, and marital satisfaction. Participants were mandated for treatment by a local court; to participate, they had to be intact couples who indicated a commitment to stay in their current relationship. They were randomly assigned to one of two treatment conditions. In the couples group, both partners attended the same group which used an eclectic cognitive-behavioral approach to modifying the violence sequence, teaching anger control, and managing conflict through problem-resolution. In the gender-specific groups, each partner attended a gender-specific group. The men's group focused on the male as perpetrator and modifying aggression, while the women's group focused on empowerment and safety. Participants took outcome questionnaires before beginning the programs, at the end of treatment, and six months later. For most participants, both treatment approaches were equally effective. However, couples with a history of alcohol abuse did significantly better in the couples group treatment.

DIAGRAM 7.9
Design Used in Comparison of Couples Groups and Gender-Specific Groups for Treatment of Spouse Abuse (a comparative or contrast group design with prospective data collection)

		Pretest		Posttest	Follow-Up
R	E_1	O	X_1	O	O
	E_2	O		O	O

E_1 = Couples group treatment.
E_2 = Gender-specific groups.
R = Random assignment to groups
Source: Brannen and Rubin 1996.

Threats to internal validity for the comparative group design are assessed in the same way as for the classical experimental design, except that all comparisons are from one group to the other. Thus, if random assignment works, selection, instability, maturation, statistical regression, and so on, are unlikely explanations of any differences in outcome between the two groups.

The comparative strategy has several advantages but also some shortcomings. One of its most attractive features is the elimination of the need for a "no-treatment" control and the various problems that accompany it. This advantage is particularly compelling with help-seeking clients, none of whom need to be deprived of service. Concerns about untoward effects on clients are not, however, necessarily eliminated. One program may be regarded by some agency personnel as inferior to the other, and there may thus be reservations about "shortchanging" clients assigned to it. If so, one could develop a crossover design, allowing the clients assigned to the presumably "inferior" service to be given, if needed, the "superior" program after the original posttest. Or the investigator may find comparison approaches that involve services that the agency staff regard as comparable, or perhaps, untested.

On the other hand, the results of a comparative design may be more palatable to many practitioners. If social work intervention does not prove more effective than a control group, as in fact was the case with the counseling for spouses of cancer patients (Toseland, Blanchard, and McCallion 1995), it is hard for many practitioners to accept the findings. When two treatment approaches, each with acknowledged merits, are compared, practitioners are more likely to accept that one may be superior to another.

A comparative test also provides a straightforward means of developing diagnostic criteria and isolating differential treatment effects. Two methods may be found to differ in their relative effectiveness according to type of client or problem, as happened with alcohol problems in the study of group treatment for domestic violence (Brannen and Rubin 1996). Or we may learn that the two interventions affect clients differently: one may be more effective in changing the client's self-concept, the other, in changing the client's behavior.

Given the lack of "no-treatment" control, the comparative design does not provide an estimate of the "absolute" effects of either intervention, that is, we do not know how either treatment compares to what clients can accomplish on their own or through unsystematic helping efforts. If one intervention proves relatively more effective than the other, one alternative explanation is that the "less effective" intervention *worked against* solution of the clients' problems and that the outcomes for the "more effective" intervention were merely the result of spontaneous remission. Suppose the results of an experiment were as follows:

Type of Intervention	Clients Showing Problem Alleviation
Group treatment	55%
Individual treatment	70%

A skeptic familiar with spontaneous remission rates might argue that close to 70 percent of clients would have improved without any treatment at all, that those receiving individual treatment did as well as untreated clients who remit spontaneously, and that those receiving group treatment were "held back" by the intervention. In the absence of a control group, this possibility is hard to assess. However, if at least one of the compared interventions has been tested successfully against a control group in a previous experiment, there is some confidence that the outcome is better than spontaneous remission. In fact, a strong developmental strategy is to test newer approaches, or refinements of tested approaches, against the best available interventions, that have established track records, so to speak.

In the comparative design, one faces another set of problems that do not arise in the classical design, problems concerning the nature of the interventions to be compared and how they are implemented. The interventions must, of course, be sufficiently distinct that one might reasonably expect differences in outcome, but at the same time they must both be appropriate for the type of problems or clients selected. Because the comparison is between different types of intervention, these should be administered with the same degree of skill. Given these requirements, the selection and deployment of practitioners raise issues not easily resolved. The ideal solution—to form a sizable pool of practitioners equally adept in both interventions and to allocate them at random to these interventions—is often not feasible. If, as is often done, practitioners are assigned to conduct one treatment on the basis of their skill with it, differences in practitioner experience, skill, and so on, become potential sources of unwanted variance. If one set of practitioners conducts both interventions, one must contend with another problem: leakage, or distinctions between the approaches being blurred by practitioners carrying over methods prescribed for one approach to the other.

Comparative Design with No-Treatment Control

The advantages of both the classical and comparative designs can be realized if a no-treatment control group is added to the latter. The result is a powerful hybrid that permits a comparison of the relative efficacy of two or more interventions and provides an estimate of the absolute effects of each.

Accordingly, if the interventions have similar outcomes, it is possible to say that both were effective (or that neither was).

Most things that are elegant are difficult and costly to create; this design fits that rule. Problems in obtaining an adequate no-treatment control must be resolved; there must be sufficient numbers of clients for at least three groups, the wherewithal to collect data for these numbers, and resources to engineer and oversee the many facets of this more elaborate design. Given the way most experiments evolve, the design is most likely to be considered when there is interest in some form of comparative study. Under these circumstances, it is usually most desirable to add one or more no-treatment control groups if it is possible to do so.

An example of a comparison group with no treatment control is an attempt to prevent tobacco use among Native American adolescents in western United States (Moncher and Schinke 1994) (diagram 7.10). Over 1000 youths in fourth and fifth grades were randomly assigned to one of three conditions. The first intervention—skills training based on life skills and social influence models of prevention—included interactive groups focused on bicultural competence, tobacco knowledge, problem-solving, and coping skills. The second intervention group received skills training plus participation in presenting community projects to prevent tobacco use. The control group received no intervention, although they were exposed to the media campaigns and community projects developed for and by the intervention conditions (an example of leakage between conditions). The youths completed questionnaires about and were tested biochemically for tobacco use at pretest, posttest, and two follow-ups. By the second follow-up, all groups increased their tobacco use, but with risk factors taken into account, the control group increased use more than the intervention conditions, which did not differ.

DIAGRAM 7.10

Design Used in Study of Tobacco Use Prevention Among Native American Youth (comparative design with no treatment control group and prospective data collection)

		Pretest		Posttest	Follow-Up	Follow-Up
	E_1	O	X_1	O	O	O
R	E_2	O	X_2	O	O	O
	C	O		O	O	O

E_1 = Skills training in tobacco knowledge, bicultural competence, problem-solving, etc.
E_2 = Skills training plus community activity.
C = No treatment control.
R = Random assignment to groups.
Source: Moncher and Schinke 1994.

Factorial Experiment

The factorial experiment is a complex form of a comparative design. It can perhaps be best understood by picturing a simple comparative design in which two interventions are compared, say short-term versus long-term treatment for marital problems. Suppose we are also interested in learning about a second contrast in treatment approach: treatment conducted by means of joint interviews with husband and wife as opposed to treatment done by means of individual interviews with each.

It would, of course, be possible to conduct another experiment in which this second contrast was studied. A factorial design provides a more economical approach: the two contrasts are examined simultaneously. In the example, the clients assigned to the short-term service are randomly divided into two equal groups: one is treated by means of joint interviews, the other through individual interviews. The same subdivision is made for clients assigned to the group scheduled to receive long-term treatment. Table 7.1 shows how the design would look if there were one hundred couples participating in the project.

An analysis of the example reveals the advantages of this design. As can be seen, the same participants are used for two sets of comparisons (long-term versus short-term and joint versus individual interviews). In effect two experiments, each with samples sizes of 100, are compressed into one, achieving considerable economy. Moreover, the researcher is able to examine *interactions* between treatment length and type of interview. For example, it may be found that brief intervention is particularly effective when used with joint interviews. In other words, it would be possible to examine the relative effectiveness of four different combinations of interventions.

TABLE 7.1

Layout for a 2 x 2 Factorial Design Testing Length of Treatment and Type of Interview: Number of Clients Receiving Each Form of Intervention

	TYPE OF INTERVIEW		
TREATMENT LENGTH	JOINT	INDIVIDUAL	TOTAL
Long term	25	25	50
Short term	25	25	50
Total	50	50	100

Finally, each contrast provides a control for the other. Thus, in the short-term versus long-term comparison, the deployment of joint and individual interviews is held constant: half the couples receive one type, half the other. In a simple (nonfactorial) comparison the couples assigned to the briefer treatment might have received a disproportionate amount of joint interviewing as a way of maximizing the clients' involvement in treatment within the available time limits. If the short-term modality then proved more effective than the long-term service, it might be impossible to tell if its greater effectiveness was due to its time-limited structure or to its reliance on joint interviews or to some combination of the two. To generalize from the example, the factorial design, as opposed to a simple comparative strategy, has the advantage of greater economy, greater informational yield (through study of interactions), and greater control over intervention components.

The example involved a comparison of two intervention variables (treatment structure and interview type) with two categories for each variable (short-term/long-term; individual/joint). The design can be extended to more than two variables and to more than two categories of each variable. A form of shorthand has been devised to describe factorial designs in terms of number of variables and number of categories of each. The design in the example is a 2 x 2 factorial (spoken of as "two by two factorial"); if a third variable, say treatment technique, had been added and that variable dichotomized (insight oriented versus supportive), the design would be called a 2 x 2 x 2 factorial. Each number represents a different contrast, and the number itself tells how many categories are in the contrast. If one of the variables had three classifications, that is, if treatment structure had been divided into short-term, moderate length, and long-term, a 3 x 2 x 2 factorial would have resulted.

In the examples given so far, the independent variables—different forms of intervention—have been active. It is also possible to use some combination of active and attribute variables that cannot be altered by the investigator. For instance, a researcher might wish to compare long-term and short-term treatment as used by practitioners with differing amounts of experience (experienced versus inexperienced). Clients could be randomly assigned to practitioners at different experience levels, but experience could not be separated very well from associated factors, such as skill. Or the researcher may wish to examine these methods with different types of clients, those with acute versus those with chronic problems. Although clients could not, of course, be randomly assigned to these conditions, the clients with each type of problem could be randomly assigned to short-term and long-term interventions.

The factorial experiment shares the basic limitations of its parent, the comparative design. The most important of these limitations—lack of data on absolute effects—can be removed through the addition of a no-treatment control group, which would produce a factorial variation of the design presented in the preceding section.

Additional limitations of the design grow out of its cost and complexity. In its simplest (2 x 2) version, four groups must be compared, which, if guidelines suggested earlier are followed, would require a sample of sixty clients at a minimum. (This number can be reduced to what might be required for a simple comparative study, say about thirty subjects, if one concentrates on the effects of the two major variables and forgoes study of interaction. If so, the design is much more economical than two comparative designs.) The simultaneous testing of two independent variables may, however, create certain complications. Each intervention becomes partially defined and hence limited by characteristics of the other. This may be an advantage for control purposes but under certain circumstances may impose undesirable rigidities that may weaken the interventions. Thus, restricting short-term intervention to individual interviews, as would be done with half the cases, might slow the pace of treatment to the point where necessary goals could not be accomplished within fixed time limits.

Because of its complexity, the design has not been frequently used in field tests of social work intervention although a number of examples can be cited. For example, Feldman, Caplinger, and Wodarski tested three methods of group work ("social learning," "traditional," and "minimal") with a sample of 701 male youths at a community center (1983). Group composition was systematically varied: some groups consisted entirely of "antisocial" boys referred from community agencies; others contained a mixture of antisocial youth and "prosocial" boys who were regularly enrolled in the center's program and were not identified as having specific behavior difficulties; a third group was made up entirely of prosocial boys. A final experimental variable concerned the amount of "experience" of group leaders: graduate social work students versus undergraduate college students who lacked prior social work training or experience. The design (a 3 x 3 x 2 factorial) permitted simultaneous tests of the general and interactive effects of three independent variables (treatment methods, group composition, and practitioner experience). The major outcome variable was an observational measure of the boys' behavior (along an antisocial-social dimension) in the groups. Although the findings revealed that treatment method made no difference in outcome, they did suggest that the groups led by the experienced practitioner did better than those led by the inexperienced. Analysis of interactive effects suggested, however, that inexperienced leaders did relatively better with youngsters in the mixed groups than in groups consisting solely of antisocial or prosocial boys.

Although factorial designs are expensive and difficult to implement in field trials, they are common in analog studies where participants are asked to respond to fictitious situations, usually through written vignettes. For example, Rabinowitz and Lukoff (1995) investigated factors that might influence assignment of clients to short-term or long-term treatment. They asked social workers to respond to case vignettes in which four factors of interest were systematically varied. The factors were client symptoms (adjustment disorder, borderline personality, or dysthymic disorder), gender (male, female), race (black or white) and educational level (college or high school) for a 3 x 2 x 2 x 2 factorial design. Thus, there were 24 different case examples generated. (Each practitioner was asked to respond to only 12 of the vignettes.) Overall, symptoms had the greatest impact, with almost all practitioners recommending short-term for clients with adjustment disorder and long-term for the borderline clients (regardless of other factors).

Nonequivalent Group Designs

When it is not possible to use random assignment to generate equivalent groups, it may still be useful to use experimental designs in which different nonequivalent groups are compared. These designs may take the same forms as equivalent group designs—prospective or ex post facto data collection, comparison of alternative interventions or no treatment control groups—but they differ fundamentally in not using random assignments to place participants in groups.

Forming Nonequivalent Groups

In forming nonequivalent groups to compare, the preferred strategy is to use natural groups if they can be located—classes, wards, residential units, caseloads of different practitioners, and so on. The researcher hopes to find groups that are "more or less alike" even though their equivalence cannot be ensured. Thus, ideally, the investigator finds two sixth-grade elementary school classes that were formed in a manner that might approximate random assignment, while avoiding classrooms where the pupils were "tracked" according to ability. An example of such a natural nonequivalent group design is Dhooper and Schneider's (1995) evaluation of a puppet show to alert children to child abuse, where they compared children in schools that did and did not agree to host the puppet show. In diagram 7.11, note the absence of the symbol for random assignment (R), indicating it is a nonequivalent group design.

DIAGRAM 7.11

Design Used in Study of a Child Abuse Prevention Program (nonequivalent experimental and control group design).

	Pretest		Posttest
E	O	X	O
C	O		O

E = Experimental group: child abuse prevention program including puppet show at participating schools.

C = Control group: no intervention control at schools that did not want puppet show.

Source: Dhooper and Schneider 1995.

Another approach to forming nonequivalent groups is assigning clients in some systematic or haphazard way, for example, alternating clients between two groups, or assigning a client to the next practitioner who has a space available, regardless of which research condition was involved. While such an approach would appear to be close to random assignment, there may be subtle differences in the order of assignment that lead to unequal groups.

Another strategy is the wait-list or overflow approach, in which clients are placed in a control or comparison condition when the caseload of the experimental program is full. This approach differs from random assignment to a wait list control in that all clients are accepted into the experimental program until it is full, while the latecomers are assigned to the other condition. Agency personnel are often willing to accept such an approach when they are unwilling to have clients assigned randomly, but it runs the risk of having insufficient clients for the comparison, and the overflow clients, being latecomers, may differ substantially from the other clients. For example, Rubin (1997) used an overflow group to evaluate a family preservation demonstration project for families referred by Child Protective Services (CPS) (diagram 7.12). An initial problem was that CPS workers might be reluctant to make the referrals if they suspected the family preservation project caseloads were full and the clients might be placed in the comparison group. A later problem was that nearly a third of the overflow group was also referred for similar services elsewhere, thus systematically contaminating the control group.

A final approach to creating nonequivalent groups is using a comparable group at a different time, for example, agency clients who applied the previous year, or students in an instructor's previous class. While some comparison group is better than no comparison, this approach creates several additional problems. Clearly, there may be seasonal or temporal differences that mean that clients in the groups are different. For example, families with children experience different stresses around holidays, during the school year, and during summer vacation. Further, groups formed at different times may experience quite different events that may affect outcome. Thus history cannot be ruled out as an alternative explanation the way it may be when data collection is taken at the same time for both groups.

DIAGRAM 7.12

Planned Design in an Evaluation of a Family Preservation Project for Families Referred for Child Abuse or Neglect (nonequivalent experimental and control group design)

	Pretest		Posttest	Follow-Up 6 MOS.	Follow-Up 12 MOS.
E₁	O	X	O	O	O
C	O		O	O	O

E_1 = Experimental group: family preservation project.
C = Control group: routine Child Protective Services (overflow comparison) (caseloads were full when family was referred).
Source: Rubin 1997.

Evaluating Alternative Explanations

In nonequivalent (or quasi-experimental) designs, the primary concern of the researcher is the possible influence of between-group differences on outcome. The groups may differ in initial characteristics (selection) or may be exposed to different external events (history) during the experiment, and any of these differences may affect outcome. If the groups are sufficiently large and heterogeneous, and if measures of change in individual members are used as outcome criteria, initial differences affecting outcome can sometimes be dealt with through statistical controls.

Suppose a patient self-government program is set up in one ward of a psychiatric hospital and another ward is used for control purposes and among criterion measures are those relating to patient hospital adjustment and discharge rate. The experimental group is found to contain a higher proportion of patients with acute disorders that may be expected to show a more rapid recovery rate. Hence, the experimental group would be likely to do better for this reason alone. The statistical analysis illustrated in table 7.2 would provide a solution for the problem.

The example provides another illustration of the use of statistical controls (see chapters 4 and 11). The potentially confounding variable, acuteness-chronicity, is controlled by examining acute and chronic subgroups separately within experimental and control conditions. As table 7.2 shows, although acute patients do better than chronic patients generally, both types fare better under the experimental condition. If such a breakdown had not been made, the experimental group would have shown a much greater degree of superiority on this variable, but it could have been argued that this favorable outcome was due to its having a higher proportion of acute patients. The use of the statistical control weakens that argument.

TABLE 7.2

Mean Change in Hospital Adjustment of Patients in Experimental and Control Wards, by Type of Disorder (hypothetical data)

	Experimental Ward		Control Ward	
	TYPE OF DISORDER		TYPE OF DISORDER	
	Acute (N = 30)	Chronic (N = 15)	Acute (N = 12)	Chronic (N = 24)
Mean change in hospital adjustment	+3.2	+.5	+2.1	−1.0

No matter how sophisticated the analysis, use of statistical control procedures has a number of limitations in nonequivalent group experiments. The groups must be sufficiently large and varied to permit meaningful statistical analysis. If the groups in the example had been very small or if they had been homogeneous—e.g., one consisting of all acute patients, the other of all chronic patients—statistical controls could not have been used. Even when these constraints are not present, statistical controls are fundamentally limited by the scope and quality of the data to which they are applied. Groups that are not randomly assigned may differ in ways not measured, and so critical data needed for control purposes may be missing. Or critical variables may be crudely measured. One can go through the motions of statistically controlling for differences, but little control may occur if the measurement is fraught with error.

Another means of reducing the influence of extraneous variables in nonequivalent group designs is to use some form of matching. Matching procedures discussed earlier can be used but are not, of course, combined with random assignment. For example, Pithouse and Lindsell (1996) evaluated an innovative family center for families whose child was identified as at risk of harm (diagram 7.13). They matched the center families with families who were receiving routine protective services, matching on variables thought to have an important influence on outcome: reason for being in protective services, race, age of parents, and family structure.

DIAGRAM 7.13
Design Used in Evaluation of a Family Center Program for Treatment of Families Whose Children Are at Risk of Abuse (nonequivalent group design with matched groups and ex post facto data collection)

		Posttest
E_1	X_1	O
E_2	X_2	O

E_1 = Experimental group: family center program.
E_2 = Experimental group: routine child protective services (matched families).
Source: Pithouse and Lindsell 1996.

The major limitation in this matching procedure is that one cannot ensure equivalence on other variables that may also be important; for example, regardless of their age or family structure, parents in the "experimental" program may have better support systems and be better motivated than those in the "comparison" program. Without random assignment, these differences cannot be equalized. Whereas matching does not need to be limited to one or two variables, it is often impractical to match for several because of the large number of cases that would be needed to find the correct matches. Moreover, while cases may be matched in terms of some metric (e.g., ratings of risk for abuse) systematic measurement error (instrumentation) may mask actual differences between the groups. For example, it could be that child protective cases in the family center who were given ratings of "severe risk" are actually in worse shape than "severe" cases in the regular services because of ethnic, ecological, or other factors not taken into account in the measurement.

Despite these limitations, matching may still be a useful device when random assignment cannot be used. Sophisticated matching techniques based on factor analysis and other multivariate procedures have been developed and may be considered when potential samples of clients are sufficiently large (Sherwood, Morris, and Sherwood 1975).

Finally, the phenomena of statistical regression may move apparently matched groups in different directions regardless of what kind of services they receive. Suppose cases in the family center were characteristically more severe than those in the routine child protective services. Cases from each program rated "moderately" severe, at the *point of matching*, may undergo different regression effects. As time passes, the ratings of the family center cases may decline toward a more severe level since a number of the cases in the moderate category would have been on temporary upswings. By the same logic, the routine service cases in the moderate category may show improvement! This phenomenon could well nullify or even reverse the effects of a successful family center program.

Nonequivalent groups are generally less useful as control devices if the experimental group was formed for the purpose of receiving the intervention. For example, there may be interest in studying the effects of a program designed to improve the communication skills of high school students. The students have "selected themselves" into the experimental group. Any group that might be found or formed for comparison would necessarily differ on motivational and other variables related to the students' self-selection into the training program. These variables could be expected, of course, to have a strong influence on outcome. Still a nonequivalent control group may have value under such circumstances. For example, if the outcome measure is likely to reflect a good deal of change due to normal maturation, a nonequivalent group of subjects may be given the same instrument at two points of time to estimate a base rate of change against which change in the experimental group can be compared.

Using natural groups introduces a different twist to threats from selection, differences due to the group itself. Recall our earlier example of the experiment involving patient self-government. With the use of statistical controls, it was possible to use a second ward to rule out certain extraneous factors that might have caused improvement in the patients' hospital adjustment. But another alternative explanation is possible. It could be argued that the experimental ward with its greater proportion of patients with acute disorders (many of whom were perhaps already recovered) had a much different atmosphere than the control ward in which most of the patients were chronic. The greater improvement of both the acute and chronic patients in the experimental ward might have been in response to this climate rather than to the institution of a self-government program. This alternative explanation could be tested by setting up the self-government program in a ward consisting largely of patients with chronic disorders. If the patients in this ward showed a degree of change in hospital adjustment similar to their counterparts in the original experimental ward, then the rival hypothesis that change was due to ward climate could be discounted.

As has been indicated, a nonequivalent group generally provides imperfect or partial control for alternative explanations. In some cases, two or more nonequivalent groups may be used—in the same study or in successive studies—to control for different sources of extraneous variation. This strategy may provide reasonably effective control through what Campbell and Stanley refer to as an "inelegant accumulation of precautionary checks" (1963:227). In principle, the design is much stronger than one using only a single nonequivalent group and may provide a degree of control comparable to that achieved by an equivalent-groups design.

In discussing explanations that are alternatives to the hypothesis, we have concentrated on selection because it interacts with other alternative explanations. For example, if two groups differ on age, we might reasonably expect them to react to the passage of time differently. In general, the interpretation of results of nonequivalent-group designs needs to be guided by the kind of logic that can be applied to evaluate the findings of uncontrolled studies. The crucial question is "What plausible alternative explanations need to be ruled out?" If the evidence for an intervention effect in the experimental group is in itself quite persuasive, a nonequivalent group may need only to supply limited data that might help rule out a rival hypothesis of questionable plausibility. In any case, even weak nonequivalent group designs provide substantial information about relative change and possible alternative explanations. The potential difficulty of attaining comparable groups should not inhibit the attempt to find useful comparison groups.

The Experimental Intervention

In any service experiment, great care needs to be given to the planning, implementation, and recording of the interventions to be tested. Because of the complexities, we take up these considerations here. The substance of our observations also applies to single-system designs.

In designing an experiment, the researcher usually begins with some conception of the intervention to be tested—the *planned intervention*, one might say. Often this intervention is not well explicated. It may be a complex and vaguely described entity such as "family preservation" or "case management" or a procedure that has never been tried. Pilot tests can help "map" interventions prior to a more rigorous testing. But with or without the aid of a pilot study, the researcher attempts to define the experimental interventions at a general level and to operationalize them through specific descriptions of what practitioners are to do in carrying them out. The end product is a set of guidelines for practitioners to use in applying the intervention.

Recently, as investigators build on previous research, some clearly explicated intervention methods are available, often with detailed treatment protocols that spell out the exact steps the practitioner should take (see, for example, LeCroy 1994). Whether the investigator uses such protocols or develops guidelines for the first time, the next step is training in use of the intervention. At a minimum, the training should involve a recorded trial of the interventions in an actual practice situation, with review and discussion among the practitioners. This step also provides a pretest of the guidelines; feedback from the practitioners can be used to clarify and amplify instructions. Moreover, by providing a sort of pretest of the interventions themselves, the training process provides a final opportunity to modify them before the experiment.

Once the experiment is under way, the implementation of the interventions should be monitored through tape recordings or other devices, with immediate feedback to practitioners concerning deviations or difficulties in implementation. Although the logistics of this process are often difficult to manage, it is important to have regularly scheduled meetings with practitioners. Rubin vividly describes the consternation—and blow to the research design—when it was discovered that practitioners had changed the duration of intervention without telling the investigators (Rubin 1997).

If the results of the experiment are to be meaningful, it is essential that accurate data be obtained on how the experimental interventions were actually carried out. It does little good to learn that a program was effective (or ineffective) if we do not know what was done. A description of the intervention as planned provides only a statement of intentions and should not be used, as it sometimes is, as a portrayal of the *intervention as implemented*. Hence, a plan for collection of data on service activities should be an integral part of the design of any experiment. Methods of data collection and measurement used to describe interventions are taken up in detail in chapter 15.

Ideally, an experiment should be implemented as planned, but often significant changes occur during its course. Components of the original intervention may prove unfeasible; practitioners will inevitably improvise, usually in the direction of what appears to be working best from their perspective. These modifications alter the working definition of the interventions. The experiment informs us about the effectiveness of the intervention as implemented and not as planned. If the program turns out to be a pastiche of improvisations and ad hoc compromises, it may offer little basis for generalization. It may have been effective, but it may defy replication. Midstream changes should be kept to a minimum.

Generalization from Group Experiments (External Validity)

The basic considerations presented earlier (chapter 6) concerning generalization from single-system experiments apply as well to group experiments. The essential difference is that a group experiment provides a broader, and usually better, foundation for generalization. Although generalization from a group design may be less precise than from single-system experiments, it is based on a larger and presumably more representative sample of clients, problems, practitioners, and interventions.

Only rarely in service experiments, however, are participating clients and practitioners selected in ways such as random sampling that would permit precise assessment of their representativeness. Hence it is usually not possible to generalize within a known margin of error to a larger population (see chapter 8). In other words, generalization usually proceeds without the help of probability theory or statistics. Instead, one must use logic, or a systematic qualitative assessment of the degree of similarity between the study context and contexts one would like to generalize to (Rosenthal 1997).

In generalizing from a group experiment, one begins with the characteristics of the clients and program studied and moves outward. Usually the findings will be most applicable to similar cases dealt with by the same or similar practitioners within the same setting. As these parameters are changed, the risk of error in generalization increases. For example, suppose that a parent-training program tested in a particular agency is found to be effective with two-parent middle-income families. A generalization involving a relatively small amount of risk would be that the program would also be effective for similar families within the same agency. Risk of error would increase if the generalization were to lower-income, single-parent families in the same agency, and would further increase if it were extended to other agencies.

The size of the sample, variability, and knowledge about its representativeness provide additional guidelines. Other things being equal, it is safer to generalize from large samples, say those exceeding a hundred cases, than small ones, say those less than thirty. Although the numbers are fewer, the same considerations apply to variations in the number of practitioners. Further, the more variable the sample, i.e., the greater the differences among participants, the greater the ability to generalize (Rosenthal 1997). In this respect, the needs of internal validity to reduce unwanted variability by limiting participants to those who meet certain criteria conflicts directly with our desire to generalize to other populations.

However, in any kind of generalization process the representativeness of the sample is always more important than its size. The difficulty with most intervention experiments in social work is that it is hard to know what the sample is representative of; this is the reason we suggest that one begin with the study at hand and attempt to relate it to similar groups. Still, certain assumptions are usually made about representativeness and these need to be examined by the cautious investigator or reader. It may be assumed, or asserted, that clients in an experiment are roughly representative of the agency's clientele because no restrictions were placed on intake to the project. It may be found, however, that intake occurred during a time of the year in which referrals from the school system were unusually heavy and that a sizable proportion of clients accepted at intake dropped out of the project and were replaced. In this way, the sample may overrepresent school problems and better-motivated clients.

As with single-system experiments, an important strategy in improving generalizability is replication (see chapter 6). Direct replication under similar experimental situations can demonstrate that the experiment was not a fluke, while systematic replication with differing clients, practitioners, settings, and so on, can demonstrate generalization to many settings. Examples of long-term programs of systematic replication through group experiments include the development of the task-centered model (Reid 1997b), support and treatment groups for caregivers of ill persons (Toseland and McCallion 1997), and home health care for the ill (Hughes 1997).

Laboratory Experiments: Analog Studies of Intervention Effects

Up to this point in the chapter, we have considered the application of experimental design to the study of intervention effects as they occur under field conditions, that is, when services to actual clients with real problems are exposed to experimental testing. As discussed earlier (chapter 4), almost any variable can be simulated and studied under laboratory conditions, including social work intervention.

In essence, an intervention method is tested under conditions that are simulated or are analogous to those characterizing actual helping efforts. Suppose, for example, that an investigator wishes to investigate how different levels of practitioner empathy affect what a person being helped reveals. An experimental study of this problem would be difficult to conduct under field conditions, for practitioners would be reluctant to manipulate the amounts of empathy they displayed with actual clients. Consequently, the researcher might attempt a simulated or analog study. Students taking the role of "clients" might be interviewed about minor "real" problems in their own lives or about fictitious but more serious problems. (In such simulations, it is wise to avoid the more serious problems that students really might have.) The students, who would not be informed about the exact purposes of the experiment, would presumably respond to variations in degree of empathy in a way that would be similar to the responses of actual clients.

There are gradations between simulated and real clients in these experiments. Closer to real clients would be recruited volunteers who might actually have problems (usually in mild form) that could be "treated" in simulations. Or "real" clients of a service program may serve as volunteers or paid participants. The client subjects may then be exposed to different interventions in a simulated service situation and asked to respond as if they were receiving help, for example, they might then be asked to put themselves in the place of clients on a videotape and rate the amount of practitioner "understanding" reflected in the tapes. The special advantage of such an approach is that one can study the effects of intervention on "clients" who may be close to actual clients in respect to socioeconomic status, educational level, degree of emotional disturbance, and other variables.

For example, Nugent (1992) conducted two analog studies of the effect of facilitative and obstructive interviewing styles. In the first, participants watched a simulated interview in which the practitioner alternated between facilitative and obstructive behaviors. Participants included professional helpers, staff at a residential treatment facility, and—most like clients—volunteers attending a conference for school personnel. They were asked to put themselves in the shoes of the "client" and record their feelings. In the second experiment, Nugent asked several volunteers to play the role of client while the practitioner varied the interviewing behaviors (the "clients," of course, did not know that the interviewing behavior was the purpose of the study). The "clients" talked about a minor personal problem they were currently dealing with. In both experiments, the observers/"clients" had positive emotional reactions when the practitioner was facilitative and negative reactions when the practitioner was obstructive. A final experiment (not actually conducted for obvious reasons) might be to vary facilitative and obstructive interviewing with a real client, to see if the client had similar reactions.

Analogs give researchers the opportunity to test intervention-like procedures in controlled experiments that might not be possible to conduct under field conditions. Moreover, in laboratory as opposed to field experiments, experimental variables can usually be more carefully implemented, their effects can be measured with greater precision, and extraneous factors can be better controlled.

But as a simulation, an analog study can only approximate the conditions of real interest—those obtaining in the field. Whereas the experiments may have a high degree of internal validity, their external validity, or the extent one can generalize from them, is always problematic. Generalizations to actual client populations may be limited by differences in characteristics between experimental "clients" (who may, for example, be young, middle-class students) and the clients for whom the interventions are intended. Even if subjects are drawn from client populations, they are only pretending to be clients in the experiment and thus may lack the motivation, distress, and problem characteristics of actual clients. Given the artificiality inevitable in an analog study of intervention, one cannot expect experimental variables to "behave" in the same way as they would in reality. Often they operate with less strength, since they lack potentiating factors, such as investment or distress, present in field situations. Consequently, a practitioner's expressions of empathy might be expected to be less convincing if evoked by a role as opposed to a genuine outpouring of feeling. On the other hand, the "problems" to which these weaker interventions are applied may be much more tractable than problems possessed by actual clients. In short, projections from the laboratory to the field can never be readily made.

Still, analog experiments can make an important contribution to the development of intervention approaches. Although a simulation may not provide an adequate basis for asserting how an intervention would work in the field, it might be able to identify promising methods and provide data useful in construction of methods for field trials. Consequently, laboratory experiments can serve a valuable exploratory function in the development of intervention approaches, and can be used to test hypotheses from practice theory. (For additional discussion of analogs, see chapter 15.)

Summary

Group experiments are quantitative designs whose purpose is explanation—to establish causality between the active independent variable and dependent variable(s)—in social work intervention research, between the experimental intervention and the outcome(s). In all designs but the single group design, two or more groups of participants are compared with the assumption that the control or comparison group represents the way things would be without intervention. The group experiment designs vary on two important elements, whether the groups are equivalent (participants are assigned using random assignment) or nonequivalent, and whether data collection is prospective or ex post facto. If the groups are equivalent, then selection (differences between groups) is an unlikely alternative explanation for the findings, and consequently there is unlikely to be interaction between selection and other alternative explanations such as maturation or statistical regression. (As with all studies, each study must be assessed for itself.) If data collection is prospective, then selection can be assessed and change can be measured, but then testing and reactivity become possible alternative explanations.

We covered five basic experimental designs with equivalent groups. The classical experimental design includes prospective measurement (a pretest and posttest), an experimental group and a control group that does not receive the intervention, and random assignment to groups. If the random assignment "works," the design is strong in ruling out most threats to internal validity. A variation that meets the ethical reservations about withholding treatment from clients is the partial crossover design: after the posttest in a classical experimental design, the clients are offered the experimental intervention and then given another posttest to assess effects.

The Solomon Four Groups design is one of the more powerful designs available. It includes two experimental groups, one with prospective measurement and one with ex post facto measurement, and two control groups, also with and without a pretest. If random assignment creates comparable groups, the Solomon Four Groups design has good control over all alternative explanations except nonspecific effects that go along with intervention.

Two of the experimental designs discussed do not use control groups but instead compare two or more interventions. In the comparative design, participants are randomly assigned to competing interventions. The factorial experiment is an efficient way to test several different variations of treatment; participants are randomly assigned to one of all possible combinations of dimensions. For example, in a 2 x 2 factorial experiment testing the effects of goal-setting and homework assignments on problem reduction, there would be four groups: (i) goals set, homework assignments given, (ii) goals set, no homework, (iii) no goals, homework assignments given, and (iv) no goals, no homework. Both comparative designs have control over alternative explanations similar to the classical experimental design, but only in relation to the compared interventions. One cannot assess what might have happened without intervention. However, in both designs, it is possible to add a no treatment control group.

Nonequivalent group designs take the same forms as the equivalent group designs (although researchers have not given them discrete labels). However, because there is no random assignment, potential differences between groups (selection) is an important alternative explanation.

In terms of generalization, group designs generally offer a better foundation for generalizing than single-system experiments. However, unless an experiment uses probability sampling techniques to select participants, one must use the logic of similarity to generalize, i.e., one must assess how similar the participants, settings, and interventions are to others. (Field designs generalize better than laboratory designs simply because more of the crucial elements are similar to agency settings.) In general, the larger the sample size and greater its variability, the greater the ability to generalize. However, an investigator must balance the desire for variability with the need to reduce unwanted variability in order to reduce threats to internal validity.

DIAGRAM 7.14
An Outline of Designs

Diagrams of Experimental Designs

The classical experimental design (pretest-posttest control group design):

		Pretest		Posttest
R	E	O	X	O
	C	O		O

A partial crossover design as a variant of the classical experimental design:

		Pretest		Pre-/Posttest		Posttest
		TIME $_1$		TIME $_2$		TIME $_3$
R	E	O	X	O		
	C	O		O	X	O

The Solomon Four Groups design:

			Pretest		Posttest
	i	E	O	X	O
	ii	E		X	O
R	iii	C	O		O
	iv	C			O

The comparative or contrast group design with prospective data collection:

		Pretest		Posttest
R	E_1	O	X_1	O
	E_2	O	X_2	O

The comparative design with no treatment control group and prospective data collection:

		Pretest		Posttest
	E_1	O	X_1	O
R	E_2	O	X_2	O
	C	O		O

Diagrams of Nonequivalent Group Designs ("Quasi-Experiments")

A nonequivalent design (no random assignment) comparing intervention to a no treatment control group, prospective data collection:

	Pretest		Posttest
E	O	X	O
C	O		O

A nonequivalent design (no random assignment) comparing two interventions, prospective data collection:

	Pretest		Posttest
E_1	O	X_1	O
E_2	O	X_2	O

O = Data collection point.
E = Experimental group.
C = Control group.
X = Occurrence of manipulated independent variable (intervention).
R = Random assignment to groups (or matching with random assignment).

8 Sampling

In the preceding chapters on research design we have made both explicit and implicit references to sampling, or the process of selecting participants for a study. In this chapter we take a closer look at the logic and methods of this process. Our purpose is to provide a general orientation to sampling in its more technical sense.

While researchers study specific phenomena—certain individuals, groups, organizations, and so on—they inevitably intend to use their data as a base for making statements about some broader class of phenomena, for example, individuals similar to those studied. Even if these statements take the form of "implications" or "speculations," there is always concern with a bigger picture. If not, there would be little point in doing the study in the first place! In research, the specific phenomenon studied is usually referred to as a *sample* (the people or things actually studied—people, behaviors, case records, cities, and so on); a single unit of a sample is called a *sampling element* or *unit*, and the process of selecting the elements is termed *sampling*. The larger class to which a sample is to be related is known as a *population*—the general group to which one wishes to generalize, for example, all persons with a drinking problem who seek help. The *sampling frame* is the group from which the sampling elements are actually selected, for example, the list of current clients at an alcoholism treatment facility. The sampling frame may be the same as the population but more often is a subset or list from which the sample is actual drawn. Regardless of the form sampling takes, the concern is always with the relation between the actual events studied—the sample—and its referent class—the population (diagram 8.1).

The Nature and Purposes of Sampling

Although social workers may not always realize it, they frequently make use of sampling methods in their practice. The social worker may ask parents concerned about their teenage daughter to describe the daughter's behavior at home; from this description—a sample of the daughter's behaviors—the social worker may tentatively diagnose the daughter as depressed. The sample of in vivo interaction between husband and wife during the interview may cause the marriage counselor to perceive their relationship as basically competitive, each trying to control and outdo the other. A supervisor may select several of a worker's case records to read before writing an evaluation of the worker. A school social worker may observe a child's behavior in the classroom and on the playground to understand better what the teacher refers to as the child's aggressive behavior. A planner at United Way may contact a number of people representing different segments of the community to serve as volunteers on a health needs assessment panel.

DIAGRAM 8.1
The Population, the Sampling Frame, and the Sample

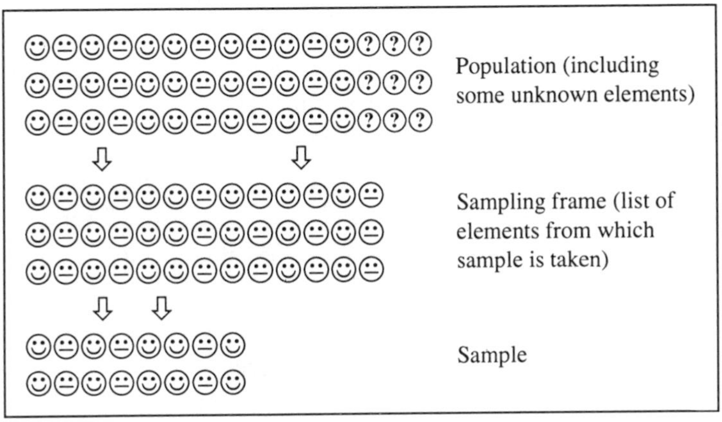

The case records and the volunteers are obviously samples since in neither case do they constitute the population from which they were drawn; that is, they are not all of the worker's records nor all of the people in the community. In the first example, the population is easily defined, that is, all of that worker's case records; one assumes the supervisor took a sample for the sake of efficiency of time and effort. How that sample was selected and which records were read would obviously be of concern to the worker being evaluated. The worker's view of the appropriate sampling method and consequently the "best" sample may not necessarily coincide with the view of a more objective observer. The worker might prefer to handpick the cases while the observer might insist on an unbiased method of selection such as random sampling.

Although the United Way planner is also concerned with efficiency, the position is very different from the supervisor who, given the time and desire, could read all of the worker's cases. First, the size of the panel of volunteers must necessarily be limited. In addition, there are the inherent difficulties of trying to identify all the segments of the community that should be represented and of identifying all the possible representatives of each segment; the population cannot be listed. In this case, sampling not only is desirable but also is the only feasible method. Doubtless, the planner would prefer a purposive sample, that is, people the planner selects as good representatives. The planner can make a list of potential representatives (the sampling frame) and then chose individuals who meet certain criteria such as knowledge about health needs and resources.

The use of sampling methods in the examples of the depressed teenager, the competitive spouses, and the aggressive schoolchild may not be so clear. Social workers, as other people do, form impressions and make diagnoses based on observed or described behavior. These behaviors are not randomly selected; they may be the most salient or problematic in the view of the observer, they may be viewed as symptoms, or they may provide examples or confirmation of an impression, diagnosis, label, or other preconceived way of organizing behavior. They are samples of the subject's behaviors in a given situation, selected (usually) because the worker is trying to assess the situation.

Bias is certainly a possibility in all these examples, but whether or not it is a problem depends on the purpose of the sample. The school social worker is looking for aggressive behaviors and therefore pays less attention to the child's other behaviors. The practitioner could erroneously use these observations to label the child and react to it as if the aggressiveness were the sum total of the child's personality. Or the practitioner could appropriately use one or more of the observed behaviors as the focus of a specific treatment plan. Bias is always a serious problem whenever one is making generalizations or assuming that a set of behaviors, events, attitudes, and so on is representative or typical of a larger population.

From the foregoing examples, it is clear that the major reason for sampling is feasibility. Often it is impossible to identify all members of a population of interest, for example, homosexuals, drug abusers, or parents of preschool-age children. Even if it were theoretically possible to identify, contact, and study the entire relevant population, time and cost considerations would often make this a prohibitive undertaking. Sampling techniques have been developed that can result in "good samples," that is, samples representative of the population. (Samples need not, however, be representative in every respect, only in those characteristics relevant to the particular study.) These techniques involve probability sampling. The use of such samples may result in more accurate information than might have been obtained if one had studied the entire population. This is so because time, money, and effort can be concentrated to produce better quality research (better instruments, more in-depth information, better trained interviewers or observers, and so on).

Samples and the Research Question

Before turning to types of sampling procedures, it is worth discussing several issues related to sampling in the context of the research question or hypothesis: whether the sample is appropriate to the hypothesis, whether it is precise, and whether it needs to be representative given the purpose of the research.

First, the research question or hypothesis should dictate the sample: are the elements sampled those appropriate for the research? For the United Way planner, the selected panel members may not represent the whole community, but they are (or certainly should be) people active in the social service community who can contribute knowledgeably about health needs, the purpose of the panel. When the practitioner observes the competitive couple, their interaction in an interview may not represent all the ways they interact, but it is a sample of their real interaction, which is what the practitioner is interested in. But are parents' reports of the daughter's behavior the most appropriate sample of what the daughter is doing, for the purpose of diagnosing her as depressed? And if the supervisor reads the social worker's case records for the purpose of assessing the worker's competence, a poor writer or someone behind on completing progress notes might argue that the written records are poor representations of what happens in cases, where the worker is empathic and skillful. In short, the elements studied should relate directly to the research question or hypothesis, or, stated another way, the population should include the sampling frame.

This may appear self-evident, but careful examination shows that in much research, the sample elements are not those expressed or intended in the hypothesis or research question. Common examples include asking wives (only) about spousal interaction (the sample is wives, while the hypothesis deals with couples) and asking parents about children's behavior. Family members, for example, frequently disagree about family functioning (Green and Vosler 1992; Kolevzon et al. 1988), testimony to the potential for distortion when the respondents are not those expressed in the hypothesis. Often, such shifts in the population from hypothesis to sample are legitimate responses to practical constraints—the use of indicators when something cannot be measured directly will be discussed in chapter 10. However, in planning or assessing a study, one must be alert to whether the hypothesis has been tested on a sample that can yield data to address the hypothesis.

Second, the converse consideration is whether the sample is specific or narrow enough for the hypothesis (or the intended hypothesis, since the problem can also lie with the conceptualization). In intervention research, the issue is called "targeting," or being accurate about who the intervention is designed to help. For example, in the study of counseling for spouses of cancer patients referred to in chapter 7, the intervention was apparently not effective—there were no differences between the those receiving the counseling and the control group (Toseland, Blanchard, and McCallion 1995). Careful analysis by the investigators suggested that the most burdened spouses did indeed benefit from the counseling, but they were a small proportion of the sample. That is, the spouses recruited for the study may not have been those who needed counseling. A sample that "targeted" highly stressed caregivers more precisely might have yielded different results (Toseland and McCallion 1997). This example illustrates several points: the potential danger of sampling "clients" who were recruited rather than clients who sought service (see chapter 7); the difficulty (and importance) of being precise in defining the population; and a fallacy that professionals can fall into, on the assumption that services will automatically be useful to anyone we define as at risk.

The third consideration is whether testing the hypothesis or research question requires a representative sample or not. Many research texts assume that representative sampling is paramount, but in our view the importance of representativeness depends on the purpose of the study and the nature of the phenomenon being studied. For example, if one is simply interested in identifying variables that may be involved in maintaining egalitarian marriages, an acceptable sample might consist of almost any set of couples known (or believed) to have an egalitarian marital relationship. If, on the other hand, one's interest is in ascertaining how frequently egalitarian marriages occur in the population, or what factors are related to egalitarian marriage, representative samples of married couples would be necessary. Representativeness is critical when one wants to estimate prevalence or incidence in the population. It is not important when one is exploring new phenomena or developing hypotheses for future testing. In most social work research—particularly intervention research—the importance of representativeness is somewhere in between. One strives for greater representativeness as the research question shifts from "does this treatment approach work at all, with anyone?" to the question "who else does this treatment approach work with?" to "does it work with everyone?"

The ability to generalize from samples to the population depends in part on the sampling frame and the type of sampling procedure. We now turn to the types of sampling procedures.

Basic Types of Samples

Samples are usually divided into two major types: nonprobability and probability. Of the two, nonprobability sampling is used more frequently in social work research. However, when it can be used, probability sampling provides a firmer basis for generalization. For these reasons, nonprobability samples are described briefly first, and probability samples are considered in greater depth in a later section.

Nonprobability Samples

In nonprobability sampling, one cannot determine the probability that an element in the sampling frame will be selected, and consequently one cannot use statistical probability techniques to generalize from a sample to a population. Most samples used by social workers (in their practice and in research) are nonprobability samples. The major advantages of nonprobability samples generally are convenience and economy, although as mentioned, at times they are the only feasible approach because a sampling frame cannot be defined. The major limitation of all nonprobability samples is that they are rarely representative and one can generalize only by using logic about similarities. The nonprobability sampling plans most frequently used are accidental, snowball, quota, and purposive.

ACCIDENTAL SAMPLES Accidental samples, sometimes referred to as availability samples or samples of convenience, are, as these names imply, made up of elements that meet requirements of the study and are selected because they are at hand and easy to obtain. This method of sampling is probably the most common. If a student is interested in social work students' attitudes toward research and sends questionnaires to all the MSW and BSW students in the local school, the sample selected is an accidental one. An investigator interested in parent satisfaction in two-parent families may select a residential neighborhood and begin knocking on doors to interview people who are at home at the time, who meet the study criteria, and who are willing to participate in the study. A social worker, wanting to study adjustment of families with a retarded child, includes in the sample all cases with a retarded child opened by a service agency during a specified period of time. (This is sometimes referred to as a time sample.)

Nearly all the studies of social work intervention mentioned in the previous chapters used accidental samples of clients: usually, the investigators included all clients at a selected agency who applied for service during the time the study was being conducted and who met the criteria for the study. Clients would be accepted into the study as they applied, until the sample was large enough.

Accidental samples have a major shortcoming. Because of biases that may be operating consciously or unconsciously, one does not know how typical the sample is of the population of interest. For example, the students' attitudes about research in the school studied may be different from those of social work students generally because of factors such as the way research is taught there, the abilities and personalities of the research teachers, and the students' interests and abilities. Similarly, clients who apply to an agency during the time of a research study may have very different problems from clients who apply at a different time of year. However, if the purpose of the research is to test new approaches to intervention, accidental samples may be sufficient, because the research question is, "does this treatment approach work at all?" or "who else does this treatment work with?"

SNOWBALL SAMPLES A variation on the accidental sample is a snowball sample. The investigator starts with a few individuals who meet the study criteria and asks them to suggest the names of additional individuals who meet the criteria; the investigator makes the same request of each new individual until enough subjects are located. Snowball sampling is particularly useful—sometimes essential—when little is known about a phenomenon or potential subjects are difficult to locate. For example, Lazzari, Ford, and Haughty (1996) wanted to study the activities and attitudes of Hispanic women who were activists in their communities. No list of such women is available. Consequently, the investigators identified a few women and asked them for the names of others, eventually identifying and interviewing 21 activists.

Snowball sampling can also be used as a research tool, to map a network and measure its density. For example, to determine the informal power structure of an organization, one might ask the director who influenced decisions, whether designated as administrators or not. One would continue asking those named until no new names were proposed. Thus, a map of the real power structure could be developed, something probably not available any other way.

The disadvantage of snowball sampling is that it clearly favors the opinions of its starting point, and it is possible to get a network that knows and supports each other while entirely missing a network of similar persons who have quite different viewpoints. These problems may be overcome by starting with clear criteria that can be described to participants and by judicious phrasing of the request for new names. However, one cannot eliminate the possibility that snowball sampling will yield a systematically biased sample.

QUOTA SAMPLES Quota sampling, like accidental sampling, takes any subjects at hand, but differs in that it tries to take into account diverse segments of the population that may be important for purposes of the study. To accomplish this, one divides the population into segments or strata based on the selected characteristics, then samples from each stratum. For example, in Toseland et al.'s (1995) study of supportive counseling for spouses of cancer patients, the investigators knew that men and women react differently to both the caretaking role and to counseling. Consequently, they included equal numbers of men and women in the study and built gender in as one of the variables in their research design. To recruit subjects, they identified possible participants from outpatient clinic records and then had a recruiter—"an enthusiastic lay person, who had recovered from cancer of the breast, and believed in the benefits of counseling" (518)—approach caretakers while they waited for their spouses at the clinic. The first 43 men and the first 43 women who agreed to participate were included in the sample.

The sample might have been improved further by stratifying the population on additional variables such as socioeconomic status, age, racial or ethnic group, diagnosis and duration of cancer, and so on. In this way, one could be sure that various segments of the population were included. Practically, however, stratification is limited to only a few variables because, as variables are added, the sampling plan becomes more complicated and difficult to implement and because the likelihood of too few elements in some subgroups increases. Since each subgroup is an accidental sample, the combined sample is accidental and may not be representative of the population.

PURPOSIVE OR JUDGMENTAL SAMPLES Purposive or judgmental samples consist of elements (respondents, cases, time segments, and so on) deliberately chosen or handpicked for the study's purposes. In this way, cases may be selected for inclusion because they are thought to be typical of what one is interested in studying. Samples selected in this manner may be especially useful when the function of a study is primarily exploratory (chapter 4). An example is Akin and Gregoire's (1997) study of how a state child welfare system treated abusive parents who are also substance abusers. Because they wanted parents who were successful, they purposively selected "extreme" cases of parents: parents who were recovering from substance abuse and had or were in the process of regaining custody of their children. Cases were picked because they were deemed to be typical successes who could talk articulately about the effect of the child welfare system on their struggles to overcome their addiction.

Like other nonprobability sampling plans, it is risky to use purposive samples for generalizing to larger populations, for we do not know to what extent the samples are representative of populations of interest. There is clearly some conscious or unconscious bias in how purposive samples are selected. Nevertheless, they can be very useful for developing theory, particularly in qualitative approaches, where cases may be selected to show differences that need to be taken account of in developing the theory.

Probability Samples

In probability samples, the likelihood of each element in the population's being included in the sample can be specified. As we discuss later, this means that the investigator can use statistical techniques to generalize to the population, that is, to estimate the "real" parameters in the population. However, probability sampling requires being able to list the elements. This is impossible for many phenomena of interest to social workers; we do not even know the number of alcoholics, battered wives, or pregnant teenagers at any one time. Even if we did know the number of alcoholics, the problem would remain of trying to list them or devise some other method of selecting a sample from all alcoholics in the United States, say, in such a way that the probability of each alcoholic's being selected can be specified.

In reality, an investigator uses a sampling frame, or a list of elements that have a possibility of being sampled and from which the sample is actually selected. We might have a list of clients at local substance abuse treatment facilities, of police cases involving domestic violence, or recent births to women under the age of 20. A probability sample drawn from such a sampling frame can be generalized statistically to the members of that sampling frame. We still have the problem of how well that sampling frame represents the population. For example, a fairly common procedure to discover social workers' opinions is to take a random sample of members of the National Association of Social Workers (NASW). The results may accurately represent NASW members, but not all social workers are members, and we must generalize with caution to "all social workers." In short, while probability samples increase the ability to generalize, unless one is reasonably certain that almost all members of the population can be listed, one must still use logic to generalize from the sampling frame to the population.

The major types of probability samples are simple random samples, stratified random samples, certain types of cluster samples, and certain types of systematic samples.

SIMPLE RANDOM SAMPLES An investigator interested in students' attitudes about an issue on a particular campus who selects "at random" (more precisely, haphazardly) students passing in front of the library does not have a random sample. (The sample obtained in this manner is accidental.) Simple random sampling (often shortened to random sampling) involves a very systematic process, which ensures that every element and every combination of elements have a specifiable chance of being chosen. In simple random sampling, each element and all combinations of elements have the same probability of being selected into the sample. To illustrate, the investigator could have obtained a list of all the students at that particular college (the sampling frame) and selected the sample in such a way that every student would have had an equal chance of being interviewed. The researcher might have done this by first numbering consecutively each name on the student list and then using a table of random numbers to decide which students to select. This would result in a random sample of students on that campus. The sampling frame would not be complete (some students might be late to register and others might have dropped out already) but would be close enough so that we would consider it a reasonable representation of the population (students at that college).

Tables of random numbers consist of rows and columns of numbers randomly generated. One uses a table of random numbers by blindly picking a starting point on a page and then going across the rows, down the columns, or diagonally to obtain numbers to be included in the sample. For example, suppose there were 1,200 students on the campus and the researcher had decided to go down the columns using the first four digits (and ignoring the last digit) in a table of random numbers set up as follows:

46880
77775
00102
06541
60697

Two students from these numbers would be selected for the sample: those numbered 10 (the third row) and 654 (the fourth row). The other three numbers in the table (4688, 7777, and 6069) would be disregarded, for they are larger than 1,200 and 1,200 was the highest number in the sampling frame. For a sample of 100, each student would have 1 in 12 chances of being selected in this manner (100/1200). If the same student were picked twice, he or she would be replaced with another random selection. Instead of using a table of random numbers, the investigator might have used a list of random numbers generated by a computer; this latter method is less tedious when large populations are involved.

An example of a simple random sample is included in a study comparing homeless families to poor families with housing (Johnson et al. 1995). The investigators sampled homeless families who were residents of a St. Louis shelter during 1989 (a nonprobability accidental sample). The comparison group was from the Public Use Microdata Sample (a public data base), which was a random sample of all St. Louis-area family households who completed the United States Census long form in 1989 (their sampling frame). (In their data analysis, they used only the families living below the poverty line.) Thus, their sample of housed families is representative of poor families in the region under study. The sampling frame—U.S. Census data—is the most complete list of a U.S. population known, yet even the Census is not a complete population list, because many people, particularly minorities, are undercounted.

Another example of a simple random sample is a study of the issues confronting African immigrants to the United States (Kamya 1997). Kamya obtained the membership lists of churches and common interest organizations that served African immigrants and took a random sample from those lists. Thus his sample is representative of persons who belong to the selected organizations, but we must use logic to assess how close his sampling frame is to the population. Clearly, immigrants who did not belong to the organizations are not represented, and they may differ substantially from those that do. In short, a random sample (like other probability samples) can be limited by its sampling frame.

Simple random samples are the simplest, most direct way of selecting a representative sample, but they require a sampling frame or list of potential participants.

STRATIFIED RANDOM SAMPLES As in quota sampling, in stratified random sampling, the population is first divided into segments or strata based on the characteristics one wants to take into account. Then simple random samples are selected from each stratum. One purpose of stratification is to ensure that diverse elements of the population considered important for the study purposes are included. In most cases, simple random sampling also accomplishes this goal. There are special cases, however, when stratified random sampling improves on the efficiency or representativeness of the sample. Generally these circumstances occur when heterogeneity exists between the strata and homogeneity within the subgroups on variables of interest in the study.

For example, if one is interested in the opinions of social workers on managed care, one might have reason to believe that administrators will view the issue very differently from direct practitioners. To ensure that the different opinions are represented, one would break the social workers in the sampling frame into these two groups, take a random sample from each group, and then combine the two subsamples. First, this guards against the possibility that no or very few administrators will be included, which is possible in simple random sampling. Second, if administrators tend to hold similar opinions to each other while the practitioners hold different opinions, the representativeness of the sample is enhanced.

In stratified random sampling it is necessary to know or have a reasonable estimate of the proportion of people in the population (and sampling frame) in each of the subgroups. One can sample from each stratum in the same proportions as exist in the population (proportionate sampling) or not (disproportionate sampling). Although it is not necessary to sample in accurate proportions (one may want to oversample administrators, for instance), it is necessary to include enough cases in each stratum to make sure each subgroup is adequately represented and to provide for further categorization, if warranted, in analyzing the data. If the strata are not sampled in the same proportions as exist in the population, then numbers in each subgroup must be weighted in generalizing from the sample to the population.

A complex stratified random sampling procedure was used in a study of development of delinquent behavior, the Rochester Youth Development Study referred to in chapters 4 and 5 (Krohn et al. 1996; Smith 1996; Thornberry, Bjerregaard, and Miles 1993). The sampling frame was students in the seventh and eighth grades of public schools in Rochester, New York, a mid-sized city. To reduce unwanted variability, the investigators set several criteria: English or Spanish was spoken in the student's home, no siblings were included in the sample, and the student was in the expected age group for the cohort. To increase variability on the main variable of interest, potential delinquent behavior, the investigators stratified the census tracts based on the adult crime rate. Students in tracts with high crime rates were oversampled (and weighted for the final analyses). Then, because age and gender were considered critical developmental influences, the students in each tract were stratified by grade level and gender. Finally, simple random samples were taken from each stratum (e.g., high crime census tract, seventh grade males; low crime census tract, seventh grade males, and so on). The result is a sample that can be generalized to the youth in the sampling frame with considerable precision yet ensures variability on delinquent behavior, age, and gender.

Stratified random sampling requires not only a sampling frame, but knowing ahead of time where each individual element will fall into the strata. Thus, in the Rochester Youth Development Study, before beginning sampling, the investigators had to know each youth's census tract, grade level, and gender. Stratified random sampling also assumes that the investigators are able to identify the correct variables for stratification, and know the approximate proportion of elements in each stratum.

CLUSTER SAMPLES For practical reasons, large-scale studies generally use cluster or area sampling rather than simple random sampling. In cluster sampling, one first divides the population by clusters, usually geographic areas or other higher-level units. In a single-stage sampling plan, one randomly selects clusters and obtains data from the elements in the selected clusters. In a multistage cluster sampling plan, one randomly selects clusters, then breaks the elements in those clusters into smaller clusters, randomly selects from the second-stage clusters, and so on. In both types, the final stage may include obtaining data from all elements, or a simple random sample of the elements in the final cluster. An example of single-stage cluster sampling would be a sample of all child welfare offices (elements) in a randomly selected state (states are the cluster). A multistage sampling plan might involve successive random samples to choose a state (first-level cluster), a child welfare office (second-level cluster), a worker (third-level cluster), and then inclusion of all the worker's cases (or a random sample of cases) in the final sample. Of course, one may select more than one sampling unit (state, office, and so on) at any stage.

Whether cluster samples are probability or nonprobability samples depends on whether random selection is used. Multistage sampling may involve both probability and nonprobability sampling since the sampling units at different stages may be selected differently. In the given example, one might choose at the first step a few states purposely selected to represent different regions of the county (nonprobability sampling), from each state randomly select an urban and a rural child welfare office (probability: stratified random), from each office randomly select a worker (probability), and from each worker select a simple random sample of cases (probability). If probability sampling is used at every stage, it is complicated but possible to specify the probability of an element's being selected into the sample.

Cluster sampling is usually preferred to random sampling of large populations, particularly if they are widely dispersed. In our example, listing all child welfare cases in the United States is a near impossible task. Even if such a list could be compiled or obtained, selecting a simple or stratified random sample from it would be a huge undertaking and collecting data from such a widely scattered sample would be extremely expensive unless mail questionnaires were used. However, a multistage cluster sampling plan makes simple random or stratified random sampling quite manageable at every level. At each level, one must be able to specify a sampling frame (a list of all states, all child welfare offices within the selected state, and so on) but not until the last, most delimited level is it necessary to list all elements (all cases on the selected worker's caseload).

An example of a single-stage cluster sample is a study of whether adolescents' choice of alcoholic beverages is associated with problem drinking and drug use (Smart and Walsh 1993). The investigators first stratified their cluster (homeroom classes in one Canadian province) by grade level and by region, then took a random sample of homerooms in each strata. All the students present on the day of administration in the selected homerooms were asked to take the questionnaire about substance abuse. In this example, the investigators needed a list of homerooms (and their location and grade level), but did not need a list of all students in school in the province.

An example of a multistage cluster sample is from an evaluation of a community's reaction to regular contact with persons with disabilities (Tice 1994). Persons with severe mental or physical handicaps were employed in a community recycling project, picking up recyclable material from residential curbs. To select the area to receive the service, one census tract in rural Ohio where the program was initiated was chosen (accidental sampling). From among the communities in this tract, two communities were randomly selected. One received the experimental recycling program, the other was the control community. Then, to sample respondents for the assessment of attitudes toward those with disabilities, a list was compiled of all adult individuals in the selected communities and one adult was randomly selected from each household (random sampling after stratifying by household).

SYSTEMATIC SAMPLES Systematic sampling involves choosing every nth element, for example, every tenth case record in an agency's files or every sixth name on the local NASW membership list. The sampling interval (in these examples, ten or six) is obtained by dividing the population by the size of the desired sample. Whether or not systematic samples are probability samples depends on how the first element is selected; probability sampling would require the first element to be randomly selected. (Note that most combinations have no chance of being selected; for this reason, some researchers question whether any systematic sample should be considered a probability sample.) In the first example, a number between one and ten would be randomly chosen to determine the first case record for the sample. Thereafter, every tenth case would be selected into the sample. Thus, the probability of a record's being chosen for the sample is one in ten initially but changes after the first record is selected to either 100 percent or zero.

Because of this changed probability, it is important to examine the files or lists beforehand to see how they are constructed. A genuinely random order would result in a random sample. Certain orders may result in a stratified sample. For example, names listed in alphabetic order may stratify the sample on ethnic origin since the "Mac's" and "Mc's" would be together and so forth. Case records filed according to closing date or type of case would be stratified by those principles. In some cases this stratification might be advantageous, but this would need to be evaluated by considering the basis for stratification in relation to the particular study. There are times when the order of the files or lists may result in biased samples. For example, a child welfare agency may keep separate records on foster parents, natural parents, and each child in the family for which the agency has responsibility. If all the records making up a "case" are filed together and in the same order (for example, foster parents first, then natural parents, and then children according to age), the systematic sample would be biased by having large families overrepresented and very possibly by having certain kinds of record (for example, foster parents) overrepresented or underrepresented. The possibility of these biased samples presents serious problems for the researcher.

Although systematic samples may or may not approximate random samples, their primary advantage is ease. When the sampling frame consists of a very large number of elements, the process of numbering the elements to take a random sample may be prohibitive. Systematic sampling avoids the necessity to construct an actual list of elements. Further, if one is sampling clients as they apply to an agency, it would be questionable to ask them to wait for service until all clients had applied and a random sample could be taken. Taking a systematic sample would permit one to offer service or begin data collection immediately.

An example of a systematic sample is a study by Bush, Epstein, and Sainz (1997) to investigate the influence of the social sciences in social work intervention theory, practice, and research. They looked at where the citations (references) had been published for articles in important social work journals. Their sampling frame was all articles in three journals, *Social Work*, *Social Service Review*, and *Families in Society* (formerly *Social Casework*) from 1956 through 1992. To get their sample, they selected all articles in the first issue of each journal every third year. In doing so, they must assume that there is no systematic difference in the first issue, that it is similar in content, type of articles, and so on, to all other issues.

COMBINATIONS OF SAMPLING PROCEDURES As several examples have illustrated, it is possible to combine sampling methods. The study of adolescents' choice of alcoholic beverage combined stratification and cluster sampling (Smart and Walsh 1993). The comparison of homeless and poor with housing used two different sampling methods (simple random and accidental) to select the groups that were compared (Johnson et al. 1995). Tice's study (1994) of community reactions to contact with persons with disabilities used accidental sampling, stratification, and random sampling within multistage cluster sampling. Such combinations are appropriate and often improve the sampling plan or make it more feasible.

However, as discussed under cluster sampling, if the sampling procedures mix probability and nonprobability sampling, then the sample is no longer representative because one cannot estimate the probability of including an element. In the study of homeless and housed, the group of housed was representative while the homeless were not. In the study of community reactions, the county selected was not representative, but at the next level of the cluster, the individuals selected were representative of the community because stratified random sampling was used.

Generalization from Probability Samples

Making statements about a larger group (population) on the basis of a smaller group studied (sample) is referred to as *generalization*. In this section we focus primarily on generalizing from representative samples in which probability theory is used to estimate characteristics of populations from samples. When nonrepresentative samples are used, generalization is guided by the logical considerations set forth in the two previous chapters. These logical considerations, developed within the context of experimental research, apply as well to naturalistic research and to thinking about sampling frames when they are not closely tied to the population. With a nonrepresentative sample, one arrives at informed speculations about larger groups based on similarities to the sample characteristics and on judgments about possible atypicalities and biases of the sample.

With representative samples, however, the process moves more systematically, as the following example shows. Suppose a democratic school of social welfare was considering changing its curriculum slightly to require a statistics course for the social work degree and decided to base the decision on student opinion. The 400-member student body is polled by asking them to indicate on a ten-point rating scale the extent to which they agree or disagree with making the statistics course a requirement: a rating of 10 would indicate maximum agreement, and a score of 1, maximum disagreement. The school decides to make the statistics course a requirement if the average (mean) student rating is over 5.5 but not to make this change if the mean score is 5.5 or below. Suppose ratings are obtained from all the students and when the scores are added together and divided by 400, the mean score is 4.9. According to the previous decision, the statistics course would not become mandatory.

Since the entire student body was contacted, we know the true population mean (a parameter)—knowing it is a rarity in social research—and consequently we do not have to estimate it from a sample mean (a statistic). Suppose, for illustrative purposes, we randomly selected from this student body a sample of 40 students and calculated the mean of these scores as 5.1. If the school decision had been based on this sample, it would have been the same as the one based on the population value: no new statistics course. Suppose three more random samples of 40 students each are drawn from the 400 students (with all students' names replaced before each sample selection), and the calculated sample means are 4.8, 4.7, and 5.7. Two things immediately become apparent: one is that most of the sample means are very close to the population mean, and the other is that if the last sample had been taken as representative of the population on the variable of interest (the student body's wishes concerning the statistics course), the opposite conclusion would have been reached and the course would have been made a requirement. If we randomly selected a large number of samples of size 40 from this population of students, calculated their means, and plotted these means on a graph, we would find that they would distribute themselves around the population mean roughly in the shape of a bell-shaped curve (called a normal curve) as in figure 8.1. This is called a sampling distribution.

In other words, most of the sample means would cluster around the population mean, and the more extreme the sample values, the less likely they would be to occur. If an infinite number of random samples of the same size is taken from the same population, the shape of the distribution of means will be a normal or bell-shaped curve and the most frequently obtained sample mean will be the population mean. This is also true of other sample statistics (standard deviations, medians, proportions, and so on)—all of which could be plotted as sampling distributions. This characteristic of random samples is basic to the notion of generalization and inferential statistics (chapter 11).

In reality, we take only one random sample and we have no way of knowing for sure whether it is similar to the population on variables of interest or whether it is dissimilar, that is, whether it is one of the extreme samples. This is so because we do not know the population values (parameters); if we did, there would be no need to obtain a sample. However, probability theory provides us with some assurance here. First, as we observed in figure 8.1, probability samples are more likely than not to be representative of, although seldom identical

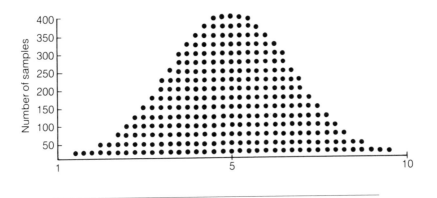

FIGURE 8.1 Sampling distribution of means of sample size 40

to, the population. Second, probability theory enables us to estimate the representativeness or accuracy of the sample. If we take our theoretical sampling distribution of means (an infinite number of samples of the same size), we can calculate a measure of variability (spread or dispersion) around the population mean called the standard error.

In effect, the standard error is the standard deviation of the sampling distribution and is a measure of sampling error. We can use the standard error, which takes into account the size of the samples, to determine the probability of obtaining samples with different values (means). According to probability theory, approximately 34 percent of the sample estimates (statistics) will fall within one standard error above the population parameter and 34 percent of the estimates will fall within one standard error below. Thus about two-thirds (68 percent) of the estimates will be within (plus or minus) one standard error (see figure 11.5). Approximately 95 percent of the sample estimates will fall within two standard errors on either side of the population parameter, and virtually all (more than 99 percent) within three standard errors. This information from probability theory permits us to make inferences about the one sample we have randomly drawn. For example, since we know that 95 percent of the sample means on a given variable will be within the values representing two standard errors on either side of the population mean, we infer that the chances are 95 percent that our sample mean is between those two values. That is, we are 95 percent confident that our sample mean is within that specified interval. (The use of the standard normal curve with its associated calculated probabilities enables us to make much finer discriminations than those given here.)

Because we do not know the population parameter, we use our sample statistic (for example, the mean) as the best estimate of the parameter. From the preceding discussion, we know that most of the time this will be an accurate estimate and further that we can specify a degree of confidence that the population parameter is within a certain range. Our illustration concerning the statistics course can be used to illuminate these concepts. Suppose the standard error (the sampling error) for the sampling distribution displayed in figure 8.1 was .3. Since we know that the population mean is 4.9, we would expect 68 percent of sample means in a sampling distribution to be between 4.6 and 5.2 (4.9 ± .3), 95 percent between 4.3 and 5.5, 99 percent between 4.0 and 5.8, and fewer than 1 percent of the sample means to be smaller than 4.0 or larger than 5.8. Thus, we see that a mean as large as the 5.7 we obtained on one of the four samples we drew initially, which would have resulted in a different conclusion if it had been used to make inferences about the school population, could be expected to occur less than 5 percent of the time. Usually there is no way of knowing if such an unlucky event has occurred, since the population parameter is rarely known. ("Unlucky" refers to the lack of representativeness, although the students at that school may have perceived another referent.)

A less technical interpretation of the foregoing may be helpful. When a study makes use of truly random sampling methods, the reader must be alert to two ways in which the sample may give an inaccurate estimation of the means, proportions, and so on, that characterize the population. First, random samples can be expected to vary within a certain range of the population value. For example the report of a poll based on a random sample may say that 55 percent of the voters in a state prefer candidate Brown over the rival but may add the qualification that this estimate may be off by as much as 4 percent. Second, there is always some chance that the sample will fall completely outside the range in which it is expected to vary. Thus not only do we expect actual voter preferences for Brown to vary between 51 and 59 percent but even that estimate has a chance of being wrong—say, one in a hundred.

It should also be noted that the sampling frame from which a random sample is drawn may not be the full or intended population. Thus a study of the attitudes of institutionalized aged may use a random sample of subjects from a particular institution. Although generalizations based on probability theory can be made about the population of the institution, one may wish to consider what the findings suggest about institutionalized aged in general. Generalization beyond the institution needs to proceed on logical grounds as would be done for a nonprobability sample.

There is also a pragmatic consideration of response rate in much social sciences research. Once an individual is selected for the sample, that individual may not be located or may refuse to participate. Such attrition obviously affects how representative the sample is of even its sampling frame. For example, in the study of African immigrants mentioned earlier, a random sample was drawn from the membership lists of relevant organizations (Kamya 1997). However, only 42 percent of those selected returned a questionnaire that could be used. We have no way of knowing how representative these respondents were of the original sample, even though that sample was representative of the original membership. Low response rates such as this generally indicate a problem in generalizing even with probability samples.

Size of Sample

Decisions about how large a sample to use involve the same considerations already discussed for group experiments in chapter 7. Generally, the larger the sample, the more representative it is likely to be and the greater the chance that the mean is close to the population mean. However, sample size may be completely irrelevant if conscious or unconscious biases are operating. For example, if a student who detests mathematics had been allowed to choose an accidental sample for the student poll concerning the statistics requirement, it might not have mattered whether 10 or 100 students were polled.

However, in the case of probability sampling, the larger the sample, the more likely it is to accurately reflect the population. This is so because, as the size of the sample increases, the sampling error decreases, indicating more cluster around the population parameter. The standard error of the mean is σ/n where σ is the estimated standard deviation of the population and n is the number of cases in the sample. Thus, as the sample size increases, the denominator becomes larger and the standard error smaller. Again, by making use of probability theory, it is possible to determine how large a sample is needed to achieve a certain degree of precision as measured by the width of the confidence interval. However, the formula requires estimates based on the investigator's judgment and consequently is of limited value for inexperienced researchers. For relatively small populations, some researchers use a sampling fraction of 1/10, which means sampling one-tenth of the population.

Intuitively, the reader will perceive that the more homogeneous the population on variables of interest, the smaller the sample needed to reflect the variability in the population. Ultimately, if all elements are the same, only one element need be selected to represent the population. In the final analysis, sample size is usually based on the researcher's judgment, with factors such as time and cost considerations, requirements of planned data analysis, and the like, being taken into account.

Sampling is, after all, only one of many considerations in the planning and implementation of a research study. For example, much of this chapter has dealt with sampling methods designed to prevent bias, but bias can enter into the study at any number of points, for example, in the underlying assumptions of the investigator, in the way data are collected, or in how the findings are interpreted. All the stages of research involve considerations of time, effort, cost, feasibility, appropriateness, desirability, what is possible, and so on. Because resources are inevitably limited, judgments and trade-offs must be made. Decisions made at one point in the research often have implications for other stages. Consequently, the sampling must be viewed within the context of the entire study, with the purpose of the research as the major guiding principle.

Summary

Sampling—selecting units to be studied from a population or a sampling frame—is usually undertaken because it is not feasible to study the entire population. Important considerations in sampling include whether the sample is appropriate and specific for the research question or hypothesis and whether the sample is representative, or, put another way, whether the investigator can generalize using knowledge of sampling error (probability) or must use the logic of similarity.

Probability sampling allows one to generalize to the population—or, more accurately, to the sampling frame—using statistical techniques, but may be difficult to conduct, and how well it represents the intended population depends on the correspondence of the sampling frame to the population. Simple random sampling, which requires a list of all elements that might be sampled, selects elements so that each element has an equal chance of being selected and all combinations of elements have an equal change of being selected. Stratified random sampling stratifies on important characteristics before sampling, while cluster sampling first organizes the elements by a larger unit, often geographical, and systematic sampling takes the nth case.

Nonprobability sampling is relatively easy and practical but allows only the use of logic to generalize and yields unrepresentative samples that may be systematically biased. Accidental sampling takes whatever elements are available, snowball sampling uses initial respondents to generate additional respondents, quota sampling stratifies by key characteristics, and purposive sampling involves deliberately selecting cases because they are thought to exemplify a desired characteristic.

9   Measurement

Measurement is as much a part of social work practice as relating to clients is. Social workers use measurement procedures in obtaining information about their clients and their problems, in developing treatment strategies, and in evaluating outcomes. Measurement procedures are used in ascertaining the needs of target populations and in evaluating the services or programs that may result. Face sheets, case records, program statistics, annual reports, and the like, contain data resulting from or summarizing these measurements.

Definition

Measurement can be defined in many different ways. The most important differences in meaning for our purposes concern how broadly or narrowly the term is used. References to measuring effectiveness, mental health, or family functioning suggest use of the term in its broadest sense, while counting the number of social workers attending a meeting or the number of agencies in a community providing homemaker service suggests a more restricted usage. In its broadest sense, measurement is used interchangeably with operationalization; in its narrower sense, it refers to the part of an operational definition that quantifies or categorizes the essence being measured.

Often, the term *measurement* is substituted for operational definition, as illustrated by: "In this study, aggression was measured as follows . . ." Viewed broadly then, measurement can be thought of as encompassing the processes necessary to define both the "what" and the "how" to observe and measure; that is, it can include the specification of the indicators selected to represent the major concepts in the study, as well as the categorization or quantification of those indicators. Criteria used to evaluate measurement procedures, such as reliability and validity, are concerned with measurement in this broader sense.

Another common but narrower way in which the term *measurement* is used focuses on the part of the operational definition that attempts to categorize or quantify the indicators. Suggested originally by Stevens (1951:1), this definition states that "measurement is the assignment of numerals to objects or events according to rules." In clarifying this definition, Kerlinger (1985) points out that in fact one measures, not objects or events, but rather indicators of the properties or characteristics of objects. For example, it would not be clients or preschool-age children that we would measure, or even be interested in measuring, but some attribute that can describe them such as their mental health, intelligence, or aggressiveness. However, since we cannot measure even these characteristics directly, we choose or develop indicators to represent them that we can measure, such as questions answered correctly or hitting other children. Generally numbers, which are numerals that have been assigned quantitative meaning, are assigned to or mapped onto the indicators.

The rules used in assigning numbers can be good or bad, and this will determine, other things being equal, whether or not the measurement is sound or poor, even meaningless. To develop good measurements, the rules or assignment or correspondence have to be tied to, or isomorphic with (that is, similar in form to) "reality." Here we are concerned with the fit between the numbers assigned to each of the preschoolers in our sample, for example, and how aggressive each one is. Of course, we cannot determine the goodness of fit precisely or directly, for we cannot know the "true value" of the amount of aggression each child possesses. What we try to do instead is to obtain some indirect evidence of fit by examining various aspects of the measurement procedure. Essentially we look at two levels of correspondence: one, the fit between the concept (say, aggression) and our indicators of it (say, hitting another child); and the second, the correspondence between the amounts or degrees of the indicator and the meaning of the numbers assigned to represent these amounts. In the first instance, we are referring to operational definitions and are concerned about validity; in the second instance, we are referring to level of measurement and are concerned about use of the appropriate measurement scale (that is, nominal, ordinal, and so on).

Role of Measurement

Measurement is a crucial part of the research process. As described in chapter 2, measurement (as operational definitions) provides a bridge between the world of concepts and the empirical world. Operational definitions of variables say what parts of observable phenomena will be measured, how they will be measured, and how they will be categorized. Measurement thus provides the definition of variables that are linked to concepts, theories, and hypotheses.

Measurement thus plays a vital role in helping us answer research questions and test hypotheses. It is a basic step in the collection and organization of data and a necessary procedure for yielding data that can be analyzed statistically. Inferences about the existence or nonexistence of relationships between variables will be made on the basis of the manipulation of measurements. Consequently, hypotheses will be accepted or rejected on the basis of analyses using measurements that may be viewed as the researcher's approximations to reality.

In addition to making hypothesis testing possible, measurement enables us to describe and classify individuals, organizations, cultures, and so on, according to their attributes. It can help us refine our conceptual definitions and gain greater objectivity in our observations. It enables us to discover relationships among variables and makes standardization possible. Measurement also allows us to communicate our research operations more precisely, which is crucial for replication, evaluation of results, and appropriate use of findings.

In the sections that follow, we will first talk about the aspect of measurement that relates to quantification: the meaning of numerals assigned to categories in the operational definition (levels of measurement). We then move to principles for ensuring that what is measured is what was intended (reliability and validity). In these discussions, we follow research convention and use the nouns "measure" and "instrument" to indicate any measuring instrument, for example, a questionnaire, test, interview, or format for observation. In chapter 10, we will take up some of the differences between these instruments when we look at a different aspect of operational definitions, how one goes about collecting the information (data collection).

Levels of Measurement

As discussed, part of the process of measurement is categorizing indicators of properties or characteristics. If we are assessing motivation to change among a group of clients, we might place them into subgroups based on their motivation: highly motivated, moderately motivated, indifferent, and resistant. Then, for convenience, we assign each category a numeral, for example, 1 for highly motivated, 2 for moderately motivated, and so on. These numerals may or may not have a meaning beyond being convenient labels for the categories. In this example, intuitively, the numerals have some additional meaning—the categories are rank-ordered on the characteristic of motivation, with category 1 (highly motivated) having the most of the characteristic and category 4 (resistant) having the least of the characteristic.

The type of categories can be classified by the extent to which the characteristics take on the properties of the number system. The more like the number system, the more meaning the numerical labels have, and the more one can use arithmetical operations. The properties of the number system usually considered in classifying categories are order, distance, and origin. There are four commonly accepted types of categories, called *levels of measurement*, or *scales*. These are, in ascending order: nominal, ordinal, interval, and ratio. At the lowest level, nominal measurement, there is no correspondence between the categories that the variable is partitioned into and the number system. The numerals assigned to various categories of the variable being measured are merely symbols or labels with no number meaning. (For this reason some methodologists do not consider the nominal level as measurement but rather as simply nominal classification.) At the highest level of measurement (ratio scales), the numbers indicate the actual amount of the property being measured; consequently, there is perfect correspondence between the attributes being measured and the characteristics or meaning of the numbers assigned to the attributes. Ordinal and interval measurement, as will be shown, fall between these two extremes.

Because the level of measurement is related to the degree to which properties being measured take on characteristics of the number system, the arithmetic operations and statistical manipulations that can be performed on data differ according to the level of measurement used. The higher the level of measurement, the more sophisticated the arithmetic operations and statistical tests that can be used. In addition, since the levels of measurement are cumulative (each higher level has the characteristics of all levels below it plus an additional characteristic), operations and tests that are appropriate at lower levels can also be used at higher levels.

Generally, because of the increased information to be obtained, researchers aim for the highest level of measurement that is appropriate for the variables of interest and that is consistent with their research purposes. At the lowest level where attributes are categorized or classified, we can obtain frequencies or "counts" of the number of cases in each category. At the next level, the data can be ordered and we can determine magnitude, that is, more or less of an attribute. Even more precise quantitative data are obtained at the two highest levels where the data are referred to as metric. Among the advantages of being able to measure variables on higher levels are precision of description, increased communicability of research operations and results, and increased possibilities for discovering and establishing relationships among phenomena.

Nominal Measurement

Nominal measurement, the lowest level of measurement, is the categorization or classification of objects or properties of objects. Individuals assigned to one category are equivalent to all others in that category on a given characteristic. However, they differ from individuals assigned to another category on that characteristic. Nothing more than difference is implied, even if numerals are used as labels for the categories. For example, individuals categorized as female differ from those categorized as male on gender, but there can be no assumption that one is better than or has more gender than the other.

In nominal measurement, numbers assigned to categories have no numerical meaning but are only names or labels for the categories (hence "nominal"). Suppose we try to classify courses in a school of social welfare according to their major emphasis and our rules call for assigning a 1 to treatment courses, a 2 to social policy courses, a 3 to research methods courses, and so on. No order can be inferred from the numbers; for example, 3 is not more or less, higher or lower, than 2. Nor can any arithmetical operations be used; for example, a 1 and a 2 do not equal a 3. (A treatment course plus a social policy course do not equal a research methods course!) However, cases within a subclass can be counted and cases in one subclass can be compared with cases in other subclasses (on other variables). For example, one could obtain frequencies for the number of treatment courses, social policy courses, and so on. One could compare the average number of students in treatment courses with the average number of students in research methods courses or one could compare the proportion of A's given in social policy courses with the proportion given in research methods courses.

Categorization is basic to all measurement. At a minimum we must be able to partition into categories or classes the attributes of a variable. We may classify people into two groups, students and nonstudents, on the basis of schooling; into several groups according to type of treatment case; into a defined number of categories describing degree of marital satisfaction; or into some large number of categories according to age. On some variables we can categorize cases only into two groups on the basis of presence or absence of some attribute.

In developing categories, we need to be concerned about only two criteria: mutual exclusiveness and exhaustiveness. To be *mutually exclusive*, categories must be unique, distinct, and unambiguous; there must be only one appropriate category for each case. For example, one cannot have age categories of 10–15 years and 15–20 years—there is an overlap and 15-year-olds could be placed in both categories. It also means that categories must be unidimensional, or at the same level of abstraction. These categories for religion are mutually exclusive: Catholic, Protestant, Jew; these are not: Catholic, Protestant, Lutheran, and Jew. Attempts to classify cases as child abuse, neglect, or sexual abuse present problems since cases may involve any two or all three. One would need to have categories for all combinations or develop a set of categories for each problem, such as presence or absence of child abuse and so on. *Exhaustiveness* refers to having a category for each case. To meet this requirement, a category called "other" may need to be added for some variables if the researcher cannot, or chooses not to, specify all possible categories. For example, one might use the following categories for marital status: married, divorced, separated, never married, and other.

Ordinal Measurement

In ordinal measurement not only are characteristics divided into categories, but also the categories can be rank ordered. Relationships of "greater than" or "less than" can be expressed. Like nominal scales, individuals classified into an ordinal category are equivalent to all other individuals classified in the same category and different from those in all other categories. In addition, those in category A have more of the quality in question than those in category B (A>B), which means that B can never be equal to or greater than A. And, if A is greater than B (A > B), and B is greater than C (B > C), then A is greater than C (A > C).

Although ordinal scales allow us to express the degree to which objects in a category possess a certain characteristic, they do not allow us to say how much they possess. For example, we might have parents rate their child care arrangement as "very satisfactory," "satisfactory," "unsatisfactory," "very unsatisfactory." The categories might be assigned numerals, with 1 = very satisfactory and 4 = very unsatisfactory. ("Very unsatisfactory" could be assigned the numeral 1; and "very satisfactory" 4; the direction does not matter so long as assignment is consistent and in rank order.) Although this ordinal scale clearly indicates degree of satisfaction, it does not permit us to infer that the distance between "very satisfactory" and "satisfactory" is the same as that between "satisfactory" and "unsatisfactory." Ordinal scales indicate only rank order, not equal intervals or absolute quantities; category 1 indicates more satisfaction than 2, but we do not know how much.

In this example, each set of parents rates their satisfaction, and it is possible for several to give the same answer. Their answers are separate from other parents', or independent. Another type of ordinal scale requires that the parents as a group be rank-ordered by satisfaction with day care. The most satisfied set of parents might be rated 1, the next satisfied 2, the third most satisfied 3, and so on.

Many variables used in social work research and practice are most appropriately measured on ordinal scales. Some examples are socioeconomic status, educational level, severity of problem, and attitude, opinion, and prestige scales.

Interval Measurement

On interval scales, not only can categories be rank-ordered, but also there are equal intervals between the categories. However, there is no natural origin or absolute zero. The commonly cited example of an interval scale is temperature as measured on the Fahrenheit or Celsius scales. (The Kelvin scale, on the other hand, is ratio since it has an absolute zero.) Western calendar time, with Christ's birth as the arbitrary origin, is also an interval scale. It is difficult to give other examples, for almost all interval scales are also ratio scales. Attempts have been made to develop interval scales in the social sciences, most notably the Thurstone method of equal-appearing intervals, but there is no consensus that these go beyond ordinal measurement.

Arithmetically, equal intervals means that the numerals assigned to categories have real meaning and can take on the operations of arithmetic. For example, the distance between 1 and 5 is the same as the distance between 53 and 57, and 3 times 5 has real meaning as 15 equal intervals. This means that common statistical operations such as addition, subtraction, multiplication, and division can be performed on the scales.

Ratio Measurement

Ratio scales have all the properties of the other three scales plus an absolute zero or natural origin. Therefore, ratio measurements indicate absolute amounts. Not only can we say that one person is different from another according to some characteristic (nominal measurement), has more or less of that characteristic (ordinal), and is so many units above or below another person on that characteristic (interval); but also we can now express the difference as a ratio by saying that one person has so many times as much of the characteristic as another person. For example, a person with six dollars has twice as much money as a person with three dollars. Weight, height, and age are usually measured on ratio scales. When we count objects, we are using a ratio scale. Social work practitioners and researchers often use ratio measurement for variables such as number of cases, interviews, problems, agencies; amount of income, welfare grant, child support (in dollars); and duration or length of interview, case, marriage, or employment.

When numerical data are grouped into categories, the result is an ordinal scale. Instead of asking respondents their exact age or income, researchers may develop age or income brackets and ask respondents where they fall, believing that the latter question is less objectionable to most people. The result is also ordinal if numerical data are collected but grouped during the analysis. Whereas the full range of statistical procedures is appropriate for ratio measurements, only those procedures that can be used with ordinal scales are appropriate for the grouped numerical data.

A few comments are in order about the common practice in social work research (indeed, in social research generally) of using arithmetic operations and statistical procedures in analysis of data derived from measurement at the ordinal level. Arithmetic operations, such as addition, subtraction, multiplication, and division, assume at least interval level data. Thus, computation of means, which requires summation and division, strictly speaking, is "inappropriate" for data based on measurement that simply asserts that A is greater than B. Yet measurement of most concepts of interest to social workers does not exceed the ordinal level, and most social work researchers will treat ordinal data as if they were at an interval or ratio level. This practice is best justified by assuming that most ordinal scales approach interval measurement to some degree. It is possible, when necessary, to test this assumption (Borgatta and Bohrnstedt 1980; Kenny 1986). To the extent that they do approach interval level, treating them as interval scales permits one to make use of a wide range of "more powerful" manipulations and tests that are possible if arithmetic operations are employed. Although this assumption and resulting practice can be defended, one must keep in mind that it invariably introduces an unknown amount of error into what analyses are performed, error that can offset the greater "power" of the arithmetic operations. Hence, ordinal data that have been extensively manipulated by procedures that assume interval level measurement (such as product-moment correlations and factor analysis) must be treated with more than the usual amount of caution.

This use of ordinal data as if they were interval applies only to ordinal scales where responses are independent, that is, how one individual is classified does not affect how another individual is classified—everyone can be "very satisfied," for example. If responses depend on each other, e.g., only one person can be first, only one second, and so on, then it is not possible to use usual arith-

TABLE 9.1
Levels of Measurement and Their Characteristics

LEVEL OF MEASUREMENT	CHARACTERISTICS	SELECTED MATHEMATICAL OPERATIONS	APPROPRIATE STATISTICS
NOMINAL	equivalence within catagory, difference between	A=A A≠ B	frequencies mode
ORDINAL	above, plus: rank order	A>B if A>B and B>C, then A>C	median range
INTERVAL	above, plus: equal intervals	A+B=B+A if A=B and AC=D, then BC=D (AB)C=A(BC)	mean standard deviation
RATIO	above, plus: true, natural zero		

metic operations. Special statistics have been devised to apply in such circumstances (for example, the Wilcoxon Matched-Pairs Signed Ranks Test, the Kendall Coefficient of Concordance, or the Kruskal-Wallis One-Way Analysis of Variance).

Criteria for Evaluating Measurement Procedures

Because of the crucial role measurement plays in research—linking theory to reality—the adequacy of measurement procedures is of great concern to researchers, evaluators of research studies, and discriminating users of research findings. The criterion of greatest importance in the evaluation of measurement is *validity*, which refers to how much an instrument corresponds to the "true" position of a person or object on the characteristic being measured. A more general way of expressing this idea is to say that validity is a gauge of how well measurement achieves its purposes. If the purpose of the consumer price index is to measure the cost of living, how well does it accomplish this goal? Much more technical definitions of validity, sometimes making use of statistical concepts, have been attempted (for example, Kerlinger 1985). But however validity is defined, it is clear that it attempts to capture an elusive property of measurement: "its truth value." For most measures of social phenomena, this value cannot be ascertained in any fundamental sense. There is usually no way of knowing the "true" characteristics of the realities of interest to us. Consequently, validity is inevitably a matter of judgment based on evidence and inference.

Traditionally, one aspect of validity has been treated somewhat separately, perhaps because it does lend itself to more precise assessment. We are referring to the consistency or *reliability* of measurement—whether it gives the same result at different times or under differing conditions. While we may not be able to determine if a measure is true, we can determine if it yields consistent or reliable results through means such as repeating the measurement or having it independently applied by two observers. If it does, we have some evidence that the instrument is achieving its purposes—at least whatever is being measured is being measured consistently. But we have come only part way: two measurements may be consistent but both may be false. If its application yields inconsistent results, then the instrument has failed an elementary test of validity, and our confidence in its capacity to achieve its purposes is lessened.

To put these ideas in concrete form, let us suppose two travelers want to be sure of the time. They consult their watches but regard them as fallible measures and so they ask a companion to give them the time. If the companion gives them a time similar to their own, they are reassured that their watches are correct. The "reliability check" has provided some proof of validity. But there is still the chance that all readings may be in error—both the travelers and their companion may have gone through a time zone without resetting their watches (reliability without validity). Obviously, if the initial check had revealed that the companion had a quite different time, the travelers would have received no confirming evidence that their watches were giving them the right (valid) time. Now it is possible that the travelers had the correct time after all, and the companion was wrong. Inconsistent results do not *necessarily* mean that an instrument is in error, but they provide no evidence that it is on the mark.

Figure 9.1 shows the relation between reliability and validity. The central bull's-eye represents the "real" concept we are trying to measure, while the shots represent results from the measurement instrument. If the shots are

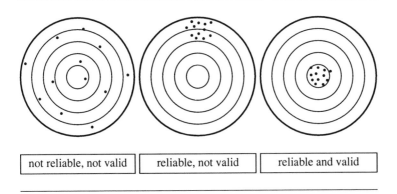

| not reliable, not valid | reliable, not valid | reliable and valid |

FIGURE 9.1
Analogy for the relation between reliability and validity

widely scattered—inconsistent results—there is no reliability and the question of validity is irrelevant. If the shots are clustered—good reliability—then we can ask if they are accurate or valid. Only if the instrument is reliable and valid will the cluster be on the bull's eye.

In addition to needing measurement procedures producing data that are correct, that is, valid and reliable, the researcher also needs to obtain data that are relevant, practical, feasible, and sensitive. *Relevance* refers to obtaining data that bear upon the research questions, the adequacy of the indicators selected, and the appropriateness of measures for respondents. As an example of appropriateness for respondents, it would be meaningless to ask respondents if they approved of pending welfare reform legislation if they knew practically nothing about it. Further, the data obtained would be misleading if they responded without the investigator's awareness of their lack of knowledge. *Practicality* and *feasibility* refer to matters such as cost in money, time, and effort and to ethical considerations in using the measurement procedures. Cost factors, which pose eternal constraints on research, need no elaboration. Procedures for the protection of human subjects intended to minimize risks to individuals often constrain what data may be collected in what manner. Instruments also need to be *sensitive*, that is, capable of making distinctions fine enough for the purposes they are to serve. In some studies, simply being able to separate individuals correctly into two groups, for example, homeless and having housing, may be sufficient. Such a crude distinction, even if free from error, would probably not be adequate in studies where quality of life is a major variable.

Because few if any measuring instruments in the social sciences meet all of these criteria, trade-offs must be made here as in other aspects of research. Efforts to increase validity and reliability are liable to be costly in terms of money, time, and effort. Increased sensitivity often lowers reliability. Because of such problems, researchers are advised to use, when possible, more than one measurement procedure for major variables.

Against the backdrop of these general considerations, we examine in more detail two central aspects of measurement adequacy: reliability and validity. Following convention we treat these aspects separately, although, as we have shown, reliability is a facet of validity. Because reliability is in fact subordinate, it is dealt with first. In discussing both aspects we draw on the typologies and vocabulary developed by Selltiz, Wrightsman, and Cook (1976) and widely used by research methodologists.

Reliability

There are different types of reliability, depending on the kind of measurement procedures used and the aspect of reliability one is interested in. The aspects most frequently considered are stability, equivalence, and homogeneity. Stability and equivalence are concerned with external consistency, and homogeneity is concerned with internal consistency. Assessing reliability requires conducting research studies designed explicitly to test the qualities of the measurement procedure (usually a questionnaire or schema for observation)—the measurement function of research design described in chapter 4. Usually these studies are naturalistic with one or two periods of data collection. Subjects should be as close as possible to those for whom the instrument is intended (even a well-tested instrument may not be reliable or valid when used with a new population). In testing the different aspects of reliability, it is assumed that the subjects or respondents remain the same, but the time, instrument, or investigator may vary, depending on the type of reliability being assessed. Generally, when stability is the concern, the time of administration varies (but not the instrument or the investigator), and when equivalence is the issue, either the instrument or the investigator varies (but not the time). When homogeneity is the concern, some items in the instruments (usually questionnaires) are compared to other items and there is no variation of other factors.

STABILITY   Stability refers to consistency of measures on repeated applications; it is assessed by repeating data collection. For example, to assess the reliability of a self-report questionnaire, the investigator would give the same group of subjects the same questionnaire at two different times. To assess reliability of an observational coding schema, the investigator would have the same coders apply the observations to one stimulus at different times, perhaps observing videotaped interaction between a parent and child. The assumption is that the characteristics measured will stay the same—the subjects' attitudes will be the same, or the videotaped interaction will be the same.

However, in reality, the variation in results between the two data collection periods reflects not only errors of measurement but also any fluctuations in the characteristic being measured. Genuine fluctuations or changes complicate attempts to assess stability of the measuring instrument. Attitudes, opinions, perceptions, and emotional states—phenomena that social workers are often interested in—are particularly subject to change.

Test-retest reliability is the most commonly used method of ascertaining reliability when the concern is stability. This method, which involves two applications of the measuring instrument, is applicable to most measurement procedures, including interview schedules and questionnaires. The results of the two measurements are compared and an index of reliability such as a coefficient of correlation can be calculated. (As will be discussed in chapter 11, the higher the correlation, the more congruent are the responses at the two times; the range is .00 to 1.00.)

An example of test-retest reliability is a measurement study by Briggs, Tovar, and Corcoran (1996). They gave the Children's Action Tendency Scale (CATS) (Deluty 1979) to 207 children aged 11 to 15. Eight weeks later, they gave the same children the CATS a second time. The correlation coefficients ranged from .29 for boys on the submissiveness subscale of the CATS (poor reliability) to .73 for girls on submissiveness (good reliability). Interestingly, girls' consistency over time was much better than boys.'

When the measuring instrument consists of a questionnaire, attitude scale, or other self-report device, several phenomena can influence the results on the retest. The measurement procedure itself can affect the characteristic being measured. For example, respondents may not have thought much about education in prisons and consequently have formed no opinion about its desirability. Being asked about it, however, might stimulate their awareness of prison conditions, possibly causing them to begin paying attention to publications or discussions about it, so that by the time of the retest they have formed definite opinions.

If the interval between the two measurements is short, respondents may remember their earlier answers and simply repeat them upon retest, which can cause an inflated reliability coefficient. On the other hand, the longer the period between the measurements, the more likely there are to be genuine changes in the characteristic one is measuring. The latter results in an underestimate of instrument reliability. This dilemma is difficult to resolve. In an effort to minimize the effects of recall and of genuine change, some researchers suggest an interval of two to four weeks between measurements.

It goes without saying that if one is interested in assessing reliability of an instrument, it is important to administer the instrument each time in as similar a manner as possible, under conditions as similar as possible. For example, very clear instructions, unambiguous wording of questions, and adequate training of interviewers and observers are important to minimize variation in administration. It may not be a fair test of an interview schedule to question a husband about marital satisfaction the first time alone and the second time with his wife present.

EQUIVALENCE Equivalence is the ability of two measures to give the same results. Equivalence may be assessed through two different types of comparisons: 1) different investigators using the same measurement procedures at the same time but independently of one another, or 2) different instruments administered at the same time.

In the first, two or more observers may watch a family planning a trip, and separately record the number of times speeches are directed to various family members; two or more case analysts may be asked to read the same case records and judge the degree of affection exhibited in the parent-child relationship. This type of reliability is generally referred to as interobserver reliability. Depending on the measurement activity engaged in by the investigators, terms such as *interjudge, interrater, interobserver,* and *intercoder reliability* are sometimes used.

If two or more investigators are to be used to observe, make ratings, code information, and so on, it is crucial to ascertain interobserver reliability after training the investigators in the use of the measuring instruments. Continued training with special attention to identified problem areas is necessary until satisfactory reliability is achieved. "Satisfactory reliability" is largely a matter of judgment. For example, a correlation coefficient of .80 or a percentage of agreement of 75 may be quite acceptable or again it may not. The determination depends largely on the purpose of the measurement procedure, the method used to ascertain reliability, and the relevance of that method to the purpose.

A frequently used, and perhaps the simplest, index of interobserver reliability is percentage of agreement. This measure, which is applicable to nominal data, is the number of agreements between observers (usually two) divided by the total number of observations (agreements and disagreements) multiplied by 100. The index is not, however, as straight forward a measure of reliability as it might appear to be. For one thing, a certain amount of agreement between observers may be due to chance. Chance agreement is especially likely to occur when most observations tend to fall in one category; for example, when coding rare behavior over time, most time periods will be coded in the category "did not occur." In any case, one may wish to use a refinement of the percentage of agreement that corrects for chance factors, such as Cohen's kappa (Cohen 1960). For example, Biggerstaff (1994) examined the agreement among oral examiners on passing or failing candidates for licensure as a social worker in Virginia. Although overall at least two examiners agreed on pass or fail in more than 90% of cases, once Cohen's corrections were applied, only 56% of the teams had adequate agreement among their members (defined as kappas between .50 and 1.0).

Another complication is that the percentage of agreement may take different forms depending on the nature of the data and other circumstances. Thus, in the example of rare behavior, a simple percentage of agreement may be artificially "high" simply because observers can readily agree on its absence. The fact that they do not agree about the occurrence of the behavior—the crucial part of the reliability test—may escape attention. In such a case the percentage of agreement may be limited to occurrence of behavior as seen by one or both observers.

If the observers were making ratings on ordinal or interval scales instead of using nominal categories, other indexes of agreement are possible, such as Kendall's tau or Spearman's rho (comparing rank orders) or the correlation coefficient r (for interval data.) The coefficients obtained by these methods (and by Cohen's kappa) can be tested for significance to see if the level of agreement is likely to have occurred by chance. In reporting interobserver reliability, it is important to indicate not only the percentage of agreement or size of the coefficient but also how it was obtained.

An example of interobserver equivalence reliability is from a study of the effects of training volunteer workers to be pleasant and cheerful to the people who came for help to an antipoverty agency (Johnson and Fawcett 1994). The interactions between volunteers and clients were observed by researchers trying to blend into the flow of the agency—sitting in the waiting room reading a magazine, browsing through clothing in the room where free clothing was kept, etc. (The volunteers signed informed consent forms and presumably knew their behavior was to be observed.) For each interac-

tion between a volunteer and client, the observers coded six types of courteous behavior as occurring, not occurring when it should, or not appropriate to the situation. To assess the interobserver reliability, at selected times,
two observers watched the volunteer at the same time, each making his or
her own judgments about courteous behavior without consulting with each
other. Agreement was calculated by "dividing the number of agreements by
the number of agreements plus disagreements" (p. 148). Percentage agreement for the different categories ranged from 85 percent to 100 percent with
an average of 95 percent.

The second type of equivalence is between different measuring instruments.
Comparisons are made between measures obtained from the same individuals
using equivalent instruments or alternate forms of an instrument administered
at the same time. Developing equivalent instruments is difficult, however, as it
involves sampling twice from all potential items that relate to what one is trying to measure in such a manner that individuals tested will be ranked in the
same way on both instruments. Thus, the difficulty of developing one instrument that adequately meets all the relevant criteria (validity, reliability, feasibility, and so on) is compounded by having to develop two such instruments.
So far, alternate forms have been developed primarily for intelligence and ability tests.

An example of equivalence reliability is in the Means-End Problem-Solving
Test (MEPS)(Platt and Spivack 1975; 1977), which tests individuals' ability to
solve problems by completing short stories that pose an emotional or social
problem. Because the stories are quite vivid, most respondents remember
their answers for some time. Hence, ten alternative forms or stories have
been developed; equivalence reliability was asssessed by having respondents complete all the stories at one time and calculating a correlation coefficient between scores on each pair of stories. Respondents generally got the
same problem-solving rating on several of the stories. Thus, an investigator
conducting an experiment with a short time between pretest and posttest
could use one of these stories at the pretest and an equivalent one for the
posttest.

HOMOGENEITY Homogeneity reliability is concerned with the internal consistency, or inter-item reliability, of a measuring instrument. It is used almost
exclusively on questionnaires where sets of questions (called scales or sub-

scales) are intended to measure the same thing, for example, the assertiveness subscale on the Children's Action Tendency Scale (Deluty 1979). The assumption being tested here is whether all the items in the scale are measuring the same characteristic.

Several procedures can be used to ascertain the degree of homogeneity. The oldest and perhaps still the most common is the split-half method. The instrument is divided into halves, analogous to alternate forms, and the degree of equivalence is ascertained by seeing if respondents get the same or similar scores on the two halves. Traditionally, the test was usually divided by putting the even-numbered items in one half and the odd-numbered items in the other half. More recently, methods have been developed for random assignment of items to halves with corresponding new methods of computing a coefficient of equivalence. The two best-known coefficients of equivalence are coefficient alpha (Chronbach's alpha) for interval scales and the Kuder-Richardson formula 20 for dichotomous items such as True/False items. As with most coefficients of reliability, .00 means no equivalence, while 1.00 means perfect equivalence among all items.

Forte and Green (1994) used Chronbach's alpha to assess the homogeneity of the Index of Peer Relations (Hudson 1982) with a sample of adolescents. Chronbach's alpha is based on the average correlations among all items. Their alpha of .94 indicated excellent internal consistency; among their subjects, the 25 items on the Index measure the same dimension.

Briggs, Tovar, and Corcoran (1996) used a different, less stringent, procedure, odd-even reliability, to assess the Children's Action Tendency Scale (Deluty 1979). Odd-even reliability is a form of split-half reliability in which the sum of the odd items is correlated with the sum of the even items. The reliabilities, calculated separately for each of the three subscales in the instrument, were .65, .82, and .84. There is some disagreement among researchers about the lower end of acceptable homogeneity (suggestions range from .60 to .80 as a minimum). It appears that items on the low scale, assertiveness, may be measuring different constructs—that is, items have different meaning to the respondent—, while those on the higher scales are more consistent with each other.

Another approach is to calculate intercorrelations between each item and between each item and the total test score. This method not only yields estimates of homogeneity but also helps pinpoint nonequivalent items.

Non-equivalent items can then be eliminated to increase the degree of homogeneity.

In general, the higher the intercorrelation, the better. However, there is a point beyond which high intercorrelations among items may be inefficient and dysfunctional. The intercorrelations can be so high that each item adds little or no additional information about the concept being measured. If there is perfect correspondence (a coefficient of 1.00), each item measures the same thing and only one item is needed; there is no point in having a whole set of questions. In assessing homogeneity, investigators must also guard against the possibility that high internal consistency is the result of some extraneous factor such as response set or social desirability, that is, the items do not measure the same thing but the respondents are giving a set of similar answers based on their overall impression of the topic or on what they perceive as acceptable answers.

Obviously, if the instrument is intended to measure several characteristics, homogeneity of the measuring instrument as a whole is not desirable. Many interview schedules and questionnaires used in social work research attempt to combine the measurement of several concepts in one instrument. For example, Tracy and Abell (1994) used a questionnaire that included a social support map, several different measures of social support, satisfaction with support, and parental coping methods. They were interested in whether structural aspects of the support system were related to perceived support and coping among poor urban parents. Even though one (long) questionnaire was used, they calculated separate measures of homogeneity for each of the measures and their subscales. Thus, they had a series of estimates of internal consistency, one for each important concept in the study.

Validity

Just as there are different types of reliability, there are also different kinds of validity, depending on evidence and procedures used. Similar types may be referred to by different terms, adding no little confusion to an already murky subject. We shall focus on three widely recognized types of validity: content, criterion, and construct.

CONTENT VALIDITY Content validity, sometimes called *face validity*, refers to the representativeness or sampling adequacy of the content of a measuring instrument. Two considerations are relevant in assessing content validity. One is the extent to which the instrument is measuring what it is intended to measure: to what extent do the questions, observed behavior, and so on, reflect the concept to be measured and not some other concept? For example, is use of food pantries part of social support? The second consideration is whether the instrument includes an adequate sample of the behavior. To what extent do the items, topics, questions, or behaviors reflect broad and representative coverage of the concept to be measured? Would a list of sources of financial assistance be a broad enough definition of social support? Both aspects are determined on a logical basis; that is, the measurement procedure is inspected and a judgment is made about it in terms of the two considerations listed. Some investigators use expert consultants to assess content validity, but each researcher and each reader can and should assess the content validity of measures used in any study.

Basic to the judgment of content validity is the notion of a theoretical universe of items reflecting the concept from which one can choose potential items. Some universes of content are more obvious than others and consequently judgments about measures of the concepts are easier to make. However, many concepts that social workers are interested in, such as parent-child interaction, marital communication, and social support, are extremely complex with difficult-to-define universes. As discussed in chapter 2, operational definitions seldom encompass all that is meant by the concept as defined abstractly. Often operational definitions also include parts of other concepts not intended to be measured. How well a concept is operationalized is a gauge of its content validity.

For example, in a checklist instrument designed to determine if parents are providing young children with a minimal acceptable standard of care, there may be agreement that an item such as "keeps harmful substances out of child's reach" would be an appropriate indicator but there may be question about "makes child's bed each day." Further, the instrument would need to be examined to ascertain if important indicators of minimal acceptable care had been omitted, for example, if providing an adequate diet was left out. The fit between the items and characteristics of subject populations would also be a matter of concern. Keeping harmful objects out of child's reach would not be relevant for children beyond a certain age.

To assess the content validity of the Social Support Survey—Clinical Form (SSS-C), Richman, Rosenfeld, and Hardy (1993) systematically compared their instrument to the content of previous literature on social support. To assess the range or sampling of content on forms of support, they identified eight forms in the literature, such as listening, emotional support, reality confirmation support, task appreciation support, tangible assistance support, and so on. They then checked that they had an item for each of the eight areas, for example, Personal Assistance: "People who provide you with services or help, such as running an errand for you or driving you somewhere" (p. 306). To assess the type of question asked, they reviewed other questionnaires as well as the literature, and compared them to their questions. For each form of support, they asked four questions: who provides the support, the recipient's satisfaction with it, the difficulty of getting more of it, and importance of that form.

CRITERION VALIDITY Criterion validity refers to whether the new measure yields similar results to established measures believed to be valid measures of the concepts. Validity is judged according to the accuracy of the predictions to the outside criterion. Establishing criterion validity requires naturalistic research in which one group of participants are assessed on two (or more) measures, the measure to be validated, and an accepted measure. Criterion validity is particularly appropriate when the purpose of the measurement procedure is to make specific predictions about individuals for selection and placement in jobs, training, or treatment programs, or to predict behavior such as child neglect. In such cases, whatever one is trying to predict (for example, success in a social work program) is the criterion used to estimate validity. It is also used to assess the usefulness of indicators, for example, whether self-report questionnaires about drinking accurately measure observed behaviors such as alcohol consumption. Finally, criterion validity is used when trying to develop a shorter form of a long, complicated instrument that already exists, such as diagnostic or intelligence tests. In these cases, the criterion for comparison might be behaviors (urine measurements) or the longer form of an instrument, such as an intelligence text.

Criterion validity is very important in social work research and in other kinds of applied research, since much of this research is concerned with predicting behavior and outcomes. It is also important in practice, where critical judgments must be made about a client's potential destructive behaviors, such as suicide, spouse abuse, or child abuse and neglect. For example, the debate about child welfare and removal of children from their homes, which receives great publicity on a regular basis, is a debate about the criterion validity of social workers' judgments. Predictive validity is critical in child maltreatment cases, where numerous instruments try (not very successfully) to predict who will abuse, while reducing both false negatives—cases judged low risk in which maltreatment subsequently occurs—and false positives—cases incorrectly identified as potential abusers (Lyons, Doueck, and Wodarksi 1996).

Criterion validity can be a straightforward, practical approach when a good external criterion such as child abuse exists. Often, however, good criterion measures do not exist for the characteristics social workers wish to measure. For example, what is a standard criterion for social support? Practitioner empathy? Self-esteem? This poses a serious challenge for the investigator who may need to supplement the criterion available with other relevant evidence. It is also a reason why it is usually recommended that investigators use several approaches to measuring important variables.

There are two types of criterion validity: *concurrent* and *predictive* validity. Both involve prediction, are determined empirically, and use an external criterion. They are distinguished by whether the criterion data exist at the same times as the results of the measurement procedure (concurrent) or whether these data come from a later time (predictive). In practical terms, concurrent validity requires a single occasion naturalistic design while predictive validity requires at least two occasions of data collection, once for the measure being tested, later for the predicted criterion measure.

Richman, Rosenfeld and Hardy (1993) assessed the concurrent criterion validity of their new instrument, the Social Support Survey-Clinical Form (SSS-C), by giving the same group of respondents at the same time two questionnaires, their SSS-C and a widely accepted measure of social support, the Norbeck Social Support Questionnaire (Norbeck, Lindesy, and Carrieri 1981). They hypothesized that there would be a high correlation between the SSS-C emotional support scales and the Norbeck affect scale, and between the SSS-C tangible assistance and personal assistance scales and the Norbeck aid variable. Correlations were between .51 and .68, acceptably high for criterion validity.

Predictive criterion validity for their human services Job Satisfaction Scale (JSS) was the concern for Koeske et al. (1994). They gave the JSS questionnaire to 68 intensive case managers who were hired to provide services for the severely and persistently mentally ill. The managers took the JSS 3, 12 and 18 months after they were hired. Job satisfaction (JSS) at 3 months was significantly related to depression, burnout, and intention to quit at 12 and 18 months. The overall JSS did not predict actually quitting, but one subscale did, the salary and promotion subscale.

CONSTRUCT VALIDITY In criterion validity, the concern is only with how well one's instrument predicts a criterion, not with why the instrument works.

Indeed, one may be measuring some phenomenon other than what was intended but may not discover this with criterion validation procedures if the predictions are reasonably accurate. Such a situation would be revealed through construct validation procedures, however, since construct validity is concerned precisely with what the instrument is measuring. Is the Job Satisfaction Scale (Koeske et al. 1994) "really" measuring job satisfaction, or is it some other concept like motivation for human service work? Does the Social Support Survey (Richman, Rosenfeld, and Hardy 1993) really measure social support or does it measure a generalized sense of well-being? The classic example of a widely accepted and still useful instrument that has poor construct validity is the intelligence test. Although it has good criterion validity in predicting performance in many arenas, it clearly does not measure something innate called "intelligence," but instead is a combination of underlying factors such as social class and reading ability.

Construct validity is generally considered to be the most important type of validity. It is concerned with the "meaning" of the instrument, with explaining individual differences in responses, and with identifying the factors or constructs that explain the variance of the measuring instrument. Since constructs (concepts) cannot be directly observed or measured, their existence must be inferred from other evidence. Generally this involves testing propositions about the relationship of the concept to other variables. Thus, in construct validity, one tries to validate not only the hypotheses but also the theory behind the hypotheses. This preoccupation with theory, explanatory concepts, and the testing of hypothesized relationships is the distinguishing feature of construct validity. It is primarily the use of empirical data as evidence that distinguishes construct validity from content validity.

According to Cronbach (1970), there are three parts to construct validation: suggesting what concepts possibly account for test performance, deriving hypotheses from the theory involving the concept, and testing the hypotheses empirically. This is nothing less than conducting an empirical study of the concepts involved in one's research. Although Cronbach's formulation indicates a time-consuming, involved process, it also suggests that any testing of hypotheses or empirical study of relationships involves construct validity. In other words, the results of any empirical testing can provide evidence of validity of the concepts involved.

In construct validation, the investigator formulates a hypothesis based on theory and the theoretical interrelation of concepts; the measurement instrument is the operational definition of one of the concepts in the hypothesis. If the hypothesis is upheld, that is confirming evidence that the instrument has construct validity. If the hypothesis is not upheld, it could be because the instrument does not measure the concept, because the hypothesized relationships do not exist, because the theory is incorrect, or because of other causes. What is important is that there is no confirming evidence that the instrument has construct validity.

There are many approaches to construct validation, or types of hypotheses that can be tested. One of the most important is the *known-groups method*. This technique involves administering an instrument to groups of people with "known" characteristics and making directional hypotheses about the differences. For example, a scale designed to measure anxiety might be tested on a group of clients in an outpatient mental health clinic who are being treated for problems of anxiety and on a group of people in the general population. A predicted finding that the clients have higher anxiety than the general population would indicate construct validity.

Convergent validity and discriminant validity are additional forms of construct validation. In convergent validity, the hypothesis is that different measures of the construct yield similar results; in discriminant validity, that the construct can be differentiated from other similar constructs. One should be able to predict which variables are correlated with the construct and how they are correlated. In addition, one should also be able to predict which variables are not correlated with the construct.

Forte and Green (1994) used known groups, convergent, and discriminant approaches to test the construct validity of the Index of Peer Relations (Hudson 1982) with adolescents. In the known groups approach, they compared a sample of adolescents in an inpatient psychiatric hospital to adolescents in regular classrooms of a school district in the same city. As predicted, the clinical group was three times as likely to report peer problems as the nonclinical youths. In the convergent approach, they correctly predicted that youths with more peer problems would also have more problems with self-esteem and depression. In the divergent approach, they made two types of hypotheses: one, that the Index of Peer Relations would be inversely associated with some characteristics, and second that it would not be associated at all with other characteristics. They found that 1) greater peer problems were related to less family cohesion and family health and 2) peer problems were unrelated to age, education, income, or number of siblings. Overall, all their hypotheses were upheld, good evidence for the construct validity of the Index of Peer Relations when used with adolescents.

Yet another important approach to construct validation is *factor analysis*, which is discussed in chapter 11. In factor analysis, a large number of items are reduced into a smaller number of factors, or items that cluster together, that is, measure the same thing. The factors generated by this analytic technique are the constructs underlying the measures. Thus, factor analysis and construct validity are very closely related. In addition, the factors or constructs can be used in further analysis; for example, relationships can be ascertained between the factors and other variables in the study.

Greenley, Greenberg, and Brown (1997) used factor analysis and convergent approaches to validate an instrument to measure quality of life for people with severe mental illness. They gave the Quality of Life Questionnaire (QLQ) to 971 people with mental illness living in communities throughout Wisconsin. In the convergent approach, they predicted that clients with higher levels of functioning, those in treatment voluntarily, and those who were employed would have higher quality of life. The results were as predicted. In the factor analysis, the investigators expected the items to cluster in seven areas thought important to life quality: living situation, finances, leisure, family, social life, safety, and health (work was omitted because so few were employed). Statistical procedures suggested that the items did cluster together, but not nearly as well as they should. The investigators concluded that some items on their questionnaire were not clear or relevant. Another interpretation might be that the particular areas they predicted were not the key underlying constructs, for example, that social life was not a discrete part of quality of life.

Each of these methods of construct validation requires a research study whose purpose is measurement, usually a single-occasion naturalistic design. Generally, a single study is not considered sufficient to definitively establish the construct validity of a measure. Usually a series of studies, often over many years, is required before a measure is accepted as "truly" measuring the underlying meaning of its concept.

Summary

The term measurement refers both to operationalization, or making the link between a concept, its variable, and observable phenomena, and to the process of quantifying or assigning numbers to what is measured.

In developing categories for classifying the characteristics we wish to measure, the classifications themselves may take on the properties of the number system to a greater or lesser degree. This degree of isomorphism is reflected in the levels of measurement, which are used to determine what statistical procedures may be used with a particular variable. The levels of measurement are in ascending order, with each higher level having all the characteristics of the levels below it. The levels, from lowest, are nominal (characteristics may be categorized as different from each other), ordinal (categories are rank-ordered), interval (equal intervals between ranked categories), and ratio (equal intervals and an absolute zero).

A second crucial aspect of a measurement is validity, or how well the instrument captures the "true" characteristics. Reliability—whether the instrument gives consistent measures under varying circumstances—should be established through research before one can address the question of whether the instrument is measuring the correct thing. Types of reliability include stability, or consistency over time (also called test-retest reliability); equivalence between two versions of the same instrument or between two observers applying the same observational form (interobserver reliability); and homogeneity, or consistency among multiple items on a scale in a questionnaire.

Validity also has three forms. Content validity, assessed by examining the measure carefully, includes whether the instrument appears on the face of it to measure the concept, and whether it includes the whole range of meanings of the concept. Criterion validity, assessed through research, determines whether the instrument yields similar results to already validated instruments measuring the same thing, either concurrently or in the future. Construct validity uses formal hypothesis testing to make theoretically based predictions about the relationship between the measure and other concepts. Common forms of construct validity include testing known-groups to be sure the instrument measures differences among them, convergent and discriminant validity to see if the measure is related to other concepts in the predicted direction, and factor analysis of multi-item questionnaire scales to see if the underlying clusters of items seem to measure the concept.

10 Data Collection

Social work researchers and practitioners obtain data by asking people questions, observing them, or using available materials such as case records, organizational budgets, or statistical data. Although their purposes and procedures may differ, both have a need to collect good data, that is, data that are relevant, reliable, valid, and sensitive. In the preceding chapter, we discussed how to evaluate data collected by various means. In this chapter we discuss commonly used methods of collecting data in social work: self-report methods such as interviews and questionnaires, observation, and use of available data.

Selecting a Data Collection Method

Data collection is the "how?" part of an operational definition, or the procedures used to collect the information that allows us to categorize characteristics. Which procedure should be used depends on the type of information the investigator wishes to measure, that is, derives directly from the hypotheses, concepts, and variables.

Like other aspects of the research process, the selection and assessment of data collection methods is a trade-off between the ideal and the practical. This section gives an overview of when a data collection procedure should be used (under ideal circumstances), while the following sections look more closely at the approaches themselves and how to use them.

To measure people's subjective attitudes and opinions, internal traits such as self-esteem, or memories of past events, the most appropriate data collection procedure is a self-report method. Compared to both observation and use of available data, self-report methods are the most direct and valid means of getting information that only the respondent knows, such as opinions, perceptions, or memories. Internal traits or other unconscious aspects of personality may be inferred from behavior, but generally self-report measures are more practical. The limitation, of course, is that the information be something the respondent is willing (or able) to share. An attitude such as homophobia or anti-Semitism may not be accessible from self-report methods unless the purpose of the measure is disguised, which may raise ethical questions.

Self-report methods vary on the amount of personal contact between the investigator and the subject, from in-person interviews to written, mailed questionnaires completed with no possible additional input from the investigator. Interpersonal contact increases the possibility of establishing rapport, making it easier to gain cooperation and in-depth information from respondents, but it also reduces privacy and increases the possibility of bias. Consequently, the ideal approach depends on the necessity of interpersonal contact to accomplish the purpose of the research. If interpersonal interaction is important to place a respondent at ease, to get in-depth information, a lot of information, or information that requires much reflection and discussion, then in-person interviews are ideal. At the other extreme, if privacy is desirable, for example, the topic is one that people will not address honestly in others' presence, then a written questionnaire filled out while alone is ideal.

To measure human beings' current behavior or characteristics of the physical environment, the most appropriate data collection method is an observational method, either directly or unobtrusively. People are often unconscious of their behavioral patterns or report socially desirable behavior as their own. Similarly, reports from others, which may get at unconscious patterns, are filtered through the biases and desires of the reporter. The only way to be certain to get actual behavior is to observe it. Similarly, the only way to assess an environment—the comfort of a group home or the structure in a classroom—is to observe it. Of course, in many situations it is simply not practical nor feasible to observe, and some other method must substitute. In such cases, the investigator (and reader) must be continually aware that the substitute—self-report, others' reports, or available data—is but a perception or indicator of the behavior or physical environment.

To get information on past events or public records of events, the most appropriate data collection method is use of available data. For past events, often the only available source of data is records such as newspaper accounts, legislative hearings, personal diaries, or physical traces of activities. These are likely to be more reliable than the memories of participants, which are colored by their emotional reactions to the events (or forgotten). However, available data that rely on human gathering includes only what those who collected them thought suitable or desirable, that is, it is not an account of "reality," but of what people perceived as important. Often, however, this may be exactly what one wishes to study, for example, the history of public opinion toward workfare.

The preceding paragraphs on ideal means of gathering data for particular types of variables assume infinite patience, time, money, and access on the part of the investigator. However, for practical and ethical reasons, the ideal method may not be feasible or even desirable and the investigator must rely on other methods, or even on indicators with relatively tenuous connection to the original concept. For example, if one wishes to assess a family's interaction patterns while quarreling, the best way to do so is through observing them interact in a situation where family members' individual interests conflict. But, it is impractical to follow family members around all day until they quarrel, and some might consider it unethical to deliberately instigate a quarrel. Consequently, an investigator might employ self-report measures on which family members assess their general perceptions of the family's interaction, or give examples of recent disagreements and how they were handled. Such self-reports are undoubtedly distorted by memory, self-interest, and genuine differences in perceptions—we know that family members agree only generally on family functioning (Green and Vosler 1992; Kolevzon et al. 1988). But if such distortions are taken into account, the self-report may be an acceptable substitute for observation—at the least, it is a practical approximation. However, in interpreting the research, it is critical to understand the limitations of such indicators—we really do not know how the family truly interacts.

The following discussions of each data collection method include additional considerations in selecting a data collection method.

Bias in Data Collection Methods

Throughout this chapter—and throughout the book—references are made to biases that may affect data collection. Before taking up specific data collection methods, it may be well to provide an overview of different forms of bias.

"Bias" in data collection refers to systematic influences that diminish the reliability and validity of the data: sources of distortion may be found either in the data collection method or in the subjects from whom data are obtained. Bias in the data collection method may be embedded in the instrument itself. Questions or items may be worded in ways that suggest certain answers or may be skewed by the assumptions on which the instrument is based. If the data collection process can be influenced by a researcher, such as an interviewer or observer, another source of bias is introduced. Such investigator bias may be less important if there is a structured format such as a standardized interview, more important if a method depends to a large extent on the information processing capacities of the collector, such as unstructured interviewing or participant observation. Whatever their specific form, instrument and collector biases usually reflect a distortion toward what is expected. Thus a researcher or practitioner committed to the theory that delinquents have poor self-concepts may follow up on interview responses that might lead to evidence of poor self-concept more assiduously than responses pointing in the contrary direction. A more dramatic example is found in the history of science. Hoping to surpass Roentgen's discovery of x-rays, Blondot, a French scientist, developed a theory of N-rays. Blondot and his followers saw N-rays everywhere and published almost a hundred scientific papers on their properties, even though subsequent experiments proved quite conclusively that nothing of the kind existed (de Solla Price 1961).

Bias in the response of subjects (or clients) is a pervasive problem in data collection. Like researchers, subjects are vulnerable to expectancy effects based on prior convictions. An adult child convinced his aging mother cannot care for herself is more likely, when interviewed, to recall examples of confusion than competence in her behavior. In addition, response to questions may be influenced by what the respondent thinks would be appropriate to reveal, would be well received, would create the proper impression, and so on—in short, by what would be the socially desirable response under the circumstances. Even a subject being observed who is aware of the observation can produce atypical, often socially desirable reactions.

Regardless of its cause, bias can seldom be completely eliminated. It can however be watched for, controlled, and taken into account in the interpretation of findings. In the discussion that follows, we will emphasize the potentialities of bias in various data collection procedures and how to minimize it, i.e., how to increase reliability and validity through data collection methods.

Self-Report Methods

Self-report methods elicit respondents' views, attitudes, and traits—literally, anything that individuals can report about themselves. A common self-report method is the interview, which may be conducted face-to-face with the respondent or over the telephone. A closely related data collection method that also relies on self-report by the respondent is the questionnaire. Unlike the interview, which is oral, the questionnaire calls for written responses and is normally self-administered. Questionnaires may be given to respondents in groups or individually, or they may be sent through the mail. Interviews and questionnaires can be developed ad hoc for particular projects or can take the form of standardized instruments, that is, instruments designed to be standard tools for measuring some phenomenon, such as anomie, marital satisfaction, alcoholic tendencies, suitability of physical environment for toddlers, and so on.

Many different types of information can be elicited through the use of interviews and questionnaires. Simple factual data, such as marital status and occupation of respondents, or number of staff and funding sources of social agencies, are easily obtained. Respondents can also be asked about present or past behavior and experiences of their own or of others. Although some behavior can be observed directly, much cannot be. Some behavior and experiences occur infrequently, are private, or have already happened. Even when observation is possible, asking respondents about behavior may be more feasible and less costly in time, effort, and money. As mentioned, information about attitudes, feelings, beliefs, perceptions, values, and future plans can be obtained only from the respondent's self-report. And while most uses of self-report methods rely on the respondent giving a conscious report, they may also tap unconscious traits or deep-seated tendencies that the respondent is not readily aware of, as Rorshach's (1942) projective "ink blot" test is intended to do.

Comparison of Self-Report Methods

Once it is clear that self-report methods should be used, the decision to use personal interviews, telephone interviews, or questionnaires depends on the purpose of the study and consequently the type of information sought, constrained by such factors as budget, time available, and characteristics, number, and geographical dispersion of desired respondents. Each method has advantages and disadvantages, discussed briefly in what follows.

WRITTEN QUESTIONNAIRES Questionnaires are pencil-and-paper instruments with a structured format that typically consists of closed-ended questions and a limited number of open-ended questions. They are usually completed independently by respondents, either privately or in groups, although they may be read aloud to respondents who have difficulty reading (if read, some of the interaction effects of interviews are relevant).

Compared to the personal interview, the questionnaire is less expensive to prepare and is easier to administer. Because the directions are incorporated in the instrument, the questionnaire requires little skill to administer and in fact is usually self-administered. Consequently, the questionnaire can be mailed to prospective respondents, a procedure that enables the investigator to survey a very large sample that is widely dispersed geographically. Mailed questionnaires or those completed in private can address sensitive topics that respondents might be reluctant to discuss with an interviewer, and bias due to the interviewer is not a factor.

A major disadvantage of mailed questionnaires is, however, that the response rate is typically low. In fact, when cost is assessed against the number of usable responses, interviews, which usually have a higher response rate, are often more cost-effective. According to Selltiz et al. (1976:297), the most important factors affecting the rate of return from mail questionnaires are: "(1) the sponsorship of the questionnaire; (2) the attractiveness and clarity of the questionnaire format; (3) the length of the questionnaire; (4) the nature of the accompanying cover letter requesting cooperation; (5) the ease of filling out the questionnaire and mailing it back; (6) the inducements offered to reply; (7) the interest of the questions to the respondent and (8) the nature of the people to whom the questionnaire is sent."

Some of these factors have implications for the design of the questionnaire, such as attractiveness, length, and ease of completion. An excellent, detailed guide to questionnaire construction is Dillman's *Mail and Telephone Surveys* (1978). Other factors are outside the control of the investigator. Questionnaires are appropriate, for example, only for rather well-educated, literate people. The length—short to encourage returns—curtails the amount of information that can be obtained. The standardized format and prearranged questions also limit the amount and kind of data, which tend to be superficial compared to interview data; for example, it is not possible to probe responses to get greater detail or clarify misunderstandings. When questionnaires are mailed, there is no guarantee that the person filling it out was the person intended. Generally respondents may have greater confidence in the anonymity of unsigned questionnaires. However, more sophisticated respondents recognize that numbered questionnaires or use of other codes indicates the existence of a master list by which they can be identified by the researcher. (These codes are often put on questionnaires by researchers to help them identify nonrespondents to send follow-up requests to in an effort to improve the return rate.)

One generally begins to become concerned about low return rate when the percentage of responders falls below 70 percent, and particularly when it is less than half. With a low return rate the question becomes, "Do the nonrespondents differ from the respondents in ways that may distort the findings of the study?" For example, a family agency sends an anonymous mailed service satisfaction questionnaire to clients who had been seen during a particular period. Of the 50 percent who respond, the overwhelming majority report a high degree of satisfaction with service. One might ask if the nonresponders were more likely to be dropouts or others with less than satisfactory service experiences. If data are available it is important to compare responders and nonrespondents on relevant measures. This is not possible, of course, if the clients' responses are anonymous, as in the example just cited. It may be possible, however, to compare respondents with known characteristics about the population. Thus if the family agency questionnaire elicited information about the amount of service clients had received, it would be possible to determine if respondents were likely to be clients who had received more than the average amount of service. One might then make use of data from other studies that might shed light on the relation between length of service and client satisfaction.

Return rates for mailed questionnaires can usually be increased through repeated mailings, which, of course can raise the cost of the study. In interpreting results researchers can bring to bear whatever evidence or assumptions they may have about nonresponse bias. For example in the family agency study, they might suggest that levels of client satisfaction might have been lower if early terminators had been better represented in the sample—assuming relevant data supported that assumption.

AN EXAMPLE OF A MAIL QUESTIONNAIRE

To study adaptation to a new country, Kamya (1997) mailed a questionnaire to 125 recent immigrants from Africa to the United States. Fifty-seven returned the questionnaire (46 percent response rate), of which 52 questionnaires were usable. Both the low response rate and the unusable questionnaires are common difficulties with mailed questionnaires. In using the mail questionnaire, Kamya had to assume that his respondents would read English well enough to understand the questions and that the person who answered the questionnaire was the one to whom he sent it, not someone else in the household and not a family effort.

Kamya's mail questionnaire included five standardized self-report instruments that measured his key variables, stress, hardiness, self-esteem, coping resources, and spiritual well-being. Appropriately, one measure, the SAFE, was developed specifically to measure stress among immigrants who are acculturating to a new culture (Mena, Padilla, and Maldonado 1987). The SAFE consisted of 24 statements that respondents rated on an ordinal scale, from 1 = not stressful to 5 = extremely stressful for the respondent. Scores were then summed (treating the ordinal data as ratio). On another of the instruments, the Coping Resources Inventory (Hammer and Marting 1987), respondents rated how often they engaged in various behaviors (also an ordinal scale). In addition to the standardized measures, Kamya included several fixed-alternative questions that he wrote himself about their decision to emigrate and the role of religion in their lives.

IN-PERSON INTERVIEWS In-person interviews consist of face-to-face contact between one or a few respondents and an interviewer. The interview can range from a totally unstructured format to a highly structured format with either open-ended or closed-ended questions.

In-person interviews can elicit information in larger amounts and in greater depth than is possible with written questionnaires. In-person interviews are particularly useful for obtaining data on topics that are complex, highly sensitive, emotionally laden, or relatively unexplored. Questions can be explained and clarified, misunderstandings identified and corrected, and fuller answers and reasons for responses elicited through probing. Almost any group of respondents (the illiterate, children, those with failing sight, those suspicious of research, and so on) can be interviewed successfully. The rapport established by an in-person interviewer is important in drawing out respondents; however, there is considerable danger of bias induced by the interviewer. In-person interviews are almost essential in qualitative research because the interviewer analyzes the information and varies the questions simultaneously with collecting the data. Further, in-person interviews give the opportunity for observation by the interviewer, as well as collection of self-report data.

EXAMPLE OF AN IN-PERSON INTERVIEW

Cooper and Pearce (1996) studied the effects of relocation on elderly long-term patients with a psychiatric disability. They interviewed patients or the staff members most directly responsible for their care, if they were too ill to respond. Interviews were structured and included standardized measures that used ordinal summated scales, for example, subjective quality of life and social support. In addition to the self-report measures, the interviewers observed the elderly persons and made ratings on their ability to conduct day-to-day activities using two summated scales, the Barthel Index (Mahoney and Barthel 1965) and the Revised Elderly Persons Disability Scale (Fleming 1994). Finally, the interviewers also made rating of the subjects' depression based on behavioral indicators (Montgomery and Asberg Depression Rating Scale (Montgomery and Asberg 1979)). The combination of in-person interview and observation by the interviewer was appropriate. The subjects could report their subjective experiences such as quality of life, but were too disabled to complete a written questionnaire. Day-to-day activities are behaviors that an outsider can observe and verify with good reliability and validity. However, in the relatively short time of an interview, the interviewers could not see the patient perform all possible activities, so they had to rely on reports from caretakers as well. Observing symptoms of depression—a subjective state—is a common approach (often used by social workers), but it is possible to overrate depression because of similar-appearing physical or medication problems.

Compared to the use of questionnaires, in-person interviewing is very time-consuming and can be very expensive, although the quality of data and quantity from each individual may offset the cost. In larger projects, interviewers and coders must be hired, trained, and supervised. Not only must salaries be paid but also travel costs since most research interviewing takes place in respondents' homes. The cost of interviewing geographically dispersed respondents is so great that large-scale studies using interviews are rare unless cluster sampling is employed. In small-scale projects, however, an investigator (or team) may be able to interview a respectable number of respondents, say from fifteen to fifty, without spending a great deal of money.

TELEPHONE INTERVIEWS Telephone interviews combine some of the advantages and disadvantages of questionnaires and in-person interviews. Like questionnaires, telephone interviews are relatively inexpensive, they permit coverage of a large number of respondents over a wide geographical area, and data can be collected in a fairly short period of time. The opportunity is available to probe, clarify questions, and correct misinterpretations. The response rate is usually greater than mail questionnaires, although the widespread use of telemarketing and political polls have reduced response rates considerably, to only about 56 percent in 1989 (McMurtry 1997).

Telephone interviews are generally shorter than in-person interviews and the amount and type of data that can be collected are more limited. Rapport is less (with less opportunity to bias the responses) and nonverbal behaviors cannot be observed. Compared to in-person interviews, respondents usually give shorter answers and are somewhat less honest with sensitive questions (deLeeuw and van der Zouwen 1988; Sykes and Collins 1988). People without telephones or with unlisted numbers present obvious problems for telephone interviews, although a sample can be generated by dialing numbers selected at random from given telephone exchange codes (random digit dialing). Moreover, respondents who live in neighborhoods considered too dangerous for interviewers to enter may be interviewed by telephone. Telephone interviews, like in-person interviews, can be planned in advance with respondents so that a block of time convenient for the respondent can be set aside. Because they are so widely used in social sciences and national opinion polling, there are several manuals on the technical aspects of large-scale telephone interviewing (Groves et al. 1988; Lavrakas 1987).

AN EXAMPLE OF TELEPHONE INTERVIEWS

Hardina and Carley (1997) used telephone interviews to evaluate a California experiment to increase the work participation of welfare recipients. Potential respondents were first contacted by mail or telephone to set up an interview. Interviews were conducted in one of three languages and lasted 30 to 45 minutes. The interviews used a structured questionnaire focusing on recent hours of work, income, welfare grants, education, and employment. Telephone interviews allowed the investigators to contact a large number of people spread over a fairly large geographic area in a short period of time. However, telephone interviews in one language proved too difficult and consequently interviews with Hmong respondents (conducted in Hmong) took place in their homes and lasted 2 to 3 hours.

Degree of Structure

Interviews and to a lesser extent questionnaires may vary in the degree of structure, or how standard they are for each respondent. They may be as unstructured as nondirective or clinical interviews, or as structured or standardized as self-administered questionnaires, or may fall somewhere in between. The more structured or standardized the instrument, the greater the likelihood that each participant is responding to the same stimulus, but the less likely that in-depth information can be collected.

Completely standardized interviews and questionnaires consist of predetermined questions and responses. That is, questions are worded in a set manner, the order of questions is always the same, and for each question respondents are given a set of fixed alternative responses from which to choose. Explanations of the study and instructions for filling out the questionnaire or responding to the interview are also standard. To construct a standardized interview schedule or questionnaire, the investigator must already have a fair amount of knowledge about the phenomenon under study. One must know not only the relevant questions to ask but also what the possible responses are. If that is the case, a completely structured or standardized format should be considered. Such an instrument produces highly comparable data that are relatively quick and easy to analyze because they are already precoded or very nearly so. This type of instrument is particularly suitable for large-scale surveys.

A particular type of structured instrument consists of published standardized measures whose psychometric properties—e.g., their reliability and validity—have been tested. We shall reserve the term "standardized instrument" for such measures. In social work, these instruments are widely used in clinical practice and research. Examples include the Family Assessment Device (FAD) (Epstein, Baldwin, and Bishop 1983), the Beck Depression Inventory (BDI) (Beck 1967), and the Index of Spouse Abuse (Hudson and McIntosh 1981). (For further discussion of Rapid Assessment Instruments, see chapter 13.) Sourcebooks for such standardized instruments include two volumes by Fischer and Corcoran, *Measures for Clinical Practice*, 2d ed. (1994a, 1994b). Because modifying them may change their psychometric properties, such standardized instruments should be used "as is," in their published forms. However, one can develop structured questionnaires that are specific to a study, and indeed can mix standardized and newly created scales within a structured interview or questionnaire.

At the other extreme are unstructured interviews in which neither questions nor responses are predetermined. The interviewer obtains information about certain topics but is free to decide the content, wording, and sequence of questions to ask respondents. Because these interviews are very flexible and open, they require knowledgeable interviewers who can control their biases. Not only must the interviewers be skilled, but also they must be clear about the purposes of the study if they are to obtain complete and relevant information. Unstructured interviews are particularly useful when little is known about the phenomenon being studied, as in exploratory research, or for the kind of indepth investigations characteristic of qualitative approaches.

AN EXAMPLE OF AN UNSTRUCTURED IN-PERSON INTERVIEW

Shaw and Shaw (1997) sought to determine how social work practitioners make judgments to themselves about whether their work with a client is going well or not. They conducted in-depth unstructured interviews with 15 British social workers. They describe the general guidelines that the interviews followed (page 70):

Each social worker talked in detail to one of the authors about two recent examples of their work, one in which they thought they did the work well and one in which they thought they performed less well. They were asked to describe the work and to say how they knew whether it went well or not. They were encouraged to identify the evidence specific to each instance of their work. They were also invited to consider whether the service users would have reached a similar or different criteria in evaluating the service received.

Semistructured interviews fall between the two extremes just discussed and combine elements of the structured and unstructured interviews. For example, a semistructured interview schedule might consist of open-ended questions with suggested probes to elicit data that respondents might not provide spontaneously. The wording of the questions and probes and the order in which the questions are to be asked are predetermined, but the response categories are not. Other variations are possible. A semistructured instrument might contain both fixed-alternative and open-ended questions; may contain specific or suggested probes; and may or may not allow the interviewer some flexibility in the wording or rephrasing of questions or in asking additional probes. Because of its versatility in being able to combine many of the advantages of both completely structured and unstructured interviews, the semistructured interview is probably used more often by social work investigators than any other type of interview. It is an appropriate and frequently used format for intake interviews as well.

Questionnaires may vary in structure much as interviews do, primarily through the use of open-ended questions. However, less structured questionnaires are generally problematic. Respondents are seldom willing to write much and what is written usually proves difficult to code. Respondents tend to be those who are highly motivated by the topic or the chance to express themselves, making the generalizability of the results suspect. Consequently, in general, open-ended questions on questionnaires are used selectively, when it is not possible to predetermine possible answers, or when respondents may desire an opportunity to make open-ended comments.

Types of Questions

Whether one uses interviews or questionnaires, the questions may be open or closed. Closed or fixed-alternative questions provide categories of responses from which the respondent chooses. Examples of fixed-alternative questions are as follows:

Do you currently have a child care arrangement? (Please circle one response)

1. Yes
2. No

If yes, how satisfactory is this arrangement? (Please circle one response)

1. Very satisfactory
2. Satisfactory
3. Unsatisfactory
4. Very unsatisfactory

What is your yearly family income (before deductions)?

1. Under $10,000
2. $10–19,999
3. $20–29,999
4. $30–39,999
5. $40–49,999
6. $50–59,999
7. $60–69,999
8. $70–79,999
9. $80–89,999
10. $90–99,999
11. $100,000 or over

To develop fixed-alternative items, the investigator needs to know what the relevant responses might be and, in some cases, how they might distribute themselves. For example, the income brackets in the third question just given would be inappropriate for a sample of families on welfare. Not only would it show a lack of sensitivity, it would also yield little variance, for virtually all responses would fall in the first two categories. Sometimes enough information can be obtained from pretests using open-ended questions to develop appropriate categories for closed questions.

Open-ended questions do not present fixed choices to respondents but allow them to answer in whatever way they choose. For example, dual career couples in one study (Smith and Reid 1986) were asked:

1. To what extent do each of you feel financially responsible for the other?
2. What are the advantages and disadvantages of the type of financial arrangement that you have?

A technique often used with open questions is going from the general to the specific through the use of probes. The same study provides an illustration of this funnel approach.

3. How do you manage family finances?
(Probe for the following if not already answered)
   a. Do you pool your incomes, do each of you manage your own money, or some combination?
   b. (If each manages own money): Who pays for what or who contributes what?
   c. Do you have separate or joint checking accounts? Separate or joint savings accounts?

Generally, fixed-alternative questions are most appropriate for factual information and open-ended questions for complex data. Closed items offer the advantage of obtaining uniform data for measurement and thus may be more reliable. Because the wording of the categories defines the dimension the investigator is interested in, the respondents are forced to make comparable responses on the dimensions of interest. For example, responses of dual-career couples to the open-ended question,"How much leisure time do you have to spend together?" may include many different dimensions: "Not enough," "About an hour a day," "We usually go out every weekend," "That's the main thing that suffers," and "We make it a point to get away together at least twice a year." If the investigator is interested in a particular dimension such as number of hours per week or the respondents' perception of the adequacy of the amount of leisure time, this interest could better be pursued through the use of a fixed-alternative question. Response categories for closed questions also help clarify what the question means. For example, the categories "single," "married," "separated," "divorced," and "widowed" help to clarify what is meant by "marital status." Another major advantage of closed questions is the ease of processing the data for analysis; fixed-alternative responses are quickly and easily coded or may even be precoded and scanned directly into a computer for statistical analysis.

Disadvantages of closed questions include the difficulty of constructing good categories for some items. If categories are not mutually exclusive and exhaustive, reliability and validity suffer. Inaccuracy results if a major category is omitted: some respondents may put their answer under "other" while some may choose the closest category instead. Another disadvantage is the superficial nature of responses to fixed-alternative questions. One may know only the level of satisfaction with child care arrangements, not why an arrangement was satisfactory or unsatisfactory to a parent. (To obtain such information, closed questions could be followed by an open question asking the respondent to explain the answer.) Respondents can be irritated if they are forced to make a choice when none of the alternatives is acceptable to them. Another serious disadvantage of fixed-alternative questions is that respondents can easily give false information without the researcher's being aware of it. For example, respondents may find it preferable to choose an alternative rather than admit they have no knowledge about the topic, or to indicate an opinion when they really have none.

Many of the advantages and disadvantages of open questions are apparent from the preceding discussion. Open-ended questions are flexible, easy to develop and administer, and, in interviews, can be used to develop rapport and encourage the cooperation of the respondent. Ambiguity, misunderstanding, and lack of knowledge are more likely to be detected; in interviews, the opportunity is available to clear them up. Respondents can provide their own frame of reference and indicate salient dimensions. In-depth information is more readily obtained through open questions.

Major disadvantages of open questions include the lack of comparability in responses, difficulty in developing categories, and time spent in coding. A great deal of effort can be expended in developing a manageable number of nonoverlapping categories for the responses, especially if more than one dimension has been tapped (see chapter 11). Sometimes a set of categories for each major dimension tapped needs to be developed for a single open-ended question. For example, on a written questionnaire, Fortune et al. (1997) asked field instructors if they had difficulties or misunderstandings with their field student, whom did they consult with and what kinds of help did they get? Their responses were coded along three different dimensions: the type of problem, who was involved in resolving it, and the outcome.

In larger projects, the people who code responses to open-ended questions must be trained until a sufficient degree of intercoder reliability is obtained, and they need to be supervised throughout the coding process. In smaller studies in which one or two people both collect and code the data, it is still advisable to have at least some items, the more difficult or more important ones, recoded for reliability purposes.

Scales

The response categories for fixed-alternative questions may be organized at any level of measurement, although as we shall see, the most common is ordinal. Fixed-alternative questions are often referred to as scales. Often, too, several related questions at the same level of measurement are grouped together and collectively referred to as a scale. Thus, a researcher may refer to "a nominal scale" meaning a fixed alternative question (or set of questions) whose response categories are at the nominal level of measurement.

For example, an investigator may wish to examine clients' perceptions of their social workers. From some exploratory interviews with clients, the investigator generates a list of descriptive statements that includes the following:

> Was warm and understanding
> Helped me get thing I needed
> Said things I didn't understand
> Gave me useful advice
> Helped me learn things about myself
> Seemed uninterested in my problems

The statements appear to be useful in getting clients to reveal their perceptions of their practitioners, but what type of fixed alternative responses should the investigator use?

The simplest method would be to use the statements on a *checklist*—or as a nominal scale. A client could be asked to indicate the statement that best describes the social worker, to check all that apply, or to make other choices, such as checking the two most descriptive statements. As the example suggests, checklists are simple and quick to complete, but they give minimal information and are subject to social desirability effects. Some clients might tend to check the more positive statements simply to avoid appearing impolite or ungrateful (a social desirability effect).

Usually, information is more useful if the answers are at least ordinal level. One approach is to have respondents *rank order* a set of items according to some criterion. To continue with our example, clients could be asked to order the set of statements from "most like" to "least like my worker." The "most like" would receive a 1, the next most like a 2, and so on, until the entire set had been ranked. The chief advantage of rank order scales is that they require the respondent to state a position on each item relative to the others. As a result respondents are prevented from limiting themselves to obvious, perhaps socially desirable, choices; and what is more, they must provide discriminations among all options given. For example, one might learn from the rank orders about the relative value accorded advice-giving compared to other intervention methods. By the same token, however, the measures of "most like," "most important," and so on, are always relative to the other items in the set ranked. Some clients might not have regarded any of the items as descriptive of their workers! Moreover, ranking is a cognitively difficult task for many people, and it is usually assumed that five or six items are about the maximum that most respondents can rank successfully (the exception is a complex procedure called Q sort, which requires respondents to put items, on cards, in piles whose sizes approximate the normal distribution). The difficulties of the task can be lessened by using a partial rank order scale. For example, respondents could rank order the three statements most descriptive or could select the "most like" or "least like" from a set of four statements.

Another common method, perhaps the most frequently used ordinal scaling approach in data collection, is to have subjects rate each item in a set separately and then to combine ratings into a total score that provides a measure of some attribute—a *summated rating* scale. Thus the investigator in our example might measure the clients' evaluation of their workers on a positive to negative continuum. Statements describing the worker in both positive and negative terms (like those given in the example) would be generated. (A total of fifteen items is usually regarded as minimal in such scaling.) The client would rate each statement on some type of numerical scale, for example, on a scale of 1 to 10 with 10 defined as "all the time" and 1 as "none of the time," or words to that effect. In this and following examples, the scales may be referred to as *anchored scales* because the descriptors provide a meaning or anchor for the responses.

Was warm and understanding
none of the time 1   2   3   4   5   6   7   8   9   10 all of the time
Helped me get the thing I needed
none of the time 1   2   3   4   5   6   7   8   9   10 all of the time

A variation would be to provide descriptive categories for the different scale points:

Was warm and understanding

never   seldom   sometimes   frequently   always

Said things I did not understand

never   seldom   sometimes   frequently   always

When descriptive categories are used, each category is given a straightforward numerical weight: always = 5; frequently = 4; and so on.

With each item rated, after giving "reverse" weight to negative items, one simply adds up the item scores to obtain a total score. (In reverse weighting, items that suggest positive characteristics of the social worker would be scored normally while the scores for the items that suggest negative characteristics would be reversed; in the example above, the responses for "said things I did not understand" would be scored always = 1, frequently = 2, and so on.)

Summated rating scales are easily administered and scored. They arbitrarily assume that each item is of equal weight, and they assume that the distance between responses is equal, i.e., they use arithmetic procedures appropriate for interval level of measurement with ordinal data. However, they tend to correlate well with scales in which more elaborate weighting methods are used. If it is important to assure that summated scales do meet the assumptions of interval data, several procedures are available to test whether respondents seem to be answering as if the categories were interval (Borgatta and Bohrnstedt 1980; Kenny 1986). On the negative side, summated scales are vulnerable to "halo" effects (the tendency to give items similar ratings) as well as "errors of central tendency" (avoiding extreme values).

It should also be noted that individual items can be treated as separate scales, whether or not ratings are summed. Thus clients' ratings of their workers in respect to their warmth and understanding could be analyzed as a variable in its own right.

A more complicated method of ordinal scale is Guttman or *cumulative scaling*, where items are structured in terms of progressive steps or stages. Such a scale requires a single dimension. In the example given, for instance, an aspect of service might involve helping the client secure employment and it might be possible to view the helping process in terms of the following succession of items:

1. Social worker discussed possibility of helping me get a job.
2. Social worker made active effort to help me get a job.
3. Social worker helped me get a job.

In such a succession, it is assumed that each scale point signifies that previous points of the scale have been passed, that is, in order for the practitioner to help the client get a job, there would ordinarily have been an "active effort," which would have been preceded by "discussion." In this manner, the score informs one exactly how far the worker proceeded in the client's eyes. Although such unidimensional scales have obvious strengths, it is difficult to apply them to complex phenomena and the progression of scale points is always open to question. (Conceivably a worker might help the client get a job without making an "active effort," at least as defined by the client.)

Instrument Construction

The type of instrument to be developed depends on prior decisions such as the specific method of obtaining data and the degree of structure. Whatever the format—a self-administered questionnaire, a semistructured interview schedule, an unstructured interview guide—a great deal of careful planning goes into procedures such as instrument development, training of interviewers, writing instructions for interviewers and respondents, and so on. The intent is to obtain reliable, valid data that will answer the research question or hypothesis.

Clarity is essential in instrument development. Concerns about clarity that have already been discussed, in formulating hypotheses or research questions and in defining concepts, are paramount at this stage. Clear, precise operational definitions of all the major concepts of the study are crucial, for they provide the basic framework for the instrument. Now the concern for clarity extends to the wording of questions, to instructions to interviewers and respondents, and to the format of the questionnaire or interview schedule.

Several suggestions can be offered for writing clear, precise, relevant questions. To begin with, the knowledge and understanding level of the respondents must be considered to develop questions relevant to them. Questions should be asked of respondents only if there is reason to believe they have the desired information. For example, one would not ask a parent if his teenage son had ever smoked marijuana. One might, however, ask the parent if he thought his son had smoked marijuana. Another example of an irrelevant question is asking about attitudes or opinions on a topic about which many of the respondents have given little thought. One should avoid professional jargon, slang words, or other words and phrases that the respondents may not understand. Questions about chemical dependencies asked of community residents might need to be worded differently from those asked of pharmacologists. Questions should be appropriate for the culture of the intended respondents; for example, as noted in chapter 3, parts of the Children's Action Tendency Scale had different meanings to Latino and Caucasian children (Briggs, Tovar, and

Corcoran 1996). One must be careful, however, not to be patronizing in the wording of questions; this is most apt to occur with certain groups like the poor or minorities.

A number of commonly used terms, which on the surface seem quite clear, must be defined more precisely for research purposes. Examples are income, employment, family, and child care arrangement. Does family mean family of origin, family of procreation, extended family, only members currently residing in the family home, or what? Do child care arrangements include regular school, parents taking care of their own children at home or at work, children taking care of themselves, siblings looking after one another, a neighbor looking in on the children occasionally, some of the above, none of the above? Possible interpretations such as these must be anticipated and specific questions developed to obtain comparable and desired information from respondents. Developing questions that are precise and short, both requirements for clarity, sometimes represents quite a challenge for the investigator.

When possible, time frames and anchor points should be provided for respondents. Instead of asking a student how often he studies in the school library, one might ask how many times he studied in the library for as long as 15 minutes during the past week, specifying when the week began and ended. One might also want estimates of the amount of time spent studying in the library each time or to ascertain if the past week was typical in this regard. Descriptions that serve as anchor points are useful to respondents (or coders) and help to improve consistency of the data.

Clarity and precision also require that questions be simple, not compound. That is, each question should ask about only one idea. Problems arise if it is not clear whether the answer refers to all or part of a question or if it is possible that the responses to the two ideas might be different. "Are you satisfied with your child care arrangement and do you plan to continue it?" is an example of a compound question that should be separated into two questions. Sometimes confusion results from a related practice—the investigator's making an implicit assumption about a phenomenon and then asking the respondent a question based on this assumption. For example, students might be asked,"Which aspects of your field placement are you dissatisfied with? your field instructor, lack of supervision, distance to the placement, lack of fit with classes." Respondents who were satisfied with their placements would have no way to respond, yet the results would misleadingly imply that all respondents were dissatisfied about something.

Although the need for unambiguous, specific, relevant questions cannot be stressed too much in the construction of any research instrument, this matter assumes even greater importance in the development of self-administered questionnaires because there is no possibility of additional clarification.

Clarity and specificity are also crucial in explanations and instructions on self-administered questionnaires and on interview schedules for the interviewer. The format of the instrument should be logical and uncluttered, with attention given to clarity in presentation. For example, one should be able to discern immediately which are instructions to the interviewer, which are questions to be asked, which are probes, whether to read response categories to respondents, where and how to record answers to each question, when the topic or frame of reference shifts, and so on. Even if solo investigators can keep details in their heads, they will need to convey their procedures to others in their written reports.

As always, an important consideration in instrument construction is avoiding bias. Questions should be worded in a neutral manner and in some cases may need to be prefaced with statements designed to cut down on social desirability effects. For example, a question might read, "Some people believe that married couples should have children if they can while other people believe it is all right for married couples to remain childless if they wish. How do you feel about this?" The layout of the instrument should also discourage bias. The order and direction of questions can influence people's responses, especially in telephone interviews (Bishop et al. 1988). Questions should discourage a string of similar responses, such as all "yeses," or checking straight down the middle or one side of a list of items. Care should also be taken to avoid bias in explaining the purpose of the study, in providing directions for respondents and interviewers, and in selecting questions to be asked.

Finally a trial run, or pretest, of the instrument with a few respondents will provide helpful feedback on such things as appropriateness and scope of the items, completion time, and administration procedures. Also a pretest can provide interviewers with practice in using the instrument.

Selection and Training of Interviewers

The persons who conduct interviews are critical to the success of the research, as they can influence refusal rate, the amount of information respondents give, bias or lack of it, and so on. Matching interviewers and respondents on such characteristics such as sex, race, age, and socioeconomic status can affect the amount of data obtained and the way people respond to questions. Generally, the rapport gained from matching must be balanced against possible bias from overidentification. Matching on relevant attributes should be considered, particularly in studies dealing with sensitive issues, but the decision will depend on a number of factors, including the rapport/overidentification equation, feasibility, and costs.

Both social workers and nonsocial workers are used as interviewers in social work research. For most studies, experienced research interviewers, whether social workers or not, are probably preferred. Studies using unstructured interviews may require interviewers with knowledge in the general area being investigated, for example, corrections or child welfare. Social workers or graduate social work students are often selected as research interviewers because of their interviewing experience. Many interviewing skills are transferable from social work to research interviews, but research interviewing is different in a number of ways, so social workers should receive training that emphasizes the differences for research purposes.

The major differences between interviewing in practice and in research flow from the different purposes of the two activities. The purpose of the social work interview is to provide service to clients; the purpose of the research interview is to obtain data for the study. Consequently, the practitioner may follow areas of client strengths and problems, while the research interviewer focuses on the information needed for the research. The practitioner is interested in establishing a professional relationship with the client; the research interviewer tries only to establish rapport to collect the necessary information. Consequently, the practitioner expresses empathy and support while the research interviewer will use minimal neutral prompts; the practitioner individualizes his or her relationship with the client, while the research interviewer attempts to present similar stimuli to each respondent. The practitioner often plans to see the client over a period of time; the research interviewer usually sees the respondent only once. Consequently, the research interviewer seldom has a second opportunity to ask questions overlooked, clarify ambiguous responses, or pursue fruitful avenues with probes. Unlike the practitioner, the research interviewer has no service to offer the client regardless of what issues the client may raise. (The one possible exception is referral if this contingency is planned for in the study.) Consequently, the research interviewer must be careful not to raise expectations for service or to slip into a "counseling mode."

Regardless of the interviewers' background and experience, training is needed in data collection for the specific study for which they are hired. The content, length, and thoroughness of training will vary depending primarily on the requirements of the study. Some of the aspects training must deal with are making contact with the prospective respondent (how to present oneself, explain the purpose of the study, handle confidentiality issues, and elicit voluntary cooperation); interviewing techniques including asking questions, probing, responding to comments and questions, remaining objective and neutral; handling various contingencies; and recording information. Role playing is a useful technique in this type of training. If interviews are to be taped, interviewers should be carefully trained in the use of tape recorders for recording interview data. Again practice is important. Because tape recorders are so common (many of the interviewers will probably own one), this training may seem unnecessary, but it is not.

An example of preparation of interviewers comes from Hayden and Goldman's (1996) study of the stress levels and need for service among families of adults with mental retardation. Five doctoral students from various social sciences departments served as interviewers. They attended six hours of classroom training and ten to twelve hours of field training. Training included viewing a videotape on interviewing, additional information on specific interviewing techniques, review of the survey instrument, observation of interviews conducted by experienced field interviewers, and being observed and receiving feedback.

The Interview in Small-Scale Studies

In the foregoing section, we assumed that the study was large enough to require a group of interviewers—hence considerations involving selection and training. Somewhat different considerations apply in small-scale studies in which the investigator does all the interviewing.

In the single case study in which the social worker takes on a practitioner-researcher role, structured dual-purpose segments that serve both research and clinical assessment purposes can be built into interviews, around the less-structured interviewing that serves primarily practice goals. For example, a practitioner can conduct assessment interviews at various points in a case to monitor progress on the client's problems. Such interviews can be semistructured, guided by specific questions the practitioner prepares in advance. For example, if the client's problem is fighting with other children, questions can be asked about the frequency and nature of fights in a given period. Considerations of clarity and the like suggested earlier apply particularly to this kind of interviewing, which serves research purposes within a practice context. The practitioner-researcher can also make use of questionnaires tailor-made for the case at hand or quickly administered standardized Rapid Assessment Instruments (see chapter 13).

And of course, investigators may do their own interviewing in small-scale studies in which research is the only activity. In any case, investigators who do their own interviewing should apply to themselves the preparatory requirements they would apply to interviewers they might hire. Self-training through pretest interviews is particularly important.

Whether conducting a single case study as a practitioner-researcher or interviewing a small sample of respondents in a research undertaking, the single investigator has to be especially alert to bias—in particular, the natural tendency to shape the interview, or what is taken from it, in the direction of the investigator's expectations. A good control for bias, and a means of giving the study greater credibility, is to tape-record the interviews and have samples of the tapes assessed by an independent reviewer.

Observation

Observation as a data-collection method entails visual monitoring of a situation, either in person or through preserved media such as videotapes. Observation may be quite informal or very systematic, and may use simple recording with pen and paper or elaborate, mechanized procedures for timing and recording data.

Whether engaged in research or not, all social workers use observation as a way of obtaining information. Observation of behavior is used to obtain descriptive information and informally to supplement or confirm data obtained by other methods. In practice, as a widow talks about the death of her husband, the practitioner may be alert to her affect (vocal quality, facial expression, whether crying or not, and so on), as well as to her words. A community organizer may be aware of the reaction a particular community leader seems to engender in others at meetings. A research interviewer may pick up clues about the quality of the interview data being obtained by observing signs of fatigue or disinterest, distracting influences, and so on.

Systematic observational methods might include having clients observe themselves or family members to monitor progress (see chapter 13). A group worker might record group interaction to help ensure all clients have a chance to participate. Researchers use observation to study individual and group behavior. Marital communication; parent-child and family interaction; children's behavior in the classroom, at camp, and in other group settings; case studies of mental institutions or social service agencies; and ethnographic research in subcultures such as gangs, hospital emergency room staff, or immigrants: these are only a few examples of research in which observation may be the primary data collection method.

For reasons that will soon be apparent, observation is a demanding, time-consuming, and often expensive method of data collection. Why then use direct observation as the primary data collection technique? Simply put, it is because observation is the best or only method of obtaining certain data. Observation is clearly the best way to study communication patterns, for example, in interaction between dyads such as parent-child or marital partners, or among group members such as families or work groups. Observation may be the best way of obtaining information about other individual or group behavior even when other data sources are possible. For example, a teacher could describe a child's hyperactive behavior in the classroom or group leaders could describe their individual leadership styles. Yet most researchers would agree that, compared to these verbal reports, direct observation would probably yield more objective, systematic data.

Observation provides direct access to phenomena under study: the investigator can see or hear what is happening. While the observer's biases and the subject's reactions to being observed are inevitable limitations, distortions inherent in data reported by others can be eliminated.

Preparation for observation involves decisions in three areas: what to observe, where and how to observe it, and how to record the data. Although we review these areas separately, the considerations in each apply to the others. As with other activities of the research process, these decisions are interdependent and overlapping. Consequently, many of the points discussed will need to be considered almost simultaneously regardless of the order in which they are mentioned.

What to Observe

The purpose of the study provides the general guidelines concerning which behaviors to observe. Operational definitions pinpoint more specifically the behaviors that will serve as indicators of major concepts in the study. The degree of specificity and precision provided by operational definitions may vary, however, by the type of observational study. Essentially, this relates to how structured the observational methods will be, which in turn depends on the state of knowledge about the behaviors to be investigated and the purpose of the study. An exploratory study using unstructured observation will not be able to specify as precisely the relevant behaviors or aspects of behavior to observe as the hypothesis-testing study using structured observation must. In fact, the purpose of an exploratory or an ethnographic study may be to ascertain what behaviors are likely given certain conditions or what aspects of behavior are relevant in certain situations. On the other hand, structured observation requires a very detailed level of specificity: that is, one must be able to ascertain exactly which acts or actions constitute each relevant behavior and which do not.

Even in unstructured field observation, the investigator should be as clear as possible about what will be observed and why. For example, is the purpose of the study to describe a particular group or organization, or is it to be able to generalize about certain kinds of group interaction or organizational behavior? Is the appropriate unit of analysis camp groups, campers, camp counselors or leaders, camper counselor interaction, or camp behavior in general? Although the focus may shift as the investigator learns more about the group, these shifts should be conscious decisions. With a particular focus of observation in mind, the investigator decides about the unit of observation—whether to record events or time periods. Some of the options and considerations are presented below.

MOLAR OR MOLECULAR LEVELS The distinction between molar and molecular concerns the level of abstraction in defining what is to be observed. "Molar" (large, generally defined units) and "molecular" (small, specifically defined units) actually reflect ends of a continuum, with any number of mid-range possibilities. Generally, narrative descriptions or ratings of behavior on scales are used with larger, or molar, units of behavior, while category systems are usually based on smaller, or molecular, units. Describing group leadership styles as democratic, authoritarian, or laissez-faire implies a very molar view of behavior. Still molar, but less so, is the description of a group leader's behavior as "played softball with the boys." A molecular unit would be a single act such as "hit the ball" or "ran to first base." Even smaller units of behavior are "gripped the bat" and "looked at the ball." In observing verbal interaction, one can use larger units of behavior, such as the entire discussion between a husband and wife on a topic or a paragraph of typescript from an audiotape. Alternatively, one could use a molecular unit such as a simple sentence or its equivalent or, smaller still, a word.

Both molar and molecular units have advantages and disadvantages. Generally, molar units are considered to have greater validity, for they tend to capture "natural" behaviors or behavioral sequences. Molecular units may segment behaviors in such a way that the units bear little resemblance to the behaviors. On the other hand, molecular units tend to be more reliable since they can be operationally defined more precisely and are more objective. Molar units involve more complex behavior and thus require more inference on the part of observers.

> An example of unstructured field observation comes from Susan Mercer's (1996) study of a Navajo nursing home for the elderly. Based on review of the Navajo culture, Mercer began the study with the assumption that care in the nursing home would be influenced by important cultural aspects such as the view of the world as a balance in harmony, obligations to family and clan, and the centrality of the home. Her broad research question was how these factors affected admissions and care. She spent five weeks on the reservation—in the facility and with residents, their families, and staff (participant observation)—and she interviewed key informants who provided information and assessed the validity of her conclusions (unstructured interviews). She recorded her observations, interactions, and events in a diary, using narrative accounts. Although she interviewed and interacted with individuals, her focus was on a limited range of topics and behavioral patterns and she recorded at the broadest molar level—general events related to admissions and care.

UNITS AS EVENTS OR TIME INTERVALS Recording for observation can be done using events—something that happens—or time intervals—a period of time during which the observation takes place. An event is a natural unit such as an aggressive act, an instance of prosocial behavior, or the use of the first-person pronoun. Construing units as events is a simple, straightforward way of proceeding with observational research. It is particularly advantageous when phenomena to be observed occur infrequently or if they would be distorted if broken into time intervals. Limitations include difficulties in ascertaining reliability, especially when it is hard to discern when events start and end and when observers overlook events because of their inattentiveness.

In using time intervals, the investigator observes the occurrence or nonoccurrence of some defined behavior within a fixed block of time. Time intervals are generally brief, usually less than 20 seconds. If the behavior—hitting, for example—occurs within the interval, the occurrence is recorded. Different aspects of behavior can be simultaneously observed and recorded, for example, hitting and swearing. Interval recording can produce a precise picture of behavior, readily quantified in terms of percents of intervals in which the behavior occurs. Reliability is easily determined since observers record observations within this same set of intervals. Diagram 10.1 illustrates a recording format and hypothetical observations for two behaviors.

DIAGRAM 10.1

BEHAVIOR	INTERVALS (10 SECONDS)																
Staring	X	X	X					X	X				X	X	X			
Headbanging				X	X					X	X						X	

X = behavior occurred during the 10-second interval

Time interval units may not be appropriate for infrequently occurring behavior. Also, they may not work well for behavior whose meaning may be lost if fragmented into brief time intervals. Human speech, for example, loses its meaning if recorded at too small a time interval. Finally, time interval observation with its need to maintain constant attention and frequent recording is a demanding task, usually not one for observers like parents and teachers, who must work observation into other activities.

Whatever is selected for observation and whatever form the observational unit takes, some plan for sampling units must usually be developed. In some circumstances, to be sure, it may be decided to try to observe the occurrence of a defined event without selectivity. For example, a parent may be instructed to observe and record tantrums whenever they occur, or a client may self-observe all instances of depressive episodes. This type of observation requires an omnipresent observer for the events in question; it tends to be used in practice applications, as the examples suggest.

Perhaps the most frequently used sampling method in observational research consists of time blocks that may be selected purposively or randomly (chapter 8). A classroom may be observed every other afternoon between 2 and 3 p.m. or at three randomly chosen hour periods during the week. Additional sampling frames may involve subjects and settings. In the observation of classrooms, for example, certain children, again purposively or randomly selected, can be observed. Different settings may be sampled, purposively, as a rule, in order to study a behavior in different situations. Assessment of unassertive behavior in a single case might involve sampling of target behaviors at work, at home, and with friends. Observation of subjects in natural versus laboratory settings (discussed below) may also be viewed as a sampling issue.

Where and When to Observe

Several additional considerations are involved in determining how the observations are to be made. These include where and under what conditions the observations will be made, who will make them, whether the subjects know they are being observed, and the degree of structure or control the investigator imposes over the observational situation. The extent to which the investigator will have options in these areas depends on the phenomenon under study and the research questions or hypotheses.

In terms of where, some phenomena, such as interaction among children of different races at camp, or a child's talking without permission in class, can be observed only in natural or field settings. Other behavior, such as proximal behavior of a young child to his parent, or communication patterns among family members, can be studied in laboratory settings. Either type of setting may provide the opportunity for obtaining descriptive data, formulating or testing hypotheses, or conducting experiments. Laboratory settings offer the distinct advantage of a high degree of control over extraneous factors. On the other hand, there may be a question about the artificiality of the behavior and the possibility that the subject's behavior might be influenced by the observation process(testing effects). The same question would apply to field observations if the subjects were aware of being observed. One might, however, expect the effect on behavior of being observed to diminish more rapidly in natural settings.

Studies vary in whether subjects know they are being observed, and how obtrusive the observer is. In social work research, subjects usually know they are being observed since their consent to be a part of the study is normally required (chapter 3). There are still some situations in which it is possible for the presence of the observer to be concealed; even when this is not possible, there may still be choices concerning the degree of obtrusiveness of the observer and concerning what is said to the subject about what is being observed.

In field observations of group behavior, a decision must be made about the extent to which the observer will participate in the group's activities. For example, as a participant observer in a hospital surgical training program, Bosk (1989) participated as a "gofer"—fetching charts, opening bandages, and so on—, as a sounding board, and as a referee in disputes, but not as a budding surgeon.

Obviously, some match between the characteristics of the group and of the observer makes observation easier, although as with interviewers too much similarity may result in overidentification. For example, Sykes would have found it difficult to be accepted in girls' gangs had she been male, but her race made less difference and she was able to gain entree to African-American, Latino, and white girls' gangs (1997). The possibilities range from only observing and not participating at all to only ostensibly participating by concealing the observer role from the group. Concealment raises questions of ethics and feasibility among others, while the pure observer role tends to keep the investigator on the outside and thus limits the data obtainable. The role of participant observer is frequently decided on as the best and most natural strategy. Usually only the fact that the participant-observer is a investigator and a very general explanation of the research purpose are conveyed to the group. (See chapter 12.)

In laboratory settings subjects must be informed about the observation and they must consent to it, but they may not be told exactly which behaviors are of interest. For example, a mother may be told that her child's play behavior is being observed when in fact it is her own behavior that is of interest. The observer may or may not be engaged in activities (treatment, doing structured tasks, group discussion, or the like) with the subjects. The observer(s) may be in the same room with the subjects in full view or may be in another room behind a screen or one-way mirror. Alternatively, the behavior may be recorded mechanically on film, audiotape, or videotape (see chapter 14). The degree of obtrusiveness of the observation depends on which of these techniques is used and how it is carried out.

The observational setting can be unstructured or structured to try to elicit or control selected behaviors. The investigator may assume the role of passive observer or may attempt to influence the behavior being observed. The investigator intervenes directly by manipulating the independent variable in field and laboratory experiments. In between, the investigator may provide structure by way of group tasks or situational tests that elicit the type of behaviors being studied.

For example, one might ask a family to plan a vacation in order to study its decision making, or might place a mother and her toddler in a strange room full of toys to observe the toddler's proximal behavior (that is, how long before it will leave its mother's side, how far it will stray from her, and so on). Sometimes the investigator simply tries to control the setting to maximize the chances of being able to observe behavior. For example, interaction between a father and his child is more likely to occur if the two are alone together in a room at the agency than if they are home with the rest of the family involved in normal daily activities.

Recording Observations

Another set of decisions that a investigator collecting data through observation must make involve how to record the observations: when to do it, whose viewpoint is taken and the amount of inference required, and the form on which observations are recorded.

The method selected for recording observational data depends to some extent on how structured the observations are. In fact, in very structured observation, the recording of data is an integral part of data collection. In such cases, observations are made and recorded almost simultaneously.

An important decision to be made about recording observational data is when it is to be done. Possibilities are on the spot, immediately after the observational period is over, or at a later time from film, videotape, or audiotape. When narrative descriptions or scales are used to summarize behavior, data are recorded after the observational period is over. Most category systems require that data be recorded on the spot or from mechanical recordings such as videotapes. There are obvious advantages to being able to code from recorded observations like videotapes. The coder can play back to catch behavior missed the first time and to check codes. Several different recording systems can be applied to the same observations. In addition, it may be easier to check interobserver, and certainly intraobserver, reliability from recordings than from observations of in vivo behavior, that is, behavior as it is occurring. A major disadvantage of recorded observation is the cost involved. If audiotapes must be transcribed before coding, the procedure is even more expensive. Audiotapes are not, of course, appropriate for nonvocal behavior and are of limited value when visual clues would help to interpret the meaning of verbal behavior. A possible disadvantage of films and videotapes compared to direct observation is the editing of behavior that may occur if the camera is not able to or does not focus on all relevant behavior at one time (see chapter 14).

Another issue is from whose viewpoint the observations are to be recorded and how much inference the observers should make. Should the behavior be coded from the standpoint of the actor (what was intended), the respondent (how that person interpreted the behavior), or a neutral bystander? Sometimes these viewpoints are the same, but often they are not. One child may lightly tap another child on the arm in an effort to get his attention, the second child may respond to the tap as if it were an aggressive act, while an observer may have seen it as a friendly gesture. Although it might not possible to know what the first child intended, the observer might be expected to make inferences about intent from observing the entire behavioral sequence. On the other hand, the degree of inference could be minimized by having the observer record only the exact movements or actions that occurred, for example, "One child moved close to the other, raised one arm, brought the arm down and let his hand drop on the other child's shoulder," and so on. This type of recording can be laborious and not very useful for some purposes. Probably most of these studies require the observer to view the behavior from the standpoint of a neutral onlooker and to make a medium degree of inference.

A third issue is the form used to record observations. The major types are narrative accounts, ratings on ordinal scales, and nominal-level category systems. As previously indicated, narratives, or written accounts of what transpired, are particularly suited to unstructured observation such as field research or participant observation. Scales with ordinal assessments of some quality are generally used with more structured observation, and time-interval and nominal category systems are used with very structured observation. Each form is next discussed briefly.

Narrative accounts are running descriptions of events and large segments of interaction. These descriptions may be limited to observed events, but generally they include the observer's interpretation of the behavior as well. These interpretations should be clearly labeled. Sometimes the observer is able to take brief notes while in the field; in some situations only "mental notes" are advisable. In either case, full field notes should be made daily after the observational period is over. Since it is impossible, and not even desirable, to record everything that occurred during the period of observation, the selection of what to record is guided by the purpose of the study; that is, the most important behaviors, interactions, or events for the study purposes are recorded as completely as possible. Descriptions of situations observed often include information about the participants, setting, purpose, social behavior, and frequency and duration. Or instead of a full, free-flowing chronological record of behavior, the narrative may be more structured and selective by focusing on critical incidents or collecting anecdotes about the behaviors of interest.

Ordinal scales can also be used to record observations of behavior. Like narratives, the scale ratings are made after the observations are completed, and they constitute a summary evaluation of specific behaviors. For example, observers might be asked to rate the degree of warmth in a parent-child relationship after having observed the parent and child together for a period of time. Generally, observers are asked to make a series of ratings covering different dimensions for the same observational period. In the example cited, other dimensions might include child's initiative in play, child's independence from parent, amount of verbal exchange, parent's attentiveness to child, parental encouragement, and so on. Scales vary in gradations; generally scales with fewer than five points result in distinctions too gross for most studies and those with more than eleven in distinctions too fine for most raters to make without great difficulty. Common biases in rating scale data result from avoidance of extreme ratings (end points of scales), the tendency to give only complimentary ratings, and the halo effect (tendency to give a subject the same rating on all scales). Although these biases cannot be eliminated completely, efforts can be made to minimize them. Clear operational definitions of the concepts to be rated are necessary prerequisites. Word definitions of the numerical scale gradations are helpful. And, of course, adequate training of the raters in the procedures—both in making the observations and in using the scales—is essential. Sometimes rank-ordering subjects, instead of rating them, can be used to minimize some of the biases. Unlike narratives, rating scales produce quantitative data which are often manipulated mathematically.

Nominal-level or category systems—in which the observer notes the occurrence of specific observations—differ from narrative accounts and ordinal scales in several ways. One of the most important is the size of the behavioral unit: category systems generally use molecular units of behavior. Instead of summarizing overall impressions of behavior during an observational period, category systems usually require the observer to code each separate or isolated behavioral unit as it is being observed. This may take the form of indicating if a particular behavior occurred during a specified time interval as illustrated earlier, tallying the number of times a behavior occurred during the interval, or coding behavioral units into previously developed categories. The system may require only the behavior of interest to be coded or it may require that additional information about the behavior be coded, such as who initiated the behavior and toward whom it was directed.

An example of a structured observational system using molecular behavioral units and time intervals for recording is from a field experiment with a sportsmanship curriculum for children (Sharpe, Brown, and Crider 1995: 406–407). In the experiment, two classes of poor urban children received an intervention that consisted of training and reinforcement in good sportsmanship and leadership during physical education, while one class received only the regular physical education curriculum. Hidden cameras recorded all interaction during two 45-minute classes each week, one gym period and one regular education period, held at the same time every Wednesday (systematic sampling of time blocks). The videotapes were later coded by three trained graduate students using computers that assisted data entry. The coders used a categorical system, recording the frequency and duration of six teacher and eight child behaviors. For selected child behaviors, individual children were observed. A child was observed for 5 minutes and then observation rotated to another child. The children to be observed were randomly selected from four groups, with groups rotated (stratified random sampling of children). Thus, although the unit of focus was the class, at times a single child was observed and assumed to be representative of the class. Examples of child behavior categories and their operational definitions include:

Student skill engagement and game play. Students are actively engaged in the actual subject-matter activity. This may include wait time involved within a particular activity, such as center fielder anticipation in baseball, or field-of-play travel in soccer or basketball.

Social response. A student or student group makes a verbal or nonverbal response to another student, peer captain, or student referee's instructional, organizational, or conflict resolution directive in the context of a game activity.

Social response, following behavior. A student simply complies with the particular student, peer leader, or student referee directive.

Social response, leadership behavior. A student emits a verbal or nonverbal response clearly designed to facilitate, help direct, or support and appropriate social response.

The behaviors were not mutually exclusive; for example, a child could be coded simultaneously for "teacher independent conflict resolution" and for "social response—leadership behavior." Clearly, although the definitions seem fairly explicit, the coders had to make inferences about the intent of the children's behavior. However, interobserver reliability was excellent (Cohen's kappa coefficient ranged from .89 to .98 with an average of .94).

Available Data

Another source of data useful for research purposes is information already collected by others for other purposes. These published and unpublished materials come in a variety of forms and from many different sources. Traditionally, social work researchers have probably made the greatest use of case records and other agency materials, statistical data from agencies and governmental sources, and historical documents. Sources used less often include mass media materials, both public and private documents such as letters and diaries. Raw data from other studies constitute another little used but potentially important source of data for social work researchers. In this section we describe briefly some of these types and sources of available data and their uses and problems.

Sources of Available Data

Sources of available data include databases of previous investigators' quantitative or qualitative data, research reports, statistical data from various organizations, agency records, public archival material, mass media, and personal documents.

Data collected by social researchers are increasingly being made available to other investigators for secondary data analysis. This is particularly true of large-scale surveys and evaluation studies. Raw data from large investigations are stored in social science data archives or data banks, usually located in universities or research centers, to be readily available to other investigators, including students. Social science data archives are facilities for collecting, processing, preserving, and disseminating computer-readable research data. One of the largest such facilities is the Inter-University Consortium for Political and Social Research (ICPSR) at the Institute for Social Research at the University of Michigan. For example, numerous investigators have obtained from ICPSR data from the ongoing National Election Studies, begun in 1952, for studies of decision making, group identification, political socialization, and the like. Other archives of particular interest to social work investigators include those based at the National Opinion Research Center at the University of Chicago, the Survey Research Center at the University of California at Berkeley, the Institute for Poverty Research at the University of Wisconsin, and the Qualitative Data Archival Resource Center (QUALIDATA) at the University of Essex in Great Britain. For example, data from the New Jersey Negative Income Tax and from the Rural Income Tax experiments are archived at the University of Wisconsin. Unfortunately, there is no central index of all existing data collections; however, one can request lists of holdings from individual research centers, often via the World Wide Web. Depending on how the data archive is funded, a nominal fee may be charged for acquisition of the data. In addition to the large-scale data banks, many university departments and computer centers have local archives for use by that university's faculty and students.

Published research reports can be an important source of data for meta-analyses, which use statistical techniques to combine the results of many studies. Because single studies often lack samples large enough to show effects, and results among studies are often conflicting, such meta-analyses are powerful ways to summarize and gain new insights from already-conducted research. Meta-analysis is described in more detail in chapter 11.

A wide variety of routinely gathered statistical data is of interest to social work investigators. Such data range from local agency statistics to national statistics compiled by public and private organizations. Several federal government agencies publish massive statistical compilations (and narrative reports) on topics relevant to social work. For example, the Bureau of Labor Statistics in the Department of Labor provides data on topics such as labor force participation, earnings, and unemployment rates; the Bureau of the Census in the Department of Commerce, on population, housing, income, and poverty data, among others; the National Center of Health Statistics in the Department of Health and Human Services, on vital statistics (birth, marriage, divorce, and death rates), health resources and expenditures, and so on; the National Center for Social Statistics, on a variety of topics such as welfare expenditures, child welfare, and juvenile delinquency. An excellent resource is the American Statistics Index (ASI), which is a comprehensive guide to the statistical publications of the United States government. The annual *Statistical Abstract of the United States: National Data Base and Guide to Sources*, summarizes these data.

National voluntary organizations such as Family Service America and the Child Welfare League compile statistical data from their member agencies. As examples, the National Association of Social Workers has information on its membership; the Council on Social Work Education, on enrollment in schools of social work; and the United Way, on community fund contributions. The National Clearinghouse on Child Neglect and Abuse, an American Humane Association project sponsored by the Office of Child Development, has statistical information on official reports of child abuse and neglect.

Local and state counterparts to many of these national public and private organizations may also be resources for statistical data. Again the data may be in published or unpublished form. For example, states have general information in Blue Books and Statistical Abstracts. Local organizations may need to be contacted for their statistical data.

Chow and Coulton (1998) used several existing data sets in their investigation of whether social conditions had worsened during the 1980s in one large urban area, Cleveland. They brought together in one data set indicators of crime (e.g., personal and property crime), family and child development (e.g., births to unwed mothers, juvenile delinquency filings), health problems related to poverty (low birthrate, infant death), and economic dependency and labor force participation (Aid to Dependent Children, general assistance cases). They drew these measures from the Uniform Crime Report from the city police, the Ohio Department of Health Vital Statistics, the local county Juvenile Court records, and the county Department of Human Services. Obviously, in doing so, they had to rely on indicators that may not measure exactly what they were interested in—social conditions in neighborhoods. They were also limited by the quality of data recorded, for example, the Uniform Crime Report includes only crimes reported to the police. And they had to define "neighborhood" as "census tract" because that was the unit for which data were available. Nevertheless, they demonstrated a transformation of social conditions: a deterioration in conditions and an increase in the interdependency among adverse conditions.

Social workers are familiar with another kind of available data: social agency records and materials. Case records have frequently been used for research purposes. Research protocols may be filled out by case analysts using these records. Write-ups of group treatment or activity group sessions; minutes of agency board meetings, committee meetings, and staff meetings; and agency reports, annual summaries, mission statements, statements of policies and procedures, staff memos, and so on, have also provided research data. Content analysis has been used with these narrative materials (see chapter 15). Although the value of agency records and documents has been recognized by social work researchers, often collecting and analyzing the data have been laborious procedures. Computerized information systems, now in most agencies, should facilitate these processes, although issues of accessibility and confidentiality continue to be difficult. Increasingly, single agency and multiagency systems are being developed, often at the state level.

An example of the use of agency records is Sullivan's qualitative study of group process using as data a social worker's detailed session notes for a long-term group of mothers at a child guidance clinic (Sullivan 1995). Starting with a theoretical perspective that group dynamics is primarily a struggle for control of the group, Sullivan focused on the worker's control. She analyzed the session notes in several ways. First, in a structured approach to the data, she constructed sociograms of each week's interactions—diagrams of who interacted with whom, who initiated each interaction, and whether the interaction was agreeable or disagreeable. Then she used qualitative abstracting to develop themes of what was going on in the group, moving from the specific behavioral details ("Betty offered to help Lorraine—refused") to a more abstract level ("Offer of help spurned") to an even more abstract theme ("A room of individuals still trying to make connections with each other, but 'baggage' prevents successful connections"). [pp. 19–20].

Public documents such as congressional hearings, laws enacted by the Congress, Supreme Court cases, state and local legislative documents, and various other historical documents are also sources of data readily available to investigators. To illustrate, Ofman (1996) used such materials in her analysis of differences between urban and rural areas in disbursement of mothers' pensions (early support programs for women with children) in Michigan from 1913 to 1928. She analyzed legislation, State Board of Corrections and Charities data, Children's Bureau statistics and publications, writings by contemporary social workers such as Edith Abbott and Sophonisba Breckinridge, and probate court records.

The mass media—newspapers, magazines, advertisements, TV, radio, films, public speeches, and so on—constitute yet another source. Such materials are usually subjected to content analysis. A related source is professional literature. For example, a number of investigators have analyzed social work journals to study phenomena such as trends in types of research, sex of authors, and the knowledge base of the profession. A favorite topic is productivity rankings among schools of social work. Typically, the affiliations of each author are noted and schools are ranked by the frequency or per capita publication rate of their faculty members (Green 1995; Kirk and Corcoran 1995; Ligon, Thyer, and Dixon 1995). Sometimes, citation rates are used—the number of times each faculty member is cited in someone else's article (Bloom and Klein 1995; Lindsey and Kirk 1992).

Personal documents such as autobiographies, diaries, and letters have seldom been used in social work research. However, Chestang (1977) used autobiographies of a number of black persons as the data for his study of the effect of race on the development of coping mechanisms as reflected in the concepts of effectance, competence, adaptation, and the family as a socializing agent.

A particular type of available data is physical evidence or traces of activities, such as empty beer cans, urinalysis, or scrap paper generated by students working on a term paper. In the social sciences, archeology concerns itself almost exclusively with physical evidence, but it can also be useful to other social science research. For example, the content and amount of garbage is a direct indicator of wealth, nutrition, and social customs. Physical evidence is useful when attempting to make inferences about the past, when other data is not available or needs to be corroborated, and when unobtrusive measurements are desirable. For example, physical evidence from garbage can be used to confirm self-reports of drinking habits or mileage on a car can verify a traveling sales person's activity. In one study of the effects of choice and personal responsibility on elderly in a nursing home, the level of activity was measured unobtrusively by putting white tape around the rims of the wheels of each resident's wheel-chair (Langer and Rodin 1976). The level of activity was measured by the discoloration of the tape; the darker, presumably the more active and engaged the individual. The major disadvantage of physical evidence is that it is usually an indicator of something else and the validity of it as an indicator is difficult to establish.

Using Available Materials as Research Data

Existing materials may be used as the data for one's study. Sometimes these are the only available data source. Investigators engaged in historical studies or exploring trends over time must rely on existing materials such as published and unpublished documents and statistical compilations. Even when it is possible to use other data, there are times when already collected data may be superior to original data that the investigator might collect. Examples are data from well-designed, large-scale evaluations and sample surveys. The research expertise and technical skills, the large field data collection operations, and other resources and facilities employed in these projects are beyond the reach of most investigators. These data provide a rich research resource. Rarely do the collectors of data in these large-scale studies exploit the data fully from all conceivable perspectives. In planning research in a particular area in which a great deal of data are needed, a researcher might be wise to try to track down potentially relevant already collected data. As already indicated, social science data archives constitute an excellent resource.

Other kinds of existing data may also be the best data source available. Although data for some statistical studies could possibly be obtained through a questionnaire survey, existing statistical data may be more accurate, reliable, and comprehensive.

Another reason for using available materials rather than collect original data is that using the existing data is more expedient and economical. Sometimes investigators prefer to collect their own data but do not have the time or resources to do so. As the costs of surveys and large-scale evaluations continue to rise and as funding for research becomes harder to get, the cost of collecting original data will increasingly become insurmountable for many investigators. Secondary data analysis is one solution. Creative use of other investigators' raw data or inventiveness in finding other available materials to test one's hypotheses or answer one's research questions may become increasingly important for many social work investigators. Secondary data analysis also provides other opportunities. For example, independent reanalyses can be conducted to check on the statistical procedures and conclusions of the original research. Older data can be reassessed by using other, perhaps newer and more sophisticated, statistical methods, or in light of new findings or theoretical formulations. Secondary researchers can address new issues or use different theoretical approaches with the existing data. Sometimes, longitudinal studies not planned by the original investigators can be executed by secondary investigators if reliable identification of the subjects exists.

On the other hand, a number of disadvantages and problems are often associated with the use of available materials as research data. An initial hurdle may be locating relevant data for one's research purposes. Obtaining the data file can also pose a problem, particularly if the original investigator still has it and is reluctant to share it for a number of reasons, including wanting to mine the data first.

Definitions of terms and adequacy of sampling and data collection methods may constitute problems with already collected data. A basic problem here is lack of information; terms may be inadequately defined or not defined at all; sampling and data collection methods may not be described in enough detail for the investigator to determine their adequacy. Does "married" mean all married persons or only those residing with their spouses? Does "employment" mean full-time employment only or both full and part time? Why are the unemployment rates for black teenagers reported by the National Urban League consistently higher than the Department of Labor's figures? Since definitions, sampling plans, and data collection techniques vary across sources and over time, investigators wanting to make comparisons or describe trends may run into difficulty.

Even when operational definitions are clear, the data may not capture the concepts the investigator hoped. While much research relies on indicators rather than measuring a characteristic directly, the problem of adequate operational definitions is ever present when the investigator must rely on others' definitions. Often the available data measures a concept only indirectly. And later the investigator may find an important alternative explanation but be unable to test its likelihood because no adequate measure of the concept is available to use as a control variable.

Data from some sources may not be consistently available. Case records, for example, may have missing face sheet information. The content of the records forms (forms completed, narrative data, and so on) and the completeness with which information is recorded vary. Such inconsistencies may present serious problems for the investigator, particularly if it results in bias such as having certain kinds of cases overrepresented or underrepresented.

An example of using agency records for research purposes is from a study of parental drug abuse on children in foster care (Lewis, Giovannoni, and Leake 1997). Investigators reviewed Department of Children and Family Service case records on each child. On a structured data collection form, they noted children's and mothers' characteristics such as gender, birthweight of child, mother's substance abuse, history of mental health problems, and reason for referral. Caseworker notes were not always consistent, so some characteristics may have been categorized incorrectly or missed. Missing data were also a problem. For example, an important indicator of health, the child's birthweight, was missing in a quarter of cases.

Problems of validity and reliability may also exist. Information on which to make informed judgments about these issues is often lacking. Adequately documented data from other investigations and well-explained statistical data are generally more easily evaluated. This evaluation may be facilitated if other research studies using these data have been reported in the literature, since such reports may comment on evidence of validity and reliability. Otherwise, the investigator will be faced with the difficult question of whether the data are what they seem. How were major terms defined? What constituted a unit? How carefully were the data collected? From whom? When? By whom? What biases are likely to be reflected in the data? Consideration of such questions help the investigator consider how appropriate the data are for the research purposes. As this discussion implies, a careful examination of the data one plans to use is a virtual necessity when using already collected data.

Other Uses of Available Data

In addition to being used as the data for one's study, existing materials have other uses in research. We indicate briefly how these data are used in the planning stage and as auxiliary data.

In planning research, the investigator reviews the literature and obtains other relevant information about the topic. Knowing what other research has been done in the area and what their findings were helps in formulating a study by indicating fruitful avenues to pursue and how to go about it. For example, the investigator may get ideas that help develop specific research questions or formulate hypotheses. Ways of obtaining the necessary data—possible sources, subjects, data collection instruments, and so on—may be suggested.

Already collected data may also be used in an auxiliary manner. They may be used to provide background information for the study and to place the research findings in context. Information from agency reports, for example, may be helpful in describing the setting and the services offered. Statistical data may indicate the extent of the problem being investigated. Research findings from previous studies may provide a basis for comparison for the results of the study. Since random samples are seldom attained, statistical information may provide a check of sorts on one's sample on demographic variables. Available data relevant to the study can also be used to supplement the findings by filling in gaps in knowledge that may help in the interpretation and in suggesting directions for further research.

Summary

Data collection refers to how the investigator goes about gathering the information that becomes variables in the research. The main methods in social work research are self-report methods, observation, and use of available data. All methods have potential for bias, and the choice of method is a balance between what is ideal, the bias involved, and what is feasible.

Self-report methods, which are ideal for measuring subjective attitudes and opinions, include interviews and written questionnaires. In-person interviews permit establishing rapport and consequently getting in-depth and personal information, but are expensive and subject to interviewer bias. Unstructured in-person interviews are almost essential when broad research questions are used—exploratory and qualitative research. Telephone interviews allow interviewing respondents who are geographically spread out, but may return more limited information than in-person interviews. For both in-person and telephone interviews, a key consideration is selection, training, and supervision of interviewers to reduce bias and ensure that each subject is presented with similar stimuli.

Written questionnaires are the cheapest self-report method. They present a standard stimulus, and allow for rapid, geographically wide-spread data collection, but have the lowest response rate and generally must be highly structured, i.e., require that the investigator know the questions and potential answers from the outset. Both open-ended and fixed-alternative (closed-ended) questions may be used in any format, but interviews lend themselves better to open-ended questions while questionnaires do not.

Observation is ideal for assessing behavior or the physical environment, but is often time-consuming, difficult, and expensive. Key considerations in observation are (a) what should be observed—small bits of behavior or larger aspects of the situation—, and events or time units; (b) where and when to observe—field or laboratory, directly or unobtrusively, with what degree of structure or control over the situation; and (c) how to record observations— when, from whose viewpoint, and whether to use narratives, ordinal scales, or categorical systems. A critical issue in all observation is reliability among observers, i.e., reducing bias among the observers.

Available data are ideal for records of past events, and are important for studying perceptions when individuals cannot be asked directly. They are also used when others make available already-collected data. Sources include archives of others' raw data, statistical reports, agency records, public documents, mass media, personal documents, and physical traces. Limitations of available data are that they often have unknown validity: they are limited by what people thought was important to save, often reflect perceptions rather than actual events, and often are indicators that cannot be verified.

11 Quantitive Data Analysis

Probably no other step in the research process is as awe-inspiring to the inexperienced researcher as data analysis. Visions of mountains of data, jumbled masses of numbers, and pages of complicated mathematical formulas may be part of the nightmare but are seldom, if ever, part of the reality. One reason is that, in a well-designed quantitative study, the question of what to do with the data has been anticipated and the analysis planned well before the data are collected. The reader will remember that, because the activities in the research process are overlapping and interrelated, with decisions at each stage influenced by earlier decisions and affecting later decisions, ideally the study should be clearly conceptualized from beginning to end during the initial planning stage. This does not mean that all steps are planned in great detail or that modifications or additions will not be made later. But it does mean that all the research procedures need to be planned with enough specificity to allow earlier steps to anticipate the requirements of later ones. For example, concepts that are not measured cannot enter into the data analysis, and the way a variable is measured will determine the kinds of analyses that can be performed with that variable.

Sometimes, however, the research study is not or cannot be so carefully planned. The plan for data analysis and interpretation may have been developed earlier only in a very global and fuzzy manner. By definition, specific hypotheses and detailed data analysis plans are not possible in most exploratory studies. Or perhaps one is using available data, data collected by someone else for another purpose. In such situations, one must plan and do the analysis under the constraints imposed by the data at hand. Regardless of when the plan for analysis and interpretation is made, it is guided by the purpose of the study.

According to Kerlinger (1985), data analysis is "the categorizing, ordering, manipulating, and summarizing of data to obtain answers to research questions" (p. 134). Analysis is accompanied by a closely related procedure, interpretation, which means to explain or find meaning. The findings of a research study are interpreted on two levels. First, the relations within the data of the study are explained. For example, a statistical test may be performed during the analysis for the purpose of ascertaining the strength of relationship between two variables. The results of this test would probably be interpreted immediately and inferences made on the basis of the study data. The second level of interpretation is the one that places the findings in broader perspective. This is done by linking one's results to other knowledge, particularly to other research findings and to theory.

The approach to analysis differs depending on the research questions, the design of the study, and the type of data collected. The major difference is between quantitative and qualitative studies (chapter 4). The major portion of this chapter is devoted to analysis of quantitative data in group designs. Analysis of data from time series designs is then considered. The chapter concludes with a discussion of meta-analysis, a method for synthesizing the results of different quantitative studies. Chapter 12 will take up qualitative methods and analysis.

Quantitative Data

Our intent is to provide the reader with a conceptual grasp of quantitative data analysis, with emphasis on what may be needed for purposes of understanding research reports. Statistical methods are discussed only in relation to research: we stress the logic underlying the use of statistical tools for research purposes rather than the computations or the statistical procedures per se. Many excellent statistics texts are available for the latter. (For example, see Blalock 1979; Craft 1990; Frank and Althoen 1994; Kanji 1994; Kobler 1985; Mendenhall, Ott, and Larson 1974; Pagano 1986; Sprinthall 1987; Weinbach and Grinnell 1995).

The reader should be warned of the authors' strong bias in favor of the use of multivariate techniques for analysis of quantitative data in social work research. Behavior of interest to social workers is typically complex. Seldom, if ever, does one type of behavior always lead to the same consequence; conversely, a given behavioral or social consequence is seldom, if ever, caused by only one condition. With the possible exception of well-controlled experiments, attempts to explain behavior or social phenomena by looking at only one possible cause are simplistic and misleading. Like Kerlinger (1985), we use the term *multivariate* to refer to more than one independent variable or more than one dependent variable or both. This broad interpretation permits the classification of techniques such as elaboration, factor analysis, and multiple regression analysis as multivariate procedures.

Quantitative data in social work research can be analyzed by hand or by computer. The decision will rest primarily on the amount of data to be analyzed and the number and types of analyses to be performed. The size of the data set depends on the number of cases or units of analysis (subjects, respondents, organizations, and so on) and on the number of variables or individual items of information collected about each case in the sample. If the number of cases is relatively small, some statistical analyses can be performed manually with calculators. However, even with a small data set, these methods are very time-consuming if a number of analyses are to be performed. Hence, except for studies in which the number of cases is very small and the analyses to be performed are few and easily done with the help of a calculator, the researcher should plan to use a computer for the data analysis.

Whether the data are to be analyzed by hand or computer, most statistical analyses require that the raw data be in the form of numerical codes. Depending on how the data were collected, much or all may already be in numerical form. Chapter 9 discussed the numeric meaning of codes (levels of measurement), while chapter 10 discussed the use of categories in the collection of data. Here we describe in more detail the steps involved in converting raw data into quantitative form for analysis.

Categorization and Coding

Data must be organized to make them usable for answering the research questions. Categories may need to be developed and the raw data placed into the appropriate categories. Generally, the categories are numbered and the raw data are assigned numbers corresponding to the appropriate category. Although the terms *categorizing* and *coding* are often used interchangeably, we use *categorizing* to refer to the process of developing categories and *coding* to refer to the process of placing data in categories.

As previously indicated some or all of the data may already be classified in this manner. The more structured data collection methods generally require that the data be recorded by using predeveloped categories and scales. Examples are fixed-alternative questions, category systems for observations, checklists, and rating scales. In some cases the respondents have coded the data; that is, they have selected particular categories for their responses. In other cases, the interviewers or observers code the data as they record it. The data may be completely precoded or may need only to have numbers assigned to categories. Open-ended responses, however, require the development of categories before the raw data can be coded. If narrative records and other unstructured materials such as those resulting from unstructured interviews or observations are to be analyzed quantitatively, these data must also be categorized. Unstructured materials present special problems in quantitative analysis, for they are difficult to categorize. This is discussed further later.

In his study of interactions between gay partners and their parents, LaSala (1997) asked the gay partners how they protected their relationship from negative reactions from their parents. Among the responses he received were the following:

a. "I respect my mother's right to feel that way and to have her opinion. I recognize that her experiences are different than mine. I can validate her feelings and not buy into them."

b. "I don't need their acceptance on this. It doesn't matter what they say. I struggled for so long I don't care what people have to say now."

c. "A level of detachment assists us in protecting ourselves from him (disapproving father). When I knew I was gay I had to maintain a detachment from the world. Learning how to get to the point that if people have a problem, it's their problem, not mine.

d. "It's my obligation to challenge her (respondent's mother) to confront her negative feelings. I was aggressive, making sure she knew we were together."

e. "My insisting that they accept the relationship and they accept my partner as part of me or else they do not have me."

f. "One of my cousins got married. We were both invited but we didn't go. I thought my parents would be embarrassed. I was also protecting my partner. He wouldn't have to deal with my aunts' or uncles' (negative) reactions."

Following an analysis of such responses, LaSala (1997) decided they formed 3 categories of coping responses: (1) Establishing emotional independence from the parents (responses a, b, and c); (2) taking an assertive stand (responses d and e); (3) distancing self from parents (response f).

If we assume that all the responses indicated only a single coping response, LaSala's categories conform to the basic rules for classification laid out in chapter 9. Two criteria for developing categories are: mutual exclusiveness and exhaustiveness. This means that it should not be possible to put a response in more than one category within each set and that every response should fit into one of the categories. In grouping data that have already been collected, it is necessary to add two additional rules: 1) categories should be set up according to the research questions and study purpose, and 2) each set of categories must be derived from one classification principle.

Obviously there are many different ways of categorizing such data. For example, one can see that in some responses (a, c, and d) either the father or the mother were mentioned specifically as a source of negative feelings. If one were interested in determining how often such mentions occurred, one could construct the following kind of code, which could be applied to each response:

Father mentioned ＿＿＿＿＿＿
not mentioned ＿＿＿＿＿＿
Mother mentioned ＿＿＿＿＿＿
not mentioned ＿＿＿＿＿＿

Both sets of codes could be used with the same responses.

Developing categories for materials such as focused interviews, field notes, case records, and minutes of board meetings presents a special challenge when the data have been collected in an unstructured manner. Here we do not have specific questions and responses to suggest classification schemes. We usually have only narrative material and often large quantities of it. Yet if the decision is made to analyze any part of the data by use of quantitative methods, those data must be put in the required form. Since unstructured methods are gener-ally confined to exploratory studies, hypotheses and precise, narrowly focused research questions are not available to guide the categorization of raw data. Consequently, we start from the broader guidelines stemming from the pur-pose of the study and try to develop more specific questions or working hypotheses based on the data collected.

For example, in a study Smith and Reid (1986) conducted on egalitarian or role-sharing marriages, in-depth interviews with a purposive sample of dual-career couples revealed that some couples who shared the major family roles before having children continued this pattern after starting a family while many others changed to a traditional division-of-labor pattern with the wife responsible for housework and child care and the husband responsible for sup-porting the family financially. Analysis of possible reasons for this pattern sug-gested the hypothesis that a couple's sharing an egalitarian ideology prior to having children tends to foster continued sharing of roles after the birth of chil-dren. The hypothesis required categorizing the data on two variables, extent of shared commitment to egalitarian ideology, and pattern of family responsibil-ities with infants or small children in the home. Since there was no specific measure of egalitarian ideology, judgments had to be made from responses indicating attitudes toward role sharing, reasons for dividing tasks and respon-sibilities the way they did, and so on.

To enhance reliability in coding unstructured data, it is particularly impor-tant to define categories as clearly as possible with the use of examples to illustrate what is meant by each category. Often specific topics or questions can be identified as containing relevant information for making ratings or other judgments for classification purposes. However, because of the way the data are collected, the same information is not always available on all cases.

Missing data and lack of comparability of data are major problems in categorizing unstructured materials for quantitative analysis.

Univariate Analysis

Once data are coded and numerals assigned to the categories, the investigator can turn to ways of summarizing the data so that they can be communicated quickly and clearly to others. Normally, the first step is univariate analysis, which summarizes one variable at a time. Univariate analysis provides useful information to the researcher in and of itself and provides the foundation for more sophisticated analysis. In this section we consider frequency distributions and statistics for summarizing and describing data on single variables.

Frequency Distributions

Usually we want to know how observations are distributed to describe the sample and to plan subsequent analyses. To do this we simply count the number of cases that fall into each category of the variables. These counts are called "frequencies" or sometimes "marginals," since they are found on the margins of the statistical tables. Marginals can be numbers representing the actual counts or can be converted into percentages. Percentages standardize the data so categories or subsamples can be compared.

If percentages are used, one needs to decide on the base, that is, what constitutes 100 percent of the cases. The most fundamental decision here is whether to use all the cases or to eliminate the ones in the missing data category. Sometimes "undecided," "don't know," and similar categories are eliminated from the base. The decision is determined according to the purpose of the analysis and should be made clear in describing the results. For example, to compare the marital status of the sample with that in another study, any missing data categories should be eliminated, for they would not be meaningful and would be confusing.

Frequency distributions can also be displayed pictorially. Sometimes it is necessary or desirable to categorize some continuous variables into fewer categories for graphic representation. For example, age might be categorized into decades. Descriptions of these graphs and how they are constructed can be found in many statistics books and manuals of publication and are not elaborated here. Butterfield (1993) has an excellent discussion on when to use what type of table, chart, or graph in social work publications. Although graphs are used most frequently in the presentation of data, they can also be a useful tool in the analysis since they may provide a different perspective on the data.

Descriptive Statistics

We can also summarize data by using numerical descriptive measures. Descriptive statistics for single variables fall into two groups: measures of central tendency and measures of variability (table 11.1).

TABLE 11.1
Outcome Ratings for Five Clients Illustrating Measures of Central Tendency and Variability (hypothetical data)

CLIENT	RATING	DEVIATION FROM MEAN	DEVIATION SQUARED
A	2	−2	4
B	2(mode)	2	4
C	6	+2	4
D	7	+3	9
E	3 (median)	−1	1
	20 ÷ 5		22 ÷ 5 (sum of squares)
	4.0 (mean)		4.4 (variance)
			$\sqrt{4.4} = 2.1$
			(standard deviation)
			7−2 = 5 (range)

MEASURES OF CENTRAL TENDENCY Measures of central tendency locate the center of the distribution; they are single numbers that characterize what is typical or average in the sample. The three measures of central tendency are the arithmetic mean, median, and mode.

The *mean* is the sum of the measurements divided by the number of measurements. Thus it is influenced by both the magnitude of the individual measurements and by the number of measurements in the set. The mean specifies the center of gravity or balance point of the distribution. It is the most stable and versatile of the measures of central tendency and is the most widely used for statistical inference. Although it technically requires interval data, it is often used, albeit inaccurately, with ordinal data.

The *median* is the midpoint of the distribution: that is, half of the measurements are above the median and half below it when the measurements are arranged in order of magnitude. If there is an odd number of measurements, the median is the middle number of the scale; if there is an even number of measurements, it is the average of the two middle observations. Although the median is not as stable as the mean, it is appropriate for ordinal data, as well as interval data. (The reader will remember the cumulative nature of measurement scales.) Medians, unlike means, can also be used for variables that have open-ended categories at the extremes such as "under 21 years old" or "over $50,000." Medians are also more appropriate for certain data in which extreme scores would distort the mean; for example, the median is usually used to summarize the income of a sample since one or more very high incomes would inflate the mean and provide a misleading picture of the income level of the sample.

The *mode* is the measurement or value that occurs with the greatest frequency. It is the least stable and least common of the three measures of data. Sometimes distributions have more than one mode, which we refer to as bimodal, trimodal, or multimodal, and sometimes there is no mode, as in a flat distribution. Often the mode is used to describe the "typical" value while the mean or median is used to describe the "average" value. Only in perfectly normal distributions do these three measures coincide.

MEASURES OF VARIABILITY Numerical summaries of data usually include a second statistic, a measure of variability or dispersion. This measure indicates how widely the measurements scatter around the central value. We mention only three measures of variability here: the range, variance, and standard deviation. Unlike our discussion of the measures of central tendency, we start with the simplest and most easily understood measure of variability. The *range* is the difference between the largest and smallest measurements. This indication of scatter is very unstable and can be misleading, for it depends entirely on the two extreme values. It is, however, a useful statistic in describing small samples.

The most useful and widely employed of the measures of dispersion are the variance and the standard deviation. The *variance* is the sum of the squared deviations of the measurements about their mean, divided by the number of measurements. That is, the mean of the distribution is subtracted from each value in the distribution, each of these deviation scores is squared (resulting in all positive numbers), the squared deviation scores are added, and this sum (called sum of squares) is divided by the number of measurements. (The calculations are illustrated in table 11.1.)

The *standard deviation* is the positive square root of the variance. In other words, the standard deviation is a measure of the average distance of values from the mean. Like the mean, it assumes interval data.

Variance and standard deviation are two of the most important concepts in inferential statistics. Variances of different sets of measurements can be meaningfully compared (the greater the dispersion, the larger the variance), but it is difficult to interpret the variance for a single set of measurements. Fortunately, this is not the case with its square root, the standard deviation. In normal or "bell-shaped" distributions, approximately 68 percent of the measurements fall within one standard deviation on either side of the mean, 95 percent within two standard deviations, and more than 99 percent within three standard deviations (see figure 11.5). This fact is useful, not only in interpreting what the standard deviation means, but also in standardizing data measured in different units to permit comparisons to be made in generalizing from samples to populations (inferential statistics). For example, if we learn that an underachieving child has scored "two standard deviations above the mean" on a standardized intelligence test, we know that his score is in the upper 2 to 3 percent of a population of children who have taken the test.

Bivariate Analysis

The purpose of the univariate analysis (just discussed) is to describe respondents or other units of analysis in terms of data collected about them or to make descriptive inferences from the sample to the population (see chapter 8). The primary purpose of bivariate and multivariate analyses is explanation, that is, determining what variables are related to what variables and how they are related. As stated previously, bivariate analysis (analyzing the relationship between two variables) is generally only the first step in the attempt to explain most of the complicated phenomena social workers are interested in. Individual and group behavior or social problems are seldom caused by a single factor; however, this does not mean that social workers are never interested in bivariate relationships.

Many of our research questions and hypotheses are posed in this manner; that is, they are concerned with the relationship between two variables. Many of our experiments seek to determine the effect of one independent variable (treatment) on one dependent variable (outcome). But generally the analysis does not end there. If a relationship is found, we want to be able to specify the conditions under which the relationship holds. For example, in which groups (age, sex, race, class, and so on) are the two variables related? With what kinds of behavior or problems is the treatment successful? Multivariate analysis (simultaneously analyzing the relationships among several variables) can help answer these questions. Accordingly, phenomena are explained better.

TABLE 11.2

Employment Status by Gender (hypothetical data)

Number of Respondents

	EMPLOYED	NOT EMPLOYED	TOTAL
Men	75	25	100
Women	25	75	100
Total	100	100	200

However, bivariate analysis, like univariate analysis, is useful not only for understanding the data but also for serving as a basis for more complicated analysis.

In general, this process of seeking explanation is guided by the study's hypotheses or questions and by the level of measurement of the variables. One conducts bivariate analyses between the independent and dependent variables, selecting the procedures appropriate for the levels of measurement of the variables (chapter 9). Because other variables are known or suspected to be alternative explanations of the relationship between the independent and dependent variables, additional bivariate analyses are conducted to determine what might be explanatory variables that should be taken into account statistically. Multivariate statistics, chosen for the level of measurement of the variables involved, then permit assessment of the conditions under which the original relation between independent and dependent variables holds—or does not hold.

Cross-Tabulations

A common bivariate approach for two nominal level variables is the cross-tabulation. The notion of tabulating data on a single variable (counting the number of cases in each category) is extended in cross-tabulation by obtaining the joint occurrence of cases in categories on two variables. The result is a contingency table. For example, in table 11.2, the upper left cell is the number of persons (75) who fell into the joint or contingent categories "men" and "employed." The frequencies obtained during the univariate analysis of these hypothetical data indicated that the sample contained an equal number of men and women (100 each) and that half the sample was unemployed. (See row and column totals or marginals.) The two-by-two contingency table reveals that the large proportion of unemployed was due primarily to the women in the sample; three-fourths of the women were unemployed, with only one-fourth of the women employed, while the reverse was true for the men.

We might also want to cross-tabulate employment status with age categories, race, and other variables that we have reason to believe may be associated with employment status. In like manner, we may want to cross-tabulate gender with other variables to see if the latter are influenced by gender. Some of the variables we cross-tabulate may have more than two categories, resulting in different size contingency tables, such as two-by-three, two-by-five, three-by-four, and so on.

Instead of (or in addition to) frequencies in the tables, we could use percentages. Decisions would have to be made about what base to use and in what direction to percentage. These decisions will depend on the research questions and what makes sense. If one of the variables can logically be considered a dependent variable, the data should be percentaged "in the direction of" the independent variable, that is, the frequencies in the categories of the independent variable become the base (divisor). Perhaps an illustration using hypothetical data will make these points clearer.

Technically, the data in table 11.3 could be converted into percentages as in tables 11.4 (gender as independent variable) or 11. 5 (attitude as independent variable). However, only table 11.4 is logical in an explanatory sense. Sex may be a determinant (independent variable) of attitude toward WORKFIRST (a hypothetical work training program), but it does not make sense to think of one's attitude as the cause of one's sex. Table 11.5 may be useful for prediction. For example, if we know that a person's attitude toward WORKFIRST was positive, we could predict that the person was probably a woman because 94 percent of those with positive attitudes are women. If one's interest is only in describing subgroups, either table 11.4 or 11.5 is correct. In cases where either variable can be considered the independent variable and either the dependent variable, tables are usually percentaged in both directions during data analysis, particularly if the researcher is interested in explaining both variables.

If we take a closer look at tables 11.4 and 11.5, we see that they give us very different information. For example, table 11.5 tells us that, of the people who had negative attitudes toward WORKFIRST, half were women. Looking at 11.4 however, we find that only 4 percent of the women in the sample had negative attitudes. It would be erroneous to conclude from table 11.5 that women were as likely as men to have negative attitudes toward WORKFIRST: table 11.4 indicates that in fact men are five times more likely to have negative attitudes. How do we prevent this type of misinterpretation? A basic rule regarding table reading will help: make comparisons in the opposite direction in which tables are percentaged. Accordingly, in table 11.4 we would compare percentages across;

for example, we would compare the 21 percent men with negative attitudes to the 4 percent women with negative attitudes. In table 11.5 we would compare

TABLE 11.3

Attitude Toward WORKFIRST (hypothetical data)

ATTITUDE	NUMBER OF RESPONDENTS		
	MEN	WOMEN	TOTAL
Positive	35	525	560
Neutral	60	100	160
Negative	25	25	50
Total	120	650	770

TABLE 11.4

Attitude Toward WORKFIRST (percentages)

ATTITUDE	RESPONDENTS	
	MEN (N = 120)	WOMEN (N = 650)
Positive	29	81
Neutral	50	15
Negative	21	4
Total	100	100

TABLE 11.5

Attitude Toward WORKFIRST (percentages)

ATTITUDE	RESPONDENTS		
	MEN	WOMEN	TOTAL
Positive	6	94	100 (N = 560)
Neutral	37	63	100 (N = 160)
Negative	50	50	100 (N = 50)

the percentages going down and would see from that table that, as attitudes become more positive, the person holding that attitude was more likely to be a woman while the opposite trend held with regard to men.

In sum, when interpreting a table, one should percentage (or standardize) on the categories of the independent variable, then compare across a category of the dependent variable.

Our illustrations have dealt with two ways of percentaging tables. There are two other ways. One is to use the total number of cases as the base. In our example, using 770 as the base, we would find that 4.5 percent of the total sample were men with positive attitudes toward WORKFIRST, 68 percent women with positive attitudes, and so on. In most studies, this additional information is of little use. Much more common are tables that assume an independent variable, as in table 11.4 or 11.5. A fourth way tables may be constructed is by giving only partial information. For example, table 11.4 might indicate only that 29 percent of the men and 81 percent of the women held positive attitudes toward WORKFIRST. These percentages can be directly compared with each other and would not be expected to add up to 100. It would be understood that the other 71 percent of the men and 19 percent of the women held either neutral or negative attitudes about WORKFIRST. This procedure assumes that there is an independent variable and highlights what the investigator sees as important.

One further point concerning the construction of tables: one always indicates the numbers that represent 100 percent, as in tables 11.4 and 11.5, the reader can then convert all percentages in the table to actual counts.

Pictorial Descriptions

Like frequency distributions for single variables, the association or relationship between two variables can be depicted in two ways: pictorially and numerically. The contingency table discussed earlier is one way of picturing association. For example, one can look at table 11.4 and "see" the kind of relationship that exists between sex and attitude toward WORKFIRST. A more refined way of picturing association is the scattergram, in which the joint occurrences of values on two variables are plotted for each subject. The relationship is demonstrated most clearly when each of the variables can take on several values, that is, has several categories, and are ordinal level or higher.

For example, suppose we had asked each respondent in a study of WORK-FIRST to rate the program on a five-point scale in which 5 was the most favorable rating and 1 the least positive. Suppose we also knew how long each respondent had been in WORKFIRST and wanted to know if people viewed the program more or less positively the longer they participated in it. For each subject we could plot the joint occurrence of these two values (that is, the subjects rating of WORKFIRST and the length of time he or she had been in WORK-FIRST) on a scattergram in which one axis is used for time in WORKFIRST and the other for rating of WORKFIRST. Figures 11.1 through 11.4 illustrate four possibilities of association between these two variables. Figure 11.1 indicates that, the longer respondents stayed in WORKFIRST, the more positive their rating of the program was likely to be. The inverse (or negative) relationship pictured in figure 11.2 shows exactly the opposite. Unlike figures 11.1 and 11.2, which show a linear (straight-line) relationship, figure 11.3 depicts a more complicated, curvilinear relationship. It indicates that participants tend to have positive attitudes about WORKFIRST when they first enter the program, that these attitudes later become less positive, but again become more positive as they stay in the program longer. (One possible explanation for this type of association is that participants enter WORKFIRST with high expectations but become disillusioned and less positive about the program if they feel their expectations are not being met. The more positive attitudes for the longer term participants may be largely due to the fact that the disillusioned had dropped out of WORKFIRST by that time and those remaining were getting what they wanted from the program.) Figure 11.4 depicts independence (no relationship); it indicates that knowing how long a participant has been in WORKFIRST does not help in the prediction of his or her rating. Thus, scattergrams indicate several things about the relationship: the shape (linear, curvilinear, J-shaped, and so on), the direction (positive or negative as indicated by the slope of the line), and the strength (as indicated by the amount of scatter: the stronger the relationship, the more the points fall on a single smooth line).

Numerical Descriptions

Just as we were able to use means and standard deviations, for example, to describe frequency distributions in terms of average values and amount of scatter, we can use numbers to describe the magnitude or strength of the association between two variables. There are a number of different measures of association. The primary factor determining the appropriate one to use is the way the two variables were measured. (See table 11.10 at the end of the chapter.) Some of the measures that can be used with nominal data are lambda, tau, the phi coefficient, and others noted in table 11.10. Examples of measures of association appropriate for ordinal data are gamma, Kendall's coefficient of concordance (W), Somer's D, and Spearman's rank-order correlation coefficient (rho). The degree of linear relationship between two variables measured on interval or ratio scales can be ascertained by using the Pearson product moment correlation coefficient (r) or the coefficient of determination (r^2). The correlation ratio eta can be used when the relationship is nonlinear. Other measures of association are available for various combinations of measurement, such as interval data for one variable and nominal data for the other. Some of the measures of association mentioned earlier are used with data cross-classified in 2 x 2 tables (for example, the phi coefficient and Yule's Q) while others are used with data in larger tables (for example, the contingency coefficient and gamma, the counterparts to phi and Q).

While all the measures mentioned provide an index of strength of relationship, some indicate additionally the direction of the relationship. Some range

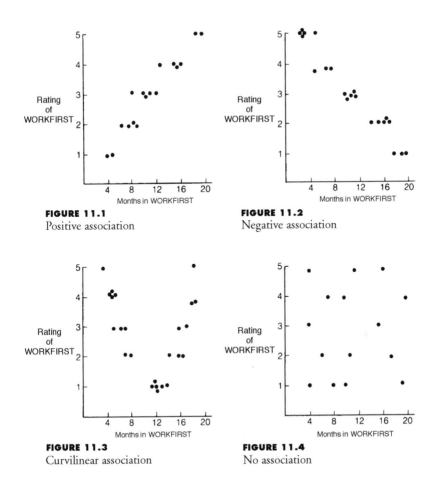

FIGURE 11.1
Positive association

FIGURE 11.2
Negative association

FIGURE 11.3
Curvilinear association

FIGURE 11.4
No association

from -1 (perfect negative association) through 0 (no association) to +1 (perfect positive association). Examples are gamma, Q, rho, and r. When variables are negatively associated, one variable is higher while the other is lower. For example, school grades are negatively associated with absences: students who get good grades tend to have fewer absences. When variables are positively associated, one is higher when the other is higher. Other measures of association vary only between 0 and 1 (for example, Kendall's W, r^2, eta, and the measures for nominal data).

The most widely used of these measures of association is the Pearson product-moment correlation (r). This measure indicates both magnitude and direction of covariation. An r may vary from -1 to +1, indicating either a perfect negative or positive correlation. Correlations that fall between .30 and .60 indicate a modest (toward .30) to moderate (toward .60) degree of association between two variables. As correlations exceed .60, we can begin to regard the degree of association as "high."

A more precise way of evaluating the strength of a correlation is to determine the amount of variance (variation) in one variable that is accounted for by the other. This can be done by squaring the correlation coefficient. Thus if the correlation is .80 we can say that one variable accounts for, or explains, 64 percent of the variance in the other. It takes then a rather high level of correlation (more than .70) to explain more than half the variance. Also it becomes clear that low correlations (less than .30) account for very little of the variance. Even though such correlations may be statistically significant, that is, not likely to be chance occurrences, their explanatory power may be practically nil. For example, suppose a researcher found a statistically significant correlation of .10 between the amount of client education and client satisfaction with service. Although the correlation might suggest a nonchance link between education and satisfaction, it would explain only 1 percent of the variance between the two variables! In other words 99 percent of the variance in client satisfaction could be due to factors other than education. It is also important to remember that the term "variance explained" refers only to the ability of one set of numbers to account for variance in another. It does not refer to causality in a substantive sense. Thus the amount of social worker experience may be highly correlated with client outcome in a study, but the findings would not be grounds for asserting the experience was responsible for better outcomes. Other factors, such as tendencies for more experienced practitioners to select the more promising cases, would need to be considered as possible explanations. Finally, r indicates only linear association. It is also possible for r to be 0 and the two variables to be perfectly correlated in a curvilinear manner. For this reason, one needs to ascertain the shape of the association, which can be done by constructing a scattergram.

Inferential Statistics

Once we have established an association through bivariate analysis, we must address the question of how "real" this finding is. As discussed in chapter 5, a common source of uncertainty in research findings is *instability*, that is, the possibility that the findings reflect some chance variation rather than some property of the phenomenon under investigation. Inferential statistics provides logic and testing procedures (tests of significance) that help us to evaluate uncertainties of this kind.

The foundations of inferential statistics and tests of significance were introduced in our discussion of sampling in chapter 8. Whether testing for associations or differences, we expect our measures and statistics to vary somewhat owing simply to sampling variability. For example, if we compared the means of an experimental group and a control group on an outcome variable after the intervention, we would not expect these two means to be identical whether or not the intervention had been effective. From the discussion in chapter 8 on random samples, we know that samples from the same population will differ by chance but that very large differences seldom occur. Thus, if the means of our experimental and control samples are very similar, we would probably attribute the small difference observed to sampling error. On the other hand, if the differences were very large, we would probably conclude that the intervention made a difference or, in statistical language, that the two groups were not (or no longer, since they should have been alike initially) from the same population. We would have difficulty, however, in trying to make decisions about differences between these two extremes. How large would the difference need to be for us to decide was a real difference and not just sampling error? Our problem is that we have sample statistics but need to know population parameters, which are numerical descriptive measures of the population. Since we do not know these parameters (if we did, we would not have used samples) and cannot engage in repeated sampling to obtain estimates of the parameters, we must make inferences about the population based on our one sample. Inferential statistics provides guidelines to help us with the decisions we must make.

Since inferential statistics is based on probability theory, there is always some risk involved in using statistical procedures to make decisions. On the other hand, no other method of making inferences from samples guarantees certainty either. Inferential statistics has, however, an important virtue that other methods do not: it tells us how much risk we are taking. We know how much reliance we can place on inferences using its procedures since all inferences are accompanied by a measure of their stability.

The notions of probability and sampling distributions of statistics were discussed in chapter 8. Figure 8.1 illustrated that the means from a very large number of random samples of the same size would distribute themselves in a normal or bell-shaped curve. This is a symmetrical curve in which the mean, median, and mode coincide and is the shape that the sampling distributions of many statistics take. In explaining the standard deviation units earlier in this chapter, it was indicated that if the horizontal axis of a normal distribution were divided into standard deviation units and lines were erected at those points, certain probabilities would be associated with these areas. Figure 11.5

illustrates this point. These probabilities hold for all normal frequency distributions of variables and for all sampling distributions of statistics taking this form. In fact, most statistical texts provide tables that give the probability of the area between the mean and any cutting point, expressed in standard deviation units. From these tables, one can calculate the probability of the area between any two lines erected along the horizontal base. Exactly 95 percent of the statistics in a normal sampling distribution would fall within 1.96 standard deviations on each side of the mean, and 99 percent within 2.56 standard errors.

Statistical Tests

Now, how do we make use of this information in making the decisions we need to about sample data? For example, how do we use it to decide if the differences we have observed are due only to sampling variability? We use it to posit and test the "null" hypothesis that our findings are explained by sampling error or chance. Only if our results would rarely occur by chance, say, less than 1 time in 20, do we rule out sampling error as the explanation and assume that our research hypothesis explains these improbable results. This process of comparing two hypotheses in light of sample evidence is called a test of significance or simply a statistical test.

Although we will use the normal distribution to explain the logic of tests of significance, it is well to keep in mind that not all test statistics assume this form, particularly with small samples. Examples of commonly used test statistics whose distributions take other forms are chi-square, t, and F. For each distribution there are tables for determining the critical areas and probabilities associated with the critical areas for tests of significance. Despite the differences in form, the logic involved in making inferences from sample data is the same.

A statistical test involves four components: a null hypothesis, a research hypothesis, a test statistic (decision maker), and a rejection region (Mendenhall, Ott, and Larson 1974). The null hypothesis is a hypothesis about the population that asserts that sampling error is the explanation for the sample data. This hypothesis may state that a parameter (the population value) is a specified value, that a parameter falls within a certain interval, that two variables are independent (unrelated), that there is no difference between two (or more) groups, and so on. We test the null hypothesis and either accept or reject it. If we accept it, we conclude that our sample results could have occurred by chance and are therefore not statistically significant. If we reject the null hypothesis we disregard it as an explanation and accept the research hypothesis or alternative hypothesis. The research hypothesis is, of course, the hypoth-

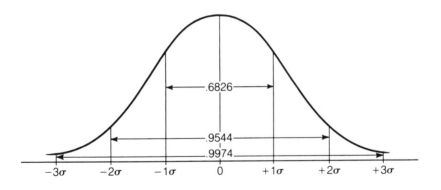

FIGURE 11.5
Normal probability distribution

esis that guides the research and the hypothesis we really want to test, but we cannot test it directly. The research hypothesis may state, for example, that a parameter is not a specified value, does not fall within a certain interval, that two variables are associated, or that two groups differ. The last may be expressed by saying the groups are from different populations as evidenced by some parameter.

The test statistic, or decision maker, is computed from the sample data, for example, from means, proportions, variances, frequency distributions, and so on. The appropriate data are plugged into a formula (the test statistic) and the result is compared to a known distribution of values. The rejection region indicates values on that distribution that are contradictory to the null hypothesis and consequently imply its rejection. Commonly used rejection regions are illustrated in figures 11.6 and 11.7, which are set up for the test of a null hypothesis of no difference between two groups (H:$\mu_1 = \mu_2$ or $\mu_1 - \mu_2 = 0$, where μ (mu) is the population mean).

Figure 11.6 shows a two-tailed test at .05 level of significance, based on a normal curve. It indicates that we will accept the null hypothesis of no difference between, say, the experimental and control groups unless the difference between the means of the two samples is large enough to fall in the rejection region, at least 1.96 standard errors from the mean of the sampling distribution of differences between means ($\mu_1 - \mu_2$). A total of 5 percent of values on a normal distribution would fall in the rejection region (2 $^1/2$% at either end). As figure 11.6 also indicates, 19 times out of 20 we would be correct in our decision but wrong 1 time in 20. We would make an incorrect decision by rejecting the null hypothesis 5 percent of the time when it was, in fact, true.

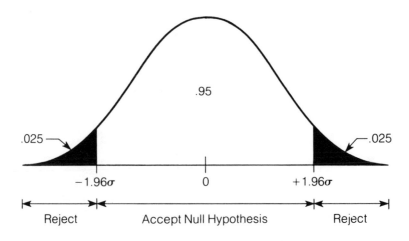

FIGURE 11.6
Rejection region for two-tailed test with *H1*: μ1 ≠ μ2, when α = .05

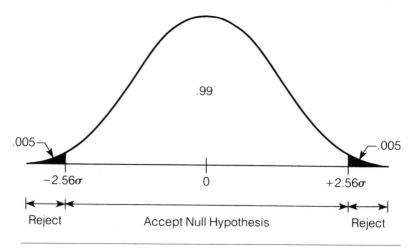

FIGURE 11.7
Rejection region for two-tailed test when *H1*: μ1 ≠ μ2, when α = .01

To minimize this risk of accepting chance differences as real, known as Type I error, we could demand even more extreme values, that is, even larger differences before we rejected the null hypothesis. Figure 11.7 illustrates how the risk of being wrong in rejecting the null hypothesis could be cut down to only 1 time in 100. However, we can also err on the other side: accepting the null hypothesis when it is, in fact, false. That is, we may fail to recognize real differences. This is called a Type II error. Unfortunately, these two types of error are inversely related for a given sample size. Researchers sometimes try to determine which type of error would be more serious for their specific study and choose the level of significance accordingly. The level of significance controls the risk of a Type I error.

The probability of Type I error is α (alpha); the probability of Type II error is ß (beta); ß is more difficult to calculate than α, partly because the calculation of ß requires one to make assumptions about the true value, that is, the value under the alternative hypothesis. Generally, researchers are more concerned about making a Type I error and want a fair amount of evidence before dismissing sampling error as the explanation. They usually set α at a low level and take whatever ß accompanies it. Table 11.6 summarizes information concerning Type I and Type II errors.

Most social work researchers appear to use the .05 level of significance. This means that they would describe findings as significant if there was only a 5 percent probability ($p = .05$) that the findings could be explained by chance. They may report findings significant at the .10 level as tendencies.

TABLE 11.6
Decision Table

DECISION	NULL HYPOTHESIS IS:	
	FALSE	TRUE
Reject null hypothesis	Correct	Type I error
Accept null hypothesis	Type II error	Correct

Source: Mendenhall, Ott, and Larson 1974.

However, there may be times when accepting the .10 level of significance is justifiable. Examples are evaluations of treatment with populations where there is little evidence that anything works or in exploratory studies where the goal is hypothesis formulation. Applying very stringent criteria in tests of significance may prevent the researcher from detecting possible clues to be pursued further. This is especially true with small samples in which results need to be more extreme (that is, larger differences or stronger associations) to permit rejection of the null hypothesis. The ability of a statistical test to reject the null hypothesis when it is false and the research hypothesis is true is called the power of the test. This term is used to refer to 1-ß, a probability statement. As Hays (1973) has observed, "it is literally the probability of finding out that H_0 [the null hypothesis] is wrong, given the decision-rule and the true value under H_1 [the alternative hypothesis]" (p. 357). As indicated, one way of increasing the power of a statistical test is to increase the sample size (see also chapter 6).

In figures 11.6 and 11.7, two-tailed tests of significance were assumed: that is, α was divided between the two tails. This is appropriate for nondirectional tests where the hypothesis stated only that some difference is to be expected, or if a research question was posed. However, if a directional hypothesis was formulated initially, then we are interested in differences in only one direction and a one-tailed test is more appropriate. For example, an investigator might hypothesize that the experimental group of adolescents who received training in independent living skills will show more gains in conducting daily activities like money management and cooking than a control group that did not receive the training. In such a case we would use a one-tailed, or directional, test in which α is concentrated in one tail. With an α of .05, the rejection region of a one-tailed test using the normal curve would be enlarged to cover the area in that tail from 1.645 standard deviations from the mean (instead of ±1.96 standard deviations at each tail). Given the same α level and the same true alternative, we would increase the power of the test by using a one-tailed test provided the true alternative lies in the direction we think it does. In other words, when a difference is predicted, as noted in chapter 2, a less stringent test is required.

Pragmatically, to test statistical significance, we use the sample data in a test chosen because of its purpose and the levels of measurement of variables. The result is compared to the probability of occurrence of all possible results (the sampling distribution) and a probability is generated (all this is usually done by computer). That probability is then compared to previously set significance level (α). If the probability of the result is equal to or less than the significance level, the result is said to be statistically significant. In doing so, we understand that we will be incorrect a certain proportion of the time, α.

THE *t* TEST One of the most common statistical tests is the *t* test, which is most frequently used to compare the means of two samples. It requires that there be two nominal-level categories and an interval-level variable. (The two categories are considered two samples for statistical purposes; the logic behind the test is a null hypothesis that the samples are drawn from the same population.) Briggs, Tovar, and Corcoran (1996) made use of this test in their effort to validate the Children's Action Tendency Scale (CATS) for Hispanic youth. (The CATS is an instrument to measure how children and youth might be expected to behave in conflict situations.) They hypothesized that boys would score higher on aggressiveness than girls. The mean aggressiveness score for boys was 11.4 and for girls, 7.9. A *t* test was used to determine if the difference between these means was sufficiently large to be statistically significant. The probability of *t* was calculated from a formula using data from the boys and girls. That probability was less than the significance level set by the investigators ($p < .01$), so the difference is statistically significant. (Readers should also note that this is an example of the "known groups" method for testing the construct validity of an instrument discussed in chapter 9.)

The *t* test assumes normally distributed populations and interval or ratio data. The *t* distribution is like a flattened normal curve; the smaller the sample, the flatter the *t* distribution. As the sample size increases, the *t* distribution approaches the normal curve. Although we could use the normal curve with its corresponding *z* statistic with very large samples, because *t* is adjusted for sample size, we use it to eliminate concern about sample size. Other statistical tests are available for comparing two samples when the assumptions of the *t* test cannot be met. For example, the Mann-Whitney U can be used with ordinal data with no assumption about the form of the population probability distribution. Siegel (1956) is an excellent reference for nonparametric procedures.

THE CHI-SQUARE TEST The chi-square test of significance is frequently used for nominal data such as that in a cross-tabulation. Holmes (1995a) used the chi-square statistic (χ^2) in a study exploring the effects of child abuse. One of his questions concerned whether or not clients with a history of child abuse differed in respect to diagnosis from clients without such a history. His analysis, using a sample of family agency clients, produced the results shown in table 11.7. Of clients diagnosed as adjustment disorders, only 2 in 10 had a history of abuse; of clients with a diagnosis of depressive disorder, 4 in 10 had such a history; of clients with a diagnosis of personality disorder, the proportion of clients with an abuse history rose to 8 in 10. The probability of the chi-square was slightly above .01. In other words, the probability of obtaining a difference in diagnosis between the two groups as large as was observed in this sample is a little over 1 in 100—a result that is easily significant at the conventional .05 (1 in 20) level.

Instead of comparing means as the *t* test does, chi-square in effect compares frequency distributions. The frequencies in each of the cells of the contingency table are used to calculate the value of chi-square. The greater the deviation of an observed frequency from its "expected" or "chance" value, the greater will be the chi-square value for the cell. Thus one would expect by chance approximately 4 clients with a history of abuse to be diagnosed as a personality disorder, given the numbers of clients in the sample with histories of abuse and with diagnoses of personality disorder. (We determine the expected or chance frequency for the cell—the one in the lower right-hand corner of the table—by multiplying the total number of clients with a history of abuse (14) by the total number of clients diagnosed as personality disorder (10) and dividing by the total number clients in the sample (32). If you perform this calculation, you will find that the precise expected frequency is 4.375. Expected frequencies for the remaining cells can be obtained in a similar manner). If we compare the expected and actual frequencies in the cell under consideration, we can see that there are a greater number of clients with personality disorders *and* histories of abuse, than chance would lead us to expect. Additional calculations would reveal that clients without histories of abuse are more likely to be diagnosed as adjustment disorders. However, we would also find that the expected and observed frequencies are virtually identical for depression.

TABLE 11.7
Relationship of Abuse as a Child to Diagnosis as an Adult

	ADJUSTMENT DISORDER	DEPRESSION	PERSONALITY DISORDER
No history of abuse	10	6	2
History of abuse	2	4	8
Total	12	10	10
$\chi^2 = 8.97$, df= 2, $p = .011$			

Source: Holmes 1995a.

When such deviations are calculated and summed over all cells, the resulting chi-square value (8.97) is sufficiently large to make the differences in diagnosis between those with and without histories of child abuse significant at the .05 level. As might be expected, the total chi-square value is evaluated in relationship to the number of cells in the table. This information is conveyed by the number of "degrees of freedom," which begins at 1 in the simplest (2 x 2) form of the contingency table. Tables showing significance levels for different chi-square values and degrees of freedom can be found in most introductory statistics texts.

The versatility of chi-square becomes apparent when we recognize that any set of data can be reduced to nominal form. For example, scores on instruments may be divided into the nominal categories of "high" and "low," with the median used as the dividing point. Although more "powerful" tests, such as the *t* test, may make fuller use of the information contained in the data, chi-square has the advantage of ease of computation, which the student researcher will appreciate. A few minutes with a pocket calculator, following a simple readily available formula, is all that is needed for most chi-squares. Moreover, the reduction to a nominal level may not waste as much information as may appear since frequently the scores are in the form of ratings or similar measurements which may provide much less than interval measurement in any case.

Evaluation of Significance Testing in Group Designs

By helping to evaluate the possibility that findings may be due to chance variation, tests of significance perform a useful function in social research. But the limitations, and possible abuses, of such tests need to be kept in mind. First of all, it must be recognized that in most social work studies, tests of significance are based on a number of challengeable assumptions. For example, relatively few such studies use random samples from large populations. Consequently, in order for tests of significance to be applied, one must assume that whatever group was studied is representative of some population of interest to the researcher. A test of significance tells us then something about the stability of findings, if the study were to be repeated with additional samples from that same population.

Keep in mind, however, that the population is actually a construction of the researcher. Actual replications of the study would doubtless make use of different populations. Given this and other assumptions, tests of significance can best be seen as providing a rough criterion that helps us separate findings to be taken seriously from those that may be considered to be unstable, aberrant, unreliable, and so on. They give us a clue to those associations and differences that may be expected to occur again if additional studies were conducted.

While significance tests provide a useful screen for the elimination of inconsequential findings, the screen is used with the smallest amount of error when the associations or differences to be tested are specified in advance. Sometimes researchers proceed with no prior hypotheses but simply look for large associations or differences and apply tests of significance to them. This procedure in effect capitalizes on chance and opens the door to Type I error. It is analogous to placing a bet on a horse after the race is underway. As we know, any set of findings will produce a few that reflect chance occurrences. In fact if we use the .05 level, about one in twenty will be considered large enough to appear stable but will actually reflect the operation of chance. Now if we search simply for large differences or associations, we are bound to find these chance events and claim them as real findings. This practice may still have some justification if the number of tests conducted is small and if due recognition is made for the increased likelihood of Type I error.

The practice can be quite misleading if a large number of findings are tested and only those that appear to be "significant" are reported without information about the number of tests run. Thus if we use the .05 level and examine 100 correlations, we are likely to discover five or so that are "significant," even if we are dealing completely with random associations among the variables.

It is important not to confuse statistical significance with theoretical or practical significance. Tests of significance deal only with numbers and are no better than the numbers we have to work with. In experiments, statistically significant differences between treated and untreated groups may reflect the operation of extraneous factors. Tests of significance help us to rule out instability but nothing else. Also whether or not differences turn out to be significant is influenced by the size of the sample. Thus if very large samples are being compared, relatively minor differences or associations may be sufficiently stable to be "significant" but may have little theoretical or practical significance. (See Pragmatic Generalization in chapter 6 and Outcome Criteria in chapter 13.) As suggested, a test of significance gives us really minimal information: is a difference or association worth taking seriously? Once that fact has been established, we are interested in knowledge that is really more important: the size of the difference or association. For instance, a researcher may report that the outcome shows a significant correlation with ratings of practitioner empathy, and much may be made of the finding. We may learn, however, that the correlation was based on a study of a large number of cases and is only .15. We know that such a correlation would explain just a little over 2 percent of the variance between the two variables (r^2 equals variance explained as noted earlier), hardly a magnitude to get very excited about! Contrary to the common notion, tests of significance should be given *greater* weight when samples are small than when they are large (Bakan 1967).

In some circumstances tests of significance are best avoided. For example, the researcher may be dealing with an entire population, say the residents of an institution, and may not be interested in extrapolations to other institutions or to points further along in time beyond the one under study. Findings should then simply be assessed on the basis of the magnitude of differences or associations. Or the researcher may have conducted an exploratory study without prior hypotheses and may have obtained a large number of findings. As noted earlier, the use of tests of significance may be misleading. The most impressive or most interesting findings can simply be reported without a significance test.

Finally we would like to stress that the complexity, or sometimes obfuscation, of the reporting of statistical tests should not prevent consumers from making their own judgments about the meaningfulness of the findings tested. Keeping in mind that tests of significance, regardless of their form, serve only to rule out chance variation as an explanation of the findings, readers can examine the size of differences or associations and, more importantly, what the measures are based on and what they appear to add up to at a substantive level. Additional discussion of issues involved in the use of tests of significance may be found in Cowger (1984) and Glisson (1985).

Multivariate Analysis

Thus far we have examined different ways of analyzing the relationship between two variables, including methods of determining whether or not a stable relationship exists and of ascertaining the magnitude of the relationship (measures of association). As previously indicated, research in social work is typically concerned with more complex relationships, those occurring among a set of variables. To deal with these more complex relationships, we must turn to different forms of multivariate analysis, which we examine in this section.

The Three-Variable Case

The simplest form of multivariate analysis involves three variables. Consideration of analysis at this level reveals basic principles that can be applied to more complex forms.

Chapter 4 introduced the notion of statistical control in examining the relationship between two variables. This technique involves the introduction of a third variable, which may be antecedent or intervening (chapter 2), to see what happens to the original two-variable relationship. Sometimes the researcher's interest is simply in eliminating the influence of a third variable from the two-variable relationship. This can be accomplished through contingency analysis with categorical data by examining the two-variable relationship separately for each category of the third variable as was done in table 4.2. With interval or quasi-interval data, a procedure called partial correlation is used. Partial correlation permits one to control (hold constant) a variable by "partialing out" or eliminating its effect on the correlation between two other variables. In the reduced correlation, the influence of the third variable has been removed from both the variables (that is, the independent and dependent variables). Partial correlation is not limited to three variables; higher order partial correlations can be calculated to control a number of variables.

Often researchers add a third variable to increase their understanding of the original two-variable relationship. This procedure is usually referred to as elaboration. By adding a second independent variable, the researcher is able to "see" the relative contribution each independent variable makes in explaining the dependent variable and also the combined effect of the two variables on the dependent variable, for example, whether they are spurious, mediating, or moderating (chapter 2). In the illustration used in chapter 4, the relationship between father absence and son's self-concept disappeared when social class was introduced into the analysis. In other words, the original relationship turned out to be spurious or "not real" since it was, in fact, due to the third, mediating, variable, social class.

As noted, sometimes the third variable is an *antecedent* variable that occurs before the independent variable, as was social class, and sometimes it is an *intervening* variable. If it is antecedent, we say it helps to *explain* the two-variable relationship. If it is an intervening variable, we say it helps to *interpret* the relationship. The following hypothetical example illustrates the latter case.

Suppose we found that children with lower IQs had higher truancy rates than children with higher IQs. Suppose we also found that children who received lower grades had higher truancy rates than children with higher grades. Further suppose that most but not all of the children with lower IQs received low grades and that most but not all of the children with higher IQs received higher grades. When we controlled grades, suppose we found no correlation between IQ and truancy rates. This would suggest that children who are not successful in school, as indicated by grades, may lose interest in school and therefore are more apt to be truant. Since IQ is related to school achievement, we say we have traced the process by which IQ affects truancy or that we have interpreted the relationship between IQ and truancy by introducing the intervening variable, school achievement. This indicates the importance of the time sequence in trying to establish causality (diagram 11.1).

Not only may a third variable cause a relationship to be reduced or elimi-

DIAGRAM 11.1

Discovering a Mediating Variable Through Partial Correlation

DIRECT CORRELATION	AFTER CONTROLLING THROUGH PARTIAL CORRELATION
IQ → truancy	IQ ≠ truancy
↘ ↗	↘ ↗
grades	grades

nated, it may also lead to intensification of the relationship within one sub-group and its reduction within another, that is, it may be a moderator or specifier variable. When this happens, we say we have specified a condition under which the relationship occurs. Conditional relationships refer to the interaction of the two independent variables. When considering such relationships, we do not need to be concerned with whether the third variable is antecedent, intervening, or concurrent.

To illustrate, suppose we find a positive relationship between quality of a training program and satisfaction with the program; that is, the higher the quality of the training program according to some specified criteria, the more satisfied trainees are with it. When the relationship is examined separately for trainees with high aspirations and those with low aspirations, it intensifies somewhat for the high aspiration group and almost disappears for the low aspiraters. In other words, higher quality programs are viewed as more satisfactory by trainees who have higher aspirations, but the quality of the program matters little to trainees with lower aspirations. Level of aspiration is a moderator that helps to clarify the original relationship by specifying a contingent relationship.

The addition of a third variable may also cause a relationship to appear where there was none. This might happen if two variables are associated in opposite directions in subgroups of a third variable. The opposite effects may cancel each other out and conceal a relationship that really exists between the two original variables. For example, there may appear to be no relationship between use of service method and client change, but it may be found that the method helps mild depressives but harms severe depressives. As Lambert, Shapiro, and Bergin (1986) suggest, this canceling out may explain lack of apparent differences between experimental and control groups in studies of the effectiveness of intervention.

We have indicated some of the effects that adding a third variable can cause in a bivariate relationship. The possibilities include having no effect, causing a relationship to disappear, clarifying a contingent relationship, and causing a relationship to emerge.

Multiple Variables

The reason that adding a third variable can have such strange and diverse consequences for the original two-variable relationship is that the latter is made up of many partial or contingent associations. For example, in the illustrations in chapter 4 (tables 4.1, 4.2, and 4.3), the total association between father absence and self-concept included partial associations between social class and father absence and social class and self-concept. One could expand that example by substituting other variables as the test variable. One might find that there is a separate relationship between father absence and self-concept for boys and girls; for white and black children; for older and younger children; for first-born, middle, and youngest children; for children with authoritarian and permissive parents; and so on. In other words, the total relationship between father absence and self-concept is composed of many partial relationships.

In general, two-variable associations or correlations are composed of many partial associations or partial correlations. Often there is an interaction between these additional variables, that is, associations may exist among them. Hence, their combined effect may not be fully additive. Not only, then, do we need to identify the various contingent associations that comprise the relationship we are interested in, but also we need to understand how these contingent relationships combine. In other words, we need multivariate techniques that permit us to analyze simultaneously the relationships among several variables.

MULTIPLE REGRESSION ANALYSIS Multiple regression analysis (sometimes called "ordinary least squares multiple regression" to distinguish it from other forms of regression) is one of the most powerful tools in this regard. It accomplishes several important analytic tasks simultaneously. First it can reveal the relative effects of a number of independent variables on one dependent variable. Second, it can provide an estimate of the strength of the effect of any given variable, while controlling for the influence of remaining variables. Finally it can tell us how much of the variance in a dependent variable is explained by the entire set of independent variables used in the analysis. An example will help clarify these functions.

Gary (1995) used multiple regression as a major analytic method in his study of African-American men's perceptions of racial discrimination. His sample consisted of a stratified random sample of 537 such men drawn from a major mid-Atlantic city. To measure the dependent variable, perceived racial discrimination (PRD), he asked the men whether or not they had experienced racial discrimination within the past year in a number of social situations—at work, from the police, at the bank, etc. The independent variables of the study consisted of factors that might be associated with PRD. These included the experience of daily hassles with parents, children, friends, etc., the experience of stressful events during the past year such as illness, racial consciousness (degree of identification with black people), sex-role identity (degree of masculine versus feminine orientation), marital status, and age. He found that each of these variables, in separate tests, were in fact associated with PRD.

However, the analysis up to this point left important questions unanswered. One kind of question concerned the independent effects of these different variables on PRD. For example, the experience of daily hassles might be strongly associated with PRD, but this relationship might be explained by an antecedent variable—experience of stressful events. That is, those men who experienced stressful events during the previous year may be more inclined to have daily hassles. If one were to control for stressful events, the relationship between daily hassles and PRD might disappear. Another kind of question concerns the amount of variance in PRD that is explained by the entire set of variables. To what extent do these variables account for changes in PRD?

Answers to these questions were obtained through a multiple regression analysis, which is reproduced in table 11.8. Our attention is first drawn to the column headed "Simple r." In this column are given the correlations between each independent variable and PRD. As indicated earlier, all showed significant associations. The last column, with the heading of "Beta," displays key results of the multiple regression analysis per se. The numbers in the column are standardized regression coefficients (beta weights). Beta weights provide a measure (in standard deviation units) of amount of change in the dependent variable that is due to an independent variable when the *effect of all other independent variables in the regression analysis are held constant or are controlled*. The larger the variable's beta weight, the stronger that variable is as a predictor of the dependent variable. These coefficients remain the same regardless of the order in which the variables are added to the regression equation. They will change, however, if one or more variables are added to or subtracted from the equation or they may also change from sample to sample.

In the example, the beta weights give us important information that could not be obtained from the simple correlations. For example, we learn that the experience of daily hassles is the strongest predictor of PRD, when the effects of other variables are controlled. In other words, hassles are not an artifact of stressful events or other variables. Also note what happens to "age" as we move from the simple correlations to the more sophisticated level of regression coefficients. At the "simple r" level, age ($r = -.286$) is outranked only by hassles in the strength of its association with PRD. We also observe that the direction of the correlation is negative, that is, older men are less likely to perceive racial discrimination than younger men. However, when other variables are controlled in the multiple regression analysis, age becomes less significant as a predictor. Its beta weight is, in fact, surpassed by that of racial consciousness, whose simple corre-

326   *Quantitative Data Analysis*

TABLE 11.8

Stepwise Multiple Regression of Perceived Racial Discrimination and Selected Variables

VARIABLE*	MULTIPLE R	R² CHANGE	SIMPLE r	BETA[b]
HASSLES OR STRESSFUL EVENTS	.393	.155	.393	.297***
MARITAL STATUS	.430	.010	−.105	−.090
RACIAL CONSCIOUS– NESS	.439	.008	.056	.106***
AGE	.449	.008	−.286	−.104
SEX-ROLE IDENTITY	.456	.006	.068	.080*

Total R^2 = .207
Adjusted R^2 -.199
P(6,530) = 23.15, p = .000

Source: Gary 1995:214
[a]A dummy code was used for marital status (married = 1, not married = 0) and employment status (employed = 1, unemployed = 0).
[b]Beta = standardized coefficients.
*$p < .05$. **$p < .01$. ***$p< .001$.

lation with PRD was much lower. (Although terms like "effect of a variable," may be used in discussing multiple regression, we need to keep in mind that the procedure is essentially correlational and hence does not provide definitive answers for questions of causality. It can help us sort out which variables are the most influential within a particular set of variables, but cannot rule out the possibility that variables not considered in the analysis will have greater explanatory power.)

Another important piece of information is provided by the "R^2" at the bottom of the table. Recall from our earlier discussion of correlation that squaring a correlation coefficient yielded the amount of variance explained by the correlation. The R^2 extends that notion to the multiple correlations that are a part of regression analysis. In the example, R^2 = .207 (or adjusted R^2,= -.199) which tells us the combination of the 6 variables included in the analysis explains approximately 20 percent of the variance in PRD. However, more than three-fourths of the variance is left unexplained by the variables, or "regression model." This is not unusual in social work research. Generally, models that can explain as much as 15 percent of the variance are considered worthwhile, and one that can explain as much as 30 percent is very good indeed.

Regardless of the amount of variance they explain, regression models are most useful if the variables they contain are linked together by a theory. In the present example, Gary develops theoretical formulations from the literature and his own findings. Readers should not be overly impressed by models that may explain a good deal of the variance but are lacking in theoretical "glue."

Data under the columns headed by "multiple R" and "R^2 change," the meaning of which readers may be able to infer from the foregoing discussion, are less important to understanding multiple regression. Such data may or may not be presented in multiple regression tables.

Going down to the footnote of the table, we see that two of the variables are coded as dummy variables, a procedure that quantifies categorical variables for use in the analysis. Thus in respect to marital status, married persons were coded 1 and the unmarried persons were coded as 0. The 1s and 0s can be used in the same way as any set of numbers in the analysis.

With the use of dummy variables, researchers can combine categorical and continuous variables in multiple regression. The dependent variable, however, needs to be continuous (ordinal or higher). Variations of multiple regression, such as logistic regression and discriminant function analysis, can be used when the dependent variable is categorical (nominal). (An excellent reference on multiple regression analysis is Kerlinger and Pedhazur ([1973]).

ANALYSIS OF VARIANCE AND COVARIANCE The t test is limited to the comparison of two means; analysis of variance (ANOVA) is used to compare three or more means. For example, a researcher may be interested in comparing the effectiveness of three different methods of treatment (or of leadership styles, work conditions, and so on). The comparison may involve a decision concerning the differences among the sample means on the dependent variable. The analysis of variance technique can answer the question: Are the differences among sample means large enough to imply a difference among the corresponding population means? Analysis of variance breaks down the total variance in the dependent measures into component variances and pits two sources of variance against each other. In the simplest case, the one-way analysis of variance (which is actually a bivariate method), the total variance is broken down into between-groups variance (presumably due to the experimental, or independent, variable) and within-groups variance (presumably due to error or randomness). The test-statistic is F; the F ratio consists of between-groups variance in the numerator and within-groups variance in the denominator. Thus, the larger the variance due to the treatment variable compared to error variance, the more likely the result will be statistically significant. As Kerlinger (1985) points out, this is what we seek to accomplish by experimental manipulation: to increase the variance between means. That is, we attempt to make the means different from one another.

For example, Caputo (1998) used ANOVA to assess the differences among black, Hispanic, and white men and women on the Income-to-Poverty Ratio (IPR), a measure of economic well-being. The probability of the calculated F-ratio was .0001, which was statistically significant (less than his criteria for significance of .05). Thus, we know that the variance between groups (black men, black women, white men, white women, and so on) is greater than the variance within each group (among the black men, among the black women, and so on).

More complicated analysis of variance techniques are multiple analysis of variance (MANOVA) and analysis of covariance (ANCOVA). MANOVA, an extension of ANOVA described above, provides an overall test of differences between two or more groups across multiple measures of the dependent variable. Often, if not usually in research, the dependent variable is measured in a number of ways. In ANOVA one would test these variables one at a time. There would be as many ANOVAs as there would be measures of the dependent variable. Such multiple tests increase the odds of obtaining a "chance" finding. MANOVA provides protection against obtaining such a spurious finding by testing all dependent measures simultaneously. In other words the test asks if the groups differ significantly, taking into account the multiple measures. If the MANOVA is significant, one can then test for specific differences using ANOVAs and t tests.

In situations where groups are measured twice, as in prospective experimental designs, ANCOVA is used to provide "statistical control" (chapter 4) for initial characteristics that may bias comparisons between groups. The technique is most commonly used in experiments in which methods of assigning subjects to groups fail to produce the desired equivalence. Thus, clients may be assigned nonrandomly to experimental and control groups in a test of a service program. The experimental group members may score higher on measures of motivation than the control group members and motivation may prove to be correlated with outcome. ANCOVA can be used to hold motivation constant in comparisons of the groups on measures of outcome.

ANCOVA can also be used in other contexts to adjust for differences between groups. In a study previously referred to, Holmes (1995a) was interested in comparing short-term treatment outcome for clients with a history of childhood abuse with those who lacked such a history. ANCOVA was used to adjust for differences between the two groups in respect to demographic and other variables (Holmes 1995b). When multiple dependent measures are used, an extension of ANCOVA—multiple analysis of covariance (MANCOVA)—is appropriate. Even more sophisticated statistics are also coming into use, for example, random regression models (RRM's) that not only control various covariates but also allow estimation of person-specific effects (Toseland and McCallion 1997).

FACTOR ANALYSIS Factor analysis is another powerful multivariate analytic technique. Like multiple regression analysis and most analyses of variance, it involves complicated computations and requires the use of a computer. Factor analysis is a method of analyzing the intercorrelations within a set of variables. This technique is used to determine the number and nature of the underlying variables called factors among a larger number of measures. It extracts from a set of measures what the measures have in common (common factor variance) and thus reduces the larger pool of measures to a smaller number of factors. Factors are constructs or abstractions that underlie the set of measures. They are empirical entities without inherent substantive meaning. Factor analysis is often used to develop and test the construct validity of measures such as scales, tests, and questionnaire items; it may also be used to reduce a large number of variables to a smaller, and hopefully more meaningful, set.

Fortune (1985b) factored the responses of 101 social work students to a questionnaire designed to measure their satisfaction with different aspects of fieldwork. Responses entered into the factor analysis consisted of student ratings of satisfaction on seven-point scales (7 = very satisfied). Examples of the items rated as well as results of the factor analysis are presented in table 11.9.

The items are organized into factors produced by the analysis. As can be seen, the analysis groups the items into clusters (*factors*). The grouping is based on solely statistical considerations—that is, on the pattern of intercorrelation among the items. The factor labels, e.g., Professional Role, are designations devised by the researchers to capture the observed statistical "glue" which joins the items. The labels may or may not correspond to whatever organizing concepts the researchers had in mind in developing the instrument. The "factor loadings" (second column) can be interpreted as correlations between given items and the factors to which they belong. Factor loadings must meet specified criteria of size—in excess of .30 for example—for the item to be considered as belonging to the factor; by the same token, high loadings, for example, in excess of .80, indicate a high degree of correlation with the factor.

TABLE 11.9

Average Item Scores and Factor Loadings for Satisfaction and Perceptions of the Field Placement

ITEM	ITEM MEAN	FACTOR LOADING
Satisfaction with field agency	5.25	
Satisfaction with field instructor	5.28	
Satisfaction with field learning	5.42	
Factor 1: School-Agency Liaison		
My contact with my field liaison bas been satisfactory to meet my learning needs.	4.10	.918
If there are problems at my field placement, I am comfortable consulting with my field liaison.	4.01	.873
When I have problems in my placement, I go to my field liaison.	3.05	.838
I am aware of the possible roles of my field liaison.	4.68	.708
Communication between the school of social work and my agency is adequate.	3.99	.663
Factor 2: Professional Role		
I have the same responsibilities as the professional staff at my agency.	5.44	.859
I am included in all agency activities that professional staff are expected to attend.	5.54	.825
I have the same privileges as the professional staff at my agency.	5.23	.779
I have been able to meet the expectations of my field placement.	6.13	.636
I agree with my agency's policies.	5.00	.457
Factor 3: Relevant Learning		
I enjoy working with the type of client I see at my agency.	5.94	.840
My field work assignments this year have been relevant to my learning goals.	5.64	.751
I was able to actively participate in designing my learning experience.	5.54	.616
Factor 4: Supervision		
My field instructor enjoys his/her role as "teacher."	5.79	.770
I have been encouraged to express new or different ideas in my practicum setting.	5.30	.654

TABLE 11.9 (*Continued*)

ITEM	ITEM MEAN	FACTOR LOADING
Factor 5: Practicality		
My agency provides adequate physical facilities (i.e., desk, office, supplies) for students.	5.11	.727
My courses this year have been relevant to my field experience.	4.75	.536
Factor 6: Evaluation Anxiety		
There is conflict between the agency and the school's policies concerning expectations for students in the field.*	4.39	.716
Having a "pass/fail" system reduces my anxiety concerning my field placement.	5.74	.668

Source: Fortune 1985b.

*Scoring is reversed (higher = less perceived conflict). On all other items, higher scores indicate more of the quality.

By grouping together measures that intercorrelate, factor analysis not only serves to reduce and organize the data, but can generate new measures for use in further data analysis. Thus in the Fortune et al. study the six scales produced by the factor analysis (table 11.9) were in turn correlated with global measures of satisfaction with field agency, field instructor, and field learning. The scales proved to correlate positively with these satisfaction variables. However, a striking exception was the lack of correlation between the School-Agency Liaison Scale and *any* of the satisfaction measures. Thus with the help of factor analytic techniques, the researchers were able to discover an intriguing pattern. While students were less satisfied with School-Agency Liaison than with other aspects of fieldwork (as can be seen from table 11.9) their relative unhappiness with this aspect had little apparent effect on their satisfaction with their agencies, their instructors, or their learning.

Limitations of Multivariate Analysis

As we indicated at the beginning of this chapter, we believe multivariate techniques hold a great deal of promise for social work research. These techniques handle the complexities of behavioral and social phenomena far better than simpler analyses that deal with two variables at a time. However, even multivariate procedures are limited in the extent to which they reflect the realities of the phenomena of interest to social workers. We mention briefly the major limitations we see in the use of multivariate analysis, particularly those procedures based on correlation methods.

First, multivariate methods are essentially tools that should be guided, or programmed, intelligently. The researcher must decide what variables go into the analyses and how the analyses are to be performed. These decisions should be informed decisions, based on the researcher's theoretical notions. Accordingly, although multivariate techniques are useful in teasing out possible causal relations, they seldom adequately control the range of extraneous factors that may be influencing dependent variables.

Second, the results of any multivariate analysis are dependent on the particular procedures or routines employed. For example, the solution selected and type of rotation used influence the results of a factor analysis. Similarly, in analysis of covariance (ANCOVA), the results may differ depending on whether the pretest scores are entered into the formula before or at the same time as the independent variable.

A third limitation has been referred to but bears repeating. When multivariate techniques are used with ordinal data, as is often the case, resulting distortions are compounded in the elaborate manipulations of the data, involving perhaps thousands of calculations that are integral to the use of these techniques.

The quality of the measures themselves usually constitutes another limitation. The imperfections of scales for measuring marital satisfaction, self-concept, group cohesion, and the like, can be clarified sometimes by multivariate techniques but cannot be corrected by them.

Finally, reproducibility is always a matter of concern. For example, the "underlying structures" in attitude, client change, or other phenomena that may be revealed by factor analytic techniques may vary considerably from sample to sample. These limitations arise, of course, in the use of simpler methods of analysis. Our essential point here is that the sophistication of analytic techniques and the complex statistical displays that often accompany them should not blind us to what—sometimes what little—is actually being conveyed by the data.

Analysis of Time Series Data

Time series data, which, broadly speaking, consist of repeated measurements over time, can be gathered on samples of all sizes and analyzed in a variety of ways. Analysis for group designs such as panel studies is beyond the scope of this text. A conceptual outline of a typical analysis is presented in chapter 5 in the study of adolescent drug involvement over time (Krohn et al. 1996). In this section we shall discuss analysis of time series data obtained in single-system designs.

Significance Testing

As was observed in chapter 6 the usual method of ruling out instability as a source of alternative explanation in single-system time series data is to "eyeball" a graph or other data display and to make a judgment about whether or not observed changes appear to be greater than those that might have occurred by chance. If changes are of great magnitude and the data base is sufficiently large, the role of chance may be reasonably discounted using this method. But often the amount of change is modest or there are few data points. The last consideration is sometimes overlooked. If there are only three or four observations during baseline and a similar number during intervention, a fairly large difference may be a chance artifact. Furthermore experimenters and others who hope that intervention will be successful may understandably overestimate the amount of change that has taken place and erroneously dismiss the possibilities of chance influences. (See Rubin and Knox [1996] for a discussion of "ambiguous" graphs.) Thus, there is a need for a systematic means of assessing chance factors in time series.

Unfortunately, however, time series data do not lend themselves to a straightforward application of standard statistical tests, such as those that have been discussed in preceding sections. The major difficulty is lack of independence between data points in a time series. Standard statistical tests are based on the assumption that data points, or sample elements, are independent of one another. For example, in testing the results of a group experiment it is assumed that the outcome for client A exerts no influence on the outcome for client B. While this assumption may apply reasonably well to the usual group study, it is hard to justify with time series data which by their very nature tend to be serially dependent or autocorrelated. In single-system studies different data points concern the same individual, hence any one value is likely to be influenced by its predecessors (serial dependency). Suppose daily observations are recorded on progress made by a mildly retarded child learning to read out loud. Data points take the form of errors made in reading passages of comparable length and difficulty. It is likely that the data would assume the shape of a learning curve: the number of errors made each day would tend to decrease at a gradual rate over time. The following series of recorded errors might in fact be obtained: 10, 9, 8, 7, 6, 5, 5, 3, 2, 0. It is obvious that how the child performs on a given day is related to his previous performance as his reading improves. Autocorrelation can be seen at a statistical level if one pairs each observation with its successor (10/9, 9/8, 8/7, 7/6, and so on). As in any correlation, the values in each pair covary.

Autocorrelation can also be negative as might occur in rapidly fluctuating behavior and need not be confined to adjacent data points, as might be the case if there is a time lag between a behavior and its consequences. Therefore, a correlation might occur between time points 1, 3, 5, 7, 9 (lag 2); 1, 4, 7, 10 (lag 3); and so on.

In addition, standard statistical tests do not take into account the trends in time series data. In figure 11.8, a marked change in trend occurs coincident with the beginning of treatment. Yet, the means for the baseline and treatment phases are similar; and the *t*-test for differences in means would not reveal a significant difference. Obviously, significance testing would need to determine changes in trends—usually referred to as a change in "slope"—as well as a change in level of magnitude. More sophisticated approaches to significance testing with time series data are available (Bloom, Fischer, and Orme 1995). These more elaborate methods, referred to generally as *time series analysis*, ascertain significance of change in slope and level with adjustments for autocorrelation found in the series.

Applications of these techniques to clinical practice have been limited by their computational complexity, which necessitates use of a computer. Another obstacle has been the requirement for more observations than would normally be obtained in a clinical case.

Simpler Approximations

Bloom, Fischer, and Orme (1995) describe a number of simpler approaches to the assessment of instability. These include the proportion frequency approach, Shewart Charts, and ordinary tests of significance, such as chi-square and *t* tests. For example, in a basic time series (AB) design, Shewart Charts (Shewart 1931) project a two-standard deviation band based on the variability of baseline data into the intervention phase. If two consecutive data points fall outside the band (and continue outside), the difference from baseline performance is considered statistically significant (at the .05 level). As these authors indicate, these procedures can lead to misleading results if data are autocorrelated. For example, Shewart Charts will give misleading results if there is uncorrected autocorrelation or a baseline trend in the direction of the intervention-phase data, for example, if a child's temper tantrums had started to decrease during baseline. Bloom, Fischer, and Orme describe both manual

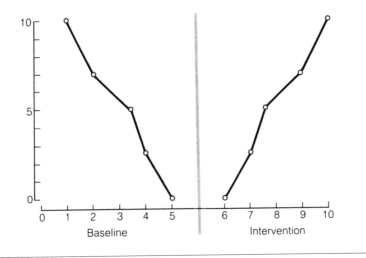

FIGURE 11.8
Contrasting trends but similar means for baseline and intervention periods

and computerized methods for identifying and adjusting for autocorrelation and other potential problems preliminary to the use of the procedures.

Such techniques can provide bench marks for assessing the magnitude of findings. Although probability values that might be ascribed to them may be approximate, the procedures offer a convenient standard for deciding which findings will be taken "seriously."

Meta-Analysis

Methods of analysis considered thus far are used to make sense of the data from individual studies. As research accumulates in given areas of knowledge, analytic methods are needed to synthesize the findings from aggregations of studies. A time-honored method familiar to all students is the narrative research review, in which a scholar examines existing studies on a topic and draws conclusions about what their findings add up to. Meta-analysis, a more recently developed method for synthesizing reported research, makes use of statistical methods for combining and analyzing data from the original studies. Since meta-analyses are being used increasingly to carry out research syntheses, it is important to understand their characteristic features as well as their strengths and limitations.

In a meta-analysis, each study provides data for analysis, much like an individual in a survey. In conducting a meta-analysis an effort is made to obtain a comprehensive, if not exhaustive, set of studies for a given topic and time period. This effort is customarily described through an explicit delineation of search procedures and criteria used for selecting studies. (It should be noted that a good narrative review might also make use of such retrieval procedures.)

In meta-analyses, data from individual studies are aggregated. For example Reid and Crisafulli (1990) conducted a meta-analysis to determine the relationship between marital conflict and child behavior problems. Thirty-one studies that examined this relationship were located. Most of these studies expressed the relationship in the form of correlation coefficients or in statistics that could be converted to such coefficients. These correlations were averaged. Thus it was found that mean correlation between measures of marital conflict and of child behavior problems for these studies as a whole was .12. It was also found that this correlation was higher for boys (.16) than for girls (.05).

In the language of meta-analysis measures of relationship between independent and dependent variables are referred to as *effect sizes*. In order to combine effect sizes from different studies, they need to be put in standardized form. Relationships expressed in terms of correlation coefficients, as in the Reid and Crisafulli meta-analysis, are already in that form. Thus a mean effect size for their 31 studies could be obtained through a simple average. Often, however, the original findings are not in standardized form.

To illustrate how such findings can be standardized, we shall perform a mini meta-analysis with two hypothetical studies. Suppose we have two experiments that test the efficacy of social skills training with delinquent youth. In the first experiment, the experimental group exceeds the control group by an average of 10 points on a scale to measure proficiency in social skills. In the second study the difference is 1.5 points, but a different skill proficiency measure with a smaller range of possible scores is used. In computing an effect size, the experimental-control differences for each study are divided by the standard deviation of either the control group or the pooled standard deviation of the control and experimental group, depending on what method of meta-analysis is being used. The result is two scores in the form of standard deviation units, that is in the form of a standard or z score. Like any standard scores, effect sizes can be averaged and used in other kinds of statistical analyses. Thus the effect size of the first experiment is .61 and the second, .41, the mean effect size of the two experiments is .51. By determining the area of the normal curve associated with such an effect size, it is possible to translate the effect size into a statement of the relative gains of treated clients compared with their control counterparts.

Such a translation indicates that an average effect size of .51 means that the average youth in the treatment programs would have a skill proficiency score greater than 69 percent of youths in the control groups.

Other variables can be generated from studies in a meta-analysis, such as the type of intervention used or the kind of research design employed. Typically studies are coded (categorized) in terms of a range of such variables, which can then be used in statistical analyses. For example suppose there were 30 skills training studies with delinquents that varied in respect to the type of training methods used. It would be possible to determine if there was a statistical relation between such variables as skill training methods and effect size.

As the foregoing suggests, one of the advantages of meta-analysis is its ability to produce precise, quantitative syntheses of findings from a collection of studies. From a narrative review one might conclude that there was evidence for the effectiveness of a particular method. A meta-analysis could inform us about the degree of effectiveness attained as well as about factors associated with the effectiveness of the method. Because of their reliance on quantitative methods, the advantages of meta-analysis become particularly compelling with large samples of studies, say in excess of 50.

Meta-analysis has certain limitations, however, which need to be kept in mind. Perhaps the most serious is the combining of highly divergent studies that may differ in respect to definitions of variables, methodology, and so on. This limitation, referred to as the "apples and oranges" problem, can take many forms. For example, the meta-analyst interested in studying the effectiveness of social skills training may find considerable variation from study to study in how social skills are defined and what social skills are tested. Moreover some studies may use as outcome measures an assessment of how well the skills were performed in a role play test. Other studies may use measures of how well the skills were implemented in actual life situations. Solutions to the problem include limiting the meta-analysis to studies that are similar in key respects or to take important variations into account in the meta-analysis itself. Thus one could do a meta-analysis on certain types of skills training programs or separate out such types in the meta-analysis. However, no solution can completely eliminate the problem of study divergence.

A second limitation is somewhat of a special case of the first—combining of studies that differ in quality. For example, studies using randomized experimental designs might be combined with those that use nonequivalent groups. If "apples and oranges" is an appropriate metaphor for the first issue, then "wheat and chaff" might do for this one. In narrative reviews studies may be differentially weighted, at the reviewer's discretion, in terms of their methodological rigor, sample size, and so on. That is, a well-designed study with a large sample may be accorded considerable weight, while small uncontrolled studies may be discounted.

In meta-analysis the problem is handled through sample selection and statistical analysis. The usual solutions parallel those of the "apples and oranges" problem—to limit the meta-analysis to studies of the same (usually the most rigorous) quality and to account for differences in quality by coding studies in terms of rigor, etc. The resulting "quality variable" is then entered into the analysis to determine if quality is correlated with effect size. The usual paucity of high quality studies limits both solutions.

The results of a meta-analysis may be misleading if it fails to include all existing research on the question addressed. A common problem here is restricting the meta-analysis to published research. Unpublished studies may be less likely to report significant findings (Strube, Gardner, and Hartmann 1985); the "file drawer problem" (as it has been called [Rosenthal 1979] because this is where unpublished studies presumably wind up) may be more important in some types of meta-analyses than others, but it is usually an issue in most. Of course, the best solution is to search assiduously for all studies relating to a particular question. Many unpublished studies, such as doctoral dissertations, may be located through computerized data bases.

Another solution—"the fail-safe N"—has been developed by Rosenthal (1979). In this procedure, one calculates the number of studies with zero effect size that would be needed to nullify a significant finding in the meta-analysis. The larger the number of such hypothetical studies that would be needed to negate the finding, the more confidence one has that the finding is indeed valid.

A final limitation pertains to meta-analyses in which effect sizes are computed for multiple measures in each study and statistical tests are performed on the resulting effect sizes. This practice may lead to "inflated n's." For example, a meta-analysis may consist of 10 studies that average 6 measures per study. In statistical testing the true sample size should be the 10 independent studies, not the 60 effect sizes, which would reflect considerable interdependence in the data. A straightforward solution to the problem is to use one effect size per study, although to do so may create other difficulties (Fischer 1990). (For fuller discussions of the methodology of meta-analysis, see Rosenthal [1984] and Fischer [1990].)

The limitations and problems cited above need to be kept in mind in conducting or evaluating a meta-analysis. The value of its contribution will depend on how they are resolved.

Summary

Analysis of quantitative data is a systematic, usually well-planned, process that is driven by three considerations: the hypotheses or research questions in a study, the level of measurement of the variables involved, and the need to rule out alternative explanations through statistical controls.

Once data are coded and categorized following rules of measurement, the first step in most quantitative studies is providing frequency counts and summary univariate statistics that describe the sample on critical variables. Statistics that summarize the typical aspects of the sample are measures of central tendency: the mean (interval level data), median (ordinal and interval), and mode (all levels of measurement). Those that describe the spread or variability of the sample include the standard deviation (interval) and range (ordinal).

Bivariate association—how much does one variable vary with another?—can be conveyed pictorially through crosstabulations or scattergrams, or can be assessed through measures of association such as the Pearson product moment correlation (r) (for interval data), Spearman's rank-order correlation coefficient (rho) (ordinal), or phi (nominal). Most such statistics indicate strength of association by higher numbers (closer to ±1.0). Many also indicate direction by pluses or minuses, with positive association (+) indicating that higher values of each variable are associated with each other and negative (-) that lower are associated with higher.

Although an investigator may hypothesize a relation between two variables, the real interest includes ruling out alternative explanations and explaining the conditions under which there is an association between independent and dependent variables. To do so requires adding additional variables to the statistical stew. Multivariate statistics use various approaches to control for or account for the effects of additional variables. Some, like ANCOVA, adjust for unwanted variations between groups when assessing changes over time. Others, like multiple regression or logistic regression, show the relationship of many variables to a dependent variable while simultaneously controlling statistically for the effects of each variable.

The associations (or differences among groups) indicated by bivariate or multivariate statistics may or may not occur in the population from which the sample is drawn. To assess the likelihood of an association being a "real" one, we use inferential statistics to estimate how likely it is that the result might occur in the population or (more realistically) in another sample. Such tests of statistical significance—for example, the F-test, t-test, or chi-square—use known sampling distributions to estimate a probability of occurrence from the sample data. A test of statistical significance tests the null hypothesis, which is essentially the opposite of the research hypothesis. For example, if the research hypothesis is that two groups will differ on some mean score, the null hypothesis states that they will have the same mean score. If the null hypothesis is rejected (based on calculations from the sample data), the research hypothesis is accepted, but with some risk of error, α, also called Type I error. Prior to conducting the statistical test, the investigator sets a criterion or significance level for α. If the calculated probability of occurrence (from sample data) is equal to or below the criterion, then the results are considered statistically significant. This significance level, or Type I error, is the risk of being wrong when rejecting the null hypothesis (i.e., the risk of being wrong when one concludes that a result is statistically significant, or that the research hypothesis is upheld). Social workers tend to use a .05 significance level (1 chance in 20 of being wrong), but .01 or .001 are common, and .10 may be used with small samples or in exploratory research.

These statistical tests are most commonly applied to group data, but variations may be applied to single-system time series designs, and specialized complex and simple tests are also available. A major problem in single-system time series designs is autocorrelation, or having measures that are dependent on each other because they come from the same system.

Meta-analysis is a statistical technique that allows compiling results from many studies to estimate overall results more systematically and precisely than traditional literature reviews. However, like most other statistical techniques, meta-analyses are only as good as the assumptions about the data and the quality of the studies.

In terms of criteria for establishing causality (chapter 4), statistical techniques can establish association, the first step. They can help rule out some alternative explanations through statistical controls, and they can specify conditions under which a relationship might hold, the third step. They cannot address the second step in establishing causality—showing that the independent variable occurred before the dependent variable; only design can do so conclusively. And by themselves, statistics cannot relate findings to theory in any meaningful way. A statistically significant association, even one well controlled through multivariate analysis, is no more than an association, and does not demonstrate causality. As with all other parts of the research process, the results of statistical analysis must be assessed in relation to other parts of the study, including the quality of the measurement, the representativeness of the sample, and the theoretical framework for the hypothesis.

TABLE 11.10
Common Statistics by Level of Measurement

LEVEL OF MEASUREMENT	MEASURES OF CENTRAL TENDENCY	MEASURES OF VARIABILITY	BIVARIATE PICTORIAL ANALYSIS	BIVARIATE MEASURES OF ASSOCIATION	TESTS OF SIGNIFICANCE	MULTIVARIATE MEASURES OF ASSOCIATION
NOMINAL	Frequencies Mode		Crosstabulation	Eta; Lambda; Tau ; Phi coefficient; Contingency coefficient; Yule's Q; Cramer's V	Chi-Square (χ^2)	Logistic Regression (dependent is nominal, independent may be nominal or interval)
ORDINAL	Median	Range	Scattergram	Gamma Kendall's coefficient of concordance (W); Spearman's rank-Somer's D; order correlation coefficient (rho)	Mann-Whitney U	
INTERVAL/RATIO	Mean	Standard deviation		Pearson product moment correlation coefficient (r); Coefficient of determination (r^2)	t-test (two-category nominal independent variable, interval dependent); Analysis of variance (ANOVA) (3+ category independent variable, interval dependent variable) (F-ratio)	Partial correlation; Multiple regression (independent may be nominal or interval, dependent must be interval) (R, R^2); Multiple analysis of variance (MANOVA); Analysis of covariance (ANCOVA); Factor analysis

12 Qualitative Research

In our earlier discussion of the methodological orientation of research (chapter 4), we presented an introduction to some of the assumptions and characteristics of qualitative approaches to inquiry. In subsequent chapters, we introduced a number of methods, such as snowball sampling and semistructured interviewing, that are used in both quantitative and qualitative studies. In this chapter we take up the distinctive methodology of qualitative research in some depth. (Before beginning the reader may first wish to review our discussion of qualitative methodology in chapter 4.)

Modes of Qualitative Research

Qualitative research is characterized by an effort to reason inductively, from the observed phenomena to concepts and theories, by flexibility in use of methods, and by an "insider" rather than "outsider" stance. In respect to the dimensions of design presented in chapter 4, qualitative research is by definition naturalistic. Samples are typically small and nonprobability. Although most studies are largely exploratory-descriptive in respect to their knowledge producing functions, most contain explanatory features and some are primarily designed to create explanatory theory. Although qualitative studies have many common features, a variety of types can be distinguished. Some of those commonly used in social work research are briefly described and illustrated below: grounded theory, ethnography, narrative, discourse analysis, and program and case evaluation. The specific qualitative methods from which they all draw will be taken up in subsequent sections. An excellent overview of qualitative research, along with considerable technical detail, may be found in Denzin and Lincoln (1994). For social work applications see Sherman and Reid (1994) and Riessman (1994).

Grounded Theory

Originally developed by Glaser and Strauss (1967), grounded theory has become a widely used method of qualitative research in social work. In addition to investigations that explicitly use grounded theory, many others use the essence of the approach implicitly and thus can also be seen as grounded theory studies. Such a study attempts to develop theory from qualitative data. The theory developed is based on (or grounded in) the data of the study. As Strauss and Corbin (1994:274) state "the major difference between this methodology and other approaches to qualitative research is its emphasis on theory development."

In typical studies, theory is developed through largely inductive methods from in-depth interviews, field observation, and analysis of documents. Use is made of theoretical sampling and methods of constant comparison (discussed in a subsequent section of the chapter). Whatever the methods of sampling or data collection, texts are produced in the form of transcripts of tape recorded interviews, field notes, and so on. These texts are then coded in order to identify patterns in the data that might lead to the development of theory. In one grounded theory study, Burnette (1994) attempted to gain insight into how the frail elderly coped with illness. She interviewed 20 elderly subjects who had one or more chronic illnesses and who lived alone. She was able to identify a number of coping strategies used by her subjects. For example, she found that while her subjects made use of social supports (relatives, friends, etc.), they did so as if they were using a precious resource that was not to be squandered. They tried to "save" their sources of support until they really needed them. Burnette was able to build such insights into a broader theory of how subjects like hers were able to manage their illnesses while remaining independent. A detailed presentation of grounded theory methodology may be found in Strauss and Corbin (1990). For applications in social work see Gilgun (1994).

Ethnography

Ethnography has its roots in anthropological studies of cultures. It is conducted through immersing one's self into a culture, which may include such continuing groups as families, youth gangs, and cottages in residential treatment centers. Participant observation is the primary data collection method augmented by other techniques, such as informal (conversational) interviewing or collection of autobiographies. There is usually emphasis on attempting to understand phenomena from the point of view of the persons studied—the "insider" viewpoint—although researchers may combine this perspective with an "outsider" view of their subjects. (This dual perspective is found frequently throughout qualitative research.)

Ethnographic methods have also been applied to the study of specific situations and settings, such as welfare offices and interdisciplinary teams. In one illustrative investigation, Goodson-Lawes (1994) studied a small number of recently immigrated Mexican and Vietnamese families over the course of the year. In carrying out her study she spent a considerable amount of time with the families, much of it in everyday activities. She served such roles as legal advocator, health care educator, translator, and homework tutor. Through this process she was able to gain intimate knowledge of how the newcomers struggled to adapt to a strange and often baffling environment.

The Davis and Srinivasan (1994) study of a shelter for battered woman was used earlier (chapter 3) to illustrate the role of theory in research. It is also an illustration of an ethnographic study. One of the authors (Srinivasan) worked in the shelter as a volunteer. To augment her on-site observations, Srinivasan had many conversational interviews with both staff and residents. The data revealed an important feature of the shelter that may not have emerged in another kind of study: although the shelter was set up to empower oppressed women, its hierarchical organization, in which the residents had little say in how things were done and had to live under rigid house rules, was inadvertently creating a new form of oppression. For additional discussion of ethnography see Atkinson and Hammersley (1994) and Sherman and Reid (1994). A relevant periodical is the *Journal of Contemporary Ethnography*.

Narratives

Narrative methods are based in the old and familiar practice of storytelling. Social work practitioners do a form of narrative when they ask clients to describe their childhoods or to tell how they became involved with drugs. In qualitative research, narratives are developed in in-depth interviews in which the researcher helps the subject reveal his or her experiences relating to certain themes. Narrative is concerned not only with the content of the stories but how they are told. How subjects present themselves, what they include or omit, how they construct and express meaning are of particular interest (Riessman 1993). Researchers attempt to identify patterns in the experiences revealed and the ways in which they are revealed.

For example, Robinson (1994) used a narrative approach in her interviews with 30 delinquent girls. At the beginning of each interview she asked the girl to "Tell me about your family." Relationships revealed in response to this question were further explored. Among the patterns revealed in the narratives was the connection between the girls' experience of sexual abuse in the home and their delinquent behavior. In another study, Martin (1994) used a form of narrative—oral history—with 15 elderly African Americans to gain an understanding of their experience of oppression and the ways they coped with it. (For further reading on narrative see Riessman [1993].)

Discourse Analysis

In discourse analysis the focus is on the study of verbal interchange—what transpires, for example, between a practitioner and client in a clinical interview. This kind of analysis, which may make use of both quantitative and qualitative methods, incorporates approaches used in the study of treatment processes in social work and related fields, and, of course, includes much more, such as analysis of human conversations in a variety of contexts (see chapter 15).

Qualitative methods may include different forms of linguistic and interpretative analyses. For example, Sherman (1994) did an intensive study of practitioner-client discourse in a single case, making use of both a quantitative scale to measure the client's affective experiencing during the session and an interpretative analysis of the events in the session that seemed to account for the client's shifts in his level of experiencing. Additional qualitative approaches to discourse analysis will be taken up in chapter 15. (For further reading on discourse analysis see Sherman and Reid [1994].)

Program and Case Evaluation

A qualitative approach to program and case evaluation does not constitute a distinct mode of inquiry, as does grounded theory or ethnography. It rather constitutes an application of these and other modes to the practical problem of assessing service delivery. However, given its potential importance in social work there is justification for considering this approach on a par with the others.

When the target is an agency program, qualitative evaluations are generally concerned with in-depth examinations of both service operations and outcomes. In studying the characteristics or outcome of a program, qualitative researchers may use participant observation, conversational and open-ended interviewing, and review of documents to gain an understanding of the services the program is actually offering.

The use of qualitative methods has a particular advantage in complex, difficult-to-define programs involving a variety of components and service providers. For example Gerstel et al. (1996) evaluated a shelter system for homeless families. Their intent was to get both the institutional side of things—what policies there were, why, how well they worked—and the consumers' views of the system—why they were homeless, what effect the shelters had, and so on. The research team conducted two years of field observation in 10 shelters "to observe the enactment of official practices, the enforcement of housing regulations, and the implementation of services" (p. 545). They also had regular contact with the homeless, shelter personnel, and county department of social services personnel. They conducted open-ended interviews with staff responsible for delivering services and with selected clients who had used the shelters. Such interviews may be able to penetrate to a depth of client and staff revelation not possible in structured interviews or self-administered questionnaires in which clients may give superficial and socially desirable responses (see chapter 14). Finally, they conducted semistructured interviews with all the people who entered transitional housing, interviews which included a life history calendar as a way of getting recollections of important life events.

Qualitative program evaluations often rely on collections of intensive case studies. The same methodology can also be applied to an evaluation of work with an individual, family, or group. In such situations, the practitioner may be thought of as a participant-observer who can record observations, maintain logs, analyze tapes of treatment sessions, and so on. He or she might also use an in-depth interview as part of a termination (or planned follow-up) session with the client(s) to gain evaluation data. In addition qualitative methods for studying the processes of change, which will be taken up in chapter 15, might be used.

Although qualitative methods can provide an in-depth, holistic, and detailed understanding of program processes and outcomes, they are usually not able to provide definitive evidence that program effects have actually occurred. Without control or comparison groups, along with quantitative measures of effects, it is difficult to assert that a program is more effective than some alternative condition. A combination of qualitative and controlled quantitative methodologies might be able to produce evaluations that could not only identify intervention effects with some degree of confidence and precision but could also produce detailed descriptions of these effects as well as the processes that brought them about. For example, Gerstel et al.'s (1996) evaluation of the homeless shelters in fact combined qualitative and quantitative data, including a sophisticated regression analysis of factors predicting length of stay in the shelter system. Other examples of evaluation studies making use of qualitative methods can be found in Sherman and Reid (1994). For further reading on the use of qualitative methods in evaluation see Greene (1994) and Patton (1990).

The approaches described above constitute only some of the forms of qualitative research of interest to social workers. Other modes of qualitative methodology, all of them overlapping with one another and with those presented above, include ethnomethodology, phenomonology, and hermeneutics. It should also be noted that much qualitative research reflects a mixture of different forms and that many studies do not carry any particular label other than some generic term such as "field study" or simply "qualitative study."

The Methods of Qualitative Research

In qualitative research, methods of sampling, data collection, and analysis do not necessarily occur in separate stages as they do in quantitative research. A qualitative investigator may begin his or her inquiry with a single case or several cases. As data are collected the investigator begins looking for patterns, themes, or organizing constructs. When these emerge, a tentative analytic framework is developed. The framework may involve the construction of categories or hypotheses or both. Further sampling and data collection may then be guided by this analytic framework, and the usefulness of the framework may be ascertained. Categories may be added or subtracted and hypotheses modified as the new data indicate. This process of sequential analysis and increasingly focused sampling and data collection may continue until the researcher is satisfied with his or her understanding of the phenomenon. A detailed example is in Gilgun's (1992) account of her research on incest perpetrators. In many respects the intertwining of these processes resembles what is done in investigative reporting. A reporter may start with a lead, interview one or two persons, develop some hunches (hypotheses) about the issue under investigation. From these hunches, the reporter may come up with some possible theories (analytic frameworks), which may lead to other contacts, interviews, and so on.

Not all qualitative research, however, is characterized by this degree of interpenetration of its methods. For example, a sample may be decided on in advance of data collection and analysis. Perhaps the general idea is that qualitative methods are applied with a good of flexibility, which usually involves some degree of looping back and forth between the processes of sampling, data collection, and data analysis. With this perspective in mind, we shall now examine some of the specific methods used in qualitative research: sampling, data collection, and data analysis.

Sampling and Generalization

As suggested earlier, qualitative research favors the use of relatively small, nonprobability samples, intensively studied. Qualitative researchers use all types of nonprobability samples discusssed in chapter 8—accidental, snowball, quota, and purposive. As noted above, sampling may occur incrementally as the study progresses. What needs to be emphasized is the role of theory in the sampling process. As Miles and Huberman point out (1994:29), samples in qualitative research are "theory-driven," that is, are more concerned with conceptual questions than with generalization to a particular population.

This principle has been most clearly articulated in grounded theory (Strauss and Corbin 1990) in which the sampling method is referred to as "theoretical sampling." In this form of sampling one initially chooses cases on the basis of the kind of theory to be developed. Initially, similar cases are chosen until they contribute no new information to the analysis, a point called theoretical saturation. Subsequently the researcher might select cases similar to the ones already studied in order to see if emerging concepts are also applicable to them. Then contrasting cases may be sampled. For example, in the study of incest perpetrators described in chapter 1, Gilgun (1992) started with married males who had been abused as children and as adults were sex abusers, then added similar men who did not have spouses available, then added abused males who were not adult perpetrators. Her purpose was to find key factors that differed, to test the hypotheses she was generating.

Theory-guided sampling may also be used to select incidents within or across cases (Miles and Huberman 1994). For example, a qualitative study might involve repeated interviews with a small sample of subjects. After the first round of interviews, the researcher may conclude that a certain kind of subject behavior, which emerged incidentally in a few cases, is of theoretical importance. Such behaviors would then be explored in the second round of interviews. The same logic would apply if a researcher realized early in a set of one-time interviews that a particular behavior not originally included in the interview guide was important. In subsequent interviews that behavior could be sampled.

Although qualitative researchers may not be interested in using their samples as a basis for describing a population, generalization is always of concern. Thus if the goal of a study is theory development, it is assumed that the theory has relevance to individuals and situations beyond those studied. Generalization in qualitative approaches is essentially a logical one, as it is indeed for most quantitative research in social work (chapter 8). In specifying the logical considerations to be used in qualitative research, Lincoln and Guba (1985), use the notion of the "transferability of findings." "Transferability is a direct function of the similarity between . . . contexts. If Context A and Context B are sufficiently congruent then working hypotheses from the sending originating context *may* be applicable in the receiving context" (p. 124).

In social work research generally we appear to build generalizations in a similar way—by extending what has been learned from a given situation to others that are similar to it while keeping in mind how the situations differ. The process yields at best tentative propositions. As Cronbach (1975:125), a well-known quantitative methodologist, once put it: "When we give proper weight to local conditions any generalization is a working hypothesis, not a conclusion." Such hypotheses may suggest what is likely or possible in a given situation. Whether or not it does occur needs to be determined in the situation itself.

Data Collection

The most frequently used methods of data collection in qualitative research are interviewing and observation. Although these methods have been discussed earlier (chapter 10), the variations of them emphasized in qualitative studies will be examined here in greater depth.

INTERVIEWING Whatever form it takes, interviewing in qualitative research gives the respondent ample opportunity to express his or her own point of view. Reports of qualitative studies are generally replete with quotes from respondents. These are, of course, obtained through the interview process. Structured or standardized interviews generally stress open-ended questions. Such questions may be used together with those asking for multiple-choice types of response, especially in studies that combine quantitative and qualitative methods, or the entire interview may consist of open-ended questions. Open-ended questions may be accompanied by "probe instructions" which indicate directions for further inquiry after the subject has responded. For example, in interviewing Asian children who have been adopted by American families, the interviewer may ask the child: "How are things at school?" A probe instruction may direct the interviewer to ask about teasing if the child does not mention it in his or her response. Less structured interviews may make use of interview guides in which the topics to be covered, and perhaps some key questions, are written out, but the order in which they are covered may vary from interview to interview. In completely unstructured interviews, interviewers may focus on certain topics but do not follow prescribed guidelines. In response to what their subjects say, they may explore areas that had not occurred to them prior to the interview.

Since the interviews permit thorough exploration of the subject's thoughts, feelings, attitudes, etc., about a particular topic, they are often referred to as "in depth." They may last longer— e.g., from 1 to 3 hours—than typical structured interviews that consist largely of short answer responses. Also subjects may be interviewed two or three times in order to secure greater depth of information. (In quantitative approaches, repeated interviews may be used but usually to track changes over time.)

Brief, informal, "conversational" interviews may be used in conjunction with participant-observation, as was done in the Davis and Srinivasan (1994) study mentioned earlier. These interviews are unstructured, often opportunistic, encounters that may occur while the researcher (as participant observer) may be involved with the subject in other activities.

Group interviews, often referred to as focus groups, may be used to augment, or take the place of, individual interviews. Essentially the group may be asked to discuss a topic or to answer specific questions. As in individual interviews, the format may vary from structured to unstructured. For example, alcoholics in recovery may be asked to reveal the kinds of things they do to avoid relapse. As Fontana and Frey (1994:365) have commented: "The group interview has the advantage of being inexpensive, data rich, flexible, stimulating to respondents, recall aiding, and cumulative and elaborative, over and above individual responses." Potential problems include the possible repressive effects of group culture and possible domination by one or two individuals. In addition to basic interviewing skills, the interviewer should ideally have some knowledge of group dynamics as well as facility in handling groups. For detailed discussion of the group interview see Frey and Fontana (1998). (See also discussion of nominal groups, in the chapter following.)

OBSERVATION Many types of observation may be used in qualitative research. The researcher may be an "outside" observer, that is, not a part of the situation being observed. For example, one might observe a classroom to gain an understanding of the interactions that may lead to disruptive classroom behavior. When the researcher becomes more a part of the situation, the term "participant observer" may be used. But this term may cover a variety of roles. The researcher may be a part of a situation in the sense that he or she may interact with others but participation may be limited to largely research activities, such as observing or having conversational interviews. Or the researcher may be a full participant in the sense of carrying out nonresearch activities similar to what others in the situation are doing, while still retaining a research role. Srinivasan's serving as a volunteer in a woman's shelter in the Davis and Srinivasan study (1994) is an example. An illustration of an even more complete welding of participant and observer roles is provided by the practitioner-researcher in a single case study.

Observation in qualitative research shares the same advantages and disadvantages of observation in general (see chapter 10). A particular advantage of participant observation as a method is that it can give the researcher firsthand experience with a situation, which opens up numerous possibilities for learning about what is really going on.

Participant observation is particularly well suited to the study of complex service systems that may involve a variety of activities by different personnel. For example, there may be interest in investigating the treatment of older residents in an institutional setting, the "processing" of children admitted to a hospital, or a community's approach to dealing with delinquent youth. While useful, data obtained from sources such as records, surveys, and structured observation might not yield a coherent, comprehensive picture of the service system. A single participant-observer, or team of observers, can observe the various facets of the system in operation and seek out data needed to put together a view of the whole. In a study of service systems the participant-observer may have conversational interviews with service providers or review records and other documents. In addition to providing a unified description of a service system, investigators can also identify flaws and trouble spots that may not surface in data obtained from official records, questionnaires, formal interviews, or other conventional means. Like the investigative reporter, the participant-observer can dig beneath surface images of what is going on. In his participant-observation study of services to senile elderly in a particular community, Frankfather (1977:111) first describes a hospital ward in terms that one might obtain from an official description. "Service A is administered by the supervising psychiatrist and chief resident, a third-year psychiatric resident. Ward staff, nurses, social workers, and attendants are organized in six teams led by first-year psychiatric residents. Patient population (including the elderly) ranges from 2 to 30 and each patient is assigned to a specific psychiatric resident and team."

A rather different (though not necessarily contradictory) impression of service A is obtained when we see it through the investigator's eyes: "The paint is filthy and peeling. . . . The room is lined with ragged, sometimes cushionless couches. . . . The remains of lunch are left lying around until dinner time. This provides some patients, usually the elderly, with an opportunity to go picking among the left-overs during the day" (p. 111).

Investigator subjectivity and bias are, of course, inherent limitations in studies based largely on participant observation. But these limitations may be well worth accepting to obtain accounts that report on facets of programs that may otherwise not be brought to light. Methods of examining and controlling such sources of error are discussed below.

Data Processing and Analysis

In qualitative research, the essential instrument is the human observer, and the essential data are words. He or she must absorb a large and complex variety of information from interviews, observations, documents, and so on, and ultimately derive meaning from them. What follows is an overview of this process. More detailed descriptions may be found in Strauss (1990), Miles and Huberman (1994), Neuman (1994), and Lofland (1995).

ORGANIZING AND CODING Key to the analytic process are methods of organizing and coding data. This process begins as data are first collected. The researcher takes notes based on observations, interviews, reading interview transcripts or other documents. These notes serve as a basis for initial coding, that is forming categories. Coding operations follow principles set forth in the previous chapter.

Note taking and coding usually lead to memos, which are more theoretical analyses written to oneself, as well as diagrams showing relationships between categories. In this process initial codes are reworked and combined into more complex codes—into axial codes (Strauss and Corbin 1990) or pattern codes (Miles and Huberman 1994). The purpose is to identify themes that can provide a meaningful description of what is being studied or become a part of a theory based in the data.

In chapter 11 we used a study by LaSala (1997) to illustrate basic coding processes. The study was, in fact, a qualitative investigation. At an initial level, the approach to coding may be similar in qualitative and quantitative methods, a point also made by the use of this particular study to illustrate coding in the context of quantitative research. In qualitative research, however, the initial coding does not stop at simple categories or definitions of points on rating scales, but rather serves as the basis for more elaborate word pictures and conceptualizations.

The LaSala study provides a good illustration. It will be recalled that LaSala was interested in exploring relationships between gay partners and their parents. In reviewing tapes of his interviews, he found discrepancies in his gay subjects' descriptions of their relationships with their parents. Many of the subjects who, at a global level, described these relationships in unqualified positive terms would also (at other points in the interview) indicate aspects of the relationship that could only be interpreted as negative. For example, a subject might say that "my parents accept our relationship," but later in a different context, might comment that "they refused to invite my partner to my sister's wedding." LaSala's initial codes noted the presence of both these positive and negative statements. As instances of these codes were compared, a more complex pattern code,"discordant information," emerged. As evidence of discordant information accumulated, LaSala wrote a memo calling attention to this pattern and putting it into a theoretical context. He observed that the parents might be sending mixed messages regarding their approval of their sons' relationships. Because it was important for the sons to view their relationships with their parents in positive terms, they might tend to ignore or minimize negative aspects. Perhaps, his memo concluded, the men were attempting to reduce "cognitive dissonance" (Festinger 1962).

The accumulation of texts, notes, codes, memos, and the like, can produce a considerable amount of material to organize. Computer software is available to store and retrieve such material. An overview of use of computers in qualitative analysis as well as review of specific programs may be found in Miles and Huberman (1994).

CONSTANT COMPARISON A useful method that may be used as a guide to both data collection and analysis is "constant comparison" (Glaser and Strauss 1967; Glaser and Strauss 1970; Strauss and Corbin 1990)—one of the key approaches in grounded theory. (Aspects of constant comparison have already been mentioned in conjunction with our discussion of theoretical sampling above.) "Significant categories are first identified during preliminary field work. Comparison groups or cases are then located and chosen in accordance with the purposes of providing new data on categories or combinations of them, suggesting new hypotheses, and verifying initial hypotheses in diverse contexts" (Glaser and Strauss 1970:292). For example, in an initial study of client satisfaction with agency services, there may be clues that the most dissatisfied clients were those who sought a concrete service from the agency but were given "counseling" instead. A group of clients who applied for concrete services might then be sought out and studied to check this hypothesis. This group might then be compared with a group that sought counseling services only, and so on.

The use of comparisons can also be made within a set of cases (or within a single case). For example, in her study of Korean adoptees, Huh (1997) was interested in developing theory relating to how the adoptees cope with teasing from other children regarding racial differences. In the process of building categories for the theory, the responses of boys were compared to those of girls, those of younger children to those of older children. Each comparison yielded new insights. Thus by comparing the responses of younger and older children, she was able to develop a progression in the maturity (and effectiveness) of the responses.

RELIABILITY AND VALIDITY As suggested in chapter 4, a potential limitation of qualitative methods is investigator bias. The unstructured nature of much of the data in qualitative research lends itself to selective recall and selective attention and to making interpretations that support one's convictions. Even if the researcher has no prior expectations about the data, he or she may develop them as the study proceeds. A potent form of bias in the analysis phase is the need to have the data "fall into place" that is, to add up to a coherent or interesting picture. As a possible picture emerges, the researcher may be tempted to look for evidence to support it and ignore evidence that does not.

In quantitative approaches such biases are addressed, albeit imperfectly, through conventional measures of reliability and validity (chapter 9). Although such standards and measures may not be used in qualitative studies, the issues they address are of concern. We would support the position of Miles and Huberman (1994) that some measure of intercoder reliability be obtained. Independent coding early in the analysis can not only determine reliability but can help sharpen the coding process by revealing different perspectives of the same phenomena. Given the volume and complexity of codes in a qualitative study, it may not be feasible to have a complete reliability check. However, it should always be possible to have a limited number of key codes applied to the same data by a second coder and to determine their percentage of agreement (see chapter 9).

Providing evidence for coding reliability also provides some evidence for the validity of the study's findings or, to use terms favored by qualitative methodologists, the study's credibility or authenticity. Additional validation can be achieved through some form of "triangulation "(Denzin 1978; Janesick 1994), in which the researcher obtains converging evidence from different methods or data sources. For example, different staff members in a hospital may be asked to comment on the kind of care received by psychiatric patients and the patients themselves might be asked to give their opinions. Or different researchers may interview the same or similar respondents. Another approach is to have the study participants read and critique the investigator's conclusions.

For example, Shaw and Shaw (1997) developed a schema of how practitioners determine whether their work is any good, and asked those they had interviewed to evaluate their conceptualization. An additional means of validation is an "audit" carried out, perhaps, by another researcher who has had no connection with the study (Huberman and Miles 1994). The auditor might ask such questions as "Was negative evidence sought for?" or "were rival explanations considered?" Even if an audit is not done, and it is not a common practice in qualitative research, the kinds of questions an auditor might ask provide a useful checklist for researchers who want to assess or improve the validity of their findings. (For a comprehensive list, see Miles (1994:279.)

Summary

Qualitative research uses flexible methods to observe phenomena and construct meaning from observations, using an inductive logical process and a stance as "insider" or both insider and outsider. It is often used to understand others' worldviews, to gain new insights on supposedly familiar phenomena, and to generate hypotheses about phenomena we do not understand. Common modes include grounded theory, narrative methods, discourse analysis, and program or case evaluation. These uses share some methodological approaches. Sampling generally aims at informing theory by selecting cases for similarities or differences that will provide new information, rather than at representativeness. Data collection is flexible and may vary throughout a study, even from moment to moment.

There is emphasis on interviewing—often unstructured or semistructured using approaches such as life history or recount of critical incidents, and on observation—often with considerable involvement through participant-observation. Data processing begins while data are being collected and often leads to changes in direction as the investigator develops hypotheses and seeks to confirm or disconfirm them. Data—written notes—are coded and organized, often using the constant comparison method from grounded theory.

Given the flexibility and heavy emphasis on the investigator's conceptual capacities, a potential problem in qualitative research is reliability and validity; methods to increase authenticity include having others review and code notes, triangulation or use of multiple methods and sources of data, and audit of results by other investigators.

An example of a qualitative study is Laseter's (1997) investigation of the labor force participation of young black men in Chicago. His conceptual framework for conducting the study was economic explanations of the labor market: demand-side explanations such as the shift to a service economy, spatial mismatch between jobs and living areas, and discrimination; and supply-side explanations such as work attitudes, dislike of low-wage jobs, and the presence of a lucrative underground economy. This framework provided the structure for his analysis once the data were collected.

Laseter, working as part of a larger project (the University of Chicago Urban Family Life Project), interviewed 18 black men aged 16 to 30 years who lived in economically depressed areas on the west side of Chicago. Men were recruited through social service agencies, a church, and finally by referral from respondents (accidental sampling augmented with snowball sampling). The interviews were semistructured around the topics of "work, the underground economy, aspirations, and perceptions of opportunity" (p. 76).

Data analysis followed standard qualitative procedures (Miles and Huberman 1994; Strauss and Corbin 1990). Laseter used three approaches to analyze themes: "looking for patterns of similarity or difference between respondents, trying to understand the strategies that respondents used to cope with events in their lives, and looking at contextual factors and intervening conditions that affected attitudes and strategies" (p. 78). He reported his findings as themes under the economic framework already mentioned, with extensive descriptions and accounts of incidents to substantiate the conclusions he reached. His findings included identifying three groups: young aspirers who were ambitious and optimistic, valued education, but usually had vague goals; young non-aspirers who had already encountered life events like fatherhood, local gangs, or drug use, whose goals were related to "whatever was available"; and older (and more experienced) workers whose goals were limited but specific to increasing their economic opportunities, often through education. For all, employment was unstable and erratic, at low-wage jobs, although some were employed full-time. The young men themselves identified two groups of non-workers, those who wanted to work but had lost hope, and those who preferred the underground economy and hanging out in the neighborhood. A barrier to work was the combination of jobs in (distant) suburban areas and, while there, pressure to conform to a different culture in dress, language, and behavior.

13 Assessment

In preceding chapters, we set forth the foundations of research methods as they are, or could be, used in social work. In the remaining chapters, we consider applications of these methods of special relevance to the tasks of social workers. A central theme is how research strategies can be employed to generate knowledge about the targets, processes, and outcomes of intervention.

Various research strategies can be applied to the task of understanding actual or potential client systems and their problems. Through naturalistic designs, researchers can study client characteristics and problems as they find them and can contribute to explanations of these phenomena. Through experimental designs, theories about human and, hence, client and system behavior can be tested, at least in the laboratory. Field experiments testing out intervention methods can add to understanding how types of clients and targets respond to methods tested. The data collection and measurement techniques that have been considered are integral to the assessment of any human system. In this chapter we concentrate on application of research methods to assessment of the client system and immediate environment in generalist practice and to the assessment of need as a basis for program planning.

Research Procedures in Assessment for Generalist Practice

In chapter 1, we saw how a scientific viewpoint could influence practice. To review these ideas in relation to assessment, a practitioner who uses an empirical perspective is likely to ground fuzzy diagnostic abstractions like "reality testing" or "enmeshment" with specific indicators, to apply research-based knowledge in an effort to understand client systems, to consider alternative theories and explanations in formulating assessments, and to use research instruments as part of the assessment process. Perhaps the most practical of these ideas is the last. We shall attempt to develop it in more detail below through a survey of kinds of instruments that can be used to measure client systems.

Assessment Interviewing

A clinical interview or portions of an interview directed at eliciting data from clients about their functioning, problems, histories and so on, normally uses methods of inquiry similar to those used in research interviewing. Although the purposes of clinical assessment and the research interview differ, both draw on the same repertoire of techniques. Thus, criteria for questions that accurately measure the concept of interest in research interviews and instruments are relevant to assessment interviewing in clinical practice. One type of confluence of research and clinical considerations is represented by the *behavioral interview*, a systematic initial interview conducted within a behavioral treatment framework (Collins and Thompson 1993; Hamilton 1993; Kanfer and May 1981; Turkat 1986). By focusing on specific behaviors, their antecedents and consequences, the interviewer attempts to develop an empirically grounded formulation of the client's problems that can serve as a guide to intervention. Principles and techniques of the behavioral interview can be broadened to apply to nonbehavioral and generalist forms of practice.

In another type of assessment interview, topics relating to client functioning, client problems, and the environment are covered through open-ended questions. The resulting data then serve as a basis for rating scales or other measurements. Examples include the Social Adjustment Scale (Weissman 1990), the HOME Inventory (Caldwell and Bradley 1984), the Family Functioning Scale (Geismar 1980), and measures of target complaints and problems (Battle et al. 1966; Mintz and Kiesler 1982; Persons 1991).

Goal Attainment Scaling

Goal Attainment Scaling (Kiresuk and Lund 1978; Kiresuk and Sherman 1968; Mintz and Kiesler 1982; Rockwood 1994) is a set of procedures for setting up goals during the assessment phase and of evaluating attainment of them at termination or follow-up. The setting of goals is a way of specifying the problems to be worked on and thus has a definite assessment function. Since goal-setting provides a direction for work, it also provides a way of structuring service. In Goal Attainment Scaling, areas of potential change in a client's life are described. For each area, different possible outcomes in terms of changes that may be achieved are identified and ordered according to levels of treatment success. Goals at many levels can be formulated, for example, family or system response to the client, or agency staff performance. This information is recorded in a guide, a portion of which is given here together with an illustration of how the scaling process works (figure 13.1).

Check whether or not the Scale has been mutually negotiated between patient and CIC interviewer SCALE ATTAINMENT LEVELS	SCALE HEADINGS AND SCALE WEIGHTS	
	Yes _X_ No __	Yes __ No _X_
	SCALE 1: Education ($w_1 = 20$)	SCALE 2: Suicide ($w_2 = 30$)
a. most unfavorable treatment outcome thought likely (−2)	Patient has made no attempt to enroll in high school. √	Patient has committed suicide
b. less than expected success with treatment (−1)	Patient has enrolled in high school, but at time of follow-up has dropped out.	Patient has acted on at least one suicidal impulse since her first contact with the CIC, but has not succeeded. √
c. expected level of treatment success (0)	Patient has enrolled, and is in school at follow-up, but is attending class sporadically (misses an average of more than a third of her classes during a week).	Patient reports she has had at least four suicidal impulses since her first contact with the CIC but has not acted on any of them.
d. more than expected success with treatment (+1)	Patient has enrolled, is in school at follow-up, and is attending classes consistently, but has no vocational goals. *	*
e. best anticipated success with treatment (+2)	Patient has enrolled, is in school at follow-up, is attending classes consistently, and has some vocational goal.	Patient reports she has had no suicidal impulses since her first contact with the CIC.

FIGURE 13.1
Goal attainment scaling

Naturalistic Observation

The practitioner or an associate (e.g., a teacher or house parent) can observe a client system in a nonlaboratory environment or "natural" setting, such as a school, a hospital ward, or a home. In this type of observation the observer attempts to be as unobtrusive as possible in order to minimize effects on the client's behavior. Observation may involve either quantitative or qualitative methods or some combination of the two.

In using quantitative methods, the practitioner usually records the frequency of a behavior during a specified time period. Various techniques for conducting this form of observation may be found in Bloom et al. (1995).

In using qualitative methods, the observer (normally the practitioner) would attempt to identify characteristics or themes of diagnostic interest. For example, in observing a disruptive child in a classroom the practitioner/observer would note the different types of disruptive behavior, the reaction of the teacher and other pupils to disruptive acts, events preceding them, the physical environment that may affect the behavior, and so on. Counting of specific behaviors would not be considered essential, although it might be done as part of a broader observational process. Notes would be taken and written up in a form of a summary. Careful observations and recording of the sequence of specific events distinguishes a qualitative empirical approach from the kind of global impressions one might obtain through casual observation. Thus, one avoids vague abstractions, such as "showed poor impulse control" but rather states concrete behaviors, such as "repeatedly tapped pencil on desk," or "bumped into desk in next row." Illustrative studies of naturalistic observation include Arndorfer et al. (1994), Peppler and Craig (1995), and Messer and Gross (1995).

Observation of Task Behavior

Clients may be asked to perform tasks in the practitioner's presence and their behavior may be observed for assessment purposes. For example, a number of approaches using interactional tasks have been devised for marital and family assessment (Filsinger 1983; Gomez and Francisco 1995; Yeh and Hedgespeth 1995). Such observational devices, which are often time-consuming to administer and score in their entirety, may be adapted for purposes of clinical assessment. In this context, the general point can be made that no instrument must be used either as designed, or in its entirety, to serve useful functions in clinical assessment.

Practitioners can develop their own tasks for assessment or evaluation purposes. A husband and wife may be asked to discuss a problem or parents may be directed to engage in a game or other activity with their child. An adolescent who has difficulty in being assertive may be able to demonstrate the problem in a role play with the practitioner. Because tasks of this kind can be shaped to the particular circumstances of the case at hand, they can often produce observations that approach the validity of those obtained through naturalistic means. Moreover, in many situations, such as family assessment, some practitioner activity, e.g., task setting, is necessary in order to set the stage for the occurrence of behavior for assessment purposes.

Client Self-Observation

Rather than the practitioner observing clients, clients can be asked to observe themselves and bring in the results. Client self-observation can take a variety of forms, including diaries, logs, questionnaires, simple devices for recording occurrences of one's own behavior or the behavior of a family member, and "self-anchoring" scales (Baumann 1995; Gingerich 1979). Often self-recording can have beneficial effects on behaviors observed (testing effects). The act of self-recording a behavior makes one conscious of it. An effort at self-control may follow. This may lead to gains prior to treatment, which complicates the use of client self-recording for assessment purposes.

Of much greater difficulty is getting clients to do the observation in the first place. A good rule is to keep it simple; another, is not to expect too much. Examples of the use of self-monitoring procedures may be found in Kanfer (1996) and Ludgate (1995).

Standardized Instruments

A standardized, self-report instrument relating to client functioning, client problems, or environmental resources and barriers is a versatile, easy-to-use tool. Although any standardized instrument, or even a battery, can be used for assessment purposes in clinical work, practitioners prefer what Levitt and Reid (1981) have called "rapid assessment instruments," or RAIs. An RAI is brief (one or two pages), quickly administered (usually in less than 10 minutes), and easily scored. As a result, an RAI can be given and, if necessary, scored within the session. Among the more commonly used RAIs are those that make up the WALMYR Assessment Scales (Hudson 1992), which includes 22 RAIs to measure a variety of client problems and characteristics; the Beck Depression Inventory (Beck 1967); the Locke-Wallace Marital Adjustment Scale (Locke and Wallace 1959); and the Dyadic Adjustment Scale (Spanier 1976). A compilation of such instruments may be found in Fischer and Corcoran (1994a; 1994b) and Gregory (1996).

RAIs serve three functions in assessment. First, they provide a compact but comprehensive survey of a problem or area, asking key questions that might not occur to the practitioner, that the practitioner may not have time to ask, or that clients may be reluctant to answer frankly, particularly in an interview with other family members present. What is of primary interest in this function is the client's responses to particular items—e.g., "Do you ever think of taking your own life?" Second, the client's test scores can be compared with averages from samples of identified populations. For example, a certain score on the Beck Depression Inventory would indicate that a client's responses resemble those of severely depressed patients. Some instruments provide "cutting scores," which serve somewhat the same function. For example, client scores exceeding a certain level may be interpreted as indicating the presence of a clinical problem. Finally, repeated administrations of an RAI can provide measures of change relating to goals of service. (Additional discussion of RAIs as measures of outcome may be found in the chapter following.) Their usefulness with nonverbal, disorganized, and resistive clients and helping marital partners better understand each other's perspectives were among more specific advantages cited by family agency practitioners in a trial use of RAIs under ordinary agency conditions (Toseland and Reid 1985). On the other hand, an RAI may not routinely add much to what has been obtained from a clinical interview, a limitation cited by practitioners in the same project.

One drawback of RAIs is that most RAIs focus on individual or family functioning, rather than on other systems or the impact of other systems on the individual. The paucity of instruments to identify levels for intervention or to measure higher-level systems makes it easy to ignore such systems. A generalist practitioner who relies solely on RAIs may inadvertently focus only on individual behaviors and problems when the overriding concern should be the systemic factors that influence the individual, and when intervention should be at other levels. Further, Meyer (1996) asserts that there are no instruments that measure psychosocial events, such as unemployment, poverty, or neighborhood violence, in such a way to encourage intervention, thus limiting the scope of practice.

Nevertheless, there are standardized instruments that can be helpful in assessing broader aspects of a client's situation, for example, Vosler's (1990) Family Access to Basic Resources (FABR) that includes financial resources and stability of both financial and other resources. Some can be used as well for measuring outcome of interventions at higher levels. For example, Moos's (1987) Social Climate Scales measure the way users view a physical environment; among the scales relevant for social work are those for family, work, classroom, treatment or task group, correctional institution, inpatient ward, and community-based treatment program.

Recording

In most cases the bulk of data relating to assessment and intervention will be recorded by the practitioner in narrative form, with such devices as client logs and RAI's providing supplementary information. Audiotaping or videotaping can also be utilized by the practitioner. Whatever style of recording is used, essential data on problems, client characteristics, system assets and limitations, intervention processes, and change need to be captured. In order to make sure the essentials are systematically preserved, some type of structured recording format is recommended.

One may use a general purpose format such as the Structured Clinical Record (Videka-Sherman and Reid 1985) or develop one to fit the situation at hand. Essentially, such a record calls for recording items of information under predetermined headings. For example, a recording format may include such headings as a) Presenting Problem; b) Historical and Contextual Factors; c) System Resources and Barriers, d) Treatment Goals; e) Principal Interventions and Immediate Outcomes; f) Client and System Situation at Termination. In a structured format, omissions of key data are less likely to occur and can be readily spotted. Moreover, the organization of data facilitates coding, analysis, and communication to others. To this base of organized, essential data, the practitioner can add detailed descriptions for specific purposes, for example, to record in detail an observation of a child.

Needs Assessment

The notion of studying communities or other human aggregations to identify and assess targets for intervention represents one of the oldest uses of research in social work. For example, the community survey provided much of the empirical grounding for the social reform movements in the earlier part of this century (Zimbalist 1955). In recent years, the expression "needs assessment" has emerged as an umbrella term to cover various old and new techniques for study of populations as a basis for program planning. Also in recent years, interest and activity in this area have been stimulated by federal requirements for needs assessments as a condition for social and mental health services.

The notion of "needs assessment" comprises a diverse variety of concepts and methods. The term "need" itself may vary from an abstract indicator of a social problem, such as the youth crime rate in a community, to requests by consumers for particular services. Need may be diversely defined by professionals, government officials, community representatives, and the recipients of service themselves. Assessment techniques may range from judgments about the sentiments of community members expressed at an open hearing to highly sophisticated statistical procedures. Nevertheless, the notion serves the practical function of grouping together a set of approaches all concerned with study of what people may require from the health and welfare system.

Although traditional needs assessments have focused on client problems and the services needed, they should be used as well to identify gaps in service delivery, impediments to client access to service, and larger-scale influences on the client situation, such as housing discrimination, local economic opportunities, and health care networks.

Following a classification developed by McKillip (1987), we take up five major categories of needs assessment methods: structured groups; key informants; surveys; use analysis; and social indicators. We discuss each method in turn and then consider likely combinations of methods.

Structured Groups

Perhaps the simplest and least expensive method of assessing need is to assemble relevant groups—of citizens, experts, and so on—and to elicit their views of need. Several common techniques will be reviewed.

COMMUNITY FORUM In using the community forum technique, planners sponsor a meeting of interested members of the community. Sometimes the community members are preselected; at other times the meeting is open to the general public. The meeting is designed to elicit the attendees' views of the needs of the community in a situation where ideas can flow comfortably. This is certainly the least scientific and systematic of the needs assessment methods. But it is effective with groups up to about 50 people (Witkin and Altschuld 1995). In fact, the forum without effective leadership or with too large a number of respondents may degenerate into a session of complaining about the local government or agency and its policies rather than a constructive discussion of the perceived needs of the community. Moreover, if the meetings are open to the general public, the respondents are self-selected and may not be representative of the community as a whole. Ideally, one should hold a series of smaller forums, either centering on specific subject areas or located within different neighborhoods in a community.

The community forum is able to elicit the input of ordinary citizens without structuring their thinking in a preconceived way. If the forum truly has an open agenda, it may provide an outlet for previously undefined community problems. Questionnaires, surveys, and agenda-controlled discussions all structure the thinking of the respondent/participant. They provide certain definitions that place boundaries on what may appear to be legitimate areas of need or problems. An open meeting provides the opportunity for a spontaneous statement of a previously unperceived need. (This advantage becomes more attractive when one considers the apparent problems with the key informant method discussed later.) Also the community forum can be good preparation for a survey, for it gives the researcher a preliminary reading of the concerns of community members, how they express these concerns, and the priorities they place on them.

FOCUS GROUPS More structured and systematic than the community forum are "focus groups." A small number of participants, eight to ten, are selected to represent a larger group, for example, tenants in a housing project or parents of mentally retarded children. The goal of the focus group interview is to elicit how participants feel about the topic and to identify the range of perspectives regarding it. Obtaining a consensus is unnecessary (Witkin and Altschuld 1995).

Views of needs can be elicited through open discussion led by a moderator who may be the needs assessor. A series of such meetings may be conducted with groups representing different constituencies. Bias in selection of participants is one source of concern. Another is possible disproportionate influence exerted by more vocal or articulate members of the group.

NOMINAL GROUPS A useful method of structuring discussions to maximize the information gained in the community forums or focus groups is the nominal group technique (Delbecq 1983; Delbecq and Van De Ven 1971). The technique evolved from research showing that structured group process enhances creativity (Thompson and Smithburg 1968) and that interaction between group members can prevent some members from openly expressing their ideas and concerns (Hairston 1979; Taylor, Berry, and Block 1958). Another performance problem with interactive groups, identified by Paulus and Dzindolet (1993), is that reluctance to outdo one another can lead to low performance levels. Their research suggested that nominal groups are able to eliminate this problem.

In running nominal groups, one typically starts by dividing persons in attendance into smaller groups. The division is made to reflect strata in the larger group, for instance, age, race, or other variables that the organizers consider relevant. Participants are asked to write down the needs they perceive in the community. A round-robin is then conducted in each group to list the concerns. Next, each item on the list is discussed and clarified but only briefly, so as to avoid influencing the original thinking behind the expression of the concern. Participants are asked to select individually a given number of concerns or difficulties and then to rank them in importance. These rankings are compiled for each small group and then discussed in the larger group.

ELECTRONIC GROUPS Use of interactive electronic techniques to conduct meetings is now widely accepted. One illustration given in Witkin and Altschuld (1995) discusses how the Pennsylvania Department of Education held an activity in which panelists had their presentations televised to seven locations within the state. Participants raised questions by means of direct connections to the studio, e-mail (electronic mail), and telephone. Same-site use includes having participants in the same room and using computers to transmit their comments. Witkin and Altschuld (1995) suggest that this technology facilitates group interaction by taking advantage of the capabilities of computers for storage, processing, and speedy transmission, while maintaining respondent anonymity and increasing the potential for rapid feedback that enables process gains, e.g., synergy and the avoidance of redundant ideas (Davidson and Davidson 1983). Networked systems of computers reduce time spent in group process and increase payoff by letting individuals who are often drowned out or intimidated by more dominant individuals to communicate anonymously (Dennis and Valacich 1993; Valacich, Dennis, and Connolly 1994). Feedback on ideas is also anonymous.

Another way to employ electronic technology is to have key informants (discussed in an upcoming section) who are widely dispersed geographically e-mail information or opinions to the needs assessor using a coding system to preserve their anonymity.

Using electronic groups for needs assessments will continue to accelerate as costs decrease and technology becomes more accessible and available and needs assessors become comfortable with its use. Its ability to preserve anonymity and quickly process data gives it advantages over other types of group interactions. It also has eliminated some of the drawbacks of group process that will be discussed in analyzing use of service. Nagasundaram and Dennis (1993) suggest that electronic brainstorming's effectiveness, when compared to nominal and verbal brainstorming groups, happens because electronic brainstorming stimulates a collection of individuals to interact with an evolving set of ideas, rather than with other individuals.

Key Informants

The key informant method involves obtaining expert opinions from a selected sample of respondents assumed to have special knowledge of the needs of the target population. Often agency practitioners themselves are chosen, as well as other community professionals in adjunct occupations. Also included may be various public officials and other community figures who represent sectors or organizations considered to have special knowledge about problems in the community. In addition respondents may include actual or potential clients or their families. Advantages of this technique are that it can be done at a modest, low-cost level, and it is usually easy to obtain a sample. Disadvantages include possible biases among key informants who might overestimate the importance of certain needs while underplaying others.

The choice of key informants should be determined by the questions to be asked or the issues to be addressed. In modest studies the sample may be quite small, a dozen or so. The design is generally descriptive-exploratory (chapter 5). The researcher is interested in generating knowledge of needs of the target population from the combined data supplied by the informants, rather than how one kind of informant differs from another. Data collection methods may range from unstructured interviews to structured questionnaires, depending on how much is known about the target population and its problems and on the size of the sample.

An example of use of key informants is provided by Miller and Solomon (1996), who used this method, along with others, to assess the AIDS/HIV-related needs of women, primarily women of color, in three low-income housing projects in Brooklyn, New York. The target population included former drug users, female partners of current and former drug users, and adolescents. Researchers drew up a list of key informants representing local health and service providers, community organizations, and churches. Respondents (interviewed over the telephone) were asked to identify the greatest needs of women in the community relating to AIDS and HIV as well as the greatest barriers to using services. Respondents were also asked to identify other knowledgeable people in the community who should be interviewed. (Note here that researchers were making use of the snowball sampling methods described in chapter 8.) Some 60 interviews were completed. The study produced a number of findings useful for program planning. For example, the informants identified the greatest AIDS/HIV related-need in the neighborhoods as education. They also viewed lack of literacy, language skills, and transportation as key barriers to utilizing AIDS/HIV-related services.

Program planners often use an informal sort of key informant survey. Instead of conducting a formal needs assessment, they may use informal one-to-one consultations with others in the community to guide their programming decisions. However, these informal procedures can be easily upgraded to small-scale needs assessment studies. The combination of a carefully chosen sample of key informants, with the use of standard questions, and systematic data analyses can provide decision makers with information that is more dependable and better organized.

In sum, the key informant approach is probably best used to provide an approximate assessment of need. In many situations, however, rough and ready approximations may provide adequate information for planning purposes.

Community Surveys

Community surveys involve giving standardized questionnaires or interviews to a sample of community members. The better surveys use probability sampling methods (chapter 8), although nonprobability methods are more common. The focus is usually on perceived needs of respondents who may be clients, members of at-risk populations, or citizens in general. In surveys of at-risk or potential client populations, emphasis is on determining needs of groups that have not received services. Such surveys generally use "descriptive" designs (chapters 4 and 5) and interviews or questionnaires (chapter 10).

Advantages of the community survey include opportunity to measure need as perceived by actual or potential consumers. In addition, assessment of need can be based on a *representative* sample of individuals. However, good surveys are expensive and require some expertise to administer. Response rates may also be low, leading to possible biases in the results. In addition, of course, they suffer from the usual problems, such as social desirability effects and response sets, found in any self-report instrument.

Use of a community survey is illustrated by the AIDS/HIV project referred to above (Miller and Solomon 1996). To obtain an estimate of need directly from potential consumers, the project planners decided to supplement their key informant study with a community survey.

A total of 212 women, mostly African American, who were at home in one housing development, were interviewed. An instrument consisting of a combination of closed and open questions was used to gather a range of demographic and attitudinal data. A number of findings with implications for program planning emerged from the survey. Although the women were concerned about AIDS/HIV, their worries about it were dwarfed by other issues, such as their children's welfare, crime, violence, and money. AIDS/HIV was not one of their daily concerns and not linked to their sense of well-being. For AIDS/HIV prevention, the women turned to friends and relatives, who might not always give them well-founded advice. Major obstacles to learning more about AIDS/HIV appeared to be disinterest and fear but the ignorance of their male partners was also seen as a barrier to the women's making use of what information they had.

Results of the survey were combined with findings from the key informant study to lay the groundwork for a program. It is important to note that their needs assessments research brought about a major shift in the thinking of the program planners. They had originally thought of the program as consisting largely of didactic workshops that would present information about risk-reduction behaviors. Their studies, however, convinced them that such an approach would not work. It lacked congruence with the women's concerns and ways of obtaining and using information. Rather it was decided to emphasize continuing support groups in which women could discuss their health and community concerns, including AIDS/HIV. Another component would be an outreach effort by peer educators who would provide women with information about prevention. There would also be educational forums on AIDS/HIV open to men as well as women. The authors note that subsequent experience with the program confirmed the validity of the change in plans.

The two studies provide an excellent illustration of how needs assessments can help planners from going off in the wrong direction and, more importantly, can provide them with basis for developing programs oriented to the actual needs and orientations of the people they are designed to serve.

Analyzing Use of Service

In analyzing service use, it is assumed that one can extrapolate from persons who have received or are receiving services to the service needs of a larger population. By examining data describing those currently receiving services, one can gain a picture of the characteristics of a potential clientele. On the basis of how often these characteristics appear in the community's population, planners can estimate the need, or demand, for services. For example, if an agency discovers that it serves many recently divorced women, it can estimate potential demand for its services by means such as a study of available data on divorces awarded by courts in the community.

Also, service utilization data from one agency can be used by another. For example, a child welfare agency may be interested in starting an international adoption program. One way of assessing need for the program would be get information on the response to an established program of this kind in a similar community.

There are several ways in which service utilization data can be collected. Perhaps the quickest is through a computerized information system, if it contains the data needed. Another way is through the use of a data sheet completed on each client the agency serves. In addition to face sheet data, information may be gathered on whatever might be helpful in assessing need, e.g., the presenting problem, treatment or services provided, frequency of treatment, duration of contact with the agency, how the client was referred to the agency, and referrals the agency made for the client.

Still another way is through analysis of case records. A disadvantage of this method is that the records may be incomplete. The researcher may end up having to disqualify many cases or to spend precious time gathering the missing data verbally from workers in the agency. Often, even this undesirable method of data collection cannot be used. In addition to the usual distortions present in any form of case recording (chapter 15), records rarely reveal who perceived the problem or need—the practitioner or the client.

A major drawback of use data is that they can simply affirm existing perceptions of need represented by the services provided and the populations already being served, rather than help the service provider develop a more nearly comprehensive picture of the needs of the community. There is little chance here for an entirely unrecognized need to show itself, for the sample, from which data are drawn, is biased by definition.

Moreover, concerns about confidentiality can interfere with the collection of data. Though it is possible for anonymity to be ensured, the sharing of any client information may be against the policy of an agency or of a private practitioner. However, to get a really balanced picture of clients under treatment, it may be necessary to tap the caseloads of all sorts of service providers. It may be particularly difficult to solicit the participation of private agencies that do not receive substantial public funds. In short, it may be quite difficult either to cover the entire population of service recipients or even to draw a representative random sample.

Because it is often necessary to compare use data with data describing the whole population to extrapolate need, one usually needs at least one other data set, such as census data. This is an important drawback. Although agencies usually collect use data routinely, the complexities of comparing use data with other data can considerably increase the cost of using this method.

Another standard against which to compare use data is similar data drawn from previous years. Comparing use data within an agency or community from year to year can allow the agency or community to develop a baseline of need and then to evaluate its performance in meeting that need each year. This is a way in which needs assessment data can be used to evaluate the effectiveness of programs.

In spite of all these difficulties, this method can be useful when its limitations are recognized and accepted. It can give the agency or community a clear sense of the needs it is already trying to meet. Various methods of analyzing the data collected can reveal the different properties of the data; it is possible that patterns might be detected and used as predictors of problems or clusters of problems that new clients may have. In other words, these patterns could be used to improve agency personnel's understanding of various problems and situations and their subsequent interventions. Problem patterns discovered through this sort of data analysis can also be useful in directing policy decisions.

Social Indicators

In its most traditional sense, "the social indicators method of assessing needs is based on the assumption it is possible to estimate the health and other human service needs of persons on the basis of the geographical, ecological, social, economic and demographic characteristics of the area in which they live" (Warheit, Buhl, and Bell 1978:240). Existing statistical information is used to analyze geographical areas in terms of social indicators thought to be indicative of certain social conditions. Sources of social indicators include education (e.g., school records dealing with student absenteeism, health, behavioral problems, results of school, district, state, and nationwide assessment programs, etc.), social services (e.g., demographic characteristics of clients, use of services, etc.), and city, region, or government units (e.g., census or demographic data, such as age, income, housing patterns, ethnicity, level of education, etc.). The use of existing records requires less time and is generally cheaper than creating new data sets (Witkin and Altschuld 1995). These geographic areas, usually census tracts, are ranked for each indicator, and then the rankings are mapped, to provide a multidimensional view of the needs of the overall area.

No attempt is made in this kind of analysis to isolate causes or effects. The aim is to demonstrate clusters of indicators that have been shown to signal the coexistence of certain social needs (Bell et al. 1983). This information can then be used to direct social planning. This information also helps to define the social and demographic boundaries in a community, making the geographical ones less relevant for planning and decision making.

A less traditional definition of social indicators includes any existing statistical data that describe important characteristics of a target population or group. In this way, any regularly kept statistics can be useful. For example, in the HIV/AIDS project referred to above (Miller and Solomon 1996), use was made of available data on the incidence of AIDS, poverty levels, and crime rates for the target communities.

The use of social indicators to plan services in the area of child and maternal health is illustrated by a study reported by Terrie (1996). The study shows how statistical information can be gathered from local, state, and federal agencies and combined into a profile useful in program planning. It also reviews how CD ROMS available from the Bureau of Census can be used in constructing such profiles in desk-top map-making. Another illustrative study is reported by Allen-Meares and Roberts (1994), who used social indicator data as a base for statistical modeling in an attempt to predict the timing and frequency of prenatal visits among adolescents and young adults.

Combining Approaches to Needs Assessment

Since each method has inherent weaknesses, a needs assessment model, particularly at the level of assessing needs of an entire community, usually contains a combination of approaches. All methods could be used at various intervals to maintain a clear picture of the ever-changing needs of the community. However, this is not financially feasible for most communities.

Since community surveys can reach such a large portion of the population, they can be particularly beneficial when used in concert with other methods. A community survey can generate a large base of information that can then be refined through the use of key informant surveys. Alternately, the community survey can be used to verify data gathered by other methods like use data, community forum, and key informant techniques.

One combination of methods that is particularly appealing, for they appear to complement one another well, is the combined use of social indicators and the community survey. Whereas the survey can be rather costly, the use of social indicators is usually relatively inexpensive. These methods also provide a good check on one another, for the social indicators provide the objective data, while the survey provides the subjective side of the picture.

Another likely combination is the use of community surveys with key informant studies, as was done in the AIDS/HIV project (Miller and Solomon 1996). Although there is no objective measure here as a check, the two subjective measures can provide a two-dimensional view of the articulated needs.

A final, but important, issue to consider is the public relations aspect of conducting a needs assessment. There are two issues here—recruiting support, and the readiness of the community to make constructive use of the data. Sometimes participants may be selected as focus group members or key informants not because of their current support but to introduce issues to them and to get potentially innovative thinking on an issue. For example, local merchants might be invited to forums dealing with a community problem of young men hanging out on street corners. Similarly, a community must be ready to "hear" and react to the information. On both counts, to maximize community involvement and to ensure that those involved could respond to the results, an HIV prevention program for Puerto Ricans living in Holyoke, Massachusetts, employed a needs assessment that involved a community forum, focus groups, and interviews with providers (Buchanan et al. 1994).

Luckily, these methods are fairly inexpensive to use. Gauging the readiness of the community or agencies to use the data is crucial. It is pointless to invest in sophisticated data collection and analysis if the results will never be taken seriously in the policy making and planning processes.

Needs Assessment as a Planning Tool

The data collection techniques of needs assessment methodology are fairly well developed; however, in viewing the methodology as a planning tool, some important weaknesses become apparent. One weakness is mentioned by Witkin (1994), who points out that few tools have been developed for use in transforming the data collected into priorities or planning guidelines. The social indicators method is perhaps the only one with an analytic technique (e.g., mapping) that does part of this job. The mental health work of Hall and Royse (1987) is a good example of combining social indicators with mapping techniques (Witkin and Altschuld 1995).

By graphically displaying the information on census tract or subcommunity maps, areas of intense need can be delineated. Even though areas of a community can be differentially described in this way, some other process is still required to set priorities for which needs are to be addressed when, and which geographic area is the best bet for intervention. Most often, the process used to make the decisions is the political process.

The lack of a stable definition of need is another weakness in the methodology. Witkin (1994) suggests that many needs assessments confuse needs with wishes. Clearly, it is often a problem within projects, as values come into conflict, and as assessors try to decide whether need equals demand or is a phenomenon that can be measured against some objective standard. Again, criteria defining need are often arrived at through political processes. This method may often be the best one.

If needs assessment methods are to be fully used in the planning process, then they must be related to program evaluation. In that way, it would be possible to learn how assessed needs were actually being met by programs developed to meet them. Feedback of this kind would not only facilitate more rational program planning but would also serve as a guide to future needs assessments. In assessing needs, it is important to distinguish populations that can be effectively served by existing programs from those that cannot be. Needs assessments may be only tenuously related to ensuing programs and tend to be even less well connected to whatever evaluations may follow. A step in the right direction is Witkin and Altschuld's (1995) three-phase plan for assessing needs that includes a preassessment phase for exploration, an assessment phase for data gathering, and a postassessment phase for utilization evaluation.

These different strands of the planning process could be knit together more closely if greater use were made of principles of developmental research or design and development strategies (see chapter 16). Use of such strategies would enable programs to be shaped through a systematic process of trial and evaluation, beginning with analysis of need.

Summary

Research methods can be central to assessment in social work, and in our opinion should be essential. Assessment for generalist practice includes: interviewing; observation of behavior in natural and structured situations; self-reports from clients; administration of standardized questionnaires that measure client behavior, resources, social climate, and physical environment; and written and media recording of problems, characteristics, and environmental factors. At the agency and community levels, needs assessment provides data for service program planning. Methods for needs assessment include structured groups, key informants, community surveys, analyses of service use, and social indicators.

From all indications, emphasis on outcome evaluation will continue to grow. Increasingly, oversight and funding agencies are requiring some form of "results-based accountability" (Weiss 1997). That is, they are stipulating that outcome data be routinely collected as evidence that programs are attaining specified goals (Hatry 1997). This trend will affect all levels of social work practice, from management of agencies and programs to individual work with clients.

Program Levels and Evaluation Designs

The outcome of social work intervention has been considered in a number of contexts, such as experimental design, the case study, data collection, and measurement. In this chapter we focus in detail on the measurement of outcome of social work *programs*. In our conception social work programs refer to systematic efforts to affect target systems—problems, individuals, families, groups, and so on. A program may involve work with a single system, for example an individual, or an aggregation of systems, as in an agencywide program for high-risk youth. The generalist view that a program can occur at different levels provides a way of integrating considerations of single case (or single group) evaluations with evaluations of larger, e.g., agencywide programs.

At the level of the work with cases (including treatment groups), the practitioner may make use of single-system designs (chapter 6) or their component methods to carry out case monitoring and evaluation. Thus, repeated application of a structured instrument may provide data about the client's progress and assist the practitioner in decision making about choice of intervention and timing of termination. Outcome measures at the close of a case may provide the practitioner with feedback about the possible effectiveness of the kind of intervention used as well as serve purposes of accountability to the agency and its funding sources. Methods useful in case monitoring and evaluation may be found in chapters on single system designs (6), measurement (9), data collection (10), qualitative approaches (12) assessment (13), intervention (15) and, of course, the remainder of the present chapter.

From evaluation of individualized programs with single clients, families, or treatment groups, we can proceed to evaluations of programs involving sizable numbers of clients. In ordinary agency contexts, considerations of outcome measurement do not change radically as we move up the ladder. Moreover, single-system designs may still be used if aggregated (as discussed below) or if the unit of study can be conceptualized as a single system, as in Gamache et al.'s (1998) study of three communities (chapter 6). However, in evaluation of larger-scale programs, the norm is to use nonequivalent and single group designs, with occasional equivalent group designs (chapter 7). Methods useful for conducting evaluations of larger-scale programs can be found in that chapter as well as those referred to in the preceding paragraph.

Different levels of evaluation can be joined in different ways. As suggested above, single-system designs can be aggregated to provide evaluations of larger programs. In this regard, Benbenishty (1997) has proposed that results of routine single-system evaluations can be computerized as a means of obtaining an ongoing evaluation of an agency's performance. Also larger scale evaluations can be conducted with attention to specific data on single systems. Particular cases of interest can then be analyzed separately.

Outcome Criteria

To evaluate outcome requires first developing outcome criteria that relate to program goals and philosophy, then specifying or operationalizing the criteria so that meaningful and feasible measures are developed. In most social work programs, outcome may be conceived of in such terms as changes in the client's behavior, attitudes, cognitions, social functioning, problems, emotional distress, environmental circumstances, and status (for example, release from care). We expand this conception, however, to include some related notions. One addition is goal attainment. Although a goal is usually defined as some type of desirable change in behavior, attitudes, and so on, it may be defined as maintenance of the status quo, particularly if the state of the target system is expected to worsen in the absence of intervention. Another addition to the notion of outcome is the relation of outcome to intervention costs, as in cost-effectiveness or cost-benefit measures. Outcome may also be thought of in terms of consumer satisfaction. For example, did the client regard the service as helpful? From these conceptions, criteria or indicators of outcome are derived.

Goals and Theory of the Program

In operationalizing outcomes for a particular program, one usually develops indicators from the program's objectives. "What is the program trying to accomplish?" is the customary initial question. To answer this question, it is usually helpful to view program objectives within the framework of the theory in which the program is based. Thus, a program of task-centered case management in the schools (Reid and Bailey-Dempsey 1995) is based on the theory that specific problems of students at risk of failure can be alleviated by tasks carried out by practitioners, teachers, parents, and students. The theory further predicts that helping clients resolve particular problems through methods prescribed by the approach will have additional benefits for them, such as engendering a more positive attitude toward teachers and increasing their problem-solving skills. As the example illustrates, examination of a program's theoretical underpinnings usually reveals that a program has multiple objectives (e.g., immediate problem resolution and enhancement of problem-solving skills) and that its goals can be ordered in a certain sequence (e.g., task accomplishment leads to problem reduction). With such a map of program goals, one can fashion criteria sensitive to a range of program outcomes. The logic applies to programs of any scope, from those used in single cases to large-scale undertakings.

This process may be difficult, particularly if the program is complex and directed toward vaguely defined objectives and lacking a well-articulated theoretical base. Additional obstacles are posed if those responsible for the program have unrealistic notions of the capabilities of the program or are unable to agree on what its goals should be.

Issues in Selecting Outcome Criteria

With consensus on program objectives, one can begin to develop criteria for assessing outcome. Some considerations when selecting criteria include unintended consequences, whose perspectives are pertinent, how short- or long-range the goals may be, durability of outcome, and cost-effectiveness.

UNINTENDED CONSEQUENCES In deriving outcome criteria, one should not be confined to the goals of a program or to its underlying theory. It is important to be aware of unintended consequences of a program, particularly of the possibility that a program may have negative effects. Thus, a wider perspective needs to be brought to bear, perhaps one informed by other theories.

For example, an individualized program may be directed at modifying the behavior of a particular child who has several siblings. The program calls for the mother to reward the child when he or she behaves in a desired way. Although the goals and theory of the program might limit attention to the mother-child dyad, it would be an oversight, we think, to confine outcome criteria accordingly. A systems perspective on family interaction, if not common sense, would suggest that the mother's rewarding one child might have consequences for her relationships with her other children. Reasonably comprehensive outcome criteria would need to take such "system effects" into account.

PERSPECTIVES OF PARTICIPANTS The meaning of outcome, and criteria for its assessment, will also vary according to the perspectives of different participants: service practitioners, collaterals, clients, and researchers. Even when outcome considerations are restricted to "objective evidence," what evidence is regarded as a valid measure of outcome and interpretations placed on it can be expected to differ according to different observers. And usually there is little basis for regarding any one vantage point as decisive. Thus the goal of a program may be to alleviate problems in psychosocial functioning. According to the practitioner's criteria, changes in surface problems, which he or she may regard as "symptoms," may be discounted. Clients may place a high degree of value on changes of this order. A researcher, making judgments on the basis of interviews with clients, may occupy an intermediate position. A collateral such as a teacher or neighbor may feel that the wrong issues altogether were addressed.

OTHER CONSTITUENCY GROUPS Nonparticipant constituency groups also have an important stake in service programs, and like participants their perceptions of legitimate goals and objectives will vary. Such constituency groups include funding sources (which may include multiple sources with conflicting aims and expectations); local, regional, state and sometimes federal regulatory and legislative bodies; other service providers; organized professional and consumer groups; and community groups such as religious organizations or businessmen's councils. In one evaluation of a public comprehensive service program for the mentally ill, constituency groups included four levels (Pulice 1994): at the central (state) level were the state legislature that authorized, regulated, and funded the program; the governor's executive staff that negotiated budgets and contracts; the central administration of the state department of mental health; and powerful consumer advocacy groups, the state Mental Health Association and the Alliance for the Mentally Ill. At the regional level were the regional state mental health administration and psychiatric hospitals, who were accustomed to autonomous operation rather than cooperation with community agencies. At the county level were powerful local governments who had no traditional and unclear new roles in the program, and county service providers. At the agency level were the agency's client groups (which often included other populations besides mentally ill), local consumers and families and their organizations, and other local service providers.

Pulice (1994) suggests that such constituency groups' stance toward evaluation can be assessed by knowing what roles they take on several dimensions: insider or outsider, professional or lay, consumer or provider, and policy maker or implementer.

Whereas differences among different actors can be reduced through the development of specific indicators of criteria, they probably cannot be eliminated completely. Outcome assessments obtained from different vantage points tend to show a considerable amount of divergence (Lambert and Hill 1994). Increasingly, and with good reason, researchers are being advised to incorporate the perspectives of more than one actor in their measures of outcome (Lambert and Hill 1994).

PROXIMAL VERSUS ULTIMATE OUTCOMES As noted, a program of intervention can be conceptualized in terms of a sequence of goals or outcomes. Task accomplishment (a proximal goal) leads to problem reduction (an ultimate goal) as in the example given earlier. A program to help patients discharged from mental hospitals become self-sufficient may use on-the-job training in a sheltered workshop as a means of securing job placements in the community. Outcomes for the job training component could be seen as subsidiary to the outcome of the job placement efforts.

Although interest may be centered in the "ultimate" criteria that culminate the sequence, indicators of outcome earlier in the sequence should not be overlooked. It is important, if possible, to obtain a picture of the chain of events that led to final outcomes. Information of this kind can provide evidence on the effectiveness of the intervention by tracing the process of its impact (chapter 6) and can also help pinpoint weak links in the chain. For example, the lack of problem change in a task-centered intervention program might be traced to the lack of accomplishment of certain tasks. Developing better or alternative tasks for the problem might be the key to improving the program. In some instances, such as programs to prevent teenage pregnancy, the ultimate goals may occur too far in the future to permit feasible follow-up. "Proximal" goals (Rossi and Freeman 1993), such as a change in the teens' sexual behavior, may serve as the best available measure.

DURABILITY Although words such as "final" or "ultimate" may be used to describe the desired end goal of a program, we seldom achieve once-and-for-all solutions. Questions about the durability of effects inevitably contribute additional complexities to decisions about outcome criteria. Usually priority is given, and with good reason, to indicators of the immediate effects of a program. There is little point in worrying about durability of gains if no gains had occurred. In most social work programs, such effects, if they are found at all, occur by the time of the termination of service or shortly thereafter. "Sleeper effects"—those that first appear some time after the end of service—do sometimes occur, but are relatively rare.

However, the durability of effects is usually accorded a high degree of importance. In fact, in some types of program, interest in durability may be paramount. The immediate effects of a program may have already been established; one wishes to learn if these effects persist over time. (A good deal of behavioral treatment fits this case.) In other situations, target problems presumably affected by the program may occur at a relatively low frequency. A fair amount of time may need to pass before one can establish that the intervention has done its work. Programs designed to reduce delinquent behavior provide examples.

Typical follow-up periods range from six months to two years post-termination, with longer periods used for some problems. Ideally the length of the follow-up period should be determined by knowledge of the typical course of the problem following intervention. For example, the relapse rate for some problems, such as alcoholism, is known to be high for a period of several years following treatment. Thus follow-ups of alcohol treatment programs may be of several years duration. For problems that may be cyclical in nature, such as depression, the follow-up period would ideally be long enough to span the likely occurrence of the next cycle.

One always hopes that changes achieved in intervention will be durable, but lack of durability, especially in long-term follow-ups, is not necessarily a cause for complete dismay. A period of sustained problem relief, for example, two years of abstinence in the life of a drug addict, can be seen in a positive light, even though a relapse occurs.

EFFICIENCY Criteria that are becoming increasingly important in our present age of managed care and other forms of financial restraint concern program efficiency, which examines the effectiveness of a program in relation to costs (Rossi and Freeman 1993). Methods of evaluating efficiency comprise *cost-effectiveness* and *cost-benefit* analyses.

In using cost-effectiveness criteria, one usually compares the costs of alternative programs in achieving a given outcome. For example, if a brief counseling program, consisting of eight interviews, was found to achieve outcomes equivalent to a longer-term program consisting of twenty interviews, the short-term program, other things being equal, could be said to be the more cost-effective. To determine the extent of the difference in cost-effectiveness, it would be necessary to calculate the actual costs of the two programs in terms of salaries paid to practitioners, etc. Note that in analysis of cost-effectiveness, only the cost of the program is converted into monetary terms (or "monetized"). As one might surmise, a precise calculation of the costs of a program would involve a number of technical accounting considerations. Approximations may suffice if the cost-effectiveness differences are large, as they might be in the example given above.

An important area for cost-effectiveness analysis in social work concerns programs that attempt to prevent institutional care, for example, care in foster homes, nursing homes, hospitals, and residential treatment centers. One purpose of such programs is to provide care in the community that is as good as, if not better than, institutional care at lower cost. Although it is difficult to apply cost-effectiveness analysis to such programs—for instance, it is difficult to determine numbers of cases prevented as well as quality of care—reasonable estimates may be convincing.

In cost-benefit analysis, both the costs and effects of the program are monetized. Obviously this method has more restricted usefulness in social work in which it is difficult to place monetary values on such outcomes as "relief of depression" and "improved marital relations." However, the method can be applied to some programs. For example, the effects of work-training programs for welfare recipients can be converted to dollar amounts based on earnings from jobs. (Obviously such programs would have other effects that could not be so converted.) If effects can be monetized, it is then possible to evaluate the program's efficiency through a *benefit-cost ratio*. To continue with the example above, let us suppose that the average costs for training and placing a welfare recipient are a $1000 per year but that the average annual savings to the government budget from reduced welfare expenditures are $3000. This would produce a benefit-cost ratio of 1 to 3, that is, for every dollar spent on job training the government would save three. Benefit-cost ratios generally rely on a number of assumptions about costs and effects, which need to be critically examined. Moreover, they need to be considered in relation to the accounting perspective used. In the example just given, a quite different benefit-cost ratio would be obtained if the accounting perspective were that of the client.

Peak, Toseland, and Banks (1995) report a study using efficiency criteria. Spouse care-givers of frail elderly veterans were randomly assigned to either support groups or a usual-care control condition. Caregivers attended weekly group meetings for 8 weeks followed by monthly meetings for 10 months. The meetings, led by an MSW social worker, were concerned with mutual support, health education, problem solving, and stress reduction. Data on health care costs indicated a cost differential of approximately $7500 in favor of the experimental cases over a year period. Veterans whose spouses participated in the support group program used fewer and less costly medical services, especially hospitalization, than those in the control group. Moreover spouses in the experimental group were less likely to see declines in the health of the veterans than spouses in the control group. Program costs were estimated at $700 per participant caregiver. The cost-benefit ratio (which was not reported) would suggest that the program saved large amounts of money without sacrificing—in fact, possibly benefiting—the health care of the veterans.

Developing Specific Indicators of Outcome

Thus far we have considered a number of sources and types of outcome criteria. We now turn to questions of depth, or to the movement from the abstract to the concrete in the development of criteria. One may begin with a global conception of outcome, such as "increased independent functioning," and attempt to fashion definitional chains encompassing an array of more specific indicators. In one chain this conception may be specified as "improvement in self-care routines," which in turn may be further specified (in part) as "increased ability to dress self." Even indicators that are fairly specific to begin with require further specification. Thus outcome in a single case study may concern reduction in a child's getting out of his seat without permission, a complex behavior that would need to be specified in terms of the rules governing the movement of children in the classroom.

In the development of outcome indicators it is important, we think, to keep certain principles in mind. First, global concepts of outcome should always be defined in terms that are as specific as possible. Global concepts such as "improvement" and "positive change" should always be so articulated, even though inherent difficulties in spelling them out may make it tempting to leave their interpretation to practitioners, judges, clients, or even readers. Second, in explicating criteria an attempt should be made to include indicators sensitive to small effects. Given the difficulties in demonstrating the effectiveness of many forms of social work intervention, the researcher should try to include indicators that relate to minor or subtle changes, goal achievements, and the like.

Finally, attention needs to be given to the practical significance of changes resulting from the program. Although it is well to measure subtle effects, it is also important to be able to identify proportions of clients who have achieved a level of change commensurate with the goals of a program. Thus, clients in an agency program may change to a statistically significant degree (when compared with a control group) but few clients may have attained adequate resolutions of the problems that occasioned service. Such paradoxical results have generated considerable interest in establishing criteria for practical or clinical significance (Bloom, Fischer, and Orme 1995; Jacobson, Follette, and Revensdorf 1984; Jayaratne 1990).

Various criteria have been suggested to determine what might be regarded as clinically significant. (For a review, see Lambert and Hill 1994.) Perhaps the most promising of these is the use of normative data. For example, one could use a standardized instrument to determine the level of depression of a client who had just completed treatment. The client's scores could then be compared with norms for nondepressed persons to see if they were now in the normal range. If so, a clinically significant degree of improvement could be readily established. At a community level, the rates of teen pregnancy in comparable neighborhoods might be used as a substitute for norms when assessing a prevention program.

Criteria of this kind are limited to problems for which good normative data exist, a shortcoming in various types of social work practice. Still the general thrust of the clinical significance movement, which calls for setting standards of decisive progress and for reporting proportions of clients who meet those standards, applies to all forms of social work practice.

From Criteria to Data

A final step in the specification of outcome measures is consideration of how data are actually derived. Although outcome measures can take the form of direct evaluations of service, as when clients are asked what they thought of a program, most measures involve gathering data about change in some target that the intervention has presumably affected. The more common means of deriving change measures are briefly reviewed.

The simplest means is to obtain retrospective estimates from clients, practitioners, or others who in effect are asked for their opinions about change in target problems, systems, and the like, since the beginning of intervention. Like most ex post facto data collection, retrospective assessments of change may suffer from respondent memory loss and the influence of recent events. The desire of respondents to see benefits from intervention may result in exaggerations of amounts of change that have occurred. To provide more information than error, these retrospective approaches should not be limited to global impressions but should rather cover aspects of change in a detailed and comprehensive manner.

A more rigorous method of deriving measures of change is prospective timing of data collection, that is, one measure of the status of the target prior is obtained prior to intervention (premeasure) and a second measure (postmeasure) following the intervention. The change score is calculated by subtracting the premeasure from the postmeasure. Thus, if a family is rated five on the Geismar Family Functioning Scale (Geismar 1980) at case opening and seven at case closing, a change score of + 2 is recorded. In principle, the procedure is the same as weighing oneself before and after a period of dieting and measuring change in terms of pounds gained or lost. Before-and-after change scores can be used to measure the amount and significance of change within a single group or to compare outcomes between different groups. In measurement of intervention outcomes, however, subtractive measures tend to be vulnerable to certain kinds of distortions. For example, extremely "poor" initial scores have greater room for improvement than scores closer to the mean (statistical regression).

In comparing the outcomes of different groups, especially those that are nonequivalent, there are advantages in incorporating both before and after scores simultaneously in the same analysis. This can be done through analysis of covariance (ANCOVA) in which the initial scores are treated as a covariate (chapter 11). In this way, the possibly biasing effects of the initial scores can be better controlled. (For an example see Pomeroy, Ruben, and Walker 1995.) As might be surmised, this method requires a fair amount of statistical sophistication and samples of at least moderate size.

An alternative to approaches outlined above are measures of change based on judges' comparisons of before-and-after data. In this method, a trained judge compares data on targets obtained before and after intervention and makes a rating of change on scales developed for the purpose. Ideally, the judges are unaware that intervention has occurred in the interim and can even be kept in the dark about which set of data was obtained before intervention and which after. In other words, judges can simply be asked to assess change between two "pictures" of a case, without knowing anything additional.

A principal advantage of this method over the preceding measures is its greater sensitivity, a particular strength in evaluation of social work intervention where changes are frequently in the "modest" range. Thus a small, but important, decrease in the intensity of a couple's quarreling may be apparent from comparing interview data obtained from the couple at different points of time, a decrease that might not be detected in retrospective or subtractive measures. The assessments of judges may, however, be based on data, such as interview protocols, that may have significant limitations. Also one sacrifices information about level: the position of a target before intervention as might be compared to general norms. These drawbacks may be more than offset by gains in sensitivity if change is difficult to detect through the use of before-and-after measures.

Still another approach, one taken in single-system designs, consists of repeated measures over time. Assessments of change are then based on evaluations of variability, level, and trend of the series of measures as discussed in chapter 6. As can be seen, such a time series is an extension of pre-post measurement. Measures are now obtained not only before and after intervention but also during its course. Since it incorporates pre-post measurement and provides in addition continual readings of the course of change during intervention, time series measurement might be seen as clearly superior. However time and costs in data collection may make them impractical to use in group experiments involving more than a small number of subjects.

Moreover, repeated measures can create their own special kinds of distortions: for example, clients may remember previous responses on a test, or their behavior may be influenced by repeated testing or observation. In addition, it may be difficult to withhold from the data collector knowledge that clients are receiving intervention, knowledge that could be a source of bias.

However, time series may be particularly helpful in evaluating change in higher-level systems, for example, the attractiveness of a group education program by graphing attendance, or the effectiveness of a publicity campaign by the number of applications for service. Such an approach may be particularly feasible if existing data like attendance and applications are used. An example is the study of coordinating police, courts, and social service responses to incidents of wife-battering, where public data on arrests and prosecutions were used to measure the community-wide impact of the program (Gamache, Edleson, and Schock 1988; chapter 6).

Sources and Types of Data

In a broad sense, the measurement of outcome comprises the various steps that take place in the translation of outcome criteria to refined data. As we have seen, they include the development of instruments, obtaining raw data from particular sources, and transforming these data into final measures of change. We now take a close look at two dimensions of major importance in this complex process: 1) data sources and 2) the types of data obtained from these sources.

Clients

Most approaches to the measurement of outcome can be traced to one ultimate source—the clients themselves. Case record data, although supplied by practitioners, are to a large extent based on client self-report. Clients are a more direct source of data when their behaviors are observed, when they are interviewed about changes in their problems or their situations, or when their evaluations of service are elicited.

A central consideration when the client is the source of data is the extent to which the amount and kind of information provided the researcher are under the client's cognitive control. At one extreme would fall measures of client opinion about a program and measures based on the client's own report of change. At the other extreme are observations of the client's behavior in a natural setting or his or her performance of a task in the laboratory. The most common devices used to collect data from clients—interviews, questionnaires, and standardized instruments—are very much under the client's cognitive control. These devices will be briefly discussed.

INTERVIEWS AND QUESTIONNAIRES Perhaps the most direct way to obtain data about how clients have fared in a program is to ask them about changes in their problems or lives that have occurred since their involvement in the program. Instruments used for this purpose include structured and semistructured interviews and self-administered questionnaires. Clients may be asked to give information about changes that have occurred or to give a picture of their current situation which can be compared to a similar picture prior to the beginning of the program.

Because the information provided is dependent on the client's memory or judgment, there is considerable opportunity for distortions or biases to affect the data. Clients, like all human beings, are limited by their ability to recall events in the past, and moreover their recall may be influenced by their own involvement in the program. Appreciation of the practitioner's efforts and a need to justify their investments of time and money may cause them to give an erroneously favorable picture of the program's impact. Social desirability effects may be additional sources of bias. If clients perceive a data collector as a representative of the program, they may give a response that would make the program look good to please their interrogator. "Polite lying" to people responsible for providing service is a natural reaction: indifferent meals suddenly become "fine" when we are asked our opinions of them by waiters and maitre d's. When clients are dependent on the program for important resources, such as income, housing, or health care, they may be reluctant to be critical because of their wish to "stay out of trouble." For these reasons it is best if outcome interviews or questionnaires are administered by researchers who are not identified with the program. Even in single-system studies conducted by practitioner-researchers, it helps to have outcome data of this type collected by someone else or at least to have clients put questionnaires into sealed envelopes.

Sample attrition or mortality may add further distortion. As noted in chapter 7, clients willing to cooperate in an outcome study are more likely to give positive evaluations than are dropouts.

Despite these limitations, client self-report data obtained through interviews and questionnaires provide a unique perspective on outcome in evaluating programs. This is especially true of programs designed to change phenomena that researchers cannot readily observe, for example, family interaction in the home. To control for biases associated with memory, social desirability and the like, an attempt should be made to pin measures to specific events and, if possible, to obtain self-report data (on initial status) prior to service as well as data relating to change—perhaps obtained by practitioners—during the course of service. If only post-service ratings are possible, clients can be asked to do retrospective ratings of how problems were before service began and then to rerate how these problems are "now," so that measures of change can be calculated, as discussed earlier. As Beutler and Crago (1983) suggest, such anchored change measures are preferable to the more common client post-service ratings of improvement which appear to be heavily influenced by the clients' current sense of well being. (Specific procedures for before-and-now ratings can be found in Beutler 1983.)

CLIENT SATISFACTION RATINGS Client ratings of satisfaction with service are measures commonly obtained from interviews and questionnaires. These measures are conceptually distinct from data relating to change, improvement, and the like. (Clients can be satisfied with a service that has produced little change in their lives, or vice-versa.) Global ratings of satisfaction with service tend to be quite positive. For example, compilations of studies of client satisfaction with mental health services have reported satisfaction rates that generally range from 70 to 80 percent (Berger 1983; Lebow 1983; Lehman and Zastowny 1983; Ruggeri 1994).

It is impossible to determine to what extent these rates reflect genuine satisfaction as opposed to sampling bias, self-justification, social desirability, and other types of distortion, but it is reasonable to suppose that they contain some amount of "exaggeration of benefit" or inflation in a positive direction. This point is illustrated convincingly by Ware (1997: 46), who found in one study of patient satisfaction with health care that 80 percent indicated that they were "completely satisfied" with the services they had received. The patients who had expressed complete satisfaction were then asked if the services could have been better. A third said that they could have been improved! Further, that third were less likely to comply with treatment regimens and more likely to change to a new provider.

Conservative interpretations of data are justified as a rule. Thus, if 20 percent of the clients receiving services say they are "very satisfied," 50 percent "satisfied," and the remaining 30 percent "dissatisfied," it would be more reasonable to conclude that an alarming number of clients had reservations about the program (almost a third expressed dissatisfaction) than to suggest that 70 percent were "satisfied customers." (A client rating of "satisfied" can almost be interpreted as a neutral response if a "very satisfied" option is available.) This is not to say that one can dismiss the possibility of negative bias in client self-reports, particularly if there is reason to suppose that clients resented an "imposed service." Well-validated measures of global client satisfaction may be found in Attkisson and Greenfield (1994).

Often more useful than ratings of satisfaction for programs as a whole are client evaluations of specific components. An example is provided by client dissatisfaction with time limits in short-term treatment (O'Connor and Reid 1986).

STANDARDIZED INSTRUMENTS Standardized client self-report measures of target problems were considered in the previous chapter in relation to their use as assessment tools. They become tools in the measurement of outcome when they are repeated over time, for example, when they are given prior to and at the end of service. Reviews of standardized instruments that can be used to measure change associated with psychotherapy and other forms of interpersonal treatment may be found in Ciminero, Calhoun, and Adams (1986), in Lambert and Hill (1994), and in Bloom, Fischer, and Orme (1995). Reviews of methods of assessing the environment, including both physical and social environments, may be found in Moos (1987) and Gregory (1996).

The primary rationale for using a standardized instrument in the study of outcome is to enhance comparability of measurement across client systems.

Measurement bias or other forms of error resulting from variation in instrument items, testing procedures, and so on, are, at least in theory, reduced. Standardized instruments have additional advantages of efficiency and economy since they require no variation from case to case. If the outcomes of an intervention program can be appropriately assessed by an available instrument, additional advantages accrue. Usually such instruments have been developed systematically by knowledgeable researchers. An available instrument may already have been used in a number of studies so that a good deal of evidence on its validity, reliability, and other measurement properties may have been gathered. Normative data in the form of scores of various groups of subjects may exist. These norms can be used for comparative purposes. Thus, if the Beck Depression Inventory (Beck 1967) were used to evaluate the outcome of a program for depressed clients, researchers could, as noted in the previous chapter, assess the severity of the degree of depression in their sample of clients before intervention by comparing initial scores of their clients to the inventory scores of a large number of depressed persons. These normative data provide "benchmark" scores indicating different degrees of depression, scores that have been validated against the diagnostic judgments of psychiatrists. Moreover, the gains made by depressed clients in one study could be compared with gains, again as measured by the Inventory, of depressives treated in other programs.

Standardized instruments may be particularly useful when the targets of intervention are relatively homogeneous. For example, if a program were directed exclusively at helping mentally retarded persons find employment, uniform questions about type of work found, wages, job satisfaction, and so forth, would make sense. If targets are relatively homogeneous and if there is an existing standardized instrument designed to measure change in that type of target, then the advantages in using a well-developed instrument may be compelling.

The advantages of standardized instruments in the measurement of outcome are counterbalanced by a number of limitations. Although a standardized instrument exposes different subjects to the same stimuli, this constancy of exposure does not guarantee that the stimuli will be interpreted in the same fashion or responded to with the same degree of accuracy. Thus subjects may vary considerably in the meanings they ascribe to "feeling blue," in how well they recall such episodes, their frankness in admitting to such feelings, and so on. Given such variation, one cannot assert that two clients with the same "depression score" are equally depressed. A high degree of equivalence between scores and phenomena measured occurs only when an instrument is responded to in a constant fashion, as would be the case in determining the daily weight of subjects with a set of accurate scales. When instrument stimuli evoke variable responses, as is the case with most standardized instruments used to measure the outcome of social work intervention, the relations of scores to phenomena measured must be assessed, and then only in approximate fashion, through complex validation procedures (see below and also chapter 9).

Since items on a standardized instrument must be cast in general terms to be applicable to a wide range of subjects and their circumstances, they are often global and vague (I feel at ease with other people: never__; sometimes __; usually__ ; always__). Not only do these items fail to provide much precise reliable information, but also their lack of specificity makes it easy for clients to exercise their biases. (See also discussion of fixed alternative items, chapter 10.)

It may be difficult to determine if in fact the instrument is measuring change in the target problem or in the client's biases. For example, a mother who paints a rosy picture of her family at the start of service and a somewhat less rosy one at its conclusion may be providing evidence of a more realistic attitude, rather than negative change in her family's behavior. Thus what might appear to be a failure of service might actually be a sign of its success. As with questionnaires and interviews, standardized instruments may be influenced by the clients' tendencies to exaggerate the benefits received from service. Because of the possibility that the instrument might be measuring something other than what it is supposed to, it is always important to examine its results in the light of other data.

For example, in the case of the mother who reported an apparent decline in family functioning, it might be instructive to examine her initial scores in relation to other evidence regarding the family's problems at the beginning of service. Her scores on the standardized instrument might be unusually positive (in relation to general norms) but at the same time she might have reported a number of family problems. Moreover the "negative" direction of her scores on the instrument might be contradicted by evidence of positive change from other measures. As the example suggests, client biases in completing standardized instruments need not necessarily mean that the results are of no use. Indeed they may be quite revealing if they can be assessed in the context of other data.

Even if they measure what they purport to measure reasonably well, standardized instruments are usually limited in their sensitivity to the range and detail of particular changes that may occur in the client systems under study. These limitations are most obvious when an instrument measures change in only one kind of target in a project that may be addressed to a variety of targets. Thus an instrument designed to measure change in an adolescent's self-concept may frequently miss the mark if self-concept is not an issue in a large proportion of cases in a program being evaluated. This lack of case relevance can result in an underestimation of intervention effects. To continue with the example, changes in self-concept may occur as a result of intervention but in not enough cases to show a statistically significant result since cases in which it was not a target may show no change.

Standardized instruments may be relevant in a general way to the change target but still not sensitive enough to capture the relatively subtle (but meaningful) changes that may result from intervention. An adolescent male may label himself (correctly) as "shy" on a standardized instrument before and after intervention but still may have made significant improvement in his ability to initiate social relationships. More generally, the change experienced by a client system may be characterized by a particular configuration that a standardized instrument or even several may not detect. Certain problems are handled a little better, there is some increase in self-confidence, conflicts in family relationships have lessened somewhat. It all may add up to substantial improvement, but no one piece of the pattern is striking enough to be detected by the instrument.

It is important to review the literature on any standardized instrument one plans to use. An author of a published instrument may report an impressive amount of data on the instrument's reliability, validity, factor structure, and so on, and such data may be, of course, quite useful in evaluating the instrument. Because the instrument is the author's own, the data may be presented in a favorable light and may need to be examined critically. It may pay to search the literature for a more objective appraisal of the instrument. (Indices to literature on specific tests may be found in Bloom, Fischer, and Orme 1995; and Murphy, Conoley, and Impara 1994.)

Particular attention needs to be given to the validity of the instrument. It is a common error to regard an instrument as "valid" simply because there is evidence that it can discriminate between groups of subjects, for example, between psychiatric patients and normals, or that it correlates with other measures, such as other standardized tests or ratings of clinicians. To reiterate a point made earlier (chapter 9), instrument validity is always a matter of degree and seldom "established" in any final sense. Instrument validity must be related to the purposes the potential user has in mind. For example, an instrument to measure perceived "powerlessness" may have shown predicted differences between middle- and lower-class subjects, but this does not mean that it can discriminate between groups of lower-class subjects. If an investigator uses the instrument to test the effects of a program with an exclusively lower-class clientele, he or she does so on faith that it can detect meaningful differences within such a clientele. Moreover, validity evidence may be based on correlations with similar instruments, which may share similar biases, or the evidence may rest on statistically significant but essentially weak associations with criterion variables. The investigator needs further to examine the fit between items used in the instrument and the subjects in the immediate study. A test of assertiveness that contains youth-oriented items, with references to dating and the like, may not provide a meaningful measure of this variable in a group of senior citizens. Similarly, normative data compiled by the instrument developers must be examined for relevance to the sample at hand.

Contrasting approaches to use of client data are from two evaluations of prevention programs. Fuscaldo, Kaye, and Philliber (1998), evaluating a teen parenting program, used standardized instruments that measured client attainment of program goals and gave them both before and after the program. The instruments included the Brief Symptom Inventory (Derogatis and Spencer 1982) to measure the young women's mental health and the Parenting Stress Inventory (Abdin 1990) to measure their parenting competence. They also used self-report data on high school graduation and employment to measure economic self-sufficiency, and pregnancy rates to measure the goal of reduction of teen pregnancy. Drisko (1998), by contrast, focused on the utilization or intermediate outcomes of two intensive family intervention programs, and used qualitative data from interviews with parents. He reported parents' subjective impressions of the staff, referral process, agency auspices, issues of confidentiality, perceptions of service, and so on. In discussing the utility of the evaluation, he reported that staff and supervisors "were surprised to see that families offered a different emphasis from that of program planners" (72).

OBSERVATION When outcome measures are based on observations of the client's behavior in natural situations or performance of structured tasks, then distortions of the kind considered above are less likely to occur. One must still be concerned with the client's reactions to being observed or tested, reactions that may produce atypical, often atypically positive, responses. Although the client's selective recall may not be an issue, the researcher must now pay attention to the representativeness of what has been observed or tested. Do the observation periods reflect a fair sample of the client's behavior? Does a role-play test of assertiveness cover typical situations in which assertive responses may be called for? If role plays are used to test changes in client behavior, e.g., the acquisition of social skills, a key concern is how well the client's behavior in the role play will correspond to behavior in actual social situations. For this reason role-play tests should be supplemented, if possible, by data obtained by observers in the client's natural situation.

Practitioners

The practitioner is frequently used as a source of data on client change. Data can usually be readily obtained from practitioners at minimal cost. Also, the practitioner has firsthand knowledge of changes in the client's life and circumstances that may be associated with intervention and, as we have noted, brings to bear a perspective informed by professional knowledge.

Outcome data may be obtained directly from practitioners by means such as questionnaires, structured recording forms, scales, or interviews. Less direct means usually involve coding of the practitioners' written narrative recordings. The more direct means are almost invariably superior, given the additional sources of error inherent in narrative recordings, although it may be necessary to use the latter in ex post facto studies (see also chapter 15).

LIMITATIONS OF PRACTITIONER DATA The most important limitation of practitioners as sources of outcome data is probably bias resulting from their involvement in the intervention. Artisans are seldom considered to be the best judges of their own work. Even if they attempt to be strictly honest in their appraisals, practitioners may be inclined to give more weight to positive changes than an objective observer might; on the other hand, their perceptions may be influenced by self-critical tendencies, with the result that gains others may see are downplayed. Since it is impossible to predict the amount or direction of these biases, one can only place a large question mark alongside the outcome data obtained from the practitioner.

Another limitation grows out of difficulties in training practitioners to apply criteria developed to assess change. Practitioners may have their own notions about what constitutes improvement, goal attainment, and the like, which they may find difficult to give up and which may vary considerably from one practitioner to the next. Moreover, the time needed to train practitioners to view change in some standard manner may be lacking. Practitioners may then be given crudely defined scales or other instruments in the naive hope that their judgments will be based on common standards. Like judges and coders, practitioners need to be given well-developed instruments and to be trained in their use.

Finally, data supplied by practitioners are limited by their own knowledge of their clients and their situations. This knowledge may be highly selective, particularly if it is limited to what clients have discussed in clinical interviews. Although clients may be more open with their practitioners than with research interviewers, what the clients reveal to their helpers can still be partial and distorted. Practitioners are in a better position if they have had the opportunity to obtain information about the client from a variety of sources, including observation of clients in interaction with others.

PARTICULARIZED INSTRUMENTS A useful tool that practitioners can use in outcome measurement is a particularized instrument for assessing outcome. (Such instruments can also be used by researchers in post-service interviews with clients or by judges who make use of a variety of case materials.) An instrument can be said to be particularized or individualized if it enables a practitioner or researcher to adapt the measure to the individual characteristics of the case. As this definition suggests, particularized instruments attempt to achieve greater sensitivity to idiosyncratic patterns of change.

A particularized instrument usually asks in effect "How much change or progress has occurred in respect to the particular problems, symptoms, goals, and the like, that are at issue in the case at hand?" For example, in the evaluation of task-centered practice (Reid 1978, 1994a), changes in target problems are rated by practitioners using 10-point scales whose values range from "considerably worse" (1) to "problem alleviated" (10) with a rating of "no change" (5) in the middle. Thus a small improvement in the financial picture of a couple with a problem of credit-card debt might be given a rating of 6. The rationale for such an approach is that it is more sensitive than a standardized instrument to the specific and often modest changes that might be associated with intervention and can capture changes for which a standardized instrument may not be available.

Although such target problem ratings may be affected by practitioner bias, the presence of bias can be assessed by obtaining second ratings from independent coders (judges) who listen to tapes of "problem reviews" conducted by the practitioners with their clients. Satisfactory correlations have been found between practitioner and coders (Reid 1978; 1994a).

Similar to the problem change measure just described are the use of "target complaints" to evaluate changes in adult outpatients in mental health settings (Battle et al. 1966; Mintz and Kiesler 1982); Persons' (1991) "case formulation" method; Gillespie and Seaberg's Individual Problem Rating [IPR] (1977; Orme, Gillespie, and Fortune 1983). Perhaps the best known and most widely used of the particularized approaches is Goal Attainment Scaling (1973, 1977; Kiresuk and Sherman 1968). (See also chapter 13.) In Goal Attainment Scaling, outcome is evaluated in terms of progress clients have made toward goals established at the beginning of service. Progress (or regression) is assessed on five point scales by practitioners, judges, collaterals, or the clients themselves. The scales may be further refined by weighting the goals according to their importance. A review of both target complaint measures and Goal Attainment Scaling may be found in Lambert and Hill (1994).

When change targets are heterogeneous, as is often the case, a standardized client self-report instrument may be too "blunt" to detect the variety of changes at issue. A particularized instrument may be needed. There may be little doubt on this score when targets are obviously heterogeneous, as would be the case in a counseling program addressed to a variety of psychosocial problems. The matter is not as clear when targets fall within the same class but still reflect considerable diversity. Marital problems are a case in point. In one situation, a problem may center on sexual difficulties; in another, on quarrels about money. A particularized instrument (whether completed by a practitioner or researcher) may be able to detect changes that would be missed by a standardized measure. A reasonable strategy is to use a combination of standardized and particularized instruments, particularly when targets, as in the example given, have some degree of similarity and standardized instruments to measure them are available.

The major limitation of particularized instruments is the reciprocal of its strength. If each case is measured on its own terms, there are obvious problems in making comparisons among cases or in giving any precise interpretation to ratings on scales used to record amounts of change. Thus the problems in one case may be trivial in comparison to those in another case. A rating of "slight improvement," made for both cases, would obviously have much different meanings. And, of course, statements about slight or considerable amounts of problem alleviation, goal attainment, symptom relief, and so on, say little about what in fact was changed. The issue does not arise, however, if cross-case comparisons are not necessary, as may obtain in single system designs.

Collaterals

Outcome data may be obtained from persons involved in a case—relatives, teachers, houseparents, and so forth—who have firsthand knowledge of the client. The idea can be extended to include persons (sometimes called "informants" or significant others) who know the client but who may not have any connection with the case; for example, clients may be asked to nominate a friend to serve this role. Since they usually have less of a personal stake in the intervention process, collaterals may be more objective in their appraisal of change than either practitioner or client. They may also have access to data, such as the client's behavior in a classroom or on a ward, that is beyond the scope of the practitioner's knowledge and that the client for any number of reasons may not be able to recall accurately.

Standardized instruments have been developed expressly for gathering information from collaterals. One of the best known is the Katz Adjustment Scale-Relatives Form (KAS-R) (Katz and Lyerly 1963). Some instruments are designed to elicit both self-report data from the clients and data from those who know the client. The Psychological Adjustment to Illness Scale (Derogatis 1976) is an example.

While collateral data can provide an important perspective on outcome, their value in a given study needs to be carefully weighed. It cannot be assumed that collaterals have no personal investment in the outcome of intervention—in some cases they may have been involved in implementing the program; in others they may have the hope or expectation that the client will improve. On close inspection, one may find that the collateral's actual knowledge of the client may be more limited than initially assumed. For example, teachers' observations of their pupils' in-class behavior have been found to suffer from a considerable margin of error (Green and Wright 1979). And, of course, the collateral's knowledge of the client is invariably confined to only certain aspects of the client's functioning. It may be even more difficult to orient collaterals than practitioners to criteria for assessing outcome since, among other reasons, there are usually more of the former. Consequently, collaterals can probably be best used if emphasis is placed on specific data pertaining to the client rather than on their global judgments about change, although these judgments may be of interest as indicators of how the results of the program are perceived by others.

Of course, collateral data are essential when a goal of intervention is a change in systems at a higher level than the client or family. A generalist practitioner may seek to change the seating pattern in a classroom, the way staff respond to requests from nursing home residents, or the number of local businesses that provide summer jobs for youths. Reports from the relevant collaterals—teacher, staff or agency administrator (or other residents!), local employers—are necessary to evaluate outcome. When collateral reports involve their own behavior or attitudes, their reports are subject to the same issues as client self-report, such as social desirability or under- or overreporting of change.

Available Data

Various kinds of previously recorded information about the client, e.g., grades, contacts with police, admissions and discharges from institutions, and so forth, may be used as the basis of outcome measures. These data, which are usually collected by persons who are not a part of the intervention program, have the advantage of being free from bias resulting from case involvement. (Routine case information recorded by practitioners and collaterals would be exceptions if included here.) Moreover, they are the best, and often the only, source of data pertaining to contacts and status changes with human service organizations, hospitals, welfare departments, correctional facilities, and the like.

As Shyne (1975) has pointed out, a first consideration in use of recorded information is its "consistent availability." Data records may contain omissions, and official criteria used for defining categories of interest such as what constitutes a police contact or job placement may vary over time. She wisely suggests that the investigator spot-check recorded information before deciding to use it.

It is also important to determine how such data were obtained, by whom, and under what instructions and what conditions. One can then indicate possible sources of bias or inaccuracy in the data. In other words, the data collection processes used to produce the information need to be looked upon in the same critical light as one would regard any method of data collection used in a study. In this respect, assessments of data quality by staff who collect and use the information may be quite instructive. The error of assuming that records labeled "official" are thereby accurate should be avoided at all costs.

It is usually possible to make some judgments about the probable validity of different kinds of available data. For example, archival data relating to cost factors, such as number of days in care or date of discharge, are likely to be reliable because close attention is usually given to anything with financial consequences, and such data can be precisely recorded. On the other hand practitioners' global judgments about clients' functioning might be of questionable value.

Research Judges and Expert Observers

Researchers play an intermediary role in the use of any source of data. Usually this role is limited to collecting data by means of observation codes, interview schedules, or other devices in which the researchers' own interpretations of the data are minimized. In this capacity, the researcher serves as a channel, albeit an imperfect one, for conveying information from the source. Researchers can be considered data sources in their own right, however, if they are expected to make use of a high degree of judgment in their assessments of the data. The product is a measure of change based on the researcher's judgment. In general, research judges make judgments about raw data supplied by a variety of sources—clients, practitioners, recorded information, and the like. The same function is sometimes performed by persons designated as coders and analysts. We use the term "judge" as a generic designation for any person responsible for making relatively complex judgments about previously collected data. One use of judges in measuring change was considered in the previous section.

When judges are used as sources of data, one places confidence in the judge's capacities to process and organize complex data and to produce measurements of acceptable reliability and validity. To help ensure that this confidence is warranted, judges may have to meet various requirements. For example, to qualify as judges, persons may need to have professional credentials or credentials plus practice experience. Special training (sometimes quite extensive) in the judgment tasks is usually needed.

Qualifications and training requirements vary considerably, however. Highly structured judgment tasks in which rules for making judgments are explicit may not require professional credentials; for example, graduate social work students may be used. Training time may be confined to a few hours if the judgment tasks are highly structured and limited. In some cases judge training and instrument development may take place simultaneously; judgment criteria are developed by having judges review raw data, make judgments about them, and write out the criteria they use. Differences in judgments and criteria are discussed in group meetings and the discussions are used as a basis for redrafts of the instrument. This process may be quite time-consuming.

Regardless of the initial shape of the instrument, training is usually continued until judges have reached an acceptable level of reliability in trial applications of the judging instrument (see chapter 9). If an adequate reliability level cannot be reached, the instrument may need to be revised or an alternative means of measurement developed.

In addition to making judgments based on already collected data, researchers may make judgments about data they themselves collect through observation, interviews, and so forth. Although the term "judge" is sometimes extended to describe this role, we prefer "expert observer" (Auerbach 1983), a designation which suggests that the researcher is functioning both as a data collector (observer) and judge (expert). The usual instrument used by expert observers is some form of assessment interview, as discussed in the preceding chapter. The interview generates data which the observer uses as a basis for ratings or other judgments concerning functioning, change, and so on. Several standardized interview schedules have been developed, as noted in the previous chapter. Risks inherent in placing faith in the skills and knowledge of the expert observer can be offset by having the expert tape-record interviews and having judges make independent ratings from the tapes.

Choice of Source and Type of Outcome Data

As a general principle of outcome measurement, one wishes to obtain, whenever possible, multiple readings of change. This principle applies to both sources and types of data.

As a rule, the client should be, we think, the primary data source. A good combination of measures would consist of one or more standardized instruments completed before and after program participation and data obtained through interviews or self-administered questionnaires. Measures based on observations of the client's behavior have particular advantages and should be used whenever possible. When service involves multiple clients, such as family treatment, data should be supplied by different members of the system, independently if possible.

Use of data from collaterals or available data should be governed by the availability of collaterals or records capable of generating accurate and pertinent assessments of change. The need for such data becomes accentuated when one must rely on the client's self-report, and particularly when there is reason to doubt the credibility of the client's own account.

Data from practitioners are readily obtainable and should be secured as a matter of course. Particularized instruments completed by practitioners may be especially useful. While costly, judges and research observers can be used to advantage when outcome criteria and presumed changes relate to complex, diverse, and subtle phenomena.

Variation in Outcome Measures

We have shown how measurement can vary in terms of data source and type. We now turn to problems that arise from the inevitable variation when different types of measures are obtained from multiple sources.

The researcher hopes, of course, that use of different measures and sources of outcome will yield similar results, but unfortunately these hopes are often unrealized. To be sure, different measures from the same source, for example, a questionnaire and standardized instrument completed by the client, are likely to give a similar picture. However, as previously noted, divergence often occurs when measures are obtained from different sources—e.g., client, practitioner, collateral, or judge,

When different outcome measures are well correlated and do not show systematic discrepancies in level, one has reasonable grounds for assuming that the scores are measuring the same phenomenon in a similar manner and hence one can combine the scores through averaging or other means. When variation among measures is a significant factor, as is often the case, a simple aggregation of data may present a misleading picture. Results from different instruments or sources are best presented separately. Disparate measures should be combined only if the results of separate analyses have been made clear.

Variation among data sources in assessments of the outcome of services is of course much more than a technical problem of measurement. As discusssed at the beginning of the chapter, different sources of effectiveness data—practitioners, clients, collaterals, and so on—may have differing conceptions of what is effective. The same applies to different actors who make judgments about these data—managers, staffs of funding agencies, and the like. Much of this divergence appears due to differences in value orientation (Lambert and Hill 1994). The notion of effectiveness inevitably incorporates a value component. For example, a divorce as an outcome of marital counseling may be viewed as the optimal solution by the husband, a disaster by his wife, as deplorable by the religious organization that funds the agency, and as regrettable but necessary by the practitioner. In addition, different sources have access to different information. Clients know details of life at home that practitioners do not have; practitioners may have information about norms of family life that clients lack, and so on. While such disparity is often viewed as a measurement issue, its roots lie in conceptual and value orientations. These differences are not always reconcilable or averageable.

Researchers can handle such discrepancies by reporting them and discussing reasons for the variation. For program people, the task is not confined to paper. Programs may need to be restructured to accommodate different value positions; often choices must be made between which goals to emphasize or pursue. For example, an adoption program for older emotionally disturbed children was effective from an agency perspective since "good homes" were found for large numbers of children who might otherwise have had to remain in an institutional setting (Reid et al. 1987). However, its effectiveness was questioned by many of the adopting parents who found raising the children more than they had bargained for. "How can the needs of such children be squared with those of the adopting parents?" was one of a number of issues raised by divergence in point of view about the effectiveness of the program.

Summary

Evaluating the outcome of social work programs is one of the most important functions of research in social work, whether the level is the single-system or a large-scale program or agency. The process of evaluation begins with determining outcome criteria that are based on the goals and theory of the service and that consider several perspectives: unintended consequences, perspectives of participants and constituency groups, immediate or long-term outcomes, and durability and cost-effectiveness of outcomes. From the criteria, one develops specific indicators of outcome that reflect the various viewpoints. Approaches to collecting data on indicators include data from clients (interviews and questionnaires, satisfaction ratings, standardized instruments, and observation), from practitioner reports, from collaterals, from available data, and from research judges. In general, although data from various sources can present divergent views, multiple sources are useful and more likely to meet the needs of the outcome assessment than a single approach.

15 Study of Intervention Characteristics

As observed in chapter 7, a study of the effects of intervention is based on the assumption that one can determine the nature of the intervention tested. Because social work interventions tend to be relatively complex, a systematic study of the nature of the intervention itself is usually needed. At a minimum, such an investigation should yield a reasonably accurate picture of the intervention or interventions tested. It is also desirable to determine how different types of intervention used may correlate with outcome.

Study of the characteristics and correlates of intervention need not, of course, occur as a part of an outcome study. For example, exploratory or descriptive studies may be conducted to formulate or depict interventions in models of practice, programs, settings, and so forth.

The need for basic descriptive data on the nature of social work intervention has long been recognized (Briar 1974). Whether one is attempting to teach intervention methods to students or to interpret social work to funding sources, empirically based knowledge of what social workers do is of vital importance.

To questions of "What does intervention look like?" can be added questions like the following: "What makes it look that way?" How do experience and training influence practice? How are social workers' activities shaped by their diagnostic assessments?

The considerable variety of forms that intervention may assume makes it difficult to generalize about research approaches. Ideally, generalizations would need to span a range in which one finds disparate activities such as interview techniques, social action, and foster care. In the review that follows, we continue our focus on activities involving generalist practice with clients but at points extend our discussion to measurement of other facets of social work practice. We include data from practitioner reports, client reports, obtrusive and unobtrusive observation, change process research, and intervention analogs.

Data from Practitioner Reports

Traditionally, investigations of social work intervention have relied on practitioner reports of their activities. Whatever variety they assume, practitioner reports may be considered to be a form of participant observation data with its particular combination of strengths (observations based on firsthand knowledge) and weaknesses (biases resulting from personal involvement). (See chapters 4, 10 and 12.) Here, we consider several of the more important approaches to gathering data from the practitioner's perspective: narratives like process recordings, systematic recording forms, analysis of critical incidents, and self-report methods.

Discursive Narratives

In considering practitioner reports, an obvious starting point is the large volume of data that practitioners themselves accumulate as part of their routine recording procedures. The data are readily available and have cost the researcher nothing to collect. Most service programs use the discursive narrative case record, which may take such form as progress notes or summarized process recording. Samples of case records (or samples from records) may be used as a basis for studying practitioner activity or other forms of intervention. Interventions may be coded with some form of a content analysis instrument (see later discussion) or reviewed in a more impressionistic fashion.

The limitations of narrative case records as a basis for measurement of intervention are well known. Incompleteness, inaccuracy, selectivity, and bias in recording are typical problems. Their summarized and uneven character usually precludes any sort of fine-grained analysis of what practitioners do.

Still, narrative records have their uses in research. They provide an excellent means of gaining an overview of the activities of a complex program. Spottiness in recording is not a problem if one wishes only to acquire a sense of the type and range of interventions taking place. In this respect, the narrative record gives one a sense of the configuration of program activities that one might not obtain from data in more atomistic form, such as the number of different types of specific interventions used. And often, of course, narrative records are the only data on intervention that can be secured, as is the case when the decision to evaluate a program is not made until the program is well along or completed. Moreover, they may be the only source of data in historical studies of intervention. A discussion of strengths and weaknesses of narrative recording and ways of improving it may be found in Graybeal and Ruff (1995).

Systematic Recording

The utility of the case record can be increased manyfold if provisions are made to build in systematic recording procedures. The resulting record can serve multiple purposes: clinical, supervisory, administrative, and research. A number of formats for systematic case recording have been developed (Corcoran and Gingerich 1994; Kagle 1984; Kane 1974; Videka-Sherman and Reid 1985; Weed 1969). These formats require the collection of specific kinds of case data organized under predetermined headings. Omissions of key data are less likely to occur and can be readily spotted (and possibly corrected) when they do. Moreover, the organization of the data facilitates coding and analysis.

For example the Structured Clinical Record (Videka-Sherman and Reid 1985) provides a means of tracking problems, goals, interventions, and outcomes in a case regardless of the service model employed. Kagle (1984) describes two useful systematic recording devices: the Chronolog, which lists activities with clients in a chronological order, and the Progress Log, which records specific attitudes, feelings, or actions that represent the client's response to service. More highly structured forms may consist of precoded items, such as checklists. A general movement in social work toward more structured forms of recording has been documented by Kagle (1993).

Structured recording can be done on a routine basis. If so, the resulting data can be incorporated as part of a computerized agency information system. See for example, Corcoran and Gingerich (1994).

Critical Incidents

The researcher may wish to concentrate on specific types of intervention that may occur now and then in the course of complex practice situations and to have reasonably full descriptions of those interventions. If so, practitioners may be asked to record incidents of the occurrence of the intervention of interest, making use of the critical incident technique developed by Flanagan (1954). The incidents (which may be recorded on cards or reported in interviews) may describe what practitioners did in designated situations and possibly their perception of the immediate consequences of their actions.

Critical incidents can be used to identify potentially effective methods practitioners use in their work. For example, Havassy (1990) asked a sample of human service managers who were considered to be particularly effective to identify successful critical incidents in their interactions with different constituencies. The data were used in an effort to develop a model of effective administrative practice. Or critical incidents can be used to build descriptions of what practitioners do. Such an application was made by Banach (1995) who asked respondents to identify critical incidents demonstrating their application of the "in-the-best-interests-of-the-child" principle.

Interviews, Focus Groups, Questionnaires

Interviews, focus groups, and questionnaires provide additional means of securing practitioner self-report data on intervention, although they can also be used, as noted above, as a means of collecting critical incidents and other events. Semi-structured interviews with practitioners are particularly useful when one wishes to obtain exploratory data on the range and variety of interventions the practitioner might use, or if other forms of data collection, such as written or tape recordings, are not feasible or would not give an adequate accounting of the practitioner's work. For example, Rooney (1985) interviewed 28 practitioners six months after they had received training in task-centered practice to determine the extent and variety of use of task-centered methods in the post-training period. Also, an interview may be the method of choice if one wishes to investigate the practitioner's rationale for his or her behavior or to elicit the practitioner's "expert" knowledge. Thus, Fortune (1985a) interviewed practitioners about criteria they used in termination. Practitioners can be interviewed about their practice in general as in the Fortune study, or about specific cases they have dealt with, as did Abramson (1988) in her study of hospital discharge planning.

Focus groups, in which a small number of practitioners identify and discuss interventions they use with a particular type of client or problem, provide an additional way to obtain practitioner expertise. For example, Loneck et al. (1996) used a focus group to learn about methods of clinical practice with mentally ill–chemically addicted (MICA) clients seen in psychiatric emergency rooms. (See also chapter 12.)

If a researcher wishes to obtain a picture of the activities of a large number of practitioners, a self-administered questionnaire may be the instrument of choice. In one study illustrating this methodology, Cocozzelli (1987) compared the theoretical orientation and the self-reported practice behavior of 199 clinical social workers through questionnaires distributed through agency administration. In another investigation, Teare and Sheafor (1995) studied tasks of social workers in a national survey by means of an original self-administered instrument (the Job Analysis Survey).

Data from Clients

Clients themselves may provide data on intervention processes, usually by means of questionnaires or interviews. A frequent purpose in collecting such data is to determine the clients' subjective perceptions of their service experiences. It may be assumed that clients are unable to give an adequate accounting of complex and technical interventions, but there may be interest in ascertaining the client's view of them for its own sake. In order for certain interventions to work, clients may need to have a cognitive grasp of what is going on or at least the interventions may need to make sense to them. In one of the earlier studies of this kind, Mayer and Timms (1970) found that working-class clients who had sought help for concrete problems were mystified by insight-oriented counseling. In a more recent study, clients were asked to identify instances of misunderstandings with their practitioners (Rhodes et al. 1994).

Clients may be also used as sources of descriptive data on program operations, particularly if other sources are unavailable or inadequate. For some services, homemakers, for example, clients may be in a better position to describe concrete aspects of the service than anyone else.

Direct and Electronic Observation

Whether obtained from practitioner or client, recollections of intervention characteristics are inherently limited: participants cannot be expected to recall the nature or sequence of complex interventions with a high degree of accuracy and, because they are emotionally involved in the process, their objectivity is always problematic. To obtain data free of these limitations, the researcher must find ways of studying practitioners in action. A principal means is through observation of actual intervention processes, either by recording with audio- or videotape, or through direct observation.

Audiotape

Audiotape recording is relatively inexpensive and in most situations does not seem to engender reactive effects of any duration. Clients normally accept recording procedures. Safeguards to client confidentiality can be spelled out in forms that clients approve and sign.

Audio recording works best, of course, when intervention consists of face-to-face interaction between practitioners and clients. This kind of recording encounters greater obstacles as one moves out into the community, for practitioners, collaterals, or other professionals may be reluctant to get involved in the recording process. Still, with some effort and ingenuity, a good deal of this communication, even including telephone calls, can be tape-recorded. Audiotapes record, of course, only vocal communication, but some reflection will reveal that most of the significant communication events in most social work intervention are reflected in language and paralanguage, including voice expressions. To the extent that important communication processes are kinesthetic (for example, body movements and facial expressions), then audio is less useful, as might be the case in family treatment sessions involving children.

The sound quality of audiotapes is an important aspect that is frequently not thought of until the researcher, to his or her dismay, discovers that precious tapes, obtained by considerable effort, are inaudible and virtually useless. It pays, literally, to have decent though not necessarily expensive equipment and to train practitioners in its use. Specifics such as testing equipment before and during the session and watching the sound level indicator should be stressed. Lapel microphones are particularly useful. If only one microphone is used, it should be omnidirectional and carefully placed so that it picks up the voices of all participants.

Videotape

Videotaping is both more expensive and intrusive. As suggested earlier, researchers should take a hard look at what its use might contribute over audio recording. When video is used, camera work becomes an important factor. One may be able to include all participants by using a fixed-camera position, but the advantages of close-ups are lost. If the camera is moved, then some selection occurs. The person operating the camera, who may be a technician, then, in effect, has a good deal of influence over which visual data are obtained.

Whatever type of tape is used, electronic recording simply reproduces the volume and complexity of the intervention processes observed. Tape preserves sense impressions and permits them to be repeated, which is a considerable advantage, but it does nothing to further the analytic process.

Direct Observation

Research observers can observe intervention processes directly as they occur. The observers may be physically present or may watch the action through one-way mirrors. Direct observers have the simple but powerful advantage of "being there." They can take into account the full range of events that may be occurring without restrictions imposed by the reports of others or the limited scope of electronic recording. However, direct observation of social work processes must contend with several obstacles. First, the presence of an observer may be distracting, especially in such forms of practice as individual and family treatment. (While one-way mirrors provide an answer, many facilities do not have this kind of equipment.) Second, it is difficult for the observer to process the complexities of live social work intervention. Observation codes, ratings, and the like must usually be kept at a simple level. Finally, since two observers are generally involved (for reliability purposes) and often must observe on repeated occasions, logistics often become troublesome. For these reasons direct observation tends to be used to observe interventions when the observers' presence is less disruptive and when electronic recording may present problems, for example, work with client or community groups.

In a study by Feldman, Caplinger, and Wodarski (1983), observers rated group leaders' style of method as "minimal," behavioral, or traditional. The observers (who were simultaneously observing and coding the boys' behavior) rated the leadership styles at four points during the project. Although these global ratings were simple, bias was controlled by keeping the observer "blind" as to which leadership style was supposed to be used. The resulting data were useful in interpreting the results of the experiment. Thus only a quarter of the "traditional-method" leaders were found to implement this method adequately; by contrast almost two-thirds of the "behavioral-method" leaders were rated as having made adequate implementation of their method (p. 220). (The findings underscore the point made in chapter 7 about the importance of measuring service inputs in an experiment.)

In this example, use of direct observers and simple ratings were appropriate to the nature of the treatment, which involved the work of numerous leaders with a groups of active boys in a context in which the observers' presence was probably not a significant distraction. When a more fine-grained analysis is desirable or when an observer's presence would be intrusive, researchers are likely to turn to indirect (electronic) means of recording.

Analysis of the Data

Audio- or videotapes of intervention with typescripts made from them provide an abundance of data that can be examined through a variety of methods—ratings, event and time interval coding (chapter 11), qualitative analysis, and so on. A common methodology involves the construction and application of coding schemes. In the context of communications data of this kind, this methodology is frequently referred to as *content analysis* (Allen-Meares 1984;

Fortune 1981; Reid and Bailey-Dempsey 1994). Content analysis may also be used of course with written records.

A principal type of instrument used in content analysis of treatment processes is referred to as an intervention typology. Such a system is designed to classify (code) discrete intervention methods, such as facilitating negotiation, providing reinforcement, or advocacy. Most research on intervention characteristics in social work has concentrated on clinical interviews, and hence most available instruments reflect that emphasis. Examples of intervention typologies related to social work intervention may be found in Hollis (1972), Reid (1978), Basso (1985), Rothman (1991), and Teare and Sheafor (1995). A typology for counseling and psychotherapy has been developed by Hill (1986), and one for family therapy by Pinsof (1986).

Intervention typologies represent only one form of content analysis. Almost any recordable aspect of practitioner intervention can be investigated through one kind of content analysis scheme or another. For example, extensive use has been made of content analysis to study practitioner skills and attributes such as empathic responding, expressiveness, and warmth. A comprehensive review may be found in Orlinsky, Grawe, and Parks (1994).

Change Process Research

In recent years considerable attention has been given to the processes of change occurring within courses of intervention, including both practitioner and client activities as well as evidence of immediate change that may result (Greenberg and Newman 1996; Reid 1990). This new approach has been referred to as "change process research" (Greenberg 1986). In the words of Elliott (1984:249), this research strategy is a "discovery-oriented approach to significant change events." The emphasis is on study of the link between specific treatment activities and specific *immediate* outcomes, for example, "change that is evident in the session" (Greenberg 1986:4). This is in contrast to the conventional practice of linking gross measures of intervention to gross measures of outcome at termination. Further, an attempt is made to isolate key events *in context* on the assumption that certain episodes of process may be critical to change while others may not be. In this strategy one rejects the "myth of homogeneous process" (Rice and Greenberg 1984) in which a given unit in a process category is seen as more or less equal to any other unit in that category regardless of the context in which it occurs. Thus, as Elliott (1983:114) observes, research on "empathy in which empathy ratings are averaged across interviews or cases are insensitive to the possibility that empathy may play a crucial role only at certain moments in a helping relationship—for example, following a new and highly intimate disclosure." This is not to dismiss the sizable body of research based on the assumption of homogeneous process but rather to say it has left untouched important areas of inquiry that may be fruitfully pursued by intensive study of change events in context.

An extended example of change process research was presented in chapter 5 to illustrate a particular kind of naturalistic study. In that study (Jones et al. 1993), it will be recalled that an attempt was made to determine the connection between the therapist's interventions and the patient's symptoms during the course of long-term psychotherapy—a good illustrations of one of the functions of change process research.

In this evolving approach, change events are investigated in depth in relatively small units of process—single sessions in small groups of cases (Rhodes et al. 1994), single cases (Davis and Reid 1988; Jones et al. 1993; Reid et al. 1987), and single episodes within sessions (Elliott 1983). Both quantitative and qualitative methods may be employed, often in combination. For example, Elliott (1983) used a mix of seventeen quantitative and qualitative techniques in his analysis of a single psychotherapeutic episode. Such mixes can combine the capacity of quantitative measures to reveal statistical patterns in objective communication data with the ability of qualitative analysis to depict contextual features and capture the more elusive complexities of process.

In change process research both practitioner and client behavior may fall within the focus of study on grounds that the intervention process is not simply a function of the practitioner's methods but is rather part of a system that comprises the practitioner, clients, and often others (Gurman, Kniskern, and Pinsof 1986). Some studies may focus on the interrelationship of client and practitioner activities (Reid and Strother 1988); others may concentrate on the client's behavior (Sherman 1994). Below are brief descriptions of some of the methods used in change process research: event analysis, Interpersonal Process Recall, task analysis, and analysis of interventions and proximal outcomes.

Event Analysis

In change process research, events can comprise a broad range of episodes and occurrences of interest to the researchers. For example, Mahrer and Nadler (1986:14) review use of "good moments," which they define as "epochs of a few seconds or more wherein the client is manifesting therapeutic process, movement, improvement, progress, or change." Although their compilation of types of good moments emphasizes client rather than practitioner behavior, the focus is on specific occurrences within an intervention context, such as "provision of personal material about self and/or interpersonal relationships or expression of insight-understanding." Analysis of such episodes is designed to illuminate the practitioner-client interactions that give rise to them and hence can be seen as integral to the study of intervention characteristics. In fact, study of specific client behaviors in relation to specific practitioner activities enables researchers to break down the artificial distinctions between the "processes" and "outcomes" of intervention. Examples of intensive study of therapeutic events can be found in Clarke (1996), Elliott (1984), Rhodes et al. (1994), Rice and Greenberg (1984), Toukmanian (1992), and Yalom (1985). A type of event used in the construction of intervention models has been referred to as "an informative event" (Davis and Reid 1988; Reid 1985), which has been defined as an occurrence or episode in a case that generates useful new thinking about ways to improve the intervention (Reid 1994a). Informative events, which are collected following review of written or taped case material, generally fall into such categories as promising techniques, inadequacies of service design, and instructive successes or failures. For example, in Naleppa and Reid's (1998) field trial of a case management model for frail elderly in the community, one of the informative events identified was the lack of provision in the service design for methods of dealing with clients' tendencies to reminisce during the interview. The protocol was revised to provide ways for the client to reminisce while still maintaining focus on the target problem. Identification of an even a single occurrence of an event can occasion a revision in the innovation. Additional examples of the use of informative events can be found in Donahue (1995) and Reid and Bailey-Dempsey (1994).

INTERPERSONAL PROCESS RECALL (IPR) IPR is a form of event analysis in which the practitioner and client together review taped selections of a treatment session (Elliott 1984). Clients may be asked to react to key events which they or the practitioners select. For example, in their use of IPR, Naleppa and Reid (1998) asked frail elderly clients to comment on interventions used by the practitioner. Was the practitioner being helpful at this point? What could he or she have done to be more helpful? IPR can also be used with practitioners who may be asked the same questions.

TASK ANALYSIS In task analysis, one attempts to determine the sequence of steps clients can (or should) use in working through a particular issue (event) in the session. Analysis of how clients actually proceed with the issue is combined with a rational analysis of possible options to produce an ideal model of how the client can solve the problem. Thus Berlin, Mann, and Grossman (1991) used task analysis to construct a model of how depressed clients can resolve dysfunctional appraisals of significant others. Practitioner interventions can then be designed to help clients implement such problem-solving models. (See also Greenberg and Newman 1996.)

Analysis of Interventions and Proximal Outcomes

In analysis of interventions and proximal outcomes, the immediate outcomes of specific interventions are examined, using such data as tapes of treatment sessions, practitioner recording, or client responses to questionnaires given at the end of the session or at regular intervals during the course of treatment. The purpose is to determine if particular kinds of interventions are more likely than other kinds to be followed by predicted short-term changes. Thus, in action-oriented approaches one might be interested in determining if certain kinds of tasks, directives, behavioral assignments, etc., were more likely to be done than others. For example, Reid (1994a) found that family members were more likely to carry out tasks at home if these tasks had been discussed and planned by the family members together in a structured problem-solving sequence than if the tasks had been simply developed in an unstructured discussion between the practitioner and family members.

Intervention Analogs

The study of social work intervention as it actually occurs must contend with a number of obstacles. Investigation of practitioner behavior in detail can be a time-consuming and costly business. The complexities of intervention are difficult to sort out, as well as the multitude of variables that affect what the practitioner does. Moreover, it may not be feasible to control for certain variables that may affect the practitioner's actions. Accordingly, if an investigator were interested in determining the effects of the client's race (black versus white) on how clients were treated, a design executed in the field would ideally require that a sizable group of practitioners treat black and white clients matched on all other influential variables.

One answer to such problems is to study intervention through use of practice analogs that the investigator can shape according to the specific purposes of the study. Thus, two case summaries can be developed, identical in all respects except that in one the client is presented as white and in the other as black. These different "cases" can be randomly assigned to practitioner-subjects who are then asked to assess and treat them as they would in their practice. The influence of the independent variable, the race of the client, can be discerned from differences in practitioner responses to different forms of the case.

In this section, we discuss common types of analogs, the validity of analogs as a substitute for study of real practice, and issues in constructing analogs.

Types of Analogs

The most common variety of analog consists of some form of stimulus material, such as a paper case vignette, a film, or videotape of an interview, to which practitioner-subjects are asked to respond as they would if confronted with such a situation in their practice. A paper case vignette is probably the most common type. For example, Johnson, Brem, and Alford-Keating (1995) presented practitioners-in-training with a case vignette of a family seeking help. The subjects received, through random assignment, different forms of the vignette. In some forms the parents were straight and in others either gay or lesbian. The subjects' responses, e.g., expected problems of children, revealed a systematic pattern of bias against gay and lesbian parents. Additional examples of such analogs can be found in Davis and Carlson (1981), Gingerich (1982), Franklin (1985), and McKenzie (1995).

To achieve greater realism and complexity, videos, role-plays, or live actors may be used to present stimulus material. For example Nugent and Halvorson (1995) used simulated interactions between a "client" and a "social worker" to present different types of "active listening" responses (in which the social worker paraphrases empathically what the client says). In one, type A, the social worker's response was neutral in respect to the client's interpretation of an event or suggested that other interpretations were possible. In the other, type B, the response assumed the accuracy of the client's interpretation. Practitioners and students who responded to a series of such presentations were asked to record their emotional states on standardized scales as if they were the client. As predicted, subjects exposed to the B type of response were more likely to have *negative* emotional reactions—anger, anxiety, and depression—than those exposed to the A type.

Validity of Analogs

As the foregoing examples suggest, analogs provide a wide variety of ways of studying practitioner behavior under controlled conditions. Measurement of practitioner behavior can be quite rigorous. For example, response alternatives can be carefully defined and then refined through pretesting. Moreover, analogs have the advantages of economy and feasibility. One does not have to collect and analyze hours of tape recording or to make any intrusions in practice situations. All these pluses must be weighed, however, against a profound limitation, and that concerns the validity of this type of instrument.

Like any instrument, the validity of an analog can be thought of in terms of its capacity to measure what it purports to measure. Since, in the present context, an analog is viewed as a way of measuring practitioner behavior in actual practice situations, the validity of an analog must be evaluated in terms of its relation to what practitioners actually do.

Like any test, an analog can be validated against some criterion measure. For an analog the criterion would be some measure of actual practitioner behavior. This kind of empirical validation has been rarely attempted with analogs, however. One reason has been that most analogs have been devised for purposes of particular studies and do not seem to be sufficiently reusable to warrant elaborate empirical validation procedures. Also it would prove quite difficult to secure the necessary measures of practitioner behavior in actual practice situations since the analogs tend to be rather specific to the kinds of case situations studied.

Usually stress is placed on content validity, which involves evaluating the analog in terms of how well its content seems to tap desired practice variables. Most of the content validity issues grow out of the artificiality of the analog situation. Whether the case takes the form of an individual client, a group, or a community, it is likely to strike the practitioner-subject as something quite different from the real thing. The information provided is limited, much more so than might be true in an actual situation, and the subject is not able to get additional information through normal processes of interaction. Variables of interest may not have the same strength on tape or on paper as they would in reality. It is one thing to react to a psychotic client in the flesh; it is quite another to react to a written description of such a client. In responding to analogs, practitioners have more time to think than they would in practice and as a result may be more inclined to give "textbook" answers. An analog may further limit the practitioner's choice of response in various ways, such as requiring him or her to select a preferred intervention among several possibilities. In addition, sampling constraints in use of analogs must be recognized. Most analogs present subjects with one or a very small number of case situations, and the sampling of practitioner responses is normally quite circumscribed.

Construct validation offers another and in some ways more decisive approach to the problem. This approach to validation is best used when the analog tests a theory-based hypothesis, preferably one for which some evidence has already been accumulated from nonanalog research. Confirmation of the hypothesis provides some evidence that the analog has, in fact, measured what it was designed to measure; otherwise, the hypothesis would not have been confirmed. The Nugent and Halvorson study (1995), just referred to, provides an example.

More generally, the usefulness for analogs is clearest when they are used in theory-related research. By confirming hypotheses, they can strengthen theories of practitioner behavior. They can also serve an exploratory function by suggesting ways of responding not accounted for by theory. In the latter case, they produce hypotheses, which need to be tested through additional research, preferably based in some part on the study of actual practice behavior.

Construction of Analogs

In research built around original analogs, the construction of the analog itself is usually the most demanding and time-consuming task of the entire study. Although the many intricacies of the process cannot be fully dealt with here, we can offer some general guidelines and a few specific suggestions that may prove helpful. Again we assume that the analog consists of a practice situation presented in writing or on tape.

It goes without saying that we should have a reasonably well-developed research question or hypothesis before beginning work on the analog, but it usually pays to think of instrumentation possibilities before coming to closure on the research problem. This step may well lead to modification of the problem or will at least test its clarity. The practice situation devised for the analog should then be constructed to achieve the researcher's purposes as they evolve from a process that involves some going back and forth between the problem and the instrument.

In developing the practice situation, one needs to build in the stimuli needed to bring forth the desired variation in responses. For example, a researcher interested in determining how social workers with a psychodynamic orientation differ from systems oriented social workers would incorporate case material that would be likely to elicit hypothesized differences in interventions. If the analog is good, it should provoke controversy among the study's subjects if they were to react to it as a group. To be avoided are situations that all subjects would handle in pretty much the same way. For this reason, analogs should usually be invented rather than rooted in actual situations. It is usually not difficult to develop fictitious analogs in the form of case summaries that will be accepted by practitioner-subjects as realistic. Presenting case material in the form of audiotape or videotape recording does not guarantee realism. Amateurish acting is often readily detected. Still the subject's awareness that the practice situation is contrived is not necessarily a fatal limitation. It need only be sufficiently "realistic" to evoke the kinds of responses a practitioner would make if it were in fact real.

Usually the problem is not so much the subject's sense that the case lacks realism as it is that the analog case material is not likely to have as strong an impact as a real-life case would. Consequently, features of the analog case that the researcher wants the subjects to react to need to be made strong and vivid. For example, if the researcher is interested in how subjects would deal with a child who is physically acting out, the child's acting-out behavior should be of a serious nature and should be described in graphic detail. If the researcher plans to compare practitioner responses to such a child with a child whose acting out is confined to a verbal level, the differences between alternative forms of the analog should be sharply delineated in this respect. The need to hit subjects "between the eyes" with strong representations of stimulus material must be balanced, however, against a need to have the case representative of practice situations to which the researcher may wish to generalize.

Subjects may use any of the forms of response applicable to questionnaires. If practitioners are given a range of interventions to choose from, it is important that these possible responses be described in specific, behavioral terms. One should avoid vague generalizations such as "give support."

Hwang and Cowger (1998) created an elaborate analog for their study of strengths in assessment and treatment planning. The analog, the case of an elderly woman confronting problems in daily living, was based on a case used for training public social service workers at a state Department of Aging. It included background information, the referral process, presenting problem (whether to continue living alone), and family involvement; a script of an interview between the client and worker; and an assessment of the client written by experienced social workers. The assessment included an equal number of strengths and deficits; their content validity was assessed by a different group of practitioners. The questionnaire asked respondents first to rate the importance of seven personal and environmental strengths and seven deficits and secondly to assess the importance of two treatment plans, counseling and service acquisition.

To determine if the analog was sufficiently realistic, 32 pretest social workers were asked how typical the case was and whether the assessment task represented knowledge and skills that they used regularly. In the study itself, 205 clinical social workers considered both strengths and deficits important but emphasized strengths slightly more. They were evenly distributed in their opinions of the importance of counseling (on a Likert scale from "least important" to "most important"), but were nearly unanimous that service acquisition was more or most important—an indication that the analog did not stimulate enough controversy in that area.

At various points in analog construction, the researcher may wish to obtain the assistance of others. An expert (or a small panel of experts) may be asked to evaluate the stimulus material for realism, to suggest varieties of possible responses, or to classify responses already selected. A pretest given to a small group (six to ten) subjects will help identify problems in interpretation of instructions and responses that reveal little discrimination.

Summary

In practice experiments, it is as important to operationally define and study the intervention as the outcome. Intervention may also be studied on its own. Methods of studying "live" practice include practitioner reports (systematic and free-form narratives, analysis of critical incidents, and other self-reports from practitioners), client reports, observation directly or through electronic recording, and change process research. Practice situations may also be simulated through analogs, which like laboratory research permit careful control of stimuli but may encounter difficulty in generalizing to practice in the field.

In chapter 15 we considered methods of studying social work intervention. A main purpose of such research is, of course, to find ways of creating better interventions. In this chapter we apply these research methods to a more direct means of improving practice: developing interventions through systematic testing and revision.

The Design and Development Paradigm (D&D)

Since the 1970s we have seen the emergence of a number of overlapping approaches for systematically designing and testing human service interventions, including developmental research (Thomas 1978, 1984); social R&D (Rothman 1974, 1980); personal practice models (Mullen 1978, 1983) and model development (Reid 1979, 1985); and design and development (Thomas and Rothman 1994). Although these approaches have differed in a number of respects, they have conveyed a basic message—effective interventions must be built systematically through a process of design, continual testing, feedback, and modification.

Perhaps the most comprehensive and best articulated of these approaches is the design and development (D&D) paradigm (Thomas 1984, 1994), which sets forth detailed guidelines for creating, testing, and disseminating human service interventions.

According to Thomas and Rothman (1994) D&D proceeds in a stepwise fashion through a set of stages that guide the generation process: (1) problem analysis and project planning; (2) information gathering and synthesis; (3) program design; (4) early development and pilot testing; (5) evaluation and advanced development (which includes more rigorous, controlled testing); and (6) dissemination (Thomas and Rothman 1994). D&D provides a direct link between research activity and improvement of service. The outcome of a D&D

endeavor is an intervention technology rather than knowledge about human behavior, as in conventional research. The self-corrective powers of research can be used in a systematic and efficient way in the process of constructing and testing interventions.

The D&D paradigm is an effort to create a systematic method of constructing and testing human service methods that parallels methods used in industry to develop new products. For example, in industry a new product is carefully designed, prototypes are created, tested, and modified, and the final product undergoes a series of tests and additional refinements before it is marketed. Or take an example somewhat closer to the human services, the development and testing of drugs is carried out through a systematic process that culminates in controlled experiments to determine the drug's efficacy—all before the drug is approved for human consumption.

As we know, most social work and other human service methods become established in a much more haphazard fashion. As a result many interventions become entrenched with their original flaws still in place. In other cases, interventions are created with little awareness of what is already available, thus becoming reinventions of the proverbial wheel. In still others, innovations may be discarded prematurely; some testing might have revealed their promise. More generally, most social work innovations, as well as many established practices, can benefit from systematic processes of design, testing, and modification. D&D provides a framework and methodology for these processes.

The D&D paradigm has been systematically applied in a number of contexts. Using a D&D strategy, Thomas et al. (1987) developed a model for working with spouses of alcohol abusers (unilateral family therapy) and then evaluated it in a controlled experiment (Thomas 1994). Rothman and his coworkers followed D&D principles in their pilot testing of a case management model (Rothman 1992; Rothman and Tumblin 1994). Reid (1994a) applied a D&D approach to the development of a specific intervention in conjoint family treatment. Other recent exemplars of the D&D paradigm include efforts to develop adaptations of the task-centered approach to problems of school failure (Bailey-Dempsey and Reid 1996; Reid and Bailey-Dempsey 1994, 1995), to social work intervention in the classroom (Viggiani 1996), to field instruction (Caspi and Reid 1996), to mediation with post-divorce couples (Donahue 1995), to treatment of families with a developmentally disabled member (Chou 1992), to case management with the frail elderly in the community (Naleppa 1995; Naleppa and Reid 1998), to group treatment of single parents in a college setting (Raushi 1994), and to group treatment of sex offenders (Kilgore 1995).

As is typical of most D&D applications the examples concern tests of innovations. However, as will be made clear below, the innovations usually tested are seldom completely novel, but rather are likely to consist of some combination of accepted and new practices applied for the first time to a specific clinical problem or population. Also as the examples suggest, D&D typically is concerned with "intervention packages" or models, although it can be applied to single interventions as in Reid (1994a).

With the exception of the work of Thomas and associates and Reid and Bailey-Dempsey, the examples were all "early stage" projects, that is, projects that completed the first four stages of the paradigm, but not stage 5 (Evaluation and Advanced Development). That is, they were not exposed to rigorous testing through controlled designs. However in all these instances, some dissemination occurred (stage 6). The lack of exposure to rigorous testing means of course that the effectiveness of the interventions has not been definitively established. Still there is justification for dissemination without such testing if the intervention shows promise (Curtis 1996) and if there is nothing in place that has been shown to be more effective. These criteria appeared to apply to all the examples. Without stage 5, of course, the paradigm becomes much more feasible for student projects and small-scale agency undertakings. We shall now present a somewhat modified version of the Thomas-Rothman D&D paradigm with particular emphasis upon the first four stages.

Problem Analysis and Project Planning

A focal point in the first stage, problem analysis and project planning, is the problems or goals for which the intervention is being developed. It is important to spell these out with as much clarity and specificity as possible. For example, in a D&D project concerned with children at risk of school failure, Bailey-Dempsey and Reid (1996) identified the problems to be addressed as difficulties in academic work, poor attendance, and disruptive classroom behavior.

Once problems or goals have been clarified, a state-of-the-art review is conducted. The purpose of this review is to determine what work has been done in relation to the problems or goals of concern. For example, what relevant interventions have been developed? Does the problem lend itself to social work intervention? The review should help justify the need for the project and provide some initial direction for its subsequent stages.

One then devises a preliminary plan, which specifies the setting, the practitioners, the approximate number of cases, and the project structure. Different kinds of project structures can be used. In one type, all cases are carried by a single practitioner-researcher. In a second, the practitioner-researchers consist of a small staff group who develop and carry out the project together. In a third, a single practitioner-researcher has primary responsibility for the project, but the bulk of the cases are carried by agency staff. (If the latter type of organization is used, it is still a good idea for the supervising practitioner-researcher to carry at least one case in order to get first hand experience with the intervention.) Additional decisions need to be made about the purposes, types and phasing of studies to be carried out. These decisions will be taken up in "Field Testing" below.

Information Gathering and Synthesis

In the information gathering and synthesis stage, an effort is made to acquire and integrate knowledge useful in designing the intervention. The state-of-the art review conducted during the previous stage should have made a beginning at this task; however, that review was concerned with determining whether or not effective methods for the problem were already available. What is needed now is a much more in-depth examination of sources that would be helpful in fleshing out the intervention to be developed.

A primary source is the research and practice literature, which may be accessed through computerized abstract services, such as SWAB (Social Work Abstracts) and PSYCHLIT (Psychological Abstracts) (see appendix 1). If a considerable amount of work has been done in a given area, it is a good idea to first access research reviews and meta-analyses (chapter 11). The purpose is to identify possible interventions or program components that might be incorporated into the service design, with priority given to interventions with empirical support. For example, in constructing a case management model addressed to problems of school failure, Bailey-Dempsey and Reid (1996) located effective methods of treating problems in academic performance, attendance, and classroom behavior. Mullen (1994) presents and illustrates a well-developed scheme for analysis of intervention components identified from the literature.

In addition to the literature (and especially when it is in short supply), information can be gained through study of "natural examples" (Thomas 1984). For example, the investigator can interview practitioners who have used interventions that might be incorporated into the design. Another source of information might be the researcher's own prior experimentation with the intervention. Often innovative ideas grow out of one's own practice.

Design

"Design" in D&D refers to the plan for the intervention. Although it makes use of previous work in the area, the design phase is basically a creative undertaking. It is here that the researcher gives shape to innovative ideas. Some design activities may involve extensions of an existing approach to a new population or problem, as with the examples given earlier of novel applications of task-centered methods. Others may consist of assembling and adapting an array of interventions from different approaches. Still others may require construction of new interventions for a problem not previously identified or for a problem that has proved resistant to existing methods.

The culmination of this stage is the creation of an *intervention protocol*, which outlines the kinds of problems to be addressed and the assessment and treatment methods to be used in attempting to resolve them. Initially the outline may be skeletal, but it should become detailed and comprehensive as testing of the intervention proceeds. Ultimately, the protocol might include a step-by-step description of procedures to be used in each interview and indications of how different contingencies are to be handled. It is important to construct a protocol even if the researcher is the sole practitioner, since one needs to know what was attempted as a basis for coming up with modifications. Besides, at some point the researcher will want to communicate the work to others.

Field Testing

Field testing may begin with informal try-outs of preliminary versions of the intervention with one or two cases. More formal field testing takes place after an intervention protocol has been devised and data collection instruments constructed or selected.

EXPLORATORY EXPERIMENTS One plan for the field test consists of an "exploratory experiment," which may be thought of as specific kind of pilot study. Such an experiment is most useful when a practice model is at an early stage of development or when it is being adapted to a novel type of problem or population. In such cases, conventional experiments with design controls that might ordinarily be used to test the effectiveness of an intervention make little sense. One cannot hypothesize, as one should in an experiment, that application of X will create Y effect, for it is not clear what X is. Moreover, the risk of obtaining negative findings is high if the intervention itself must be made with considerable trial and error, and if there is uncertainty about what to measure and how. These findings may result in the abandonment of promising intervention strategies or, as is more usually the case, the cessation of further testing of them, before either the intervention or means of evaluating it have been adequately developed.

Of course, not all models need to pass through this stage. A full model may not have been field-tested, but its key components may have been, so adequate mapping of the intervention and probable outcomes may be possible from the outset. If so, then a controlled study of its effects (stage 5) may be a logical next step. This course of model development is likely to be rare in social work, where there has been little testing of specific intervention components.

The exploratory experiment consists essentially of a preliminary trial of the model on a small scale. In projects the second author has conducted or supervised, 6 to 10 cases (or 2 or 3 groups) has been the norm although larger numbers may be used (see for example Thomas 1994). The practitioners themselves supply data through devices such as structured recording forms, ratings, audiotapes, and reports of critical incidents (chapter 15). Clients or other actors in the practice situation may take standardized instruments before and after the intervention or be interviewed, perhaps making use of methods of Interpersonal Process Recall (chapter 15). In addition, it is desirable, as noted earlier, that the researchers themselves become participant-observers (as either a practitioner or supervisor) to acquire firsthand data on the operations of the intervention.

Feedback from practitioners would be a part of some of the methods described above. Additional information can be obtained from practitioners through conferences or supervisory sessions during the field test. In some cases formal debriefing interviews with practitioners after completion of the projects may be indicated.

From a D&D perspective, two types of data are emphasized in the initial field trial. One type consists of summary evaluation data. How well on the whole did the intervention achieve its goals? Did it appear to be more effective with certain kinds of clients or problems than with others? (See chapter 13.) Since the studies lack controls, it is not possible to determine effectiveness in a definitive way. However, as Curtis (1996) has pointed out, interventions may achieve levels of success short of the kind of "probable" or "established" effectiveness that can be achieved through use of controlled studies. There may be "tentative evidence" that the intervention is effective or enough evidence to consider the intervention "promising." These lesser levels may be attained, as Curtis argues, with small numbers of cases and without controls, as is the case in the kind of initial field testing we are discussing.

For example, Donahue (1995) field-tested a task-centered mediation model for divorced or separated couples with problems concerning child visitation. The goal of the intervention was to enable the couples to work out an agreement which would remain in place for at least 3 months. Seven of the 10 project cases met this criterion. Making use of available information about success with this kind of mediation problem, Donahue was able to conclude that the intervention showed "some promise," but was less effective for couples where there was "intense, overt conflict" (p. 154). The next step in development would be to construct and test methods that might be effective for highly conflicted couples.

The second type of data is concerned with the processes of the intervention and related changes in the problem. Here the purpose is to fill out and correct the rough map laid down in the preliminary formulation of the intervention. What specific methods were used? Did some work better than others? Were there omissions or shortfalls in the service design? Some questions concern feasibility. Are practitioners able to do the suggested operations? If not, why not? Other questions concern the range and variation of expected events. What kind of case situations were encountered? What methods, of those suggested, were used most frequently and what did they look like in actual use? Still other questions are related to possible effects of specific procedures. Because design controls are not used, it is not possible to obtain definitive answers to questions concerning the effectiveness of the practitioners' activities. Nevertheless, one can gather evidence that permits tentative judgments to be made. For example, is the use of an intervention followed by expected changes in the client's behavior? How do practitioners, clients, and collaterals assess the effectiveness of particular interventions?

A secondary, though still important, purpose of the experiment is to test and refine data collection and measurement procedures. Through this process, one hopes to devise research methods that are maximally sensitive to the practice operations and outcomes of interest in the intervention.

Data analysis, which makes use of both quantitative and qualitative methods, attempts to lay the base for intervention revisions. The processes by which data influence a reworking of the intervention are not completely clear, for they are interwoven with such imponderables as the ability to synthesize information and to use it for creative ends. Some aspects can, however, be described.

Much of the analysis is directed toward understanding, distilling, and ordering the mass of events that occurred during the field test. Key tools used in data collection and analysis are the methods of change process research discussed in the previous chapter. Analysis of informative events is particularly important. For example, through the use of informative events innovative interventions, perhaps stimulated by the intervention but not specified as a part of it, can be identified, evaluated, and, if it seems promising, incorporated into the next version of the intervention. Unanticipated problems can be described and new guidelines written to handle them. The data may well generate hypotheses for further research. Some of these hypotheses may be translated into tentative intervention guidelines. For example, an analysis of interventions and proximal outcomes (chapter 15) suggest that a certain procedure does not work well with a particular type of client. Pending a more definitive test of this hypothesis, the intervention might be revised to suggest that the procedure in question be used cautiously with this type of client and discontinued if adverse effects appear. Through analysis and application of findings, the researcher puts together a revised version of the initial intervention.

CASE STUDIES AND SINGLE-SYSTEM DESIGNS   An alternative to the exploratory experiment are either case studies or single-system designs. If the latter are used, they usually take the form of simple time series (AB designs). In most instances better controlled designs, e.g., withdrawal or multiple baseline, are more appropriately used further along in the D&D process, when more rigorous testing of a developed intervention is in order. If more than one study or design is used, results of early cases can be used to make midcourse corrections in the intervention protocol. If the intervention does not change radically during testing, data from the cases can be aggregated. In some service designs the intervention can be broken down into different components, each of which can be tested separately through one or more studies.

The number of cases to be selected will depend on the originality and complexity of the intervention as well as on the goals and resources of the researcher. Results from a single case can be informative. It can detect flaws in the service design, suggest how the design can be improved, and provide an initial test of data collection instruments. Payoff from the field test increases with each additional case. Methods of data collection and analysis are virtually the same as those used in the exploratory experiment described above.

RECORDING   Good recording is essential to capture key types of data described above. If possible, interviews with clients should be tape recorded. In addition to tape recording, or in place of it, use can be made of structured recording forms (Reid 1992; Videka-Sherman and Reid 1985). Such forms enable focused recording (either through check-offs or short answers) of key interventions, immediate client changes, and terminal outcomes (chapter 15).

Evaluation and Advanced Development

In this stage of the D&D paradigm, the intervention is put through a more rigorous test of effectiveness. Ideally some form of controlled experiment is used. Examples may be found in Bailey-Dempsey and Reid (1996) and

Thomas (1994). Demonstrated efficacy (if such turns out to be the case) provides a much stronger base for dissemination than the promise the intervention might have shown in the pilot test. Even then effectiveness findings from a single experiment, especially one conducted by the developers of an intervention, must be viewed with some degree of skepticism. Additional experimental testing by more disinterested researchers is always desirable (although seldom done). Normally further development of the intervention takes place as a result of the more rigorous test.

For example, the case management model for children at-risk of school failure proved to be effective during the school year in which it was used but gains did not persist during the year following (Reid and Bailey-Dempsey 1995). Accordingly the service delivery plan was altered to provide additional help to children who needed it over a span of several school years. Additional developmental work may be needed on particular components of the intervention or on the intervention as a whole if it is adapted to new problems or populations.

Dissemination

The sixth and final stage of the D&D process, dissemination, occurs ideally after the intervention has been rigorously tested in stage 5. However, as noted earlier, an argument can be made for dissemination prior to rigorous testing. First, models of intervention that have completed step 4 have been systematically designed, tested in a field trial, and redesigned in light of the test. They have attained a measure of "developmental validity," which refers to "the extent to which interventions in an intervention have been adequately used on a trial basis and have been tested developmentally" (Thomas 1985:54).

If the model is intended to supply a need in practice that is not currently being met with interventions with any *greater* degree of developmental validity, then there is a justification for its implementation in practice and even its dissemination, in the absence of a controlled experiment. Because D&D is generally not used if tested methods are already available, interventions shaped by the D&D process generally are better tested (i.e., have greater developmental validity) than alternatives. If they prove promising, such interventions *should* be tested more rigorously, but pending such a test, there is justification for giving them preference over counterparts that have not gone through a developmental process. Moreover, as Curtis (1996) points out, dissemination of preliminary field trials can stimulate others "to try new ideas and to add their insights into the investigation" (p. 118).

In some circumstances the researcher may decide that the intervention is not ready for dissemination. The field trial may have been very limited, e.g., to a single case, or it may have raised troubling issues in service design. The decision might be to conduct a second field trial.

If it is decided that some form of dissemination is in order, the first step normally entails a write-up of the project. The report sets forth the intervention originally tested, the methods of data collection and findings relating to apparent effectiveness and possible improvements, the changes to be made in the approach in light of the field test, and, of course, the limitations of the study, e.g., the lack of a rigorous test of the effectiveness of the model. A key part of the report (although it may be placed in the appendix) is an intervention protocol, one that has been revised in light of the field test. Dissemination may take many forms. More limited dissemination may be confined to agency staff or to fellow students, e.g., presentations or poster-sessions. More extensive dissemination, e.g., publication in a professional journal, should be considered if field tests have been substantial *or* if the intervention proves to be distinctive enough—well developed and highly original—to command a larger audience.

Illustration

Naleppa and Reid (1998) made use of the D&D paradigm in the construction and testing of task-centered case management model for work with the frail elderly in the community (see also Naleppa 1995). In the initial stage, *Problem Analysis and Project Planning*, the problem was defined as needs of the frail elderly, especially those that, if unmet, might likely result in long-term care. Difficulties relating to health, mental capacity, and finances were among the more prominent. A state-of-the-art review revealed that there were a number of case management models for work with the frail elderly but little in the way of tested models that provided practitioners with specific guidelines and practice methods. The project plan called for the construction and testing of a model in a particular hospital setting. Four case managers from this setting agreed to participate. The senior author and primary researcher (Naleppa) would also carry a case. An exploratory experiment, consisting of approximately 10 cases, was planned. In the next stage, *Information Gathering and Synthesis*, the literature was searched to identify intervention methods that might be used in the model. It was decided initially that the task-centered model (Reid 1992), which seemed well-suited for the problem, would provide the main framework for the approach. The literature on task-centered work with the frail elderly was reviewed to identify specific procedures. Further search of the literature revealed additional intervention approaches that seemed useful in work with this population, notably Rothman's (1992) model of case management core functions and a framework for autonomy decisions proposed by Collopy (1988). Finally a focus group approach (chapter 15) was used to elicit natural examples from the case managers who would be participating in the project.

In developing the design for the intervention (stage 3) the methods identified in the previous stage were organized into a protocol for the case managers to use. The case managers themselves participated in the creation of the design. (If at all possible practitioners who will be implementing a service approach should have a part in its construction.)

A field trial of the model (stage 4) was then planned and implemented. The practitioners received 6 hours of training in the approach prior to carrying cases. In the field trial, which lasted about 3 months, data were collected on 10 cases. Data collection ended after a case had received 5 or 6 sessions. Although most cases would require long-term monitoring, the model was focused on helping clients identify and resolve initial (referral) problems.

A number of instruments were used, including measures of mental and functional status, and forms for recording needs, problems, goals, and tasks. On the forms the case managers could record progress made on each client problem as well as on tasks for clients, caregivers, and practitioners. Interviews were tape recorded.

Analysis of informative events served as an initial means of accessing the data on intervention processes (chapter 15). The session tape recordings were reviewed to identify such events, selected in this study because they provided useful factual information about the model, raised questions, or provided insight into the intervention process. In addition one event per case was analyzed by means of Interpersonal Process Recall (IPR). Preselected segments of session recordings were played back to clients and case managers, and responses were elicited. For example, with clients a practitioner intervention might be identified and the client might be asked if he or she thought it was helpful or how it might have been improved upon.

As noted, data on task completion and problem changes were routinely collected as part of the implementation of the model. Of particular interest was whether a change in the problem took place immediately after completion of the tasks. Outcome data suggested that the model offered promise as a means of serving the frail elderly in the community. In all cases except one there was clear improvement in initial problems. Almost three-quarters of the tasks were completely achieved. Problem improvement tended to follow task accomplishment.

The analyses of process data revealed several aspects of the model that could be improved and suggested specific improvements. For example, excessive reminiscing by the client proved to be an obstacle in some cases. Through use of event analysis and the IPR, successful ways of handling the obstacle were identified, e.g., the obstacle appeared to best resolved when the practitioner clearly led back to the topic while giving the client time to leave the past and re-enter the present. Another example entailed more extensive revisions. It was found that the case managers were carrying out certain functions, e.g., helping clients with grief work, that did not fit well into the core methods of the task-centered approach. The modification was to develop intervention modules that could be used to supplement the task-centered methods. These revisions were among the many that were incorporated into a revised version of the case management model. Unlike conventional research, the main product was not a set of findings and implications but rather a revised intervention model. In other words the findings and their implications were utilized by the researchers themselves to improve the intervention they had tested.

A more rigorous evaluation of the approach, one using a controlled experimental design (stage 5), has not yet been carried out. However, given the lack of tested and manualized case management approaches for the frail elderly and given the promise shown by the model, dissemination (stage 6) seemed to make sense. Dissemination efforts thus far have included the publication of a journal article and several workshops in this country and abroad. Meanwhile additional testing of the model, using another exploratory experimental design, has been undertaken.

In an example using a single-system design, Rogers (1997) developed a model designed to resolve an obstacle often encountered in the treatment of children with Attention Deficit Hyperactivity Disorder—parents who are reluctant to participate in the treatment of their child. (The model could also be applied to reluctant parents of children with other types of problems.) Rogers developed the model as a part of a course on clinical evaluation and tested it with a single family. Among her findings were informative events that suggested that the family's guilt and shame over the disorder were important dynamics in the initial contact. These findings were used as a basis for model development. "Extremely sensitive techniques must be utilized to avoid exacerbating these feelings in the parents and to engage them in moving toward active change" (p. 25). A next step in model development would be to devise such techniques and specify how they might be used. It would not necessarily be assumed that all reluctant parents would have these feelings, but rather that such feelings would be likely to occur frequently enough to warrant the development of appropriate methods of helping parents deal with them constructively.

Summary

An important contribution to social work practice is design and development, or developing new approaches through systematically testing and revising promising approaches. One approach, the design and development (D&D) paradigm (Rothman and Thomas 1994), includes six stages: problem analysis and project planning, information gathering and synthesis, design, field testing, evaluation and advanced development, and dissemination. These steps can be used to develop, test, and modify new practice approaches in areas where there is insufficient knowledge of effective interventions.

Appendix 1

The Library Research Process

MARY JANE BRUSTMAN

In theory, the library research process is very simple and straightforward. The researcher arrives at the library with a topic to research. Relying on previous knowledge of the library and the use of materials found in or through the library, the researcher is able to proceed through the stages of the library research process: (1) understanding and focusing the topic clearly; (2) outlining a search strategy including specific bibliographic resources to be searched; (3) searching and identifying potentially useful research materials; (4) efficiently gaining access to those materials; and (5) evaluating them. The reality for many researchers, especially students, is quite different. Inexperienced researchers often arrive at the library without having clearly defined the topic, a topic about which they as yet know very little. They are unfamiliar with the different kinds of library research resources available or with specific sources, and lack knowledge about, or experience in, selecting, locating, and evaluating the materials.

Library research to the inexperienced researcher may seem like an overwhelming task. The purpose of this chapter is to lay out a systematic method for successfully carrying out that process. General principles of searching will be discussed as will the types of resources which can be effectively used in the search process. Key reference materials in social work, in related fields, and in the broader social sciences will be described.

The ultimate goal of the library research process is to obtain relevant research materials. During the first three stages noted above, effort is concentrated on the creation of a selective bibliography of sources tailored to the particular research project. The bibliography is constructed by systematically searching the relevant literature. During this search, researchers should seek out materials which provide general background knowledge on the topic and explain what research has already been done. They should develop an awareness of what information is known about the topic, whether there are findings that are widely accepted in the field, what research methods have been used, and whether or in what areas there is a need for more study (Engeldinger and Stuart 1990: 369). A summary of this survey is often referred to as the *literature review*.

The library search process involves intensive use of library reference resources. These resources either provide discrete pieces of information such as background, definitions, or factual data, or they refer the researcher to other materials, such as books or articles on a subject. Reference resources serve different functions in the course of the search process. To understand and focus the topic the researcher should consult encyclopedias, handbooks, and general books on the topic; relevant terminology should be explored in thesauri and dictionaries. To form a strategy for the library search the researcher should consult local library guides, research guides, and the reference librarian. The researcher should use the library's catalog to identify relevant books, reports and documents, and use indexes and abstracts to identify journal articles, newspaper articles, statistical sources, and additional documents. Handbooks and indexes can provide further statistical and factual material. The research materials themselves are accessed primarily through the library's catalog, and, secondarily, through library services designed to utilize sources external to the library. Each of these types of sources will be described later in this chapter.

As the search proceeds, these reference resources are comprehensively mined for useful information. This is not, however, a linear step-by-step process where the search strategy and literature needed are determined at the beginning and followed throughout the search (Simpson 1993 preface). It is rather an interactive process. As the researcher progresses through the search and reads encyclopedia articles, books, journal articles, handbooks, etc. the topic becomes more clearly understood and focused. Both the topic and the research strategy may be repeatedly modified based on a better understanding of the subject matter. As this new knowledge is gained, the researcher may need to revisit some resources which have already been searched.

The process of doing research is affected by the nature of the literature being searched and by communication methods used within a particular field of study. The body of literature in social work is steadily growing, but remains small when compared to many related fields like psychology, health, or sociology. The field of social work has developed from a professional, applied, and practical tradition, and its somewhat smaller proportion of empirical research continues to reflect this. Other fields like psychology, health, and sociology contain much more of this rigorous research material. To access the abundant information in related fields which is useful for the social work researcher, it is important that the researchers think expansively, in an interdisciplinary way. They should begin first by searching the literature of the social work field and then broaden out to appropriate reference tools for finding material in other fields.

Journals are the primary source of current research information in the social work field. DeVilley (1987) notes that more detailed specialized analyses are found in journals as well as exposure to a greater variety of viewpoints. Conference papers and reports are also often sources of current research. Books provide much more in-depth information on theory and practice, synthesize and interpret previous research, and frequently include excellent background information. Books tend to focus less on reporting the latest research, and the information in them is generally less current. Current practice and policy information in the social work field are now widely available in electronic formats as well.

Selection of information sources is critical not only because of the huge number of publications resulting from the *information explosion* of the past few decades, but because of the many and growing number of formats of publication as well. At the present time these include print, CD-ROMs, the Internet, on-line sources, computer disks, microforms, videos, and others. In the midst of this information overload the issue becomes one of evaluation and selection. While there may be too much information on many social work topics, there is not necessarily too much useful information.

Researchers need to develop methods of determining which materials will most likely be valuable. The most important characteristic is relevance to the research topic. The researcher should look at the type of publication. If it is an article, is it published in a research journal? If it is a book or report, is it from a reputable publisher? Does it appear to be sufficiently current? Once the item is actually in hand, the reader can then further evaluate its usefulness and quality. Criteria for evaluating authority, currency, accuracy, methodology, and point of view are discussed below, under "Evaluation."

The literature review demands time, persistence, and flexibility. The researcher must have the persistence to stay with the research process through many obstacles. Sometimes it takes many searches with many different search strategies or in numerous sources to identify needed information. Sometimes there is no research which has been published precisely on a topic, and in this case "knowledge drawn from research on related topics can be productively brought to bear" (Yegidis and Weinbach 1996:56). This may include information on closely related topics or subtopics as well as information included within works on a broader topic. Sources on other topics may also provide ideas for the research methodology.

The student's ally through the library research process is the reference librarian. Among the many ways the reference librarian can provide assistance are in finding information to refine and define a topic to suit the research process, locating background information, identifying reference materials to assist in building the bibliography, providing guidance in evaluating what materials will be most useful, and helping to locate the resources when the bibliography is complete. This can also involve coaching in developing a research strategy, investigating terminology, and locating or accessing further or alternate resources outside the home library. As Kuhlthau (1994 :58) notes, librarians are an "information source" and a "means of access to information." A librarian can often identify difficulties with the search process and offer advice that will lead to needed information.

Resources for Review of the Literature

1. Consult encyclopedias, handbooks, general books for background material on the topic; explore relevant terminology in thesauri and dictionaries.
2. Consult research guides, in-house library guides, and/or the reference librarian to form a search strategy.
3. a. Use the library catalog to locate books and reports.
   b. Use indexes and abstracts to identify journal articles (as well as newspaper articles and government publications).
   c. Use handbooks and indexes and abstracts to provide statistical and other factual material.
[Note: Increasingly, useful information is being found on the Internet and other electronic sources.]

Getting Started with the Search Process

The researcher begins the search by reading an overview of the topic and breaking it into appropriate subtopics. Major authors, thinkers, theories, issues, events, and government actions should be noted, and a basic chronology constructed. All unfamiliar terms should be carefully defined. The researcher should think about the following questions: Are primary or secondary materials more appropriate? How much information is needed? How much is available? What quality? How much time is available to do the research? What disciplines may be involved? (Beaubien, Hogan, and George 1982). In addition, the researcher needs to consider whether the search will involve current materials only or if older materials may be valuable.

Students can greatly increase the efficiency of their search by defining, narrowing or broadening a topic at the earliest stages of the research process, and they should continue to do so throughout the search. The student reads and evaluates material that has been identified thus far and "attempt(s) to integrate it into the framework of the project" (Simpson 1993 :18). If too much information has been identified, narrowing the scope of the project should be considered. If there is interesting information in one direction, perhaps the project should be refocused. If there is too little information on the topic, a broader topic might be explored. Properly defining and limiting the topic is critical. As noted in DeVilley (1987:17) too broad a topic will result in "hours of floundering," too narrow in "serious frustration." The amount and quality of material available on a given topic may also affect the viability of a particular topic for student research. In doing an extensive project, like a thesis, the researcher may want to consider whether the subject has already been sufficiently studied.

Background Information

A careful survey of background information on the topic can help define the topic and bring it into focus. In fact, the value of a careful background survey cannot be overstated. It lays the groundwork for both better quality research and more efficient research. Many student researchers begin a research project with only a vaguely defined topic. While they are aware of the need for "some books" or "some articles," they seldom have a clear idea of what specific materials they require or how to proceed in finding them (Ready 1987).

General background information is usually found in encyclopedias, handbooks, and general books on the topic. An encyclopedia is often the best first step. An *encyclopedia* is a volume, or set of volumes, containing articles covering a specified range of topics. Encyclopedias may be general in nature (covering all fields of knowledge) or limited to a particular subject. Encyclopedias usually give an overview of the topic, place it in context, note issues involved, and provide a basic chronology. A brief bibliography of important writings on the topic is often appended. Encyclopedias constitute an especially good starting point for those who are unfamiliar with their topic.

The *Encyclopedia of Social Work* does an excellent job of orienting researchers to most social work topics. It provides an overview of more than 240 social welfare topics, focusing on the United States in the past, present, and future. It covers social issues and problems, institutions, human development, research, the profession, etc. Most entries provide background, current state of the issue, dimensions of the topic, how the issue fits in the social work field, a bibliography, and, if applicable, policy issues involved and the federal government role. Entries are written by respected practitioners and scholars in the field. Published in print as a 3-volume set, it is also available on CD-ROM.

Encyclopedias in other fields may also provide valuable background information for social work research projects. For instance, some of the topics covered in the *Encyclopedia of Sociology* are drug abuse, community health, death and dying, family violence, marriage, homelessness, and poverty. The *Encyclopedia of Psychology* provides coverage of mental health, including such topics as research methods, types of therapy, mental disorders, tests, and major figures in the field. Encyclopedias with interdisciplinary coverage of certain populations, such as the *Encyclopedia of Gerontology*, or specialized encyclopedias or handbooks on legal, medical, and educational topics may also be useful. New reference sources and newer editions of older sources are continually being published.

There are many other kinds of sources of background material. The *Social Work Almanac* contains overviews with facts and statistical information on the U.S. population, children, education, health, crime, older adults, welfare, etc. Other sources of background material include articles which review the literature, research, or current developments on a topic and general books in the field. For further refining topics, top journals in a particular area of study, annual reviews, and collections of meeting papers may also be helpful.

Notes should be kept of all useful information from background materials. Anything photocopied should have a complete citation written on it to avoid later difficulties in finding the item again or in constructing the bibliography.

Useful Encyclopedias for Background Information

Birren, James E. et al., eds. 1996. *The Encyclopedia of Gerontology.* San Diego, Calif.: Academic Press. 2 vols.

Borgatta, Edgar F., Marie L. Borgatta, et al., eds. 1992. *Encyclopedia of Sociology.* 4 vols. New York: Macmillan.

Corsini, Raymond J. et al., eds. 1994. *Encyclopedia of Psychology.* New York: Wiley, 4 vols.

Edwards, Richard L. et al., eds. 1995. *Encyclopedia of Social Work.* 19th ed. 3 vols. Washington D.C.: NASW. (Also available on CD-ROM as part of the Social Work Reference Library.)

Ginsberg, Leon. 1995. *The Social Work Almanac.* 2d ed. Washington D.C.: NASW. (Also available on CD-ROM as part of the Social Work Reference Library.)

If suitable encyclopedias, dictionaries, annual reviews, or thesauri are not known to the researcher, he or she should consult the reference librarian, a local

library guide, the library's catalog, or a research guide. Use of the library catalog is discussed under "Finding Books and Reports." Research guides are discussed below under "Developing the Bibliography."

Terminology

In reviewing the terminology used for a research project, the researcher
should have three goals: (1) to define terms already known; (2) to make sure
that the accepted terminology in the topic area is employed (i.e., that used by
writers in the field and, therefore, that which will be used by catalogs, indexes,
etc.); and (3) to make sure that all relevant terms are included in the search
strategy. Terms may be used in a distinctive way within a discipline so the
researcher should consult a discipline-specific dictionary if any unfamiliar
terms are encountered.

Terminology is critical when using print or electronic reference resources.
Access to traditional print sources is usually dependent on the use of *controlled
vocabulary* (a list of subject headings). In catalogs, indexes and abstracts, and
other reference sources, subject headings are assigned by an editor to form an
index or to establish consistency throughout the bibliography or database. In
print sources, usually these provide the only access other than author or title.

Computers are very literal about the terms and instructions they are given.
If key terms are not included in the search, then the computer may miss
important articles or other resources. The researcher should begin with what
seem to be the most relevant, most focused terms and their synonyms, but be
prepared with a list of all important terms within the subject area. For example: many reference resources for human services use the term *family violence*:
using a less-used term, *domestic violence*, may cause the researcher to miss relevant literature. If the researcher uses the term *family violence*, and is really
looking for information on the narrower term, *spousal abuse*, then many of the
items retrieved will be beyond the scope of the researcher's topic. Conversely,
if the term *child abuse* is used and the researcher really wants information on
family violence, a considerable amount of useful information will not be discovered.

The *Social Work Dictionary* is a key source of social work and social welfare
terminology. Published by the National Association of Social Workers
(NASW), it contains more then 3000 terms on various aspects of social work.
The definitions in this dictionary define terms as they are used in the profession. Here again, there are useful dictionaries in related fields such as mental
health, psychology, sociology, public policy, etc., which define similar terms as
they are used in each discipline.

Useful Dictionaries for Social Work Topics

Barker, Robert L., ed. 1995. *The Social Work Dictionary*. 3d ed. Washington D.C.: NASW.

Harris, Diana K. 1988. *Dictionary of Gerontology*. New York: Greenwood Press.

Johnson, Allan G. 1995. *The Blackwell Dictionary of Sociology: A User's Guide to Sociological Language*. Cambridge, Mass.: Basil Blackwell.

Slee, Virgil, Debora Slee, and Joachim Schmidt. 1996. *Health Care Terms*. 3d ed. St. Paul: Tringa Press.

Sutherland, Norman S. 1996. *The International Dictionary of Psychology*. 2d ed. New York: Crossroad.

[Note: This is a very selective list. There are many other dictionaries in the human services, psychology, sociology, and health, as well as generally in the social sciences.]

Thesauri contain lists of terms used as subject headings (also known as *descriptors)* in indexes, abstracts, and databases. Although thesauri do not define terms as would a dictionary, they do provide lists of terms, along with notes about their scope (topical coverage), related terms, broader terms and narrower terms. Some thesauri are associated with particular reference sources or databases. Some examples of these are *Thesaurus of Psychological Index Terms* (the thesaurus for *Psychological Abstracts*, *PsycLIT* in CD-ROM format, or PsycINFO on-line), *Thesaurus of Sociological Indexing Terms* (associated with *Sociological Abstracts*, or *Sociofile* on CD-ROM or on-line). Others, like *Contemporary Thesaurus of Social Sciences Terms and Synonyms*, are designed for general use rather than for a particular reference source. There is no useful thesaurus specific to the social work field.

The following example is excerpted from *Thesaurus of Psychological Index Terms* (Walker 1997: 41):

Child Abuse

SN Abuse of children or adolescents in a family, institution, or other setting.
  B Crime
    Family violence
  N Battered child syndrome
  R Abandonment
  ↓ Abuse reporting
    Anatomically detailed dolls
    Child abuse reporting
    Child neglect
    Child welfare
    Emotional abuse
    Failure to thrive
    Munchausen syndrome by proxy
    Patient abuse

   Pedophilia
   Physical abuse
↓ Sexual abuse
Child Advocacy
Use Advocacy

Note: SN = scope note, what is contained under a topic; B = broader terms which may be employed; N = narrower terms; R = related terms. "Abuse reporting" and "Sexual abuse" are more specific terms.

Thesauri often include "UF" (used for, meaning used instead of the term listed), "see" (indicating another term is used instead), "see also" (indicating another term which might also be useful). The researcher should note the terms which most accurately represent their topic. Broader, narrower, and related terms should be recorded for possible use if the terms originally selected don't prove fruitful when searching catalogs, indexes, and abstracts. Some databases include an on-line thesaurus.

Useful Thesauri for Social Work Topics

Booth, Barbara. 1996. *Thesaurus of Sociological Indexing Terms*. San Diego, Calif.: Sociological Abstracts.

Diliberti, Wendy and Margaret Eccles, eds. 1994. *Thesaurus of Aging Terminology*. 5th ed. Washington D.C.: American Association of Retired Persons.

Knapp, Sally. 1993. *Contemporary Thesaurus of Social Science Terms and Synonyms*. Phoenix: Oryx Press.

Picon, Alice and Gwen Sloan, eds. 1990. *PAIS Subject Headings*. 2d ed. New York: Public Affairs Information Service.

Walker, Alvin Jr., ed. 1997. *Thesaurus of Psychological Index Terms*. 8th ed. Washington D.C.: American Psychological Association.

Developing the Bibliography

After general background information and terminology have been investigated thoroughly, the researcher is ready to outline a research strategy. The researcher should by now be fairly clear about the focus of the topic and have answered questions about the research materials sought: the quality, quantity, currency, primary or secondary nature, time available to do the search, and disciplines involved. The last concept is important; the researcher should have an awareness of what other fields of study are likely to contain useful information.

The next step is to make decisions about what reference tools should be used to find the articles, books, reports or other materials that are needed. The first place to look is the library's catalog, which in electronic format is commonly referred to as an *OPAC*. Following this the researcher will want to select indexes and abstracts which will aid not only in identifying specific articles, but other materials as well. Many libraries have in-house guides (specific to their library) which will help with research in particular subject areas. In addition, research guides which list encyclopedias, dictionaries, handbooks, bibliographies, indexes and abstracts, and factual and statistical sources in particular fields are available. Linda Beebe (1993) has written an excellent guide to writing in the human services which includes a chapter devoted to social work library resources; Pam Baxter (1993) has produced an exhaustive guide to sources in psychology, as has Stephen Aby (1997) for sociology. Unfortunately, as of this writing, there is no current comprehensive guide to the sources of social work. The next two sections of this chapter will assist the researcher in selecting a few useful sources with which to begin.

Guides to Library Sources in Social Work and Related Fields

Aby, Stephen H. 1997. *Sociology: A Guide to Reference and Information Sources.* 2d ed. Englewood, Colo.: Libraries Unlimited.

Baxter, Pam M. 1993. *Psychology: A Guide to Reference and Information Sources.* Englewood, Colo.: Libraries Unlimited.

Beebe, Linda, ed. 1993. *Professional Writing for the Human Services.* Washington D.C.: NASW.

Herron, Nancy L., ed. 1996. *The Social Sciences: A Cross-Disciplinary Guide to Selected Sources.* 2d ed. Englewood, Colo.: Libraries Unlimited.

The researcher should keep in mind in compiling lists of articles, books, and reports to examine, that the goal is to be selective, not comprehensive. The bibliography should be tailored to fit the project being worked on.

Finding Books and Reports

The researcher begins developing the bibliography by searching for books and reports. At least some of these items should be scanned *as they are selected*. This will alert the researcher to new terminology, issues, concepts, directions for research, etc. If the topic being researched is still not sufficiently defined the researcher may want to use books and reports as a way to find further background information. Books are valuable as resources for research papers because many have very comprehensive information on a topic. They often provide in-depth information, information on theory and practice, and synthesis and interpretation of previous research. Books are also sources of literature

reviews, i.e., summary narratives of the research that has previously been produced. Book length bibliographies or lists of sources are also available on some
topics. As noted before, they are, however, not usually as up-to-date as journals.
When focusing on one topic, books are also referred to as *monographs*.

In addition to books, reports are another good source of general (and sometimes specific) information on a topic. They often focus on a particular problem and provide comprehensive information such as history, factual material,
analyses of issues involved, and alternative solutions or policies.

The first stop for finding books and reports is the library's catalog. In addition to books and reports, the catalog usually lists government publications,
journals (but not individual articles), electronic media, and audio-visual materials. There are a number of critical concepts to keep in mind when using the
library catalog. The library catalog is made up of *records*, each one corresponding to an item in the library's collection. Each record contains a listing of the
author, title, publisher, date, subject headings, and often other information
such as notes about contents. If the user already is aware of a particular item to
search for, this is a *known item* search. When looking up a known item, use the
title if possible; this is usually the most individual attribute of a book or report
and will be the quickest way to retrieve the information.

Unless already familiar with a particular author or book title, the researcher
will probably initiate the search using subject headings. The researcher may
want to consult a thesaurus such as *Library of Congress Subject Headings* (or
Sears List of Subject Headings, which is more commonly used in smaller
libraries) to learn which terms are used and which broader, narrower, and
related terms are suggested. These thesauri (which most libraries place near the
library catalog) will also indicate how headings can be subdivided by aspects of
the topic, for instance, geographically. Many electronic catalogs are also search-
able by *keywords* (i.e., words that are not in themselves formal titles, authors, or
subject headings, but instead merely occur somewhere in the title, author, subject headings, notes, etc.)

Many students attempt to do comprehensive searches on fairly narrow topics. For instance, searching for information using the term *substance abuse*,
when really looking for information on *alcohol abuse*, or *alcohol* when they really
want *alcohol abuse treatment*. The result can be a large number of books or other
resources to review and evaluate. In general, the researcher should use the nar-
rowest term(s) which accurately reflect the material being sought. If this strategy does not yield sufficient information, the researcher should then expand the
search to include broader terms which encompass the original concept or narrower terms covering one of its subtopics. If information is not adequate there,

then related terms should be considered. (Hint: once useful books have been identified, the user should examine the subject headings in the catalog record to make sure that relevant headings have been included in the search.)

Journals titles can be searched on a library catalog; individual articles usually cannot be searched. The researcher must identify the journal name and at least some information on volume or date before coming to the catalog.

Subject Headings for Library Catalogs

Miller, Joseph, ed. 1997. *Sears List of Subject Headings.* 16th ed. New York: H. W. Wilson.

U.S. Library of Congress. 1997. *Library of Congress Subject Headings.* 20th ed. Washington D.C.: L of C.

Once books or reports have been identified, the researcher should note *at least* the title, author, and call number (location where the material will be found on the shelf). The call number will be used to find the book or report in the user's own library. The title and author will be convenient to have if the item needs to be looked up again, either in the catalog or in some other reference source.

If researchers want to look for books beyond their own library's collection, many libraries offer services such as *WorldCat* database (from OCLC FirstSearch) or *RLIN* for on-line and Internet access to records of library materials owned by libraries throughout the United States as well as much international material. Some electronic databases (like *PsycLIT*, which is discussed under "Finding Journals") are also useful for identifying books. Many individual libraries make their catalogs available on the Internet. Libraries have access to vast networks for borrowing materials for their patrons from other libraries. This service, called Interlibrary Loan or ILL, takes varying amounts of time depending on the arrangements the library has made and the types of materials being sought.

Finding Journal Articles

Journals, whether they are produced in print, microform, CD-ROM, or on the Internet, are the most important source of current research in the field of social work. They are generally of two kinds. *Research journals* publish articles by scholars detailing their research or analyzing or synthesizing the work of other scholars. Also, they may identify issues or problems and propose solutions to them. They are characterized by having bibliographies of references, having sound research methodology, and contributing to the knowledge base of a field. Articles to be published in research journals are usually selected by editorial boards or reviewers, often with the authors remaining anonymous during the selection process. Articles in research journals are the basic building blocks of most social work research papers.

While *popular journals* (like *Time*, *Newsweek*, or *Ms.*, for example) do not meet the above criteria, they do have a place in some research papers. For example, if a researcher wants to see how the media handles an issue or how the public perceives a government program, using some popular journals might be appropriate. Both research journals and popular journals serve an important function: they expose the researcher to a greater variety of viewpoints than do books (DeVilley 1987: 19). It is very important to distinguish between the two type of journals, and know when the use of each is appropriate.

There are a number of methods, both informal and formal, for identifying relevant journal articles. Among the informal methods are personal communication and noting items found in footnotes from other articles. The most common formal methods are utilizing indexes and abstracts and performing a citation search. The focus in this chapter is on the two formal methods.

INDEXES AND ABSTRACTS For most researchers, particularly researchers unfamiliar with their topical area, the primary method for finding journal, magazine, and newspaper articles will be the use of *indexes and abstracts*. Most indexes and abstracts are reference sources which provide subject, author, and title access to the literature of a field. Electronic sources permit additional access, including searching by *freetext* (any word appearing in a record in the database) and manipulation of and coordination of terms.

Almost without exception, when looking for journal articles for a social work research paper, it is a good idea to start with social work sources. Any information found there will more likely reflect the social work point of view, and is likely to be focused well for research papers in the social work field.

One hundred and ten journals plus dissertations in social work are covered in the basic *abstracts* of the field. These are entitled *Social Work Abstracts* in print form and *SWAB* in electronic form. Abstracts are summaries of the contents of an article or dissertation; usually they are written by the author of the original work. *Social Work Abstracts* has comprehensively indexed and abstracted more than thirty years of journal articles and dissertations in the field. In the print version, each issue has author and subject indexes which are cumulated annually. Citations from the past twenty years (more than 26,000 abstracts) are available on CD-ROM and on-line. It is in electronic format that most researchers prefer to search.

Electronic databases, like *SWAB*, typically contain thousands of *records*, each record representing one article (or in some cases, book or report or video, etc.). Each record is divided into many *fields*, usually including author(s), title, name of journal (or in the case of a book or report, name of publisher), author affiliation, publication date, volume and pages where applicable, an abstract (usually written by the author), *descriptors* (in a print source referred to as subject headings). Some databases have no abstracts; in that case they often have other notes to indicate contents. Electronic resources usually permit the following operations which greatly enhance the researcher's ability to refine a search: combination of terms and access to new terms; coverage of many years in one operation; ability to search for various forms of a term (known as *truncation*); ability to specify date(s) and language desired; and capability to print, download, or mail results to an e-mail account.

In order to combine terms, the searcher uses *Boolean* searching. In Boolean searching, the use of connectors enables the searcher to instruct the computer on the relationship between or among inputted terms. The most commonly used connectors are *and* and *or*. In the example of a search on *child abuse* and *foster care*, if *and* is used as a connector between *terms* (*child abuse and foster care*), the search software "understands" that the searcher only wants the record retrieved if both concepts are included in that record. If the connector, *or*, is used, then if *either* one of the concepts is included in the record, it will be retrieved. Thus *and* limits or refines retrieval, while *or* expands and broadens a search. This capability to manipulate terms to produce a refined list of sources is the most powerful advantage of electronic sources.

New terms can be accessed as they appear in titles and abstracts, before they appear as subject headings. For instance, when the name of a new concept develops, like "Temporary Assistance to Needy Families," computer searching will allow access to articles using the phrase in titles or abstracts before subject headings have been assigned.

Truncation allows for retrieval of multiple forms of terms. For instance, *alcohol** (if * is the truncation symbol in a particular database) will retrieve *alcohol, alcoholic, alcoholics, alcoholism*, etc. However, truncation must be used with caution. For example, *minor** will retrieve both *minor* or *minors* plus *minority* or *minorities*. Searches may be further refined by limiting the parameters of certain fields. For instance, the search could be limited to particular years of publication or particular languages.

As previously noted, a major advantage of electronic databases is their cumulative nature. All of the abstracts in *Social Work Abstracts* since 1977 are available on one CD-ROM (or, in the case of on-line use, one database). This is very efficient because the researcher doesn't have to search multiple volumes. It also facilitates looking at all the work of one author or completing a citation when not all the information is known. An additional and useful feature of many electronic sources is that, in some libraries, they may be accessed from many points, both internal and external, to the library.

Print indexes and abstracts frequently have one surprising characteristic in their favor: the print version often is published more often than the CD-ROM and thus is more up to date. This is true of *SWAB*, where the CD-ROM version is published twice yearly compared to the print version's four times. Where currency is vital the researcher should look for the latest print issue to update the CD-ROM. (Note: the on-line version is also updated quarterly.)

Much as with the library catalog search, the researcher should think about the search as it proceeds, examining descriptors to look for additional terms when reviewing results. The researcher should never take "no matches" for an answer when searching indexes and abstracts, but should instead look at the terminology and construction of the search, check thesauri, and consult the reference librarian. There will almost always be relevant information, whether on aspects of the topic, on closely related topics, or on methodology used in the research. It is important to develop a good search strategy *before* the search begins, to refine it as the search proceeds, and to *check all relevant* bibliographic search resources. The researcher should be sure to focus the search as much as possible so that it results in a manageable number of citations.

Once the researcher has completed the initial search of *Social Work Abstracts* then he or she should think in interdisciplinary terms. What other subject fields are likely to provide good information on this topic? If the researcher is working on any topic in the field of mental health, *Psychological Abstracts* should be searched. When researching anything related to children, the researcher should consider *ERIC*, anything to do with youth problems, *Sociological Abstracts*, and so forth.

If there is any kind of a policy component to the research, *PAIS International* (print, CD-ROM, on-line) should be utilized as well. Kemp and Brustman (1997) compared the usefulness of various CD-ROM databases for social policy research. *PAIS International*, the public policy database, was an excellent source for all topics tested. *SWAB* proved to be a poor source of social policy articles, but many other specialized databases like *Ageline* or *ERIC* were very good for policy literature in their area(s) of specialization. The researcher should also consider whether the topic warrants using other specialized sources, for instance, indexes to newspapers or to government documents.

Many libraries purchase CD-ROMs like *SWAB*, *PAIS International*, and other databases from the same vendor so that searching is done in the same manner. There are literally hundreds of indexes and abstracts available. Consult a librarian or research guide to help you identify useful ones for your project.

Once articles have been identified, the researcher needs to search the library's catalog by the *titles of the journals* needed. The catalog record will indicate what years the library holds. Libraries usually use one of two methods for shelving journals, by call number or alphabetically by title. Sometimes the software for electronic databases will tell the searcher which journals indexed and abstracted there are owned by the library. (Note: Increasingly, databases are offering full text documents and articles. Individual libraries may subscribe to services which provide these; ask the reference librarian at your library.)

Major Indexes and Abstracts for Identifying Journal Articles: Social Work, Related Disciplines, and the Social Sciences

[note: most of these databases include items other than journal articles. many of these cd-rom databases are also available on line. Access at individual libraries will vary.]

Ageline. (CD-ROM). Washington D.C.: American Association of Retired Persons. 1978+. Literature on aging, including journal articles, books, book chapters, government publications, organization publications, reports and audiovisual materials. Also available on-line.

ERIC. (CD-ROM). Rockville, Md.: U.S. Department of Education, Office of Education Research and Improvement, ERIC Processing and Reference Facility. 1966+. Literature on education and related disciplines, including journal articles, books, dissertations, government documents, organization publications. Also available on-line and corresponds to the print sources, *Current Index to Journals in Education* and *Resources in Education.*

MEDLINE. (CD-ROM). Bethesda, Md.: U.S. National Library of Medicine, MEDLARS Management Section. 1966+ Literature on medicine and related disciplines, including journal articles only. Also available on-line.

PAIS International. New York: Public Affairs Information Service. 1915+. Literature on public policy and public affairs including journal articles, books, government materials, organization publications, reports. Also available on-line and CD-ROM, 1976+.

Psychological Abstracts. Washington D.C.: American Psychological Association. 1927+. Professional and clinical literature in psychology and related disciplines, including journal articles, books, and book chapters. Also available on-line as *PsycINFO* and on CD-ROM as *PsycLIT,* 1974+.

Social Sciences Citation Index. Philadelphia: Institute for Scientific Information. 1969+. Literature of the social sciences, including journal articles. Also available on-line and on CD-ROM, 1986+.

Social Sciences Index. New York: H.W. Wilson. 1974+. Literature of the social sciences, including journal articles. Included in *International Index (to Periodicals),* 1907–65 and *Social Sciences and Humanities Index,* 1965–74. Available on CD-ROM 1983+ , also on-line and on CD-ROM with abstracts as *Social Science Abstracts,* 1983+.

Social Work Abstracts. Washington D.C.: National Association of Social Workers. 1965+. Professional and clinical literature in social work, including journal articles and dissertations. Also available on-line and on CD-ROM as *SWAB,* 1977+.

Sociological Abstracts. San Diego, Calif.: Sociological Abstracts, Inc. 1953+. Literature of sociology, including journal articles and dissertations. Also available on-line and on CD-ROM as *Sociofile*, 1974+.

CITATION SEARCHING The second most commonly used method of finding useful journal articles is *citation searching*. Virtually all scholarly work contains citations to other research. Citation searching provides a means to track future articles which reference a source and, therefore, follow the development of an idea or topic of research. In citation searching the researcher begins with the author of a known relevant article (or book, report, etc.) This author is looked up in the *citation index* portion of an index such as *Social Sciences Citation Index* to see which later *articles* are listed which *cite* the original source. An article is said "to cite" the source if it has the "cited" source in its reference list or bibliography. In this way the researcher finds out about subsequent articles that review the source, discuss a particular point of research, or correct errors.

Most novice researchers begin with a thorough literature search employing catalogs, indexes, and abstracts. Many specialists begin with the citation search. They are more easily able to do this because of their familiarity with important books and articles in their particular area of study. Both the experienced and the inexperienced researcher can benefit from employing both strategies. Novices can use the citation search to find further useful sources; specialists can use indexes and abstracts to extend the search to publications beyond their discipline's mainstream, to related fields, or to sources overlooked by other scholars. Where a truly comprehensive search is required, searching of indexes and abstracts *and* citation searching should both be done to provide the best results (Engeldinger and Stuart 1990).

Other Sources

Law and Government Materials

Government documents are materials produced by federal, state, and local governments. If they originate in the executive branch of government, they will include reports, studies, regulations, factual materials, manuals, etc. From the legislative branch they may be reports, hearings, laws, etc. The judicial branch primarily produces court cases.

While government documents provide information of all kinds, they are particularly useful for policy research. If a research project has a *federal* policy angle the researcher may want to search GPO, the federal government publications database, on CD-ROM (or its print equivalent, the *Monthly Catalog of U.S. Government Publications*). In completing a search of the library's catalog and *PAIS International* the researcher should already have identified many of the documents that are relevant to the topic; GPO or *Monthly Catalog* offer more comprehensive searching of documents literature if needed. (A word of caution when checking to see if your library owns these materials: some libraries don't include federal documents in their catalog or they may be difficult to find there. Ask the reference librarian for assistance.)

Government documents include program or policy information right from the source, the agency which implements the policy or the congressional committee which formulates it. Government reports, evaluations, studies, etc., can provide a wealth of information on policy planning and evaluation. In conducting research many students working on policy projects will also be interested in information related to laws, regulations, court cases, etc. Most libraries will have resources where you can look up a law as a distinct entity or in code form (i.e., combined with other laws on the same or similar topics). Other useful sources can be legislative history, reports, hearings, etc.

Secondary sources may also be useful. Legal resources include dictionaries, encyclopedias, and subject-oriented resources of various kinds. Indexes and abstracts provide access to legal journals. As a general rule, there will be much more material on a federal policy or law than on state ones. It is therefore generally much easier to write a paper on a topic which is primarily federal. Full text legal information is widely available in electronic sources, both on-line and via the Internet.

Sources of Government and Legal Information

GPO. (CD-ROM). Washington D.C.: U.S. Superintendent of Documents, Government Printing Office, 1976+. (CD-ROM title varies by vendor. Also available on-line.)

U.S. Superintendent of Documents. *Monthly Catalog of United States Government Publications*. Washington D.C.: U.S. Superintendent of Documents, Government Printing Office, 1995+.

Statistical and Factual Sources

Many projects benefit by support from statistical and factual information. *Statistical Abstract of the United States* is often an excellent starting point for statistical information. This source, produced by the U.S. government, offers tables of data collected by the federal government. It also has information on the bottom of each table clearly identifying the source of the material. There are many more sources for U.S. government, state/local government, and private organization statistics. *American Statistics Index* indexes federal government statistics and *Statistical Reference Index* state and organization statistics. *Social Work Almanac* also has handy statistical and factual material. The Internet is replete with good statistical sites. Many related fields have a wealth of useful statistical sources; health is a good example.

There are also many factual sources useful for research projects. One notable item in the social work and psychology fields is the *Diagnostic and Statistical Manual of Mental Disorders* (DSM-IV). This provides descriptions, diagnostic features, and other information on hundreds of mental disorders.

Useful Statistical and Factual Sources

American Psychiatric Association. 1994. *Diagnostic and Statistical Manual of Mental Disorders.* 4th ed. Washington D.C.: APA.

American Statistics Index. Bethesda, Md.: Congressional Information Service. 1973+. Available also as part of the CD-ROM, *Statistical Masterfile.*

Ginsberg, Leon. 1995. *The Social Work Almanac.* 2d ed. Washington D.C.: NASW.

U.S. Bureau of the Census. *Statistical Abstract of the United States.* Washington D.C.: U.S. Government Printing Office, 1878+.

Statistical Reference Index. Bethesda, Md.: Congressional Information Service. 1980+. Available also as part of the CD-ROM *Statistical Masterfile.*

Internet

The *Internet* is a system of networks which allow a user at a computer in one location to access files on computers at other locations. *Web browsers* are software that permit users to easily access and search the Internet. The Internet is a very rich source of information for certain topical areas of social work. Directory information, funding information, information on specific programs like self-help programs and policy material are good examples. There is a proliferation of public sites (for example, the Administration for Children and Families or the Social Security Administration) and private organization sites (for example, National Association of Social Workers or Children's Defense Fund) which provide excellent up-to-date information on topics related to social welfare. One of the difficulties of using Internet resources is evaluating the quality of the material. Anyone can put information on the Internet. While researchers may be able to weigh the authority of the author or the seeming reliability of the information, they usually cannot rely on publisher reputation or the refereeing process (discussed previously under "Finding Journals"). Searchers can, however, note if the contents are current and how often they are updated, and the quality of the site in terms of organization and balance or bias in viewpoint.

Searching the Internet is becoming increasingly sophisticated, often utilizing search techniques similar to the sophisticated software of CD-ROM searching. Generally there are two ways to go about searching on the Internet, beginning with a search engine (for a subject, person, or organization search) or starting with a known Internet site on a topic and examining the links to sources that have been placed there. If the latter option is possible and quality sources have been selected, this will be a much more efficient method of searching.

Citing the Work of Others

Carter noted three purposes for references in scholarly writing: (1) to show how the new contribution advances previously reported research; (2) to provide information on what is already known on a topic; and (3) to provide sources for finding additional information (Beebe 1993 citing Carter). References in the text should be used when the researcher is quoting another source or paraphrasing the words of another. In addition the *Publication Manual of the American Psychological Association*, also known as the *APA Manual* (1994b: 294), states that, "The key element of this principle is that an author does not present the work of another as if it were his or her own work. This can extend to ideas as well as written words." The National Association of Social Workers echoes this in its *Code of Ethics*. Social workers should take credit for "work actually performed" and should "acknowledge the work" of others (1995: 24).

The *APA Manual* offers exhaustive coverage of how to cite references and construct bibliographies as well as other aspects of preparing manuscripts for term papers or publication. While the manual covers citing of electronic sources and gives some examples, electronic citing is not yet fully standardized. Electronic formats keep changing. Researchers should adapt forms which are already in use, keeping in mind that citing is for (1) crediting the author(s); and (2) assisting the next researcher in finding the information.

Guides to Citing and Scholarly Ethics

American Psychological Association. 1994. *Publication Manual of the American Psychological Association*. 4th ed.. Washington D.C.: APA. (Versions also available on the Internet.)

National Association of Social Workers. 1996. *Code of Ethics*. Washington D.C.: NASW.

Accessing Materials

Typically, information identified in reference sources leads to books, journals, dissertations, reports, or government publications. These materials come in a variety of formats, for instance print, microform, on-line, or the Internet. Researchers should first check their library's catalog to determine if the materials are owned by the library. Individual libraries sometimes have some materials which are not in the general catalog or are more difficult to find. If materials cannot be located, the reference librarian should be consulted.

If materials are not owned by the library, there are several options for electronically accessing the full text of documents. These include full text databases, document delivery services, and the Internet. If needed materials are not available full text on-line or via the Internet, the library's interlibrary loan service should be employed.

Evaluation of Materials

Once materials have been obtained, the researcher will want to evaluate their usefulness. During the search process the researcher used criteria to determine the *potential usefulness* of materials identified. Once the materials are in hand, the same questions should be asked again. The researcher will probably not be able to answer all of these questions for every source, but there is now much more information for evaluation:

- Source: Was the article published in a research journal? (Criteria for identifying research journals are covered earlier in this chapter under "Finding Journal Articles.") Or was it published by a reputable publisher or a government agency?
- Authority: What is the authority of the source? Do the authors have relevant credentials? Is it written on a scholarly level?
- Currency: Is the information sufficiently current for the research being conducted? This may be determined not only by publication date, but by reading the text and noting the dates of the bibliographic references.
- Accuracy: Does it appear to be accurate? Does the information in the source accord with other knowledge the researcher has on the topic?
- Viewpoint: Does the presentation seem balanced or biased? This is best judged by the researcher's growing knowledge of the topic.
- Methodology: The researcher will want to examine the research methodology. Do the methods seem sound? Is there scholarly documentation of information?

Summary

In reading this chapter, the researcher has studied processes to define and focus a topic for research, to formulate a search strategy and select appropriate reference sources to search, to search and identify potentially useful sources, to locate published materials, and to evaluate those materials for usefulness in the research project. While library research is presented as a step-by-step systematic process, the researcher should remember that it is also an interactive process. The topic, the terminology, the research strategy, and the specific sources employed should be continuously modified by the researcher's growing knowledge of the subject and the resources available on that subject.

The researcher should remain open to a wide range of resources in social work, related fields, and in the broader social sciences. On many topics, this will constitute a large amount of material. The researcher should master techniques for selection and evaluation, both for compiling a bibliography of the best materials available, and for efficiency in time and effort. And, very importantly, the researcher should be persistent and recognize that it takes time to do quality research. Lastly, the researcher should take advantage of the help the reference librarian can provide.

Appendix 2

Guidelines for Preparing Research Reports

In this appendix we present guidelines for writing a research report. The guidelines first take up reports of quantitative studies, then discuss modifications for qualitative research. We assume that the report will take the form of a term paper or a journal article, although the guidelines should also be helpful in preparing other kinds of research products, such as reports to funding agencies. We have in mind a document ranging in length from about 10 to 25 typewritten pages, including tables, figures, and references.

To a certain extent, the report should be geared for its audience. A research report for an agency board of directors may focus less on technical aspects of research methods and more on recommendations for agency service than one intended for a research course instructor. A report intended for journal publication usually focuses more than the agency report or course paper on placing the study in the larger context of other research and in developing conclusions that contribute to a wider body of knowledge. An article intended for a social work practice journal will highlight the practice implications, while that intended for a research journal may include more sophisticated discussion of the sampling or data analysis issues. Despite the need to keep the audience in mind while writing, there is a set of core content that should be included in all research reports.

The guidelines outline one variation of a conventional structure for presenting the kind of reports we have described. There are, of course, many other variations, some of which will be mentioned in the course of our discussion.

Front Matter: Title, Author(s), and Acknowledgments

The title of the report should be clear, concise, and precise, without overgeneralizing (see chapter 3) or assuming inside knowledge of the agency or study. The reader should be able to tell immediately what the report is about.

"Authors" should include all those who made major contributions to the conceptualization, conduct, or writing of the study. The order of the authors indicates responsibility; the person who made the most contribution to conceptualization and conduct of the study is normally the first (senior) author. If all authors contributed equally, the authors' names may appear in alphabetical order with a note in the acknowledgments saying that all were equal. (If there will be several reports, many investigators rotate whose name appears first.) In large projects, those who made susidiary contributions, for example, interviewers, coders, or data analysts, are not included among the authors, but may be thanked in the acknowledgments.

"Acknowledgments" must include the funding source (often with the grant name and number) if the research is funded. If the report is one of several from a single study, that fact and the citations of other reports must be included. Other content that may go in the acknowledgments includes approval by Institutional Review Boards, support from an agency or other body, and thanks to nonauthors who made contributions to the study, such as manuscript reviewers, editors, or research staff.

Presenting a Research Report

Statement of the Problem

The usual way to begin a research report is with some discussion of the problem to which the study is addressed. In social work reports, the problem may not be initially presented in terms of research questions or hypotheses but rather as a social issue, e.g., substance abuse by pregnant women, the development of ethnic identity on the part transracially adopted children, and the like. As the examples suggest, the problem is usually introduced in the specific terms that defined the study to be reported. That is, if the study concerned housing problems of the homeless mentally ill, one would begin with a discussion of that problem, and not issues concerning homelessness, housing, or mental illness in general.

Discussion of the problem can be quite brief—a few paragraphs may suffice—but there is often question about how much and what to include. A useful question is: What do readers need to know in order to understand the problem, to place it in an appropriate context, and to appreciate its significance?

The amount of attention given to these factors depends on the nature of the problem and the assumptions about the audience to whom the report is primarily directed. If the problem involves concepts or theoretical formulations that are likely to be unfamiliar to readers, some explanation of these ideas is in order. The significance of some problems will be self-evident and need not be belabored; the importance of others has to be made clear. If the report is intended for a social work audience, the relevance of the problem to social work practice should be articulated if it is not obvious.

Review of the Literature

The next step is to review literature directly related to the problem area. Priority should be given to prior studies that have led to the current research. Theoretical and other kinds of literature may be included if they are relevant to the study. If a large amount of research has been done in the area, the writer may need to generalize about existing empirical knowledge.

The review should not consist of a string of paragraphs, each presenting a capsule summary of a different study. Rather, it should organize findings pertinent to different aspects of the study, with emphasis on identifying gaps in knowledge that the the study will address. The review should be as succinct as possible and directly focused on the questions or hypotheses of the study. Again, the focus is on what the reader needs to know about directly relevant previous work, not on the breadth of reading done by the author.

Study Questions (or Hypotheses)

The questions or hypotheses to be addressed by the study is the focus of this section. Depending on what was presented in the discussion of the problem and review of the literature, there may need to be some explication of relevant theory and key terms. This section presents the focus of the study, so clarity is particularly important.

In some reports this section may precede the review of the literature. In others it may consist of a paragraph at the end of the review.

Research Methodology

The methods section sets out the methodology of the study. It usually includes descriptions of the research design, the sampling plan, data collection procedures, and measurement instruments. Information on the validity and reliability of the measurement instrument(s) used and on characteristics of the setting may be included. Aspects of methodology that may better be understood in conjunction with presentation of the findings may be deferred until results are actually presented.

The most common shortcoming in this section is insufficient or unclear presentation of the study's methods. The researcher's own intimate familiarity with these methods may breed insensitivity to the reader's ignorance of them. As a result, the study methodology may be presented in an indirect, cryptic manner. An excellent device to avoid this is for researchers to put themselves in the position of readers who know nothing about the study.

It is particularly important to provide a clear picture of the connection between the research question and the data obtained. In order to accomplish this, the investigator should provide some description of the study's measurement instrument, including sample questions. Ideally, the actual instrument or key portions of it should be included as an appendix, but this is usually not feasible for reports published in professional journals. In any case, the steps by which the data were obtained from the instrument should be delineated. If there are many variables, it may help clarify measurements to present the independent and dependent variables separately. If the hypotheses are complex, it may also be advisable to restate the research question or hypothesis in operational language, indicating the quantitative basis for measurement. For example, a hypothesis may be stated as a prediction that certain scores will be correlated or that statistically significant differences between sample groups will be found on the dependent variable.

Findings

While all the findings of a study need not be reported in an article-length report, all important results that bear on the research questions or hypotheses should be set forth. The two principal formats for presenting the findings are data displays and narratives.

DATA DISPLAYS A useful first step in beginning work on findings is to prepare tables, graphs, figures, or other *data displays* that will form the core of the presentation. The narrative portion of the findings section can then be organized according to these displays.

The first principle in displaying data is to present them in a manner that can be readily understood, given the information provided up to that point in the report. In tabular data displays, the most widely used form, this criterion is met by providing a descriptive title for the table and labels for columns and rows. Data displays should be clearly labeled so that a reader can understand the table without referring to the text. (See, for example, Butterfield 1993 and the tables presented in chapter 11.)

The purpose of a data display is to communicate information to the reader in a clear and concise manner. If a display has achieved this purpose efficiently, there should be no need to repeat the information it contains in the text of the report. Textual commentary on data displays should be used to emphasize the main points of the data or to draw attention to characteristics of the data that might be overlooked. For example, one might summarize a table: "The most frequent intervention techniques were reframing and confrontation" rather than stating "Reframing was used by 52% of practitioners, praise by 15%, confrontation by 38%," and so on.

In keeping with the purpose of data displays—to enhance the reader's understanding—complex displays should be used only if absolutely necessary. Indeed, displays should not be used at all to communicate basic information that can be expressed more simply in the text.

NARRATIVES The narrative presentation of research findings should follow a logical sequence. Data describing characteristics of research participants or respondents (demographic data) often are presented first, as a means of defining the group to which the findings relate. Then, a convenient way to proceed with the description of findings is in the order of the research questions or hypotheses presented earlier. Findings not anticipated by these questions or hypotheses can then be introduced.

It may be necessary to describe additional measurement procedures as well as analytic methods. The amount of detail and explanation necessary to present the data analysis techniques varies. Routine data processing procedures that are of no consequence to the study's findings certainly do not need to be reported. For example, informing readers that the data were coded, entered into the computer, and analyzed adds nothing of value to the report.

Common statistical techniques, such as standard measures of association to measure the strength of a relationship between variables, are neither explained nor referenced. It is good practice, however, to clarify their function so the essential meaning of the statistical findings can be grasped. In describing a correlation between expenditures for social work services and the patient discharge rate in mental health facilities, for example, the report might state: "The correlation coefficient between expenditures and the discharge rate was .76, which suggests a relatively high degree of association between these two variables." Specialized methods that are not in common use should be explained, however.

The usual practice in this section is to present the study's findings and clarify them if necessary, but not to discuss them at length. There may be reasons to deviate from this format, however. For instance, if a study produces a number of findings, some of them may be discussed when presented, and the next section can focus on those that are to be emphasized.

Discussion

The discussion section, usually headed simply "discussion," is primarily concerned with pulling together and interpreting the findings reported in the previous section. Although the discussion should focus on the hypotheses tested or questions answered, not all findings need be mentioned. The discussion can focus on those the investigator considers the most important.

The content of the discussion section varies according to the nature of the findings and what has been previously said about them. In most studies, the findings are sufficiently complex, ambiguous, or puzzling to warrant some explanation of what was in fact learned about the sample studied.

In the process of discussing the findings, usually some attempt is made to summarize those thought to be central, even at the risk of some repetition from the findings section. However new findings should not be introduced.

A good deal of attention is usually given to developing possible explanations for key findings. For example, the length of social work treatment may be found to be positively correlated with clients' outcomes. Does this mean that greater amounts of treatment played a causative role in the outcome, or does it mean that clients who were getting better on their own tended to remain in treatment longer? Tests of rival hypotheses or other evidence or argument that can be brought to bear on this point should be presented. If hypotheses were not confirmed, reasons for their failure should be elucidated. There should be discussion of unexpected findings and possible reasons for them. Inconsistencies in the findings should be noted, and, if possible, resolved.

In examining such relationships and determining the meaning of the findings, possible sources of bias or error in sampling, data collection and measurement should be pointed out. For example, were the interviewers' perceptions influenced by knowledge of the study's hypothesis? Is it possible that clients were giving socially desirable responses?

While the findings may not "prove" or "establish" a great deal, they may "provide evidence for," "suggest the possibility that," or "raise questions about." With such qualified language, points can be made that readers will find useful but not misleading. Authors often do not push either their imaginations or their data far enough. Ultraconservative interpretations of findings may have the dubious advantage of avoiding criticism, but they also may fail to extract useful ideas and suggestions from the findings.

The interpretation of results may be strengthened or qualified by references to related literature, using sources reviewed earlier in the report or introduced in this part in order to connect the findings of the study to the results of other investigations. Introducing other authors' findings in this section is also appropriate when the study's findings have been serendipitous or were not covered in the literature referred to in the introduction.

The limitations of a research study, particularly major shortcomings that may affect how the findings are interpreted or applied, should be made explicit. A major limitation of most social work studies concerns the lack of representativeness of the sample. More important atypicalities of the sample can be pointed out. While generalization in a statistical sense may not be possible, the results should have some degree of application to other populations and situations. Those for which the study may have relevance can be noted. Limitations may be set forth in the course of discussing the findings, as illustrated above, at the end of the discussion, or in a separate section.

Implications and Recommendations

Implications and recommendations refer to ways in which the findings of the study may affect other domains, such as theory, research, policy, and practice. In journal articles, implications and recommendations may be used interchangeably. The term "recommendations" is likely to be used in reports addressed to particular decision makers (such as key agency staff members) who might be able to initiate them. (For the sake of simplicity we shall refer only to implications.) Implications, especially those relating to theory and research, may be made in the discussion section. Another variation is to present them in a short "Conclusion" section at the end of the article.

Implications for practice and policy represent a synthesis of research findings and desirable goals. If the goals are generally accepted, it may not be necessary to be explicit about them. If the goals are controversial, then the assumptions should be stated clearly. For example, Huh (1997) found that participating in activities relating to Korean culture appeared to help Korean adoptees increase their ethnic identities. Since efforts to increase the ethnic identities of intercountry adoptees may not be universally seen as desirable, Huh's suggestion that social workers help such adoptees engage in cultural activities was based on her clearly expressed assumption that a heightened sense of ethnic identity was desirable for such adoptees.

In discussing implications, the primary focus should be on what the audience for the report will be interested in or should know. Extensive suggestions for improvements in research methodology will interest a research audience but not a practice or agency audience. And while the writer should not fear stating obvious conclusions, conclusions that are too broad or obvious are not helpful to the reader. For example, in most circumstances, a statement like "more research is needed" is so obvious and unspecific that it adds little to the report.

References

The reference section should list all material cited (referred to) in the text. It should not include material that is not cited. The style of references and in-text citations (or footnotes) should follow the style preferred by the agency, course instructor, or journal. If given a choice, authors should select an easy, flexible system such as the styles of the American Psychological Association (APA 194a), the NASW Press (Beebe 1993), or the University of Chicago Press (1993).

Reporting Qualitative Research

The main difference in reporting qualitative and quantitative research, in our view, occurs in the findings section of the report. In a report of a qualitative study there should be a statement of the problem, a review of the literature, and a description of the methods of the study. In the findings section, of course, one finds words instead of numbers. In presenting the findings of a qualitative study, one concentrates on setting forth the main themes or patterns that emerged from the analysis. In fact, the section may be subdivided according to the themes discussed. Themes are developed with supporting detail including quotes from subjects. In order to do justice to the themes, a good deal of narration may be required. Sometimes other parts of the report, especially the methods section, are kept excessively brief to compensate. This does not make for a balanced report, in our judgment. Methods should be as well described in a qualitative as in a quantitative investigation.

Numbers may be used to specify how many subjects fit a particular pattern, although expressions like "the majority" or "only a few" are more likely to appear when specification is needed. Excessive use of numbers, e.g., "two said this, three said that, and one said something else," can impede the flow of the narrative and obscure important themes.

Because the themes incorporate a good deal of interpretation, a separate discussion section may not be necessary. Findings may be followed with an implications or conclusion section.

Contents of a Research Report

I. Statement of the Problem
II. Review of the Literature
    A. Important concepts and previous research
    B. Gaps in current knowledge that this study will address
III. Hypotheses or Research Questions

IV. Research Methodology
    A. Research design
    B. Sampling plan
    C. Data collection procedures, including setting
    D. Measurement instruments
        1. Description of instruments and which concept/variables they measure
        2. Reliability and validity of instruments
V. Findings
    A. Description of sample
    B. Data addressing hypotheses or research questions
        1. Quantitative reports organized by hypotheses or questions with data displays: tables, charts, diagrams interwoven with narrative that highlights or explains data displays.
        2. Qualitative reports organized by themes interwoven with evidence for themes/conclusions in form of quotes, description, etc.
VI. Discussion
    A. Highlights of main findings
    B. Explanation or meaning of findings
    C. Linkage to current state of knowledge, literature
    D. Limitations of study and how they affect results
VII. Implications or recommendations
VIII. References
IX. (Optional) Appendixes

Note: Section headings in a report may reflect content of the study.

Glossary

α (alpha), *see* **Type I error.**

ß (beta) — (1) In significance testing, the probability of accepting the null hypothesis when it is in fact false, also called Type II error; a false positive. (2) In multiple regression, a statistic that measures the contribution of each independent variable to the dependent variable on a standard scale so that the relative contributions can be compared; also called beta weights.

μ (mu) — In inferential statistics, a population parameter, mean of the population data.

σ (sigma) — In inferential statistics, the standard deviation of population data.

AB design, *see* **Basic time series design.**

ABAB design, *see* **Withdrawal-reversal design.**

Accidental sample — A nonprobability sample selected by including anyone at hand or available who meets specified criteria, for example, all clients who apply during one week. Also called availability or convenience sample.

Active variable — A variable whose categories can or do change for an individual; phenomena are deliberately altered as in experimental treatment; contrasts with attribute variable.

Alternative explanations — Other explanations than what is hypothesized; explanations for the relationship between two variables other than that the independent variable caused the dependent variable; also called rival hypotheses and threats to internal validity.

Analog — A simulation of a real situation, for example, written case summaries as a stimulus for practitioners to record interventions.

Analysis of covariance (ANCOVA) — A statistical procedure that compares scores for the same individuals at two (or more) times while controlling for the initial set of scores.

Analysis of variance (ANOVA) — A statistical test for significance of the differences of means for three or more groups (one interval-level variable, one nominal level).

Anchored scales — Scales whose points are described by "anchors"—illustrations, descriptions, etc.; *see also* **Self-anchored scales.**

Antecedent variable — In time sequence, a variable which occurs prior to the independent variable.

A phase — In a single-system time series experiment, the phase during which data about the intervention target are collected many times over time, without intervention; if it occurs prior to intervention, it is also called the baseline.

Association — A condition in which two variables are related or "go together" in some systematic way, also called "covariation"; *see also* **Hypothesis of association.**

Attribute variable — A variable whose categories do not change for a given individual; measurement is imposed without altering the phenomenon; contrasts with active variable.

Autocorrelation — In time series designs, when a score at one time predicts or is correlated with a score at a later time; also called serial dependency.

Available data — An approach to collecting data that uses material already collected for other purposes; common sources include databases, published material, statistics gathered by agencies, mass media, and physical traces.

B phase — In a single-system time series experiment, the time period when intervention occurs while data about the intervention target are collected over time; also called the intervention phase.

Baseline — (1) In a single-system time series experiment, the phase prior to intervention when data about the intervention target are collected many times over time; also called the A phase. (2) Generally, data collected before a change in conditions.

Basic time series (AB) design — A single system time series design with one phase during which data on the target condition are collected without intervention (baseline or A phase); during the second phase, intervention occurs while data collection continues (intervention or B phase). Dimensions: field experiment, single system, explanatory, prospective, repeated occasions (time series), quantitative.

Before and after design or measure — Colloquial term for group design or measurement in which data on the dependent variable are collected once before intervention begins (prospective measurement) and again when intervention ends.

Beta weight, *see* ß (beta).

Bivariate analysis or statistics — Statistics that analyze the relation between two variables.

Central tendency — Univariate statistics that summarize the central or average characteristics of values for variables in a sample; includes the mean, median, and mode; contrasts with measures of dispersion or variability.

Chi-square (χ^2) — A statistical test for significance of the joint occurrence of two nominal variables (tests the association in a crosstabulation table).

Classical experimental design — A group experimental design with a pretest and posttest; subjects are randomly assigned to a control group (no intervention) or experimental group (which receives intervention). Design dimensions: substantially controlled experiment with random assignment to groups; prospective repeated data collection; multiple groups; explanatory function; quantitative.

Closed question, *see* **Fixed alternative question**.

Cluster sample — A sample selected in several stages: first, clusters — higher level units, usually geographically based — are sampled, then individual elements within the selected clusters. Cluster sampling yields a probability sample if all stages use probability sampling. For example, random sampling may be used to select (U.S.) states, then counties within the selected states, then individuals within the selected counties. May include many stages and different sampling procedures.

Coding — The process of placing data into categories; may also include assigning numerals to open-ended responses or using a coding format to record observations.

Comparative design — A group experimental design with at least two groups that receive different experimental interventions; if subjects are randomly assigned to the groups, is substantially controlled. Also called comparison or contrast group design. Design dimensions: multiple groups; explanatory function; quantitative.

Comparison group — In a group experiment that compares interventions, a group that receives one of the forms of intervention; also called contrast group.

Concept — Abstraction or symbol that represent similarities or common characteristics in phenomena; theory organizes concepts in systematic ways; also called a construct.

Conceptual definition, *see* **Nominal definition**.

Concurrent validity — A form of criterion validity: whether an instrument yields similar results as a valid measure that occurs at the same time; assessed by giving the new and the valid measure of the same concept to one group of people at the same time.

Constant comparison — In qualitative data analysis, an approach that stresses comparing new cases to previous material for the purpose of developing new insights and patterns; a key component of grounded theory.

Construct validity — In measurement, whether the measure gets at the underlying meaning or constructs in the concept; the degree to which a measure relates to other variables in ways hypothesized from theory. Assessment requires inference, theoretical prediction, hypothesis testing; common procedures include known-groups, convergent and discriminant validity, and factor analysis.

Content analysis — A method of systematically analyzing written or electronically recorded material by developing and applying categories.

Content validity or **face validity** — In measurement, representativeness or sampling adequacy of an instrument; includes: a) whether, on the surface or face of it, the instrument appears to measure what was intended; b) whether the entire range of meanings of the concept are included (sometimes called sampling validity). Assessed through judgment by experts.

Contingency table, *see* **Crosstabulation**.

Control group — In a group experiment, a group used to demonstrate what might happen under normal conditions; usually, a group which receives no intervention and serves as a contrast to the experimental group.

Convergent and discriminant validity — In measurement, an approach to construct validity which tests the hypothesis that a new measure is associated with other measures of the concept (i.e., the measures converge) and that the new measure is not associated with measures of different concepts (i.e., that it can be discriminated from other concepts).

Correlational design — A naturalistic design in which data are collected from a group of subjects at one point in time with no attempt to alter phenomena; also called cross-sectional or survey. Dimensions: group, naturalistic, single occasion.

Correlation coefficient, *see* **Pearson product-moment correlation coefficient** (r).

Covariation, *see* **Association**.

Criterion validity — In measurement, whether an instrument yields similar results as something known (or assumed) to be a valid measure of the concept (an outside criterion); includes concurrent validity where the criterion is simultaneous and predictive validity where the criterion occurs in the future.

Cross-sectional design, *see* **Correlational design**.

Crosstabulation — In statistics, a table showing the joint occurrence of cases on two variables; a cell contains the number of cases that fall into both category x on variable A and category y on variable B; also called contingency table and crossbreaks.

Curvilinear relationship — A relationship between variables that, if drawn on a graph, would be curved, for example, learning is low if anxiety is low or high, while learning is greatest when anxiety is moderate; contrast with linear.

Data analysis — The process of synthesizing raw observances to demonstrate patterns. Data analysis may be quantitative using, for example, descriptive and inferential statistics, or it may be qualitative, for example, the constant comparative method.

Deductive reasoning or logic — Reasoning from the abstract to the concrete, from theory to observable phenomena.

Degrees of freedom — In statistical significance testing, the number of values that can vary in a given formula, needed to interpret the probability of a given result; abbreviated *df*.

Dependent variable — In an explanatory chain, the variable thought to be caused or affected by another (independent) variable.

Descriptive design — A study whose purpose or function is to delineate the characteristics of phenomena and to show their relationship or association; contrasts with exploratory, measurement, and explanatory on the design dimension of purpose.

Descriptive statistics — Statistics that summarize the distribution of values on variables in a sample; includes measures of central tendency and measures of dispersion; contrasts with inferential statistics.

Design — The overall plan or strategy by which hypotheses or research questions are answered.

Directional hypothesis, *see* **One-tailed hypothesis.**

Discourse analysis — Analysis of verbal interchanges such as client-practitioner sessions.

Discriminant validity, *see* **Convergent and discriminant validity.**

Effect size — In meta-analysis, a measure of the relationship between an independent and dependent variable, based on the data from a single study but standardized so that many studies may be compared.

Empirical practice — Social work practice characterized by the use of: empirical referents (operational definitions for practice concepts), use of well-explicated practice models when available, research-based knowledge and technology, and research methods as part of practice (e.g., gathering data to test hypotheses, assessment instruments, evaluation).

Equivalence reliability — A form of reliability: the ability of two measures to give the same results; includes two forms (1) different investigators use the same instrument, and (2) different versions of the same instrument. Also called interjudge, intercoder, interrater, interobserver, etc., reliability.

Equivalent group designs — A class of group designs that uses random assignment to place subjects in groups and consequently has the possibility to control selection as an alternative explanation for results. Also called true experimental designs.

Ethnography — An approach to qualitative research where the investigator is immersed in a culture or setting; usually includes participant observation, interviews, and extensive note-taking focused on careful "thick description."

Experimental design — A class of research designs in which the researcher alters or manipulates the independent variable; contrasts with naturalistic design in the design dimension of investigator control over phenomena; is a strong design for establishing time priority.

Experimental group — In a group experiment, a group that receives the intervention of interest, usually compared to a control group that does not.

Explanatory design — A study whose purpose or function is to understand causes so one may make predictions; contrasts with exploratory, measurement, and descriptive on the design dimension of purpose.

Exploratory design — A study whose purpose or function is to seek preliminary understanding or to develop hypotheses, used when little is known about a topic; contrasts with measurement, descriptive and explanatory on the design dimension of purpose.

Ex post facto data collection (or measurement) — Data are collected for the first time "after the fact": one (or more) measurements are taken only after the occurrence of the independent variable; also called retrospective, contrasts with prospective data collection on the design dimension of timing of data collection.

External validity — Representativeness or generalizability: capacity of a research study to provide results that apply to other situations and people.

Extraneous variable — A variable that is not part of a hypothesis but which does or may affect the relationship among variables in the hypothesis; often unknown, may be referred to as an alternative explanation for results.

Face validity, *see* **Content validity.**

Factor analysis — A statistical technique that examines underlying commonalties and differences among items; often used for establishing construct validity of summated scales on questionnaires or similar measures.

Factorial design (or factorial experiment) — A group experimental design that compares different combinations of attributes or characteristics of interventions, with subjects randomly assigned to combinations. For example, a 2 x 3 x 2 factorial design might include two types of case management, three levels of intensity of intervention, and two types of service; clients would be randomly assigned to one of the 12 possible combinations. Design dimensions: multiple groups; explanatory function; quantitative.

Field experiment — A research experiment conducted in the normal environment for that activity, e.g., agency, home, street; contrasts with laboratory experiment.

Fixed alternative question or item — A question that has categories of responses from which the respondents choose; also called closed-ended question or multiple choice question; contrasts with open-ended question.

Focus group — A method to elicit information in which representatives of a selected population are brought together to discuss a topic in a semi-structured format; often used in program evaluation and needs assessment.

Follow-up - In research designs, a point of data collection after the posttest (in group designs) or after treatment has ended (in time series designs).

F-ratio — A statistical test for determining significance, used with several statistical approaches including analysis of variance and multiple regression.

Frequency distribution — In statistics, a tabulation of the number of times each value (category) of a variable occurs in a sample.

Generalization — Making inferences from the study to other people and situations. Includes (a) making inferences about a larger group from the people actually studied (making statements about the population from the sample) and from the study situation to other situations and (b) pragmatic generalization or feasibility and cost-effectiveness. Generalization to a population or situation may be done based on logic (for nonprobability sampling) or on the statistics of probability theory (for probability sampling). Also called external validity of a study.

Grounded theory — A method of conducting qualitative research developed by Glasser and Strauss (1967) that aims to build theory by identifying themes and patterns in the data; *see also* **Constant comparison; Theoretical sampling.**

Halo effect — On instruments with multi-item scales, the tendency of respondents to choose the same rating without differentiating responses.

Heterogeneous group — A sample that includes individuals who differ from each other on the main variables of interest; contrasts with homogeneous on the design dimension of composition of sample.

History — A threat to internal validity or alternative explanation: specific environmental events which may influence phenomena and be mistaken as the cause of the dependent variable, for example, a father returns home at the same time child starts treatment.

Homogeneity — A form of reliability for questionnaires with many items that are intended to measure a single concept: the ability of each item in the scale to give similar results as other items. Also called internal consistency or inter-item consistency; common methods of testing are split-half reliability and Chronbach's alpha.

Homogeneous group — A sample that includes individuals who are the same on the main variables of interest; contrasts with heterogeneous on the design dimension of composition of sample.

Hypothesis — A statement of the relation between two or more variables/concepts; a conjecture about reality.

Hypothesis of association — A hypothesis that predicts two variables are associated or vary together in a systematic way.

Hypothesis of difference — A hypothesis that predicts that two or more groups differ in a systematic way.

Hypothesis testing — The process of testing propositions derived from theory against reality; characteristic of the scientific approach to knowledge.

Independent variable — In an explanatory chain, the variable thought to cause or influence another, dependent, variable.

Inductive reasoning or logic — Reasoning from the specific to the abstract, from observable phenomena to theory.

Inferential statistics — Statistics used to make inferences from sample data to the population, used (1) to assess probability that sample descriptive statistics accurately represent the true population data, and (2) to estimate the probability that bivariate and multivariate associations are true associations and not due to chance.

Instability — Chance variation or random fluctuation in a measure: can act as a threat to internal validity or as source of uncertainty in generalizing from a sample to population.

Instrument — Any device used to measure or collect data on a variable, e.g., questionnaire, test, coding format, observation format; also called a measure.

Instrumentation — A threat to internal validity or alternative explanation: systematic biases introduced by the measuring instruments, "decay" in instruments, or changes in the measurement procedures that might explain the results rather than the presumed cause.

Interaction effects - In multivariate data analysis, when two variables combined have a different effect on the dependent variable than each variable separately, for example, the second variable may have an effect only under certain categories of the first variable; *see also* **Moderator variable**.

Internal consistency, *see* **Homogeneity**.

Internal validity — The capacity of a research design to isolate the effects of the independent variable by controlling for extraneous variables or alternative explanations.

Interval level (scale) of measurement — Measurement in which the categories of a variable have equal intervals or distances between categories; for example, the distance between 10 and 15 is the same as between 41 and 46.

Intervening variable — In time sequence, a variable which occurs between the independent and dependent variables.

Intervention phase — In a single-system time series experiment, the time period when intervention occurs while data about the intervention target are collected over time; also called the B phase.

Inverse relationship, *see* **Negative association**.

Judgmental sample, *see* **Purposive sample**.

Key informant method — A method of data collection in which individuals are selected for interviews or focus groups on the basis of the knowledge of the topic under study.

Known-groups — In measurement, an approach to construct validity that tests the hypothesis that a new measure will discriminate between groups known to be different on similar concepts, for example, does a research test distinguish between experts and neophytes?

Laboratory experiment — A research experiment conducted in an artificial setting such as a psychology laboratory; contrasts with field experiment.

Level of significance — In statistical testing, the probability set by the investigator for a Type I error, the risk of rejecting the null hypothesis when it is true (and accepting the research hypothesis when it is not true); colloquially, the probability that a result is produced by chance, or the risk of being wrong when asserting that a result is statistically significant.

Levels (or scales) of measurement — The extent to which categories of a variable take on properties of the number system; the levels, in hierarchical order, are nominal, ordinal, interval, and ratio.

Likert scale — A questionnaire format developed by Rensis Likert in which a statement is followed by ordinal closed-ended responses with equal-appearing intervals, for example, "strongly agree," "agree," "disagree," and "strongly disagree;" normally, a large pool of items is generated, the most relevant are selected based on testing, and the relevant items are summed in a summated scale.

Linear relationship — A relationship between variables that, if drawn on a graph, is a straight line; e.g., as one variable gets higher, the other changes at a constant rate; contrasts with curvilinear and interactive.

Matching with random assignment — In assigning subjects to groups after they have been included in a study, subjects are matched on key characteristics and then randomly assigned to groups.

Maturation — A threat to internal validity or alternative explanation that includes the normal effects due to the passage of time, for example, reduction in grief over time, or normal maturation processes among adolescents.

Mean — A measure of central tendency for interval (or higher)-level frequency distributions: the arithmetic average (sum of all values divided by the number of values); symbolized as $\bar{x}$.

Measure — (1) Any device used to measure or collect data on a variable, e.g., questionnaire, test, coding format, observation format, also called an instrument; (2) The act or process of collecting data or assigning characteristics to categories; (3) Generally, a statistic that is the result of measurement and data analysis, for example, a measure of association.

Measurement — (1) An operational definition: what and how the indicators of a variable are measured in a study, the link between a concept and raw data, as in "we measured aggression by . . ."; (2) the assignment of numerals to characteristics or categories of variables, with the meaning of the numeral designated as level of measurement; (3) the result of data collection, a score or result; also called a measure.

Measurement design — A study whose purpose or function is to develop or test a measurement instrument, for example, to establish reliability or validity; contrasts with exploratory, descriptive, and explanatory on the design dimension of purpose.

Median — A measure of central tendency for ordinal (or higher)-level frequency distributions: the mid-point of a distribution, at which half the scores fall higher and half lower.

Mediator variable — A third variable that accounts in full or in part for the relationship between the independent and dependent variables; also called mediating variable.

Meta-analysis — A statistical method of synthesizing data from many studies: effect sizes are developed by standardizing data from the individual studies; may include analysis of investigator-developed variables such as the quality of the study or type of intervention or problem.

Mode — A measure of central tendency for nominal (or higher)-level frequency distributions: the value that occurs with greatest frequency.

Moderator variable — A third variable that affects the relationship between the independent and dependent variables so that the relationship is different for different values of the third variable, that is, it specifies the conditions under which a relationship holds; also called modifier or specifier variable.

Mortality — A threat to internal validity or an explanation in group designs: when groups are compared over time, effects due to different rates or types of dropouts. For example, less disturbed clients may drop out of one treatment and but not another.

Multiple analysis of variance (MANOVA) — A statistical test for significance of the differences of several means taken from the same subjects (several interval-level dependent variables, one (or more) nominal level variables).

Multiple baseline design — A single system time series design that repeats the same design (usually an AB design) for three or more targets, with intervention lagged so the second target continues its baseline while intervention begins on the first, and so on. Systems and targets may be one system with three problems, one system with one problem in three circumstances, or three systems with similar problems. Dimensions: experiment, explanatory, prospective, repeated occasions (time series), quantitative.

Multiple intervention effects — A form of nonspecific effects (a threat to internal validity) in which a combination of factors cause an effect, rather than the independent variable alone; for example, therapeutic improvement may be due to homework assignments combined with a supportive environment, not homework by itself.

Multiple regression — A statistical approach that examines the effects of many independent variables on an interval-level dependent variable while simultaneously controlling for the effects of all independent variables.

Multistage probability sample, *see* **Cluster sample.**

Multivariate analysis or statistics — Statistics that analyze the relations among three or more variables.

Narrative — An approach to qualitative research where subjects are asked to develop a narrative or tell a story, usually about some aspect of their lives; the narratives are typically analyzed for content, presentation, and how subjects construe meaning.

Naturalistic design — A research study in which phenomena are studied "as they lie" with no attempt at alteration; contrasts with experimental design as part of the dimension of investigator control over phenomena.

Needs assessment — A naturalistic study carried out for the purpose of identifying and assessing potential targets for intervention, for example, to assess the feasibility of a new service, or to determine the needs of the elderly.

Negative association — In bivariate statistics, a relationship between two ordinal or higher-level variables in which higher values of one variable are associated with lower levels of the other; often symbolized with a minus sign (-). Also called inverse relationship.

Nominal definition — A definition of a concept using abstract terms or other concepts; also called conceptual or theoretical definition; contrasts with operational definition.

Nominal group technique — A structured format for eliciting and ranking ideas in small groups, often used in program evaluation and needs assessment.

Nominal level (scale) of measurement — Measurement in which the categories of a variable are based on qualities or differences (only); numerals may be used to designate categories but have no arithmetic meaning. Categories must be: unidimensional (measures one thing, or on same conceptual level), mutually exclusive (an individual fits into one category only), and exhaustive (each individual can fit into a category).

Nondirectional hypothesis, *see* **Two-tailed hypothesis.**

Nonequivalent group designs — A class of group designs that does not use random assignment to place subjects in groups and consequently has limited ability to rule out alternative explanations for results. Also called quasi-experimental designs.

Nonequivalent treatment and control group design — A group experimental design with an experimental group (which receives intervention) and a control group (no intervention) and subjects are assigned to groups without random assignment. Design dimensions: uncontrolled experiment; multiple groups; explanatory function; quantitative.

Nonprobability samples — A class of samples in which the chance of selecting a given individual is unknown; contrasts with probability samples.

Nonspecific effects — A threat to internal validity or alternative explanation: in experiments, nonspecific elements which go along with treatment but are not intended as part of it, for example, people feeling better only because someone paid attention to them. Also multiple intervention effects when something unintended is part of or goes along with treatment, such as one treatment conducted in a cheerful room, a contrasting treatment in a shabby room. Also called placebo effects or excluded intervention elements.

Normal curve — In statistics, a symmetrical, bell-shaped distribution in which the mean, median, and mode coincide with the center and a standard proportion of observations lies between the mean and a given standard deviation; for example, 68.26 percent of all observations lie between +1 and -1 standard deviations, 95.46 percent between ±2 standard deviations, and 99.73 percent between +3 and -3 standard deviations. Also called normal distribution.

Null hypothesis — In testing for statistical significance, the hypothesis actually tested, which states that there is no association or no difference or that the sample mean is identical to the population mean; colloquially, the "opposite" of the research hypothesis. If the null hypothesis is accepted, the logical conclusion is that sample results occurred by chance.

One-tailed hypothesis — A hypothesis that predicts the direction of association or difference, for example, "Group A will score higher than Group B." Also called directional hypothesis, contrasts with nondirectional or two-tailed hypothesis.

One-tailed test of significance — A procedure in significance testing when only one possible end (tail) of a probability distribution is considered, used when the direction of a difference was hypothesized (directional hypothesis).

Open-ended question — A question that allows respondents to answer in any way they wish; no choices of answers are offered; contrasts with fixed-alternative question.

Operational definition — The specific definition of how a variable will be measured in a particular study, including what will be measured (the content) and how it will be measured (data collection and measurement procedures).

Ordinal level (scale) of measurement — Measurement in which the categories of a variable can be rank ordered; for example, "more (or less) of a quality;" numerals used to designate categories indicate rank order, for example, 1 is greater than 2, 2 is greater than 3, and 1 is greater than 3.

Panel design — A group research design in which data are collected from the same group of participants on repeated occasions over time with no attempt to alter phenomena; contrasts with trend design where participants are replaced at each data collection point.

Parameter — Any numerical summary measure based on data from a population; contrasts with a statistic, which is based on data from a sample: for example s represents the standard deviation of a sample, while σ (sigma) represents the standard deviation of the population.

Partial crossover design — A group experimental design with subjects randomly assigned to experimental and control group. After the posttest is completed, the control group receives the experimental intervention (the "crossover") and a second posttest is conducted on the control (now experimental) group. Design dimensions: substantially controlled experiment with random assignment to groups; prospective repeated data collection; multiple groups; explanatory function; quantitative.

Participant observation — A data collection method in which the investigator becomes immersed in the activities of those observed, as a participant; common in qualitative research.

Pearson product-moment correlation coefficient (r) — A bivariate statistic indicating the strength and direction of linear association between two interval-level variables; runs from -1.0 (perfect negative association) through 0.0 (no association) to +1.0 (perfect positive association). The square of r (r^2) is the amount of variance in one variable accounted for by the other.

Pilot study (or test) — A preliminary trial with subjects who will not be in the planned study, used to test new instruments, data collection procedures, or intervention plans.

Placebo effects, *see* **Nonspecific effects**.

Placebo group — In a group experiment, a form of control group that receives an alternative intervention that includes nonspecific effects, for example, a discussion or support group that does not include the experimental intervention. Allows an estimation of the effects of the experimental intervention beyond the nonspecific effects.

Population — The larger group to which one wants to generalize; the universe of people or things that meet the specifications of interest for a study.

Population parameter, *see* **Parameter**.

Positive association — In bivariate statistics, a relationship between two ordinal or higher-level variables in which higher values of one variable are associated with higher levels of the other; often symbolized with a plus sign (+).

Posttest — In group experimental designs, the first data collection point after the end of the intervention; the "after" in a before-and-after design.

Power analysis, *see* **Statistical power analysis**.

Predictive validity — In measurement, a form of criterion validity: whether a measure yields similar results as another measure of the concept that occurs in the future, for example, whether a risk-detection instrument accurately predicts child-neglect.

Pretest — (1) In group experimental designs, a data collection that occurs before intervention begins and thus makes the design prospective; the "before" in a before-and-after design. (2) A trial before the planned study, to assess the feasibility of instruments, data collection procedures, or interventions; also called pilot study.

Probability sample — A class of samples that permit specifying the chance or probability that each individual will be selected for the sample.

Prospective data collection (or measurement) — Data are collected at least once before the occurrence of the independent variable; contrasts with retrospective or ex post facto on the design dimension of timing of data collection.

Purposive or judgmental sample — A nonprobability sample in which individual sampling elements are hand-picked to be typical of some characteristic, e.g., "best outcome," "typical case," or "known expert" (key informant).

Qualitative design (or research) — A research study characterized by the investigator as "insider"; a flexible research question which is refined as study continues; data collection methods that vary to suit the needs of the moment; data analysis begun while data is collected; data analysis which uses logic; and a philosophical assumption that subjective, holistic experience is valid knowledge. Contrasts with quantitative design on the dimension of methodological orientation.

Quantitative design (or research) — A research study characterized by the investigator as "outsider"; specific hypotheses or questions that remain constant throughout the study; data collection planned in advance, applied in a standard manner, and analyzed later; data analysis using statistical techniques; and a philosophical assumption that knowledge requires objective standards to control biases. Contrasts with qualitative design on dimension of methodological orientation.

Quasi-experimental design, *see* **Nonequivalent group design.**

Quota sample — A nonprobability sample that first categorizes elements on key characteristics, then uses accidental sampling methods to select elements until a specified number (quota) is reached in each category.

r, see **Pearson product-moment correlation coefficient** (*r*).

Random assignment — Use of probability (chance) methods to assign subjects to groups that are to be compared after the participants have been included in the study: each individual has an equal probability of being in a given group and every possible combination of people has an equal probability of being in a given group; increases the likelihood that characteristics that might influence the dependent variable are equally distributed among the groups.

Random sample — A probability sample selected so that each individual and all possible combinations of individuals in the sampling frame has an equal probability of being included in the study. Also called simple random sample.

Range — A measure of variability for ordinal (or higher)-level frequency distributions: the difference between the highest and lowest score recorded in the sample.

Ratio level (scale) of measurement — Measurement in which the categories of a variable are equal distances apart and there is a natural origin or absolute zero (there cannot be any "minus" of the quality).

Reactive effects or reactivity — A threat to internal validity or alternative explanation: in experiments, effects due to an interaction of being measured (testing) and receiving the intervention, for example, treatment is effective only because the client's anxiety was reduced by pretest interviews; more generally, any change resulting from use of measurement procedure.

Regression, *see* **Multiple regression; Statistical regression.**

Rejection region — In statistical testing, the values of a statistical test's sampling distribution at which the null hypothesis will be rejected as improbable; the size of the rejection region depends on the level of significance, for example, if the significance level is .05, the 5% of values that are least likely to occur will be in the rejection region.

Reliability — Consistency of a measurement instrument, or getting the same results at different times or under different conditions; includes stability, equivalence, and homogeneity reliability.

Replication — A repetition of a study to ensure that the results were not due to error.

Representativeness — How accurately the sample represents the entire population (all people with the designated characteristics). Probability samples are normally more representative than nonprobability samples.

Research design, *see* **Design.**

Research hypothesis — In testing for statistical significance, the hypothesis that there is an association, or difference; the hypothesis that is accepted when the null hypothesis is rejected; normally, the same as the hypothesis that a study seeks to test.

Research question — Guiding question about the relationship among variables/concepts, used when not enough is known to formulate hypotheses.

Retrospective data collection (or measurement), *see* **Ex post facto data collection.**

Rival hypothesis, *see* **Alternative explanations.**

Sample — People or things actually studied; the sample is made up of sampling elements selected from the sampling frame.

Sampling — The process of picking people or things to be studied.

Sampling distribution — In statistics, the pattern of results that would occur if an infinite number of random samples were taken from a population; a common sampling distribution is the normal or bell-shaped curve.

Sampling element (or unit) — A single member of the population.

Sampling error — The extent to which values in the sample differ from those in the population; the difference between a sample statistic and the population parameter (usually, the true but unknown value).

Sampling frame — The group of people or things from which the sample is drawn, usually a subset of the population.

Scattergram (or scatterplot) — A graph showing the joint occurrence of values of two ordinal-level variables for each case.

Scientific approach to knowledge — Approach to understanding characterized by reason (systematic logic) and by empiricism (observation of the real world); contrasts to experience, intuition, and authority as ways of understanding phenomena.

Selection — A threat to internal validity or alternative explanation: in group designs, unintended systematic differences or biases between groups, differences that affect the dependent variable; for example, the experimental group may have more motivated clients.

Self-anchored scales — Points of the scale are defined or anchored by the client or respondent. For example in a self-anchored scale for depression, the respondent might define "1" as "I feel great"; a "3" might mean "I feel so-so"; and a "5" might mean "I feel so rotten I can't get out of bed."

Self-report methods — An approach to collecting data that relies on respondents' reports of their behavior, attitudes, or traits; includes written questionnaires, in-person interviews, and telephone interviews.

Simple random sample, *see* **Random sample.**

Single-system design — A class of research designs that study a single unit such as an individual, family, group, or community; if the unit is of a higher level, the data are treated as coming from a single unit. Also called single-case, n=1, and idiographic design.

Slope — On a graph or chart, the rate at which a line rises or falls when covering a given horizontal distance; if it slopes upward (as one variable is greater, the other is greater), it is referred to as positive, if downward, it is negative.

Snowball sample — A nonprobability sample that selects individuals by requesting participants to nominate other individuals; useful when it is difficult to locate a sample or when studying networking.

Social desirability — The tendency of participants to give answers or behave in a way they believe that the investigator wants, that is expected of them, or that puts them in a desirable light, rather than their true beliefs or behaviors.

Social indicator analysis — An approach to needs assessment that uses existing statistics on social problems as indicators of social conditions and needs.

Solomon Four Groups Design — A group experimental design developed by Solomon (1949) with subjects randomly assigned to four groups: an experimental group that receives both a pretest and posttest, an experimental group that receives only a posttest, a control group that receives both a pretest and a posttest, and a control group that receives only a posttest; permits assessment of reactivity and testing as well as differences between control and experimental groups. Design dimensions: controlled experiment with random assignment to groups; prospective repeated data collection; multiple groups; explanatory function; quantitative.

Split-half reliability — A form of homogeneity reliability for summated scales that is calculated by comparing respondents answers to half the items with their answers to the other half.

Spurious variable — A variable whose relationship to another variable is shown to be false, or due to some other factor.

Stability or test-retest reliability — In measurement, whether a measuring instrument gives the same results at different times. Assessed by applying the same measurement instrument to the same stimulus at different times, e.g., one group of people takes the same self-esteem questionnaire three weeks apart.

Standard deviation (sd) — A measure of variability for interval-level frequency distributions: amount of spread around the mean, calculated as the positive square root of the variance; can be used to compare samples and in inferential statistics to infer probability of a result.

Standard error — In inferential statistics, the standard deviation of a sampling distribution.

Statistic — Any numerical summary measure based on data from a sample; contrasts with a parameter which is based on data from a population; for example, $\bar{x}$ represents the mean of a sample while μ (mu) represents the mean of the population.

Statistical power analysis — A method of determining the smallest sample size necessary to demonstrate that associations are not due to chance, i.e., are statistically significant.

Statistical regression — A threat to internal validity or alternative explanation: the tendency of extreme scores to move toward the middle at subsequent measurements.

Statistical significance — A relation between two or more variables that is unlikely to be due to chance; calculated by plugging the sample data into a formula, calculating the probability of the result, and comparing that probability to a criterion level set earlier. For example, if the criterion is .05 (due to chance 5 of 100 times) and the sample results could occur 5/100 times or fewer, the results are said to be statistically significant.

Stratified random sample — A probability sample in which the elements of the sampling frame are divided into categories based on key characteristics, then a simple random sample is taken from each category.

Summated rating scale — A series of questions tapping a single concept whose responses are on the same ordinal scale (for example, 1 = most positive, 5 = most negative); the responses are summed to yield a single score.

Survey design, *see* **Correlational design.**

Systematic sample — A sample selected by taking every nth case (e.g., every 10th or 56th case). If the first case is selected at random, may be considered a probability sample.

Testing — A threat to internal validity or alternative explanation: effects due to the subjects' reaction to being tested (measured) that might be cause for a change rather than the presumed cause, the effect one data collection might have on results of subsequent data collections; for example, a questionnaire motivates someone to study the subject matter.

Test-retest reliability, *see* **Stability reliability.**

Test statistic — In testing for statistical significance, the formula used to determine the probability that the sample result occurred by chance; common test statistics include chi-square, t-test, and F-test.

Theory — A coherent system of ideas or concepts that organizes knowledge to help understand reality.

Theoretical sampling — A sampling plan used in some qualitative research, where cases are selected on the basis of their ability to contribute to theory development by disproving or elaborating the theory; a component of grounded theory.

Threat to internal validity — Alternative explanation for results; explanations for the relation between two variables other than that the independent variable caused the dependent variable; some threats may be ruled out or prevented by the design of a study; also called source of extraneous variation, alternative explanation, or rival hypothesis.

Time priority — Establishing that one variable occurred before the other. A necessary (but not sufficient) condition for establishing causality, preferably demonstrated through prospective data collection and experimental design.

Time series design — A class of single system research designs in which data on the same variable are collected at many points over time.

Trend — (1) A group research design in which data are collected on repeated occasions with no attempt to alter phenomena but from a new group of participants each time; contrasts with panel design that uses same group of people. (2) In time series designs, a pattern of successive measurements that increases or decreases; having a recognizable slope. (3) A finding that falls just short of being statistically significant.

t-test — A statistical test for significance of the difference between two means (one interval-level variable, one nominal level).

Two-tailed hypothesis — An hypothesis that predicts only an association or difference, without specifying the direction, for example, "A and B will vary together." Also called nondirectional hypothesis, contrasts with directional or one-tailed hypothesis.

Two-tailed test of significance — A procedure in significance testing when both ends (tails) of a probability distribution are considered, used when the hypothesis predicted a difference but not the direction of the difference (nondirectional hypothesis).

Type I error — In significance testing, the probability of rejecting the null hypothesis when it is in fact true, also called α (alpha) or the significance level; a false negative.

Type II error — In significance testing, the probability of accepting the null hypothesis when it is in fact false, also called ß (beta); a false positive.

Undifferentiated data collection (or measurement) — When all data are collected at one time and one cannot distinguish the independent and dependent variables based on time priority; contrasts with retrospective and prospective data collection on the design dimension of timing of data collection.

Univariate analysis or statistics — Statistics used to describe and summarize one variable at a time; includes frequencies, measures of central tendency, and measures of variability; contrasts with multivariate statistics.

Validity — Whether a measurement instrument captures what was intended, the "true nature" of the concept or the quality; includes content, criterion and construct validity.

Variability — Variation in measurements: (1) in time series designs, the fluctuation of repeated measures over time; (2) in univariate statistics, the amount of spread or dispersion around a measure of central tendency; includes the range, variance, and standard deviation; contrasts with measures of central tendency; also called dispersion.

Variable — A concept or part of a concept that is actually studied. A variable must include two or more values (e.g., presence and absence of treatment).

Variance — A measure of variability for interval (or higher)-level frequency distributions: the amount of spread around the mean, calculated as the sum of the squared deviations (distance) from the mean, divided by the number of measurements.

Withdrawal-reversal design (ABAB) — A single-system time series design with four phases: a baseline phase with no intervention (A), an intervention phase (B or intervention phase), a phase during which intervention is withdrawn (stopped) or reversed (pre-existing conditions reinstated) (A), and a second intervention phase (B). Data on the target condition are collected at multiple intervals throughout all phases. Design dimensions: experiment, single-system, explanatory, prospective, repeated occasions (time series), quantitative.

Working statement of the problem — A statement of the research problem that includes enough detail to guide the research study; usually includes concepts, variables, their operational definitions, and hypotheses.

References

Abidin, Richard R. 1990. *Parenting Stress Index Short Form.* Charlottesville, Va.: Pediatric Psychology Press.

Abramson, Julie S. 1988. Participation of elderly patients in discharge planning: Is self-determination a reality? *Social Work* 33 (5): 443–448.

Aby, Stephen H. 1997. *Sociology: A Guide to Reference and Information Sources.* 2d ed. Englewood, Colo.: Libraries Unlimited.

Acierno, Ron and Cynthia G. Last. 1995. Outpatient treatment of obsessive compulsive disorder by self-directed graded exposure and response prevention. *Psychotherapy in Private Practice* 14 (3): 1–11.

Akin, Becci A. and Thomas K. Gregoire. 1997. Parents' views on child welfare's response to addiction. *Families in Society* 78 (4): 393–404.

Albaek, Erik. 1995. Between knowledge and power: Utilization of social science in public policy making. *Policy-Sciences* 28 (1): 79–100.

Allen-Meares, Paula. 1984. Content analysis: It does have a place in social work research. *Journal of Social Service Research* 7: 51–68.

Allen-Meares, Paula and E. Roberts. 1994. Associations of social integration variables with prenatal care use by adolescents and young adults. *Journal of Social Service Research* 19 (3/4): 23–47.

American Psychological Association. 1994a. Guidelines to reduce bias in language. In *Publication Manual of the American Psychological Association.* Washington D.C.: APA.

American Psychological Association. 1994b. Publication Manual of the American Psychological Association. 4th ed. Washington D.C.: APA.

Ammerman, R. T. and M. Hersen, eds. 1995. *Handbook of Child Behavior Therapy.* New York: Wiley.

Anderson, Carol M., Douglas J. Reiss, and Gerard E. Hogarty. 1986. *Schizophrenia and the Family: A Practitioner's Guide to Psychoeducation and Management.* New York: Guilford Press.

Argyris, Chris and Donald A. Schon. 1974. *Theory in Practice: Increasing Professional Effectiveness.* San Francisco: Jossey-Bass.

Arndorfer, Richard E., Raymond G. Miltenberger, Scott H. Woster, Angela K. Rorvedt, et al. 1994. Home-based descriptive and experimental analysis of problem behaviors in children. *Topics in Early Childhood Education* 14 (1): 64–87.

Atkinson, Paul and Martyn Hammersley. 1994. Ethnography and participant observation. In *Handbook of Qualitative Research,* edited by N. K. Denzin and Y. S. Lincoln, q.v.

Attkisson, C. Clifford et al., eds. 1978. *Evaluation of Human Service Programs.* New York: Academic Press.

Auerbach, Arthur H. 1983. Assessment of psychotherapy outcome from the viewpoint of expert observer. In *The Assessment of Psychotherapy Outcome*, edited by M. J. Lambert, E. R. Christensen, and S. S. DeJulio, q.v.

Aylward, A. Michele, Patrick J. Schloss, Sandra Alper, and Charles Green. 1995. Improving direct-care staff consistency in a residential treatment program through the use of self-recording and feedback. *International Journal of Disability, Development, and Education* 43 (1): 43–53.

Bailey-Dempsey, Cynthia and William J. Reid. 1996. Intervention design and development: A case study. *Research on Social Work Practice* 6 (2): 208–228.

Bakan, David. 1967. *On Method: Toward a Reconstruction of Psychological Investigation*. San Francisco: Jossey-Bass.

Bales, Robert F. 1976. *Interaction Process Analysis: A Method for the Study of Small Groups*. Chicago: University of Chicago Press.

Banach, M. 1995. In whose best interest? Decision-making in child welfare. DSW dissertation, Columbia University, New York.

Barlow, David and Michael Hersen. 1984. *Single-Case Designs: Strategies for Study of Behavioral Change*. 2d ed. New York: Pergamon Press.

Basso, Robert. 1985. Teacher and student problem solving activities in educational supervisory sessions. *Journal of Social Work Education* 23: 67–73.

Bateson, Gregory. 1958. *Naven*. Stanford, Conn.: Standford University Press.

Battle, C. C., Stanley D. Imber, Rudolph Hoehn-Saric, Anthony R. Stone, Earle H. Nash, and Jerome D. Frank. 1966. Target complaints as criteria of improvement. *American Journal of Psychotherapy* 20: 184–192.

Baumann, Urs. 1995. Assessment and documentation of psychopathology: Nosology and research methods in psychiatry. *Psychopathology* 28 (Supplement 1): 13–20.

Baxter, Pam. 1993. *Psychology: A Guide to Reference and Information Sources*. Englewood, Colo.: Libraries Unlimited.

Bearbien, Anne K., Sharon A. Hogan, and Mary W. George. 1982. *Learning in the Library: Concepts and Methods for Effective Bibliographic Instruction*. New York: Bowker.

Becerra, Rosina M. and Ruth E. Zambrana. 1985. Methodological approaches to research on Hispanics. *Social Work Research and Abstracts* 21 (2): 42–49.

Beck, Aaron. 1967. *The Beck Depression Inventory*. San Antonio: Psychological Corporation.

Beebe, Linda, ed. 1993. *Professional Writing for the Human Services*. Washington D.C.: NASW Press.

Belcher, John R. 1994. Understanding the process of social drift among the homeless: A qualitative analysis. In *Qualitative Research in Social Work*, edited by E. Sherman and W. J. Reid. New York: Columbia University Press.

Belcher, John R., Alwida Scholler-Jaquish, and Mike Drummond. 1991. Three stages of homelessness: A conceptual model of social workers in health care. *Health and Social Work* 16 (2): 87–93.

Bell, Roger A., Martin Sundel, Joseph F. Aponte, Stanley A. Murrel, and Elizabeth Lin, eds. 1983. *Assessing Health and Human Service Needs*. New York: Human Sciences Press.

Benbenishty, Rami. 1997. Outcomes in the context of empirical practice. In *Outcomes Measurement in the Human Services*, edited by E. J. Mullen and J. L. Magnabosco, q.v.

Berger, Michael. 1983. Toward maximizing the utility of consumer satisfaction as an outcome. In *The Assessment of Psychotherapy Outcome*, edited by M. J. Lambert, E. R. Christensen, and S. S. DeJulio, q.v.

Berleman, William C. and Thomas W. Steinbrun. 1967. The execution and evaluation of a delinquency prevention program. *Social Problems* 14 (Spring): 413–423.

Berlin, S. B., K. B. Mann, and S. F. Grossman. 1991. Task analysis of cognitive therapy for depression. *Social Work Research and Abstracts* 27: 3–11.

Besa, David. 1994. Evaluating narrative family therapy using single-system research designs. *Research on Social Work Practice* 4 (3): 309–325.

Beutler, Larry E. and Marjorie Crago. 1983. Self-report measures of psychotherapy outcome. In *The Assessment of Psychotherapy Outcome*, edited by M. J. Lambert, E. R. Christensen, and S. S. DeJulio, q.v.

Beyer, J. M. and H. M. Trice. 1982. The utilization process: A conceptual framework and synthesis of empirical findings. *Administrative Science Quarterly* 27: 591–622.

Biggerstaff, Marilyn. 1994. Evaluating the reliability of oral examinations for licensure of clinical social workers in Virginia. *Research on Social Work Practice* 4 (4): 481–496.

Bishop, George F., Hans-Juergen Hippler, Norbert Schwarz, and Fritz Strack. 1988. A comparison of response effects in self-administered and telephone surveys. In *Telephone Survey Methodology*, edited by R. M. Groves et al., q.v.

Black, James A. and Dean J. Champion. 1976. *Methods and Issues in Social Research*. New York: Wiley.

Blalock, Hubert. M. Jr. 1979. *Social Statistics*. 2d ed. New York: McGraw-Hill.

Bloom, Martin. 1975. *The Paradox of Helping: Introduction to the Philosophy of Scientific Practice*. New York: Wiley.

Bloom, Martin, Joel Fischer, and John G. Orme. 1995. *Evaluating Practice: Guidelines for the Accountable Professional*. 2d ed. Boston: Allyn and Bacon.

Bloom, Martin and Waldo C. Klein. 1995. Publications and citations: A study of faculty at leading schools of social work. *Journal of Social Work Education* 31 (3): 377–387.

Blythe, Betty and Andre Ivanoff, eds. In press. *Integrating Practice and Research in Human Services: Progress, Innovations and Methods*. New York: de Gruyter, Aldine.

Blythe, Betty J. and Antoinette Y. Rodgers. 1993. Evaluating our own practice: Past, present, and future trends. *Journal of Social Service Research* 18 (1/2): 101–119.

Borgatta, Edgar F. and George W. Bohrnstedt. 1980. Level of measurement: Once over again. *Sociological Methods and Research* 9 (2): 147–160.

Bosk, Charles. 1989. The fieldworker and the surgeon. In *In the Field: Readings on the Field Research Experience*, edited by C. D. Smith and W. Kornblum. New York: Praeger.

Bowen, Gary L. 1994. Estimating the reduction in nonresponse bias from using a mail survey as a backup for nonrespondents to a telephone survey. *Research on Social Work Practice* 4 (1): 115–128.

Bradshaw, William. 1996. Structured group work for individuals with schizophrenia: A coping skills approach. *Research on Social Work Practice* 6 (2): 139–154.

Brannen, Stephen J. and Allen Rubin. 1996. Comparing the effectiveness of gender-specific and couples groups in a court-mandated spouse abuse treatment program. *Research on Social Work Practice* 6 (4): 405–424.

Briar, Scott. 1974. What do social workers do? *Social Work* 19: 386.

Briggs, Harold, Daniel Tovar, and Kevin Corcoran. 1996. The Children's Action Tendency Scale: Is it reliable and valid with Latino youngsters? *Research on Social Work Practice* 6 (2): 229–235.

Brothers, Kevin J., Patricia J. Krantz, and Lynn E. McClannahan. 1994. Office paper recycling: A function of container proximity. *Journal of Applied Behavior Analysis* 27 (1): 153–160.

Buchanan, David, Edna Apostol, Dalila Balfour, and Carmen Claudio et al. 1994. The CEPA project: A new model for community-based program planning. *International Quarterly of Community Health Education* 14 (4): 361–377.

Burnette, Denise. 1994. Managing chronic illness alone in late life: Sisyphus at work. In *Qualitative Studies in Social Work Research*, edited by C. K. Riessman, q.v.

Bush, Irene R., Irwin Epstein, and Anthony Sainz. 1997. The use of social science sources in social work practice journals: An application of citation analysis. *Social Work Research* 21 (1): 45–55.

Butterfield, William H. 1993. Graphics. In *Professional Writing for the Human Services*, edited by L. Beebe, q.v.

Caldwell, B. M. and R. H. Bradley, 1984. *Home Observation for Measurement of the Environment*. Little Rock: University of Arkansas.

Campbell, Donald T. and J. C. Stanley. 1963. *Experimental and Quasi-Experimental Designs for Research and Teaching*. Chicago: Rand McNally.

Caputo, Richard K. 1998. Economic well-being in a youth cohort. *Families in Society* 79 (1): 83–92

Caspi, Jonathan and William J. Reid. 1996. The task-centered model for field instruction: An innovative approach. Paper read at Annual Program Meeting, Council on Social Work Education, February 11, 1996, Washington D.C.

Chapin, F. Stuart. 1955. *Experimental Designs in Sociological Research*. Rev. ed. Cambridge: Harvard University Press.

Chestang, Leon W. 1977. Achievement and self-esteem among black Americans: A study of twenty lives. Ph.D. dissertation, University of Chicago.

Chou, Y. C. 1992. Developing and testing an intervention program for assisting Chinese families in Taiwan who have a member with developmental disabilities. Ph.D. dissertation, University of Minnesota.

Chow, Julian and Claudia Coulton. 1998. Was there a social transformation of urban neighborhoods in the 1980s? A decade of worsening social conditions in Cleveland, Ohio, USA. *Urban Studies* 35 (8): 1359–1375.

Ciminero, Anthony R., Karen S. Calhoun, and Henry E. Adams, eds. 1986. *Handbook of Behavioral Assessment*. 2d ed. New York: Wiley.

Clarke, Katherine M. 1996. Change processes in a creation of meaning event. *Journal of Consulting and Clinical Psychology* 64 (3): 465–470.

Cocozzelli, Carmelo. 1987. A psychometric study of the theoretical orientations of clinical social workers. *Journal of Social Service Research* 9: 47–70.

Cohen, Jacob. 1960. *Statistical Power Analysis for the Behavioral Sciences*. New York: Academic Press.

Collins, Frank L. and J. K. Thompson. 1993. The integration of empirically derived personality assessment data into a behavioral conceptualization and treatment plan: Rationale, guidelines, and caveats. *Behavior Modification* 17 (1): 58–71.

Collopy, B. J. 1988. Autonomy in long-term care: Some crucial distinctions. *The Gerontologist* 28: 655–672.

Coohey, Carol. 1996. Laura Epstein: Interviewed by Carol Coohey on February 2, 1995. *Reflections*, Summer 1996, 57–72.

Cook, Thomas D. and Donald T. Campbell. 1979. *Quasi-Experimentation: Design and Analysis Issues for Field Settings*. Chicago: Rand-McNally.

Cooper, Brian K. and Ariel A. Pearce. 1996. The short-term effects of relocation on continuing-care clients with a psychiatric disability. *Research on Social Work Practice* 6 (2): 179–192.

Corcoran, Kevin and Joel Fischer. 1987. *Measures for Clinical Practice: A Sourcebook*. New York: Free Press.

Corcoran, Kevin and Wallace J. Gingerich. 1994. Practice evaluation in the context of managed care: Case-recording methods for quality assurance reviews. *Research on Social Work Practice* 4 (3): 326–337.

Coulton, Claudia and Julian Chow. 1992. Interaction effects in multiple regression. *Journal of Social Service Research* 16 (1/2): 179–199.

Cowger, Charles. 1984. Statistical significance tests: Scientific ritualism or scientific method? *Social Service Review* 58: 358–372.

Craft, John L. 1990. *Statistics and Data Analysis for Social Workers*. 2d ed. Itasca, Ill: Peacock.

Craig, Kenneth D., ed. 1996. *Advances in Cognitive-Behavioral Theory*. Thousand Oaks, Calif.: Sage.

Cronbach, Lee J. 1975. Beyond the two disciplines of scientific psychology. *American Psychologist* 30: 116–127.

Cronbach, Lee J. 1970. *Essentials of Psychological Testing*. 3d ed. New York: Harper and Row.

Curtis, G. C. 1996. The scientific evaluation of new claims. *Research on Social Work Practice* 6 (1): 117–121.

Davidson, Christine V. and Ronald H. Davidson. 1983. The significant other as data source and data problem in psychotherapy outcome research. In *The Assessment of Psychotherapy Outcome*, edited by M. J. Lambert, E. R. Christensen, and S. S. DeJulio, q.v.

Davis, Inger P. 1975. Advice-giving in parent counseling. *Social Casework* 56: 343–347.

Davis, Inger P. and William J. Reid. 1988. Event analysis in clinical practice and process research. *Social Casework* 69 (5): 298–306.

Davis, Larry E., Li Chin Cheng, and Michael J. Strube. 1996. Differential effects of racial composition on male and female groups: Implications for group work practice. *Social Work Research* 20 (3): 157–166.

Davis, Liane V. and Bonnie E. Carlson. 1981. Attitudes of service providers toward domestic violence. *Social Work Research and Abstracts* 17:34–39.

Davis, Liane V. and Meera Srinivasan. 1994. Feminist research within a battered women's shelter. In *Qualitative Research in Social Work*, edited by E. Sherman and W. J. Reid, q.v.

Delbecq, Andre L. 1983. The nominal group as a technique for understanding the qualitative dimensions of client needs. In *Assessing Health and Human Service needs*, edited by R. A. Bell et al., q.v..

Delbecq, Andre L. and Andrew H. Van De Ven. 1971. A group process model for problem identification and program planning. *Journal of Applied Behavioral Science* 7: 446–492.

deLeeuw, Edith D. and Johannes van der Zouwen. 1988. Data quality in telephone and face-to-face surveys: A comparative meta-analysis. In *Telephone Survey Methodology*, edited by R. M. Groves et al., q.v.

Deluty, R. H. 1979. Children's Action Tendency Scale: A self-reported measure of aggressiveness, assertiveness, and submissiveness in children. *Journal of Consulting and Clinical Psychology* 47: 1061–1071.

Dennis, Alan R. and Joseph S. Valacich. 1993. Computer brainstorms: More heads are better than one. *Journal of Applied Psychology* 78 (4): 531–537.

Denzin, Norman K. 1978. *The Research Act: A Theoretical Introduction to Sociological Methods*. 2d ed. New York: McGraw-Hill.

Denzin, Norman K. and Yvonna S. Lincoln, eds. 1994. *Handbook of Qualitative Research*. Thousand Oaks, Calif.: Sage.

DePoy, Elizabeth, Janice P. Burke, and Laurie Sherwen. 1992. Training trainers: Evaluating services provided to children with HIV and their families. *Research on Social Work Practice* 2 (1):39–55.

Derogatis, L. 1976. *Scoring and Procedures Manual for PAIS*. Baltimore: Clinical Psychometric Research.

Derogatis, L. R. and P. M. Spence. 1982. *The Brief Symptom Inventory: Administration, Scoring, and Procedures Manual*, vol. 1. Baltimore: Clinical Psychometric Research.

de Solla Price, Derek J. 1961. *Science Since Babylon*. New Haven: Yale University Press.

DeVilley, Gemma. 1987. Systematic literature searching as a conceptual framework for course-related bibliographic instruction for college freshmen. In *Conceptual Framework for Bibliographic Education: Theory Into Practice*, edited by M. Reichel and M. A. Ramy. Englewood, Colo.: Libraries Unlimited.

Dhooper, Surjit and Phyllis L. Schneider. 1995. Evaluation of a school-based child abuse prevention program. *Research on Social Work Practice* 5 (1): 36–46.

Dillman, Don A. 1978. *Mail and Telephone Surveys: The Total Design Method*. New York: Wiley.

Donahue, Kevin M. 1995. Developing a task-centered mediation model. Ph.D. dissertation, State University of New York, Albany.

Drake, Brett and Gautam N. Yadama. 1996. A structural equation model of burnout and job exit among child protective services workers. *Social Work Research* 20 (3): 179–187.

Drisko, James W. Utilization-focused evaluation of two intensive family preservation programs. *Families in Society* 79 (1): 62–74.

Due, Linnea. 1995. *Joining the Tribe: Growing Up Gay and Lesbian in the 1990s*. New York: Anchor.

Dukes, Richard L., Jodie B. Ullman, and Judith A. Stein. 1995. An evaluation of D.A.R.E. (Drug Abuse Resistance Education), Using a Solomon Four-Group design with Latent Variables. *Evaluation Review* 19 (4): 409–435.

Eichler, Margrit. 1988. *Nonsexist Research Methods: A Practical Guide*. Boston: Allen and Unwin.

Elliott, Robert. 1983. That in your hands: A comprehensive process analysis of a significant event in psychotherapy. *Psychiatry* 46: 113–129.

Elliott, Robert. 1984. A discovery-oriented approach to significant change in psychotherapy: Interpersonal process recall and comprehensive process analysis. In *Patterns of Change: Intensive Analysis of Psychotherapy Process*, edited by L. N. Rice and L. S. Greenberg. New York: Guilford Press.

Engeldinger, Eugene A. and Paul H. Stuart. 1990. The library in social work research: A review of social work research textbooks. *RQ* 29 (3): 369–379.

Epstein, Nathan B., Lawrence M. Baldwin, and Duane S. Bishop. 1983. The McMaster Family Assessment Device. *Journal of Marital and Family Therapy* 9 (2): 171–180.

Ewalt, Patricia L. and Janice Kutz. 1976. An examination of advice giving as a therapeutic intervention. *Smith College Studies in Social Work* 47: 3–19.

Feldman, Ronald A., Timothy E. Caplinger, and John S. Wodarski. 1983. *The St. Louis Conundrum: The Effective Treatment of Antisocial Youths*. Englewood Cliffs, N.J.: Prentice-Hall.

Ferguson, Kirsten L. and Margaret R. Rodway. 1994. Cognitive behavioral treatment of perfectionism: Initial evaluation studies. *Research on Social Work Practice* 4 (3): 283–308.

Festinger, Leon. 1962. *A Theory of Cognitive Dissonance*. Stanford: Stanford University Press.

Filsinger, Erik E. 1983. Choices among marital observation coding systems. *Family Process* 22: 317–335.

Fischer, Joel. 1973. Is casework effective? A review. *Social Work* 18 (1): 5–20.

Fischer, Joel. 1990. Problems and issues in meta-analysis. In *Advances in Clinical Social Work Research*, edited by L. Videka-Sherman and W. J. Reid, q.v.

Fischer, Joel and Kevin Corcoran. 1994a. *Measures for Clinical Practice.* 2d ed. Vol. 1: *Couples, Families, and Children.* New York: Free Press.

Fischer, Joel and Kevin Corcoran. 1994b. *Measures for Clinical Practice.* 2d ed. Vol. 2: *Adults.* New York: Free Press.

Flanagan, J. C. 1954. The critical incident technique. *Psychological Bulletin* 51: 327–58.

Fleming, R. W. 1994. *The Revised Elderly Persons' Disability Scale: Validity, Reliability, and Usefulness.* Sydney: University of Western Sydney.

Fontana, Andrea and James H. Frey. 1994. Interviewing: The art of science. In *Handbook of Qualitative Research*, edited by N. K. Denzin and Y. S. Lincoln, q.v.

Forte, James A., David D. Franks, Janett A. Forte, and Daniel Rigsby. 1996. Asymmetrical role-taking: Comparing battered and nonbattered women. *Social Work* 41 (1): 59–73.

Forte, James A. and Robert G. Green. 1994. The reliability and validity of the Index of Peer Relations with a clinical and nonclinical sample of adolescents. *Journal of Social Service Research* 19 (1/2): 49–65.

Fortune, Anne E. 1981. Communication processes in social work practice. *Social Service Review* 55: 93–128.

Fortune, Anne E. 1985a. Planning duration and termination of treatment. *Social Service Review* 59 (4): 647–661.

Fortune, Anne E. et al. 1985b. Student satisfaction with field placement. *Journal of Social Work Education* 21: 92–104.

Fortune, Anne E. and Mary L. McCarthy. 1992. Predicting MSW student performance in field. Paper read at 38th Annual Program Meeting of the Council on Social Work Education, Kansas City, February 29-March 3, 1992.

Fortune, Anne E., Jacyln Miller, Amy F. Rosenblum, Bonita M. Sanchez, and Carolyn Smith. 1997. Support for field instructors under two models of agency-university liaison. Unpublished paper. State University of New York, Albany.

Fortune, Anne E. and William J. Reid. 1973. *Through the Looking Glass: Reflections on Runaway Youth.* Chicago: Travelers Aid Society.

Frank, Harry and Steven C. Althoen. 1994. *Statistics: Concepts and Applications.* Cambridge: Press Syndicate of the University of Cambridge.

Frankfather, Dwight. 1977. *The Aged in the Community.* New York: Praeger.

Frankfort-Nachmias, Chava and David Nachmias. 1992. *Research Methods in the Social Sciences.* 4th ed. New York: St. Martin's Press.

Franklin, Donna L. 1985. Differential clinical assessments: The influence of class and race. *Social Service Review* 59: 44–61.

Franks, David D. 1989. Power and role-taking: A social behaviorist's synthesis of Kemper's power and status model. In *The Sociology of Emotions: Original Essays and Research Papers*, edited by D. D. Franks and E. D. McCarthy. Greenwich, Conn.: JAI Press.

Fraser, Mark W., Peter J. Pecora, and David A. Haapala. 1991. *Families in Crisis: The Impact of Intensive Family Preservation Services.* Hawthorne, N.Y.: Aldine De Gruyter.

Frey, Diane E., Thomas J. Kelbley, Lisa Durham, and Jacqueline S. James. 1992. Enhancing the self-esteem of selected male nursing home residents. *Gerontologist* 32 (4): 552–557.

Frey, J. H. and A. Fontana. 1998. *The Group Interview.* Newbury Park, Calif.: Sage.

Fuscaldo, Diane, Jacqueline W. Kaye, and Susan Philliber. 1998. Evaluation of a program for parenting. *Families in Society* 79 (1): 53–61.

Gamache, Denise J., Jeffrey L. Edleson, and Michael D. Schock. 1988. Coordinated police, judicial, and social service response to woman battering: A multiple-baseline evaluation across three communities. In *Coping with Family Violence*, edited by G. T. Hotaling, D. Finkelher, J. T. Kirkpatrick, and M. Straus. Newbury Park, Calif.: Sage.

Garfield, Sol L. and Allen E. Bergin, eds. 1986. *Handbook of Psychotherapy and Behavior Change*. New York: Wiley.

Garvin, Charles D., Audrey D. Smith, and William J. Reid. 1978. *The Work Incentive Experience*. Montclair, N.J.: Allanheld, Osmun.

Gary, Lawrence E. 1995. African American men's perceptions of racial discrimination: A sociocultural analysis. *Social Work Research* 19 (4): 207–217.

Geertz, Clifford. 1973. Thick description: Toward an interpretive theory of cultures. In *The Interpretation of Cultures*, edited by C. Geertz. New York: Basic Books.

Geismar, Ludwig L. 1980. *Family and Community Functioning*. 2d ed. Metuchen, N.J.: Scarecrow Press.

Gerstel, Naomi, Cynthia J. Bogard, J. Jeff McConnell, and Michael Schwartz. 1996. The therapeutic incarceration of homeless families. *Social Service Review* 70 (4): 543–572.

Gibbs, Leonard and Eileen Gambrill. 1996. *Critical Thinking for Social Workers: A Workbook*. Thousand Oaks, Calif: Pine Forge Press.

Gilbert, J. P., R. J. Light, and F. Mosteller. 1975. Assessing social innovations: An empirical base for policy. In *Evaluation and Experiment*, edited by C. A. Benjnett and A. A. Lumdsaine. New York: Academic Press.

Gilgun, Jane F. 1992. Hypothesis generation in social work research. *Journal of Social Service Research* 15 (3/4): 113–135.

Gilgun, Jane F. 1994. Hand into glove: The grounded theory approach and social work practice research. In *Qualitative Research in Social Work*, edited by E. Sherman and W. J. Reid,, q.v.

Gillat, Alex and Beth Sulzer-Azaroff. 1994. Promoting principals' managerial involvement in instructional improvement. *Journal of Applied Behavior Analysis* 27 (1): 115–129.

Gillespie, David F. and James R. Seaberg. 1977. Individual Problem Rating: A proposed scale. *Administration in Mental Health* 5: 21–29.

Gingerich, Wallace A. 1979. Procedure for evaluating clinical practice. *Health and Social Work* 2: 105–130.

Gingerich, Wallace A., Mark Kleczewski, and Stuart A. Kirk. 1982. Name calling in social work. *Social Service Review* 56: 366–374.

Glaser, Barney G. and Anselm L. Strauss. 1967. *The Discovery of Grounded Theory: Strategies for Qualitative Research*. Chicago: Aldine.

Glaser, Barney G. and Anselm L. Strauss. 1970. Discovery of substantive theory: A basic strategy underlying qualitative research. In *Qualitative Methodology*, edited by W. Filstead, q.v.

Glisson, Charles. 1985. In defense of statistical tests of significance. *Social Service Review* 59: 377–386.

Gogineni, Aruna, Ruth Alsup, and David F. Gillespie. 1995. Mediation and moderation in social work research. *Social Work Research* 19 (1): 57–63.

Gomez, Clavelina and Javier F. Francisco. 1995. Two types of family assessment. *Family Process* 34 (3): 363–364.

Goodson-Lawes, Julie. 1994. Ethnicity and poverty as research variables: Family studies with Mexican and Vietnamese newcomers. In *Qualitative Research in Social Work*, edited by E. Sherman and W. J. Reid, q.v.

Grasso, Anthony J. and Irwin Epstein, eds. 1992. *Research Utilization in the Social Services*. New York: Haworth Press.

Graybeal, Clay T. and Elizabeth Ruff. 1995. Process recording: It's more than you think. *Journal of Social Work Education* 31 (2): 169–181.

Green, Glenn R. and J. E. Wright. 1979. The retrospective approach to collecting baseline data. *Social Work Research and Abstracts* 15 (3): 25–31.

Green, Robert C. and Nancy R. Vosler. 1992. Issues in the assessment of family practice: An empirical study. *Journal of Social Service Research* 15 (3/4): 1–19.

Green, Robert G. 1995. The 1990s publication productivity of schools of social work with doctoral programs: "The times, are they a-changin'?" *Journal of Social Work Education* 31 (3): 388–401.

Greenberg, David H. and Marvin B. Mandell. 1991. Research utilization in policy making: A tale of two series (of social experiments). *Journal of Policy Analysis and Management* 10 (4): 633–656.

Greenberg, Leslie S. 1986. Change process research. *Journal of Consulting and Clinical Psychology* 54: 4–9.

Greenberg, Leslie S. and Frederick L. Newman. 1996. An approach to psychotherapy change process research: Introduction to the special section. *Journal of Consulting and Clinical Psychology* 64 (3): 435–438.

Greenberg, Leslie S. and William M. Pinsof, eds. 1986. *The Psychotherapeutic Process: A Research Handbook*. New York: Guilford Press.

Greene, Jennifer C. 1994. Qualitative program evaluation: Practice and promise. In *Handbook of Qualitative Research*, edited by N. K. Denzin and Y. S. Lincoln, q.v.

Greene, Roberta R., Nancy P. Kropf, and Nancy MacNair. 1994. A family therapy model for working with persons with AIDS. *Journal of Family Psychotherapy* 5 (1): 1–20.

Greenley, James R., Jan Steven Greenberg, and Roger Brown. 1997. Measuring quality of life: A new and practical survey instrument. *Social Work* 42 (3): 244–254.

Gregory, Robert J. 1996. *Psychological Testing: History, Principles, and Applications*. 2d ed. Boston: Allyn and Bacon.

Grinnell, Richard M. Jr., ed. 1988. *Social Work Research and Evaluation*. 3d ed. Itasca, Ill.: Peacock.

Grinnell, Richard M. Jr., ed. 1997. *Social Work Research and Evaluation: Quantitative and Qualitative Approaches*. 5th ed. Itasca, Ill.: Peacock.

Groves, Robert M., Paul P. Biemer, Lars E. Lyberg, James T. Massey, William L. Nicholls II, and Joseph Waksberg, eds. 1988. *Telephone Survey Methodology*. New York: Wiley.

Gurman, Alan, David P. Kniskern, and William M. Pinsof. 1986. Research on marital and family therapies. In *Handbook of Psychotherapy and Behavior Change*, edited by S. L. Garfield and A. E. Bergin, q.v..

Hairston, Creasie Finney. 1979. The nominal group technique in organizational research. *Social Work Research and Abstracts* 15 (3): 12–17.

Haizlip, Shirlee Taylor. 1994. *The Sweeter the Juice: A Family Memoir in Black and White*. New York: Touchstone.

Hall, O. and D. Royse. 1987. Mental health needs assessment with social indicators: An empirical study. *Administration in Mental Health* 15 (8): 36–46.

Hall, R. U., ed. 1971. *Behavior Management Series*: Part II, *Basic Principles*. Lawrence, Kansas: H & H Enterprises.

Hamilton, Seward E. 1993. Identifying African-American gifted children using a behavioral assessment technique: The gifted children locator. *The Journal of Black Psychology* 19 (1): 63–76.

Hammer, A.L., and S. Marting. 1987. *Coping Resources Inventory*. Palo Alto, Calif.: Consulting Psychologist Press.

Hardina, Donna and Michael Carley. 1997. The impact of increased allowable work hours on two-parent families receiving welfare. *Social Work Research* 21 (2): 101–109.

Hatry, Harry P. 1997. Outcomes measurement and social services: Public and private sector perspectives. In *Outcomes Measurement in the Human Services*, edited by E. J. Mullen and J. L. Magnabosco, q.v.

Havassy, Henry M. 1990. Effective second-story bureaucrats: Mastering the paradox of diversity. *Social Work* 35 (2): 103–09.

Hawkins, Catherine A. and Raymond C. Hawkins II. 1996. Alcoholism in the families of origin of MSW students: Estimating the prevalence of mental health problems using standardized measures. *Journal of Social Work Education* 32 (1): 127–134.

Hayden, Mary F. and Jon Goldman. 1996. Families of adults with mental retardation: Stress levels and need for services. *Social Work* 41 (6): 657–667.

Hays, William L. 1973. *Statistics for the Social Sciences*. 2d ed. New York: Holt, Rinehart, and Winston.

Hepler, Juanita B. 1994. Mainstreaming children with learning disabilities: Have we improved their social environment? *Social Work in Education* 16 (3): 143–154.

Hill, Clara E. 1986. Verbal response modes category systems. In *The Psychotherapeutic Process: A Research Handbook*, edited by L. S. Greenberg and W. M. Pinsof, q.v.

Hogarty, Gerard E. 1993. Prevention of relapse in chronic schizophrenic patients. *Journal of Clinical Psychiatry* 54 (supplement 3): 18–23.

Hogarty, Gerard E., C. M. Anderson, D. J. Reiss, S. J. Kornblith, D. P. Greenwald, C. D. Javna, and M. J. Madonia. 1986. Family psychoeducation, social skills training, and maintenance chemotherapy in the aftercare treatment of schizophrenia. *Archives of General Psychiatry* 43: 633–642.

Hollis, Florence. 1972. *Casework: A Psychosocial Therapy*. 2d ed. New York: Random House.

Holmes, Thomas R. 1995a. History of child abuse: A key variable in client response to short-term treatment. *Families in Society* 76 (6): 349–359.

Holmes, Thomas R. 1995b. A history of childhood abuse as a predictor variable: Implications for outcome research. *Research on Social Work Practice* 5 (3): 297–308.

Horvath, A. O. and L. S. Greenberg. 1989. Development of the Working Alliance Inventory. *Journal of Consulting and Clinical Psychiatry* 36: 223–233.

Howe, K. R. 1988. Against the quantitative-qualitative incompatibility thesis or dogmas die hard. *Educational Researcher* 17: 10–16.

Huberman, A. Michael and Matthew B. Miles. 1994. Data management and analysis methods. In *Handbook of Qualitative Research*, edited by N. K. Denzin and Y. S. Lincoln, q.v.

Hudson, Walter W. 1982. *The Clinical Measurement Package: A Field Manual*. Homewood, Ill.: Dorsey.

Hudson, Walter.W. 1990. *Computer Assisted Social Services*. Tempe, AZ: WALMYR Publishing.

Hudson, Walter W. 1992. *WALMYR Assessment Scales Scoring Manual*. Tempe, Ariz.: WALMYR.

Hudson, Walter W. and S. R. McIntosh. 1981. The assessment of spouse abuse: Two quantifiable dimensions. *Journal of Marriage and the Family* 43: 873–888.

Hudson, Walter W. and Steven L. McMurtry. 1997. Comprehensive assessment in social work practice: The Multi-Problem Screening Inventory. *Research on Social Work Practice* 7 (1): 79–98.

Hughes, Susan. 1997. Impact of expanded home care models. *Social Work Research* 21 (3): 165–172.

Huh, Nam Soon. 1997. Korean adoptions. Ph.D. dissertation. Albany: State University of New York.

Hwang, Sung-Chul and Charles D. Cowger. 1998. Utilizing strengths in assessment. *Families in Society* 79 (1): 25–31.

Jacobson, Neil S., William C. Follette, and Dick Revensdorf. 1984. Psychotherapy outcome research: Methods for reporting variability and evaluating clinical significance. *Behavioral Therapy* 15: 336–352.

Janesick, Valerie J. 1994. The dance of qualitative research design: Metaphor, methodolatry, and meaning. In *Handbook of Qualitative Research*, edited by N. K. Denzin and Y. S. Lincoln, q.v.

Jayaratne, Srinika. 1990. Clinical significance: Problems and new developments. In *Advances in Clinical Social Work Research*, edited by L. Videka-Sherman and W. J. Reid, q.v.

Jensen, Carla. 1994. Psychosocial treatment of depression in women: Nine single-subject evaluations. *Research on Social Work Practice* 4 (3): 267–282.

Johnson, Alice K., Kay Young McChesney, Cynthia J. Rocha, and William H. Butterfield. 1995. Demographic differences between sheltered homeless families and housed poor families: Implications for policy and practice. *Journal of Sociology and Social Welfare* 22 (4): 5–22.

Johnson, Michael D. and Stephen B. Fawcett. 1994. Courteous service: Its assessment and modification in a human service organization. *Journal of Applied Behavior Analysis* 27 (1): 145–152.

Johnson, M. E., C. Brems, and P. Alford-Keating. 1995. Parental sexual orientation and therapists' perceptions of family functioning. *Journal of Gay and Lesbian Psychotherapy* 2 (3): 1–15.

Jones, Enrico E., Jess Ghannam, Joel T. Nigg, and Jennifer F. P. Dyer. 1993. A paradigm for single-case research: The time series study of a long-term psychotherapy for depression. *Journal of Consulting and Clinical Psychology* 61 (3): 381–394.

Jones, Reginald L., ed. 1991. *Black Psychology*. New York: Harper and Row.

Kagle, Jill Doner. 1984. Restoring the clinical record. *Social Work* 29: 46–50.

Kagle, Jill Doner. 1993. Record keeping: Directions for the 1990s. *Social Work* 38 (2): 190–196.

Kamya, Hugo A. 1997. African immigrants in the United States: The challenge for research and practice. *Social Work* 42 (2): 154–165.

Kane, Rosalie A. 1974. Look to the record. *Social Work* 19: 412–419.

Kanfer, Frederick H. 1996. Motivation and emotion in behavior therapy. In *Advances in Cognitive-Behavioral Therapy*, edited by K. Craig, q.v.

Kanfer, Frederick H. and W. Robert May. 1982. Behavioral assessment: Toward an integration of epistemological and methodological issues. In *Contemporary Behavior Therapy: Conceptual and Empirical Foundations*, edited by G. T. Wilson and C. M. Franks, q.v.

Kanji, Gopal K. 1994. *100 Statistical Tests*. London: Sage.

Kaplan, Abraham. 1964. *The Conduct of Inquiry: Methodology for Behavioral Science*. San Francisco: Chandler.

Katz, M. and S. Lyerly. 1963. Methods for measuring adjustment and social behavior in the community: Rationale description, discriminative validity and scale development. *Psychological Reports* 13: 503–535.

Kazdin, Alan E. 1981. Drawing valid inferences from case studies. *Journal of Consulting and Clinical Psychology* 49: 183–192.

Kees Martin, Sally S. and F. Scott Christopher. 1987. Family guided sex education: An impact study. *Social Casework* 68 (6): 358–363.

Kemp, Barbara E. and Mary Jane Brustman. 1997. Social policy research: Comparison and analysis of CD-ROM resources. *Social Work Research* 21 (2): 111–120.

Kennedy, Wallace A. 1995. Phobia. In *Handbook of Child Behavior Therapy*, edited by R. T. Ammerman and M. Hersen, q.v.

Kenny, Graham K. 1986. The metric properties of rating scales employed in evaluation research: An empirical examination. *Evaluation Review* 10 (3): 397–408.

Kerlinger, Fred N. 1985. *Foundations of Behavioral Research*. 2d ed. New York: Holt, Rinehart, and Winston.

Kerlinger, Fred N. and Elazar J. Pedhazur. 1973. *Multiple Regression in Behavioral Research*. New York: Rinehart and Winston.

Kiecolt, K. Jill, and Laura E. Nathan. 1985. *Secondary Analysis of Survey Data, Quantitative Applications in the Social Science*. Beverly Hills: Sage.

Kilgore, Dennis K. 1995. Task-centered group treatment of sex offenders: A developmental study. Ph.D. dissertation, State University of New York, Albany.

Kiresuk, Thomas J. 1973. *Goal Attainment Scaling at a County Mental Health Service: Evaluation*. Special monograph. Vol. no. l.

Kiresuk, Thomas J. and Sander H. Lund. 1978. Goal attainment scaling. In *Evaluation of Human Service Programs*, edited by C. C. Attkisson et al., q.v.

Kiresuk, Thomas J. and Robert E. Sherman. 1968. Goal attainment scaling: A general method for evaluating comprehensive mental health programs. *Community Mental Health Journal* 4: 443–453.

Kirk, Stuart A. 1990. Research utilization: The substructure of belief. In *Advances in Clinical Social Work Research*, edited by L. Videka-Sherman and W. J. Reid, q.v.

Kirk, Stuart A. and Kevin Corcoran. 1995. School rankings: Mindless narcissism or do they tell us something? *Journal of Education for Social Work* 31 (3): 408–414.

Klein, Waldo C. and Martin Bloom. 1995. Practice wisdom. *Social Work* 40 (2): 799–807.

Kobler, Heinz. 1985. *Statistics for Business and Economics*. Glenview, Ill.: Scott, Foresman.

Koeske, Gary F. 1992. Moderator variables in social work research. *Journal of Social Service Research* 16 (1/2): 159–178.

Koeske, Gary F., Stuart A. Kirk, Randi D. Koeske, and Mary Beth Rauktis. 1994. Measuring the Monday blues: Validation of a job satisfaction scale for the human services. *Social Work Research* 18 (1): 1–64.

Koeske, Randi D. and Gary F. Koeske. 1989. Working and nonworking students: Roles, support, and well-being. *Journal of Social Work Education* 25 (3): 244–256.

Kolevzon, Michael S., Robert G. Green, Anne E. Fortune, and Nancy R. Vosler. 1988. Evaluating family therapy: Divergent methods, divergent findings. *Journal of Marital and Family Therapy* 14: 277–286.

Kotlowitz, Alex. 1991. *There Are No Children Here: The Story of Two Boys Growing Up in the Other America*. New York: Anchor Doubleday.

Krassner, Madelyn. 1986. Effective features of therapy from the healer's perspective: A study of curanderismo. *Smith College Studies in Social Work* 56 (3): 157–183.

Krathwohl, David R. 1985. *Social and Behavioral Science and Research*. San Francisco: Jossey-Bass.

Krohn, Marvin D., Alan J. Lizotte, Terence P. Thornberry, Carolyn Smith, and David McDowall. 1996. Reciprocal causal relationships among drug use, peers, and beliefs: A five-wave panel model. *Journal of Drug Issues* 26 (2): 405–428.

Kuhlthau, Carol C. 1994. *Teaching the Library Research Process*. Metuchen, N.J.: Scarecrow Press.

Lambert, Michael J. and Allen E. Bergin. 1994. The effectiveness of psychotherapy. In *Handbook of Psychotherapy and Behavior Change*, edited by S. L. Garfield and A. E. Bergin, q.v.

Lambert, Michael J., Erwin R. Christensen, and Steven S. DeJulio, eds. 1983. *The Assessment of Psychotherapy Outcome*. New York: Wiley.

Lambert, Michael J. and Clara E. Hill. 1994. Assessing psychotherapy outcomes and processes. In *Handbook of Psychotherapy and Behavior Change*, edited by S. L. Garfield and A. E. Bergin, q.v.

Lambert, Michael J., David A. Shapiro, and Allen E. Bergin. 1986. The effectiveness of psychotherapy. In *Handbook of Psychotherapy and Behavior Change*, edited by S. L. Garfield and A. E. Bergin, q.v.

Langer, E. J. and J. Rodin. 1976. The effects of choice and enhanced personal responsibility for the aged: A field experiment in an institutional setting. *Journal of Personality and Social Psychology* 34 (2): 191–198.

LaSala, Michael C. 1997. Coupled gay men: Their relationships with their parents and in-laws. Ph.D. dissertation, State University of New York, Albany.

Laseter, Robert L. 1997. The labor force participation of young black men: A qualitative examination. *Social Service Review* 71 (1): 72–88.

Lavrakas, Paul J. 1987. *Telephone Survey Methods: Sampling, Selection, and Supervision*. Newbury Park, Calif.: Sage.

Lazarus, R. S. and S. Folkman. 1984. *Stress, Appraisal, and Coping*. New York: Springer.

Lazzari, Marceline M., Holly R. Ford, and Kelly J. Haughty. 1996. Making a difference: Women of action in the community. *Social Work* 41 (2): 197–205.

Lebow, Jay L. 1983. Research assessing consumer satisfaction with mental health treatment: A review of findings. *Evaluation and Program Planning* 6: 211–236.

LeCroy, Craig W., ed. 1994. *Handbook of Child and Adolescent Treatment Manuals*. New York: Lexington Books.

Lehman, Anthony F. and T. R. Zastowny. 1983. Patient satisfaction with mental health services: A meta-analysis to establish norms. *Evaluation and Program Planning* 6: 265–274.

Levine, Robert V., Todd Simon Martinez, Gary Brase, and Kerry Sorenson. 1994. Helping in 36 U.S. cities. *Journal of Personality and Social Psychology* 67 (1): 69–82.

Leviton, L. C. and R. F. Boruch. 1980. Illustrative case studies. In *An Appraisal of Educational Program Evaluations: Federal, State and Local Levels*, edited by R. F. Boruch and D. S. Cordray. Washington D.C.: U.S. Department of Education.

Leviton, L. C. and E. F. Hughes. 1981. Research on the utilization of evaluations: A review and synthesis. *Evaluation Review* 5 (4): 525–48.

Levitt, John L. and William J. Reid. 1981. Rapid assessment instruments for social work practice. *Social Work Research and Abstracts* 17: 13–19.

Lewis, Mary Ann, Jeanne M. Giovannoni, and Barbara Leake. 1997. Two-year placement outcomes of children removed at birth from drug-using and non-drug-using mothers in Los Angeles. *Social Work Research* 21 (2): 81–90.

Lewis, Oscar. 1959. *Five Families: Mexican Case Studies in the Culture of Poverty*. New York: Basic Books.

Liebow, Elliot. 1993. *Tell Them Who I Am: The Lives of Homeless Women*. New York: Penguin Books.

Ligon, Jan, Bruce A. Thyer, and Danny Dixon. 1995. Academic affiliations of those published in social work journals: A productivity analysis, 1989–1993. *Journal of Education for Social Work* 31 (3): 369–376.

Lincoln, Yvonna S. and Egon G. Guba. 1985. *Naturalistic Inquiry*. Beverly Hills: Sage.

Lindsey, Duncan and Stuart A. Kirk. 1992. The role of social work journals in the development of a knowledge base for the profession. *Social Service Review* 66 (2): 295–310.

Locke, Harvey J. and Karl M. Wallace. 1959. Short marital-adjustment and prediction tests: Their reliability and validity. *Marriage and Family Living* 21: 251–255.

Lofland, J. 1995. Analytic ethnography: Features, failings, and futures. *Journal of Contemporary Ethnography* 24 (1): 30–67.

Loneck, Barry, Steven Banks, Bruce Way, and Ernest Bonaparte. 1996. An empirical model of therapeutic process for clients with dual disorders in a psychiatric emergency room. Unpublished paper. State University of New York, Albany.

Loneck, B. and B. Way. 1997. Using a focus group of clinicians to develop a research project on therapeutic process for clients with dual diagnosis. *Social Work* 42 (1):107–111

Ludgate, John W. 1995. *Maximizing Psychotherapeutic Gains and Preventing Relapse in Emotionally Distressed Clients.* Sarasota, Fla.: Professional Resource Press/Professional Resource Exchange, Inc.

Lyman, Susan B. and Gloria W. Bird. 1996. A closer look at self-image in male foster care adolescents. *Social Work* 41 (1): 85–96.

Lyons, Peter, Howard J. Doueck, and John S. Wodarski. 1996. Risk assessment for child protective services: A review of the empirical literature on instrument performance. *Social Work Research* 20 (3): 143–155.

Magen, Randy H. and Sheldon D. Rose. 1994. Parents in groups: Problem solving versus behavioral skills training. *Research on Social Work Practice* 4 (2): 172–191.

Magura, S. and B. S. Moses. 1986. *Outcome Measures for Child Welfare Services: Theory and Applications.* Washington D.C.: Child Welfare League of America.

Magura, S., B. S. Moses, and M. A. Jones. 1987. *Assessing Risk and Measuring Change in Families: The Family Risk Scales.* Washington D.C.: Child Welfare League of America.

Mahoney, F. I. and D. W. Barthel. 1965. Functional evaluation of the Barthel Index. *Maryland State Medical Journal* 14: 61–65.

Mahrer, Alvin R. and W. P. Nadler. 1986. Good moments in psychotherapy: A preliminary review, list, and some promising research avenues. *Journal of Consulting and Clinical Psychology* 54: 10–15.

Marcenko, Maureen O. and Michael Spence. 1995. Social and psychological correlates of substance abuse among pregnant women. *Social Work Research* 19 (2): 103–109.

Martin, Ruth R. 1994. Life forces of African-American elderly illustrated through oral history narratives. In *Qualitative Research in Social Work*, edited by E. Sherman and W. J. Reid, q.v.

Massimo, Valerie. 1996. A study of two approaches to training child welfare employees. Unpublished paper. State University of New York, Albany.

May, Edgar. 1964. *The Wasted Americans: Cost of Our Welfare Dilemma.* New York: Harper and Row.

Mayer, John E. and Noel Timms. 1970. *The Client Speaks: Working-Class Impressions of Casework.* New York: Atherton Press.

McCall, Dwight L. and Robert G. Green. 1991. Symmetricality and complementarity and their relationship to marital stability. *Journal of Divorce and Remarriage* 15 (1/2): 23–32.

McCallion, Philip and Ronald W. Toseland. 1995. Supportive group interventions with caregivers of frail older adults. *Social Work with Groups* 18 (1): 11–25.

McCarney, Stephen B. 1995. *The Attention Deficit Disorders Evaluation Scale (ADDES).* 2d ed. Columbia, Mo: Hawthorne Educational Services.

McGrew, J. H., G. R. Bond, L. Dietzen, M. McKasson, and L. D. Miller. 1995. A multisite study of client outcomes in assertive community treatment. *Psychiatric Services* 46: 696–701.

McKay, Mary McKernan, Ruth Nudelman, Kathleen McCadam, and Jude Gonzales. 1996. Evaluating a social work engagement approach to involving inner-city children and their families in mental health care. *Research on Social Work Practice* 6 (4): 462–472.

McKenzie, F. R. 1995. A study of clinical social workers' recognition and use of countertransference with adult borderline clients. DSW dissertation, Loyola, Chicago.

McKillip, Jack. 1987. *Need Analysis: Tools for the Human Services and Education*. Newbury Park, Calif.: Sage.

McMurtry, Steven L. 1997. Survey research. In *Social Work Research and Evaluation*, edited by R. M. Grinnell Jr., q.v.

McNeece, C. A., D. M. DiNitto, and P. J. Johnson. 1983. The utility of evaluation research for administrative decision-making. *Administration in Social Work* 7: 77–87.

Meadow, Diane. 1988. Preparation of individuals for participation in a treatment group: Development and empirical testing of a model. *International Journal of Group Psychotherapy* 38 (3): 367–385.

Melidonis, Greer G. and B. H. Bry. 1995. Effects of therapist exceptions questions on blaming and positive statements in families with adolescent behavior problems. *Journal of Family Psychology* 9 (4): 451–457.

Mena, F. J., A. M. Padilla, and M. Maldonado. 1987. Acculturative stress and specific coping strategies among immigrant and later generation college students. *Hispanic Journal of Behavioral Sciences* 9: 207–225.

Mendenhall, William, Lyman Ott, and Richard H. Larson. 1974. *Statistics: A Tool for the Social Sciences*. North Scituate, Mass.: Duxbury Press.

Mercer, Susan O. 1996. Navajo elderly people in a reservation nursing home: Admission predictors and culture care practices. *Social Work* 41 (2): 181–189.

Messer, Stephen C. and Alan M. Gross. 1995. Childhood depression and family interaction: A naturalistic observation study. *Journal of Clinical Child Psychology* 24 (1): 77–88.

Meyer, Carole H. 1996. My son the scientist. *Social Work Research* 20 (2): 101–104.

Miles, Matthew B. and A. Michael Huberman. 1994. *Qualitative Data Analysis*. 2d ed. Thousand Oaks, Calif.: Sage.

Milgram, Stanley. 1963. Behavioral study of obedience. *Journal of Abnormal and Social Psychology* 67:371–378.

Milgram, Stanley. 1965. Some conditions of obedience and disobedience to authority. *Human Relations* 18: 57–75.

Miller, Deborah L. and Mary Lou Kelley. 1994. The use of goal setting and contingency contracting for improving children's homework performance. *Journal of Applied Behavior Analysis* 27 (1): 73–84.

Miller, Robin L. and Elizabeth E. Solomon. 1996. Assessing the AIDS-related needs of women in an urban housing development. In *Needs Assessment: A Creative and Practical Guide for Social Scientists*, edited by R. Riviere, S. Berkowitz, C. C. Carter, and C. G. Ferguson. Washington D.C.: Taylor and Francis.

Mintz, Jim and Donald J. Kiesler. 1982. Individualized measures of psychotherapy outcome. In *Handbook of Research Methods in Clinical Psychology*, edited by Philip C.Kendall and James N. Butcher. New York: Wiley.

Mizrahi, Terry and Julie S. Abramson. 1994. Collaboration between social workers and physicians: An emerging typology. In *Qualitative Research in Social Work*, edited by E. Sherman and W. J. Reid, q.v.

Moncher, Michael and Steven Schinke. 1994. Group intervention to prevent tobacco use among Native American youth. *Research on Social Work Practice* 4 (2): 160–171.

Montgomery, S. A. and M. Asberg. 1979. A new depression scale designed to be sensitive to change. *British Journal of Psychiatry* 134: 302–309.

Moos, Rudolf. 1987. *Social Climate Scales: A User's Guide*. Palo Alto, Calif.: Consulting Psychologists Press.

Mullen, Edward J. 1978. The construction of personal models for effective practice: A method for utilizing research findings to guide social interventions. *Journal of Social Service Research* 2 (1): 45–63.

Mullen, Edward J. 1983. Personal practice models. In *Handbook of Clinical Social Work*, edited by A. Rosenblatt and Diane Waldfogel. San Francisco: Jossey-Bass.

Mullen, Edward J. 1994. Design of social intervention. In *Intervention Research*, edited by J. T. Rothman and E. J. Thomas, q.v.

Mullen, Edward J., Robert Chazin, and David Feldstein. 1972. Services for the newly dependent: An assessment. *Social Service Review* 46: 309–322.

Mullen, Edward J. and Jennifer L. Magnabosco, eds. 1997. *Outcomes Measurement in the Human Services: Cross-Cutting Issues and Methods*. Washington D.C.: NASW Press.

Murphy, Linda L., Jane Close Conoley, and James C. Impara, eds. 1994. *Tests in Print IV: An Index to Tests, Test Reviews, and the Literature on Specific Tests*. Lincoln: Buros Institute of Mental Measurements, University of Nebraska.

Nagasundaram, Murli and Alan R. Dennis. 1993. When a group is not a group: The cognitive foundation of group idea generation. *Small Group Research* 24 (4): 463–489.

Naleppa, Matthias J. 1995. Task-centered case management for the elderly in the community: Developing a practice model. Ph.D. dissertation, State University of New York, Albany.

Naleppa, Matthias J. and William J. Reid. 1998. Task-centered case management for the elderly: Developing a practice model. *Research on Social Work Practice* 8 (1): 63–85.

National Association of Social Workers. 1995. Code of Ethics. Washington D.C.: NASW.

Neuman, W. Lawrence. 1994. *Social Research Methods: Qualitative and Quantitative Approaches*. 2d ed. Boston: Allyn and Bacon.

Norbeck, J., A. Lindsey, and V. Carrieri. 1981. The development of an instrument to measure social support. *Nursing Research* 30: 264–269.

Norton, Dolores G. 1993. Diversity, early socialization, and temporal development: The dual perspective revisited. *Social Work* 38 (1): 82–90.

Nugent, William R. 1992. The affective impact of a clinical social worker's interviewing style: A series of single-case experiments. *Research on Social Work Practice* 2 (1): 6–27.

Nugent, William R. 1993. A series of single case design clinical evaluations of an Ericksonian hypnotic intervention used with clinical anxiety. *Journal of Social Service Research* 17 (3/4): 41–69.

Nugent, William R. and H. Halvorson. 1995. Testing the effects of active listening. *Research of Social Work Practice* 5 (2):152–175.

O'Connor, Richard and William J. Reid. 1986. Dissatisfaction with brief treatment. *Social Service Review* 60: 526–537.

Offer, D., E. Ostrov, and K. I. Howard. 1982. *The Offer Self-Image Questionnaire for Adolescents: A Manual*. Chicago: Michael Reese Hospital.

Ofman, Kay Walters. 1996. A rural view of mothers' pensions: The Allegan County, Michigan, Mothers' Pension Program, 1913–1928. *Social Service Review* 70 (1): 98–119.

O'Hare, Thomas. 1996. Court-ordered versus voluntary clients: Problem differences and readiness for change. *Social Work* 41 (4): 417–422.

Orlinsky, David E., Klaus Grawe, and Barbara K. Parks. 1994. Process and outcome in psychotherapy—Noch Einmal. In *Handbook of Psychotherapy and Behavior Change*, edited by S. L. Garfield and A. E. Bergin, q.v.

Orme, John, David F. Gillespie, and Anne E. Fortune. 1983. Two-dimensional summary scores derived from ratings of individualized clients' problems. *Social Work Research and Abstracts* 19 (3): 30–32.

Orme, John G. and Terri Combs-Orme. 1986. Statistical power and Type II errors in social work research. *Social Work Research and Abstracts* 22: 3–10.

Pagano, Robert R. 1986. *Understanding Statistics on the Behavioral Sciences.* 2d ed. St. Paul: West.

Pakiz, Bilge, Helen Z. Reinherz, and Rose M. Giaconia. 1997. Early risk factors for serious antisocial behavior at age 21: A longitudinal community study. *American Journal of Orthopsychiatry* 67 (1): 92–101.

Patton, Michael Q. 1990. *Qualitative Evaluation and Research Methods.* 2d ed. Newbury Park, Calif.: Sage.

Paulus, Paul B. and Mart T. Dzindolet. 1993. Social influence processes in group brainstorming. *Journal of Personality and Social Psychology* 64 (4): 575–586.

Peak, Terry, Ronald W. Toseland, and Steven M. Banks. 1995. The impact of a spouse-caregiver support group on care recipient health care costs. *Journal of Aging and Mental Health* 7 (3): 427–449.

Pelz, D. C. 1978. Some expanded perspectives on use of social science in public policy. In *Major Social Issues: A Multidisciplinary View,* edited by M. Yinger and S. J. Cutler. New York: Free Press.

Pepler, Debra J. and Wendy M. Craig. 1995. A peek behind the fence: Naturalistic observations of aggressive children with remote audiovisual recording. *Developmental Psychology* 31 (4): 548–553.

Persons, J. B. 1991. Psychotherapy studies do not accurately represent current models of psychotherapy: A proposed remedy. *American Psychologist* 46: 99–106.

Phillips, Bernard. 1985. *Sociological Research Methods: An Introduction.* Homewood, Ill.: Dorsey Press.

Phillips, D. 1987. Validity in qualitative research: Why the worry about warrant will not wane. *Education and Urban Society* 20: 9–24.

Pinsof, William M. 1986. The process of family therapy: The development of the family therapist coding system. In *The Psychotherapeutic Process,* edited by L. S. Greenberg and W. M. Pinsof, q.v.

Pinsof, William M., Lyman C. Wynne, and Alexandra B. Hambright. 1996. The outcomes of couple and family therapy: Findings, conclusions, and recommendations. *Psychotherapy* 33 (2): 321–331.

Pithouse, Andrew and Sarah Lindsell. 1996. Child protection services: Comparison of a referred family center and a field social work service in South Wales. *Research on Social Work Practice* 6 (4): 473–491.

Platt, Jerome J. and George Spivack. 1975. *The MEPS Procedure Manual.* Philadelphia: Hahnemann Medical College and Hospital.

Platt, Jerome J. and George Spivack. 1977. *Measures of Interpersonal Cognitive Problem-Solving for Adults and Adolescents.* Philadelphia: Hahnemann Medical College and Hospital.

Pomeroy, E. C., A. Rubin, and R. J. Walker. 1995. Effectiveness of a psychoeducational and task-centered group intervention for family members of people with AIDS. *Social Work Research* 19 (3): 129–192, pp. 142–152.

Potocky, Miriam and Thomas P. McDonald. 1996. Evaluating the effectiveness of family preservation services for the families of drug-exposed infants: A pilot study. *Research on Social Work Practice* 6 (4): 524–535.

Pulice, Richard T. 1994. Qualitative evaluation methods in the public sector: Understanding and working with constituency groups in the evaluation process. In *Qualitative Research in Social Work,* edited by E. Sherman and W. J. Reid, q.v.

Rabinowitz, Jonathan and Irving Lukoff. 1995. Clinical decision making of short- versus long-term treatment. *Research on Social Work Practice* 5 (1): 62–79.

Raushi, Thaddeus M. 1994. A task-centered model for group work with single mothers in the college setting. Ph.D. dissertation, State University of New York, Albany.

Reid, William J. 1978. *The Task-Centered System*. New York: Columbia University Press.

Reid, William J. 1979. The model development dissertation. *Journal of Social Service Research* 3: 215–225.

Reid, William J. 1985. *Family Problem Solving*. New York: Columbia University Press.

Reid, William J. 1990. Change process research: A new paradigm? In *Advances in Clinical Social Work Research*, edited by L. Videka-Sherman and W. J. Reid, q.v.

Reid, William J. 1992. *Task Strategies: An Empirical Approach to Social Work Practice*. New York: Columbia University Press.

Reid, William J. 1993. Fitting the single-system design to family treatment. *Journal of Social Service Research* 18 (1/2): 83–99.

Reid, William J. 1994a. Field testing and data gathering on innovative practice interventions in early development. In *Intervention Research*, edited by J. Rothman and E. J. Thomas, q.v.

Reid, William J. 1994b. Reframing the epistemological debate. In *Qualitative Research in Social Work*, edited by E. Sherman and W. J. Reid, q.v.

Reid, William J. 1997a. Evaluating the dodo's verdict: Do all interventions have equivalent outcomes? *Social Work Research* 21: (3) 5–18.

Reid, William J. 1997b. Research on task-centered practice. *Social Work Research* 21 (3): 132–137.

Reid, William J. and Cynthia Bailey-Dempsey. 1994. Content analysis in design and development. *Research on Social Work Practice* 4 (1): lol–ll4.

Reid, William J. and Cynthia Bailey-Dempsey. 1995. The effects of monetary incentives on school performance. *Families in Society* 76 (6): 331–340.

Reid, William J., Cynthia Bailey-Dempsey, Elizabeth Cain, Toni V. Cook, and John D. Burchard. 1994. Cash incentives versus case management: Can money replace services in preventing school failure? *Social Work Research* 18 (4): 227–236.

Reid, William J. and Alida Crisafulli. 1990. Marital discord and child behavior problems: A meta-analysis. *Journal of Abnormal Child Psychology* 18: 105–117.

Reid, William J. and Timothy Donovan. 1990. Treating sibling violence. *Family Therapy* 17 (1): 49–59.

Reid, William J. and Anne E. Fortune. 1992. Research utilization in direct social work practice. In *Research Utilization in the Social Services*, edited by Anthony J. Grasso and Irwin Epstein. New York: Haworth Press.

Reid, William J., Richard M. Kagan, Allison Kaminsky, and Katherine Helmer. 1987. Adoptions of older institutionalized youth. *Social Casework* (March): 140–149.

Reid, William J. and Barbara L. Shapiro. 1969. Client reaction to advice. *Social Service Review* 43: 165–173.

Reid, William J. and Pamela Strother. 1988. Super problem solvers: A systematic case study. *Social Service Review* 62 (3): 430–445.

Rhodes, Renee H., Clara E. Hill, Barbara J. Thompson, and Robert Elliott. 1994. Client retrospective recall of resolved and unresolved misunderstanding events. *Journal of Counseling Psychology* 41 (4): 473–483.

Rice, Laura N. and Leslie S. Greenberg, eds. 1984. *Patterns of Change: Intensive Analysis of Psychotherapy Process*. New York: Guilford Press.

Rich, Robert F. 1977. Uses of social science information by federal bureaucrats: Knowledge for action versus knowledge for understanding. In *Using Social Research in Public Policy Making*, edited by Carol H. Weiss. Lexington, Mass.: Lexington Books.

Richey, Cheryl A. and Vanessa G. Hodges. 1992. Empirical support for the effectiveness of respite care in reducing caregiver burden: A single-case analysis. *Research on Social Work Practice* 2 (2): 143–160.

Richman, Jack M., Lawrence B. Rosenfeld, and Charles J. Hardy. 1993. The Social Support Survey: A validation study of a clinical measure of the social support process. *Research on Social Work Practice* 3 (3): 288–305.

Riessman, Catherine Kohler. 1993. *Narrative Analysis*. Newbury Park, Calif.: Sage.

Riessman, Catherine Kohler, ed. 1994. *Qualitative Studies in Social Work Research*. Thousand Oaks, Calif.: Sage.

Rife, John C. and John R. Belcher. 1994. Assisting unemployed older workers to become reemployed: An experimental evaluation. *Research on Social Work Practice* 4 (1): 3–13.

Ripple, Lillian. 1960. Problem identification and formulation. In *Social Work Research*, edited by Norman A. Polansky. 1st ed. Chicago: University of Chicago Press.

Robinson, Robin A. 1994. Private pain and public behaviors: Sexual abuse and delinquent girls. In *Qualitative Studies in Social Work Research*, edited by C. K. Riessman, q.v.

Rockwood, Kenneth. 1994. Setting goals in geriatric rehabilitation and measuring their attainment. *Reviews in Clinical Gerontology* 4 (2): 141–149.

Rogers, Polly. 1997. Single-case design and development: Overcoming obstacles in treatment of childhood ADHD. Unpublished paper. Albany: State University of New York.

Rooney, Ronald H. 1985. Does in-service training make a difference? Results of a pilot study of task-centered dissemination in a public social service setting. *Journal of Social Service Research* 8: 33–50.

Rorschach, H. 1942. *Psychodiagnostics: A Diagnostic Test Based on Perception*. Translated by P. Lemkau and B. Kronenburg. (originally published 1921), ed. Berne: Huber (U.S. distributor, Grune and Stratton).

Rosen, Aaron. 1994. Knowledge use in direct practice. *Social Service Review* 68 (4): 561–577.

Rosenthal, James A. 1997. Pragmatic concepts and tools for data interpretation: A balanced model. *Journal of Teaching in Social Work* 15 (1/2):113–130.

Rosenthal, Robert. 1966. *Experimenter Effects in Behavioral Research*. New York: Appleton-Century Crofts.

Rosenthal, Robert. 1979. The file drawer problem and tolerance for null results. *Psychological Bulletin* 86: 638–641.

Rosenthal, Robert. 1984. *Meta-Analytic Procedures for Social Research*. Beverly Hills: Sage.

Rossi, Peter and Howard Freeman. 1993. *Evaluation: A Systematic Approach*. 4th ed. Beverly Hills: Sage.

Rothman, Jack. 1974. *Planning and Organizing for Social Change: Action Principles from Social Science Research*. New York: Columbia University Press.

Rothman, Jack. 1980. *Social Research and Development in the Human Services*. Englewood Cliffs, N.J.: Prentice-Hall.

Rothman, Jack. 1991. A model of case management: Toward empirically based practice. *Social Work* 36 (6): 520–528.

Rothman, Jack. 1992. *Guidelines for Case Management: Putting Research to Professional Use*. Itasca, Ill.: Peacock.

Rothman, Jack and Edwin J. Thomas, eds. 1994. *Intervention Research: Design and Development for Human Service*. New York: Haworth Press.

Rothman, Jack and A. Tumblin. 1994. Pilot testing and early development of a model of case management intervention. In *Intervention Research: Design and Development for Human Service*, edited by J. Rothman and E. J. Thomas, q.v.

Rubin, Allen. 1997. The family preservation evaluation from hell: Implications for program evaluation fidelity. *Children and Youth Services Review* 19 (1/2): 77–99.

Rubin, Allen and Earl Babbie. 1993. *Research Methods for Social Work*. 2d ed. Pacific Grove, Calif.: Brooks/Cole.

Rubin, Allen and Karen S. Knox. 1996. Data analysis problems in single-case evaluation: Issues for research on social work practice. *Research on Social Work Practice* 6 (1): 44–65.

Ruggeri, M. 1994. Patients' and relatives' satisfaction with psychiatric services: The state of the art of its measurement. *Social Psychiatry Psychiatric Epidemiology* 29:212–227.

Schilling, Robert F., Steven P. Schinke, Maura A. Kirkham, Nancy J. Meltzer, and Kristine L. Norelius. 1988. Social work research in social service agencies: Issues and guidelines. *Journal of Social Service Research* 11 (4): 75–87.

Schinke, Steven P., G. J. Botvin, and G. J. Orlandi. 1991. *Substance Abuse in Children and Adolescents: Evaluation and Intervention*. Newbury Park, Calif.: Sage.

Secret, Mary and Martin Bloom. 1994. Evaluating a self-help approach to helping a phobic child: A profile analysis. *Research on Social Work Practice* 4 (3): 338–348.

Selltiz, Claire, Lawrence Wrightsman, and Stuart W. Cook. 1976. *Research Methods in Social Relations*. 3d ed. New York: Holt, Rinehart, and Winston.

Sharpe, Tom, Marty Brown, and Kim Crider. 1995. The effects of a sportsmanship curriculum intervention on generalized positive social behavior of urban elementary school students. *Journal of Applied Behavior Analysis* 28 (4): 401–416.

Shaw, Ian and Alison Shaw. 1997. Game plans, buzzes, and sheer luck: Doing well in social work. *Social Work Research* 21 (2): 69–79.

Sherman, Edmund. 1994. Discourse analysis in the framework of change process research. In *Qualitative Research in Social Work*, edited by E. Sherman and W. J. Reid, q.v.

Sherman, Edmund and William J. Reid, eds. 1994. *Qualitative Research in Social Work*. New York: Columbia University Press.

Sherwood, Clarence D., John W. Morris, and Sylvia Sherwood. 1975. A multivariate, nonrandomized matching technique for studying the impact of social interventions. In *Handbook of Evaluation Research*, edited by E. L. Struening and M. Guttentag. Beverly Hills: Sage.

Shewart, W. A. 1931. *Economic Control of Quality of Manufactured Products*. New York: Van Nostrand Reinhold.

Shilts, Randy. 1987. *And the Band Played On: Politics, People, and the AIDS Epidemic*. New York: St. Martin's Press.

Shulman, Lawrence. 1992. *The Skills of Helping Individuals, Families, and Groups*. Itasca, Ill.: Peacock.

Shulman, Lawrence. 1993. Developing and testing a practice theory: An interactional perspective. *Social Work* 38 (1): 91–97.

Shyne, Ann W. 1975. Exploiting available information. In *Social Work Research: Methods for the Helping Professions*, edited by Norman A. Polansky. 2d ed. Chicago: University of Chicago Press.

Siegel, Sidney. 1956. *Nonparametric Statistics for the Behavioral Sciences*. New York: McGraw-Hill.

Simpson, Anthony E. 1993. *Information-Finding and the Research Process: A Guide to Sources and Methods for Public Administration and the Policy Sciences*. Westport, Conn.: Greenwood Press.

Smart, Reginald G. and Gordon W. Walsh. 1993. Do some types of alcoholic beverages lead to more problems for adolescents? *Journal of Studies on Alcohol* 56 (1): 35–38.

Smith, Audrey D. and William J. Reid. 1986. *Role-Sharing Marriage.* New York: Columbia University Press.

Smith, Carolyn. 1996. The link between childhood maltreatment and teenage pregnancy. *Social Work Research* 20 (3): 131–141.

Smith, Carolyn and Susan B. Stern. 1997. Delinquency and antisocial behavior: A review of family processes and intervention research. *Social Service Review* 71 (3): 382–420.

Smith, J. K. and L. Heshusius. 1986. Closing down the conversation: The end of the quantitative-qualitative debate among educational researchers. *Educational Researcher* 15 (1): 4–12.

Smith, Mary, Sheldon Tobin, and Ronald Toseland. 1992. Therapeutic processes in professional and peer counseling of family caregivers of frail elderly. *Social Work* 37 (4): 345–351.

Solomon, R. L. 1949. Extension of control group design. *Psychological Bulletin* 46: 137–150.

Spanier, Graham B. 1976. Measuring dyadic adjustment: New scales for assessing the quality of marriage and similar dyads. *Journal of Marriage and the Family* 38: 15–28.

Sprinthall, Richard C. 1987. *Basic Statistical Analysis.* 2d ed. Englewood Cliffs, N.J.: Prentice-Hall.

Stein, L. I. and M. A. Test. 1980. Alternative to mental hospital treatment: I. Conceptual model, treatment program, and clinical evaluation. *Archives of General Psychiatry* 37: 392–397.

Sternberg, Juliet A. and Brenna H. Bry. 1994. Solution generation and family conflict over time in problem-solving therapy with families of adolescents: The impact of therapist behavior. *Child and Family Behavior Therapy* 16 (4): 1–23.

Stevens, S. 1951. Mathematics, measurement, and psychophysics. In *Handbook of Experimental Psychology,* edited by S. Stevens. New York: Wiley.

Stosny, Steven. 1994. "Shadows of the Heart": A dramatic video for the treatment resistance of spouse abusers. *Social Work* 39 (6): 686–694.

Strauss, Anselm and Juliet Corbin. 1990. *Basics of Qualitative Research: Grounded Theory Procedures and Techniques.* Newbury Park, Calif.: Sage.

Strauss, Anselm and Juliet Corbin. 1994. Grounded theory methodology: An overview. In *Handbook of Qualitative Research,* edited by N. K. Denzin and Y. S. Lincoln, q.v.

Strube, M. J., W. Gardner, and D. P. Hartmann. 1985. A critical appraisal of meta-analysis. *Clinical Psychology Review* 5: 63–78.

Subramanian, Karen. 1991. Structured group work for the management of chronic pain: An experimental investigation. *Research on Social Work Practice* 1 (1): 32–45.

Subramanian, Karen. 1994. Long-term follow-up of a structured group treatment for the management of chronic pain. *Research on Social Work Practice* 4 (2): 208–223.

Sullivan, Nancy. 1995. Who owns the group? The role of worker control in the development of a group: A qualitative research study of practice. *Social Work with Groups* 18 (2/3): 15–32.

Sykes, Gini. 1997. *8 Ball Chicks: A Year in the Violent World of Girl Gangsters.* New York: Anchor.

Sykes, Wendy and Martin Collins. 1988. Effects of mode of interview: Experiments in the UK. In *Telephone Survey Methodology,* edited by R. M. Groves, P. P. Biemer, L. E. Lyberg, J. T. Massey, W. L. Nicholls II, and J. Waksberg. New York: Wiley.

Task Force on Social Work Research. 1991. *Building Social Work Knowledge for Effective Services and Policies: A Plan for Research Development.* Washington D.C.: National Institute for Mental Health.

Taylor, D. W., P. C. Berry, and C. H. Block. 1958. Does group participation when using brainstorming facilitate or inhibit creative thinking? *Administrative Science Quarterly* 3: 23–47.

Teare, Robert J. and Bradford W. Sheafor. 1995. *Practice-Sensitive Social Work Education: An Empirical Analysis of Social Work Practice and Practitioners.* Washington D.C.: Council on Social Work Education.

Terrie, E. Walter. 1996. Assessing child and maternal health: The first step in the design of community-based interventions. In *Needs Assessment: A Creative and Practical Guide for Social Scientists*, edited by R. Reviere, S. Berkowitz, C. C. Carter, and C. G. Ferguson. Washington D.C.: Taylor and Francis.

Test, Mary Ann. 1996. Programs of assertive community treatment for adults with severe mental illnesses—and beyond. Paper read at a Symposium on Psychosocial Intervention Research; Social Work's Contribution, September 5–6, 1996, at National Institutes of Health, Bethesda, Maryland.

Test, Mary Ann and L. I. Stein. 1980. Alternative to mental hospital treatment: II. Social cost. *Archives of General Psychiatry* 37: 409–412.

Thomas, Edwin J. 1978. Mousetraps, developmental research, and social work education. *Social Service Review* 52: 468–483.

Thomas, Edwin J. 1984. *Designing Interventions for the Helping Professions.* Beverly Hills: Sage.

Thomas, Edwin J. 1985. The validity of design and development and related concepts in developmental research. *Social Work Research and Abstracts* 2 (1): 50–55.

Thomas, Edwin J. 1994. Evaluation, advanced development, and the unilateral family therapy experiment. In *Intervention Research: Design and Development for Human Service*, edited by J. Rothman and E. J. Thomas, q.v.

Thomas, Edwin J. and J. Rothman. 1994. An integrative perspective on intervention research. In *Intervention Research*, edited by J. Rothman and E. J. Thomas, q.v.

Thomas, Edwin J., C. Santa, D. Bronson, and D. Oyserman. 1987. Unilateral family therapy with the spouses of alcoholics. *Journal of Social Service Research* 10: 145–60.

Thompson, Victor A. and D. W. Smithburg. 1968. A proposal for the study of innovation in organization. Huntsville: University of Alabama.

Thornberry, Terence P., Beth Bjerregaard, and William Miles. 1993. The consequences of respondent attrition in panel studies: A simulation based on the Rochester Youth Development Study. *Journal of Quantitative Criminology* 9 (2): 127–158.

Tice, Carolyn. 1994. A community's response to supportive employment: Implications for social work practice. *Social Work* 39 (6): 728–736.

Toseland, Ronald W., Christina G. Blanchard, and Philip McCallion. 1995. A problem solving intervention for caregivers of cancer patients. *Social Science and Medicine* 40 (4): 517–528.

Toseland, Ronald W. and Philip McCallion. 1997. Trends in caregiving intervention research. *Social Work Research* 21 (3): 154–164.

Toseland, Roland W. and William J. Reid. 1985. Using rapid assessment instruments in a family service agency. *Social Casework* 66: 547–555.

Toukmanian, Shake G., ed. 1992. *Psychotherapy Process Research: Paradigmatic and Narrative Approaches.* Newbury Park, Calif.: Sage.

Tracy, Elizabeth M. and Neil Abell. 1994. Social network map: Some further refinements on administration. *Social Work Research* 18 (1): 56–60.

Tracy, Elizabeth M. and James K. Whittaker. 1990. The social network map: Assessing social support in clinical practice. *Families in Society* 71 (8): 461–470.

Tran, Thanh V. and Leon F. Williams. 1994. Effect of language of interview on the validity and reliability of psychological well-being scales. *Social Work Research* 18 (1): 17–25.

Tripodi, Tony. 1992. Differential research utilization in macro and micro social work practice:

An evolving perspective. In *Research Utilization in the Social Services*, edited by A. J. Grasso and I. Epstein, q.v.

Tripodi, Tony, Phillip Fellin, and Henry J. Meyer. 1983. *The Assessment of Social Research.* 2d ed. Itasca, Ill.: Peacock.

Turkat, Ira D. 1986. The behavioral interview. In *Handbook of Behavioral Assessment*, edited by A. R. Cimeron, K. S. Calhoun, and H. E. Adams, q.v..

University of Chicago Press. 1993. *The Chicago Manual of Style.* 14th ed. Chicago: University of Chicago Press.

Valacich, Joseph S., Alan R. Dennis, and Terry Connolly. 1994. Idea generation in computer-based groups: A new ending to an old story. *Organizational Behavior and Human Decision Processes* 57 (3): 448–467.

Videka-Sherman, Lynn and William J. Reid. 1985. The structured clinical record: A clinical evaluation tool. *The Clinical Supervisor* 3:45–62.

Videka-Sherman, Lynn and William J. Reid, eds. 1990. *Advances in Clinical Social Work Research.* Silver Spring, Md.: NASW Press.

Viggiani, Pamela A. 1996. Social worker—teacher collaboration: Intervention design and development. Ph.D. dissertation, State University of New York at Albany.

Vosler, Nancy R. 1990. Assessing family access to basic resources: An essential component of social work practice. *Social Work* 35 (5): 434–441.

Vosler, Nancy R. 1996. *New Approaches to Family Practice: Confronting Economic Stress.* Thousand Oaks, Calif.: Sage.

Walker, Alvin G., ed. 1997. *Thesaurus of Psychological Index Terms.* 8th ed. Washington D.C.: American Psychological Association.

Wallace, David 1967. The Chemung County evaluation of casework service to dependent multi-problem families: Another problem outcome. *Social Service Review* 41: 379–389.

Ware, John E. Jr. 1997. Health care outcomes from the patient's point of view. In *Outcomes Measurement in the Human Services*, edited by E. J. Mullen and J. L. Magnabosco, q.v.

Warheit, George J., Joanne M. Buhl, and Roger A. Bell. 1978. A critique of social indicators analysis and key informants survey as needs assessment methods. *Evaluation and Program Planning* 1: 239–247.

Watzlawick, Paul, Janet Helmick Beavin, and Don D. Jackson. 1967. *Pragmatics of Human Communication.* New York: Norton.

Weed, Lawrence I. 1969. *Medical Records, Medical Education, and Patient Care: The Problem-Oriented Record as a Basic Tool.* Cleveland: Case Western Reserve University Press.

Weinbach, Robert W. 1988. Agency and professional contexts of research. In *Social Work Research and Evaluation*, edited by R. M. Grinnell Jr., q.v.

Weinbach, Robert W. and Richard M. Grinnell, Jr. 1995. *Statistics for Social Workers.* 3d ed. New York: Longman.

Weiss, Carol H. and Michael J. Bucuvalas. 1980. *Social Science Research and Decision-Making.* New York: Columbia University Press.

Weiss, R. W. 1997. Outcome perspectives. In *Outcomes Measurement in the Human Services*, edited by E. J. Mullen and J. L. Magnabosco, q.v.

Weissman, Myrna M. 1990. Social Adjustment Scale. Manuscript, College of Physicians and Surgeons, Columbia University, New York.

Wells, Kathleen and David E. Biegel. 1991. *Family Preservation Services: Research and Evaluation.* Newbury Park, Calif.: Sage.

Whittaker, James K., Jill Kenny, Elizabeth M. Tracy, and Charlotte Booth, eds. 1990. *Reaching High-Risk Families: Intensive Family Preservation in Human Services.* Hawthorne, N.Y.: Aldine De Gruyter.

Whyte, William Foote. 1981. *Street Corner Society.* 3d ed. Chicago: University of Chicago Press.

Wiener, Lori S., Elizabeth DuPont Spencer, Robert Davidson, and Cynthia Fair. 1993. National telephone support groups: A new avenue toward psychosocial support for HIV-infected children and their families. *Social Work with Groups* 16 (3): 55–71.

Williams, Robert L. 1980. The death of white research in the black community. In *Black Psychology,* edited by R. L. Jones, q.v.

Wilson, G. Terence and Cyril M. Franks, eds. 1982. *Contemporary Behavior Therapy: Conceptual and Empirical Foundations.* New York: Guilford Press.

Witkin, Belle R. 1994. Needs assessment since 1981: The state of practice. *Evaluation Practice* 15 (1): 17–27.

Witkin, Belle R. and James W. Altschuld. 1995. *Planning and Conducting Needs Assessments: A Practical Guide.* Thousand Oaks, Calif.: Sage.

Yalom, Irving D. 1985. *The Theory and Practice of Group Psychotherapy.* 3d ed. New York: Basic Books.

Yegidis, Bonnie L. and Robert W. Altschuld. 1995. *Planning and Conducting Needs Assessments: A Practical Guide.* Thousand Oaks, Calif.: Sage.

Yeh, Lois S. and Joanne Hedgespeth. 1995. A multiple case study comparison of normal private preparatory school and substance abusing/mood disordered adolescents and their families. *Adolescence* 30 (118): 413–428.

Zimbalist, Sidney. 1955. Major trends in social work research: An analysis of the nature of development of research in social work, as seen in the periodical literature, 1900–1950. Ph.D. dissertation, Washington University, St. Louis.

Zuravin, Susan J. and Diane DePanfilis. 1997. Factors affecting foster care placement of children receiving child protective services. *Social Work Research* 21 (1): 34–42.

Author Index

Subject Index